The SAGE Handbook of
Consumer Culture

Sara Miller McCune founded SAGE Publishing in 1965 to support the dissemination of usable knowledge and educate a global community. SAGE publishes more than 1000 journals and over 800 new books each year, spanning a wide range of subject areas. Our growing selection of library products includes archives, data, case studies and video. SAGE remains majority owned by our founder and after her lifetime will become owned by a charitable trust that secures the company's continued independence.

Los Angeles | London | New Delhi | Singapore | Washington DC | Melbourne

The SAGE Handbook of
Consumer Culture

Edited by
Olga Kravets, Pauline Maclaran,
Steven Miles and Alladi Venkatesh

SAGE reference
Los Angeles | London | New Delhi | Singapore | Washington DC | Melbourne

SAGE

Los Angeles | London | New Delhi
Singapore | Washington DC | Melbourne

SAGE Publications Ltd
1 Oliver's Yard
55 City Road
London EC1Y 1SP

SAGE Publications Inc.
2455 Teller Road
Thousand Oaks, California 91320

SAGE Publications India Pvt Ltd
B 1/I 1 Mohan Cooperative Industrial Area
Mathura Road
New Delhi 110 044

SAGE Publications Asia-Pacific Pte Ltd
3 Church Street
#10-04 Samsung Hub
Singapore 049483

Editor: Matthew Waters
Editorial Assistant: Colette Wilson
Production Editor: Anwesha Roy
Copyeditor: Rosemary Campbell
Proofreader: Derek Markham
Indexer: Cathryn Pritchard
Marketing Manager: Alison Borg
Cover Design: Wendy Scott
Typeset by: Cenveo Publisher Services
Printed in the UK

Library of Congress Control Number: 2017942557

British Library Cataloguing in Publication data

A catalogue record for this book is available from the British Library

ISBN 978-1-4739-2951-7

Contents

List of Figures and Tables

FIGURES

TABLES

Notes on the Editors and Contributors

THE EDITORS

Olga Kravets is a Senior Lecturer at Royal Holloway of London. She holds a PhD in Economics from the University of Sydney, Australia. Her research interests lie with the historical, socio-cultural, and political aspects of consumer culture and markets in transitional societies. Her previous research examined classed consumption, materialities of marketing, and the intersection thereof with politics and state ideologies, and it has been published in the *Journal of Marketing*, *Journal of Macromarketing*, *Journal of Marketing Management*, *Ephemera*, *Journal of Material Culture*, *Business History Review* as well as edited books.

Pauline Maclaran is Professor of Marketing & Consumer Research at Royal Holloway University. Her research interests focus on cultural aspects of contemporary consumption, and she adopts a critical perspective to analyse the ideological assumptions that underpin many marketing activities, particularly in relation to gender issues. Her work also explores socio-spatial aspects of consumption, including the utopian dimensions of fantasy retail environments. She is a Co-editor in Chief of Marketing Theory, a journal welcoming alternative and critical perspectives in marketing and consumer research. Her most recent book, co-written with Professor Cele Otnes, is entitled, *Royal Fever: The British Monarchy in Consumer Culture* (California University Press).

Steven Miles is Professor in Sociology at Manchester Metropolitan University, UK, Head of the Research Centre for Applied Social Sciences and author of *Retail and the Artifice of Social Change* (Routledge, 2016). His particular interest is in the role of consumption in impacting on questions of identity, both at the individual level and that of the city. His key publications include *Consumerism as a Way of Life* (Sage, 1998), *Youth Lifestyles in a Changing World* (OUP, 2000) and *Spaces for Consumption: Pleasure and Placelessness in the Post-Industrial City* (Sage, 2010). Steven is currently Editor-in-Chief of the *Journal of Consumer Culture*.

Alladi Venkatesh is Professor of Management and Informatics, and Associate Director, Center for Digital Transformation, University of California, Irvine, USA. He is also Honorary Professor at the Stockholm School of Economics. Professor Venkatesh's publications have appeared in major journals, *Management Science*, *Journal of Marketing*, *Journal of Consumer Research*, *Communications of the ACM*,

Marketing Theory, *International Journal of Research in Marketing*, *Journal of Marketing Management* and others. In 1998, he received the best paper award from the *Journal of Consumer Research*. He was the founding co-editor of *Consumption Markets & Culture*, which was founded in 1996.

THE CONTRIBUTORS

Kate Bayliss is a Research Associate at the School of Oriental and African Studies at the University of London. She has worked for many years on privatisation and public sector reform with particular reference to water and energy in developed and developing countries. Her research interests in this area include the impact of globalisation and financialisation on the provision of basic services.

Shona Bettany is a Professor of Marketing and Consumer Research at Liverpool John Moores University. Her research focuses on Consumer Culture, bringing a predominantly critical feminist material-semiotic lens to child, animal and sexuality studies. Her work is published in the *Journal of Business Research*, *European Journal of Marketing*, *Journal of Marketing Management*, *Advances in Consumer Research* and *Consumption Markets & Culture*. She has completed funded research for the Academy of Marketing, the ESRC and the Leverhulme Trust. When not writing she is a keen socialite in and around the bars in the Leeds LGBT zone of Lower Briggate, and often found walking her whippet in the local parks.

Alan Bradshaw teaches and learns at Royal Holloway, University of London and also at Stockholm University.

Benedetta Cappellini is a Senior Lecturer in Marketing at Royal Holloway, University of London. Her research interests are in food consumption, material culture and family consumption. She has published her research in several academic journals including *Sociology*, *The Sociological Review*, *Consumption Markets & Culture*, *Journal of Business Research* and *Journal of Marketing Management*. She has recently co-edited the text *The Practice of the Meal: Food, Families and the Marketplace* (Routledge).

Indranil Chakraborty is a doctoral candidate at the Faculty of Information and Media Studies, Western University, Canada. His thesis titled ‘Laborers of a Flat World’, examines the impact of globalisation on the work and life experiences of service workers in India’s Information sector. His research interests are in the areas of technology, work, labour, neoliberalism, political theory and global studies. Previously, he worked as a journalist in India for ten years.

Andreas Chatzidakis is a Senior Lecturer in Marketing at Royal Holloway University of London. His research focuses on the intersection of consumption with ethics and politics, including projects such as consumer-oriented activism in post-2008 Athens and the role of care and relationality in everyday consumption. His work also explores identity-based and spatial politics in contemporary consumer culture, drawing on disciplines such as human geography and psychoanalysis.

Marie-Emmanuelle Chessel is Historian and Research Professor at Sciences Po and CNRS (Centre for the Sociology of Organisations, Paris, France). Her work focuses in particular on Christian actors in the consumer world and in employer milieus, especially on the role of religion in women and men's organisations. Marie-Emmanuelle Chessel has published *Consommateurs engagés à la Belle Epoque. La Ligue sociale d'acheteurs* (Presses de Sciences Po, 2012) and *Histoire de la consommation* (La Découverte, 2012). In 2016 she also edited, with Denis Pelletier, *Entreprises et religion*, a special issue of the journal *Entreprises et Histoire*.

Franck Cochoy is Professor of Sociology at the University of Toulouse Jean Jaurès and a member of LISST-CNRS, France. He works in the field of economic sociology, with a focus on the human and technical mediations that frame the relationship between supply and demand. He has conducted several projects and case studies in such areas as the role of marketing, packaging, self-service, trade press and so on. His most recent articles in English have appeared in *Consumption Markets & Culture*, the *Journal of Marketing Management* and *Marketing Theory*.

Bernard Cova is Professor of Marketing at Kedge Business School. He acts as Visiting Professor at Bocconi University, Milan. A pioneer in the Consumer Tribes field since the early nineties, his work on this topic has been published in – among other places – the *Journal of Consumer Research*, *European Journal of Marketing*, *Journal of Business Ethics*, *Marketing Theory* and *Organization*. He has collaborated through action research programmes with companies such as Alfa Romeo, Citroën, Ducati and Macif.

Daniele Dalli is Professor of Marketing at the University of Pisa. His field is consumer research and he has published in – among other journals – the *International Journal of Research in Marketing*, *Marketing Theory*, *Journal of Business Ethics*, *Managing Service Quality* and *Management Decision*.

Anisha Datta is an Associate Professor of Sociology at King's University College at Western University, Canada. Her research interests include consumer culture, neoliberalism, social theory, political economy, social inequality, comparative sociology, South Asia – India, and Global Studies. Some of her published essays are – The 'Other' in Sociological Canons: Reading the Trinity through Critical Post-Colonial Lens (2012), Fair's Unfair: Simulations of Consumption and Career in Indian Advertising (2008) and Modernity, Gender and Political Allegory in 'Third World' Literature: The Case of *Streer Patra* (2007).

Janice Denegri-Knott is Associate Editor of *Marketing Theory* and Director of the Centre of Promotional Cultures and Communication at the Faculty of Media and

Communication at Bournemouth University, England. Her research interests span from conceptualising and documenting digital virtual consumption and its practices, the emergence of media technology, the socio-historic patterning of consumption and more generally the subject of power in consumer and marketing research. She has published extensively on what stimulates consumers' desire to acquire digital virtual goods and how consumers' come to assign value to their digital virtual possessions. She has done consultancy work for a range of media companies, such as *The Daily Telegraph*, *ITV* and *Channel 4*.

Sophie Dubuisson-Quellier is Research Professor at Sciences Po and CNRS, and deputy director of the Center for the Sociology of Organizations in Paris, France. Her research is situated in the field of economic sociology, and her focus is on the social construction of consumers and markets. Her aim is to understand how consumers' economic behaviour is progressively shaped by the relationship between corporations' practice, government, and social movements. She recently published *Ethical Consumption* (Fernwood Publishing, 2013) and *Gouverner les Conduites* (Presses de Sciences Po, 2016). Her work has appeared in several academic journals, such as *Organization Studies*, *Journal of Consumer Culture*, *Sociologia Ruralis* and *International Journal of Consumer Studies*.

Ben Fine is Professor of Economics at the School of Oriental and African Studies, University of London, holding honorary positions at the University of Johannesburg and the Institute for Social and Economic Research, Rhodes University. Recent books include *From Political Economy to Economics: Method, the Social and the Historical in the Evolution of Economic Theory* (awarded the 2009 Gunnar Myrdal Prize) and *From Economics Imperialism to Freakonomics: The Shifting Boundaries Between Economics and Other Social Sciences* (awarded the 2009 Deutscher Prize), both with Dimitris Milonakis, 2009; *Marx's Capital*, with Alfredo Saad-Filho (6th edition, 2016), and *Theories of Social Capital: Researchers Behaving Badly* (2010). He is Chair of the International Initiative for Promoting Political Economy, IIPPE, and is a member of the Social Science Research Committee of the UK's Food Standards Agency.

Eileen Fischer is a Professor of Marketing and the Max and Anne Tanenbaum Chair of Entrepreneurship and Family Enterprise at the Schulich School of Business at York University. She studies how consumers and entrepreneurs navigate markets as they strive to achieve their goals, and how their actions affect both firm- and market-level dynamics. Her work has been published in *Journal of Consumer Research*, *Journal of Retailing*, *Journal of Business Venturing*, *Journal of International Business*, *Entrepreneurship: Theory and Practice*, *Consumption Markets & Culture*, *Research Policy* and a range of other outlets.

Güliz Ger is Professor of Marketing and Director of the Center for Research in Transitional Societies at Bilkent University. She has also taught as a visiting professor in numerous universities around the world. She serves as an Associate Editor for the *Journal of Consumer Research* and is on the editorial boards of various journals. Her publications have appeared in journals such as the *Journal of Consumer Research*, *Consumption Markets & Culture*, *Journal of Material Culture* and in edited books. Her research interests involve the sociocultural and global dimensions of consumption and markets, particularly in transitional societies/groups, such as the historicity of specific consumer cultures in different geographies.

Rossella Ghigi is Associate Professor of Sociology at the University of Bologna (Italy). She holds a PhD in sociology and a DEA in history of the body (EHESS, Paris). Her research interests include the sociology of beauty, gender socialisation and education, and body modification in the consumer culture. She is currently working on the social invention of cellulite, cosmetic surgery, children's fashion and gendered representations in the mass media. She is the author of a number of essays in Italian, French and English on cosmetic surgery, gendered social dynamics during adolescence, the demographic consequences of economic crisis in Italy, as well as articles on the medicalisation of ugliness, the social construction of femininity and masculinity and feminist theory.

Olga Gurova (PhD, Cultural Studies) holds the position of Assistant Professor at the Department of Culture and Global Studies, Aalborg University, Denmark. She previously served as the Academy of Finland Research Fellow at the Department of Social Research, University of Helsinki (Finland) and as a researcher at Helsinki Collegium for Advanced Studies (Finland), National Research University – Higher School of Economics (Russia), University of Michigan at Ann Arbor (USA), University of Illinois at Urbana-Champaign (USA) and Central European University (Hungary). Her research interests include cultural studies, sociology of consumption and everyday life, fashion studies, socialist and postsocialist cultures, social-network analysis, qualitative methods of social research and innovative methods of teaching. She is the author of *Fashion and the Consumer Revolution in Contemporary Russia* (Routledge, 2015) and *Soviet Underwear: Between Ideology and Everyday Life* (New Literary Observer, 2008).

Jay Handelman is Associate Professor and the Commerce '77 Fellow in Marketing at Smith School of Business at Queen's University in Canada. His research focuses on the market-level dynamic that emerges through the interaction of a variety of social actors, including consumers, marketers, and activists. Examining these interactions contributes to an understanding of how markets form and change. His work has been published in the *Journal of Consumer Research*, *Journal of Marketing*, *Journal of the Academy of Marketing Research* and other outlets.

Vicki Harman is a Senior Lecturer in Sociology at the University of Surrey. Her research interests include family life, gender, social class and ethnicity. She has published her research in academic journals including: *Sociology*, *Ethnic and Racial Studies*, *Identities: Global Studies in Culture and Power*, *Young Consumers* and *Families, Relationships and Societies*.

Benoît Heilbrunn is Professor of Marketing at ESCP Europe and IFM (French Institute of Fashion). He has a background in philosophy and semiotics. His research interests includes branding, design, consumption, and material culture. He has written many books including *Market Mediations: Semiotic Investigations on Consumers, Objects and Brands* (Palgrave Macmillan, 2015).

Vera Hoelscher is currently a PhD Researcher in Marketing and Human Geography at Royal Holloway University of London and holds an MA Marketing from the same university. Her work explores the shared offline and online spaces of ethical consumption communities. She is particularly interested in the qualitative differences between these spaces and how these underpin narratives of resistance in urban settings and beyond.

Mehita Iqani is Associate Professor in Media Studies at the University of the Witwatersrand in Johannesburg, South Africa. She is the author of *Consumer Culture and the Media: Magazines in the Public Eye* (2012) and *Consumption, Media and the Global South: Aspiration Contested* (2016), as well as several journal articles on topics linked to race, class, gender, sexuality and their discursive construction in consumer media.

Eminegül Karababa is an Associate Professor of Marketing at the Middle East Technical University, Turkey. Her research interests include the historical development of markets and consumer cultures and value creation processes in contexts of consumption and markets. She is currently researching sustainable consumption of Nature Based Solutions as part of a European Commission grant. Her research is published in journals such as *Economic History Review*, *Journal of Consumer Research*, *Marketing Theory*, *Consumption Markets & Culture* and *Journal of Historical Research in Marketing*. She is as an Associate Editor for *Consumption Markets & Culture* and serves on the editorial board of *METU Studies in Development*.

William Kilbourne, PhD, received his degree from the University of Houston in 1973. He is a Professor Emeritus of Marketing at Clemson University, and his research interests are in materialism, globalisation, inequality and environmental issues in marketing. Most recently, his attention has been directed to developing, both theoretically and empirically, the role of a society's Dominant Social Paradigm in environmentally relevant consumption behaviour and in materialistic values. The research agenda entails the cross-cultural comparison of both environmental and materialistic values. He has published 60 articles in refereed journals and more than 100 papers in national and international conferences.

Erika Kuever is Assistant Professor of Marketing at the University of Southern Denmark. She holds a PhD in Anthropology from Indiana University and an MSc in Anthropology and Development from the London School of Economics. She has done research in Beijing, China; Siem Reap, Cambodia; and Bloomington,

Indiana. Her primary research focuses on consumption and consumers in China, with a specialisation in citizenship and consumer rights, but she has also written on Chinese nationalism, LEGO Friends, and the cultural marketing strategies of the Church of Scientology. Her current research project is about Chinese tourism in Denmark.

Alev Kuruoğlu is a Postdoctoral Researcher at the University of Southern Denmark, Department of Marketing and Management. Her research interests include the entwinement of markets and material culture in generating affect and in shaping social imaginaries. Her dissertation research investigates the multi-actored and politically contentious processes of circulation and market formation, in the context of the market for Kurdish music in Turkey. Her other research includes the tactility and affectivity of analogue media, gender performance and normativity in online communities, and the role of religion in shaping leisure practices. Her publications have appeared in *Consumption Markets & Culture* and edited books.

Gretchen Larsen is a Senior Lecturer in Marketing at Durham University. Gretchen's research is located within interpretive and critical consumer research, at the intersection of consumption, markets and the arts. In particular, she seeks to understand how the position of the consumer in a socio-cultural world is constructed, performed, interpreted and questioned through the arts. This research examines the importance of arts and music consumption in helping consumers make sense of their world, and how those involved in producing and distributing arts (marketers, artists, policy makers) can ensure that these benefits are delivered.

Eleftheria J. Lekakis is a Senior Lecturer in Media and Communications at the University of Sussex. She has a PhD from Goldsmiths College and an MSc from LSE, both in media and communications, as well as a BSc in Political Science from the University of Crete. Eleftheria's research interest concern the relationship between communication, culture and consumption with an emphasis on alternative forms of consumption (previously) and resistance to consumer society (recently). Her monograph Coffee Activism and the Politics of Fair Trade and Ethical Consumption in the Global North takes on the question of ethical consumption as a form of political participation in times of globalisation. Following that, she has worked on the relationship between consumption and nationalism, while she is currently researching anti-advertising and subvertising activism and forms of creative resistance.

Alexandre Mallard is Director of the *Centre de Sociologie de l'Innovation* at the *École des Mines ParisTech, PSL Research University*. Originally trained as a sociologist of science and technology, he now works in the field of economic sociology. He has conducted research on sales activity, on very small businesses and on the rise of network interactions in the corporate environment. His current research projects investigate the social inscription of innovation, at the crossroads between economic sociology and political science.

Linda L. Price is the Philip H. Knight Chair and Professor of Marketing at the University of Oregon. Linda combines qualitative and quantitative methodologies to examine consumer and collective identity, adaptation, social influence and network interactions. She has published books, chapters and over 70 articles in leading consumer, marketing and social science journals that have garnered over 15,000 citations. Linda has taken a leadership role in marketing and consumer theory and research, serving on numerous editorial boards, policy boards, foundations, conference programme committees and co-chairing several conferences and doctoral symposiums. She served as President of ACR, helped launch JACR, now serves as President of the AMA Academic Council and has been selected as incoming co-editor of *Journal of Consumer Research*. Linda has also received many honours and awards for a lifetime of mentoring and scholarship.

Pierre McDonagh (PhD, Cardiff) is Professor of Marketing at University of Bath, England. He has worked in Universities in Ireland, Scotland, Wales, England and the US. Pierre's research primarily focuses on the (im)possibility of sustainability within the prevailing order and oppositional counter culture. He has published widely on the interactions among markets, marketing and society; dark marketing; critical marketing; and transformative consumer research. Pierre serves as Associate Editor for the *Journal of Macromarketing* (US), and on the editorial boards of the *Journal of Marketing Management* (UK), *Consumption Markets & Culture* (US), *Recherche et Applications en Marketing* (FRA).

Paul R. Mullins is Professor in the Department of Anthropology at Indiana University-Purdue University, Indianapolis (IUPUI); Docent in Historical Archaeology at the University of Oulu (Finland); and Past-President of the Society for Historical Archaeology (2012–2013). He is the author of *Race and Affluence: An Archaeology of African America and Consumer Culture* and *The Archaeology of Consumer Culture.*

Cele C. Otnes is the Anthony J. Petullo Chair of Business Administration at the University of Illinois at Urbana-Champaign. She holds courtesy appointments in the department of Advertising and the department of Recreation, Sport & Tourism, and is an Adjunct Professor at the Norwegian School of Business and Economics. Her research focuses on how micro, macro, and marketplace factors shape consumption rituals such as gift-giving, holidays and culturally-embedded occasions. She is the co-author with Pauline Maclaran of *Royal Fever: The British Monarchy in Consumer Culture* and with Elizabeth H. Pleck of *Cinderella Dreams: The Allure of the Lavish Wedding* (both by the University of California Press). Her research appears in the *Journal of Consumer Research, Journal of Consumer Psychology, Journal of the Academy of Marketing Science, Journal of Advertising*, *Journal of Retailing* and other journals and edited volumes. Her current research explores consumers' quests for tranquility-inducing products, services, and experiences, with funding from the Marketing Science Institute and the Transformative Consumer Research initiative. She served as treasurer, executive board member and conference co-chair for ACR's North American and European conferences. She serves on the editorial review boards of the *Journal of Consumer Research, Journal of Service Research* and

Journal of Current Issues and Research in Advertising. She regularly appears on the Illinois 'List of Teachers Ranked as Excellent by Their Students.' She twice received the Outstanding Teaching Award in the College of Media.

Jessica Paddock is a Lecturer in Sociology at the University of Bristol. Her research is informed by sociological approaches, which are employed to understand the interaction of everyday life practices, natural resource use, food consumption and social differentiation in the context of environmental change. Her work also includes interdisciplinary collaborations across the social and natural sciences, particularly while working as a Research Associate at the Sustainable Consumption Institute, University of Manchester, UK, and with the Sustainable Places Research Institute at Cardiff University, UK, where she was awarded her doctorate in 2012.

Maurice Patterson is a Lecturer in Marketing at the University of Limerick. Maurice's key research interest centres on the relationship between consumption, embodiment and identity, and his work uncovers the role of body-related consumption in the pursuit of individual identity projects and its connection to marketplace cultures. The work acknowledges how cultural capital endowments systematically structure consumer preferences and thwart explicit social mobility goals. It also addresses the representation of gendered bodies in advertising, and subsequent interpretation by consumers.

Daniela Pirani is a PhD candidate in Marketing at Royal Holloway, University of London. Her research interests are in food culture and consumption, queer studies and advertising. She has a paper on post-feminism veganism forthcoming in *Feminist Media Studies.*

Andrea Prothero (PhD Cardiff) is Professor of Business and Society at University College Dublin, Ireland. Prior to UCD Andy lectured at universities in Wales and Scotland. Andy's research explores the area of marketing in society and sustainability marketing has been a key focus since the early 1990s. Andrea was Guest Editor of a special issue on *Green Marketing* in the *Journal of Marketing Management* in 1998, and of two issues of the *Journal of Macromarketing* in 2014 and 2015. She currently serves as Associate Editor for both the *Journal of Macromarketing* and the *Journal of Marketing Management.*

Mary Robertson is Economic Advisor to the Leader of the Labour Party. She previously worked as a lecturer in international business at the University of Greenwich and a postdoctoral research fellow at the University of Leeds. She has a PhD in economics from SOAS, University of London, and has studied at the Erasmus Institute of Philosophy and Economics, and Balliol College, Oxford. Mary's research interests include housing, privatisation, neoliberalism and financialisation.

Roberta Sassatelli is Professor of Sociology at the University of Milan (Italy) where she teaches consumer culture, sociological theory and visual methods. She has previously taught at the University of East Anglia (Norwich, UK) and the University of Bologna (Italy). Her research focuses on the theory of consumer action, the sociology of consumer practices and the politics of contemporary consumer culture as well as the sociology of leisure and sport, body and emotions, sexuality and gender. She is also working on visual studies and ethnography. She has done empirical research on ethical consumption, consumer movements, health and active leisure, consumption and class boundaries, lifestyles and the economic crisis, fashion and gender, local food and quality food circuits, the sharing economy and collaborative consumption. Among her recent books in English you may find *Consumer Culture: History, Theory and Politics* (Sage, 2007); *Fitness Culture: Gyms and the Commercialisation of Discipline and Fun* (Palgrave, 2010 [2014 paperback]). Her last book on the crisis, middle-classes and consumption in Italy has just appeared in Italian. Her works are translated into Spanish, Portuguese, German, Greek, Czech, Finnish, Polish, Korean and Chinese. She has been visiting fellow at Caltech (US), Birkbeck College (UK), UNE (Australia) and the University of Gastronomic Sciences (Bra, Italy).

Brett Scott is a journalist, campaigner and the author of *The Heretic's Guide to Global Finance: Hacking the Future of Money* (2013). He works on financial reform, alternative finance and economic activism with a wide variety of NGOs, artists, students and start-ups, and writes for publications such as *The Guardian, New Scientist, Wired Magazine* and *CNN.com*. He produced the 2016 UNRISD report on blockchain technology and is a Senior Fellow of the Finance Innovation Lab, an Associate at the Institute of Social Banking and an advisory group member of the Brixton Pound. He tweets as @suitpossum

Stefan Schwarzkopf is Associate Professor at Copenhagen Business School and specialises in historical-sociological approaches to the study of markets, marketing and consumption. He has a PhD in Modern History from Birkbeck College, University of London. Among his publications are an edited volume on post-war motivation research and the consumer researcher Ernest Dichter. His work has been published in *Theory, Culture & Society*, *Marketing Theory*, *Organization*, *Management & Organizational History*, *BioSocieties*, *Journal of Macromarketing* and in *Business History*. Recently, he has developed a particular interest in 'economic theology' as the study of the interplay between formalised religion, theological concepts and economic organisation.

Sanjay Srivastava is Professor of Sociology at the Institute of Economic Growth, Delhi University North Campus and India-based director of the MS Merian – R. Tagore International Centre of Advanced Studies in the Humanities and Social Sciences. His publications include *Constructing Postcolonial India: National Character and the Doon School* (1998), *Asia: Cultural Politics in the Global Age* (2001, co-authored), *Sexual Sites, Seminal Attitudes: Sexualities, Masculinities and Culture in South Asia* (2004, contributing editor), *Passionate Modernity, Sexuality, Class and Consumption in India* (2007), *Sexuality Studies* (2013, contributing editor) and *Entangled Urbanism: Slum, Gated Community and Shopping*

Mall in Delhi and Gurgaon (2015) From 2012–2016, he was co-editor of the journal *Contributions to Indian Sociology*.

Meltem Türe received her PhD in marketing from Bilkent University in Turkey in 2013. She is currently working at Skema Business School – Université Lille in France as an Assistant Professor of Marketing. She conducts research in various domains including object disposal and sustainability, materialism, ethics and moral consumption, value and value co-creation and health and food consumption. Her research has been published in journals such as the *Journal of Consumer Research*, *Journal of Business Research*, *Consumption Markets & Culture*, and *Marketing Theory*.

Tuba Üstüner is an Associate Professor of Marketing at Colorado State University. Her expertise includes marketing strategy, branding, business marketing, marketing in less industrialised countries and gender and social class. She has published in leading marketing journals such as the *Journal of Consumer Research*, as well as *The Harvard Business Review*. Tuba has received numerous awards for her research and teaching. Before joining Colorado State University, Tuba was an Associate Professor at the City University of London.

Baskin Yenicioğlu is an Assistant Professor of Marketing at Istanbul Bilgi University. There he teaches at undergraduate, MBA and PhD levels and runs the Interactive Marketing MA programme. Before joining Bilgi, Baskin worked at Henley Business School in the UK leading the Strategic Marketing subject for the executive post-graduate programmes. And before even that, for as long as he can remember, he has been very much interested in consumers and brand worlds, and how these worlds collide through digital technologies. He would like to grow up to be a househusband.

Detlev Zwick is an Associate Professor of Marketing and faculty in the Graduate Program in Communication & Culture at York University, Toronto. His research interests are cultural and social theories of consumption and critical cultural studies of marketing and management practice. His works have been published widely in marketing, communication, media culture, and sociology journals, as well as in several edited collections. His edited volume (with Julien Cayla) entitled *Inside Marketing* (Oxford University Press, 2011) explores marketing practice as ideological work.

1

Introduction

Olga Kravets, Pauline Maclaran,
Steven Miles and Alladi Venkatesh

The question of consumer culture emerged as a major focus of research in the 1990s, partly in response to the Conservative governments of the 1980s' political emphasis on consumption and the resurging critique of consumerism. Titles such as *The Consumer Society* (Baudrillard, 1998), *Consumer Culture and Postmodernism* (Featherstone, 1998), *The World of Consumption* (Fine and Leopold, 1993), *Consumer Culture* (Lury, 1996) and *Consumer Culture and Modernity* (Slater, 1997) are among the recognised classics that defined the contours of the subject. Consumer culture has now established itself as a core concern across the social sciences, the humanities and business studies. In such a rich and contested cross-disciplinary arena, there is no one accepted definition of what the term 'consumer culture' means, and how it is understood varies as widely as the many disciplines that pursue the phenomena of consumer and consumption in a society. The disciplinary engagements diverge in their concerns with regard to the social, cultural, aesthetic, political, economic and ethical aspects and implications of consumption. Broadly speaking, however, consumer culture is used to refer to the intensification of consumerism along with increasing prominence of consumption as social, cultural and economic activity that has come about with free-market capitalism and that is characteristic of late modernity, or what many refer to as postmodernity. The term also refers to the significance of the market in governing social worlds, including through beliefs, values, and meanings created around commodities and acts of consumption in relation to lifestyle and identity. As Roberta Sassatelli (2007: 193) astutely observed, the term is 'imprecise and analytically wanting'. It intends to capture an abstract notion that in the current political economic system, the sphere of consumption is overriding the relations of production in ordering society as a whole. Also, the term's use often implies the idea that there is in fact a variety of socio-historically situated and differently institutionalised consumer cultures. What is more, the term aims to describe actual mundane individual and collective consumer practices from buying to fantasising about goods, as well as the commercial practices that shape and facilitate everyday consumption. In *Consumer Culture: History, Theory and Politics*, Sassatelli (2007) teases out these diverse levels of the notion, and, most notably, offers a comprehensive overview of the genesis and development of consumer society as a distinctive kind of society. In particular, drawing on an impressive array of theoretical and empirical work, she carefully outlines how consumer culture was brought about by popular, social-scientific, and institutional discourses and activity around the main dichotomies of production versus consumption, rationality versus irrationality, and freedom versus oppression. This volume aims to complement such definitive work by bringing together multiple, often conflicting in terms of basic assumptions, disciplinary approaches to studying consumer culture, thereby demarcating the subject thematically, methodologically and epistemologically. The goal here is to provide an instructive resource for scholars and students, from whatever discipline in which the key dimensions of consumer culture are critically discussed.

The *Handbook* emerges from the proposition that the breadth and diversity of consumer culture which overlaps several disciplines, including business studies, economics, sociology, anthropology, cultural and media studies, psychology, geography, history and politics, has not been fully enough explored. Above all, a divide persists between those approaching consumer culture as a psycho-economic phenomenon (e.g., psychology and behavioural economics) with a focus on decision-making patterns, and those who seek to understand consumer culture from a social scientific perspective (e.g., sociology and anthropology) with an emphasis on cultural meanings and sociality. Yet, most theories emanating from sociological or anthropological sources fail to take account of the market and the marketing system itself. They tend to look at the social categories of consumers or marketing output (advertising and promotional materials), largely ignoring the institutional dynamics of markets and that many interactions take place between consumers and marketers. In contrast, business scholars have tended until recently to focus on the micro aspects of the consumer-marketer exchange process and marketing practices, often bracketing considerations of a broader context. Given such divergent foci, it is scarcely surprising that business scholars, social scientists and humanities scholars remain largely unaware of each other's work on consumer culture. The *Handbook* seeks to bridge this divide by bringing together scholars from across the relevant disciplines and inviting a critical reflection on perspectives, assumptions and methods privileged within their respective approaches to consumer culture.

In the past three decades, the rise of neoliberal ideology and associated policies not only translated into an ever greater expansion of market logic into various spheres of social, cultural and personal life, but also exalted the 'consumer' as a primary form of agency in society (Harvey, 2005). Increasingly people are addressed primarily as consumers across social domains and institutions, including education, health care, and politics, and often accept unquestionably market solutions for social ills and improvements. A great plethora of mundane activities, forms of self-expression, and enjoyment are now coded as consumption (Graeber, 2011). Indeed, ideals of happiness and a good life for an individual, as well as prosperity and democracy for a society, are articulated predominantly in terms of consumer choice, consumer spending and consumer satisfaction. Accordingly, studies of consumers by business scholars, previously dominated by micro-economic- and cognitive-psychology-inspired approaches, seek to place consumers within their social worlds and to unpack cultural aspects of identity and group formation (Fitchett et al., 2014). This macro viewpoint conceptualises consumers as socially connected beings who seek to explore, identify and experience the world through consumption, rather than merely as rational, economic agents, who carefully process the information around potential purchase decisions. Attention has now shifted to how consumers actually behave in their everyday lives, and to the subjective, emotional and social dimensions of consumption (Bocock, 1993). Although this shift highlights the need for cross-disciplinary approaches to consumer culture, these studies have rarely reached a broader non-business audience. Similarly, scholars from social science and humanities backgrounds have appeared sceptical of more business-oriented approaches for fear of selling out and compromising the scientific status of their work. Consequently, this current volume seeks to bring different disciplines into a conversation with each other and showcase the range and variety of consumer-culture-related scholarship. The contributions illuminate various aspects of consumer culture through the juxtaposition of primary interests and key perspectives on consumption within distinct fields of study. As such, the collection foregrounds disciplinary strengths and competences as well as exposing the disciplinary biases and blind spots that hinder building a holistic understanding of consumer culture.

The *Handbook* consists of six key sections, each containing specific disciplinary foci. Recognising that disciplinary boundaries are often a matter of structural arrangements, reward and funding systems, the division into sections is based mainly on a disciplinary perspective reflected in a contribution, rather than authors' institutional affiliations. We open with sociology and introduce approaches that have proved foundational in conceptualising the notion of consumer culture. The second part considers consumer cultures in historic and anthropologic perspectives across various geographies, especially in countries like Russia and China that provide contrasting contexts to the accepted western capitalist model of markets. The third part covers contemporary thinking in business studies from an interpretive consumer research perspective. This body of scholarship borrows theories from both sociology and anthropology to look at the intertwining of marketing activities with consumer culture. Part 4 draws on media and cultural studies to focus on aspects of representation and the subjectivities created through acts of consumption. The fifth part explores object-subject relations and materiality in consumer culture, showing that objects have agency also and are not just empty containers into which we as consumers pour meaning. We conclude the volume with a section on the politics of consumption to highlight and interrogate the increasing intensification of neoliberal ideology and the logics of late capitalism that define consumer culture today.

PART 1: SOCIOLOGY OF CONSUMPTION

The first section discusses the emergence of consumer culture and, indeed, the emergence of research into its development. There is a historical thread running through the section, as contributors consider classic sociological theories of consumption and reflect on changes in the approaches and scope in studying consumer culture. Each of the four chapters illustrates how social structures, relations and values are reproduced and constructed in everyday life through practices and places of consumption. A range of arenas of consumption, food, art, financial services, public goods and elements of class and consumer subjectivity are thus considered through this lens.

The opening chapter sets the scene with a discussion of the emergence of modern consumer culture. Steven Miles documents how the nature of consumption has changed over the last twenty years, bringing a heightened individualisation and sense of precarity that in turn fuels a quest for community and experiences that fill a perceived void. He considers key conceptual developments that have significantly impacted on the field of sociology, such as prosumption, authenticity and online forms of consumption. Using Airbnb as a case study, he undertakes an in-depth exploration of the tensions created by these developments and teases out their implications for studies of consumption.

Given the increasing complexities of consumer culture, Ben Fine, Kate Bayliss and Mary Robertson argue for more sophisticated and interdisciplinary theoretical perspectives. To this end they detail the systems of provision (SoP) approach to consumer culture, an approach that looks at the full chain of activities underpinning the material production and cultural significance of different goods. Using this theoretical lens, the authors then explore two largely ignored areas, namely the privatisation of public goods and financialisation, the proliferation of which is implicated in the consolidation of new neoliberal subjectivities. Overall, by analysing consumption within the chain of processes and structures around it, the SoP approach allows for more nuanced understanding, including policy impact and outcomes.

In 'The Making of the Consumer' Marie-Emmanuelle Chessel and Sophie Dubuisson-Quellier also set consumption in its wider context, this time by taking an historic perspective. Their chapter documents the ways in which market actors, the State and civil society, as well as consumers themselves, have contributed to the social making of consumers. As part of this analysis, the authors unpack how representations of the consumer are rooted in specific political or moral projects and show that consumption is a social and political practice with an impact way beyond the domestic sphere.

The final chapter in this section foregrounds a key concern of sociology, namely class inequalities and, more specifically, how consumption delineates class. Jessica Paddock revisits Bourdieu's treatise on distinction before discussing key modifications of this work and accompanying debates around the erosion of distinction implied by the increasing choice in consumer goods. She then interrogates contemporary practices of distinction, encapsulated in the phenomenon of cultural omnivorousness, and reflects on how the impetus towards sustaining class differences persists across fields of consumption such as art, music, home décor and food.

PART 2: GEOGRAPHIES OF CONSUMER CULTURES

The second part is inherently concerned with context, recognising that consumer cultures differ considerably from place to place, while also acknowledging a central role of consumption in societies and regions across the world. All the chapters attend to the historic and geographic diversity of consumer cultures, elucidating the divergence and convergence of consumption practices, as well as the political-economic and ethical implications thereof in an unevenly globalised world.

In 'Debunking the Myths of Global Consumer Culture' Güliz Ger and colleagues methodically unpick taken-for-granted assumptions to reveal ideological blind spots common to studies of global consumer culture. The authors highlight the need to historicise both the process of globalisation and seemingly global consumption practices. The chapter calls attention to inequalities at play in local/foreign cultural encounters and the persisting reification of us/other boundaries in many consumer studies. In the main, the authors argue for a critical approach that is reflexive of the ways research into global markets and consumption might 'sanctify neo-colonial and neoliberal might and boundaries' across geographies.

Taking up this challenge, Olga Gurova opens her chapter with the question of whether it is appropriate to apply categories such as 'consumer culture', 'consumer society' and 'culture of consumption' to consumption in socialist Russia. With the significance of historical context upheld, she outlines the main dimensions of socialist consumer consumption, thereby lending support to the idea of a multiplicity of consumer cultures created along the diverse paths towards modernity that various regions have followed.

In the next chapter, Sanjay Srivastava focuses on another non-western context, this time in relation to urban developments in India and the changing nature of relationships between the state, citizens and capital. He uses this context to explicate the increasingly tangled relations between consumption and self-making that spur the cultures of privatisation and individuation. His ethnographic study aptly traces the shifts in the public imagination from savings as a national good to consumption as a personal goal, as well highlighting how the spatial transformations that characterise new urbanism (e.g., gated communities) are also producing new subjectivities.

In 'Consumption and Consumer Rights in Contemporary China' Erika Kuever picks up both the previous chapter's ethnographic perspective and its concern with the role of a state in a consumer culture. She offers a rich account of how the Chinese party-state promotes consumption through the construction of a consumer welfare apparatus, while also producing neoliberal subjects tasked with the responsibility of assuring their own safety in a complex and, at times, outright dangerous market.

The final chapter, by Andreas Chatzidakis and Vera Hoelscher, returns us to the spatial context of consumption and the domination of cityscapes by various corporate interests, with their concomitant encroachment on public space. Elaborating on movements such as urban gardening and time banks, the authors discuss the ways various physical and digital spaces interact to mediate and accelerate consumerism as well as shape modes and forces of consumer resistance.

PART 3: CONSUMER CULTURE STUDIES IN MARKETING

Part 3 provides an overview of scholarship that is often referred to as consumer culture theory (CCT) or interpretive consumer research, a research area within the field of marketing that illuminates socio-cultural aspects of marketing and consumer behaviour.

Chapters in this section illustrate key theoretical frameworks in this subfield by unpacking topics of sustained interest to consumer researchers such as identity construction in the marketplace, gift-giving, market-mediated forms of sociality and consumer activism.

Linda Price commences the section by reflecting on the growth of consumer culture theory in business schools from the 1980s onwards, as part of the neoliberal surge that saw the formation of many new scholarly fields. She bases her reflections on her own participation in the consumer culture theory community, or as she describes it, her 'seat on a sideline'. Reviewing the CCT community's origin myths, she insightfully relates her own experiences of the transition to a socio-cultural focus on the consumer, using these to ponder deeper issues around the construction of academic communities and subfields.

Gretchen Larsen and Maurice Patterson then focus on consumer identity projects, highlighting the increasing authority of consumption as it replaces traditional social categories. Identity work necessitates the skill to deploy (or resist) products and brands in a way that shows understanding of the cultural meanings and discourses surrounding them. Thus, as the authors demonstrate, achieving distinction and difference relies increasingly on an individual's ability to negotiate the material and symbolic offerings of the market. However, identity projects can be precarious and there are often limitations placed on consumers to engage in such identity play in the first instance. Many market-based choices that offer new aspirational lifestyles, may also carry the risk of making mistakes that result in failure or stigma.

Cele Otnes continues this section with another key topic in consumer culture studies, gift-giving. She tracks the theoretical development of this important body of research and how six streams of scholarship shape contemporary understandings of gift giving, streams that have both broadened and diluted the definition and scope of gift-giving. Using examples of gift exchange stemming from her own kinship and friendship circles as a rationale, she proposes reconciling these six streams and puts forward a research agenda to reinvigorate gift giving research both in consumer culture theory and beyond.

Bernard Cova and Daniele Dalli cover another key theoretical focus in consumer culture studies, namely consumer tribes and marketplace subcultures. Whereas traditional consumer research (from a cognitive psychology and economic perspective) has always privileged the individual consumer, Cova and Dalli emphasise the collective construction of value. They explore George Ritzer's notion of prosumption in this context, arguing that prosumption communities challenge traditional boundaries between the market and work.

The final chapter in this section, by Jay Handelman and Eileen Fischer, continues this collective emphasis. They concentrate on a fourth major theme in consumer culture research, consumer activism and how movements mobilise to contest the actions of marketers as well as to bring about cultural change. Handelman and Fischer question some existing assumptions about activism, arguing that these lead to neglect of the contextual characteristics that shape activism. They propose a future research agenda that includes examining heterogeneity within activism, as well as broadening the categories of actors considered relevant to activism, and looking at social institutions that inform activism.

PART 4: CONSUMER CULTURE IN MEDIA AND CULTURAL STUDIES

The fourth section probes into forms, regimes and functions of representations, the attendant types of consumer subjectivity, and their positions within contemporary socio-economic systems. The chapters in this section focus on a range of representational enterprises (advertising, social media and marketing research) to discuss the ways in which social values, norms and boundaries are established and reproduced, contested and ruptured, as images move through the circuits of popular culture.

In the opening chapter, Mehita Iqani posits that contemporary consumer culture cannot be conceptualised apart from the media economies, and identifies key theoretical and empirical concerns of today's global 'mediated consumer culture'. The author then argues that in form and content, the media sells consumerism as a set of values, while refracting the power dynamics shaped by colonial history and continuing global structural inequality.

Daniela Pirani, Benedetta Cappellini and Vicki Harman discuss advertising and its long-standing role in propagating the entrenched gender norms and values. Undertaking an analysis of studies on gender roles and food practices, they consider the context, as well as the implied gaze, in which the identified representations take place. In other words, as they argue, particular contextual conditions give rise to certain representations. The authors present an intriguing study of gender characters found in food advertising and suggest that the variety notwithstanding, these characters tend to reinforce traditional gender roles and power dynamics in the family.

The themes of gender, power and (self)representation are brought together by Rossella Ghigi and Roberta Sassatelli in their chapter exploring the body as a principle site for the expansion of consumer culture. Building on the authors' earlier empirical studies on fitness culture and cosmetic surgery, the chapter provides an important reminder about the role played by two contentious dynamics, aesthetisation and rationalisation, in fuelling both consumerism and the beauty-cosmetic industrial complex. The authors unpack the neoliberal notion of the self as an enterprising project across three arenas of body surface modification: fashion, body art and cosmetic surgery.

Continuing the theme of neoliberalisation, Detlev Zwick and Janice Denegri-Knott highlight how modern marketing encloses the subject as consumer and the commons as (creative, cognitive, etc.) capital. They argue, therefore that marketing can be understood as a technology of enclosure (i.e., plundering the commons) and that consumers, acting both individually and socially become a form of resource capture, especially through what is termed 'big data marketing'. The authors illustrate how marketing employs various technologies of surveillance, government and entanglement that mask its desire to enclose and control, making it appear to be its exact opposite in the eyes of consumers, often claiming to liberate and empower them.

PART 5: MATERIAL CULTURES OF CONSUMPTION

The fifth section looks at the relationship between persons and things, and the processes of material articulations in consumer culture. Together the five chapters in this section discuss what defines materialities of consumption and illuminate various guises of the material dimensions of socio-symbolic aspects of consumption. Overall, the section illustrates how consumer society is constructed through seemingly prosaic material objects, people's relations to these objects, and practices around them (e.g., curating, collecting, gifting, disposing, and so on).

Opening the section, Paul Mullins undertakes a detailed examination of the concept of materiality, highlighting key theoretical strands and how the concept of materiality avoids subject/object dualisms, as well as problematising the notion of consumer agency. Arguing that a material culture perspective extends our knowledge of the ways things shape experience, Mullins contends that the notion of materiality pushes scholars to systematically examine the bodily, imagined and visual experiences of material things.

The second chapter in this section, by Shona Bettany, interrogates subject/object relations more closely, looking at how this long-established dichotomy has been treated in interpretive consumer research and exposing some of the political and ideological assumptions that endure therein. Bettany's chapter explores in some depth work that challenges those assumptions around three main questions: what is agency? what is/becomes an object/subject? and what is a relation? In doing so, she foregrounds new theoretical avenues that hold much promise for future insights into the materialities of consumer culture.

Then Franck Cochoy and Alexandre Mallard discuss Actor Network Theory (ANT) and its contribution to material culture studies. They introduce the concept of 'consumer cultivation' to signify the ways in which consumers are framed by a wide range of market actors, including market-things, like shopping trolleys. Based on a relational conception of action and an emphasis on innovation, the authors highlight the processes through which consumer–product encounters occur, and how this collective work shapes consumption. For these authors, consumption is realised through the mutual tasks of shaping products and cultivating consumers.

The fourth chapter by Benoit Heilbrunn gives a very comprehensive overview of the many ways that material objects impact on our environment and the different theoretical strands that help us understand this impact. Looking at the semanticisation of objects, he explores various semiotic, philosophical and anthropological perspectives around the symbolic sign systems that objects may convey. The aestheticisation and romanticisation of objects play a key role in contemporary consumer culture, with design activities increasingly endowing objects with existential values.

The last chapter in this section is by Brett Scott, a campaigner, former broker and author of *The Heretic's Guide to Global Finance: Hacking the Future of Money*. Pondering on the implications of the drive toward a cashless society, he stresses the importance of resisting 'the digital panopticon' that seeks profit maximisation for the few and at the expense of the many who it will exclude.

PART 6: THE POLITICS OF CONSUMER CULTURE

The final section cuts across disciplinary boundaries as the authors bring a political economy perspective to explore the ways in which markets, commodities and consumers – and the networks of relations in which they are embedded – are a part of a political-economic system. What is more, in today's late capitalist societies, social membership is largely defined by one's consumptive, rather than productive role; indeed, according to Bauman (1998), citizenship hinges upon ability to consume, and those who are unable or unwilling to consume are deemed to be failing in their civic duty. Building on this understanding that consumption is always already politically structured and inextricable from the conditions of production, state policies and politics, the chapters explore consumption as a site of modern governance and discuss the possibilities and limits of political, ethical and generally transformative praxis through consumer culture.

Stefan Schwarzkopf provides a wide genealogy of the concept of choice, seeking to trace the historical, cultural and political circumstances of how choice became reified as a social policy aim in its own right. The author clarifies a common conflation of the terms 'choice' and 'decision' before offering a comprehensive historical-philosophical account of the meanings and origins of 'choice', particularly focusing on how the notion acquired a more empowering and proactive meaning – having choice and being offered a choice – that underscores its reification as an organising principle in a modern society. The key insight to be derived from this rich contribution is that the concept of choice is the outcome of a deliberate and highly politicised invention.

In 'Are you Neoliberal Fit?', Anisha Datta and Indranil Chakraborty note that political economy tends to be invoked primarily in the discussions of consumption or rather 'feeding' the poorest populations of this world. Yet, the authors state, to understand today's consumerism along with such 'bizarre phenomena' as produce wastage on an industrial scale by food manufacturers, researchers must interrogate the ideology and discourses that define the consumption cultures of the middle classes. The authors then proceed to explicate 'a neoliberal self', a mode of subjectivity effectuated by the neoliberal structural and policy changes, and discuss attendant patterns of consumption and the ever worrying individualisation of life that these patterns enact.

The next chapter considers the possibilities of systemic transformation in the context of sustainability, as it increasingly turns into an institutional economic doctrine from being mainly a social concern. Pierre McDonagh, William Kilbourne and Andrea Prothero argue that the political aspects of consumption become notable under conditions of limits to economic growth. Thus, framing sustainability as a mere trend, even if a mega one, constrains understanding of its significance and impact. They propose a new political economy approach as a way to capture and examine the politics of sustainability as an economic doctrine.

In the current political climate marked by the rise of populist nationalism, Eleftheria Lekakis's 'Buying into the Nation: The Politics of Consumption and Nationalism' is particularly resonant. She urges us to critically interrogate the popular wielding of consumption as a political tool to fight injustices, arguing that it can be used to advance conservative, nationalistic politics just as effectively as to express progressive political sentiments. The author goes on to systematically unpack the relationship between nationalism and consumption, and outlines the four key areas of study: ethnocentric consumption, economic nationalism, consumer nationalism, and commercial nationalism.

The *Handbook* closes with a chapter by Alan Bradshaw who offers a useful exposition of the construction of the consumer in consumer culture research. In order to do this he revisits debates on the consumer as manipulated dupe versus the consumer as liberated identity-seeker. Then, introducing us to two new texts on the topic, one by Holly Lewis and the other by Alison Hume, he discusses how neither side in these debates is convincing and that both serve to mystify and naturalise broader class antagonisms. In conclusion, Bradshaw shows how analysing a commodity trail can reveal hidden labour in supply chains that can be used to imagine new forms of global solidarity.

CONCLUSION

We hope this *Handbook* provides scholars and students with a substantive reference point from which to further develop their interest in consumer culture. The sections included here present a broad audit of the major paradigms, key topics, and varying concerns pertaining to the subject, and set these within their socio-historical contexts and background disciplines. Many contributions draw on the latest research and thinking, demonstrating a remarkable breadth of empirical contexts and depths of ideas in the myriad world of consumer culture studies. The volume reflects contemporary debates – for example, implicating the study of consumption and the consumer within the current political economy and neoliberal ideology therein – and many contributors point out the areas requiring future research, as well as considering how the field overall is likely to develop. The *Handbook* is by no means an exhaustive compilation of material on the subject, instead it is intended to be a cultural panopticon, offering a view over a wide range of discussions on consumer culture across swathes of the humanities, social sciences, and business studies.

REFERENCES

Baudrillard, J. 1998. *The Consumer Society: Myths and Structures*. Sage, London.

Bauman, Z. 1998. *Work, Consumerism and the New Poor*. Open University Press, Milton Keynes.

Bocock, R. 1993. *Consumption* (Key Ideas). Routledge, London.

Featherstone, M. 1998. *Consumer Culture and Postmodernism*. Sage, London.

Fine, B. and Leopold, E. 1993. *The World of Consumption*. Routledge, London.

Fitchett, J.A., Patsiaouras, G. and Davies, A. 2014. 'Myth and ideology in consumer culture theory' *Marketing Theory*, *14*(4), pp. 495–506.

Graeber, D. 2011. 'Consumption' *Current Anthropology*, *52*(4), pp. 489–511.

Harvey, D. 2005. *Neoliberalism: A Brief History*. Oxford University Press, Oxford.

Lury, C. 1996. *Consumer Culture*. Polity Press, Cambridge.

Sassatelli, R. 2007. *Consumer Culture: History, Theory and Politics*. Sage, London.

Slater, D. 1997. *Consumer Culture and Modernity*. Polity Press, Cambridge.

PART I

Sociology of Consumption

2

The Emergence of Contemporary Consumer Culture

Steven Miles

The sociology of consumption perhaps reached something of a zenith in the late 1990s to early 2000s. At least the case for arguing that consumption was worthy of critical sociological investigation in its own right appeared to have, to all intents and purposes, been won. The sociology of consumption was the product of the realization that consumption shapes social relations and social meanings in as fundamental a way as production. It was upon this basis that consumption established itself as a legitimate focus for the sociological imagination, and a whole raft of books, articles and conceptual contributions reflected as much (see for example Edwards, 2000; Miles, 1998; Slater, 1997). In practice the significance of consumption as a focus for sociological exploration was often manifested around notions of identity: in other words the sociological significance of consumption was often addressed either directly or indirectly through the role it played in relation to the construction of an individual's identity in the broader context of the relationship between structure and agency. Yet new forms of consumption, notably online, have helped to blur the nature of this relationship even further. As such, the time is clearly ripe to take stock and reflect upon what scholars of consumption more generally can learn from both the insights and oversights of the sociology of consumption.

The first thing to note about consumption, as this collection indicates so graphically, is that it is a quintessentially cross-disciplinary phenomenon, so in that sense singling out the purely sociological is a counter-productive task. No single discipline can, of course, claim to present the authoritative account of consumption. And yet, on the other hand, as a sociologist I would like to make particular claims for the benefits to be had from adopting a sociological perspective on the consuming experience. In what follows, rather than claiming I have my fingers on the pulse of where exactly the sociology of consumption currently situates itself (for this is not something 'it' claims to do in any kind of a unified fashion), I want to consider some key conceptual developments in the sociology of consumption, namely around prosumption, authenticity and online forms of consumption, before reflecting specifically on Airbnb, as a means of understanding some of the key tensions of what it means to be a consumer in the twenty-first century. In short, in what follows I will argue that the consumption experience tells us something important about the basis upon which our society operates and how our sense of our selves is compromised in the process.

CONSUMPTION, THE DIGITAL AND INDIVIDUALIZATION

The nature of consumption can be said to have changed profoundly in the course of the last twenty years. A primary cause of this change is undoubtedly the sheer presence of the digital in our everyday lives. For example, Stillerman (2015) notes that more than a billion people purchased a smartphone worldwide in 2013 or, in other words, smartphones are owned by at least 1 in 7 of the world's population. But it isn't simply the fact that consumers own such products in such vast numbers that is sociologically interesting. What's more important is the changing ways in which consumers consume. In this context Asano (2013) discusses the way in which the mobile phone and the internet radically changed both the way in which young people communicate and how it is they consume to the extent that they have produced what can be described as a 'full-time intimate community' in which virtual relationships are permanently 'on' and accessible. We consume our devices and these devices, in effect, determine who it is we are and how we relate to the world around us. Mobile phones, from this point of view encourage a particular pursuit of pleasure, and young people, in particular, reap the status or cultural capital associated with belonging to particular consumption communities. Consumption effectively *becomes* community. Gaming is a good example of how this process works and yet of the paradoxes it entails. Brock (2017) thus talks about how the consumption of games, rightly or wrongly, tends to be described as a rational escape from reality or as some kind of attempt to relieve oneself from the harsh realities of everyday life and how such analyses may underestimate the complex inner worlds and self–other relationships that have such a complex and profound impact on the consuming experience. The point here is that such communities have significant implications not just for the society in which we live, but importantly for how the individual consumer relates to that society.

The (arguably illusory) community-giving dimensions of new forms of consumption are possible insofar as the use of the media itself has become invisible (see Bjur et al., 2014) in the sense that how consumers use mobile phones, for example, has become so integrated into the way that we live that we, as consumers, barely notice it. The above reflects a broader process, reminiscent of the work of Baudrillard (1983) perhaps, in which we increasingly depend upon mediated representations of reality, despite being well aware that the content of such representations is essentially faked. As such, authenticity becomes 'a currency in the communicative relation between producers and audiences' (Enli, 2015: 1). This opens up the possibilities for consumption as an ever more ideological entity. In other words, the more we as consumers feel that consumption provides us with the choice to escape, the more we are tied to the system from which we are escaping.

The new forms of consumption that are available appear to accentuate the above process. They are often experiential in nature. So for example, the experience of visiting an Apple Store has long been about far more than just buying an Apple product. Such stores do not even offer a counter where the consumer would traditionally be expected to make their purchase. In a sense when you enter the Apple Store (or you could argue even when you are tapping on the Apple keyboard as I am as we speak) you are entering an Apple theme park in which the logical outcome is your reassertion of your belonging to the (less than) exclusive Apple family. Such developments can be said to reflect the pronouncements of Pine and Gilmore (1999) who argued that in difficult economic times the best way to create added value is to create experiences that consumers interpret as individuals: the individual pays more for something that he or she feels and experiences personally. A good example of this is the recent gaming-related leisure trend for 'Escape Rooms'. Get locked up in a room for an hour, meet the challenge of various puzzles physical trials and escape from the place you didn't need to be locked up in in the first place. You, the consumer, effectively become the actor in your own play and you construct a memorable commodified experience in the process. What's sociologically interesting about all this is that you are pulled in by the experience of something unique that isn't unique at all. Consumer capitalism has reinvented itself in such a way that the consumer is apparently the perpetuator of his or her own ideological demise.

It's in light of the constant reinvention of consumerism as a way of life that Ogino (2013) therefore talks about how the consumer society 'is no longer the precursor of a new society' but is now the very root of society itself' (p. 105) and goes on to discuss this transition in the context of Japanese internet and manga cafes which provide many, often jobless, individuals with a communication-based identity – a place, built upon consumption, where they feel that they belong. In this sense, consumption is no less significant to a person's identity than it may or may not have been back in the late 1990s when the sociology of consumption was arguably in its prime. Indeed, it could be argued that the ability of consumption to help us feel part of something is ever more insidious. There is a far greater range of ways to belong, most noticeably online. The question is whether or not to feel like you belong to a virtual group (or indeed one based around a café) constitutes any kind of belonging at all and indeed whether this sense of belonging is necessitated precisely because our society offers fewer 'authentic' means of establishing this sense of belonging. What appears to have changed then is the way that relationships around consumption are constructed, to the extent that Ogino argues, consumption is now part and parcel of an everyday human survival strategy. In other words, what constitutes 'the right to live' has radically changed in contemporary society. As such, internet and manga cafes are not in themselves a problem, they constitute a coping mechanism we use to deal with the demands society puts on us as individuals. We are obliged to partake in the worlds that consumption provides for us. They provide an escape, but that escape does no more than intensify our dependence on the freedoms that consumption allegedly provides.

Perhaps the best way of understanding the above transition is through an understanding of the process of individualization which might well be said to be at the core of the consumer 'society': the process by which intermediate social groups such as the workplace, family, religion and class are increasingly weakened. This weakening creates a situation in which an individual's everyday experience becomes increasingly precarious. The responsibility for his or her existence falls more and more squarely on his or her own shoulders. His or her life becomes more and more a personal responsibility. For Roland Robertson (2013) individuals' lives have become riskier due to the influences of globalization and the effect of neoliberal politics. The problem here is that the process of individualization, and the role that consumption plays therein, has indeed unleashed the individual. This is certainly anxiety-inducing in the example of nursing care provision, for example, creating all kinds of uncertainties for the individual consumer and his or her family, but it could also be said, at least in some senses, paradoxically to be liberating in its effect. But there may be something slightly more sinister in operation in here. The more trivial example of the Escape Rooms that I referred to above can indeed be said to constitute an example of prosumption, whereby the consumer actively partakes in an experience which he or she simultaneously produces as well as consumes. By doing so the lines between the two are blurred and more onus is put on the ability of the consumer to produce his or her own experience along the way. In effect, the individual consumer becomes the conduit for his or her own consumer-driven definition. He or she ties him- or herself to the consumer-driven world that he or she is surrounded by.

PROSUMPTION AND THE SHARING ECONOMY

Debates over the nature of prosumption have emerged as one of the most important areas of debate in the sociology of consumption. A particularly significant contribution in this regard was an article in which Ritzer and Jurgenson (2010) debate the extent to which the existence of prosumption constitutes a new form of prosumer capitalism: is the fact that capitalism obliges consumers to work towards the satisfactions that consumption provides something new? Ritzer and Jurgenson come to the conclusion that the capitalist economy has always been defined by prosumption and that prosumption only feels more important now because recent social and technological developments such as social media and what might be described as user-generated web such as Facebook, YouTube and Twitter are so prevalent. In other words, the world of consumption we are experiencing now isn't radically different to what came before, it is simply an extension of pre-existing patterns. However, in some respects the emergence of prosumption has created a set of circumstances in which the consumer is freer: he or she is liable to find space online which they find comfortable and which in turn produces a profit for the producer. Thus Ritzer and Jurgenson use the example of YouTube which doesn't need to control the quality of the videos it uploads: the consumer constructs the grounds upon which profit is made and thus does the job for them. Ultimately however, the concern here is that capitalism is characteristically adaptable and likely to use what might be described as an illusory freedom to its own economic ends.

If we accept that prosumption is an increasingly key dimension of the consuming experience we also need to reflect on the broader context in which consumption operates. A key focus of this discussion has been on the emergence of the so-called sharing economy, at the heart of which allegedly lies a more collaborative form of consumption. The suggestion here is that consumers may be moving towards an age in which the excesses and waste of the consumer society are being challenged. Thus authors such as Botsman and Rogers (2010) point towards 'an emerging economic groundswell' characterized by collectivity and community. For Botsman and Rogers (2010) collaborative consumption 'puts a system in place where people can share resources without forfeiting cherished personal freedoms or sacrificing their lifestyle' (p. xxi). What lies behind what Botsman and Rogers describe as a 'hyper-evolution' is again, internet and mobile technology, which promotes a constant reflexivity and adaptation. This in turn apparently brings us together through non-territorial communities. So although the world continues along a path of self-destructive growth a new kind of consumer is allegedly emerging that boasts a communitarian mindset. Acquisition is therefore no longer the sole goal. At times however, Botsman and Rogers' claims for collaborative consumption verges on the willfully optimistic:

> We believe we will look back and see this as a time when we took a leap and re-created a sustainable system built to serve basic human needs – in particular, the needs for community, visual identity, recognition and meaningful activity – rooted in age-old market principles and collaborative behavior. Indeed, it will be referred to as a revolution, so to speak, when society, faced with grave challenges, started to make a seismic shift from an unfettered zeal for individual getting and spending towards a rediscovery of collective good. (2010: 224–225)

The problem here as Tom Slee (2015) points out is that this is in fact the same old consumer capitalism dressed in slightly new clothes. For Slee the sharing economy, as demonstrated through Lyft, TaskRabbit, Uber and many other examples of companies that could reasonably be said to have liberated the consumer, actually serves to extend harsh free-market practices into previously protected areas of our lives. Although from this point of view there are examples of innovative non-commercial sharing initiatives that can be said to be changing the nature of consumption such as car-sharing, bike-sharing and green taxi services, for example, the impact of the sharing technology in general is to extend the tentacles of capitalism. The utopian ideals of a sharing economy are not played out in reality: what is played out in reality is a hyper-capitalism. And it is this which the sociology of consumption is at least part tasked to understand.

So what does all this mean for consumption on the ground and how have sociologists sought to interpret such experiences? Yates (2016) looks at the experience of sharing within households. He notes the trend for smaller households, and in particular for solo living which could be perceived to threaten traditional notions of community and civil society through the normative discourses about how to live that they inspire. As Yates points out, sharing isn't simply about the sustainability of consumption but about how such consumption implicates boundaries, governance and futures, and herein lies the real challenge for the sociology of consumption. What is interesting here is perhaps how and why the experience of consumption is played out in particular ways.

THE PRACTICE OF CONSUMPTION

It is worth noting that one of the more recent and important trends in the sociology of consumption has been to focus on practices in light of Warde's (2014) influential contention that the Cultural Turn has 'run its course' and that an alternative needs to be found. Thus, '[t]heories of practice provide a competing alternative approach which contests the colonization of consumption by models of individual choice and cultural expressivism'. For Warde then, theories of practice provide 'a lens to magnify aspects of common social processes which generate observable patterns of consumption' (p. 279). Noting that theories of practices have tended to emphasize structure over agency, Warde makes the case for them providing a means by which change can actually be understood. In order to achieve this, argues Warde, we need to move beyond an understanding of deliberative personal choices to understand 'the creation of norms, standards and institutions which produce shared understandings and common procedures' (p. 295). So, for example, Maguadda (2011) seeks to understand the circuits of practice involved in the consumption of digital music. The article highlights the insights to be had from an approach that focuses on the interaction between people and material objects. As Maguadda (2011: 33) puts it, 'In the present case, we have seen that changes in the way people consume music are inherently connected with more general processes of mutual co-shaping of objects, cultural values and embodied activities'. But the truth is that theories of practice have tended to over-egg the minutiae of the consumer experience. For example, the area of food consumption has received considerable attention from this perspective, but it remains debatable as to whether this body of work has transformed our understanding of the sociological significance of consumption. Practice theory might well be criticized for getting overly tied up in the micro, and the suspicion that the bigger structural picture has been somewhat neglected as a result still remains.

CONSUMPTION AND CRIME

Some of the most interesting interventions into the sociology of consumption (broadly defined) as regards with the balance between structure and agency have been made by scholars who have been concerned with the relationship between consumption and crime. Hayward's (2004) contribution on the relationship between crime, consumer culture and the urban experience is particularly significant in this regard, though this has, perhaps regrettably, had more of an impact on criminology circles than it has on the sociology of consumption. Hayward notes that people's sense of relative deprivation is the product of a blurring of the distinction between 'having' and 'being' in contemporary society. From this point of view people feel excluded not because they don't own particular products but because they are excluded from the identity-giving qualities that these products offer. As Hayward (2204: 161) puts it, 'In late modern society, need and desire have transmogrified and as a consequence we now face a situation in which individual expectations are seen in terms of basic rights and are therefore no longer fettered by traditional or economic or social restraints'. Consumers, are those who define themselves through what they do and don't consume in a society founded upon a culture of unfulfilment. From this perspective, the potential for resistance within the consumption experience is limited. Thus Hall et al. (2008) found that none of the young people involved in criminal activity that they interviewed saw themselves as 'socially excluded'. Rather, they went about the process of reflecting their own fantasized identities back to themselves: they did what they had to do to locate themselves symbolically in the day-to-day hierarchies in which they existed. Consumption was the means by which they achieved this. But the problem is, as Hamilton (2012) suggests, 'in a cruel irony, the consumption choices that are driven by a desire to mask poverty instead only serve to further stigmatize' (p. 85). Forms of consumption that are highly prized in some quarters are sources of shame in others. In effect then, consumers over-identify with consumer goods. Criminal activity can thus be seen as an effort to rectify this situation: to assert control over a culture that is otherwise so obviously inaccessible. From a sociological point of view what's interesting here is that social groups define themselves through what it is they *cannot* attain. In a sense then the sociology of consumption is as much about what you cannot consume as what you can. In this context, there are grounds for arguing that social scientific approaches to consumption more broadly, need to embrace a more sophisticated understanding of emotions, sensations and imaginations. Such a realization highlights the potential damage caused by sieving consumption off into disciplinary silos.

Sasha Newell's (2012) work on the relationship between crime, consumption and citizenship on the Ivory Coast sheds further light on the symbolic and practical value of consumption. Newell discusses how young men use brand-name clothing, accessories and technology in order to present a particular version of themselves; a performative version that amounts to an illusion of wealth. These young men are successful insofar as they appear to be so. In this scenario the performance is more important than any notion of authenticity. What this tells us is that perhaps consumption is less and less restrained in terms of the meaning people carry through it. Nobody believes that Newell's young men are rich but their consumption patterns give them an aura of respectability and authority that is immaterial to their class position. From a sociological perspective then, consumption is complex and despite appearances to the contrary, deeply socially divisive. Newell's work also obliges us to think about the broader global 'system of exclusion' in which consumption operates, and the extent to which the concentration of wealth is such that the only way in which the excluded can partake of consumption is through an illusory process of belonging that potentially excludes them more than it ever includes.

GLOBALIZATION AND CONSUMPTION

It is important to remember the broader global context in which consumer cultures have emerged, as Newell's work demonstrates so effectively. As such, Joel Stillerman (2015) discusses the emergence in recent years of an increasingly complex set of circumstances and patterns of advertising, marketing and branding which are in turn related to market segmentation, emotion and experience. Stillerman makes the important point that consumers can be both the subjects and the objects of consumption. So, for example, he goes on to discuss work on the impact of consumption on Ecuador's Otavalo Indians (see Colloredo-Mansfield, 1999). Colloredo-Mansfield discusses how it was that a segment of Otavalo traders became prosperous during the 1980s and 1990s as a direct result of them travelling to Europe and the US to sell native crafts. This process had the effect of leading to a resurgence in native culture, as evidenced through traditional festivals, dress and craft production, but also resulted in a widening class divide between between poor Otavalans dependent upon farming and those who were able to maximize the value of 'authentic' rituals. It is in this context that Stillerman goes on to develop the notion of intersectionality which he argues allows for 'an integrated understanding of how class, gender, race, sexuality and age work together in shaping consumption' (2015: 190). For Stillerman the concept of intersectionality prevents us from reducing individuals to single positions and allows us to focus instead on the broader influences that may affect a person's social positions. Meyer and Milestone's (2011) discussion of advertising is equally informative insofar as they discuss the process by which the transitional norms associated with gendered advertising are being challenged: not least by the trend for men's bodies in adverts. The point here is that such advertising needs to appeal to heterosexual men without alienating them sexually in the process. The effect of forms of consumption or their representation are not always entirely predictable. Class or race, for example, do not straightforwardly determine someone's experience of consumption and this is a process that the sociology of consumption has increasingly tried to come to terms with.

AIRBNB: ESCAPE AND THE CONTEMPORARY CONSUMER

As a means of exploring some of the tensions of the contemporary consumer to which I have referred to above I want to briefly interrogate what is perhaps one of the single most important developments in the contemporary consuming experience: namely the emergence of Airbnb. Since being founded in 2008 Airbnb has emerged not only as a global phenomenon that arguably constitutes a paradigm shift in the production of tourism, but it has also fundamentally changed the nature of the relationship between the tourist industry and the consumer. And yet despite this transformation, social scientific analyses of Airbnb have tended to focus on its consequences for the so-called 'sharing economy' and for the provision of a previously unavailable entrepreneurial tourism offer. In what remains of this article I want to begin to highlight what it is the Airbnb experience means for the consumer and what that experience tells us about what it means to be a consumer in an increasingly mobile world.

In their book *Tourism Mobilities*, Sheller and Urry (2004) talk about how it is that places are 'made and remade by the mobilities and performances of tourists and workers': the extent to which 'the playfulness of place' is also about the ways in which places themselves are always 'on the move' (p. 1). From this perspective places are subject to multiple contestations. A key part of this process lies in the fantasization of place. But in contrast to a process in which brands tend to produce particular lifestyles or generic play opportunities such as theme parks, hotel offers and budget airlines, Airbnb does something very different. Although its success is at least partly dependent on the value of its umbrella brand, beneath that surface lies something different in which the tourist experience is not so much pre-fabricated or fixed but consumer-driven and created, thereby making tourist places increasingly dynamic (see Hetherington, 1997; Sheller and Urry, 2004). Airbnb manifests a unique combination of performances played out through the relationship between the consumer and the Airbnb property and its owner. For advocates of the sharing economy, Airbnb is a shining example of the economic benefit to be found in collaboration where collaboration didn't exist before. Indeed, for Slee (2015: 31), 'It has shown that a personal visit – human-level-contact – is a viable alternative to the impersonal and uniform mass-produced anonymity of the corporate tourist industry'.

The Airbnb proposition is a relatively straightforward one. The consumer goes onto the website or via the Airbnb app and checks out the available accommodation in the area or place of his or her choice. The kind of choice available to the consumer is different to what it would have been in the past because Airbnb specializes in providing non-hotel accommodation. The experience of Airbnb is dependent upon normal people opening up their spare rooms, second homes and the like, to members of the public for overnight stays. Such accommodation is competitively priced compared to the hotel sector and succeeds partly because it appears to offer something above and beyond the homogenous hotel visit. The Airbnb experience is more than just a review site: it allows the consumer to book and he or she has the confidence to do so because of the affirmations provided by the Airbnb community. After the visit is completed the property owner reviews the visitor and vice versa. It is at the review stage where the sharing economy is at its most telling. There is an unwritten obligation to be positive: to be negative would undermine the equilibrium upon which the Airbnb experience is founded.

But what is perhaps most interesting about the Airbnb experience is the *kind* of experience which it seeks to promote. To visit an Airbnb property is to experience 'real life'. The Airbnb experience is sold as an authentic experience in which the consumer becomes a resident of two communities: the Airbnb community and the community where the accommodation resides – the latter has been a key theme of Airbnb's TV and cinema advertising. A useful way of understanding all this is perhaps through the lens of the work of Colin Campbell (1987). My focus here then is on the scope for imaginary-pleasure seeking that the Airbnb experience provides (see also Urry, 2006). As Campbell puts it, '... individuals do not so much seek satisfaction from products, as pleasure from the self-illusory experiences which they construct from their associated meanings. The essential activity of consumption is thus not the actual selection, purchase or use of products, but the imaginative pleasure-seeking to which the product lends itself' (p. 89). For Campbell then pleasure is a 'quality of experience' as opposed to a state of being' (p. 60). Perhaps the key point here then is Campbell's contention that consumption isn't simply about signification and engenders feelings and desires which are in turn embodied in beliefs and values (see Dunn, 2008). For Dunn, in turn, commodities are effectively aesthetic objects: they occupy a consumer's consciousness through their materiality or sensuousness, 'Hence, explaining the attractions, motivations, and effects of consumption depends foremost on showing how commodities function as desirable aesthetic objects in the perception and imagination of consumers' (Dunn, 2008: 83). From this point of view the 'aesthetic' is to do with a notion of 'sensual experience'. The experiential nature of consumption is such that the commodities themselves do not give us pleasure, it is our experience of them that does so and it is through our daydreaming as consumers that we are self-illusionary in this way (Dunn, 2008: 101).

My contention then is that Airbnb is uniquely positioned to promote precisely this kind of consumption and that as a model for a new mode of consumption it constitutes something of a test case. The experience of arriving at a mystery property, discovering a hidden key and opening a world of escape that is yours and yours alone for the weekend is a peculiarly imagination-driven process that depends as much on the version of the place you are visiting you have in your mind as it does on the physical place set before you. Airbnb presents to the world a promise of novelty: it provides the anticipation of a unique experience: an experience that the consumer is obliged to live to the full on its receipt. To not fulfill the imagination is to be a disappointed consumer, and such a state is not something that can be countenanced in a consumer-driven society.

The Airbnb experience is in Campbell's terms a 'disillusioning' experience: by aspiring to visit a new place the consumer attaches a degree of dream pleasure to it and thus associates with the planned visit a realization of that dream. 'The visible practice of consumption is thus no more than a small part of a complex process of hedonistic behavior, the majority of which occurs in the imagination of the consumer' (1987: 89). According to Campbell then what this is not is reflective of an insatiable desire to acquire objects, it is more about people's desire to experience in reality what they have already enjoyed in their imaginations. Airbnb provides a physical space within which this appears to be possible. Airbnb presents itself as a space in which we can counteract our dissatisfaction with the everyday by convincing ourselves that it must be possible to experience something better in reality. In actual fact that point can never be reached: the Airbnb experience offers hope but not resolution. Of course, the paradoxical nature of their consumption experience, notably in the context of tourism, is not a new phenomenon. For example, Stephenson Shaffer (2004) talks about the performative nature of backpackers who engage in 'a carefully choreographed performance of a self who strives towards "authenticity"' (pp. 139–140) and yet in the process reconstructs an obligatory and thus, inevitably in some respects at least, a homogenous rite of passage. In their hunt for meaningful experiences these backpackers are in danger of emptying out the meaning of their endeavors.

It is in this light that my concerns regarding Airbnb arise. The way in which Airbnb provides its version of 'imaginary space' is to construct a space where consumption is always imaginary and yet rarely fulfilled. On the surface, the ability to consume the settings that Airbnb provides appears to be revolutionary and liberating in its effect, freeing the consumer from the constraints of McDonaldized prescription (Ritzer, 1993) – but actually it reinforces a form of control. Perhaps it is the case that Airbnb offers a paradigm shift in the nature of the production-consumption experience, and one that, on the surface at least, appears to place more power in the hands of the consumer. But there are caveats to be found here. The trust and community engendered in the Airbnb community is ultimately fabricated. It is unlikely that the average consumer engages with real life any more through Airbnb than he or she would by visiting a hotel. As Slee (2015) points out:

> Most of Airbnb's money comes from exchanges where the host and guest may never meet except to exchange a key. And if the host takes advantage of one of the cluster of management services that are growing up around Airbnb listings, even that may never happen. (pp. 37–38)

The Airbnb community is thus in itself a façade, as indeed is the sharing economy it purports to reflect. Airbnb may mimic the kinds of social intimacies we would more readily associate with the past which we aspire to rekindle: notably a society that is more connected, respectful and communicative (Botsman and Rogers, 2011), but this is in fact a marketing proposition that feeds the imagination more than it does anything to alter or to challenge the status quo. In fact, the very success of Airbnb depends on its ability to maintain that status quo. Note the endless array of press stories critiquing the social implications of the economic model Airbnb embodies, as well as the criticism that what Airbnb does threatens the sustainability of cities through the process of gentrification and the ability of owners to offer multiple accommodation options. Each one undermines the ability of people to live in the city of their choice because those who can afford a weekend visit in a luxury apartment are pricing them out of the market.

In effect then, the Airbnb narrative is on the one hand one of personal adventure and authenticity, and on the other one of corporate cynicism and smoking mirrors. What purports or at least purported to be an informal economic arrangement offering genuine experience is actually highly professionalized so that what the consumer is offered is actually a *version* of reality. In my own experience such places are often the product of the owner's amateur design imaginations: of what they imagine it is people want to consume. And of course, this is all about maximizing markets, about providing what is ultimately a homogenized experience that purports to be individually-driven. As Slee (2015) puts it, '... despite [Airbnb's] talk of community, the only logic it seems to understand is that of the free market: the right of property owners to do what they want with their property' (p. 41). Furthermore, as Botsman and Rogers (2011) point out, the myth of the sharing economy presented by Airbnb is very different to the realities that exist beneath that surface. So what does Airbnb tells us about changing forms of consumption and their sociological significance? At one level yes Airbnb presents an illusion of a sharing economy whilst extending the divisiveness of the market it has created. At another it demonstrates just how much work is to be done to understand the way in which the social relationships that underpin our consuming experiences are so tied up with the complex engineering of the self.

CONCLUSION

It would be very easy to pigeon-hole the contemporary consumer as little more than an inevitably disappointed authenticity-seeker. But consumers do not react in predictable ways, and however much we might like to generalize about the sociological significance of consumption, the consumer is always 'unmanageable' in the sense that he or she is so hard to pin down or legislate for (see Edensor, 2000). What is more, as Gabriel and Lang (2006) argue, in a world of increasing social inequality the pursuit of happiness through consumption is now a much less plausible project than it was in the past. Perhaps Bauman (1998) was right when he said that consumer choice represents the foundation of a new concept of choice in contemporary society, and that our position in society is most likely to be defined by the degree to which we are unable to take advantage of such freedoms. In this sense we are all 'flawed consumers': unable to fulfill the requirements of a society in which the symbols of consumption are so prevalent. But perhaps there is another way to look at all this. Perhaps the sociology of consumption could do more to understand the depths of meaning that are attached to the consuming experience. Consumption is not merely an act or an activity, it is a process of meaning construction that is intimately engaged with the social and cultural understandings that the individual brings to each experience (see Rakic and Chambers, 2012). Indeed, as Illouz (2009: 397) points out, '… the emotions that drive consumption or are intertwined with it, are no less the result of the imagination as the result of concrete social relationships'. And perhaps the sociology of consumption has struggled to come to terms with this tension. Ultimately, it could be said that the challenge that the sociology of consumption faces now is the challenge it faced twenty years ago. The existence of the sociology of consumption constitutes a recognition that consumption is effectively a key 'mediation phenomenon' (Holland, 1977): a focal point for unearthing and demystifying many of the uncertainties and tensions of everyday life. And yet still disciplinary boundaries continue to get in the way (see Archibald, 1976). Consumption is a deeply sociological phenomenon and yet it is so much more than that. As this Volume demonstrates, it not only represents a fundamental plank upon which our society operates but it also serves to both support and undermine human beings' existence on a daily basis. What is more, in an age where the consumer's experience in all its diverse forms appears to be more and more about survival than it is about self-expression, there is a profound need for a sociology of consumption that aspires to intervene in such a way that it not only sheds light on the nature of the consumer society in which we live, but also aims to make a genuine difference to that society in the process.

REFERENCES

Archibald, W.P. (1976) Psychology, sociology and social psychology: bad fences make bad neighbours, *British Journal of Sociology*, 27(2): 115–129.

Asano, T. (2013) Network, community and culture. In A. Elliott, M. Katagiri and A. Sawai (eds) *Japanese Social Theory: From Individualization to Globalization in Japan Today*, London: Routledge, pp. 179–195.

Baudrillard, J. (1983) *Simulations*, New York: Semiotext(e).

Bauman, Z. (1998) *Work, Consumerism and the New Poor*, Buckingham: Open University Press.

Bjur, J., Schroder, K.C., Hasebrink, U., Courtois, C., Adoni, H. and Nossek, H. (2014) Cross-media use: unfolding complexities in contemporary audiencehood. In N. Carpentier, K.C. Schroder and L. Hallett (eds) *Audience Transformations: Shifting Audience Positions in Late Modernity*, London: Routledge, pp. 15–29.

Botsman, R. and Rogers, R. (2010) *What's Mine is Yours: How Collaborative Consumption is Changing the Way We Live*, London: Collins.

Brock, T. (2017) Video consumption: the apophatic dimension, *Journal of Consumer Culture*, 17(2): 167–183.

Campbell, C. (1987) *The Romantic Ethic and the Spirit of Modern Consumerism*, Oxford: Basil Blackwell.

Colloredo-Mansfield, R. (1999) *The Native Leisure Class*, Chicago: Chicago University Press.

Dunn, R.G. (2008) *Identifying Consumption: Subjects and Objects in Consumer Society*, Philadelphia: Temple University Press.

Edensor, T. (2000) Staging tourism: tourists as performers, *Annals of Tourism Research*, 27(2): 322–344.

Edwards, T. (2000) *Contradictions of Consumption: Concepts, Practices and Politics in Consumer Society*, Buckingham: Open University Press.

Enli, G. (2015) *Mediated Authenticity: How the Media Constructs Reality*, Oxford: Peter Lang.

Gabriel, Y. and Lang, T. (2015) *The Unmanageable Consumer*, London: Sage.

Hall, S., Winlow, S. and Ancrum, C. (2008) *Criminal Identities and Consumer Culture: Crime, Exclusion and the New Culture of Narcissism*, London: Willan.

Hamilton, K. (2012) Low-income families and coping through brands: inclusion or stigma? *Sociology*, 46(1): 74–90.

Hayward, K. (2004) *City Limits: Crime, Consumer Culture and the Urban Experience*, London: Glasshouse.

Hetherington, K. (1997) In place of geometry: the materiality of place. In K. Hetherington and R. Munro (eds) *Ideas of Difference*, Oxford: Blackwell, pp. 183–199.

Holland, R. (1977) *Self and Social Context*, London: Macmillan.

Illouz, E. (2009) Emotions, imagination and consumption: a new research agenda, *Journal of Consumer Culture*, 9(3): 377–413.

Maguadda, P. (2011) When materiality 'bites back': digital music consumption practices in the age of dematerialization, *Journal of Consumer Culture*, 11(1): 15–36.

Meyer, A. and Milestone, K. (2011) *Gender and Popular Culture*, Cambridge: Polity Press.

Miles, S. (1998) *Consumerism as a Way of Life*, London: Sage.

Newell, S. (2012) *The Modernity Bluff: Crime, Consumption, and Citizenship in Côte D'Ivoire*, Chicago: University of Chicago Press.

Ogino, M. (2013) Structuralism, post-structuralism and thereafter. In A. Elliott, M. Katagiri and A. Sawai (eds) *Japanese Social Theory: From Individualization to Globalization in Japan Today*, London: Routledge, pp. 94–110.

Pine II, B.J. and Gilmore, J. (1999) *The Experience Economy: Work is Theatre and Every Business is a Stage*, Boston: Harvard Business School Press.

Rakic, T. and Chambers, D. (2012) Rethinking the consumption of places, *Annals of Tourism Research*, 39(3): 1612–1633.

Ritzer, G. (1993) *The McDonaldization of Society*, London: Pine Forge.

Ritzer, G. and Jurgenson, N. (2010) Production, consumption, prosumption: the nature of capitalism in the age of the digital 'prosumer', *Journal of Consumer Culture*, 10(1): 13–36.

Robertson, R. (2013) Prelude: risk and reflexive modernization. In A. Elliott, M. Katagiri and A. Sawai (eds) *Japanese Social Theory: From Individualization to Globalization in Japan Today*, London: Routledge, pp. 11–113.

Sheller, M. and Urry, J. (2004) *Tourism Mobilities: Places to Play, Places in Play*, London: Routledge.

Slater, J. (1997) *Consumer Culture and Modernity*, Cambridge: Polity Press.

Slee, T. (2015) *What's Yours is Mine: Against the Sharing Economy*, London: OR Books.

Stephenson Shaffer, T. (2004) Performing backpacking: constructing 'authenticity' every step of the way, *Text and Performance Quarterly*, 24(1): 139–140.

Stillerman, J. (2015) *The Sociology of Consumption: A Global Approach*, Cambridge: Polity.

Urry, J. (2006) Preface: places and performance. In C. Minca and T. Oakes (eds) *Travels in Paradox: Remapping Tourism*, Oxford: Rowman and Littlefield, pp. vii–xi.
Warde, A. (2014) After taste: culture, consumption and theories of practice, *Journal of Consumer Culture*, 14(3): 279–303.
Yates, L. (2016) Sharing, households and sustainable consumption, *Journal of Consumer Culture*, published online: September 22, DOI: https://doi.org/10.1177/1469540516668229

3

The Systems of Provision Approach to Understanding Consumption[1]

Ben Fine, Kate Bayliss and Mary Robertson

INTRODUCTION

It is now over twenty years since Fine and Leopold (1993) first detailed the systems of provision (SoP) approach. Developed as a response to traditional 'horizontal' views of consumption, whereby discipline-specific factors were used to explain consumption across a range of goods and contexts, the approach seeks to examine consumption vertically and in its concrete specificity by looking at the full chain of activities underpinning the material production and cultural significance of different goods. As such, the approach avoids over-generalising the relevance of particular factors, instead recognising that any instance of consumption is shaped by a shifting array of context-specific determinants. This requires a fundamentally interdisciplinary outlook, eclectically but systematically drawing on concepts and theories from different disciplines in an inductive fashion determined by the issue at hand.

In addition to seeking a vertical and genuinely interdisciplinary perspective on consumption, the SoP approach was motivated by a perceived need to bridge the material and the cultural, by acknowledging that discursive practices are constitutive of consumption, but that such practices are in turn constrained by material circumstances. This outlook was originally driven by dissatisfaction with both neoclassical utility theory and postmodernism, with each being overly subjectivist in its own peculiar ways. However, the approach has since been developed as part of a broader interest in material cultures and the co-constitution of consumption practices and meanings through material and cultural determinants. The SoP approach defines such determinants broadly, encompassing not just the circumstances of material production, but also the social characteristics of different consumers and the broader context within which consumption takes place. The suggestion is that the material culture of consumption needs to be located in terms of the modes of provision as a whole and not simply by virtue of the more immediate relationship between consumer and consumed. Accordingly, what was eventually to become the 10Cs approach to the material culture of consumption was developed.

This chapter elaborates on the development of the SoP approach in terms of these specific theoretical stances. But this contribution is also concerned to push the study of consumption further in two otherwise heavily neglected areas. One is to branch out to incorporate public consumption, an area traditionally neglected in consumption studies, though achieving growing prominence by virtue of the spread of commodification through privatisation in the neoliberal period. The other – also a product of the neoliberal era – is to address the increasing influence of finance and financialisation on consumption practices and consumers. For, whilst the impact of financialisation has not been overlooked in the literature, its analysis has tended to be situated at a general level, emphasising consumption on credit (cards or mortgages, for example), or the creation or consolidation of new neoliberal subjectivities around the financial (mis)calculations of households in pursuit of aspirations to consume – admirably summed up in the notion of privatised Keynesianism by Crouch (2009). Unsurprisingly, we take a more nuanced view in light of the SoP approach, viewing the impact of financialisation on (the material culture of) consumption as highly differentiated from one item of consumption to another (and, indeed, from one country to another).

This chapter is structured as follows. In the next section we set out the origins and content of the approach, emphasising its development from critique of rational choice theory and postmodernism to become a framework for investigating material cultures. In the subsequent section we outline how the approach is applied in practice, incorporating a discussion of what we have termed the 10Cs, showing how these are used to characterise consumption cultures. In the penultimate section we look at some existing applications of the approach and make the case for extending it to public consumption and financialisation. The final section concludes.

ELABORATING THE SOP APPROACH

Background

The SoP approach was in part a response to the perceived collective failings of consumer theory across the social sciences. For example, the longstanding analysis of consumption around mainstream economics, based on utility-maximising individuals, was rejected by Fine and Leopold (1993) for its narrowness and reductionism. Differences in consumption across goods were at most accounted for by derived elasticities of income and prices but without otherwise explaining why variations occur or how they change over time and place. Producers (and production) might be deemed to play an independent role in consumption through manipulative advertising in shaping consumer preferences, or through imperfectly competitive pricing in distorting their fulfilment. But the burgeoning concerns over postmodernist subjectivities, let alone more traditional determinants of consumption across the social sciences, such as emulation and distinction, remained notable for their absence.

These were taken as a critical point of departure by Fine and Leopold. Whilst for neoclassical economics, the subjectivity of the consumer has been tied to a mechanically applied optimisation of a given utility function (across objects of consumption with given meanings), the postmodern consumer is subjectively capable of endless and unlimited reinvention of the objects of consumption and the subject's own identity. In this parallel universe to orthodox economics, reference to the material properties (and provisioning) of commodities tends to evaporate by giving way to deconstruction of the meanings of consumption to consumers created through their own inventiveness in construal. But, for Fine and Leopold, the subjective interpretations of consumption associated with the rampant postmodernist attention to symbolic meanings were themselves interpreted as being negligent of both material and social determinants of those meanings.

This, then, sets the background in general terms of the state of consumer theory in the early 1990s when the SoP approach was initiated. Across the two extremes of neoclassical economics and postmodernism, Fine and Leopold also found a common set of deficiencies shared by consumer theory more generally. First, the study of consumption had been heavily organised around a disciplinary division of labour to the extent that one or more 'horizontal' theories were applied within each discipline – utility theory for economics, semiotics for postmodernist study, emulation and distinction for sociology, and so on, usually with specific examples of consumption taken as a universal analytical norm. It was no accident, for example, that the postmodernist invention of the deconstructing consumer should focus on the more fantastic as opposed to the more mundane items of consumption and those subject to heavy advertising or cultural prominence, the better to be able to provide the raw materials for deconstruction. Other approaches also tended to presume that specific factors of interest would be of general applicability across consumption instead of asking whether some factors are significant for some consumption goods and consumers in some instances but not in others (although this was, unsurprisingly, a key element for those engaged practically in studying consumer behaviour in general and the impact of advertising and marketing in particular). In formulating the SoP approach, the idea was rejected that these separate, generally mutually inconsistent (by method and concept), and unworldly, horizontal theories could be stacked to give a general theory universally applicable to all goods.

Second, then, it was recognised that the varieties of factors that make up the study of consumption across the social sciences could be integrated, if not, as previously indicated, as a general all-encompassing theory (in some respects, the dream of those engaging practically or academically in consumer studies in management, business and commerce). Instead, focusing on particular commodities, the SoP approach proceeds inductively according to the weight of presence, mode of combination and specific (historical and social) context involved. There are, for example, different issues for consumption by reference to gender, not least in clothing, and the factor of fashion correspondingly has a different presence for men than for women. Further, the water system is different from the housing system by virtue of what is provided as well as by national and other contextual considerations.

The idea that consumption needed to be understood more closely in relation to its attachment to production was beginning to emerge across different fields in the late 1980s. In the production of food, the notion of commodity chains that linked consumption to food processing, distribution and agriculture was developing as a way to make sense of the food industry (Lang and Wiggins, 1985, cited in Jackson et al., 2004). This chain approach could be extended beyond simple producer–consumer relationships to a wider exploration of corporate power and agricultural production systems.

In housing in the UK, the work of Michael Ball (1983) established a link between the role of landed property and housing tenure. Ball persuasively argued that these issues needed to be located in relation not only to one another but also to the chain of activity running from access to landed property through the processes underpinning provision of, and access to, housing by consumers. Ball's structures of provision approach originally served to argue that researchers interested in the incidence and impact of state subsidies on housing outcomes, especially distribution, needed to take into account considerations beyond tenure balance because the way that housing was provided determined the characteristics of different tenures. Such an approach to the housing system suggested that other items of consumption should be similarly regarded as belonging to integral chains of activity that were specific to themselves.

The diverse elements that combine to shape consumption are brought together for the SoP approach. By adopting a 'vertical' analytical framework, the chain of activity connecting production to consumption for particular commodities becomes decisive in differentiating between items of consumption. Distinctions need to be made not only in their material properties and meanings to consumers, but also in how they are provided. In a nutshell, energy, housing, fashion and food *systems* are all distinctive by virtue of the structures, relations, processes and agencies of provision of which they are comprised.

SYSTEMS OF PROVISION IN DETAIL

Each SoP consists of the multiplicity of factors that lead to and shape consumption. These are wide-ranging and will vary across commodities, locations and over time. More specifically, a SoP can be specified as the combination of the material processes of provision and the material cultures associated with the commodity, which uniquely engage with one another in specific instances, making context paramount in specifying SoPs.

Consumers enter SoPs not as the representative agents found in neoclassical economics, nor as limitlessly versatile postmodern subjectivities; rather, consumers are differentiated by social characteristics that have a bearing on consumption. Thus, patterns of consumption will be affected by gender, age, income level, location, occupation and (un)employment, race and ethnicity, and so on, but in different ways and with different outcomes according to the specific SoP itself. We need to bring such social categories to bear in identifying norms of consumption specific to each SoP, and in explaining how they are reproduced or transformed.

One aspect of such norms is systematic patterns of consumption themselves, by level and quality of consumption across different social, and not just income, strata. This involves what might otherwise be called a standard of living or, more exactly, livings, contingent upon who gets how much of what. Standards of living and consumption both rise and shift with affluence and other factors, with the latter demonstrated in the wake of technological change (and electronic goods, for example, not least mobile phones and the like).

A second aspect is the material culture of consumption attached to each SoP with the meanings of consumption to consumers, variously distributed across different social strata, etc, just as the variability of levels and quality of consumption themselves and the contexts within which such consumption occurs. One of the purposes of the SoP approach is to draw out how these two different aspects of consumption norms are related to one another. Examples include questions such as: Why are there gender differences in what is consumed and how it is interpreted? Why does owner-occupation become the preferred form of housing tenure? And what are the implications for the provisioning and meaning of consumption with the privatisation of public services, on the one hand, not least as they become purchased through credit, on the other?

Of course, such questions are far from new and were, to some extent, the meat and drink, of postmodernist studies in deconstructing the meanings of consumption. Significantly, Fine (2002), in thoroughly extending Fine and Leopold (1993), takes account of developments in the field of consumer studies, with the SoP approach increasingly influenced by, and contributing to, what can be termed the study of the material culture of consumption. For this, how consumption is furnished is perceived to interact with how it is interpreted.[2] With reference to the study of consumption, material culture has emerged as in other fields, not least in response to the rise of the material practices and consequences of neoliberalism and a corresponding waning of the influence of postmodernism. Discursive practices have become increasingly perceived to be a consequence of material circumstances (although also giving rise to a proliferation and sequence of post-postmodernisms of various hues). As a consequence, the SoP approach has no longer relied upon its origins by simply presenting itself in terms of departure from the two subjectivist extremes of rational choice and postmodernism. It has also focused on how to address the relationship between the material and the cultural in terms of the practices and meanings associated with consumption and the relationships between the two. It is not just the factors involved in the delivery of a service or the inputs into a good that constitute the SoP; also relevant is the culture and meaning with which a good or commodity is associated, for both consumers and providers alike. Goods and services have cultural significance associated with modes of provision, as has been readily recognised, for example, in terms of the meanings of water contingent upon public or private delivery systems (which are themselves each subject to considerable variation). Thus, water provision sits astride discourses around basic needs, human rights and poverty alleviation as well as cost recovery, commercialisation and privatisation (see for example Ahlers, 2010; Bakker, 2007; Swyngedouw, 2005; UN-Water, 2012; UNDP, 2006).

A key example of the way in which our relationship with goods, services and commodities is culturally and socially mutually dependent is illustrated in the paradox of the recent parallel expansion of both unhealthy diets and healthy eating campaigns, not least in light of the 'epidemic' of obesity. This demonstrates that there is considerable complexity in the way in which information is translated into 'knowledge' and culture, and the ways in which these turn into behaviour. The provision of a good or a service or of information does not necessarily mean these will be used as intended or anticipated. The SoP approach recognises that the cultural perceptions and identities of the users will be significant in the consumption and production processes, and these are heavily influenced if not rigidly determined by the material practices attached to the corresponding SoP, and not simply at the point of consumption itself.

The cultural content, or system, attached to a good is related not only to the material system of provision but also to wider cultural influences (for example, gender, class, age and nationality). Each SoP is attached to its own integral cultural system and this cultural system derives content from each and every material aspect of the SoP but in ways that are not rigidly predetermined nor necessarily immediately obvious. What is absented can be as striking as, for example, the simple knowledge in the case of water in England and Wales that almost as much as one-third of bills go towards paying interest and dividends (Bayliss, 2014). Indeed, much consumer politics targets bringing knowledge of the how of production (such as sweated or child labour) to the attention of the consumer!

In such analysis, consumers are acknowledged to be reflexive. They are not passive recipients either of what they consume or how they perceive it. As a way of engaging with the material culture of consumption, Fine (2013b) grouped the characteristics of material culture under ten headings (known as the 10Cs) as follows, with these being mutually constitutive of corresponding cultural systems of SoPs in diverse and specific ways.

1. *Constructed* – the cultural systems attached to consumption are constructed in that they are influenced by the material practices of the SoP. Commodities have associated meanings for consumers, which may be variably responsive to what they know of the chain of provision, and its distinctive material properties. These may also be subject to change and to manipulation (for example, drinking a particular brand of bottled water may project a certain image as well as quenching one's thirst; buying a house in some locations may be a financial investment as well as a place to live).
2. *Construed* – objects of consumption are endowed with qualities construed by consumers. These can float free from the material properties of the (provision of the) objects of consumption themselves but are framed by the SoP. The process of construal is influenced by a multiplicity of factors and these are contextually driven. Sources of experience and knowledge are reacted to or against and imbued with meaning rather than simply received passively by the consumer. Status, emulation and distinction are longstanding examples of socially-determined construal of consumption, but these wax and wane with material provision itself.
3. *Commodified* – to greater or lesser degrees, cultures may be influenced by commodification, even if the good is not. In the UK, even supposedly non-commodified provision, such as the health service, may be understood in commodified terms with, for example, pressure for greater cost efficiency. Either non-commercialised aspects of a good can be used as a selling point (for example, good as home-made) or, the opposite, in claiming to be at the forefront of technology (currently common in motor cars). Thus, the processes of commodification serve to frame how the commodity is construed (for example, value for money) as well as alternative ways of thinking and interpreting what is consumed (as in some sense embodying qualities that are removed from the market pursuit of profitability).
4. *Conforming* – regardless of what choices the consumer makes, meanings to them are influenced by the circumstances of provision, whether social, as opposed to private, housing is seen as a right or as a dependency for example. To coin a phrase, consumers construe but not in circumstances made by themselves.

5 *Contextual* – cultures of consumption differ in time and place, and what is consumed is not only located in specific circumstances (high or low price, good or bad quality) but are associated with particular and variable meanings to the consumer (for example, an item of clothing may have different significance depending on the situation). One person's necessity may be another's luxury and the distinction may change over time, location and across income levels.
6 *Contradictory* – different agents and forces compete to give content to the cultural systems and these may provide a stimulus in opposite directions (for example, compulsions to spend and to save; to eat and to diet).
7 *Chaotic* – material cultures draw together (or not) a multiplicity of practices and influences across a multiplicity of dimensions which are reflected on by households going about their daily life, and so will be riddled with inconsistencies if not incoherence. This does not mean that there is no rationale but that these may differ and lead to tensions with unpredictable, occasionally extreme, outcomes, as with eating disorders, credit card abuse, addiction, and so on.
8 *Closed* – there is unequal participation in SoPs and unequal and differentiated roles in constructing cultures (for example, in the financial sector, while everyone may be involved, the process of intervention is both by and for an increasingly powerful financial elite with a corresponding loss of democratic accountability and rise in inequality; and for trade-marking, standards, branding, regulations, etc., all shape cultures, but only a select few are involved in their making).
9 *Contested* – different cultures of consumption may come into conflict, for example with the Occupy movement or with global protests against the privatisation of water. Contestation may also occur in terms of the conditions attached to the material practices along the SoP chain.
10 *Collective* – contestation, like provision, is usually collective. While individuals may carry out acts of dissent, collective action is likely to be a more successful form of contestation but, more generally, consumption is not a simple act of individual subjectivity.

The relevance and usefulness of the different 10Cs for dissecting material cultures will vary depending on the type of good, the SoP and the reason for which it is being investigated.

APPLYING THE SOP APPROACH

While the SoP approach offers advantages over traditional approaches to consumer theory, by virtue of being firmly anchored in real-world practices, it is also demanding in requiring the specification of the complexity and diversity of goods and of the societies in which they are consumed. When it comes to practical application, the SoP approach does not offer a blueprint because, by their nature, SoPs are unique. The SoP approach, then, is necessarily heavily inductive in application, leaving researchers to identify the nature, scope and content of particular SoPs in practice – do we have a food system and, if so, at regional, national or global levels, or separate food systems across these locations and different foods?

Given its inductive nature, the application of the SoP approach in practice is not simple, not least in identifying where one SoP begins and another ends. Indeed, it is possible to question whether the approach is legitimate at all given the interactions across different SoPs, whether within broader groups, such as food systems, or narrower groups, for example sugar, meat and dairy systems. In a sense, though, this is to revisit the horizontal/vertical dualism in the study of consumption. This is itself acknowledged within the SoP approach that both seeks to identify integral forms of provisioning whilst also acknowledging that these interact with one another. SoPs also share common horizontal factors, even if integrating them differently in extent and manner, at both national and international levels and across conditions such as equity and quality of provision, labour market conditions and macroeconomic impacts.

In principle, each SoP needs to be addressed by reference to the material and cultural specificities that take full account of the whole chain of activity, bringing together production, distribution (and access), and the nature and influence of the conditions under which these occur. This is not to say that *every* element in the chain of provision plus every relevant contextual or 'horizontal' factor needs to be thoroughly investigated before SoPs can be identified and specified. In practice, the way SoPs are identified will depend on the question at hand. Investigating sources of salmonella in chicken points to the poultry system, whereas diet as a contributory factor to an epidemic of obesity suggests attention to the food system as a whole.

For research purposes it is usually necessary to shine a spotlight on the elements of the SoP that are of particular relevance to the issue under consideration. Recent applications of the approach, for example to housing, Robertson (2014) and water, Bayliss (2014), have focused on finance and financialisation, attempting to redress the relative neglect of the growing encroachment of these on social and economic life in analyses of consumption, although there is a healthy new field studying the financialisation of everyday life (Bayliss et al., 2017; Fine, 2013a; Langley, 2008; van der Zwan, 2014). In investigating housing and financialisation, some elements of the housing SoP will be more relevant than others (which is compatible with recognising interlinkages and mutual determination), while other important elements of the SoP (such as Housing Associations, DIY, repair and maintenance, architecture, etc.) are less relevant for many issues. Similarly, an assessment of the financialisation of water will focus on the relations between agents in the context of the flow of funds, including investment, pricing, debt and dividends. In contrast, an investigation into, say, environmental issues relating to water would focus on different elements of the SoP.

In specifying SoPs, we draw freely upon standard ways of conceptualising and theorising across the social sciences by appeal to the following general, overlapping categories:

a *Structures* – broadly, this includes the historically evolved and socially-specific institutional forms of provisioning, not least patterns of ownership, control and delivery. There may be structural divisions between public and private supply as well as demand, structures in access by price and quality, and so on. Other elements that shape the structures of provision include the institutional mechanisms of provision including the regulatory and legal framework.

b *Processes* – each SoP is shaped by the interaction of the activities of labour and consumers, of service providers, of the state, but also by wider processes such as commodification, decentralisation, globalisation, commercialisation, and so on. It may be that a public sector structure of provision is subject to the process of privatisation so it is important to specify the dynamics of each SoP, how its structures and processes interact and may be in tension across one another.

c *Agents/agencies* – SoPs are determined by the participants in the processes of production through to consumption. Incorporated are those who produce and those who consume, but also wider bodies such as trade unions, consumer groups, regulators and those who affect delivery of finance, investment, technology, and so on. Agencies reflect and interact with both structures and processes, again either reproducing or transforming in tension or conformity with one another. The entry point for analysing the SoP is typically the consumer who will engage with other agents in diverse ways, depending on the good or service in question. For example, the way a consumer buys food will be different from purchasing a house or paying a water bill. And these will vary across location and over time.

d *Relations* – structures, processes and agents/agencies are necessarily far from neutral, contingent upon who exercises power, and how, and with what purpose (and meaning to participants). So the relations upon which SoPs are founded are differentiated by the roles of capital (or state as employer) and labour in production and other commercial (or non-commercial) operations through to the relational norms by social characteristics that are attached to levels and meanings of consumption. Significantly, the relations attached to and underpinning SoPs are crucial in understanding what and how conflicts arise and how they are or are not resolved. For example, the pricing decisions of a private producer will be shaped by the activities of competitors, by labour issues, the regulatory framework and, as a condition of survival, the imperative of profitability. The same criteria do not always apply in the case of public provision, and the ways in which the criteria are specified and contested are also different.

APPLICATIONS AND EXTENSIONS

Existing Applications and Support

Over a decade ago the SoP approach was described by Leslie and Reimer (1999, p. 405) as 'perhaps the most comprehensive elaboration of production-consumption relations', and has also been seen as one of the main approaches to the study of consumption, and cited as such in Jackson et al. (2004, p. 8). Early applications of the approach to food and fashion (Fine and Leopold, 1993; Fine et al., 1996; Fine, 1998) have, for example, been supplemented by work on home furnishings by Leslie and Reimer (1999), fur coats by Skov (2005), denim jeans by Brooks (2015), boy's clothes in late-Victorian England by Rose (2010), food supply chains by Seyfang (2008) and obesity by Greenhalgh (2014).

The framework was also adopted, and succinctly summarised, in a report by the OECD (2002) in analysing consumption patterns of energy, water and waste management, with a view to improving sustainability. The study aimed to approach environmental policy by considering the whole system of provision rather than simply looking at adjusting consumption patterns, stating:

> The systems of provision approach analyses consumption as an active process, with actors seeking certain lifestyles, and constructing their identity by selective consumption and practices. The 'systems of provision' is defined as the chain that unites particular systems of production with particular systems of consumption, focusing on the dynamics of the different actors (producers, distributors, retailers as well as consumers). In this light, it becomes clear that by the way governments design and transform energy, water and waste systems can either enable or obstruct household behaviour towards sustainable consumption. (p. 8)

For the OECD, consumer behaviour regarding the environmental impact is shaped by beliefs, norms and values within households and embedded in social practices. The 2002 Report continues:

> The *systems of provision* framework for understanding consumption patterns stresses the importance of exploring the mechanisms that shape everyday practices related to commodities and

> services and the extent to which they can be seen to support or impede sustainable consumption behaviour. In this light, household consumption is not the sum of individual behavioural patterns, each consciously motivated and evaluated by the actor. Instead, household consumption is a whole set of behavioural practices that are common to other households … They are social practices carried out by applying sets of rules and shared norms. They are also connected to production and distribution systems (technological and infrastructure network) that enable certain lifestyles that connect consumers to one another. (p. 8)

This application of the SoP approach to understanding the environmental impacts of energy and consumption is taken further in the work of Van Vliet, Chappells and Shove (2005) and is also a theme of the work of DEMAND, one of six centres funded by UK Research Councils to address end-use energy demand reduction.[3] Other emerging applications include infrastructure (Brown and Robertson, 2014), transport (Williams, 2014) and sustainable consumption (Spaargarn, 2003).

Incorporating the Public Sector

Evidently, the remit of the SoP approach is expanding from its initial focus on the provision of food, clothing and other sectors and issues in the context of capitalist commodity production for private consumption. The earlier narrowness of the application of the SoP approach in part reflected the limitations of consumer theory in its overgeneralisation from particular types or aspects of consumption and a tendency to exclude consumption deriving from state-provided services. These traditionally were seen as part of social policy or the welfare state and, hence, distinct from consumption as such.

More recently, the application of the SoP approach has been expanded to include the provision of public goods and services, dubbed public sector SoPs (PSSoPs). The innovation in this approach is the application of SoP to areas which do not traditionally form part of consumption studies and which have often been provided by the state. Public or collective consumption, addressed in Fine (2002), has to some degree been overlooked because it did not meet the ethos of the subjectivities of the postmodern consumer. This is in part because it raises particular challenges where consumption is not necessarily commodified (and extension of the SoP approach to non-commodity production is itself engaged cautiously), and in part because of the paradoxical consequence of consumption becoming public, leading to it no longer being seen as consumption as such, most notably in its becoming part of the welfare state (as with health, education, public housing, etc.) (Fine, 2005).

However, to some extent, the latter aspect has been thrust into prominence with the privatisation of PSSoPs, the commercialisation and (re)commodification of state provision, and the neo-liberalisation of consumption, indeed of everyday life, often with a corresponding recasting of the patient, student, tenant, etc., as client or consumer. Clearly, consumer studies cannot broach such issues unless it allows for transitions between forms of consumption (from the public to the private sector, for example, against the erstwhile movement in the opposite direction with welfarism), both materially (how provision occurs) and culturally (how provision is understood). This is all itself part and parcel of a deeper transformation in modern capitalism, associated with the neo-liberal period (and consumer) in which *financialisation* has come to the fore (see below).

For orthodox consumer theory, effectively all government provision tends to be seen as equivalent to private provision or seen as distinct from (private) consumption altogether by being alternatively designated as social policy and/or as belonging to the welfare state. But such goods and services can also be understood as being attached to their own SoPs. A theory of social policy must accommodate a variety of structural determinants and how they interact across structures, agencies, processes, relations and institutions to give rise to a diversity of shifting outcomes.

However, virtually all SoPs necessarily incorporate some element of state involvement or regulation as even private provision cannot prevail in a totally disembodied market. The extent of public sector involvement varies considerably across countries even for the same good. Thus, for example, water is provided entirely by private companies at present in England and Wales but is subject to state regulation of tariffs and quality. Other countries have water delivery services that remain entirely within the public domain.

The extent of state involvement varies, then, not just in terms of provision but also with the state as regulator and/or provider of finance. The state can be involved in a variety of ways along the chain of provision, reflecting both material and cultural, including political, factors. These have been expressed traditionally in terms such as aspirations for universal coverage (as with health, education and housing) or as a response to market imperfections whether as externalities or economies of scale and scope. For many (PS)SoPs, with the objective of universal access or provision, there are significant issues of production and distribution, concerning, for example, spatial differentiation in provision.

The essence of the SoP approach can be applied to public as with private consumption in that each of the elements of a SoP is attached to an integral and distinctive system – the health system, the education system, and so on. Modes of provision themselves are attached to particular cultural associations and predispositions, with, for example, certain preconceptions associated with the suitability or otherwise of privately provided education or health services (attitudes that do themselves have to be contextualised and explained).

Recognising diversity allows for greater understanding of the issues which are historically-specific and depend on comparative location. This stands in stark contrast with orthodox economics, which interprets decisions over the respective roles of the public and private sectors in terms of market and state failures. In orthodox economics, for example, the supposed presence of what may be termed externalities may be deemed to require state regulation. However, the nature of such 'failures' is itself sector-specific and requires a deconstruction of the nature and attributes of a good or service. Also needed is an understanding of the structures, relations, processes and agencies from production through to consumption that give rise to what are, or are not, deemed to be or to count as externalities (see below).

Finance, Financialisation and (PS)SoPs

If the provision of public goods and services has been significantly altered in recent years by privatisation, with consequent and varied impacts on consumption, one pervasive, though differentiated, attribute of privatisation has been the increased role and influence of finance in social and economic provisioning – a phenomenon captured by the term 'financialisation' – for details on financialisation and its material culture, see Fine (2013a). The SoP approach, by incorporating analysis of structures and processes, is well equipped to address these changing modes and patterns of production and consumption, and the interaction between them.

With neoliberalism in general, and privatisation in different forms in particular, finance has become increasingly prominent in accounts of SoPs, affecting private consumption (not least in the use of credit as a means to fund) and state provision (extent and forms of state financing, for example). Where there is a perceived welfare element to delivery, the issue of finance inevitably raises corresponding issues of subsidy and equity that are liable to be contested. But it would be inappropriate to confine such issues to their redistributive role alone. As is readily apparent, the extent of privatisation and financialisation of state provision is highly diverse across sectors and countries. So there is differentiation by these factors alone in the SoPs. But, equally, how such differences in these factors affect outcomes is diverse, contingent upon how they are located within the SoP as a whole. There have been, for example, differences in mortgage finance across countries and differences in how these have affected overall levels of, and access to, housing provision. Locating SoPs within the context of social policy brings in wider issues, such as income transfers (or subsidies including tax relief and means tests), but state financing features in the delivery of many goods, not just social policy, including, for example, agriculture. Bringing SoP analysis into areas with state financing and subsidy requires inquiry into the role of the state and the nature of its redistributive and other functions.

Along with chains of production, the chains of finance are also significant within SoPs. For example, privatisation has been promoted as a source of additional investment finance. However, private investment can be costly for the state due to the need to repay private financiers with a profit margin. The UK experience of the Private Finance Initiative shows how private capital has benefited greatly from the subcontracting of services that were previously provided by the state (Vecchi et al., 2013). Finance is a major factor in the relations within and across the different elements of SoPs. The presence or intervention of finance shapes processes of provision and the behaviour of other agents. More than this, however, financial agencies are often proactive in trying to shape SoPs in favourable directions, as is most obviously demonstrated by the aggressive promotion of owner-occupation and mortgages by the US subprime mortgage lenders.

Financialisation in the past three decades has transformed public provision in many sectors and locations into a private asset, from the sale of social housing to the privatisation of water. The result is that provision is subject to the vagaries of stockholder and asset value, which has encouraged speculation, sell-offs, and sub-contracting at the expense of direct production. Nonetheless, the impact of financialisation has been different across and within SoPs. For housing for example, the rise of mortgage finance and owner-occupation has been pervasive, although the extent has been uneven in itself and in its impact upon forms, levels and distribution of housing. With the supply of water in England and Wales, the financialisation of ownership of provision has gone more or less unnoticed by consumers. The commodity-specific outlook of the SoP approach makes it well equipped to comprehend such variegation.

There is, furthermore, some purchase in addressing social policy (and its privatisation) not only where there is material provision (as with education, housing, etc.) but also where there is not, other than indirectly, as with pension funds and social security for example. This can be done, though, in a sense, by 'top-slicing' the SoP approach and applying it without the underpinnings of the sectorally-specific system of provision itself. This depends on whether two crucial but mutually dependent elements of the (PS)SoP approach can be deployed in isolation from consumption itself. These are the appeal to consumption 'norms' and the application of the 10Cs in addressing the cultures of social policy. In the case of pensions, for example, although not directly related to consumption as opposed to sources of revenue to fund it, pension norms and pension cultures can both be examined through the SoP approach, not least as state and collective forms of provision have given way to the private and individualised (and the corresponding creation of financial citizens and responsibilities). Pensions shift in how they are provided, who gets what and how this is perceived in terms of collective and individual responsibilities.[4]

Such an emphasis upon the SoP approach for social policy, especially pension provision, has the advantage of critically departing from the two main ways of approaching social policy currently – the welfare regime approach of Esping-Andersen (1990) and the new welfare economics arising out of mainstream, imperfect-information economics (with each emphasising risk in its own way).[5] From the perspective of the SoP approach to social policy, both of these suffer, if in very different ways, from unduly homogenising over contextually-specific policies and practices that are differentiated by programme and country. This is so whether by appeal to ill-fitting ideal types of welfare regimes or more or less efficient incorporation of marginalised if optimising individuals into a situation of one type of market imperfection or another. Moreover, both implicitly eschew earlier political economy approaches to social policy and the welfare state that locate it in terms of the contradictory tensions between and within economic and social reproduction.

CONCLUSION

The SoP approach encompasses a considerably broader frame of analysis for consumption than most sector-specific research (and, in many ways, the approach offers a synthesis of such research, or at least of the factors covered by it, in focusing upon the rooted realities underpinning consumption and its cultures). It places consumption on the broader terrain of provisioning, where it belongs, particularly if we are to understand the shifting incidence and integration of the public and the private in norms of consumption and the corresponding impact of financialisation on who gets to consume what, how and with what meanings.

By locating consumption in the context of a chain of processes and structures brought about by relations between agents, the SoP approach opens the way for a more grounded interpretation of consumption, including policy impact/outcomes. First, SoPs are complex and they are context- and sector-specific, integrating relations across a multiplicity of agents with a diversity of structures, relations and processes. Each SoP is unique but that is not to say that there are not cross-cutting themes that can be observed, for example, in relation to financialisation. Although, in principle, the SoP approach displays some degree of neutrality towards the theory that should be deployed, and allows for theoretical differences across those who deploy it, the approach is not without theoretical implications. These include a commitment to systemic, interdisciplinary analysis that is able to finesse the relationship between theory and specificity.

Second, the material culture of a commodity clearly affects consumption patterns due to the different material nature of different goods as well as the cultural values attached to them. Yet, major ideological shifts, for example, towards greater individualisation of society and expanded presence and influence of finance have influence across numbers of SoPs.

Third, policy outcomes are case-specific. The complex web of structures, agents, processes and relations means that the same policy will lead to different outcomes in each context, depending on the prevailing SoP in which it is implemented.

Fourth, history is significant. The prevailing state of affairs rests heavily on past forms of provision and the way in which these have informed the continuing evolution of both material and cultural aspects of provision.

Fifth, the state has a multi-faceted role in incorporating diverse agencies including branches of government, from central to local. Its influence goes beyond the obvious interventions such as sector policy, encompassing a range of policy channels, including environmental and financial legislation. Privatisation does not reduce the role of the state but changes it, usually from that of direct provider to regulator and enabler. State subsidies and cross-subsidies, sometimes implicit, affect the social equity of policy outcomes.

Finally, privatisation and financialisation are transforming consumption in the UK and elsewhere, making their incorporation into consumption studies imperative. Goods production and service delivery are now subject to the vagaries of shareholders that are interested in asset values, from the sale of social housing to the privatisation of water. Rather than serving consumption as such, pursuit of profitability is diverted towards financial engineering.

The SoP approach received considerable critical acclaim when first applied to the food and clothing sectors in the 1990s. Broadening the scope to what is traditionally known as the public sector can further our understanding of the parameters that shape the SoPs, with significant insight into the way in which these affect outcomes, particularly with regard to social equity, with implications for social policy. Application of the approach can be used to deepen understanding of the profound implications for consumption of privatisation and financialisation and situate these in the wider context of economic and social reproduction.

Notes

1 Research for this paper was supported by the project Financialisation, Economy, Society and Sustainable Development (FESSUD), which is funded by the European Union under Framework Programme 7 [contract number 266800]. See http://fessud.eu/

2 For more on the material culture of financialisation, see the Special Issue introduced by Bayliss et al. (2017).

3 www.demand.ac.uk

4 Note that, despite being vital to the consumption of a major section of the population, pensions have been too mundane to be the subject of consumer theory!

5 See Fine (2014).

REFERENCES

Ahlers, R. (2010) 'Fixing and Nixing: The Politics of Water Privatization' *Review of Radical Political Economics* 42(2), pp. 213–230.

Bakker, K. (2007) *An Uncooperative Commodity: Privatizing Water in England and Wales*, Oxford: Oxford University Press.

Ball, M. (1983) *Housing Policy and Economic Power: The Political Economy of Owner Occupation*, London: Methuen.

Bayliss, K. (2014) 'The Financialisation of Water in England and Wales' FESSUD Working Paper Series, No. 52, http://fessud.eu/wp-content/uploads/2015/03/Case-study-the-financialisation-of-Water-in-England-and-Wales-Bayliss-working-paper-REVISED_annexes-working-paper-52.pdf

Bayliss, K., B. Fine and M. Robertson (2017) 'Introduction to Special Issue on the Material Cultures of Financialisation' *New Political Economy* 22(4), pp. 355–370.

Brooks, A. (2015) 'Systems of Provision: Fast Fashion and Jeans' *Geoforum* 63(July), pp. 36–39.

Brown, A. and M. Robertson (2014) *Economic Evaluation of Systems of Infrastructure Provision: Concepts, Approaches, Methods* iBuild/Leeds Report, https://research.ncl.ac.uk/ibuild/outputs/9940_iBuild_report_v6.pdf

Crouch, C. (2009) 'What Will Follow the Demise of Privatised Keynesianism?' *The Political Quarterly* 8(S1), pp. S302–S315.

Esping-Andersen, G. (1990) *The Three Worlds of Welfare Capitalism*, Princeton: Princeton University Press.

Fine, B. (1998) *The Political Economy of Diet, Health and Food Policy*, London: Routledge.

Fine, B. (2002) *The World of Consumption: The Cultural and Material Revisited*, London: Routledge.

Fine, B. (2005) 'Addressing the Consumer' in Trentmann (ed.) (2005).

Fine, B. (2013a) 'Towards a Material Culture of Financialisation', FESSUD Working Paper Series, No. 15, http://fessud.eu/wp-content/uploads/2013/04/Towards-a-Material-Culture-of-Financialisation-FESSUD-Working-Paper-15.pdf

Fine, B. (2013b) 'Consumption Matters' *Ephemera* 13(2), pp. 217–248, http://www.ephemerajournal.org/contribution/consumption-matters

Fine, B. (2014) 'The Continuing Enigmas of Social Policy' prepared for the UNRISD project on Towards Universal Social Security in Emerging Economies, UNRISD Working Paper 2014-10, http://www.unrisd.org/Fine

Fine, B. and E. Leopold (1993) *The World of Consumption*, London: Routledge.

Fine, B., M. Heasman and J. Wright (1996) *Consumption in the Age of Affluence: The World of Food*, London: Routledge.

Greenhalgh, J. (2014) 'A Systems of Provision Perspective on Obesity' Media Rhetoric, Centre for Health, Technologies, and Social Practice, University of Leeds, http://thesp.leeds.ac.uk/2014/04/greenhalgh-a-systems-of-provision-perspective-on-obesity-media-rhetorics/

Healey, M. and B. Ilbery (eds) (1985) *The Industrialisation of the Countryside*, Norwich: Short Run Press.

Jackson, P., P. Russell and N. Ward (2004) 'Commodity Chains and the Politics of Food' Cultures of Consumption, and ESRC-AHRB Research Programme, Working Paper, No. 18, http://www.consume.bbk.ac.uk/working_papers/jackson.doc

Lang, T. and P. Wiggins (1985) 'The Industrialisation of the UK Food System: From Production to Consumption' in Healey and Ilbery (eds) (1985).

Langley, P. (2008) *The Everyday Life of Global Finance: Saving and Borrowing in Anglo-America*, Oxford: Oxford University Press.

Leslie, D. and S. Reimer (1999) 'Spatializing Commodity Chains' *Progress in Human Geography* 23(3), pp. 401–420.

OECD (2002) 'Sector Case Studies Series Household Energy & Water Consumption and Waste Generation: Trends, Environmental Impacts and Policy Responses' Report by Working Party on National Environmental Policy, Organisation for Economic Cooperation and Development, Paris.

Robertson, M. (2014) 'Case Study: Finance and Housing Provision in Britain' FESSUD Working Paper Series No. 51, http://fessud.eu/wp-content/uploads/2013/04/Case-Study_-Finance-and-Housing-Provision-in-Britain-working-paper-51.pdf

Rose, C. (2010) *Making, Selling and Wearing Boy's Clothes in Late-Victorian England*, Aldershot: Ashgate.

Seyfang, G. (2008) 'Avoiding Asda? Exploring Consumer Motivations in Local Organic Food Networks' *Local Environment* 13(3), pp. 187–201.

Skov, L. (2005) 'The Return of the Fur Coat: A Commodity Chain Perspective' *Current Sociology* 53(1), pp. 9–32.

Spaargarn, G. (2003) 'Sustainable Consumption: A Theoretical and Environmental Policy Perspective' *Society and Natural Resources* 16(8), pp. 687–701.

Swyngedouw, E. (2005) 'Dispossessing H_2O: The Contested Terrain of Water Privatization' *Capitalism, Nature, Socialism* 16(1), pp. 81–98.

Trentmann, F. (ed.) (2005) *The Making of the Consumer: Knowledge, Power and Identity in the Modern World*, Oxford: Berg.

UN-Water (2012) 'Managing Water under Uncertainty and Risk' *The United Nations World Water Development* Report, no. 4.

UNDP (2006) 'Beyond Scarcity: Power, Poverty and the Global Water Crisis' Report by United Nations Development Programme, http://www.undp.org/content/dam/undp/library/corporate/HDR/2006%20Global%20HDR/HDR-2006-Beyond%20scarcity-Power-poverty-and-the-global-water-crisis.pdf

van der Zwan, N. (2014) 'Making Sense of Financialization' *Socio-Economic Review* 12(1), pp. 99–129.

Van Vliet, B., H. Chappells and E. Shove (2005) *Infrastructures of Consumption: Environmental Innovation in the Utility Industries* London and Sterling VA: Earthscan Publications Ltd.

Vecchi, V., M. Hellowell and S. Getti (2013) 'Does the Private Sector Receive an Excessive Return from Investments in Health Care Infrastructure Projects? Evidence from the UK' *Health Policy* 110(2), pp. 243–270.

Williams, D. (2014) 'Social Practice Theory and Sustainable Mobility: An Analysis of the English Local Transport Planning as a System of Provision', PhD, University of the West of England.

4

The Making of the Consumer: Historical and Sociological Perspectives

Marie-Emmanuelle Chessel and
Sophie Dubuisson-Quellier

While economics have, to a large extent, participated in the invention of the consumer as a category of knowledge, the discipline has paid little attention to the conditions of the production of his/her identity. Instead, it has largely assumed that each individual consumer has a set of preferences and values whose determination is outside the realm of economics. By contrast, the social sciences and particularly history, sociology and anthropology have devoted many studies to furthering the understanding of how consumers' desires, needs, expectations, rather than preferences, develop. While some have focused primarily on individuals' social group or trajectory to gain insight into how they consume (Bourdieu, 1984), others have shown more interest in the ways in which consumers, their identities and their tastes are the product of specific techniques, activities and actors within societies. This chapter is a review of these social science studies.

In our analysis we are particularly interested in the ways in which not only market actors but also the State and civil society, as well as consumers themselves, contribute to the social making of consumers, in both the modern and contemporary periods, and in various geographical regions. Research in history, sociology and anthropology has enabled us to broaden the spectrum of actors and knowledge contributing to the making of consumers, from the Middle Ages up to the contemporary period, in China as much as in the West, and in the Soviet Union and countries of the East as much as in the USA (Berghoff and Spiekermann, 2012; Charpy et al., 2016; Chessel, 2012a; Trentmann, 2016).

This chapter first considers market actors themselves who develop techniques to create specific representations of consumers on which commercial offers can be based. We then consider research on the role of the State and of civil society in the construction of consumers' identities. These studies show the extent to which such representations are rooted in specific political or moral projects, so that consumption is determined as a social and political practice with an impact way beyond the domestic sphere. To illustrate this, we investigate surveys on consumption. Finally, in the last part of this chapter we examine research that explores the forms of consumers' capacities and autonomy. We show that the construction of the consumer requires that he or she be given agency, which in return produces effects on the construction of the representation of consumers themselves.

MARKET PROFESSIONALS AND INTERMEDIARIES

Initially the sociology of consumption represented consumers in terms of their social trajectories (Bourdieu, 1984) or their identity formation (Douglas and Isherwood, 1979), without necessarily taking into account the role of the market itself in the construction of the relationship with consumption. By contrast, more recent studies, inspired by the sociology of techniques and innovation, have shown close interest in the activities that produce representations of the consumer, attributing desires and preferences to them, and seeking to orientate their choices. These are the activities of various types of professionals (Barrey et al., 2000) as producers and service providers, who do what sociologists have called market work (Cochoy and Dubuisson-Quellier, 2013). These activities range from building up knowledge about the consumer, during the stage of product design, to the organization of the consumer's encounter with the offer, downstream, through the definition of the characteristics of the offer. They therefore involve the techniques of marketing as well as those of design, merchandising, packaging and retailing. But this market work also produces various elements, qualities, categories and nomenclatures, along with different prices and brands, guides and references to help consumers choose and match product offers with consumers' identities. Market work is particular insofar as it rationalizes the market encounter to a significant degree, by seeing consumers from the point of view of their ability to choose. In short, consumers can choose only between those products and services that market professionals have put together for them. The market relationship with consumers is therefore particularly important in this commercial work, where various market mechanisms have to be devised and set up (Callon et al., 2007) such as labels, prices, messages and advertisements, all of which will guide consumers towards the offers designed by these professionals.

Some of this work and these mechanisms for creating consumers operate upstream from the market world, when the products or the market representation are designed. For instance, in the years around 1800, factory draughtsmen were instrumental in the transformation and diffusion of objects of daily life, such as fabrics, wallpaper, porcelain tableware, and so on. They participated in the new economy of appearances that was being established under the impetus of new technical processes. Their job was both to copy and to invent motifs that were printed on dresses or vases, and they were partially responsible for the profusion of images, colours and visual devices that gradually became a feature of urban life (Millet, 2015; Roche, 1994, 2000).

In the twentieth century, industrial designers designed objects of daily life, particularly small household appliances. By producing the shapes of electric irons or vacuum cleaners, they participated in the daily life of consumers in the 1960s

(Leymonerie, 2016). In the fashion industry, certain actors served as mediators between consumers and producers. Some women created 'bureaux of stylists' which disseminated information on the season's fashion as ready-to-wear clothing became common (Maillet, 2013). Some of these specialists were also experts who explored ways of getting to know markets and consumers. This was the case for example in the 1930s around the London School of Economics, and Paul Lazarsfeld in the US, and the Gesellschaft für Konsumforschung (GfK) in Germany (Brückweck, 2011; Conrad, 2004; Schwarzkopf, 2016).

To a large extent, the marketing techniques of mass consumption were developed to further knowledge about the market. Yet, when they were developed in the early twentieth century, they served above all to sell large quantities of products resulting from agricultural surplus production in the US (Cochoy, 1998). Underpinned essentially by a logic of supply, the rationalizing of the commercialization of these massive quantities of agricultural products forged very imprecise representations of consumers. But as these marketing techniques developed, segmentation of the demand became a strategic tool for controlling competition. Firms and marketing specialists in universities defined consumers with multiple identities. Their aim was less to improve their knowledge of the market than to enable the offer, in the context of saturated markets, to find new outlets. Marketing should thus be understood less as a technique aimed at telling 'the truth' about the market and consumers, than as an approach to promote the sale of what has already been produced, on the basis of stable relations between products and the demand. Marketing performs the market (Callon, 2007); insofar as it brings into existence the reality that it helps to describe and to produce (Araujo and Kjellberg, 2009; Araujo et al., 2010; Callon, 1998). To this end, it uses various remote techniques to represent consumers and analyse markets, typical of market studies (Dubuisson-Quellier, 2010; Heiskanen, 2005), such as survey or focus groups (Grandclément and Gaglio, 2011). Consumers' expectations are thus constructed as multiple realities (Kjellberg and Helgesson, 2006) that often compete with one another (Dubuisson-Quellier, 2013a) and that enable the various market operators to talk on their behalf in order to design the offer that they need.

Along with marketing, advertising is another set of techniques with performative dimensions. Advertising was provided by various actors even before advertisers became professionals in the twentieth century (Chessel, 1998; Marchand, 1985). In 1646, with pomp and ceremony, King Louis XIV and cloth manufacturers, supported by Mazarin, launched refined 'Dutch-like' sheets made in France. They contributed to establishing the royal manufacture of Sedan and used a publicity campaign to certify the products of the royal seal. After the French Revolution, in a new context filled with uncertainty for commerce, the manufacturer and merchant Guillaume Ternaux organized a vast publicity campaign around Sedan sheets, to reassure his customers. In 1798 he positioned himself, without saying so, in the continuation of the Ancien Régime under which articles had been certified (Gayot, 2008). Eighteenth-century retailers, particularly in the semi-luxury industry that promoted the spread of new materials, also used publicity (Berg and Clifford, 1998; Coquery, 2004).

In the nineteenth and twentieth centuries, retailers did not always need publicity professionals to tell them where to set up their shops and to help them produce innovative advertising (Miller, 1981). Jules Ouaki, for instance, who founded the maxi-discount shop Tati in Paris in the 1950s, invented a brand, or more precisely a name and colours – pink and white checks – to symbolize his business (Zalc, 2012).

From the twentieth century, advertisers, as artisans of consumers' desires, also produced mediations to foster a relationship between products and consumers (Hennion et al., 1989). These mediations were based on particular representations of consumers (McFall, 2011), developed by professionals at advertising agencies. The definitions framed the relationship that advertisers were supposed to establish between consumers and products, with the intention of developing forms of attachment between the two (Ariztia, 2015).

Yet the performativity of operations carried out by these different professionals cannot be based solely on their representations of consumers. It is also connected to the production of a large number of market devices that organize the encounter between products and consumers, which also channel it around the choices that have been made as regards both product quality and consumer profiles (Cochoy, 2010). Some authors have paid particular attention to market architectures, to gain insight into their contribution to the making of consumers' competences. They have highlighted various 'trade revolutions' (Daumas, forthcoming 2018b). In seventeenth-century England, relations between consumers and merchants took place in a context of lasting social relations, those between an aristocratic family, its suppliers, and its servants (Whittle and Griffiths, 2012). In eighteenth-century Paris these relations played out inside aristocrats' residences, where traders delivered their goods directly to their noble consumers (Coquery, 1998). In the mountains and then the countryside, up until the nineteenth century, goods trading – from clothes to books, watches or handkerchiefs – revolved around the pedlar's visit (Fontaine, 1993). Then in mid-nineteenth century Paris, shop windows were invented, and with them all sorts of architectural innovations intended to display products in public and private spaces (Charpy, 2008, 2010).

The nature and form of consumers' engagement in trade relations were therefore never independent of commercial devices. The trade relationship developed to a very large extent through the staging of the specific features that the two parties grant to this singular relationship within the market context. This point has been remarkably well illustrated by the work of Michelle de La Pradelle (2006). In the case of trading at outdoor markets in the 1990s, she describes how merchants and consumers recompose the depersonalization that everyone believes characterizes the market relationship, by engaging in personalized interactions that are artificially staged to a greater or lesser degree.

Likewise, the analysis of the diversity of market architectures suggests designers' intention to invite consumers to engage in the relationship in different ways. The 'cosy', welcoming and hyper-selective nature of some shops, inspired by nineteenth-century boutiques, builds a commercial relationship with consumers that is intentionally dense, enhanced with various services, and not simply a transaction (Miller, 1981). Some cheap department stores use pale lighting and a very simple system of stacking products to suggest that the relationship is above all economic and devoid of costly artifices (Dubuisson-Quellier, 2007). This diversity of commercial structures and their evolution in time contribute, in turn, to modifying and diversifying consumers' competencies.

The evolution of commercial *agencements* shapes the roles and competences of traders and consumers alike. Paul Du Gay (2004) describes, for example, the development of self-service in early twentieth-century English shops. Introduced in a context where the price war demanded new solutions to cut costs, self-service required consumers to adapt. Faced with these new sales techniques, consumers were initially hostile, to some extent, and complained about having to do the work of salespersons and shop assistants. New techniques and new knowledge contributed to the accessibility of merchandise, as new types of shelf space were designed, along with sign-posting intended to guide consumers and to channel their choices and their actions in the shop (Cochoy, 2016). A nomenclature was developed to enable consumers to identify categories of products so that they could learn to be familiar with them and to adopt them, while other objects became indispensable, such as shopping carts (Cochoy, 2009). A mediated relationship gradually set in between consumers and products. It is the outcome of a fairly long process that started in the nineteenth century, which stemmed directly from the progressive development of various devices used to organize selling: counters, cash registers, labels, shelves, and packaging. With the advent of shopping malls (Cohen, 2003), supermarkets (Daumas, 2006), urban commercial development (Mallard, 2016), and e-commerce websites (Licoppe, 2008), it became usual for customers to adapt constantly and to acquire new competencies. Today, market professionals organize the conditions of expression of consumers' choices in highly controlled and often optimized conditions, based on objectives of profitability of economic strategies rather than customer satisfaction.

Research has moreover shown the wide diversity of market devices framing the expression of consumers' choices. None of these devices is neutral or insignificant; on the contrary, they often reflect the competition and power struggles between the different agents involved in the supply and the commercialization of products or services. Susan Strasser's work shows, for example, that when packaged cereals gradually replaced the sale of products in bulk, it reflected producers' wish to build a more direct relationship with consumers through the guarantees of a brand, and thus to ensure that the seller alone could not control the relationship with consumers (Strasser, 1989). The making of the consumer is thus also the product of power relations between the actors of the supply: those upstream who do not wish those downstream to have a monopoly on the control of consumers' needs and expectations (Schleifer and De Soucey, 2015). Market devices populate the entire market, and each of them contributes in its own way to shaping consumers' practices and identities, whether it be a question of brands, of packaging (Cochoy, 2002), of shopping bags (Hagberg, 2016) or of loyalty cards (Araujo and Kjellberg, 2009). We even find them unexpectedly in various different worlds, as recent studies on evangelical churches and their promotional practices recently showed (Luca, 2012; Yip and Ainsworth, 2016).

To account for the systematic way in which these market operations and devices shape consumers' behaviours in markets, Michel Callon proposed the notion of market *agencement*. The term refers to the articulation of human and non-human actors that enables the circulation of products, from the people who design them down to those who use or consume them, by making possible the operations of calculation and adjustment that this implies (Callon, 2013). We owe to Lucien Karpik the construction of a framework for interpreting the various types of device in markets. Karpik (2010) classified them according to the size of the market, the regimes of coordination that they supported, and the forms of consumer involvement. His analysis enables us to see the consumer as an individual whose autonomy and engagement in markets are largely organized by the commercial activity itself. Circulation in market spaces, the identification of products and of their properties, their commensurability and their singularization, are operations that consumers perform with equipment consisting not only of physical means but also of principles of calculation and of nomenclatures provided to them by market actors. The identities and competences of consumers cannot be conceived of today in any way other than as a product of market work rooted essentially in competitive power relations and strategies of economic control (Dubuisson-Quellier, 2013a).

THE MAKING OF THE 'GOOD CONSUMER'

The making of the consumer is not only the product of market techniques; alongside market specialists, other actors also construct consumer figures. Social reformers seek to know and to educate consumers, while the State, the law and civil society contribute to forging a specific status for the consumer, that of consumer-citizen (Trentmann, 2006).

Whether they are sent by the central government or come from reformist groups wishing to transform society through philanthropy or legislative reform, those that we propose here to call 'researcher-reformers' are important actors in the construction of the consumer figure. Social inquiries have existed since the Middle Ages (Dejoux, 2014), but they took on particular importance in the nineeenth century (Bulmer et al., 1991; Kalifa, 2010; Karila-Cohen, 2008). In this context, surveys on consumers' budgets preceded and sometimes prepared the first market surveys (Schwarzkopf, 2016). Underpinned by a particular ideology, especially from 1860, Frédéric Le Play's monographic studies painted a picture in France of ideal families (Baciocchi and David, 2005–2006). We see emerging a normative portrait of working-class families that were supposed to save, to manage their budgets correctly, and to avoid consuming too much alcohol (Deluermoz, 2012; Kalaora and Savoye, 1989; Lhuissier, 2007). As these methods of surveying budgets, known as Leplaysian, have had an influence in other countries, such as China for example (Gamble and Burgess, 1921), they are particularly interesting comparative sources (Conrad and Triebel, 1985).

In the twentieth century, Catholic communities, especially those that were organized in the framework of Catholic Action – the participation of the laity in the apostolate of the hierarchy – were also major producers of surveys that were not devoid of normative advice (Lhotte and Dupeyrat, 1937; Pelletier, 1995). In the UK and the USA, as well as Japan and Eastern Europe, reformers carried out social surveys and studied consumer practices, especially regarding food (Bulmer et al., 1991; Converse, 1987; Thomann, 2015). Some of these researchers had the status of social scientists, such as Phyllis H. Williams, research assistant in sociology at the Institute of Human Relations (Yale University) in the 1930s. Williams published a book for social workers, nurses doing home visits, teachers and doctors who needed to know the community of Italian immigrants in the USA better. She described their lifestyle and criticized the richness of their diet, which was very different from that of Southern Italy (Trentmann, 2016: 598–599; Williams, 1938). The worlds of social reform and of the social sciences were indeed closely entangled in the first half of the twentieth century. American empirical sociology owed a great deal to social workers, who were very often women, like Phyllis H. Williams (Fitzpatrick, 1990; Platt, 1996; Silverberg, 1998).

These surveys contributed to the making of consumers, but in a very different sense to that of market professionals. Here it is not a question of creating consumers' needs to sell products, but of normatively framing their behaviors. In this respect, the State and civil society have also regularly sought to define moral and citizen-related obligations of consumers (Chatriot et al., 2004; Dubuisson-Quellier, 2016). It is especially in particular contexts where resources were rare and countries experienced economic difficulties, as in times of war or economic crisis, that States appeal to consumers' duties as citizens. In many countries, the making of the citizen seems to be closely articulated to that of the consumer, not only because the State plays a fundamental role in consumer societies (Strasser et al., 1998) by defining a legal status for the consumer, but, more importantly, because consumption appears as a process through which consumers fully occupy the political space (Daunton and Hilton, 2001). The notion of 'pocketbook politics' (Jacobs, 2005) defines citizens' engagement through economic behaviour that has to match the community's expectations (Trentmann, 2009). Consumers are thus regularly invited to adapt their practices according to economic and political situations. During World War I, in both the USA and the UK, governments asked citizens to reduce their consumption so as not to worsen shortages, and thus to participate in the war effort. During World War II, a federal bureau created specifically to combat inflation even asked consumers to watch prices (Cohen, 2003). After the war, women consumers in France were also called on to combat inflation (Pulju, 2011). The consumer became an actor in public policy-making and the market became an arena in which individuals could express their citizenship.

Consumption was thus also a driver of growth during the New Deal in the USA. It was even during this period that a real social contract was entered into between the State and citizen-consumers, aimed at basing both economic prosperity and democratic life on mass consumption. In *A Consumers' Republic*, Lizabeth Cohen describes how the 'citizen-consumer' of the 1930s morphed after World War II into a 'purchaser-citizen' to serve the national interest, by supporting the new mass consumption economy. This was not only the outcome of commercial trends but also revolved around urban development policies in the 1950s which segmented the population along the lines of class and race. These policies moved the white middle classes into suburban residential areas by assisting them in buying homes and cars, and by creating shopping malls devoted to them (Cohen, 2003). By facilitating access to credit for consumption and home ownership, the US government made consumption rather than savings the main driver of its economy. This contrasted with other countries such as France, where savings were encouraged (Trumbull, 2014).

The Chinese government also opted for consumption when it changed its economic policies after 1979. Aware of the failure of the planned economy in improving lifestyles, the authorities revised their priorities. Production was henceforth to be turned more towards the satisfaction of immediate desires for consumer goods.

To sustain growth, buy social peace and ensure its longevity, the Party placed its bets on a Chinese consumer society. Initially this regime was based on exports but then, from the 2000s, it started to rely on the domestic demand. Consumers and especially the middle classes were thus encouraged to consume (Davis, 2000; Gerth, 2010; Guiheux, 2011).

Civil society – especially the non-profit and activist world – has also played an active part in morally framing consumption (Dubuisson-Quellier, 2013b, 2013c). Since the emblematic cases of revolutionary boycotts against the British Empire in the eighteenth century in the USA, and then 'free produce' approaches of the abolitionist movements in the early nineteenth century which proposed goods not produced with slave labor, there has been a significant political tradition in civil society consisting in making the consumer an agent of change (Glickman, 2009). From this tradition sprung the US and European *consumer leagues* that developed at the turn of the twentieth century, with the mission of making consumers responsible for their purchases, and protecting women's labor rights (Chessel, 2012b). They thus embodied two forms of consumer mobilization: both as agents of political change and as a social group that can benefit from these changes. At the same time, in the UK, consumers defended 'free trade' (Trentmann, 2009). Although they did not entirely move away from their ambiguous position, the consumer movements that developed in the 1930s in the US and in the 1950s in Europe specialized in defending consumers' rights and interests (Hilton, 2009). Organizations such as the Consumers' Union in the USA, the Consumers' Association in England, the *Union Belge des Consommateurs* in Belgium, and the *Union Fédérale des Consommateurs* in France invented and disseminated techniques for testing products, with the idea of training consumers to make better choices (Aldridge, 1994; Mallard, 2000). This new representation of consumers, often largely institutionalized by governments themselves, served to defend their interests and was behind many laws passed to protect consumers (Chatriot et al., 2006; Trentmann, 2001; Trumbull, 2006). Indeed, states are themselves very proactive in building representations of the good consumer by designing a large set of public instruments, from taxes, to public campaigns, labeling and more recently nudges, aiming at orienting consumers' decisions towards common good objectives, such as public health or the preservation of the environment (Dubuisson-Quellier, 2016).

In post-war Poland, textile workers and the trade-union, Solidarność which formed *de facto* the largest consumer movement, even if they spoke as workers, demanded that socio-economic resources be distributed equitably (Mazurek and Hilton, 2007). In western countries, from the 1990s and 2000s, civil society organizations developed actions that targeted consumers, providing them with labels (Bartley et al., 2015). Consumers were invited to engage in 'individualized collective action', that is, to manifest their political engagement by either boycotting or on the contrary 'buycotting' certain types of product (Micheletti, 2003). These movements thus proposed numerous types of protest or resistance, or else engagement in forms of alternative consumption or in sustainable community movements (Dubuisson-Quellier, 2013c; Forno and Graziano, 2014).

Market actors, researcher-reformers, government authorities and militant organizations all construct 'figures' of normative consumers. It is in this framework that the consumer usually appears as a woman, the shopper whom people notice in the streets of London, or the 'housewife' that advertising wants to appeal to, that the reformer wants to educate, that government wants to control, and that activist organizations want to enroll (Chessel, 2011; de Grazia and Furlough, 1996; Rappaport, 2000). Thus, the shoplifter in department stores in France, the UK or the USA who appeared at the end of the nineteenth century was almost always a woman; she represented the dangers of middle-class female consumption (Abelson, 1989; Roberts, 1998). On the other hand, the consumer as an economic figure – *homo economicus* – was always a man and was never considered dangerous (Donohue, 1999). Let us now move away from these normative figures and look at the practices of ordinary men and women. Do consumers not also contribute to the making of themselves? What can be said of their agency?

THE CONSUMER'S 'AGENCY'

The framing of consumption by the market, civil society and the State may suggest that the consumer is a passive individual whose acts are largely the product of multiple framings. This view was spread by voices critical of consumption, which tended to see it as being essentially manipulated by marketing and advertising that, they claimed, were capable of stripping consumers of their free will. Advertising messages allegedly alienated consumers and maintained the working classes in a state of dependence on mass consumer products (Marcuse, 1991), thus reducing products to the state of signs mirroring social identities, devoid of substance (Baudrillard, 1996). These studies were set in a long tradition of moralizing writings (Trentmann, 2016).

In *The Theory of the Leisure Class*, Thorstein Veblen (1899) described how the upper classes in ancient societies compelled themselves to invest heavily in ostentatious consumption intended to show their rank and power in society. As this norm spread from the top down, their servants and then the lowest ranks of society adopted the same modes of consumption. The sociologist Maurice Halbwachs (1913) similarly showed the propensity of working-class households to increase the share of spending on clothes as soon as their income increased, in order to integrate into society more fully. But he emphasized that consumption should not only be read from the angle of imitations and adaptations between social classes; it is above all a strong marker and identification of class. He thus showed that the working classes' consciousness stemmed precisely from their understanding that, with regard to consumption, their employers did not have to make the same sacrifices as they did. Moreover, the family played a crucial role as the consumer unit par excellence, there where class identity was expressed, inculcated and maintained. It was probably Pierre Bourdieu who proposed the most thorough analysis of the forms of discipline that the social structure exerted on consumption practices. Inspired by Veblen and by Halbwachs, Bourdieu showed the links between lifestyles and the maintenance of positions in society. From his point of view, the manifestation of taste and above all of disgust, through consumption practices, was one of the main factors in the construction and maintenance of social relations of domination and submission. Material goods, he argued, make it possible to make these tastes visible and thus to participate in the construction of social hierarchies (Bourdieu, 1984). Individuals develop a class identity shaped in a habitus, thus constructing and stabilizing the positions of social groups as much as do individual consumption practices. While Bourdieu's analyses of cultural goods strongly reflect the period in which they were set, the importance of the social group in the diffusion of certain consumption practices remains strong to this day, as the middle classes' role in spreading organic farming and 'good food' attests (Johnston et al., 2011).

The persistence of particularities related to social groups is clearly highlighted by historians, even though they tend to qualify the determinisms (Daumas, 2018a). Under the Ancien Régime, when one was part of the 'people of Paris', one's dwelling was poor, in a single room in which it was impossible to feel really 'at home'. Despite the introduction of new objects – for instance porcelain tableware, mirrors and razors – lifestyles were linked to a particular relationship with precariousness (Roche, 1987). The risk of extreme poverty was an incentive to build safety nets, including by buying and selling goods, as needed (Fontaine, 2008). In the nineteenth century the workers studied by Leplaysian researchers used all sorts of strategies to be able to eat: they could glean vegetables or use bartering (Lhuissier, 2007). At the end of the nineteenth century, small farmers gradually adopted the urban model of consumption, but their practices remained widely diverse and particularities did not disappear. Rural populations still consumed a large amount of their own production (Daumas, 2015).

These popular practices were perpetuated in Paris in the early twentieth century, in a period when there was a broadening of the consumption of goods, notably through the development of credit intended for the working classes. These classes maintained specific practices, notably the use of goods as a means of saving, or by tinkering to extend the life-span of objects (Albert, 2012, 2014). Ethnographic studies show that in the past, and still today, low-income households devise solutions to live 'from day to day' and to manage. They count money and time, adapt their spending according to their income, travel far to obtain the cheapest goods, or use their social network (Cottereau and Marzok, 2012). In contemporary China we find the persistence of working-class consumption practices alongside a new extremely rich population. In Shanghai, which in the 1990s recovered the commercial activity that it had known in the early twentieth century, standardized spaces of mass retailing coexist with quasi-rural markets (Guiheux, 2010).

We thus discover consumers' capacity for 'bricolage', their re-appropriation of objects (de Certeau, 1984; Lüdtke, 1994) or their willing to negotiate the recommendations they receive while consuming (Plessz et al., 2016). This was for instance how the middle classes invented a new way of using, arranging and displaying goods in the nineteenth century. Being bourgeois was not solely a matter of owning goods; it was also one of 'making personal use of them that was consistent with collective practices'. Middle-class consumers protected their dwellings with locks, displayed their ornaments in cabinets, stored their documents in secretaires, kept their jewelry in boxes, and became enthusiastic collectors of objects. In this way, consumers contributed to their own social making (Charpy, 2010). In the twentieth century, it was through their 'bricolage' and their use of goods that European consumers constructed a common material culture, around, for example, the bicycle or the computer (Oldenziel and Hård, 2013).

We now know from studies on men and women's daily lives that consumption was not absent in the Soviet Union and Eastern European countries before the 1990s. Consumers here could also be active in particular contexts (Kott, 2001; Pence and Betts, 2008; Reid and Crowley, 2000). Life in the Soviet Union in the 1930s demanded resourcefulness and luck, in order to maintain normal life in exceptional conditions (Fitzpatrick, 1999). More broadly in East Europe, consumers were neither puppets nor heroes, but they did contribute to transforming the socialism of daily life through their resourcefulness within the framework of a normed system (Ragaru and Chapelle-Popacean, 2010; Zakharova, 2015, 2016).

In other words, consumers are also made through their own practices, and they constantly negotiate the norms they encounter in an ongoing play with market actors. By setting up market architectures, marketers structure the relationship between products and consumers that does not exist in the absolute. By researching and commenting on their research, social reformers shape consumer figures and norms, all the while providing valuable information on popular practices. By creating a framework, actors of the State facilitate or limit acts of consumption – an extreme example of which we see in contemporary China. The technological and general framework cannot be transformed by consumers; it is for instance impossible to heat one's apartment if the infrastructure is absent.

Yet consumers do not necessarily conform to the multiple injunctions aimed at them. Through 'bricolage', adaptation and negotiation they survive on wages below the breadline, articulate consumption and savings, maintain ostentatious consumption even when such practices are frowned upon, and come to terms with nutritional or environmental norms to choose their food. Normative and practical discourses must therefore be distinguished, even if they are intrinsically interlinked in reality. This dissociation is one contribution by recent studies on consumption, which are now focusing as much on practices and objects as on normative discourses (Crossick, 2000; Daumas, 2010; Trentmann, 2016).

ACKNOWLEDGMENTS

We would like to thank Jean-Claude Daumas and Frank Trentmann for their helpful comments on a first draft of this chapter.

REFERENCES

Abelson, E. (1989) *When Ladies Go a-Thieving: Middle-Class Shoplifters in the Victorian Department Store*. New York: Oxford University Press.

Albert, A. (2012) 'Working-class consumer credit during the Belle Epoque: Invention, innovation, or reconfiguration?', *Annales HSS*, 67(4), 731–763.

Albert, A. (2014) 'Consommation de masse et consommation de classe. Une histoire sociale et culturelle du cycle de vie des objets dans les classes populaires parisiennes (des années 1880 aux années 1920)'. Thèse de doctorat d'histoire, Université Paris I.

Aldridge, A. (1994) 'The construction of rational consumption in Which? magazine: The more blobs the better?', *Sociology*, 28(4), 899–912.

Araujo, L. and Kjellberg, H. (2009) 'Shaping exchanges, performing markets: the study of marketing practices'. In P. Maclaran, M. Saren, B. Stern and M. Tadajewski (eds) *The SAGE Handbook of Marketing Theory*. London: Sage, pp. 195–218.

Araujo, L., Finch, J. and Kjellberg, H. (eds) (2010) *Reconnecting Marketing to Markets*. Oxford: Oxford University Press.

Ariztia, T. (2015) 'Unpacking insight: How consumers are qualified by advertising agencies', *Journal of Consumer Culture*, 15(2), 143–162.

Baciocchi, S. and David, J. (2005–2006) 'Esquisse pour une autre anthologie', *Les Etudes sociales*, 142–143–144, 7–17.

Barrey, S., Cochoy, F. and Dubuisson-Quellier, S. (2000) 'Designer, packager et merchandiser: Trois professionnels pour une même scène marchande', *Sociologie du Travail*, 42(3), 457–482.

Bartley, T., Koos, S., Samel, H., Setrini, G. and Summers, N. (2015) *Looking Behind the Label: Global Industries and the Conscientious Consumer*. Bloomington, IN: Indiana University Press.

Baudrillard, J. (1996 [1968]) *The System of Objects*. London: Verso.

Berg, M. and Clifford, H. (1998) 'Commerce and the commodity: Graphic display and selling new consumer goods in eighteenth-century England'. In M. North and D. Omrod (eds) *Art Markets in Europe, 1400–1800*. Aldershot: Ashgate, pp. 187–200.

Berghoff, H. and Spiekermann, U. (eds) (2012) *Decoding Modern Consumer Societies*. New York: Palgrave Macmillan.

Bourdieu, P. (1984) [1979]) *Distinction: A Social Critique of the Judgement of Taste*. London: Routledge and Kegan Paul.

Brückweck, K. (ed) (2011) *The Voice of the Citizen Consumer: A History of Market Research, Consumer Movements, and the Political Public Sphere*. Oxford: Oxford University Press.

Bulmer, M., Beale, K. and Sklar, K.K. (eds) (1991) *The Social Survey in Historical Perspective, 1880–1940*. Cambridge: Cambridge University Press.

Callon, M. (1998) *The Laws of the Market*. Oxford: Blackwell.

Callon, M. (2007) 'What does it mean to say that economics is performative?' In D. Mackenzie, F. Muniesa, and L. Siu (eds) *Do Economists Make Markets? On the Performativity of Economics*. Princeton, NJ: Princeton University Press, pp. 311–357.

Callon, M. (2013) 'Qu'est-ce qu'un agencement marchand?' In M. Callon, M. Akrich, S. Dubuisson-Quellier, et al. *Sociologie des agencements marchands*. Paris: Presses des Mines, pp. 325–440.

Callon, M., Millo, Y. and Muniesa, F. (2007) *Market Devices*. London: Wiley-Blackwell.

Certeau (de) M. (1984 [1980]) *The Practice of Everyday Life*. Berkeley: University of California Press.

Charpy, M. (2008) 'Amateurs, collectionneurs et chineurs parisiens au XXe siècle. Le commerce des apparences du passé, entre centre et périphérie'. In I. Paresys (ed) *Paraître et apparences en Europe occidentale du Moyen Age à nos jours*. Lille: Presses Universitaires du Septentrion, pp. 369–388.

Charpy, M. (2010) 'Le théâtre des objets. Espaces privés, culture matérielle et identité bourgeoise. Paris, 1830–1914'. Thèse de doctorat d'histoire, Université François-Rabelais de Tours.

Charpy, M., Dubuisson-Quellier, S. and Guiheux, G. (2016) 'Un monde de choses', *La Vie des idées*, 18 novembre 2016. ISSN: 2105-3030. URL: http://www.laviedesidees.fr/Un-monde-de-choses.html

Chatriot, A., Chessel, M.-E. and Hilton, M. (eds) (2004) *Au nom du consommateur. Consommation et politique en Europe et aux États-Unis au XXe siècle*. Paris, La Découverte.

Chatriot, A., Chessel, M.-E. and Hilton, M. (eds) (2006) *The Expert Consumer: Associations and Professionals in Consumer Society.* London: Ashgate.

Chessel, M.-E. (1998) *La Publicité. Naissance d'une profession*. Paris: CNRS Editions.

Chessel, M.-E. (2011) 'The gender of consumption in 1900: Women and men in the Ligue sociale d'acheteurs', *L'Année sociologique*, 61(1), 125–149.

Chessel, M.-E. (2012a) *Histoire de la consommation*. Paris: La Découverte.

Chessel, M.-E. (2012b) *Consommateurs engagés à la Belle Epoque*. Paris: Presses de Sciences Po.

Cochoy, F. (1998) 'Another discipline for the market economy: Marketing as performative knowledge and know-how for capitalism'. In M. Callon (ed) *The Laws of the Market*. Oxford: Blackwell, pp. 194–221.

Cochoy, F. (2002) *Une sociologie du packaging, ou l'âne de Buridan face au marché*. Paris: PUF.

Cochoy, F. (2009) 'Driving a shopping cart from STS to business, and the other way round: On the introduction of shopping carts in American grocery stores (1936–1959)', *Organization*, 16(1), 31–55.

Cochoy, F. (2010) 'How to build displays that sell: the politics of performativity in American grocery stores (Progressive grocer 1929–1946)', *Journal of Cultural Economy*, 3(2), 299–315.

Cochoy, F. (2016) *On the Origin of Self-service*. London: Routledge.

Cochoy, F. and Dubuisson-Quellier, S. (2013) 'The sociology of market work', *Economic Sociology – the European Electronic Newsletter*, 15(1), 4–11.

Cohen, L. (2003) *A Consumers' Republic: The Politics of Mass Consumption in Postwar America*. New York: A. Knopf.

Conrad, C. (2004) 'Observer les consommateurs. Etudes de marché et histoire de la consommation en Allemagne, des années 1930 aux années 1960', *Le Mouvement Social*, 206, 17–39.

Conrad, C. and Triebel, A. (1985) 'Family budget as sources for comparative social history', *Historical Social Research*, 33, 45–66.

Converse, J. (1987) *Survey Research in the United States: Roots and Emergence, 1890–1960*. Berkeley: University of California Press.

Coquery, N. (1998) L'hôtel aristocratique: le marché du luxe à Paris au XVIIIe siècle. Paris: Publications de la Sorbonne.

Coquery, N. (2004) 'The language of success: Marketing and distribution semi-luxury goods in eighteenth-century Paris', *Journal of Design History*, 17(1), 55–74.

Cottereau, A. and Marzok, M.M. (2012) *Une famille andalouze: ethnocomptabilité d'une économie invisible*. Paris: Bouchene.

Crossick, G. (2000) 'Introduction', in N. Coquery (eds) *La Boutique et la Ville. Commerces, commerçants, espaces et clientèles (XVIe–XXe siècles)*. Tours: Presses de l'Université François Rabelais.

Daumas, J.-C. (2006) 'Consommation de masse et grande distribution', *Vingtième siècle. Revue d'histoire*, 3, 57–76.

Daumas, J.-C. (2010) 'S'approprier les choses. Consommateurs et consommation en France au XIXe siècle (1800–1914). Perspectives de recherche'. In A. Escudero Gutiérrez, J.-C. Daumas, G. Chastagnaret and O. Raveux (eds) *Los niveles de vida en España y Francia (siglos XVIII–XX). In memoriam Gérard Gayot*. Publicaciones de l'Universidad de Alicante.

Daumas, J.-C. (2015) 'La consommation dans les campagnes françaises dans les années 1880–1914: un régime de transition'. In N. Marty and A. Escudero (eds) *Consommateurs, consommation XVIIe–XXIe siècle, regards franco-espagnols*. Alicante-Perpignan, Publications de L'Université d'Alicante/Presses Universitaires de Perpignan.

Daumas, J.-C. (2018a forthcoming) *La vie matérielle. Une histoire de la consommation, France XIXe–XXIe siècle*. Paris.

Daumas, J.-C. (2018b forthcoming) *Les révolutions du commerce. France, XVIIIe–XXe siècle*. Besançon: Presses Universitaires de Franche-Comté.

Daunton, M. and Hilton, M. (eds) (2001) *The Politics of Consumption: Material Culture and Citizenship in Europe and America*. London: Bloomsbury Publishing.

Davis, D.S. (eds) (2000) *The Consumer Revolution in Urban China*. Berkeley: University of California Press.

Dejoux, M. (2014) *Les enquêtes de Saint Louis. Gouverner et sauver son âme*. Paris: Presses Universitaires de France.

Deluermoz, Q. (2012) 'Les bas-fonds en chair et en chiffres? Le budget leplaysien du chiffonnier Nieiri (1849)', *Les Etudes Sociales*, 155, 47–73.

Donohue, K. (1999) 'What gender is the consumer? The role of gender connotations in defining the political', *Journal of American Studies*, 33(1), 19–44.

Douglas, M. and Isherwood, B. (1979), *The World of Goods: Towards an Anthropology of Consumption*. London: Allen Lane.

Dubuisson-Quellier, S. (2007) 'The shop as market space: The commercial qualities of retail architecture'. In D. Vernet and L. de Wit (eds) *Boutiques and Other Retail Spaces: The Architecture of Seduction*. London: Routledge, pp. 10–23.

Dubuisson-Quellier, S. (2010) 'Product tastes, consumer tastes: The plurality of qualifications in product development and marketing activities'. In L. Araujo, J. Finch and H. Kjellberg (eds) *Reconnecting Marketing to Markets*. Oxford: Oxford University Press, pp. 74–93.

Dubuisson-Quellier, S. (2013a) 'From qualities to value: Demand shaping and market control in mass market'. In J. Beckert and C. Musselin (eds) *Constructing Quality: The Classification of Goods in the Economy*. Oxford: Oxford University Press, pp. 247–267.

Dubuisson-Quellier, S. (2013b) 'A market mediation strategy: How social movements seek to change firms' practices by promoting new principles of product valuation', *Organization Studies*, 34(5–6), 683–703.

Dubuisson-Quellier, S. (2013c) *Ethical Consumption*. Halifax: Fernwood Publisher.

Dubuisson-Quellier, S. (eds) (2016) *Gouverner les conduites*. Paris: Presses de Sciences Po.

Du Gay, P. (2004) 'Self-service: retail, shopping and personhood', *Consumption, Markets and Culture*, 7(2), 149–163.

Fitzpatrick, E. (1990) *Endless Crusade: Women Social Scientists and Progressive Reform*. New York: Oxford University Press.

Fitzpatrick, S. (1999) *Everyday Stalinism. Ordinary Life in Extraordinary Times: Soviet Russia in the 1930s*. Oxford: Oxford University Press.

Fontaine, L. (1993) *Histoire du colportage en Europe, XVe–XIXe siècles*. Paris: Albin Michel.

Fontaine, L. (2008) *L'économie morale. Pauvreté, crédit et confiance dans l'Europe préindustrielle*. Paris: Gallimard.

Forno, F. and Graziano, P.R. (2014) 'Sustainable community movement organisations', *Journal of Consumer Culture*, 14(2), 139–157.

Gamble, S.D. and Burgess, J.S. (1921) *Peking: A Social Survey Conducted under the Auspices of the Princeton University Center in China and the Peking Young Men's Christian Association*. New York: George H. Doran Co.

Gayot, G. (2008) 'Du logo d'entreprise royale à la libre enseigne de magasin. La publicité pour les draps fins en France de 1646 à 1830'. In D. Margairaz and P. Minard (eds) *L'information économique XVIe–XIXe siècle*. Paris: Comité pour l'histoire économique et financière de la France, pp. 115–139.

Gerth, K. (2010) *As China Goes, So Goes the World: How Chinese Consumers are Transforming Everything*. New York: Hill and Wang.

Glickman, L. (2009) *Buying Power: A History of Consumer Activism in America*. Chicago: University of Chicago Press.

Grandclément, C. and Gaglio, G. (2011) 'Convoking the consumer in person: The focus group effect'. In D. Zwick and J. Cayla (eds) *Inside Marketing: Practices, Ideologies, Devices*. Oxford: Oxford University Press, pp. 87–114.

Grazia (de), V. and Furlough, E. (1996) *The Sex of Things: Gender and Consumption in Historical Perspective*. Berkeley, CA: University of California Press.

Guiheux, G. (2010) 'Shangaï, société de consommation'. In N. Idler (eds) *Shangaï*. Paris: Robert Lafont.

Guiheux, G. (2011) 'La construction d'un sujet consommateur dans la Chine urbaine', *Monde chinois*, 27, 101–111.

Hagberg, J. (2016) 'Agencing practices: a historical exploration of shopping bags', *Consumption, Markets and Culture*, 19(1), 111–132.

Halbwachs, M. (1913) *La Classe ouvrière et les niveaux de vie. Recherches sur la hiérarchie des besoins dans les sociétés industrielles contemporaines*. Paris: Alcan.

Heiskanen, E. (2005) 'The performative nature of consumer research: Consumers' environmental awareness as an example', *Journal of Consumer Policy*, 28(2), 179–201.

Hennion, A., Méadel, C. and Bowker, G. (1989) 'The artisans of desire: The mediation of advertising between product and consumer', *Sociological Theory*, 7(2), pp. 191–209.

Hilton, M. (2009) *Prosperity for All: Consumer Activism in an Era of Globalization*. Ithaca and London: Cornell University Press.

Jacobs, M. (2005) *Pocketbook Politics: Economic Citizenship in Twentieth-Century America*. Princeton, NJ: Princeton University Press.

Johnston, J., Szabo, M. and Rodney, A. (2011) 'Good food, good people: Understanding the cultural repertoire of ethical eating', *Journal of Consumer Culture*, 11(3), 293–318.

Kalaora, B. and Savoye, A. (1989) *Les inventeurs oubliés. Le Play et ses continuateurs aux origines des sciences sociales*. Seyssel: Champ Vallon.

Kalifa, D. (2010) 'Enquête et "culture de l'enquête" au XIXe siècle', *Romantisme*, 3(149), 3–23.

Karila-Cohen, P. (2008) *L'État des esprits. L'invention de l'enquête politique en France (1814–1848)*. Rennes: PUR.

Karpik, L. (2010) *Valuing the Unique: The Economics of Singularities*. Princeton: Princeton University Press.

Kjellberg, H. and Helgesson, C.-F. (2006) 'Multiple versions of markets: Multiplicity and performativity in market practice', *Industrial Marketing Management*, 35(7), 839–855.

Kott, S. (2001) *Le communisme au quotidien. Les entreprises d'Etat dans la société est-allemande*. Paris: Belin.

La Pradelle (de), M. (2006) *Market Day in Provence*. Chicago: Chicago University Press.

Leymonerie, C. (2016) *Le temps des objets. Une histoire du design industriel en France, 1950–1970*. Saint-Etienne: Cité du Design.

Lhotte, C. and Dupeyrat, E. (1937) *La préparation du futur foyer de la jeune travailleuse. Une enquête de la JOCF*. Paris: Jeunesse Ouvrière Chrétienne Féminine.

Lhuissier, A. (2007) *Alimentation populaire et réforme sociale. Les consommations ouvrières dans le second XIXe siècle*. Paris: Editions de la Maison des sciences de l'homme.

Licoppe, C. (2008) 'Understanding and reframing the electronic consumption experience: The interactional ambiguities of mediated coordination'. In T. Pinch and R. Swedberg, *Living in a Material World*. Cambridge MA: MIT Press, pp. 317–340.

Luca, N. (2012) *Y croire et en rêver. Réussir dans le marketing relationnel de multiniveaux*. Paris: L'Harmattan.

Lüdtke, A. (ed) (1994) *Histoire du quotidien*. Paris: Editions de la MSH.

Maillet, T. (2013) 'Histoire de la médiation entre textile et mode en France: des échantillonneurs aux bureaux de style (1825–1975)'. Thèse de doctorat d'histoire, EHESS.

Mallard, A. (2000) 'La presse de consommation et le marché. Enquête sur le tiers-consumériste', *Sociologie du Travail*, 3, 391–410.

Mallard, A. (2016) 'Concerning urban consumption: On the construction of market agencements for retail trade', *Consumption Markets & Culture*, 19, 56–70.

Marchand, R. (1985) *Advertising the American Dream: Making Way for Modernity, 1920–1940*. Berkeley: University of California Press.

Marcuse, H. (1991 [1968]) *One-dimensional Man: Studies in the Ideology of Advanced Industrial Society*. Boston: Beacon Press.

Mazurek, M. and Hilton, M. (2007) 'Consumerism, solidarity and communism: Consumer protection and the consumer movement in Poland', *Journal of Contemporary History*, 42(2), 315–343.

McFall, L. (2011) 'A "good, average man": Calculation and the limits of statistics in enrolling insurance customers', *The Sociological Review*, 59(4), 661–684.

Micheletti, M. (2003) *Political Virtue and Shopping*. London: Palgrave Macmillan.

Miller, M.B. (1981) *The Bon Marché: Bourgeois Culture and the Department Store, 1869–1920*. Princeton: Princeton University Press.

Millet, A. (2015) 'Les dessinateurs de fabrique en France (XVIIe–XIXe siècles)'. Thèse de doctorat d'histoire, Université Paris 8-Université de Neuchâtel.

Oldenziel, R. and Hård, M. (2013) *Consumers, Tinkerers, Rebels: The People Who Shaped Europe*. Basingstoke: Palgrave Macmillan.

Pelletier, D. (1995) 'Engagement intellectuel catholique et médiation du social. L'enquête monographique de Le Ply à Lebret', *Mil Neuf Cent*, 53, 25–45.

Pence, K. and Betts, P. (eds) (2008) *Socialist Modern: East German Everyday Culture and Politics*. Ann Arbor: University of Michigan Press.

Platt, J. (1996) *A History of Sociological Research Methods in America 1920–1960*. Cambridge: Cambridge University Press.

Plessz, M., Dubuisson-Quellier, S., Gojard, S. and Barrey, S. (2016) 'How consumption prescriptions affect food practices: Assessing the roles of household resources and life-course events', *Journal of Consumer Culture*, 16(1), 101–123.

Pulju, R. (2011) *Women and Mass Consumer Society in Postwar France*. New York: Cambridge University Press.

Ragaru, N. and Capelle-Popacean, A. (eds) (2010) *Vie quotidienne et pouvoirs sous le socialisme. La consommation revisitée*. Paris: Karthala.

Rappaport, E.D. (2000) *Shopping for Pleasure: Women in the Making of London's West End*. Princeton: Princeton University Press.

Reid, S.E. and Crowley, D. (2000) *Style and Socialism: Modernity and Material Culture in Post-war Eastern Europe*. Oxford: Berg.

Revue des politiques sociales et familiales. (2017) *Joindre les deux bouts. Enquêtes d'ethnocomptabilité*, n° 123, p. 139.

Roberts, M.L. (1998) 'Gender, consumption, and commodity culture', *American Historical Review*, 103(3), 817–844.

Roche, D. (1987 [1981]) *The People of Paris: An Essay in Popular Culture in the 18th Century*. Berkeley: University of California Press.

Roche, D. (1994 [1989]) *The Culture of Clothing: Dress and Fashion in the Ancien Regime*. Cambridge: Cambridge University Press.

Roche, D. (2000 [1997]) *History of Everyday Things: The Birth of Consumption in France, 1600–1800*. Cambridge: Cambridge University Press.

Schleifer, D. and De Soucey, M. (2015) 'What your consumer wants: Business-to-business food advertising as a mechanism of market change', *Journal of Cultural Economy*, 8(2), 218–234.

Schwarzkopf, S. (2016) 'In search of the consumer: The history of market research from 1890 to 1960'. In D.G. Brian Jones and M. Tadajewski (eds) *The Routledge Companion to Marketing History*. London: Routledge, pp. 61–83.

Silverberg, H. (ed) (1998) *Gender and American Social Science: The Formative Years*. Princeton: Princeton University Press.

Strasser, S. (1989) *Satisfaction Guaranteed: The Making of the American Mass Market*. New York: Pantheon Books.

Strasser, S., McGovern, C. and Judt, M. (1998) *Getting and Spending: European and American Consumer Societies in the Twentieth Century*. Cambridge: Cambridge University Press.

Thomann, B. (2015) *La naissance de l'Etat social japonais: Biopolitique, travail et citoyenneté dans le Japon impérial (1868–1945)*. Paris: Presses de Sciences Po.

Trentmann, F. (2001) *Bread, Milk and Democracy: Consumption and Citizenship in Twentieth-Century Britain*. London: Berg Publishers.

Trentmann, F. (2006) *The Making of the Consumer: Knowledge, Power and Identity in the Modern World*. London: Berg Publishers.

Trentmann, F. (2009) *Free Trade Nation: Commerce, Consumption and Civil Society in Modern Britain*. Oxford: Oxford University Press.

Trentmann, F. (2016) *Empire of Things: How We Became a World of Consumers, from the Fifteenth Century to the Twenty-First*. London: Allen Lane; New York: Harper Collins.

Trumbull, G. (2006) *Consumer Capitalism: Politics, Product Markets and Firm Strategy in France and Germany*. Ithaca: Cornell University Press.

Trumbull, G. (2014) *Consumer Lending in France and America: Credit and Welfare*. New York: Cambridge University Press.

Veblen, T. (1899) *The Theory of the Leisure Class: An Economic Study of Institutions*. New York: Macmillan.

Whittle, J. and Griffiths, E. (2012) *Consumption and Gender in the Early Seventeenth-Century Household: The World of Alice Le Strange*. Oxford: Oxford University Press.

Williams, P.H. (1938) *South Italian Folkways in Europe and America: A Handbook for Social Workers, Visiting Nurses, School Teachers, and Physicians*. New York: Russell and Russell.

Yip, J. and Ainsworth, S. (2016) '"Notre objectif: procurer un service d'excellence à tous ceux qui viennent à l'Eglise!" Le marketing des mega-églises à Singapour'. In P. Bourdeaux and J. Jammes (eds) *Chrétiens évangéliques d'Asie du Sud-Est. Expériences locales d'une ferveur conquérante*. Rennes: Presses Universitaires de Rennes, pp. 285–304.

Zakharova, L. (2015) 'How and what to consume: Patterns of Soviet clothing consumption in the 1950s and 1960s'. In T. Vihavainen, and E. Bogdanova (eds) *Communism and Consumerism: The Soviet Alternative to the Affluent Society*. Leiden: Brill, pp. 85–110.

Zakharova, L. (2016) 'Was the Soviet telephone a medium of secondary orality? Some evidence from Soviet films of the 1930s–1970s', *Russian Journal of Communication*, 8(2), 183–194.

Zalc, C. (2012) 'Tati, ou l'invention du maxi-discount textile (1945–années 1980)', *Revue Européenne des Migrations Internationales*, 28, 11–26.

5

Consumption, Class and Taste

Jessica Paddock

INTRODUCTION

This chapter charts the sociological consideration of class and taste and their bearing on consumer practice. Indeed, since the Cultural Turn and the rise of post-industrial neoliberal free market capitalism, traditional class categories have been understood as ceasing to resonate, due to a blurring of boundaries between working- and middle-class occupations and the cultures that go with them (Crompton, 2008; Savage, 2000). This begs the question as to whether there remain any pronounced differences between classes today. To answer such a question, we must consider on the one hand how differences between social groups find means of expression, while on the other, equip ourselves with the tools necessary to observe and understand these manifestations.

For Douglas and Isherwood (1996), consumer goods produce, reflect and make stable the categories of our culture. In this way, consumption is understood to offer a lens through which to delineate class, and is a perspective closely aligned with the sociology of Pierre Bourdieu. For Bourdieu, one's disposition or worldview is acquired through the habitus, which structures one's tastes across fields; most predominantly in art and music but also in clothes, food, and even styles of furniture. That is, class can be read and understood through the analysis of consumption (Saunders, 1990; Warde et al., 1999). Taking Bourdieu's treatise on distinction as a starting point, this chapter outlines key concepts underlining Bourdieu's framework, and then explores contemporary incarnations and modifications of this key contribution (Bennett et al., 2009; Lamont, 1992; Silva and Warde, 2010; Southerton, 2002).

Beginning with a key departure marked by Mennell (1985), that increasing the variety of consumer goods leads to diminishing contrasts between these goods and the people consuming them, the chapter notes how this has triggered lively debate as to the relevance of Bourdieu's framework in explaining the relationship between consumption, class and taste today. Chiefly, the chapter presents the critical dialogue that has developed around Peterson and Kern's (1996) theory of cultural 'omnivorousness', and considers whether or not snobbish behaviours have given way to broad appreciation of diverse cultural forms. If not, I draw on the most contemporary debates in the field to suggest there *may* be new and emerging ways that distinction is expressed and the associated advantages accrued by social actors.

CLASS, CONSUMPTION AND CONSUMER CULTURE

The decline of manufacturing industry and rise of consumerism over the last century led some in Britain to argue that class serves as a less meaningful descriptive category for marking social divisions than it once was (Bauman, 2009; Clark and Lipset, 1991; Pahl, 1989). Pakulski and Waters (1996) even proclaimed class a redundant category, going as far as to proclaim the 'death' of class. Replacing class is a notion of the self as being made reflexively in interaction with the institutions of what Giddens (1991) terms 'high' modernity. As post-Fordist production and flexible specialisation bring with it the means to both create and respond to demand for rapidly changing styles in clothes, furniture and even cars, the rising middle classes were thought to have entered a period in which they were enjoying freedom of expression through the cultivation of lifestyle projects, rather than adopting a style out of custom or habit (Featherstone, 2007). Indeed, these postmodern perspectives have provided analyses that fundamentally question the relevance of class in shaping identities (Appignanesi and Bennington, 1989; Hebdige, 1988). With consumerism offering new opportunities for self-cultivation through choices made in the marketplace, class is considered an outmoded way of understanding differences between social actors and groups. Moreover, to explain systems of social inequality and injustice, further facets of one's identity and their intersectionality are thought to better account for the multidimensional layers that reproduce or deny privilege. Class, therefore, is thought not to satisfactorily account for all aspects of one's identity, and comprehending identity requires consideration of race, ethnicity, gender, physical and/or mental (dis)ability, religion and sexual orientation as well as class (although this chapter does not offer such an analysis, see Andersen and Hill-Collins, 2015). Amongst recognition of the multiplicity of identities and changing social structures and spaces of lifestyles, class may be less easily recognised (Crompton, 2008).

Indeed, rather than social position clearly determining which form was for whom, the great divide between popular ('low culture') and consecrated forms ('high' culture) is broken down as consumers playfully engage across forms and genres that were previously highly stratified (Storey, 2015). While this can be taken as evidence that class differences in consumption have somewhat dissolved, this has sparked interest in the idea that class may be structuring consumption in alternate ways. Some argue that class may even have a stronger effect upon consumption, if with the decline in industrial manufacturing; consumption takes the place of production as a linchpin of identity formation (Saunders, 1990). Whichever perspective we might consider most convincing, consumption was indeed considered a significant force in shaping an organising contemporary life (Warde, 1994, 2017). Yet, warning against overstating the primacy of individualised consumer decision-making, Warde (1997) argues that there is less choice (and less of the anxiety that goes with it) to be observed in consumer practices than is inferred by Bauman's (1988) suggestion of a new form of consumer freedom. Indeed, our socio-economic position limits the options available to us, determining choices we make as consumers (Lury, 2011). For this reason, Tomlinson and Warde (1993) were able to accurately predict the social class of a person by the contents of their shopping basket, yet this was only possible after they somewhat re-drew the boundaries of class membership by considering the possibility that the middle classes were internally differentiated. That is, the tastes of managers were discernible from the tastes of the self-employed, professionals and routine white-collar workers. It is perhaps no surprise that the class schema developed from the work of Goldthorpe and colleagues at the Nuffield College during the 1980s and 1990s was updated and codified into the National Statistics Socio-Economic Classification (NS-SEC), which continues to focus upon the divisions within as well as between classes, placing social actors in one of seven class groupings according to individual employment position. While this remains the most validated measure of class, this schema is thought by some not to do justice to the complexity of class today, and much work has ensued in fathoming the shape and boundaries of class structure in contemporary Britain.

Bourdieusian understandings of class have been championed for they go beyond measures of income and wealth, incorporating variables such as education, social networks and lifestyle, thus recognising the interplay between economic, social and cultural capital (Bennett et al., 2009; Crompton, 2008). This 'cultural class analysis' (Atkinson, 2011, 2016) offers a point of analytic intersection with further axes of differentiation, such as gender (Skeggs, 1997). The 'Great British Class Survey' (GBCS) was conducted in 2011 and reported in Savage et al. (2013), who claim to have forged a way for the new phase of class analysis, generating a whole new model of social class that considers the interaction of economic, social and cultural capitals achieved by the method of latent class analysis. In doing so, they find a clear 'elite' class, discovering that social and cultural privilege may indeed help in securing their position at the top of British society. Moving down the scale they find the 'established middle class' and the 'traditional working class', which more readily fit Goldthorpe's schema. New class groupings such as the 'technical middle class' who are more socially restricted than the established middle classes, and have low engagement with highbrow culture. 'New affluent workers' are less well-off, yet relatively economically secure, and have tastes that conform to what they call 'emerging' cultural capital. This is a concept developed in order to capture new and more cosmopolitan modes of cultural consumption – such as gig attendance and appreciation for ethnic cuisine – evolving along more contemporary lines, as the classical division between highbrow/lowbrow breaks down. 'Emergent service workers' better capture young urbanites making their way with little economic capital, but with high emerging cultural capital, and strong social connections. At the bottom end of the scale, they find evidence of a 'precariat', who are lacking in all forms of capital, offering sharp contrast to the 'elite' grouping. While Savage et al. (2013) do not intend to compete with the NS-SEC, they suggest that their model offers an alternative that seeks to 'shed more light on how cultural and social boundaries operate in Britain' (p. 243).

In this way, we can see that Bourdieu has had an enormous influence on the study of social differentiation, taste and consumption, despite some calls to uphold the Weberian distinction between class and status (Chan and Goldthorpe, 2007). For this reason, the chapter outlines the Bourdieusian approach in some detail before discussing key critical modifications and debates regarding how these can be used to understand consumer culture today.

UNDERLINING KEY CONCEPTS

Habitus, Field and Capitals

For Bourdieu, the habitus is a deeply structured cultural grammar; a set of unconscious rules that serve the perpetuation of its conditions over time. It inculcates 'reasonable' and 'common sense' forms of social action (Bourdieu, 1990: 55). As a 'structured structure' (ibid., p. 53) the habitus provides form for the social actor to become socialised into a set of appropriate dispositions. As a 'structuring structure', life chances are transformed and perpetuated into subjective ones, in turn, reifying the objective structure of the status quo. The habitus is formative, presenting a set of reasonable practices, such as attaining higher education, appreciation of certain kinds of art and literature, or sporting activities, to those positioned within the corresponding habitus to which these practices have become normal and common-sense. One develops 'stylistic affinity' (Bourdieu, 1984: 173) to that which has become reasonable and normal within that habitus, and commensurate with its economic affordances, thus accounting for the perpetuity of these forms of style over time. In other words:

> being the product of a particular class of objective regularities, the habitus tends to generate all the 'reasonable', 'common sense', behaviours (and only these) which are possible within the limits of these regularities, and which are likely to be positively sanctioned because they are objectively adjusted to the logic characteristic of a particular field whose objective future they anticipate. At the same time 'without violence, art or argument' it tends to exclude all 'extravagances' ('not for the likes of us'), that is, all the behaviours that would be negatively sanctioned because they are incompatible with the objective conditions. (Bourdieu, 1990: 55–6)

It is this recognition of the structural and cultural elements shaping one's location in the social field that makes Bourdieu's concept of 'position' appropriate to the study of contemporary class relations. It is where we see the logic of limits at work as social actors are thought to gain a sense of their place through an orientation to others and their practices. The habitus is a sphere of activity around which there circulates 'a practical anticipation of what the social meaning and value of the chosen practice or thing will probably be, given their distribution in social space and the practical knowledge the other agents have of the correspondence between goods and groups' (Bourdieu, 1984: 466–7). These are not deliberative and conscious actions, they are felt, embodied and actioned without thinking. We might think of the limits of habitus working through what makes us feel comfort or discomfort in some social occasions, or manifested in our preferences of dislike for some foods, music, ways of dressing, films and television programmes or home furnishings.

The power of the habitus to impose limits derives from a wider structure – the field. This is defined as a network or configuration of relations between positions in that field (see Bourdieu and Wacquant, 1992: 97). Fields are bounded spheres of activity identifiable through their shared principles and knowledges, and are arenas for struggle over resources defined as 'capitals' – economic, social, cultural and symbolic. Economic capital underpins all other capitals, for this 'is first and foremost a power to keep necessity at arm's length' (ibid., p. 55). All other forms of capital tend to conceal that this lies at their root (Bourdieu, 1986 [2011]: 89). Then, the most sought after resource in the field – once one is free from economic necessity – is 'cultural capital', which can manifest in the form of long-lasting dispositions of the mind and body, in the form of cultural goods, for instance, in books and instruments, or appear in an institutionalised state in the form of an educational qualification. Social capital refers to the social network or group, membership of which provides its affiliates with the benefits of mobilising collectively owned capital (Bourdieu, 1989). This is where one's social connections to others come to really matter.

It is the mal-distribution of access to these capitals across the field that forms the centre of Bourdieu's critique of domination. In sum, the field is the battleground for the struggle to acquire capital, while the habitus simultaneously imposes limits upon one's likelihood of pursuing advancement in the field. To the three forms of 'capital' outlined above, Bourdieu adds a fourth – symbolic capital. This is the form that 'capital' takes when it is misrecognised; when there is a failure to recognise the 'specific logic' in misrecognising 'the arbitrariness of its possession and accumulation' (Bourdieu and Wacquant, 1992: 119). For Bourdieu, this lies in the subjective recognition of certain commodities, relationships or practices as worthy. Relating these dynamics to the reproduction of gender inequalities, Skeggs (1997) notes that such processes lead to the celebration of some qualities, while others are disparaged and vilified.

Distinction and Homologies of Taste

Bourdieu was not the first to explore the relationship between class and consumption. As Warde (1997) summarises, the classical sociology offered by Marx, Weber and Simmel tied consumption patterns to class positions, seeing consumption as an expression of social hierarchy. Inequalities in access to resources figure consumption as a resource for class struggle. Going further, Veblen's (1994) *The Theory of the Leisure Class*, originally published in 1899, provides a commentary on what he observes as 'conspicuous consumption' – a form of consumptive display that characterised the practices of the American aspirational classes. Ultimately, it was the open display of free time and care taken to show wastefulness – 'because one could afford to' – that was seen to reflect pecuniary status. The most comprehensive examination of social class and taste, however, is Bourdieu's (1984) *Distinction: A Social Critique of the Judgement of Taste*. This study is based on a survey questionnaire carried out by extended interview and ethnographic observations in 1963 and 1967–68 administered to a sample of 1217 people in Paris, Lille and a small provincial town in France.

This work was founded upon a premise that; 'taste classifies, and it classifies the classifier. Social subjects, classified by their classifications, distinguish themselves by the distinctions they make, between the beautiful and the ugly, the distinguished and the vulgar, in which their position in the objective classifications is expressed or betrayed' (Bourdieu, 1984: 6). Here, cultural consumption is seen to figure prominently in fulfilling the social function of marking and legitimating social differences between social subjects. In understanding how such a system operates, he suggests that the 'science of taste and of cultural consumption' (ibid.), as seen in the taste for, say, jazz music, may most often be justified by the refusal of other forms, such as country music.

To comprehend the nature of distinctive practices, and the ways that different systems of dispositions express themselves, Bourdieu subjected the entire set of survey data to multiple correspondence analysis. These questions involved probing for respondents' preferences in painting, music, radio programmes and books, among many others in order to discern patterns, or homologies of taste. Homologies are sets of correspondences that exist relationally both within and across fields, where it becomes possible to recognise the interrelationship between someone's taste for one item and another. There is a link between the cultural domains of food consumption and home decor as each body is the bearer of signs that are unconsciously registered by the social actor and by onlookers.

> [T]he seemingly most immediate 'elective affinities' are always partly based on the unconscious deciphering of expressive features, each of which only takes on its meaning and value within the system of its class variations ... Taste is what brings together things and people that go together. (Bourdieu, 1984: 241)

Described as a 'resemblance within a difference' (Bourdieu and Wacquant, 1992: 106) homologies consist of tastes that unite people from within a particular habitus or 'world view' across fields. In *Distinction*, Bourdieu suggests that art and cultural consumption fulfil 'a social function of legitimating these very social differences' (1984: 7). Such a system of differences is clearly delineated in the case of food, for the 'body is the most indisputable materialization of class taste' (ibid., p. 190). Ways of feeding and caring for the body reveal the deepest of dispositions of the habitus. The working classes are distinguished by the 'inclusion of salty, substantial, clearly masculine foods' (ibid., p. 382). These include soup, meat and cheese. The working-class meal is characterised by 'elastic' and 'abundant' dishes brought to the table. There is also an avoidance of dishes that involve the measuring of portions. Instead, the soup or the casserole is brought to the table and served with a ladle – a way of eating that does not restrict portion size or the potential for second helpings. All dishes are brought to the table at the same time, and stirring spoons shared to save labour – the ceremonious over-use of cutlery and plates is considered an affectation. On the contrary, the bourgeoisie 'is concerned to eat with all due form' (ibid., p. 196). In the bourgeois habitus there is an expression of order, propriety and restraint that is as applicable to eating as it is to dressing. Crumbs are brushed from the table before dessert is served. The meal marks aesthetic refinement, with focus on quality over quantity and style over function. For the working classes, food is seen to belong to the realm of 'substance' and 'being', and for the bourgeoisie to the realm of 'form' and 'appearance'. The practice of eating, even within the family home is considered privy to distinction wherein clear homologies of taste can be observed, a dynamic that Atkinson and Deeming (2015) find is transposable to Britain today.

While to document the widespread influence of Bourdieu's work is far too large a task to rehearse here, Silva and Warde (2010) provide such a resource in their classification of reflections by key scholars whom either fully adopt, partially critique and even completely repudiate the theoretical schema outlined above. Below, the chapter turns to discuss key studies that have utilised Bourdieu's toolkit of concepts in delineating the prevalence and meaning of distinction for consumer culture.

CRITICAL DEVELOPMENT AND AMENDMENTS

'Distinction' After Bourdieu

Having conducted 160 in-depth interviews with successful French and American upper-middle-class men, Lamont (1992) provides a startling portrait of their means of separating themselves from the lower classes. Whilst paying some homage to the work of Bourdieu (1984), her work is suggestive of some neglect of his work in the moral dimensions of boundary formation between and within social classes. Above all, Lamont (1992) pays close attention to the discourses of boundary formation, particularly in relation to cultural refinement, success in the workplace and conspicuous consumption. Lamont's concept of 'boundary work' is situated around three boundary nodes – socio-economic, cultural and moral – which has since been operationalised in the UK by Southerton (2002) in his community study of class identification in a new southern English town. The least affluent respondents' narratives are revealing of a sense of distinction gained from asserting one's sense of economy over extravagance. For those having experienced short-range social mobility, cultural boundaries were drawn through expression of an aversion to a common culture of being 'rough', while looking after one's garden was presented as a mark of cultural distinction over those whose gardens were a 'mess'. Professionals living on the most prestigious streets of the town make references to tacit cultural tastes shared with friends who 'know the difference between Australian and French red wine' and whose embodied social differences mark them as separate from those who have 'always got a cigarette in their hand' (p. 185).

Key insights drawn out by Bourdieu's *Distinction* are applied to a vast number of empirical contributions. More recent contributions range from those that chart the efforts of the Russian upper class to gain social capital through the demonstration of 'culturedness' over ostentatious display of wealth (Schimpfossl, 2014), to the maintenance of female friendships (Mellor et al., 2010), sexuality and fandom (Harman and Jones, 2013) and wine drinking (Brierley-Jones et al., 2014). Furthermore, studies that follow Bourdieu's method of Multiple Correspondence Analysis – a statistical methods used to establish the pattern of relationships of several categorical dependent variables – come to map the tastes of consumers in the same way as Bourdieu (Kahma and Toikka, 2012), while others explore the social attitudes of consumers. Deeming (2014), for example, reveals sharp contours and differences in attitudes and tastes among British consumers according to class divisions, and finds evidence across fields of food, clothing and social life. Most importantly, Deeming (2014) suggests that a contemporary British working class 'taste for the necessary' is akin to that of Bourdieu's 1960s France. Looking towards the forms of emerging cultural consumption mentioned above, Portwood-Stacer (2012) theorise abstention from popular social media such as Facebook as conspicuous display.

Forty years after Bourdieu's *Distinction*, the most comprehensive appraisal of its contemporary relevance remains that of Bennett et al. (2009), who explore the role played by cultural capital in producing and maintaining patterns of social differentiation and inequality in Britain. By involving further categories of social differentiation in their analysis, they engage with much of the mounting critique of Bourdieu's (1984) work that had appeared across Europe and the USA. While addressing Bourdieu's neglect of categories such as ethnicity (Bryson, 1996; DiMaggio and Ostrower, 1992; Erickson, 1996; Lamont and Molnár, 2002); age and gender (Reay, 1998; Silva, 2005; Skeggs, 1997), they also question the extent to which Bourdieu dramatised differences in preferences for particular consumer goods and leisure activities that may in fact have highlighted differences and distinctions between classes. On the other side of this critical coin, Lahire (2008) contends that Bourdieu may have even neglected to focus upon the tastes and preferences that were common to all classes.

With reference to class and distinction, Bennett et al. (2009) find that contemporary cultural advantage is not so much pursued in order to gain advantage in the social field through 'snobbishness', but is accrued via the competencies of the social actor to bridge and bond between cultural worlds. Also, systemic patterns of cultural taste and practice were, without doubt, found across and within fields. Echoing Bourdieu's observation that bourgeois alimentary tastes are organised around restraint and delicacy, the exercised and cultivated body is found to be an instrument of social classification – through sport, exercise, diet management and maintenance. They also find that visual art markedly differentiates a set of exclusive tastes, indeed more than any other cultural field such as music or film, as participation in this field is dominated by the better-off, despite increasing availability of visual art forms through initiatives to widen access to museums and art galleries. This echoes what Grenfell and Hardy (2007) find when they chart museum and art gallery usage across Europe and the US. Turning to issues of widening access, the next section explores the view that increasing availability of cultural goods democratises their consumption, drawing particularly on examples from culinary culture.

Changing Tastes and the Problem of Variety

In 'All Manners of Food' Mennell (1985) accounts for the development of table manners and notions of propriety around eating. Indeed, the increased security of food supply enjoyed in the eighteenth century was thought to bring the need to impose controls over appetite, and members of court society embraced this as a way to differentiate and distinguish themselves from the lower classes, moderating appetites with the consumption of delicate and refined dishes. To be restrained and to have 'proper' manners, then, became associated with the ability to select and discriminate among foodstuffs. Moreover, the development of haute cuisine in France during the seventeenth and eighteenth centuries formed a hierarchy of tastes that allowed for further lines of demarcation. 'Good taste' was then marked by one's proficiency in navigating, discriminating and accessing cultural goods emerging across the French gourmet foodscape. However, as food become more abundant – as afforded by processes of industrial production and globalisation – Mennell saw this increased variety as evidence for the diminishing contrast between classes and the foods they respectively consumed.

Taking umbrage with this thesis, Warde (1997) explores the effects of social and cultural change on British food habits from 1968 to 1992, considering how people are advised about what to eat as well as the patterns of individual and domestic practices of food purchasing and preparation. Competing rationales that pervade in legitimating choice for one type of cuisine over another are characterised by four antinomies of taste. These comprise oppositions between novelty/tradition, health/indulgence, economy/extravagance and care/convenience. These provide a systematic basis for analysing data pertaining to contradictory guidance about food offered by the mass media, social contacts and government. Indeed, despite the food abundance noted by Mennell, Warde observes the persistence of nuanced differences in food tastes between classes, suggesting it may be more suitable to speak of increasing variety and *increasing* contrasts.

Tensions surrounding the view of contemporary consumer culture as characterised by distinction on the one hand and widening cultural participation on the other, is well documented by debates in 'cultural omnivorousness' (Peterson and Simkus, 1992). Here, proponents of the omnivorousness thesis observe wide engagement with cultural genres as a sign of a more democratic cultural field. With groups of the highest social status sampling from 'low' as well as 'high' cultural forms, the forms of distinction illustrated by Bourdieu are thought to be outmoded. This is not to say that the privileged are seen to like everything indiscriminately, but that they are open to a wide variety of forms, as low-brow to high-brow forms make for a mixed cultural repertoire. For example, DiMaggio and Mukhtar (2004) find a greater interest among elites in folk forms, visual arts and jazz music. This clearly offers some contention to Bourdieu's theory of distinction by challenging the notion that tastes are homologous across forms within the confines of one's habitus. Crucially, not all scholars have taken widening participation as a sign of the breakdown of traditional distinction in consumer culture, some have understood omnivorous taste as an example of a new form of distinction and snobbery (Johnston and Baumann, 2010; Warde et al., 2007). Indeed, distinct patterns of inclusion and exclusion have been found among 'omnivores'. Bryson (1996), for example, finds that when it comes to musical taste, heavy metal, rap and country music tend to be avoided by those who claim to like a wider variety of music. Highbrow snobbery is replaced with highbrow omnivorousness (Peterson, 2005). Pointing to the social advantages gained from hiding one's privilege under a guise of wider cultural engagement, Emmison (2003) suggests that the ability to appeal to wide variety of tastes can be a boon for social mobility, which requires the social actor to switch comfortably between milieus. This echoes what Bernstein (1971) identified as the ability of the middle classes to participate and converse in wider social circles, as they possessed an elaborated linguistic code. Speaking the language of all classes ensures comfort across habitus. As Lizardo and Skiles (2012) have convincingly argued elsewhere, aesthetic boundaries have been transposed onto consumer goods not intentionally designed in this way. The sheer volume of cultural goods and forms available under postmodern conditions render omnivorousness a contemporary variant of the distinctive aesthetic disposition (Holt, 1998; Wright, 2010). Further variants have been noted with reference to cosmopolitanism in eating practices (Cappeliez and Johnston, 2013), rap music (Cheyne and Binder, 2010) and more general activities and genres, such as taste in music, the arts, books and television (Ollivier, 2008).

Giving an example of such dynamics and their effect, Johnston and Baumann (2010) argue that the appearance of democracy across the gourmet foodscape serves to hide subtler means of conferring status, and serve to reproduce privilege by obscuring inequalities. They do so by analysing the discourse of 'foodies' – both through the discursive framing of popular gourmet food magazines in the USA and across 30 interviews with self-professed 'foodies'. The selectiveness (hard to find) of the ingredients listed accomplish distinction, rather than the explicit exclusion of consumers on the grounds of price. Operating under the guise of food democracy, distinction is drawn out via two dominant frames: (1) authenticism and (2) exoticism. Firstly, authenticism is achieved by understated and restrained appeals to geographic specificity, simplicity, personal connection and historicism. Reference to the origins of certain foodstuffs – brandishing the most local of olive oil – and the simplicity of dishes come to be valorised by drawing on examples of small-scale production of 'unschooled' cookery 'from mama's kitchen' (Johnston and Baumann, 2007: 181). As a technique of validation, a sense of historicism is found through the connection of foods to their cultural tradition. This, Johnston and Baumann suggest, requires a high degree of cultural capital in the form of a highly specialised gastronomic knowledge (most commonly obtained from gourmet food writers) alongside a deep seated understanding of and conviction as to why so-called 'authentic' foods are finer than their industrially produced counterparts. Secondly, exoticism is framed through reference to the exciting and unusual. The more it can offend a mainstream taste-bud the better, while excitement is bred through breaking food norms. The apparent democratisation of food as elucidated by proponents of the omnivorousness thesis (Peterson and Kern, 1996) is said to conceal these relations of distinction, allowing omnivores to both 'have their cake and eat it'. The 'having it' is represented by the consumption of superior goods, the 'eating it' constituting the guise of a democratised food culture while they remain the very arbiters of such 'omnivorous' good taste.

Concurrent with the findings of Warde et al. (1999) discussed above, Johnston and Baumann (2007) discover that their respondents only refer obliquely to a preference for expensive and inexpensive food. Instead, they focus on 'brow spanning food' (ibid., p. 195). This refers to the foods that may expand one's horizons and invite us to move out of our comfort zones by tasting new or more exotic foods. They suggest that the 'foodie' understands food consumption as a matter of cultural and symbolic importance and not solely the concern of sustenance, while simultaneously abhorring the term 'foodie' when aligned with traditional snobbery. They instead prefer to see themselves as pursuing excellence in food. On the other hand, we might question the democratic availability of such excellent food and entertain the notion that the choices made by those we might call 'foodies' are highly selective and distinctive. The ways in which they position themselves in relation to others can mark positions of superiority in the field of food consumption practice, and even come to dominate ideas of proper food, proper eating (Paddock, 2016). In this way, their interests and their foodways shape the foodscape in ways that are unrecognisable and non-relatable to those who enjoy less social, cultural and economic capital than their more privileged counterparts (Guthman, 2008; Paddock; 2015; Slocum, 2007).

In this way, exposing the limits to omnivorous openness to popular culture, Warde et al. (2008) remind us that dislikes are perhaps even more revealing than preferences. Similarly noting that there are parameters to aesthetic toleration, Ollivier (2008) identifies four different modes of openness to objects and practices – humanist, populist, practical and indifferent. None of these suggest the disappearance of cultural boundaries, nor do they suggest the levelling out of taste hierarchies, for omnivores would certainly not exist if there were no such boundaries to cross. The debate would be non-existent, while it is immediately clear that the debate over the presence of the cultural omnivore and the persistence of a hierarchical view of tastes in cultural consumption is ongoing.

Appeals for progress in this field encompass calls for methodological advance through greater qualitative inquiry. Indeed, Warde et al. (2007) note that studies of cultural omnivorousness have traditionally relied upon survey methods. Noting what he calls incomprehensibly broad categories of musical genres carved for the purposes of survey research, Atkinson (2011) suggests that much qualitative and even ethnographic work is to be done if we are to properly understand the complexities of social positioning around tastes for various cultural forms, as well as varieties within genres, and their meaning to consumers. Furthermore, this project is central to challenging the view that consumer culture, since the Cultural Turn, is characterised by individualisation, reflexivity and indiscriminate omnivorous taste not tied to socio-economic structures.

How class, status and privilege interact with taste hierarchies and orientations has formed a renewed focus in research concerned with distinction and omnivorousness in cultural consumption. Friedman (2012) has challenged dominant representations of the 'omnivore' by focusing on an emerging form of cultural consumption – comedy consumption. He provides an account of the inconsistent taste profiles of those who are socially mobile and consequently unsure of their cultural identity. He argues that upwardly mobile might be better described as 'culturally homeless' than 'culturally omnivorous' in their taste orientation. A special issue of the journal *Poetics*, published in December 2015 is further testament to the desire to move debates forward towards such qualitative specifications (Jarness, 2015), alongside consideration of the material advantages secured from an engagement with distinctive forms of emerging cultural capital (Mears, 2015). Crucially, these perspectives draw attention to Bourdieu's emphasis upon not only what is consumed, but in how the principles of the aesthetic are appropriated and displayed, and to what effect.

CONCLUSION: DEMOCRACY OR DISTINCTION?

In charting the relationship between consumption, class and taste, this chapter has considered the core underpinning concepts developed by Pierre Bourdieu, as related to his seminal study of consumption in France in the 1960s '*Distinction: A Social Critique of the Judgement of Taste*' (1984). Showing how insights from this key work have since been taken forward, we arrive at contemporary debates surrounding the relevance of class as a means to characterise identity, tastes, preferences and practices of consumption. While examples indicated and discussed are by no means exhaustive, this chapter has signalled how class has come to be understood through consumption. Receiving much empirical attention over the last two decades is the idea of the alleged democratisation of taste, on the one hand, and the observation that the wide appreciation of a variety of genres makes for a new mode of distinction, on the other (Warde et al., 1999). In this way, an Arnoldian view of culture as 'the best that has been thought and said' – see Raymond Williams's famous essay 'Culture is Ordinary' (1989) – a view that has associated high culture with a snobbish disposition, has translated into another form, rather than disappearing completely. Through the appreciation of a wide variety of cultural goods and genres, the elite and privileged have the means to hold on to distinctive modes of consumption under the guise of variety and even simplicity (see Paddock, 2015).

Nonetheless, the problem of accounting for variety in cultural consumption remains. That is, the view that omnivorousness is really distinction in action, operating under a veil of cultural openness, is based on the understanding that goods being consumed across classes appear the same, but that qualities of consumption differ. To make an example of food, we might proclaim the democratisation of food culture when observing the ubiquitous consumption of hamburgers across class groups. Distinction is maintained through the quality of ingredients – specialty cheeses and higher grades of meat. How the burger is assembled and where it is consumed may also add to this distinctive performance. But what can we make of instances where the very same goods are being eaten, worn and listened to across social groups? In a most recent special issue dedicated to such a question, Friedman et al. (2015) bring together accounts seeking to carve the way forward in bringing some resolution to such debates by means of a focus upon emerging cultural capital.

Doing so will no doubt require a fuller understanding not only of what sorts of goods are consumed across class divisions, but to consider the ways in which such goods are appreciated. Indeed, we may turn to Warde's (2013) account of consumer practice as phases of acquisition, appropriation and appreciation when exploring the extent to which differentiation manifests in consumer practice performance across social groups. Doing so would require not so much innovation, but what Atkinson and Deeming (2015) refer to as the need for methodological pluralism in this field. More extensive engagement of the social scientific methodological toolkit will no doubt add further fuel to the fire that debates the persistence of Bourdieusian-style distinction or a re-drawing of the boundaries through which social actors draw boundaries between themselves and others through consumer culture.

In this way, capturing and making sense of today's ever-shifting consumer culture and its relationship to the mechanisms of taste hierarchy, class structure and politics of domination continues to demand further methodological attention and analytic imagination to bring forth fresh insights.

REFERENCES

Andersen, M.L. and Hill Collins, P. (2015) *Race, Class and Gender: An Anthology*, 9th edition. Boston (MA): Cengage Learning.

Appignanesi, L. and Bennington, G. (1989) *Postmodernism*. London: Free Association Books.

Atkinson, W. (2011) The context and genesis of musical tastes: Omnivorousness debunked, Bourdieu buttressed. *Poetics* 39(3): 169–86.

Atkinson, W. (2016) *Beyond Bourdieu*. Cambridge: Polity Press.

Atkinson, W. and Deeming, C. (2015) Class and cuisine in contemporary Britain: The social space, the space of food and their homology. *The Sociological Review* 63(4): 876–96.

Bauman, Z. (1988) *Freedom*. Milton Keynes: Open University Press.

Bauman, Z. (2009) Memories of Class (Routledge Revivals): The Pre-history and After-life of Class. London: Routledge.

Bennett, T., Savage, M., Silva, E., Warde, A., Gayo-Cal, M. and Wright, D. (2009) *Culture, Class, Distinction*. London: Routledge.

Bernstein, B. (1971) Class, Codes and Control, Vol. I. Theoretical Studies towards a Sociology of Language. London: Routledge & Kegan Paul.

Bourdieu, P. (1984) Distinction: A Social Critique of the Judgement of Taste. London: Routledge.

Bourdieu, P. (1986 [2011]) Forms of capital. In: I. Szeman and T. Kaposy (eds) *Cultural Theory: An Anthology*. Oxford Blackwell, 81–94.

Bourdieu, P. (1989) Social Space and Symbolic Power. *Sociological Theory* 7(1): 14–25.

Bourdieu, P. (1990) *The Logic of Practice*. Stanford CA: Stanford University Press.

Bourdieu, P. and Wacquant, L. (1992) *An Invitation to Reflexive Sociology*. Chicago: University of Chicago Press.

Brierley-Jones, L., Ling, J., McCabe, K.E., Wilson, G.B., Crosland, A., Kaner, E.F.S. and Haighton, C.A. (2014) Habitus of home and traditional drinking: A qualitative analysis of reported middle-class alcohol use. *Sociology of Health & Illness* 36(7) 1054–76.

Bryson, B. (1996) 'Anything but heavy metal': Symbolic exclusion and musical dislikes. *American Sociological Review* 61(5): 884–99.

Cappeliez, S. and Johnston, J. (2013) From meat and potatoes to 'real-deal' rotis: Exploring everyday culinary cosmopolitanism. *Poetics* 41(5): 433–55.

Chan, T.W. and Goldthorpe, J.H. (2007) Social stratification and cultural consumption: Music in England. *European Sociological Review* 23(1): 1–19.

Cheyne, A. and Binder, A. (2010) Cosmopolitan preferences: The constitutive role of place in American elite taste for hip-hop music 1991–2005. *Poetics* 38(3): 336–64.

Clark, T.N. and Lipset, S.M. (1991) Are social classes dying? *International Sociology* 6(4): 397–410.

Crompton, R. (2008) *Class and stratification*, 3rd edition. Cambridge: Polity.

Deeming, C. (2014) The choice of the necessary: Class, tastes and lifestyles: A Bourdieusian analysis in contemporary Britain. *International Journal of Sociology and Social Policy* 34(7/8): 438–54.

DiMaggio, P. and Mukhtar, T. (2004) Arts participation as cultural capital in the United States, 1982–2002: Signs of decline? *Poetics* 32(2): 169–94.

DiMaggio, P. and Ostrower, F. (1992) Race, Ethnicity, and Participation in the Arts: Patterns of Participation by Hispanics, Whites, and African-Americans in Selected Activities from the 1982 and 1985 Surveys of Public Participation in the Arts. Washington (DC): Seven Locks Press.

Douglas, M. and Isherwood, B. (1996) *The World of Goods: Towards an Anthropology of Consumption*. London: Routledge.

Emmison, M. (2003) Social class and cultural mobility: Reconfiguring the cultural omnivore thesis. *Journal of Sociology* 39(3) 211–30.

Erickson, B.H. (1996) Culture, class, and connections. *American Journal of Sociology* 102(1): 217–51.

Featherstone, M. (2007) *Consumer Culture and Postmodernism*. London: Sage.

Friedman, S. (2012) Cultural omnivores or culturally homeless? Exploring the shifting cultural identities of the upwardly mobile. *Poetics* 40(5): 467–89.

Friedman, S., Savage, M., Hanquinet, L. and Miles, A. (2015) Cultural sociology and new forms of distinction. *Poetics* 53: 1–8.

Giddens, A. (1991) *Modernity and Self-identity: Self and Society in the Late Modern Age*. Stanford CA: Stanford University Press.

Goldthorpe, J.H., Llewellyn, C. and Payne, C. (1980) *Social Mobility and Class Structure in Modern Britain*. Oxford: Clarendon Press.

Grenfell, M. and Hardy, C. (2007) *Art Rules: Pierre Bourdieu and the Visual Arts*. Oxford: Berg.

Guthman, J. (2008) Bringing good food to others: Investigating the subjects of alternative food practice. *Cultural Geographies* 15(4): 4317–447.

Harman, S. and Jones, B. (2013) Fifty shades of ghey: Snark fandom and the figure of the anti-fan. *Sexualities* 16(8): 951–68.

Hebdige, D. (1988) Hiding in the Light: On Images and Things. London: Routledge.

Holt, D.B. (1998) Does cultural capital structure American consumption? *Journal of Consumer Research* 25(1): 1–25.

Jarness, V. (2015) Modes of consumption: From 'what' to 'how' in cultural stratification research. *Poetics* 53: 65–79.

Johnston, J. and Baumann, S. (2007) Democracy versus distinction: A study of omnivorousness in gourmet food writing. *American Journal of Sociology* 113(1): 165–204.

Johnston, J. and Baumann, S. (2010) Foodies: Democracy and Distinction in the Gourmet Foodscape. New York: Routledge.

Kahma, N. and Toikka, A. (2012) Cultural map of Finland 2007: Analysing cultural differences using multiple correspondence analysis. *Cultural Trends* 21(2): 113–31.

Lahire, B. (2008) The individual and the mixing of genres: Cultural dissonance and self-distinction. *Poetics* 36(2–3): 166–88.

Lamont, M. (1992) Money, Morals, and Manners: The Culture of the French and American Upper-middle Class. Chicago: University of Chicago Press.

Lamont, M. and Molnár, V. (2002) The study of boundaries in the social sciences. *Annual Review of Sociology* 28: 167–95.

Lizardo, O. and Skiles, S. (2012) Reconceptualizing and theorizing 'omnivorousness': Genetic and relational mechanisms. *Sociological Theory* 30(4): 263–82.

Lury, C. (2011) *Consumer Culture*, 2nd edition. Cambridge: Polity Press.

Mears, A. (2015) Girls as elite distinction: The appropriation of bodily capital. *Poetics* 53: 22–37.

Mellor, J., Blake, M. and Crane, L. (2010) When I'm doing dinner parties I don't go for the Tesco's cheeses: Gendered class distinctions, friendship and home entertaining. *Food, Culture & Society* 13(1): 115–34.

Mennell, S. (1985) *All Manners of Food: Eating and Taste in England and France from the Middle Ages to the Present*. Oxford: Blackwell.

Ollivier, M. (2008) Modes of openness to cultural diversity: Humanist, populist, practical, and indifferent. *Poetics* 36(2–3): 120–47.

Paddock, J. (2015) Invoking simplicity: 'Alternative' food and the reinvention of distinction. *Sociologia Ruralis* 55(1): 22–40.

Paddock, J. (2016) Positioning food cultures: 'Alternative' food as distinctive consumer practice. *Sociology* 50(6): 1039–55.

Pahl, R. (1989) Is the emperor naked? Some questions on the adequacy of sociological theory in urban and regional research. *International Journal of Urban and Regional Research* 13(4): 709–20.

Pakulski, J. and Waters, M. (1996) The reshaping and dissolution of social class in advanced society. *Theory and Society* 25(5): 667–91.

Peterson, R. (2005) Problems in comparative research: The example of omnivorousness. *Poetics* 33(5–6): 257–82.

Peterson, R. and Kern, R. (1996) Changing highbrow taste: from snob to omnivore. *American Sociological Review* 61(5): 900–7.

Peterson, R. and Simkus, A. (1992) How Musical Tastes Mark Occupational Status Groups. In M. Lamont and M. Fournier (eds) *Cultivating Differences: Symbolic Boundaries and the Making of Inequality*. Chicago (IL): University of Chicago Press, 152–68.

Portwood-Stacer, L. (2012) Media refusal and conspicuous non-consumption: The performative and political dimensions of Facebook abstention. *New Media & Society*, 15(7): 1041–57.

Prieur, A. and Savage, M. (2013) Emerging forms of cultural capital. *European Societies* 15(2): 246–67.

Reay, D. (1998) Rethinking social class: Qualitative perspectives on class and gender. *Sociology* 32(2): 259–75.

Saunders, P. (1990) *Social Class and Stratification*. London: Routledge.

Savage, M. (2000) *Class Analysis and Social Transformation*. Buckingham: Open University Press.

Savage, M., Barlow, J., Dickens, P. and Fielding, A. (1992) *Property, Bureaucracy and Culture: Middle-class Formation in Contemporary Britain*. London: Routledge.

Savage, M., Devine, F., Cunningham, N., Taylor, M., Li, Y., Hjellbrekke, J., Le Roux, B., Friedman, S. and Miles, A. (2013) A new model of social class? Findings from the BBC's Great British Class Survey experiment. *Sociology* 47(2): 219–50.

Schimpfossl, E. (2014) Russia's social upper class: From ostentation to culturedness. The British Journal of Sociology 65(1): 63–81.

Silva, E. (2005) Gender, home and family in cultural capital theory. *The British Journal of Sociology* 56(1): 83–103.

Silva, E. and Warde, A. (2010) *Cultural Analysis and Bourdieu's Legacy: Settling Accounts and Developing Alternatives*. London: Routledge.

Skeggs, B. (1997) *Formations of Class and Gender.* London: Sage.

Slocum, R. (2007) Whiteness, space and alternative food practice. *Geoforum* 38(3) 520–33.

Southerton, D. (2002) Boundaries of 'us' and 'them': Class, mobility and identification in a new town. *Sociology* 36(1): 171–93.

Storey, J. (2015) *Cultural Theory and Popular Culture: An Introduction*, 5th edition. Essex: Pearson.

Tomlinson, M. and Warde, A. (1993) Social class and change in eating habits. *British Food Journal* 95(1): 3–8.

Veblen, T. (1899 [1994]) *The Theory of the Leisure Class: An Economic Study of Institutions*. New York: Dover Thrift.

Warde, A. (1994) Consumption, identity-formation and uncertainty. *Sociology* 28(4): 877–98.

Warde, A. (1997) Consumption, Food, and Taste: Culinary Antinomies and Commodity Culture. London: Sage.

Warde, A. (2013) *Cultural Consumption, Classification and Power*. London: Routledge.

Warde, A. (2017) *Consumption: A Sociological Analysis*. London: Palgrave Macmillan.

Warde, A., Martens, L. and Olsen, W. (1999) Consumption and the problem of variety: Cultural omnivorousness, social distinction and dining out. *Sociology* 33(1): 105–27.

Warde, A., Wright, D. and Gayo-Cal, M. (2007) Understanding cultural omnivorousness: Or, the myth of the cultural omnivore. *Cultural Sociology* 1(2): 143–64.

Warde, A., Wright, D. and Gayo-Cal, M. (2008) The omnivorous orientation in the UK. *Poetics* 36(2–3): 148–65.

Williams, R. (1989) Resources of Hope: Culture, Democracy, Socialism. London: Verso.

Wright, D. (2010) Cultural capital and tastes: The persistence of distinction. In: J. Hall, L. Grindstaff and M. Lo (eds) *Handbook of Cultural Sociology*. New York: Routledge, 275–84.

PART II

Geographies of Consumer Culture

6

Debunking the Myths of Global Consumer Culture Literature

Güliz Ger, Eminegül Karababa, Alev Kuruoğlu, Meltem Türe, Tuba Üstüner and Baskin Yenicioğlu

INTRODUCTION

Globalization and global markets are typically considered in terms of production and supply chains across the world. However, globalization and its specific local encounters transform and are transformed by the consumption of goods and imaginaries as profoundly as production. Global capitalism may well be driven more significantly by new forms of consumption than by production (Comaroff and Comaroff 2005; Friedman 2005). Hence, consumption studies and marketing/consumer research have a lot to contribute to the understanding of globalization and global markets. However, cross-fertilization among disciplines has usually been scarce (see Richard Wilk's work for an exception) – for example, between anthropology and economics and political economy, between consumption studies and marketing/consumer research, or between micro and macro perspectives. Analyses of global capitalism and consumption, or neoliberal markets and consumer behavior have typically been conducted within disciplinary and sub-disciplinary boundaries. For example, macro-processes of accumulation in the world economy are more often analyzed by political scientists and economists whereas consumption patterns and consumer behavior are studied by marketing/consumption researchers, and the challenges globalization poses, such as rising inequality or ethnic violence are explored by anthropologists and sociologists. Contrary to the disciplinary focus in academia, Robertson and White (2005) point to the multidimensionality of global phenomenon in the real world: each and every phenomenon have cultural, social, political, and economic aspects. Thus, they argue that 'globalization is a site upon which relationships between disciplines are being restructured' (p. 347). The embeddedness of these multiple dimensions make it even more difficult to explain global markets and consumption with the compartmentalized approach in disciplines and sub-disciplines. Interrogating the grip of disciplinary (and micro-macro) boundaries, this chapter reviews several key domains of the literature critically, revealing assumptions, myths and ideologies that seem to have shaped scholarship on global consumer cultures.

The earliest theses about global consumption can be grouped into two opposing camps, with one group defining globalization as a process of emulation, while the other arguing that it is a process of resistance. Each camp had their respective predictions of global outcomes. While the former camp predicted that the end of globalization will be global homogenization, the latter one suggested that it will be heterogenization (Featherstone 1990; Ger 2017; Wilk 1995, 1998). Criticisms and debates on these views yielded diverse arguments. Over time these arguments converged on the highly influential accounts of hybridity and global flows (Appadurai 1990; Burke 2009; Hannerz 1987, 1992, 1996; Pieterse 2001 and 2009). Currently, from a sociocultural perspective (Tomlinson 1999), globalization is regarded in terms of 'complex connectivity' that widens, deepens and accelerates the social interactions across the planet. There are particular flows that make this connectivity possible. Appadurai (1990) defines these flows as mediascapes, finanscapes, ideoscapes, ethnoscapes and technoscapes. These flows facilitate the formation of particular hybrid consumption patterns and objects (Ger and Belk 1996). Moreover, globalization entails extensive reflexive global consciousness (Beck 2000; Tomlinson 1999). Accordingly, social processes and ways of life, including consumption and market relations, come to entail local manifestations of global patterns, representing 'glocalization' or 'sameness-within-difference' (Robertson 1995; Robertson and White 2005) and 'structures of common difference' (Wilk 1995, 2010). Such complex connectivity 'in one form or another is impacting on the lives of everyone on the planet' (Beynon and Dunkerley 2000, p. 3).

Given that global consumer culture is now a critical force in everyone's lives, it is important that we understand what it is and how it impacts us. One way to go about doing this could have been to revisit and summarize all that has been said on globalization so far (see Ger 2017 for such a review). This chapter is not going to take this path. Rather, our focus is on what is 'unsaid'. We will identify and debunk and/or question the taken-for-granted assumptions about and myths of the global consumer culture literature.

The first step towards this goal is to remind ourselves that we as academics are not outside of the grips of ideologies that surround our work. Ideologies shape individuals' belief systems and assumptions and consumers are not always reflexive of the impact of ideology (Wilk 2006 a,b,c). Interestingly, much like the consumers, we, the researchers, sometimes fall for the very same pitfalls. We do not always give due attention to what ideologies are being manifested in the concepts we use in our work. We are not always aware of how they might be shaping our thinking as scholars.

Following, we question and expose some of the myths, narratives, ideologies and assumptions researchers take for granted when they discuss and study consumption in a global world. First, we take issue with the myth that globalization is a recent condition. We argue that globalization is not a condition but a process and it is neither recent nor linear. It is shaped by historical socio-cultural and economic forces with different powerful centers shaping the process at each era. Next, we question the extent to which the encounter of the local cultures with the foreign is playful. We draw attention to the inequalities at play in hybridization and its valorization – the colonial gaze and the status games inherent in consumption of cultural differences, which can re-enforce rather than eradicate boundaries. Then, we take issue with one of the most important flows of globalization: immigration. We argue that immigrant consumption is not only about acculturation. We debunk the ideologies that structure our findings within the acculturation literature and argue that a more nuanced and critical understanding of immigrant consumption requires seeing immigrants as people, focusing on their different life worlds as opposed to lumping all same country of origin people together as one group such as Mexican Americans or British Pakistanis. Next, we deliberate how researchers approach morality and belief in the less privileged/non-Western context in comparison to the dominant/Western contexts. We contend that scholars operate with theoretical and methodological blinders which (un)intentionally reify the dualisms (e.g., us/others, West/rest) that reinforce cultural boundaries by highlighting some beliefs/moralities as superior to and less extreme than others. Finally, we interrogate to what extent the age of digitally networked technologies emancipate the complex connectivities of globalization from the powerful grip of market structures. We underscore the architecture of the digital panopticon and the underlying market realities which can still turn participatory moments into commodities for the profit of a few.

DEBUNKING THE MYTH THAT GLOBALIZATION IS A RECENT CONDITION

Scholars influential in consumption studies (e.g., Giddens 1990; Levitt 1983; Ritzer 1996) have placed globalization as a novel condition specific to the late twentieth century – as global markets, standardized products, or global orders of labor, production, governance, and military. This global condition is defined as transnational integration within which people are connected with a shared economic and cultural network of relationships, shaped by a globally shared consciousness. On the other hand, historians note the presence of global interactions from antiquity onwards and thus argue that globalization is a process and not a condition (Armitage 2004; Featherstone 1990; Hopkins 2002; Stearns 2010). Rather than arguing for or against the existence of such a condition at a specific time, historians argue that we should scrutinize globalization as a process, explaining the transformation of local into global via interactions among societies through migration, trades, diseases, wars and conquests. That is, contingencies and the processes of local societies converge in cultural, institutional, structural and psychological terms (Eisenstadt and Schluchter 1998; Stearns 2010). Research in consumer culture often focuses on current globalization processes – such as glocalization, hybridization, acculturation, and formation processes of global consumer subjectivities and consumer cultures – under conditions such as neoliberal economic order, intense migration, globally diffused digital technologies, and shifting global economic centers. However, there are two main advantages of debunking this myth of the recency of globalization and having a historical perspective.

The first advantage is to see how past patterns of global interactions form the present global markets and consumer cultures (Kjeldgaard and Ostberg 2007; Pieterse 2009; Wilk 2006c). The second advantage is to build novel understandings of how interregional or global interactions co-constitute past markets and consumer cultures in different geographies (Karababa 2015; Karababa and Ger 2011). Such a perspective will help identify the formation processes of global markets and consumer cultures under different contexts far from contemporary milieu and provide a deeper conceptualization of global formations of markets and consumer cultures.

Foundations of globalization go back as early as 3000 BCE when agriculture, urban markets, migrations and trade grew (Hopkins 2002; Stearns 2010; Pieterse 2012). Migration and trade were two important interactions – taking different shapes in different eras – between societies operating for thousands of years. The migrations in 1000 BCE resulted in a one-way interaction: immigrants who went to very far lands rarely returned to their former homes. In this period, the localism of previous ages was slowly disappearing. Connections among different regions were becoming possible through, for example, land and sea trade in the Persian Gulf and India or the exchange of precious stones and flint among east European societies.

After 1000 BCE, the emergent empires in Asia, Europe and the Middle East secured trade routes (Stearns 2010). As a result, the Silk Road and the Spice route circulated commodities across far lands. Treasured commodities such as silk from China were sold to the upper classes of the Roman Empire or the elites of Persia, the Middle East, or India. The Chinese silk changed the tastes of the upper classes and created a craze in the upper echelons of the Roman Empire, if not among the ordinary people. However, there were no such Western goods that captured the fantasy of the Chinese elite. Yet, during the period, value systems, arts, religions and social institutions did not accompany the material flows (Pieterse 2012; Stearn 2010). We have to note that for a long while, the West was not the dominant center of flows, it was located at the periphery, on the receiving side. Looking back into the history of commodity chains reveals multiple shifts in the center–periphery relations throughout time. Especially worthy of study are the shifts in the production, marketing and consumption practices along the global commodity chains, reflecting the power relations between different regions and their influence on the formation of global markets (Dicken 2007).

By 1000 CE, interregional convergence started to blossom, giving pace to the formation of an interregional consumer culture. Adventurers, missionaries and merchants were actors of global processes, traveling to the far lands. The 'seven wonders of the world' had been created and the curious traveled to far lands founding ancient tourism (Stearns 2010). Most of the recorded travel was from the west to the east. After 1000 CE, consumers in the west were interested in exotic goods, medicinal herbs and precious goods from the east (Stearns 2010). Indian calico, china, sugar, silver items, mirrors were some of the goods traveling between regions of Asia, Africa, the Middle East and Europe. During this period, Arab merchants were active in interregional trade, linking the Middle East with the Indian Ocean. Arabic became the lingua franca of the Indian Ocean.

In the sixteenth century, the new technologies and resulting discoveries of the new lands expanded the scope of the interregional trade. Mobile diasporic networks, as a specific social and economic formation also created connections between the cities sprouting on the trade routes (Hopkins 2002). Consumption depended on international trade and developed extensively in China and the Middle East (Stearns 2006). Eurasian realms like the Spanish, Ottoman, Chinese and Safavid empires experienced consumer cultures where commodities including the exotic and luxurious were spreading beyond the elites, and fashion and leisure were commercialized (Clunas 2004; Karababa 2012; Karababa and Ger 2011; Minowa and Witkowski 2009). Also a consumer subject interested in nature, science and aesthetics was forming in different parts of the Mediterranean (Febvre 1977; Karababa 2015).

Later during the eighteenth century, colonialism introduced new ways of interaction. Procedures installed by religion, law, education, labor and military service in the colonized regions were used to transform the 'undesirable' qualities of the local into 'desirable' ones (Canniford and Karababa 2013). As a practice of imperial globalization (Hopkins 2002), colonization engendered the exchange of people, goods, ideas and technologies, which were transferred from one colony to another. International companies like the East India Company, missionaries and migrants were other actors who had a catalytic effect in the interaction between the colonizers and the colonized. While imperial order was introduced to the colonies, new belief systems, tastes, practices, products, languages, the local and the global started to enmesh. Today's glocalization may well date back to this period. The strong asymmetry of power between the colonizer and the colonized defined the nature of interaction and highlighted the separation between the colonial West and the local other.

The nineteenth century's modern nation state, industrial revolution, integrated communication systems and liberal ideology positioned the West as a dominant power, the center and the locomotive of globalization (Giddens 1990; Hopkins 2002). Mass production imposed standardization rather than difference, which used to be an important precondition of trade (Hopkins 2002). The characteristics of Western society began to diffuse to the globe.

These early forms of interactions were shaped under conditions changing from milieu to milieu such as changes in the density and direction of migration, technologies of transportation, production and communication, government institutions, economic institutions, religious and moral discourses, and trade networks. Globalization has been a process where the relative dominance of actors from the East and the West, of peoples from different societies has been shifting over time.

In addition, like today, history witnesses globalization as a cyclical and reversible process (James 2009). Previous incidences of globalizations came to an end as a result of wars, financial crises and globalization of violence, where at times people move away from global settings to more secure places (James 2009). Therefore, we need to challenge the myths of globalization as a condition as well as a linear progression.

'EATING THE OTHER': QUESTIONING THE MYTH OF PLAYFUL ENCOUNTERS OF THE LOCAL AND THE GLOBAL

Globalization is often linked to hybridity. This is a world 'where reggae emerges from the slums of Kingston, and mixes with hundreds of other local musical styles, in a kind of creative ferment that leads to Australian Aboriginal reggae played with a didgeridoo and Japanese Rastafarians winning Jamaican DJ competitions' (Wilk 2006a: 6–7). Local cultures have absorbed and appropriated outside influences into ways that 'fit' their own histories (Wilk 2006a).

Such an account, at first glance, suggests a playful encounter of 'local' cultures with global flows, wherein 'new meanings and modes of expressing them can be born', and 'foreign cultural influences need not involve only an impoverishment of local and national culture' (Hannerz 1987: 555) – but rather may give people new means of managing and representing 'their own culture' (Ger 1999). Moreover, hybridization has long taken place, in nature and among cultures (Pieterse 2001). Critics have argued that hybridity is a 'plaything of the elite', yet Pieterse notes that it is in fact the lower-classes that mix and match the most – exemplifying such cases as rap by Turkish minorities in Germany. While the mimicry of colonizers can be a reproduction of their hegemony; hybridity can also destabilize – what Bhabha calls 'sly civility' – through such interventions (1985a, 1985b) as irony or civil disobedience. Yet, hybridity that is consumed through (mainstream) market/spaces does not necessarily indicate or lead to an eradication of the divide across classes, or ethnic/religious/gender identities within or across national borders. Rather, as Pieterse notes, the contingency of boundaries is more common than ever.

The fact that some (and not all) *melanges* stand out as 'hybrids' is indicative of inequality at play: selection of what becomes mixed and matched and what is valorized as such. A particular 'global gaze' is influential in choosing what becomes the object of preservation/cross-pollination/(re)presentation. Critical perspectives on hybridity and global flows argue that more often than not, the very process of 'hybridizing' itself is not only an affirmation of boundaries but also serves the verifying dominance of the 'mainstream' – as in an imagined 'Western' – order. The 'obsession' with boundaries (Pieterse 2001), on behalf of the 'West' as well as the 'rest' is what is problematic.

These boundaries are intimately linked to (a historical development of) inequality within as well as amongst locales and cultures. Shohat has argued, 'A celebration of syncretism and hybridity per se, if not articulated in conjunction with questions of hegemony and neo-colonial power relations, runs the risk of appearing to sanctify the *fait accompli* of colonial violence' (1992: 109). Ahmed (2000) cautions that the conditions of the meeting and mixing of the two are not equal. Rather, the 'other' is transformed in a way that (re)produces and commodifies the divide between the 'us' and the 'stranger'. With this transformation, the stranger is now familiarized and thus no longer someone to be feared, but rather someone whose difference needs to be celebrated. The white-dominant subject, argues bells hooks, relates to the body and practices of the non-mainstream 'Other' as 'an alternative playground where members of dominating races, genders, sexual practices affirm their power-over in intimate relations with the Other' (hooks 1992: 23). Root (1996) deems such consumption of cultural differences as 'cannibalistic' and Heldke (2001) has termed practices of culinary adventurousness as 'food colonialism' – an act of 'consuming' the other without necessarily showing any interest in or concern for the origins of the food; as well as the 'selection' process whereby certain foods are chosen, exoticized and commodified. Heldke notes, moreover, that the process of writing cookbooks may reproduce colonial hegemonies: recipes are gathered without crediting the work of the locals that goes into the preparation process; and foods that did not exist in the 'local' setting may be 'fabricated' (Narayan 1995).

The 'Other', in its edible and palatable form, serves as an essentialized mystical and emotional resource for the West, which in modernity has been deprived of its 'authenticity.' Importantly, this is also the perspective through which those who were colonized/exoticized came to understand themselves (Cook and Harrison 2003; see also Fanon 1967; Said 1978). Difference and strangeness, thus, are not necessarily constitutive of resistance against the global and colonial forces and flows, but rather are commodified (Grossberg 1995; Turgeon and Pastinelli 2002) and inverted, by the Others towards themselves.

Wilk (1995, 2006a) has conceptualized that this (co)construction and commodification of that difference is common throughout the world, in a way that he terms 'replication of diversity' (Wilk 1995: 118). Local dramas are played out in the global stage, through what Wilk terms 'structures of common difference'. In other words, 'cultures become different in uniform ways' (Wilk 1995: 118). Such process is not divorced from colonialism – the (formerly) colonized have become complicit in their self-production as commodities. This points us towards another important process: the process whereby those in the third world/less affluent world/'East' *cast* the Western/imperialist gaze upon themselves and (re)present and (re)imagine their (non-mainstream) bodies, cultures, practices as consumable resources or as open to becoming consumed and/or 'hybridized' by 'Western' influence.

Beauty is one field in which the colonial gaze is both projected upon and internalized by subjects. Mears (2010), in her ethnography on the world of high-fashion modelling, draws attention to the 'imperial gaze' on women, and notes how 'darker' bodies, when employed by the fashion industry at all, are 'posed and styled in exotic juxtaposition to the normatively white female body' (Mears 2010: 24). Wilk (1995), in his account of beauty contests in Belize, indicates that Belizean pageant contestants partially conform to local ideals of beauty, but also notes that 'an intimate awareness of the global gaze' (p. 127) shapes the way that the pageant plays out, and the way that beauty is defined and judged.

Another Belizean example is that of 'authentic' Belizean food: an invention literally 'cooked up' by Belizeans and foreign entrepreneurs, primarily to serve to tourists (Wilk 2006a). The Belizean local 'culture' has not only become commodified – it has been constructed and produced as 'local' in the first place. Certain elements of 'culture' get selected, invented and appropriated for production, preservation and consumption, be it by the 'foreigners' who are looking to find the exotic-authentic or by the locals who are trying to cultivate such experiences for tourists/outsiders, or even for themselves. Difference becomes a matter of 'style' within consumer culture in a way that occludes (past and present) antagonisms and violence (Ahmed 2000).

The consumption of the 'Other' – i.e., both the consumption of 'Western' products by the less developed world, and the consumption of the exotic East by the West – can serve similar purposes: status and display of capital. In the context of the 'East', the West is consumed as an indicator of having attained a 'normal', modern and middle-class status (e.g., Kravets and Sandikci 2014; Liechty 2002). In the 'West,' the exotic other affords avenues of displaying cultural capital through knowledge and appreciation of other cultures. In both cases, there is a display (and also a building) of cultural capital involved: people learn how to mix and match, how to arrange and organize (e.g., Holt 1998; Üstüner and Holt 2010). But in effect, these objects of consumption serve to produce and consolidate differences and boundaries (while sometimes offering the illusion that boundaries are crossed.) Ahmed (2000) argues that 'this perception of objects as *having* difference is itself an effect of the very processes of production and exchange embedded in consumer culture' (Ahmed 2000: 116). Accessing these differences or 'exotic' objects and controlling their circulation (Altglas 2014) is often a means through which the affluent build upon their status – being 'cosmopolitan', and knowing how/what to consume in terms of the *exotic* in the developed world is now a source of prestige.

Discussions on cosmopolitanism also tie into issues of mainstreamness–otherness and the constitution of the nation as an imagined community. Cosmopolitanism, as a political commitment, entails an openness to diversity and the possibility of being changed by encounters with the Others (Skrbiš and Woodward 2013). Yet, Ahmed notes that while cosmopolitanism/multiculturalism discourse on the one hand is about incorporating 'strangers' (migrants, minorities, etc.) into the nation – the us/we – it also serves as a reminder that 'we' have to live with 'them', thus reproducing the boundaries. She argues that multiculturalism also involves 'fetishizing' the stranger and her/his strangeness. This also relates to Said's conceptualization of Orientalism, that 'Europe' is produced through Orientalist discourse – the very notion that the Orient is what Europe is not. The us/we is similarly produced through this 'differentiation of familiar and strange' (Ahmed 2000: 97).

Through this critical lens, we question the playfulness that is attributed to consuming 'other' cultures – the myth of hybridity can easily occlude the colonial gaze that is inherent in seemingly innocent 'adventures' such as consuming 'food from other cultures' or appreciating 'the bridging of the East and the West' in music, arts and literature. While hybridity can indeed lead to economic benefits for some, what we as researchers need to remember, is how the colonizer's gaze continues to shape the way the 'non-West' perceives, (re)presents, produces, and consumes itself. To detect this gaze, then, is also to reveal inequality and dominance, as it plays out in the world scene – sometimes in contexts as seemingly innocent as food.

DEBUNKING THE MYTH THAT IMMIGRANT CONSUMPTION IS ALL ABOUT ACCULTURATION

Immigration is one of the most important forces of globalization. Today over 243 million people are living in a country different than their country of origin (United Nations Population Division). What is critical, at least for globalization scholars, is the extent of increase in immigration. The number of people who are starting a new life in a country different than their country of origin has been growing at an increasing rate. This increase is not only a manifestation of the expanding world population. Yes, there are more people living in the world in the 2010s compared to the 1800s; but more importantly, as a percentage, immigration is increasing even faster than the increase in world population. In 1995 immigrants made up 2.8% of the world's population. In 2005 they were 2.95% and in 2015 they were 3.3% of the world's population. All the political, economic and social indicators suggest that this trend will continue in the coming years. There will be more people living in a country different than their country of origin.

Given this trend, sociologists and marketing scholars have investigated immigration as an important social phenomenon. But the two literatures' foci have been diametrically opposite. On the one hand, the sociology of immigration literature is mostly interested in immigrants' and their children's educational and economic advancement trajectory (see Portes and Zhou 1993 for a quick review and introduction of the theory of segmented assimilation), and the structural drivers of xenophobia (Bohman 2015; Jaime-Castillo et al. 2016; Mierina and Koroleva 2015).

Marketing scholars' focus, on the other hand, have been mostly on uncovering how immigrants' consumption choices manifest and are manifested by the acculturation processes. So marketing scholars were able to engage with the topic of immigration from the perspective of immigrants' lived experiences, a perspective which is mostly lacking within the sociology literature.

However, as opposed to using a sociological lens to study immigrants' experiences, marketing scholars have mostly borrowed from the psychology literature. Almost all marketing studies on immigration engage with, what they call, the 'acculturation theory'. Acculturation theory was first developed within the psychology literature by Berry (1980). Its goal was to uncover immigrants' attitudes towards their host countries and categorize potential acculturation outcomes. Berry and colleagues uncovered four such outcomes: assimilation, separation, integration and marginalization. This theory was later adapted by Consumer Culture Theorists (Arnould and Thompson 2005) to understand immigrant *consumer* acculturation. Immigrant consumer acculturation is defined as 'the general process of movement and adaptation to the consumer culture environment in one country by persons from another country' (Peñaloza 1994: 33). Over the last two decades much valuable work has been conducted and published within the consumer acculturation literature. Due to space limitations, it is impossible to summarize those studies here with due diligence. But it is important to note that thanks to the consumer acculturation literature our understanding of immigrants' and host country citizens' consumer experiences is growing. We have moved away from the universalistic framework offered by Berry. We now know that acculturation is not an attitude-outcome. It is a process. There are antecedents and outcomes to this process. It is shaped by various socio-cultural structures and conditions. Outcomes are not solid. Neither do they fall in particular universalistic categories. Immigrants move between various possible identity positions.

Having said that, the accumulated work on immigrant consumers has very much been ideologically shaped by the acculturation theory's framework; limiting the marketing scholars' ability to develop a critical perspective. A simple etymology of the term *acculturation* reveals that the very early uses of the term indeed manifests a colonial ideology. According to the *Oxford English Dictionary* the word originated in the US around 1800s. The first use of the term surfaced in 1880 in the journal *Introduction to the Study of the Indian Languages*. Here acculturation is defined as a 'civilizing' force of the West: 'The force of acculturation under the overwhelming presence of millions of civilized people', by which the authors imply the Western colonialists 'wrought great changes'. Next it was used in *Popular Science Monthly* in 1888: 'We consider it a mistake to believe that an acculturation to our civilized ways is a thorough civilization'. Here the author implies that it is not enough to 'acculturate to the' West's 'civilized' ways. One can acculturate. But this does not mean that one will be civilized. Only people from the West are truly civilized. Interestingly this is a view still shared by some in the West in response to the refugee crisis in Europe. The next case is found in the *Journal of Negro History* in 1938: 'The overwhelming importance of the institution of slavery as the predeterminating factor in the influence and acculturation of the Negro …'. This quote does not really need much explanation in our view in terms of what the author implies by acculturation.

Very much reflective of the early uses of the term, the *Oxford English Dictionary* defines acculturation as 'adoption of or adaptation to a different culture, especially *that of a colonizing, conquering, or majority group*' (our emphasis). There are two critical assumptions hidden in this definition.

First, it assumes that acculturation means adoption or adaptation. Consumer culture researchers have been much aware of the first assumption. Indeed, the second wave of acculturation studies is named post-assimilationist to highlight its break away from the first wave of studies which focuss on 'how much' as opposed to 'how' immigrants acculturate (Luedicke 2011). These studies acknowledge that adoption is not the only outcome. Indeed, many studies argue that rejection, or pendulism (Askegaard, Arnould and Kjeldgaard 2005), or hybrid identities (Oswald 1999) are potential acculturation outcomes. But interestingly, all marketing studies which focus on immigration start with the question of how immigrant consumers acculturate to their new host countries. Even though the studies acknowledge rejection, they treat it as only a negative case. Rejection is never the sole focus.

Neither do marketing scholars study immigrants as people, rather they study them as consumers. One could argue that they are consumer researchers so it makes sense that they focus on consumers. But if the marketing scholars could think of immigrants as people, they would then start seeing sociological differences between them. Immigrants might be from the same country of origin, but they might not belong to the same social class. They might not be endowed with the same level or extent of cultural capital. They might not have the same religion. They might not even have the same race. What if social class, religion or race is the driving factor behind immigrants' rejection of (or their feelings of being rejected by) their host country cultures. Üstüner and Holt (2007) claims that social class (economic, cultural and social capital) indeed makes a difference in acculturation outcomes; but much like other studies, they focus on how migrants acculturate and treat the 'shattered identity project' of two young second-generation squatter women in Turkey merely as a negative case. As a result, with the exception of those two Turkish women, most of the respondents in marketing studies are playful and ironic, seamlessly moving from one identity position to another. But then, when one reads about what has been happening in Europe recently, one starts wondering why the second-generation immigrants in the Parisian banlieue or the Belgian suburbs do not playfully oscillate between various identity positions.

The second assumption hidden within the definition of acculturation is that it involves a clash between two cultures, with the powerful, colonizing, conquering culture winning over the powerless, colonized and conquered one. In consumer culture literature the scholars acknowledge that there could be a cultural conflict between the host and home cultures. They study conflict (Luedicke 2015). But when they do, they assume that it is a clash between *equal* but different cultures. In doing so, they miss the power dynamics that are in play between the immigrant-receiving West and the immigrant-sending East. For example, Askegaard, Arnould and Kjeldgaard (2005) do not engage with colonial theory even when they are studying colonized immigrants (Greenlanders) in a colonizing host country (Denmark). In the tables they bury the colonial history under boxes titled 'discursive elements from the home culture', 'discursive elements from the host culture'. When scholars study conflict they study it using *a*historical, universalistic models which focus on the issues surrounding the 'interpretation and coordination' of relationships between immigrants and indigenes, as opposed to underlying historical factors that shape those interpretations (for example, see Luedicke's (2015) work on conflict between Turkish immigrants and Austrian indigenes).

If the marketing scholars were to strip themselves from these assumptions, they would have more to contribute to our general understanding of immigration and the immigrant experience. Their research would be more historical, cultural and sociological. They would no longer allow the research to take shape under the burdens of the psychology literature on immigrants' attitudes (Berry 1980, learning theory and the literature on assimilation. They would reject the use of universalistic relationship models (such as that of Fiske's) in explaining conflict. They would be able to break away from the ideology that has been shaping their work. Only then could they develop a more critical approach that represents and explains what is going on in the Parisian banlieues and the Belgian suburbs.

If marketing scholars could see immigrants as people and not only as consumers, they would be able to understand their experiences better. They would start seeing differences amongst the same country of origin people. They would distinguish between their different backgrounds and upbringings. They would uncover the different forces that brought immigrants to their host countries in the first place. They would then understand how those differences shape immigrants' lives and the ways in which they use consumption goods and experiences to negotiate their lives and expectations in their host countries.

DEBUNKING THE MYTH OF THE MORAL 'US' AND RELIGIOUS 'OTHERS'

Across the world, we are witnessing the reinforcement of boundaries and enunciation of difference in increasingly common ways (Pieterse 2001; Wilk 1995): a global political scene promoting division against connection (e.g., increasing support for conservative/nationalist politicians), seeming disintegration of global entities (e.g., the 'doom' of the EU, recent debates about the functionality of UN), and fear on a global scale triggered by world-wide terror attacks and waves of immigrants. Belief, as moral principles and religious orientation, has come to be used to normalize such divisions and deal with the fear of 'the other.' The ideologies and myths surrounding belief can polarize the world by constructing some moralities as superior to and less dangerous than others. And while, as social scientists, we have celebrated the hybridity of local/global belief systems, morality and religion, it is unlikely that our research is devoid of such constructions. Reflecting on the myths on which we build our research is crucial to reveal how we come to celebrate some moralities and scrutinize others and, hence, contribute to divisions and dualisms that we want to demolish.

Consumer research provides rich insights into how global culture manifests itself in moral consumption practices. Consumption blurs the lines between the sacred and the profane (Kozinets and Sherry 2004; Muñiz and Schau 2005; O'Guinn and Belk 1989) and spiritual practices, goods and festivities become de- and re-contextualized as they move across borders (Coskuner-Balli and Ertimur 2015; Ger and Belk 1996; Kimura and Belk 2005). Global consumption culture can revive and transform sacred practices by attaching them to new products and services (Sandikci and Ömeraki 2005). Yet, while we celebrate hybridization of belief through global–local encounters, we might, as Zigon (2007) suggests, actually be telling the story of how we think belief must be (rather than is) in different localities. The myths implied by our research move beyond being informative 'clues to the spiritual potentialities of the human life' (Campbell and Moyers 1991: 5) to skew our research on globalization.

A type of colonial, (auto)orientalizing gaze is inherent in this research as some consumer groups are allowed secular spirituality for divorcing ancient practices from their religious dogmas, while others remain in the sphere of the sacred and traditional. Studies in Western contexts have explored various modes of market-mediated secularized morality (e.g., consumer resistance, sustainability and green consumption, prosumption) and pursuit of enlightened spirituality in a global consumer culture. The reflexive consumer portrayed in these studies displays a future-orientation as she projects the global consequences of her consumption and she can turn away from a materialistic lifestyle in favor of a more spiritual one (Black and Cherrier 2010; Ekström 2015). For the non-Western 'others', religion is usually displayed as the main force that shapes the emerging markets (Mittelstaedt 2002) or the attention shifts from practices of consumers to policy-makers. In the former case, 'the other' has a rather limited and religion-based reflexivity to adopt or contest Western practices and moralities. The latter reveals the struggles of policy-makers to adapt Western sustainability guidelines and practices in their countries (Carrete et al. 2012; Ekström 2015) but fails to capture local forms of consumer reflexivity. Hence, local meanings and practices of sustainability for some consumer groups (see, for instance, Türe (2014) for a discussion of how Turkish consumers prevent waste by giving their disposable things to others), as well as local historical socio-economic contexts that nurture such differences, are lost to us (Ekström 2015). In either case, the myth that enlightened consumption practices, which are claimed to transcend the bounds of institutionalized religions, flow 'from West to East' is reinforced. This stance overlooks the argument (Grove 1990) that 'contemporary' ideologies of environmentalism might actually have originated from the early globalization cycles, as Western colonizers learned from the colonized 'others' new ways to relate to nature.

Another myth reinforced in global consumption research is that belief and morality translate as religion in most non-Western contexts. The popularity of research on *halal* consumption (Kamarulzaman et al. 2015) or Islamic brands (Izberk-Bilgin 2012) insinuates such an (internalized) dominant gaze. Researchers, with a Durkhemian stance that the moral is the social (Zigon 2007), also regard these societies through the lens of religious orientations dominant in their geographies. This conceals other types of moralities and socials (e.g., secular morality or non-religious spirituality) that are also prevalent in these contexts. In other words, focusing on religion, scholars tend to disregard alternative moralities and co-existing socials. Then, over-representation of religion as the major response to globalization in some parts of the world contributes to the myth of 'religiously extremist' peripheries against which the moral superiority of the Western centers is built. The ghost of neo-jihadism – Islam against global forces (Buck-Morss 2003; Friedman 2006; Huntington 1993) – ever-present in most research on Muslim consumers across the globe is a case in point.

Conversely, by treating religion-based consumption as a micro-level phenomenon in Western cultures, we might be missing the revival of religion as a global phenomenon (Thomas 2005). The recent rise of conservative ideologies and the popularity of fundamentalist politicians in Europe and the US affirm the conclusion O'Guinn and Belk (1989) reached 25 years ago. They pointed to the rise of The New Right: 'anti-elite, anti-intellectual, anti-big government, socially nostalgic, and [which] believes in material blessings for those who "love the lord and live right." ... The ideological label attached to the common foe is secular humanism' (p. 229). Such rare observations indicate (see also Ger 2013) that religion matters not just in 'developing' countries but also in 'developed' ones. That is, focusing too much on the differences of belief obscures the similarities across contexts. For instance, consumption patterns of a woman in a headscarf, beyond *halal* products or religious clothing, or how similar she can be to 'secular' women has not received much research attention. It also locks the consumption of some parties in the domain of enlightened spirituality and others solely in the domain of religion, making some moralities more visible or superior than others.

For researchers to really celebrate theoretical and methodological diversity and to understand the local consumers' experiences, it is crucial to be aware of the ideologies that contaminate their research. We have identified above some of the myths: the West is the center for non-religious forms of enlightened spirituality and reflexive morality; religion is the major domain through which 'the others' practice morality and unite against the global forces; and religious consumption is a micro-level phenomenon in Western contexts. These myths, in addition to reinforcing the dualities (e.g., East/West, modern/Islamist) that we, consumer researchers, claim to demolish, prevent us from 'studying explicitly and analyzing local concepts of morality' (Zigon 2007, 131). Debunking these myths and adopting an inclusive view of belief in a global world require us to be open to diverse consumer experiences in different localities and look for similarities as well as differences. It requires resisting the temptation to use Western culture as reference – as 'the culture' (Waters 2001) – and to refrain from taking some moralities for granted in some contexts. We can, instead, try to bring in a broader critical view of globalization by tracing West-to-West or East-to-East global flows (see Tacey's (2013) study on how the Bateks in Malaysia negotiate the flow of Eastern and Western belief systems in their territory). This way, we can answer new questions such as 'how do global flows create different shades of belief in different localities?' or 'what are the counterparts of, for instance, infidel brands in the West or secularized moralities in the Middle East?' Producing and exploring such questions, in return, will help debunk the myths of morality and reflexivity in globalization research.

QUESTIONING THE MYTH OF EMANCIPATORY POWER OF THE DIGITAL ON GLOBAL CULTURAL FLOWS

Facilitated by digital networked technologies, the impact of globalization is now free from the constraints of temporal/spatial chasms. Connected through digital networks, global flows – of people, media, ideas, money, technology and things (Appadurai 1990) have seen an unprecedented acceleration and penetration into everyday consumption practices. But does this mean that now it is digitized globalization that mythically transforms Bauman's (2003) '[hu]man with no bonds' into human with no boundaries? Are consumers now in full control of what gets to flow across borders or are they only being offered a simulation of it? We think it is neither; yes, there are structural control mechanisms laid as traps that can lead consumers to just where the market wants them to be, yet if we can lay bare a roadmap of this digital world for consumers they can choose where they go and what to see.

Before the digitally connected world, global consumer culture flows were largely dictated through explicit knowledge retained, categorized and distributed by the more powerful agents in the global socio-economic system – dare we say the corporation? Then at the turn of the millennium, the world wide web started to be used in a transformative way – as a platform where knowledge is not only created and published by individuals but also modified and shared by networks of users in an open, participatory and collaborative fashion. Such knowledge is tacitly distributed among participants of a network where 'no one knows everything, everyone knows something, [and] all knowledge resides in humanity' (Levy 1997: 20). This is a socio-technological network, where human and non-human cultures interact based on varied agendas and infrastructures as they create and co-create meanings in the digitally connected world (Yenicioglu and Christodoulides 2013). Such borderless and participative interactions aim at expanding the experiences, knowledge and market power of participants and thus fundamentally disturb the established knowledge asymmetry democratizing the creation and sharing of the once dormant tacit knowledge. There are of course instances where the powers that be, freaking out about the loss of control they are faced with, erect borders in an attempt to limit such interactions. However, technologically savvy consumers not only find easy ways over, under, or around these borders, but also share such roadmaps with other network participants.

Consumers, as interpretive agents, may therefore gain this accolade once and for all within the global meaning-making system through this digital 'revolution'. Far from being the 'fragile flower that globalization tramples on' (Tomlinson 2003), consumers may now more than ever actively engage in the interplay of global cultural flows through socio-technological networks, continuously deterritorializing and reterritorializing the global village they live in, unifying global culture and generating diversity within it at the same time. As local everyday realities are continuously infiltrated by distant influences, perspectives and practices, global consumer culture becomes ever more rhizomic – a borderless plane of sameness in a constant flux.

Yet from a structural point of view, such a rhizome can be an architectural nightmare – 'a space that is equally impossible to live and to leave' (de Certeau 1997). Traditionally, local (such as the state) and global (such as the media and the brand) institutions negotiated socio-cultural policies that regulated individuals' interactions with global cultural flows. A panoptic architecture governs the level of cultural reflexivity of its always visible local inmates through an invisible (but always present) consumer culture ideal. The digitally networked socio-technological rhizome, on the other hand, is argued to be working with a different panoptic architecture. In the age of digital connectivity, it is not the threat of visibility, but rather the threat of invisibility that is designed to govern the interactions of participants (Bucher 2012). Power of agency in global cultural negotiations comes with an obligatory responsibility to be connected to the network. The number and level of interactions among human as well as non-human actors determine which cultural flows are going to be visible and hence important in negotiating local cultural meanings. Although digital global cultural flows seem to be in a constant flux with no apparent anchorage in a given local reality, there is an architectural structure to what is being visible and what is not for different participants of the socio-technological network. Facebook's Newsfeed for example is built according to an architectural algorithm which identifies the 'important' news items that are being shared within a network, 'relevant' to individual users. Such architectures are also dynamic and in a constant flux, changing shape as participants interact within the network. The panopticon requires actors to be visible and interact at all times in order to be in the know and also have a say in what others should know, or risk losing their agency in global cultural flows. Iqani and Schroeder (2015) call this constant penetration of the distant into the local, this global flow of digital interactions, hypervisibility.

Is this hypervisibility, this obligation to interact, this responsibility in self-reflection, and this urge to invite the distant in, just another form of spectacle dazzling the consumers with a false pretense of power and emancipation then? Or is it really moments of true participatory agency in constructing an interactive and evolving global consumer culture?

The digitally connected world neither offers a mythical emancipatory trapdoor for consumers nor does it magically hide in plain sight just another domination apparatus of the marketplace. It is for sure more powerful to be able to see the ordinary distant in all its glory and share one's own everyday realities with the world. The displacement of power to 'mediate', away from the usual suspects and towards individual actors, coupled with the growing importance of visibility, is opening up even the most private experiences of individuals to the public gaze as contributions to an evolving global culture (Lunt and Livingstone 2013).

But we should not underestimate the architecture of the digital panopticon and the underlying market realities that may more easily turn these participatory moments into commercially viable commodities for the profit of a few than the true negotiations of global cultural flows and local consumer identities. As technological systems semi-autonomously and ubiquitously permeate global cultural terrains, they may lose their ultimate objective (i.e., progressing quality of life) and instead turn into irrational and meaningless sign systems (e.g., the selfie). Fascinated and petrified at the same time by the spectacle, actors may come to accept the simulated culture (re)produced by hyperreal technological images as an immovable reality of life. Without an understanding of the consequences of global socio-technological interactions, individual agencies and creativity may develop into a perpetual reproduction of symbols of distinctions, divisions, and inequalities.

If we prefer global consumer culture to be signified in more than passively consumed commodities, in collectively transformed values, beliefs, and acts of its participants, unified for the improvement of global social welfare yet diversified to celebrate local realities, then our research needs to go beyond duly hailing or blaming digital networked technologies. Instead we need to expose their architecture and the consequences of that architecture for different actors such as the visible and the less visible or the bordered-out. We need to reflect on the participative opportunities and constraints offered by digital networked technologies and see beyond the veil of the sheer volume, variety, and velocity of global cultural flows therein.

CONCLUSION: CALL FOR HISTORICAL AND CRITICAL REFLEXIVITY AND CROSS-DISCIPLINARITY FOR STUDIES OF GLOBAL CONSUMER CULTURES

We have seen why what we call myths are myths and how easy and prevalent it is to fall prey to these myths that color our thinking as we study global consumption. Researchers tend to pay much more attention to positioning research questions and conceptualizations within ongoing debates in a particular (sub)discipline than considering what ideologies are being manifested in these very same research questions and concepts. While most scholars would acknowledge that our approaches and theories are themselves embedded in the neoliberal marketized world and its dominant ideologies, explicating and/or eliminating their manifestations and the consequences thereof have not been a widespread research practice. Thus, the obvious but difficult to exercise caveat is to be reflexive of latent ideologies at work in our scholarship; to consider how the political and academic milieu and its (sub)disciplinary scope shape the ways in which we think about globalization and consumption.

Like any other reflexivity exercise, researchers need to systematically consider their preferred interpretations and explanations, and their implications. If globalization is not a recent condition but a nonlinear process, then while developing conceptual models and arguments, researchers need to remind themselves of the underlying historical processes. We need to study consumption in dialogue with history studies and in relation to the historical processes of escalation and diminution of globalization – to its continuities and discontinuities.

If local–global encounters are not always playful but always laden with power relations, then while studying these encounters, researchers need to be aware of the history and politics of how a particular consumption object became an 'object of desire' in a foreign context, and which gaze this 'becoming' serves to validate. In other words, we need a cautious approach to the celebration of hybridity, so that we can unpack how privilege, inequality and domination – at the global scale – are reproduced through everyday acts and adventures.

Similarly, marketing and consumption researchers can uncover fresh ground if they study immigrant or 'local' or 'cosmopolitan' consumers as people with their specific social, religious, racial, ethnic positions and histories. Hence, moving beyond an acculturation lens and to a focus on the power struggle between the receiving and sending cultures and its manifestations in the immigrants' lives would enhance understanding of the interrelationships between immigration and markets/consumption in the global arena.

Correspondingly, if belief and morality have globally become references for solidifying socio-cultural divisions, then scholars must take care to question the taken-for-granted superiority of the center's moralities, and not to over-represent the import of religion or miss other shades of belief-morality in periphery contexts. In order to do so, we need to look for similarities as well as differences between and/or within our research contexts. Moreover, researchers need to be able to explore consumption and morality in different localities without necessarily using the West as the reference culture in interpreting observations.

Finally, if the volume, variety and velocity of digital networks draw a veil over the underlying market realities, in order to better understand the consequences of global digital connectivities, researchers would do well to study the underlying mechanisms and structures governing the distributed knowledge that is being generated by local participants all over the world. To understand the emancipatory possibilities as well as the barriers, we also need to investigate the divide between the visible and the invisible participants as well as the ways in which collaborative governance may work to weed out disinformation, manipulation and power games by the few.

Globalization amplifies awareness of a first (class) world and the experience of exclusion from it as well as social and economic polarization (de Koning 2009). Neoliberal policies widen global inequality and invite fundamental instability – witness new social movements (Pieterse 2005). If global inequality is dire, if the exigency of boundaries, across classes and contexts is more common than ever (Pieterse 2001, 2005), Appadurai's widely cited flows 'have to be located in global and local histories of inequality and dominance' (de Koning 2009: 194). Flows involve symbolic translations across sites rather than mechanistic movement along inert passages (Rajagopal 2001). In these renditions, disjunctures in flows are used to the advantage of the powerful in global networks. Dominant 'global structures of common difference' (Wilk 1995) such as market institutions and their consumerist ideology define what types of diversity and hybrids will diffuse and what kinds will be curbed.

Similarly, if inequality and power struggles govern global markets and consumption, consumer culture studies (Arnould and Thompson 2005) and material culture studies (Miller 2008, 2010) have to also be located in global and local histories of dominance. Researchers need to attend to the embeddedness of consumer identity and practices or the materiality and objectification of social relations, respectively, within the historical and current socio/cultural/political relations between the North and South, the center and periphery, or the dominant and the dominated.

Furthermore, the vulnerabilities as well as the complexities of globalization imply that disciplines need to speak to each other. These vulnerabilities include inequality (Pieterse 2005), ethnic/religious/national forms of violence (Friedman 2005), anti-globalization movements (Graeber 2005), and transnational criminal networks, business scandals and the commodification of human bodies (Comaroff and Comaroff 2005). Arguably, such liabilities are linked to the elevation of 'market imperatives ("the spirit of neoliberalism") to new heights where human dimensions are lost from view' (Edelman and Haugerud 2005: 158). In order to give voice to the human dimensions, as well as for a fundamental understanding of the phenomenon in the first place, researchers need to cross disciplinary boundaries and study global consumption from the perspective of social, moral/religious and political, as well as economic and cultural angles. Hence, we call for a willingness to engage with disciplines and perspectives other than our own – to cross the boundaries of thinking – in theorization and research, as we study consumption across geographic boundaries. Arguably, studies of global consumption would benefit greatly from, particularly, subaltern studies, postcolonial studies, new social movements (including resistance to globalization) and human rights studies. Researchers of global consumer culture should confront the macro-processes and structures as well as the micro-structures and processes they tend to focus on. This has become more critical today, given the world political stage in 2017.

In sum, the prevalence of global dominance relations and the elevation of market imperatives call for both greater researcher reflexivity and deeper and sincere engagement with disciplines other than our own, whatever 'our own' might be. We, researchers, have a responsibility not to sanctify neocolonial and neoliberal might and boundaries. Instead we have a responsibility to try to avoid the myths and traps in our choice of topics to study, in deciding how to study them, and in developing conceptualizations and explanations. Such responsibility invites research interests in historicizing, domination and power struggles, the unabridged lives of consumers as people, with shades of moralities and similarities as well as differences of different local cultures, market structures and governance structures of digital networks.

REFERENCES

Ahmed, S., 2000. *Strange Encounters: Embodied Others in Post-coloniality*, Routledge, London and New York.

Altglas, V., 2014. *From Yoga to Kabbalah: Religious Exoticism and the Logics of Bricolage*, Oxford University Press, Oxford, UK.

Appadurai, A., 1990. Difference and disjuncture in the global cultural economy. *Theory, Culture and Society*, *7*(2), 295–310.

Armitage, D., 2004. Is there a pre-history of globalization? In D. Cohen and M. O'Connor (eds), *Comparison and History: Europe in Cross-National Perspective*, pp. 165–176, Routledge, New York.

Arnould, E.J. and Thompson, C.J., 2005. Consumer culture theory (CCT): Twenty years of research. *Journal of Consumer Research*, *31*(4), 868–882.

Askegaard, S., Arnould, E.J. and Kjeldgaard, D., 2005. Postassimilationist ethnic consumer research: Qualifications and extensions. *Journal of Consumer Research*, *32*(1), 160–170.

Bauman, Z., 2003. *Liquid Love*, Polity Press, Cambridge.

Beck, U., 2000. *What is Globalization?* Polity Press, Cambridge.

Berry, J.W., 1980. Acculturation as varieties of adaptation. In Amado M. Padilla (ed.), *Adaptation: Theory, Models and Some New Findings*, pp. 9–26, American Association for the Advancement of Science, Washington, DC.

Beynon, J. and Dunkerley, D. (eds), 2000. *Globalization: The Reader*, Routledge, New York.

Bhabha, H.K., 1985a. Sly civility. *October*, *34*, 71–80.

Bhabha, H.K., 1985b. Signs taken for wonders: Questions of ambivalence and authority under a tree outside Delhi, May 1817. *Critical Inquiry*, *12*(1), 144–165.

Black, I.R. and Cherrier, H., 2010. Anti-consumption as part of living a sustainable lifestyle: Daily practices, contextual motivations and subjective values. *Journal of Consumer Behaviour*, *9*(6), 437–453.

Bohman, A., 2015. It's who you know: Political influence on anti-immigrant attitudes and the moderating role of intergroup contact, *Sociological Research Online*, *20*(3), Article number 6.

Bucher, T., 2012. Want to be on the top? Algorithmic power and the threat of invisibility on Facebook. *New Media & Society*, *14*(7), 1164–1180.

Buck-Morss, S., 2003. *Thinking Past Terror: Islamism and Critical Theory on the Left*, Verso, New York.

Burke, P., 2009. *Cultural Hybridity*, Polity Press, Cambridge.

Campbell, J. and Moyers, B., 1991. *The Power of Myth*, Anchor, New York.

Canniford, R. and Karababa, E., 2013. Partly primitive: Discursive constructions of the domestic surfer. *Consumption Markets & Culture*, *16*(2), 119–144.

Carrete, L., Castaño, R., Felix, R., Centeno, E. and González, E., 2012. Green consumer behavior in an emerging economy: Confusion, credibility, and compatibility. *Journal of Consumer Marketing*, *29*(7), 470–481.

Clunas, C., 2004. *Superfluous things: Material culture and social status in early modern China*, University of Hawaii Press, Honolulu.

Comaroff, J. and Comaroff, J.L., 2005. Millennial capitalism and the culture of neoliberalism. In M. Edelman and A. Haugerud (eds), *The Anthropology of Development and Globalization*, pp. 177–188, Blackwell: Malden, MA.

Cook, I. and Harrison, M., 2003. Cross over food: Re-materializing postcolonial geographies. *Transactions of the Institute of British Geographers*, *28*(3), 296–317.

Coskuner-Balli, G. and Ertimur, B., 2015. Creating hybridity: The case of American yoga. In K. Diehl and C. Yoon (eds), *NA-Advances in Consumer Research*, Vol. 43, 494–497, Association for Consumer Research, Duluth, MN.

de Certeau, M., 1997. *The Capture of Speech and Other Political Writings*, University of Minnesota Press, Minneapolis.

de Koning, A., 2009. *Global Dreams: Space, Class, and Gender in Middle-Class Cairo*, American University in Cairo Press, Cairo.

Dicken, P., 2007. *Global Shift: Mapping the Changing Contours of the World Economy*, Sage, London.

Edelman, M. and Haugerud, A. (eds) 2005. *The Anthropology of Development and Globalization*. Blackwell, Malden, MA.

Eisenstadt, S.N. and Schluchter, W., 1998. Introduction: Paths to early modernities: A comparative view. *Daedalus*, *127*(3), 1–18.

Ekström, K.M., 2015. *Waste Management and Sustainable Consumption: Reflections on Consumer Waste*, Routledge, London.
Fanon, F., 1967. *Black Skin, White Masks*. Pluto Press, London.
Featherstone, M., 1990. Global culture: An introduction. *Theory, Culture & Society*, *7*(2), 1–14.
Febvre, L., 1977. *Life in Renaissance France*, Harvard University Press, Cambridge, MA.
Friedman, J., 2005. Globalization, dis-integration, re-organization: The transformations of violence. In M. Edelman and A. Haugerud (eds), *The Anthropology of Development and Globalization*, pp. 160–168, Blackwell, Malden, MA.
Friedman, T.L., 2006. *The World is Flat: The Globalized World in the Twenty-first Century*, Penguin, London.
Ger, G., 1999. Localizing in the global village: Local firms competing in global markets. *California Management Review*, *41*(4), 64–83.
Ger, G., 2013. Islamic marketing at the nexus of global markets-religions-politics and implications for research. *Marketing Theory*, *13*(4), 493–499.
Ger, G., 2017. Consumption in the web of local and global relations of dominance and belonging. In M. Keller, B. Halkier, T.A. Wilska and M. Truninger (eds), *Routledge Handbook on Consumption*, 121–134, Routledge, London.
Ger, G. and Belk, R.W., 1996. I'd like to buy the world a coke: Consumptionscapes of the 'less affluent world'. *Journal of Consumer Policy*, *19*(3), 271–304.
Giddens, A., 1990. *The Consequences of Modernity*, Stanford University Press, Stanford, CA.
Graeber, D., 2005. The globalization movement: Some points of clarification. In M. Edelman, and A. Haugerud (eds), *The Anthropology of Development and Globalization*, 169–172, Blackwell, Malden, MA.
Grossberg, L., 1995. The space of culture, the power of space. In I. Chambers and L. Curti (eds), *The postcolonial question: Common skies, divided horizons*, pp. 169–188, Routledge, London.
Grove, R., 1990. The origins of environmentalism. *Nature*, *345*(May), 11–14.
Hannerz, U., 1987. The world in creolisation. *Africa*, *57*(04), 546–559.
Hannerz, U., 1992. *Cultural Complexity: Studies in the Social Organization of Meaning*, Columbia University Press, New York.
Hannerz, U., 1996. *Transnational Connections*, Routledge, London.
Heldke, L.M., 2001. Let's cook Thai: Recipes for colonialism. In S.A. Inness (ed.), *Pilaf, Pozole, and Pad Thai: American Women and Ethnic Food*, pp. 175–198, University of Massachusetts Press, Amherst, MA.
Heldke, L.M., 2003. *Exotic Appetites: Ruminations of a Food Adventurer*, Routledge, New York.
Holt, D.B., 1998. Does cultural capital structure American consumption? *Journal of Consumer Research*, *25*(1), 1–25.
hooks, b., 1992. *Black Looks: Race and Representation*, South End Press, Boston.
Hopkins, A.G., 2002. The history of globalization – and the globalization of history? in A.G. Hopkins (ed.), *Globalization in World History*, pp. 11–46, Pimlico, London.
Huntington, S., 1993. The clash of civilizations? *Foreign Affairs*, *72*(3), 22–50.
Ian, C. and Michelle, H., 2003. Cross over food: Re-materializing postcolonial geographies. *Transactions of the Institute of British Geographers*, *28*(3), 296–317.
Iqani, M. and Schroeder, J.E., 2015. #selfie: Digital self-portraits as commodity form and consumption practice. *Consumption Markets & Culture*, *19*(5), 1–11.
Izberk-Bilgin, E., 2012. Infidel brands: Unveiling alternative meanings of global brands at the nexus of globalization, consumer culture, and Islamism. *Journal of Consumer Research*, *39*(4), 663–687.

Jaime-Castillo, A.M., Marqués-Perales, I. and Álvarez-Gálvez, J., 2016. 'The impact of social expenditure on attitudes towards immigration in Europe', *Social Indicators Research*, *126*(3), 1089–1108.

James, H., 2009. *The Creation and Destruction of Value: The Globalization Cycle*, Harvard University Press, Cambridge, MA.

Kamarulzaman, Y., Veeck, A., Mumuni, A.G., Luqmani, M. and Quraeshi, Z.A., 2015. Religion, markets, and digital media seeking halal food in the US. *Journal of Macromarketing*, *36*(4), 400–411.

Karababa, E., 2012. Investigating early modern Ottoman consumer culture in the light of Bursa probate inventories. *The Economic History Review*, *65*(1), 194–219.

Karababa, E., 2015. Marketing and consuming flowers in the Ottoman Empire. *Journal of Historical Research in Marketing*, *7*(2), 280–292.

Karababa, E. and Ger, G., 2011. Early modern Ottoman coffeehouse culture and the formation of the consumer subject. *Journal of Consumer Research*, *37*(5), 737–760.

Kimura, J. and Belk, R.W., 2005. Christmas in Japan: Globalization versus localization. *Consumption Markets & Culture*, *8*(3), 325–338.

Kjeldgaard, D. and Ostberg, J., 2007. Coffee grounds and the global cup: Glocal consumer culture in Scandinavia. *Consumption, Markets and Culture*, *10*(2), 175–187.

Kozinets, R.V., and Sherry Jr, J.F., 2004. Dancing on common ground: Exploring the sacred at Burning Man. In G. St. John (ed.), *Rave Culture and Religion*, pp. 287–303, Routledge, New York.

Kravets, O. and Sandikci, O., 2014. Competently ordinary: New middle class consumers in the emerging markets. *Journal of Marketing*, *78*(4), 125–140.

Levitt, T., 1983. The globalization of markets. *Harvard Business Review* (May–June), 92–102.

Levy, P., 1997. *Collective Intelligence*, Plenum Trade, New York.

Liechty, M., 2002. *Suitably Modern: Making Middle-class Culture in a New Consumer Society*, Princeton University Press, Princeton, NJ.

Luedicke, M.K., 2011. Consumer acculturation theory: (Crossing) conceptual boundaries. *Consumption Markets & Culture*, *14*(3), 223–244.

Luedicke, M.K., 2015. Indigenes' responses to immigrants' consumer acculturation: A relational configuration analysis. *Journal of Consumer Research*, *42*(1), 109–129.

Lunt, P. and Livingstone, S., 2013. Media studies' fascination with the concept of the public sphere: Critical reflections and emerging debates. *Media, Culture & Society*, *35*(1), 87–96.

Mears, A., 2010. Size zero high-end ethnic: Cultural production and the reproduction of culture in fashion modeling. *Poetics*, *38*(1), 21–46.

Mierina, I. and Koroleva, I., 2015. Support for far right ideology and anti-immigrant attitudes among youth in Europe: A comparative analysis, *Sociological Review*, 63, 183–205.

Miller, D., 2008. *The Comfort of Things*. Polity: Cambridge.

Miller, D., 2010. *Stuff*. Cambridge: Polity.

Minowa, Y. and Witkowski, T.H., 2009. State promotion of consumerism in Safavid Iran: Shah Abbas I and royal silk textiles. *Journal of Historical Research in Marketing*, *1*(2), 295–317.

Mittelstaedt, J.D., 2002. A framework for understanding the relationships between religions and markets. *Journal of Macromarketing*, *22*(1), 6–18.

Muñiz, A.M. and Schau, H.J., 2005. Religiosity in the abandoned Apple Newton brand community. *Journal of Consumer Research*, *31*(4), 737–747.

Narayan, U., 1995. Eating cultures: Incorporation, identity and Indian food. *Social Identities*, *1*(1), 63–86.
O'Guinn, T.C. and Belk, R.W., 1989. Heaven on earth: Consumption at Heritage Village, USA. *Journal of Consumer Research*, *16*(2), 227–238.
Oswald, L.R., 1999. Culture swapping: Consumption and the ethnogenesis of middle-class Haitian immigrants. *Journal of Consumer Research*, *25*(4), 303–318.
Oxford English Dictionary, http://www.oed.com/.
Peñaloza, L., 1994. Atravesando fronteras/border crossings: A critical ethnographic exploration of the consumer acculturation of Mexican immigrants. *Journal of Consumer Research*, *21*(1), 32–54.
Pieterse, J.N., 1994. Globalisation as hybridisation. *International Sociology*, *9*(2), 161–184.
Pieterse, J.N., 2001. Hybridity, so what? The anti-hybridity backlash and the riddles of recognition. *Theory, Culture & Society*, *18*(2–3), 219–245.
Pieterse, J.N., 2005. Global inequality: Bringing politics back in. In C. Calhoun, C. Rojek and B. Turner (eds), *The SAGE Handbook of Sociology*, 423–441, Sage, London.
Pieterse, J.N., 2009. *Globalization and Culture: Global Mélange*, Rowman and Littlefield Publishers, New York.
Pieterse, J.N., 2012. Periodizing globalization: Histories of globalization. *New Global Studies*, *6*(2), 1–25.
Portes, A. and Zhou, M., 1993. 'Segmented assimilation and its variants', *The Annals of the American Academy of Political Social Science*, *530*(November), 74–96.
Rajagopal, A., 2001. *Politics after Television: Hindu Nationalism and the Reshaping of the Public in India*, Cambridge: Cambridge University Press.
Ritzer, G., 1996. *Sociological Theory*, Tata McGraw-Hill Education, New York.
Ritzer, G., 2007. *The Blackwell Companion to Globalization*, Blackwell, Oxford.
Robertson, R., 1995. Glocalization: Time-space and homogeneity-heterogeneity. In M. Featherstone, S. Lash and R. Robertson (eds), *Global Modernities*, pp. 25–44, Sage, London.
Robertson, R. and White, K.E., 2005. Globalization: Sociology and cross-disciplinarity. In C. Calhoun, C. Rojek and B. Turner (eds), *The Sage Handbook of Sociology*, 345–366, Sage, London.
Root, D., 1996. *Cannibal Culture: Art, Appropriation, and the Commodification of Difference*, Westview Press, Boulder, CO.
Said, E., 1978. *Orientalism*, Vintage, New York.
Sandikci, Ö. and Ger, G., 2010. Veiling in style: How does a stigmatized practice become fashionable? *Journal of Consumer Research*, *37*(1), 15–36.
Sandikci, Ö. and Ömeraki, S., 2005. Globalization and rituals: Does Ramadan turn into Christmas? *NA-Advances in Consumer Research*, *34*, 610–615.
Shohat, E., 1992. Notes on the 'post-colonial'. *Social Text*, (31/32), 99–113.
Skrbiš, Z. and Woodward, I., 2013. *Cosmopolitanism: Uses of the Idea*, Sage, London.
Stearns, P.N., 2006. *Consumerism in World History: The Global Transformation of Desire*, Routledge, London.
Stearns, P.N., 2010. *Globalization in World History*, Routledge, London.
Stiglitz, J.E., 2002. *Globalization and its Discontents*, Penguin, London.
Tacey, I., 2013. Tropes of fear: The impact of globalization on Batek religious landscapes. *Religions*, *4*(2), 240–266.
Thomas, S.M., 2005. *The Global Resurgence of Religion and the Transformation of International Relations*, Palgrave Macmillan, New York.
Tomlinson, J., 1999. *Globalization and Culture*, University of Chicago Press, Chicago.

Tomlinson, J., 2003. Globalization and cultural identity. In A. McGrew and D. Held (eds), *The Global Transformations Reader: An Introduction to the Globalization Debate*, pp. 269–278, Polity Press, Cambridge.

Türe, M., 2014. Value-in-disposition: Exploring how consumers derive value from disposition of possessions. *Marketing Theory*, *14*(1), 53–72.

Turgeon, L. and Pastinelli, M., 2002. 'Eat the world': Postcolonial encounters in Quebec City's ethnic restaurants. *Journal of American Folklore*, *115*(456), 247–268.

United Nations Population Division, International Migration Report 2015, http://www.un.org/en/development/desa/population/migration/publications/migrationreport/docs/MigrationReport2015.pdf

Üstüner, T. and Holt, D.B., 2007. Dominated consumer acculturation: The social construction of poor migrant women's consumer identity projects in a Turkish squatter neighbourhood. *Journal of Consumer Research*, *34*(4), 41–56.

Üstüner, T. and Holt, D.B., 2010. Toward a theory of status consumption in less industrialized countries. *Journal of Consumer Research*, *37*(1), 37–56.

Waters, M., 2001. *Globalization*, Routledge, London and New York.

Wilk, R., 1995. Learning to be local in Belize: Global systems of common difference. In D. Miller (ed.), *Worlds Apart: Modernity through the Prism of the Local*, pp. 110–133, Routledge, London.

Wilk, R., 1998. Emulation, imitation, and global consumerism. *Organization & Environment*, *11*(3), 314–333.

Wilk, R., 2006a. *Home Cooking in the Global Village: Caribbean Food from Buccaneers to Ecotourists*, Berg, Oxford.

Wilk, R., 2006b. Bottled water: The pure commodity in the age of branding. *Journal of Consumer Culture*, *6*(3), 303–325.

Wilk, R., 2006c. Consumer culture and extractive industry on the margins of the world system. In J. Brewer and F. Trentmann (eds), *Consumer Cultures: Global Perspectives*, Berg, Oxford.

Wilk, R., 2010. Consumption in an age of globalization and localization. In K. Ekstrom and K. Glans (eds), *Beyond the Consumption Bubble*. Routledge Interpretive Marketing Research, New York.

Yenicioglu, B. and Christodoulides, G., 2013. Internet technologies and branding. In L. Moutinho, E. Bigne, and A.K. Manrai (eds), *The Routledge Companion to the Future of Marketing*, pp. 268–282, Routledge, London.

Zigon, J., 2007. Moral breakdown and the ethical demand: A theoretical framework for an anthropology of moralities. *Anthropological Theory*, *7*(2), 131–150.

Consumer Culture in Socialist Russia

Olga Gurova

INTRODUCTION

Socialist consumption has become a focus of recent research in history, historical sociology and cultural studies. In this chapter I will discuss socialist consumption meaning, first and foremost, consumption in the Soviet Union and, in particular, in Russia, in the period between 1917 and 1985/1991: 1917 is the year of the Bolshevik Revolution, which led to the establishment of the Soviet Union; 1985 is the year when the restructuring (*perestroika*) of the economic, social and cultural system began and caused the dissolution of the Soviet Union; 1991 is the year when the dissolution of the Soviet Union was formally enacted. Many arguments regarding the Soviet Union are relevant to other socialist societies of Eastern and Central Europe, yet there are also differences that are beyond the attention of this chapter because of such a focus.

For consumer culture studies the term '*socialist consumer culture*' has been problematic until recently. Don Slater, for instance, stated that although consumption is universal and cultural, consumer culture is 'unique and specific: it is the dominant mode of cultural reproduction developed in the west over the course of modernity. Consumer culture is in important respects *the* culture of the modern west' (Slater, 1997: 8, emphasis in the original text). Slater admitted, however, that '[n]or is the consumer culture a purely western affair' (ibid: 9), but the purpose of this elaboration of his was to explain that in non-Western societies consumer culture develops thanks to Western influence, in the form of and as a means of advancement of Western markets, businesses and ways of life (Slater, 1997: 8).

This perspective has been both supported (for instance, in Sassatelli, 2007) as well as criticised, primarily by researchers of non-Western consumer cultures (for example, Karababa and Ger, 2011; and see also Ger et al.'s Chapter 6 in this volume).

Typical criticism is that the concept of consumption – and also of modernity – has tended to be monopolised for the Anglophone west (Clunas, cited in Reid, 2002: 213). Scholars who study socialist Russia add that 'there is a tacit assumption that, being communist, eastern bloc countries – and the Soviet Union, above all – could not, by definition, be consumer societies' (Reid, 2002: 213) because '[c]onsumer society has traditionally been associated with the capitalist economic system' (Chernyshova, 2013: 11). Such an attitude may partially explain the lack of interest or vibrant discussion on socialist consumption in consumer culture studies. In other areas, this tacit assumption pushed scholars to analyse the relevance of the consumer culture concept as applied to socialist societies. Recently, there has been a surge in scholarly research on consumer culture in the Soviet Russia and other socialist countries. In fact, it has been argued that not only was consumer culture present in socialist economies, but it also played an important part in and was promoted by socialist regimes (Chernyshova, 2013: 11).

An important note about the categories of analysis should be made. If 'consumption' is a universal phenomenon and exists in every single culture, then 'consumer culture' and 'consumer society' (these terms are often used interchangeably, see Sassatelli, 2007) are rooted in particular geographical and historical context and are considered as categories belonging to modern Western society, as discussed above. Recently, such an approach has been reconsidered; the idea of a multiplicity of consumer cultures has been put forward by scholars, who have claimed a 'diversity of trajectories' towards consumer modernity (de Grazia, cited in Randall, 2008: 158). Perhaps, the use of another category – 'culture of consumption', which is an anthropological category that does not imply binaries and hierarchies, can be considered as a step in the same direction (Tikhomirova, 2007).

Academic studies of the Soviet consumer from a cultural perspective were quite scarce during the Soviet times. Starting from the 1970s onwards social historians Vera Dunham and Sheila Fitzpatrick explored culture and consumption from the point of view of everyday practices in the Soviet Union in the 1930s–1950s. Back then, the access to archives in the Soviet Union was hindered or even forbidden for scholars, therefore foreign scholars based their research on published literary sources or on interviews with émigrés from the Soviet Union. Since the 1990s and the dissolution of the Soviet Union, studies of Soviet consumption started to bloom in the context of social and cultural history, cultural studies, historical sociology and sociology of consumption, because a new post-Soviet consumerism, which came fast and was sudden, forced scholars to understand its origin (Reid, 2009: 4). These studies used various sources, from archives to in-depth interviews and visual data, and a number of methodologies, from discourse analysis to oral history. They often drew from social theory and such authors as Michel de Certeau, Michel Foucault, Norbert Elias, Roland Barthes, among others. Thus Svetlana Boym (1994) wrote a book on the archaeology of practices of daily life in the Soviet Union. Elena Osokina (1998, cited in English, 2001) published an insightful investigation into the organisation of a system of provision in the Soviet Union in the 1930s. Jukka Gronow (2003) wrote a book on consumer culture, commodities, retail and advertising in the 1930s. Among other topics that were scrutinised are the archaeology of Soviet things (Buchli, 2000), peculiarities of commodities in socialist culture (Kravets, 2013), style and socialism

(Crowley and Reid, 2010), everyday life and civilising process (Volkov, 2000), fashion and social distinctions (Tikhomirova, 2007, 2010; Zakharova, 2010, 2013), cars (Siegelbaum, 2008), summerhouses (Lovell, 2003), Soviet advertising (Cox, 2006; Tolstikova, 2007), marketing strategies under socialism (Kravets and Sandikçi, 2013), the ideology of fashion and representations of femininity (Vainshtein, 1996), and DIY practices (Gerassimova and Chuikina, 2009; Golubev and Smolyak, 2013; Gurova, 2009; Orlova, 2009; Smolyak, 2014). During the first decade of the twenty-first century historians published several monographs devoted to Soviet retail trade (Hessler, 2004; Hilton, 2012; Randall, 2008). Also, Djurdja Bartlett (2010) wrote a monograph on socialist fashion, and Natalya Chernyshova (2013) issued a book on different aspects of consumer culture in the Soviet Union in the 1970s. During the past several years, Natalia Lebina (1999, 2009, 2014), a social historian, has published several explorations of the micro-history of daily life in the Russian language. A current trend in the studies of the Soviet consumer culture is to investigate it from the point of view of the history of technology or sensory history, as new angles on consumer culture are introduced. New sources and topics are being presented and social science concepts continue to be actively used by the scholars producing interdisciplinary research.

In this chapter I focus on the concept of socialist consumption, looking at the emic categories that help to understand life in Soviet society from the point of view of the culture itself (cf. Geertz, 1973). I am doing so by looking at meta-discourse of the studies of the Soviet consumer culture across a number of disciplines, including social and cultural history, cultural studies and historical sociology. I look at several elements of the consumer culture, including production, retail trade and culture of selling, the ideology of consumption, commodities, social structure and everyday consumer practices. This chapter enforces the assumption that consumer culture is a global phenomenon that is rooted in the sociocultural, economic and political circumstances of different regions.

The structure of the chapter is as follows. First, I will focus on the concepts related to the production of consumer goods in Soviet society, then I will proceed to the ideology and dominant discourses on consumption. After that I will consider socialist retail trade and the culture of selling. Then I will focus on identities and, after that, on everyday practices of consumption. In the discussion section I will pay attention to the existing debate on the peculiarities of socialist consumer culture in the Soviet Union. In conclusion, I will summarise the characteristics of the socialist consumer culture and give a brief scope of potential dimensions for future research.

PRODUCTION OF CONSUMER GOODS: 'SHORTAGE SOCIETY' AND 'STORAGE SOCIETY'

Socialism (1917–1985/1991) is referred to the economic system under which the state was the owner of the means of production and played a crucial role in the regulation of all spheres of life (Verdery, 1996). Hence the production and distribution of consumer goods were concentrated in the hands of the state and were not regulated by market mechanisms and consumer demand. Production was privileged over consumption during the entire Soviet period. Private production and private trade were illegal during most of the socialist time, with the exception of the period of the New Economic Policy of the 1920s and for the group of collective farmers who could legally sell at farmers' markets throughout the entire Soviet period.

The state based production on the calculation of 'rational' or 'reasonable' needs instead of the 'wants' of the consumers (Reid, 2002: 219). Besides, the state focused its efforts on heavy industry (so-called Group A) and not on the production of consumer goods (Group B). Natalya Chernyshova illustrates this with numbers: in the 1950s heavy industry was allocated 90% of all means of production, and light industry – only 10%. In the 1970s the ratio was 74% to 26% (Chernyshova, 2013: 27; and see also Gronow 2003: 121).

As a result, the centrally planned Soviet economy was in such a situation whereby demand for consumer goods was chronically higher than supply. Therefore, Janos Kornai (1992) called the Soviet economy '*the shortage economy*'. The term 'shortage' embraces a large group of phenomena, including tension on the market due to demand exceeding supply, a lack of consumer goods and queuing for consumer goods (Kornai, 1992; Osokina, 2001). The key concept applied to socialist society in the literature is the '*society of shortage*'. Sometimes shortages were relative, when the goods actually existed but not where and when they were needed (Chernyshova, 2013: 21), and sometimes shortages were absolute, which resulted in rationing and coupons being introduced several times during the entire Soviet period (Verdery, 1996: 21).

The 'society of shortage' is the dominant paradigm in the interpretation of the Soviet reality, which, however, has been recently criticised by historians and cultural studies researchers. They argue that, first, there were different periods in the history of Russia, including those which could be seen as periods of relative abundance. Julie Hessler, for instance, distinguished three periods in the development of the Soviet economy: crisis mode, normalising mode and normal mode. The crisis mode prevailed up until World War II, with the exception of the period of the New Economic Policy of the 1920s and in the pre-war years of 1933–1938. During the crisis there was rationing and centralised control; during the normalising period the economy moved towards consumer choice and flexibility. After World War II (WWII) the normalising mode turned into a normal mode (Davies, 2010; Hessler, 2004). Natalya Chernyshova argues that during the Khrushchev (1953–1964) and Brezhnev (1966–1982) years the regime paid increased attention to the mass production of consumer goods and, as a result, living standards rose. However, Chernyshova adds that 'no-one in their right mind would dispute the existence of shortages in the USSR' (Chernyshova, 2013: 3).

Second, Ina Merkel (2006: 268–269), in talking about the GDR, continues the criticism of the term 'shortage' emphasising that there is no such thing as a shortage as such; it is a relative term. What is perceived as a shortage differs from culture to culture, among the social classes and historically. In Merkel's opinion, the label 'society of shortage' is a term of the binary West vs East discourse, and she considers the case of Germany, which can be extended to other socialist countries. In this discourse the West becomes coloured, whereas the Eastern European countries appear as black and white, or grey. The term 'society of shortage' also intends a logical misinterpretation, because shortage leads to frustration, greed and envy. But Merkel emphasised that in such societies consumers expressed and used fantasy, creativity, improvisation and enjoyment as coping strategies, which we will discuss further in this chapter in the section on do-it-yourself culture. In line with this criticism, shortages were seen as anomie, but they also could be seen as social glue that bonded people together in opposition to the state (Crowley and Reid, 2010: 10).

Another view on the Soviet economy was suggested by Sergei Oushakine who criticised the 'shortages approach' and suggests looking at it from a different angle, putting forward the concept of a '*society of storage*'. According to Oushakine, Soviet society, being focused on production, in fact, produced too many goods, there was an overstocking of certain commodities which were unwanted, from the 1940s onwards. It was not a shortage of things but rather a 'steady increase of the volume of commodities that did not enter the process of consumption' (Oushakine, 2014: 206). Oushakine noted that over thirty years inventory in industry and trade grew by 1122%, increasing from 2.929 billion Russian roubles in 1940 to 32.873 billion roubles in 1970. In 1985 the amount of inventories 'accumulated only by state enterprises that were involved in material production amounted to 80 percent of national income' (Oushakine, 2014: 207). This condition was caused by many factors, including peculiarities of organisation of planning in a centralised economy, flaws in the transportation system of goods, flaws in statistics and the calculating of demand, a snail-paced reaction to demand, and, in general, peculiarities of the understanding of where demand comes from – not from consumer desire, as in a market economy, but as a result of centralised state planning (Oushakine, 2014: 209–212; Osokina, 2001).

Thus these two major concepts – 'society of shortage' and 'society of storage' describe the situation in the economy, which shaped the structural conditions in the Soviet consumer culture. These concepts make it clear that the planned economy formed conditions in which supply rarely met demand.

IDEOLOGY OF CONSUMPTION: BETWEEN MATERIALISM AND DE-MATERIALISATION

The state played a crucial role in the regulation of consumption in the Soviet Union through a number of means, one of which was establishing the dominant discourse on consumption. The approach of the state to the discourse on consumption was to a large extent didactic; the state formed a particular type of a citizen – a Soviet Man – and transmitted a particular set of ideas and practices corresponding to the ideology. The discursive level of consumption under socialism was discussed in literature in the context of the following topics: mythologies of consumption (Boym, 1994), philosophical ideas behind socialist consumption (Vihavainen and Bogdanova, 2015), ideologies of consumption (Gurova, 2006, 2015), fashion, taste and women's magazines (Bartlett, 2010; Gradskova, 2007, 2011; Vainshtein, 1996) and advertisements as discourse (Tolstikova, 2007).

The discursive level of consumption was studied with the use of category '*ideology of consumption*', where ideology is understood as a set of dominant discourses transmitting ideas about consumption and promotion through various forms of cultural production or cultural artefacts (magazines, newspapers, TV, cinema, material objects) (see Gurova, 2006; Vainshtein, 1996).

There were several major changes in the ideology of consumption during the socialist period. After the Revolution of 1917 and during the early 1920s the dominant discourse promoted through the official media was based on the idea of *asceticism* and the idea that individuals should be free from the oppression of material things. The ideology was aimed at rejecting the ideals of the pre-revolutionary past, and criticised petty-bourgeois materialism, philistinism and the class character of consumption (Boym, 1994; Vihavainen and Bogdanova, 2015). At the same time, there was an idea of satisfying everyone's needs, although only basic needs due to lack of resources. Such phenomena as fashion and beauty were defined according to revolutionary principles. Fashion should be functional and utilitarian and should transmit the values of a new socialist culture. Beauty should be 'natural', whereas makeup was seen as an artificial 'scab' on the body (Gurova, 2006).

In the 1930s, after the revolutionary experiments, the ideology changed, and material prosperity became a goal. Stalin recognised the importance of consumption (Gronow, 2003: 120), socialism was linked to consumerism and consumerism was seen as a positive force for building socialism (Randall, 2008: 36, 43). The logic of this change can be explained by a new contract that was established between the state and the emerging middle class, which required a stable life with consumer goods after years of revolutionary upheavals (Dunham, 1979). The new ideals were relative abundance, equality and cultural life. The key discursive concept was *culturedness (kul'turnost')* as an orientation towards relatively high standards of individual consumption (Volkov, 2000). Culturedness linked a set of consumer practices to the status of a cultured person, who should master civilising practices such as using a fork and knife, following fashion, wearing makeup, having some knowledge of literature and music, and, in general, being a skilful modern consumer. In line with new ideas of relative abundance, the media started building a 'dream world' of the new consumer culture, publishing articles about and pictures of products which, in fact, were not available in the stores, that is why Sheila Fitzpatrick (1999: 90, 93) calls this period 'virtually a consumer-goods pornography' or 'la vie en rose, Soviet style' and Jukka Gronow (2003) named one of the chapters of his book 'Soviet consumption amidst general poverty'. The attitude towards fashion and beauty changed to be more tolerant. Although the discourse promoted ideas of equality, it also constructed hierarchy, for instance, attention was given to a group of shock workers, so-called Stakhanovites, who were rewarded by the regime with material goods for achieving success in their labour (Volkov, 2000).

In the 1950s and 1960s, when the country was rebuilding itself after WWII, under Khrushchev, the middle class became numerous and embraced broader population and the masses were invited to participate in consumption (Chernyshova, 2013: 45). On the one hand, there was criticism of the consumerist ideals of Stalin's times. On the other hand, consumption was legitimated as a part of the Soviet middle-class lifestyle and also as a force in political competition with the West in times of the Cold War. The key discourse was a discourse on *Soviet taste* that played the role of a regulatory mechanism of consumer behaviour for a country, which became more open to international influences through various international events, the import of consumer goods, and increasing in- and outbound tourism (Gorsuch, 2011: 4–5; Gurova, 2006; Vainshtein, 1996; Zakharova, 2013). The good taste of a Soviet person meant consumption according to the principle of moderation and simplicity (Vainshtein, 1996). Consumer habits were linked to the inner self, and excessive consumption as well as exaggerated following of Western fashion was considered a sign of a corrupted self (Gurova, 2006). Although cosmetics were legitimised in the middle-class lifestyle and produced in the Soviet Union, the official discourse was still often critical towards them, interpreting them as a Western fashion (Lebina, 2014: 111).

In the 1970s–mid-1980s, the state promoted an ambivalent attitude towards material objects in such a way that it both supported the further evolving of consumerism and material expectations, or criticised materialism and philistinism. The ideology was aimed at creating a 'post-materialistic world' (Gurova, 2006) in which there would be relative abundance of goods, which signalised to people in the country and to the rest of the world about success of the socialist system, but in which Soviet people, at the same time, were expected to maintain an indifferent attitude towards consumer goods. In other words, people should not be obsessed with things, but neither was a lack of material comfort acceptable (Gurova, 2006; Paretskaya, 2010). Fashion was considered as a legitimate part of the Soviet people's lifestyle. Although symbolic functions of fashion were acknowledged, in comparison to bourgeois societies, the Soviet people were supposed to not be keen on buying new things because the old ones are out of fashion. Following Western fashion was tolerated, but extreme manifestation were condemned and criticised (Yurchak, 2008).

Thus the media participated in a top-down approach to the construction of a consumer culture in socialist states and enhanced the paternalistic role of the state through the creation of dominant discourses. The ascetic values in the discourse co-existed with abundance, which sometimes gets ahead of reality, stimulating the development of consumption. At the same time, the state was eager to control consumer patterns, to limit those patterns of consumption, which could be defined as excessive since they did not correspond to the ideals and norms of socialist society.

RETAIL TRADE AND SHOPPING IN A 'SELLERS' MARKET'

Soviet trade was in the focus of several monographs covering the periods of the late nineteenth to the early twentieth century (Hessler, 2004; Hilton, 2012), the 1930s (Gronow, 2003; Osokina, 2001; Randall, 2008) and the late Soviet times (Ivanova, 2017).

As for the history of formats, before the revolution there existed merchants' rows, as well as privately owned or cooperative stores, which after the revolution were closed down or nationalised and transformed into large-scale state-owned retail outlets (Hilton, 2012), among which were department stores from the first half of the century and universal stores (*universam*) from the second half. There were also specialised stores selling food and non-food items throughout the entire period. The politics of the Bolsheviks after the revolution of 1917 can be described as aiming at the democratisation of consumption, and the purpose was to create a retail trade that corresponded to the ideas of a socialist society, which was self-proclaimed as classless. According to Marjorie Hilton, the motto of the Soviet retail trade was 'Everything for everybody'. Despite this goal, the stores were stratified as the (scarce) goods were allocated unevenly for different groups of consumers, thus creating hierarchies of stores and of consumers. For instance, during whole Soviet period there were 'closed' (limited-access) stores. In the first half of the 1930s stores named *Torgsin* (an acronym derived from '*Torgovlia s inostrantsami*' translated as 'Trade with foreigners') sold food and other scarce goods (Osokina, 2001). In the second half of the century there were *Beriozka* (Birch) stores selling luxury or hard-to-get goods for foreign currencies, which were unavailable to ordinary citizens, and for precious metals (Ivanova, 2013, 2017). The access of the consumers to the stores was based on their profession and position at work: 'the closer to important material production one worked, the better were the provisions and one's living standards' (Gronow, 2003: 124). Anna Ivanova cited underground writer Iuz Aleshkovskii, who satirically wrote that *Beriozka* stores, an attractor of consumer desire in the late Soviet times, 'destroy people's faith in our classless society' (Ivanova, 2013: 259).

Not only retail formats were changed, but in-store practices too. The transformation of the culture of selling was achieved through a campaign aimed at building 'cultured trade', in which 'cultured' should be applicable to both sides – salespersons and customers. This campaign was launched in the mid-1930s and was in line with the ideas of culturedness (*kul'turnost'*) discussed above. Cultured Soviet trade meant a 'modern, rational, and hygienic retail environment where employees provided consumers with attentive and friendly customer service, new retail amenities and services, creative displays, and a wide variety of goods' (Hessler, 2004; Randall, 2008: 39).

Interestingly, the modernisation of new retail spaces was largely based on the Western experience, learnt when the Soviet delegation travelled to the US and Western Europe and studied the organisation of retail (Gronow, 2003). As Jane Randall notes, the Soviet leaders 'did not turn to Lenin or Marx and Engels in order to rethink their retail operations; rather, they looked abroad' (Randall, 2008: 46). The American department store Macy's served as one such example for socialist leaders. They picked both small practices, for instance, the way men's shirts were displayed on open shelves, each size on a separate shelf, to larger principles, such as self-service or the creation of a comfortable atmosphere for the client, who was motivated to spend time in the shop with many additional services (Gronow, 2003; Oushakine, 2014). These new principles were applied in the so-called 'model stores', for instance in GUM (Main Universal Store) and TsUM (Central Universal Store) in Moscow. These stores also experimented with home deliveries and telephone orders, additional tailoring services, and so on (Gronow, 2003: 87; Hilton, 2012; Randall, 2008).

The hierarchy of salesperson vs customer also changed, which affected the culture of selling. Before the revolution the stores' owners were interested in profit or in forcing customers to buy what they did not necessarily need. Therefore, they could cheat the clients, while after the revolution the idea was to give salespersons the status of workers who should be cultured, well-mannered and reliable. The purpose was to upgrade the position of retail workers by redefining their relation to consumers (Hilton, 2012: 236). The type of market that has been formed in socialist countries has been called the '*sellers' market*' (Kornai, 1992). By 'sellers' market' was meant the peculiar regimen of the market, in which immediate access to the consumer goods was considered as the most important resource of this market. Since the seller possesses this resource, it gives him/her power and puts the consumer into a subordinate position in such a way that the consumer has to invest his/her efforts, time and money, into gaining information and getting access to the goods. S/he also has to adapt their own needs and desires to the shortages of the consumer market. As a result, in fact, the culture of selling in Soviet Russia evolved in a direction opposite to what was intended, meaning a notorious lack of attention of sales workers to customers, lack of friendliness, boorishness, etc.

The Soviet consumers, however, had their 'weapon' against the sellers. Consumers were expected to express their agency through the practice of *complaints*, a powerful mechanism of consumers' feedback, which was institutionalised in the 1920s and existed throughout the Soviet period (Bogdanova, 2015; Hilton, 2012). Complaints were made in a 'Book for complaints and suggestions' available in every single store and in the form of letters to the press. Consumers were seen by the state as 'productive', actively involved in the process of consumption. The complaints thus could be seen as a form of consumer citizenship in the Soviet Union (Randall, 2008: 14, 134). As for the selling culture, rudeness was the most common problem and the target of complaints, in which the sales workers were portrayed as 'petty tyrants of the counter who wielded undue power in obstructing their [customers'] rightful access to goods and who verbally abused or ignored them' (Hilton, 2012: 251; see also Bogdanova, 2015). Another typical complaint was 'cheating in weighing': a salesperson could press a finger on scale to add weight. Elena Bogdanova describes a caricature illustrating this practice in which a customer says to sales worker: 'Pack your finger also, since you have weighed it!' (Bogdanova, 2015: 119). Consumers complained about the lack of goods, poor service, boorishness and the indifference of sales assistants, the poor quality of consumer goods, queues, etc. (Bogdanova, 2015: 121). The culture of selling thus produced an atmosphere of conflicts and anxieties, which along with shortages and queues sometimes made the experience of customers not so pleasurable.

The practice of shopping was defined in socialist terms as a matter of meeting material needs. Soviet scholars looked at shopping from the point of view of efficiency: how much time it takes for the consumers to get to the store or how much time they spend in queues, and how this experience can be made more efficient (Gurova, 2014). Sales workers did not serve but 'issued the goods' and also 'satisfied consumers' requests' (Hilton, 2012: 236), and the consumer 'procured' commodities (Fitzpatrick, 1999). In Soviet culture, shopping was not considered to be in the framework of leisure and pleasure. However, recently it was argued that this does not mean that Soviet society was a world without pleasure, which was in general an integral part of the planned future of socialist society – that is, of communism. Pleasure can also be found, if not in the process of purchasing goods, then in the result of obtaining not easily available commodities (Crowley and Reid, 2010: 3) which were sacral 'trophies' because of their scarcity (Chapman, 2013a: 27).

Marketing mechanisms, such as advertisements, were primarily used in the socialist Russia for didactical purpose. Advertising was considered as 'agitational and educational media' which 'elevates' and 'publicises the regime's achievements' and promotes its policy (Hilton, 2012: 196, 212; Kravets and Sandikçi, 2013: 473; Tolstikova, 2007: 46). Therefore, the purposes of advertisement were to cultivate and teach the Soviet consumer to appreciate novelties (Gronow, 2003: 86), to inform about rational and proper modes of consumption (Reid, 2002: 218) and to fight backwardness (Kravets and Sandikçi, 2013: 479). Since early Soviet advertisement was produced by artists, it was considered as art that could beautify the face of the cities (Tolstikova, 2007: 48). Recently scholars reframed socialist consumption in terms of pleasure and desire, as I mentioned above, stating that desire should not be neglected in understanding the Soviet consumer culture. Advertising, thus, also channelled desire, formed a 'proper' attitude to desirable objects and promoted the state as the main provider of material welfare (Golubev, 2016).

In general, many marketing strategies used in the Soviet Union were similar to the ones used in the West, however, they were aligned with principles of state policy rather that with demand and profit. For instance, Olga Kravets and Özlem Sandikçi explore the marketing strategies of the cosmetic trust TeZHe in the 1930s and illustrate what kinds of strategies were utilised. The trust aimed at growing varieties of perfumes and other products (a sign of abundance); introduced the names of the products after current events (promotion of events); differentiated prices, offering lower price items in order to provide everyone with basic necessities; used different packages for the same items or repackaged old products, sometimes attracting renowned artists to producing the pack materials; utilised novel ways of displaying commodities (not to stimulate the desire but to inform customers about new goods); and used mail order and travelling salesmen to distribute goods (Kravets and Sandikçi, 2013: 463). There were also other marketing tools used by retail traders, such as holiday bazaars, product tie-ins, and additional in-store services, for instance, tailoring and carrying out alterations of clothes (Chernyshova, 2013: 38; Hilton, 2012: 221).

Since the stores often did not offer what consumers needed, in addition to 'first' or 'official' economy and legal trade there was the so-called 'second economy', an unofficial, illegal or semi-legal trade (Fitzpatrick, 1999; Verdery, 1996). This kind of trade was labelled as '*black market*', a powerful sociocultural phenomenon in Soviet Russia. Black market goods were hard-to-earn often foreign products not available in stores, for instance, jeans or nylon stockings. Sellers on the black market (*fartzovshchiki, spekulianty*) obtained goods from abroad, from foreigners coming to Russia or from 'closed' stores and sold these goods to customers with the purpose to making a profit. The black market thus was a form of market economy in socialist society. Although it was illegal, the state turned a blind eye towards such activities because they maintained its stability (Lebina, 2014: 141–142).

In sum, the logic of the transformation of the retail trade illustrates the development of mass consumption in the Soviet Union. Particular tendencies that formed consumer culture in the Soviet Union were the state regulation of retail trade, the democratisation of retailing, and, at the same time, a differentiation in provision and access to consumer goods. Informal unofficial trade as an element of market economy complemented the state-regulated retail system.

COMMODITIES AS 'THINGS-AS-COMRADES'

Commodities are seen in literature as items embodying values of a culture; they are not mute and can speak (Crowley and Reid, 2010: 9). Commodities in a socialist economy, when compared to commodities in a market economy as described in the studies, are usually depicted as the ones without a 'scab of beauty,' because they were not supposed to seduce a customer with their appearance (Bartlett, 2010; Degot', 2005; Gurova, 2015). Soviet consumer culture was aimed at establishing a radically new relationship between people and material objects, which was not a relationship of alienation as in capitalist society, but of friendship. Therefore, socialist things were called 'friends' or 'comrades' to people, not slaves to them (Bartlett, 2010: 18; Kravets, 2013: 422). Scholars apply the metaphor '*things-as-comrades*', depicting Soviet material objects and arguing that in a socialist society, use value prevailed over symbolic value which resulted in a relatively 'plain' non-commercial aesthetic and rational attitude to things. Ekaterina Degot' depicts a Soviet thing as 'warm, friendly with no obsessing toward the surface, honest, truthful, modest ... Isn't it a description of a perfect human being?' she asks (Degot', 2005: 202; Gurova, 2015; Kravets, 2013).

The prevalence of use value was seen not only in the design of the products but also in the packaging – the goods in stores could be wrapped in greyish or brownish paper that was supposed to first and foremost protect a product rather than seduce a customer. A similar utilitarian approach existed in shop-windows, which had to be 'honest and informative' (Randall, 2008: 56). Nevertheless, the significance of symbolic values had been gradually increasing, and in the post-WWII period Soviet commodities absorbed new qualities such as stylishness and a nice design, and therefore embodied an ability to satisfy not only the needs but also the fantasies of the consumers (Golubev, 2016).

In the Soviet consumer culture, there was a specific group of commodities, which on the one hand, were luxurious and, on the other hand, were accessible to the wider population. These goods were introduced in the 1930s, when the ideology of asceticism was replaced by the ideology of culturedness. Among these goods were items that related to pleasure and luxury rather than to needs and necessity, such as champagne, cognac, caviar, chocolate and perfume. Jukka Gronow (1997) called such products '*democratic luxury*'. As he explains,

> Champagne was sold and drunk in great qualities ... Caviar sandwiches were on offer at almost every café in museums, theatres or concert halls. .... [I]t was not only the long queues in front of the shops and the almost chronic shortages of many everyday commodities which characterized the Soviet culture of consumption. The culture was also deeply permeated by the spirit of common and plebeian luxury. (Gronow, 2003: x)

The luxurious commodities 'trickled down' from a lifestyle of pre-revolutionary nobility, as the Bolsheviks envisioned it. These were goods supposed to be consumed for holidays and other celebrations; many of them were meant for women. The spread and popularity of these goods were in line with the general idea of democratisation of consumption. Because they were cheaper versions of more expensive and fine commodities, the concept of '*Soviet kitsch*' was also applied to interpret them (Gronow, 1997).

There was hierarchy of commodities in the Soviet consumer culture. This hierarchy was between locally produced and imported consumer goods (in particular, from the West), with the latter occupying a higher position and serving as an object of desire for the Soviet consumer (Chernyshova, 2013). The paradox was that in the official media discourse all things Western were criticised as products of bourgeois and capitalist society, but the daily life situation was more complicated. For instance, in the 1930s, when Soviet leaders went to the US to learn about the organisation of retail trade, they brought back to the country equipment for producing American hamburgers. The hamburgers were sold in kiosks in Moscow and could have become 'an ideal, "socialist" solution to mass catering for the "busy man" in Soviet cities', but the war (WWII) disrupted that plan (Gronow, 2003: 74). In the 1950s and 1960s, when Soviet designers visited the Dior company in France, they had to adopt a double language. On the one hand, in the public discourse, when speaking about French haute couture they used the politically approved clichés 'bourgeois fashion exaggerations,' but in the professional discourse and in internal reports they justified the positive effect of visiting France for Soviet design (Zakharova, 2010: 100).

Fashion as a mechanism of the aging of commodities was not inbuilt in the socialist economy to the same extent as in the capitalist system (Gronow, 2003: 145). Djurdja Bartlett supports this view, distinguishing 'official socialist dress' – representations of fashion in official media, at exhibitions and congresses and fairs (Bartlett, 2010: 8). This official socialist dress did not change fast and was a 'prisoner of time', always looking a bit out of fashion and therefore called '*congealed*' fashion (Bartlett, 2005: 141–142). In contrast with official socialist dress, so-called 'everyday dress', actually worn by consumers, belonged to a different – faster – modernity. It was more exposed to fashion, especially after WWII, when standards of living were rising, the interest in fashion was growing and new fashion trends were coming to the country via media, films, magazines or with imported goods (Bartlett, 2010: 11).

Thus, commodities in the Soviet consumer culture were characterised by the prevalence of use value over symbolic value in the official discourse, whereas in the second part of the century and in daily life the importance of symbolic function became more significant.

CONSUMPTION AND DISTINCTIONS IN 'CLASSLESS' SOCIETY

As already mentioned, Soviet society was a self-proclaimed classless society in which the individual had to be 'firmly embedded into the social collective' (Gronow, 2003: 146). According to the principle of collectivism, it was desirable not to stand out from the crowd. However, in the second half of the twentieth century a desire to be different, to show personal uniqueness, to be differentiated from a group of similar people was growing in the Soviet culture, that is, the tendency towards individualisation became of greater importance (Kharkhordin, 1999: 13, 337).

Consumption in the Soviet Union held the function of social differentiation. Officially, the socialist class system in 1936 was proclaimed to consist of three classes: workers, collective farm workers (*kolkhozniki*) and the intelligentsia. In addition, there was the party nomenclature, which were not distinguished as a separate class but were regarded as serving the people and as a 'part of the people', although their status as consumers was very different. By the Brezhnev era the class system seemed to comprise of the two classes only, whereby the intelligentsia no longer belonged to a class of their own, but were seen as an 'extra-class social stratum' (Chernyshova, 2013: 106–107). As studies show, the elite, including the party nomenclature, enjoyed privileged access to 'closed' food stores and also to clothing and furniture shops, special spas and hotels, larger apartments, cars and motorcycles, easy access to train and plane tickets, and so on (Chernyshova, 2013: 106; Gronow, 2003: 149; Tikhomirova, 2010: 285). At the same time, the Soviet elite did not show off their luxury and enjoyed it in secret (Bartlett, 2006: 180).

As for the middle class, it was not an emic category of Soviet culture, but an analytical tool that was applied to it. Soviet sociologists, when studying social structure in the Soviet society, analysed mostly professional and generational differences (Gurova, 2014). In the eyes of Western scholars after the 1930s Soviet society was gradually becoming more hierarchic and stratified, and the political elite was joined by the middle class (Dunham, 1979: 4; Gronow, 2003: 12–13). Sheila Fitzpatrick includes non-party Bolsheviks, educated professionals, shock workers, artists, scientists, and more, in the category of the Soviet middle class (Fitzpatrick, 1999: 252–254; Gronow, 1997: 60). Jukka Gronow (1997: 66) argues that only with slight exaggeration it could be claimed that only one class existed in the Soviet Union, a huge middle class, consisting both of well-to-do workers and educated specialists, and the so-called intelligentsia. This middle class escalated in the 1950s and 1960s, unifying all those people who had adopted a rather homogeneous conception of the 'good life', with modest material prosperity and a limited number of luxuries (Gurova, 2015). For instance, in the second half of the century the Soviet middle-class lifestyle comprised a one-family apartment, consumer durables, such as a refrigerator and a television (Reid, 2002), novel technological appliances, home- and kitchenware (Chernyshova, 2013), a summerhouse (Lovell, 2003), sometimes a car (Siegelbaum, 2008), vacations (Gorsuch, 2011), and the cultural consumption of literature, the theatre, cinema, and so on (Stites, 1992).

As for poor citizens, this topic is yet to be uncovered. However, Mervin Matthews offers a socioeconomic analysis of poverty in the Soviet Union, which was a well-hidden phenomenon, using very scarce statistical data and interviews with émigrés, and noticing that poverty did not only mean lack of financial resources (60% of the budget of the poor went on food), but also lack of social connections and networks (Matthews, 1986).

Gender differences were discussed in the context of a 'gender contract' in Soviet society, which reflects the roles carried out by the genders that were officially proclaimed as being equal (Gradskova, 2007). In the Soviet Union, the main roles of women were that of a worker and a mother; women as consumers also became a legitimised role in the second half of the century. In fact, consumption and household labour were naturalised as women's activities (Reid, 2002: 220). Such gender-sensitive issues as beauty and body, fashion and images of femininity were discussed in studies from the point of view of specific practices and their changes during the Soviet times (see, for instance, Gradskova, 2007, 2011). Masculinity and such consumer practices as alcoholism, drug use, fashion and sex were considered in relation to the concept of 'Soviet manhood' (Miller, 2013). Other significant forms of social distinctions were youth subcultures, among which great attention was given to *stiliagi*, the stylish youth who appeared on the streets of Soviet cities at the end of the 1940s to the early 1950s. These were younger people focused on consuming Western, mostly American, cultural and material products (Tsipursky, 2013). They were defined as 'youth-as-victims-of-Western-influence' by the dominant discourses and viewed as evidence of Westernisation (Pilkington, 1994: 48). *Stiliagi* were the consumers of the 'Imaginary West' – Western music, foreign clothes, creating a mix of Soviet and Western imagination (Yurchak, 2008: 175). They also belonged to a global movement of counter-cultures whereby the younger generation was searching for a new identity after WWII in both socialist and capitalist contexts (Tsipursky, 2013). Another group that got scholarly attention was the *hippies* (Risch, 2005).

In sum, despite the fact that Russia was a self-proclaimed classless society, consumption there served as a symbolic means of constructing identity with tendencies towards the growth of the middle class, individualisation and the use of consumption for self-expression.

CONSUMER PRACTICES IN EVERYDAY LIFE

Soviet daily practices and practices of consumption have been topics of great interest for scholars (Boym, 1994; Dunham, 1979; Fitzpatrick, 1999; Gerasimova and Chuikina, 2009; Golubev and Smolyak, 2013; Gurova, 2009; Lebina, 1999, 2009, 2014; Ledeneva, 1998; Tikhomirova, 2010). I distinguish consumer practices related to the obtaining, use and discarding of consumer goods – this approach is known as a study of '*the cultural biography of things*' (Gurova, 2009, 2015; Smolyak, 2014; cf. Kopytoff, 2005).

Firstly, as mentioned above, commodities in Soviet society were not just bought but were 'procured'. Among the practices of obtaining consumer goods from the market, queuing was one of the most common (Chapman, 2013b). One could queue in a store. There were other types of queues, for instance, an ordinary citizen could buy a car by 'registering on the waiting list at his or her workplace' (Ivanova, 2013: 246). In such a way, one could buy furniture or home appliances, and also get an apartment from the state. Such queues as the ones for an apartment, a car or for a furniture set could last for several months or years. Queuing was one of the symbols of the delay that existed in the Soviet culture between the commodity and the customer (Chapman, 2013b: 21). Because of the shortages, ordinary people often went out with a so-called 'just in case' bag (*avos'ka*), in case something was available in a store. The practice of forced purchase (*vynuzhdennaia pokupka*) made due to availability instead of a consumer's intention was a typical consumer practice (Gurova, 2014). *Blat* was a significant practice in obtaining goods through social capital – personal networks and connections with someone who had access to these goods (Fitzpatrick, 1999: 78; Lebina, 2014: 132; Ledeneva, 1998). Another common practice was travelling to shop from one city to another where there was better provision – yet another way of overcoming differences in provisions in various areas of the Soviet Union (Chernyshova, 2013).

Secondly, *do-it-yourself practices*, as scholars have proved, were of crucial importance in the Soviet Union because of the discrepancy between the needs and wants of consumers, on the one hand, and what was offered to them in stores, on the other hand. These practices were also widespread because of the nature of Soviet commodities that had to be fine-tuned according to the desires of consumers (Gerasimova and Chuikina, 2009; Golubev and Smolyak, 2013; Gurova, 2009, 2015; Kravets, 2013; Lebina, 2009; Orlova, 2009; Smolyak, 2014; Vasilyeva, 2012; Widdis, 2009). Discourse on do-it-yourself practices was popular throughout the entire Soviet period. Soviet citizens sewed and knitted clothes, prepared canned food that they had grown on their allotments, manufactured furniture and repaired technical appliances. Although these practices were considered to be 'home economy', many used resources from their workplace and used their work time to accomplish these tasks (Smolyak, 2014; Vasilyeva, 2012). Soviet society has been called by scholars the '*repair society*' because of the proliferation of practices such as the producing, repairing, mending and refashioning of material objects. In order to adjust materiality to their desires, Soviet people used lots of so-called 'little tricks' or improvisations known as '*bricolage*' (Gerasimova and Chuikina, 2009: 68). These tricks revealed the multifunctionality of material objects and the 'practical knowledge' of Soviet people. For instance, Galina Orlova gives an example from a letter from a reader published in the magazine *Nauka i zhizn'* (*Science and Life*). This reader 'discovered "new career paths for a fan" and proposed some "straightforward adaptations" to broaden an ordinary room fan's talents by turning it into mixer, electric drill, and a grindstone, while also not preventing it from fulfilling its original calling' (Orlova, 2009: 80). Such DIY practices challenged oppositions between production and consumption, manual and intellectual activities, work and leisure, invention and routine (see Kravets, 2013: 429; Vasilyeva, 2012: 28–29). Although reminiscent of a pre-modern time, these practices were not considered as a sign of backwardness in the Soviet consumer culture, but rather a sign of being modern and progressive. Besides being a straight response to institutional constraints, they were commonly seen by scholars as practices that worked against the dominant discourse (Widdis, 2009), as practices of 'resistance' to structural conditions (Gurova, 2009) or, instead, as 'acts of self-protection' because they are focused more on minimising the harm to individuals' everyday lives than on confronting the regime (Shevchenko, 2002: 163). Olga Kravets notes that this DIY work was 'not Martha Stewart craft hobby as self-actualisation, neither was it a bohemian act of self-expression and/or creative resistance, nor purely a practice of austerity driven money saving. Rather, the nature of objects (*polufabrikat*) simply demanded work of re-design and individualisation' (Kravets, 2013: 430). Emma Widdis, however, talks about the pleasure gained from making things with one's own hands, redefining Soviet DIY as a sensory experience (Widdis, 2009).

As for the discarding of things, even if the use value was lost, things were supposed almost never to be thrown away in the Soviet consumer culture. They could be hoarded and stored in upper shelves of wardrobes, balconies, garages or in summerhouses in case their owner needed them some day. When material objects lost their use or symbolic value they were not sent to a trash can, but instead were transformed into something new with other functions (Gurova, 2009, 2015). For instance, as Galina Orlova illustrates:

> The frame of an old lampshade can make a fine stand for a soldering iron; an automobile tire, a pen for chicks; a holey bucket, a container for root vegetables; a broken soap holder, a clothes brush; and a steel spring from a broken piece of upholstered furniture, the moving part of a press for photo prints. (Orlova, 2009: 81–82)

DISCUSSION: IS SOVIET CONSUMER CULTURE A CONTRADICTORY TERM?

The categories 'consumer culture' and 'consumer society' were not emic categories and were rarely used in Soviet society. Nevertheless, scholars applied them, sometimes interchangeably, and also utilised other terms. They talk about 'Soviet consumer culture' (Randall, 2008: 3), 'a mass consumer society' (Crowley and Reid, 2010: 11; Randall, 2008) or even 'a modern working class consumer society' (Hilton, 2012: 231).

There are three views on how to approach the question about whether Soviet Russia could be considered a consumer society. According to the first point of view, Soviet Russia can be called a consumer society yet with certain limitations. For instance, if the key criterion of belonging to a consumer society is the quantity and quality of the produced and purchased goods, the Soviet Union did not constitute a mass consumer society since the Soviet consumer purchased only basic, necessary goods (Hessler, 2004: 229; Hilton, 2012: 269). At the end of the day, it was a culture of shortage that required certain consumer strategies of procuring and hoarding rather than one of boundless and conspicuous consumption (Reid, 2002: 216).

According to the second point of view, Russian society can undoubtedly be called a consumer society or a consumer culture, but 'not a carbon copy' of its Western counterpart (Reid, 2009: 4). The case of the Soviet Union illustrates an alternative way of organising modern mass consumption, which is defined by the fact that consumer culture in the Soviet Union was not formed by a market, but by the state, 'from above', because the state made decisions about basically everything, including even goods' paper-wrapping and packaging (Gronow, 2003: 8). Nevertheless, despite this difference, consumption became an important channel through which attributes of modern societies such as individualisation, privatisation, aesthetisation of life and commercialisation made their way into Soviet society (cf. Chernyshova, 2013: 9).

There is another approach in defining a consumer society, which is based on the identity of the Soviet person as a consumer. According to this point of view, despite the fact that production was a prevalent sphere and professional identity was important, Soviet citizens were recognised as consumers. In certain periods the state promoted the identity of a consumer as an important part of the identity of a Soviet man. Consumers themselves objectified this status on a daily basis in many ways, for instance, when procuring goods, making complaints or participating in black market activities (Bogdanova, 2015; Hilton, 2012: 269; Randall, 2008). The agency of a Soviet consumer was especially visible in the practices of the 'second economy' and the 'home economy'. Therefore, it is important to acknowledge that the Soviet consumer culture was also constructed 'from below'.

Another important question is related to periodisation: when the Soviet consumer culture emerged. A periodisation of Soviet history has been established, and scholars usually focus on a particular period, observing what was happening to consumer culture at that particular time. There were several significant time points in the evolution of the Soviet consumer culture. After 1917 private property was abolished, which, along with other reforms, created conditions for a new Soviet consumer culture. In the 1920s there was a period when private production and private trade were legal and this noticeably affected consumption. The 1930s was the period when a new socialist consumer culture was crystallised (Randall, 2008: 14), standards of living changed, along with infrastructural transformations (Gronow, 2003: 139). In the 1950s there was a 'consumer turn', when material, ideological and an economic base for mass consumption was created (Crowley and Reid, 2010: 11; Golubev and Smolyak, 2013; Reid, 2009; Tikhomirova, 2010: 286). The 1970s was the period of 'consumer revolution' and rapid growth in private consumption. The Soviet consumer came of age in this decade (Chernyshova, 2013: 1, 3; see also Reid, 2009: 4). In the beginning of the 1990s, when private property and a market economy were restored, a new post-socialist consumer culture emerged.

CONCLUSION

This chapter has argued that consumer culture is a global phenomenon and has emphasised the peculiarities of consumer culture that was formed in socialist times in Russia. Russia can serve as a case for further comparative research with other consumer cultures formed in countries with non-market economies. A number of elements constituting consumer culture were discussed, namely, production, ideology of consumption, retail trade, commodities, social structure and consumer practices. Looking at these elements from the cultural perspective, we can define the key characteristics of the socialist consumer culture which I summarise further.

The Soviet Union was distinctive in proclaiming the prevalence of production over consumption and in the significance of the role of the state vis-à-vis market and consumer demand. Soviet society was called a 'shortage' or 'storage' society because of the limited choice of commodities available for consumers in stores. Shortage is a relative term given that along with periods of crisis there were times of relative abundance and expanding individual consumption. Soviet society was a mass consumption society. What is peculiar about it is that the state played such a strong role in the regulation of mass production and mass consumption. In addition to a planned and centralised economy there was a 'second' or an informal, semi-legal or illegal economy functioning according to the principles of market economics. The state often turned a blind eye to such practices because they compensated for the flaws in the official socialist market.

The ideology of consumption transmitted through the dominant official discourse was ambivalent. On the one hand, it was critical towards commodity fetishism, philistinism, petty-bourgeois attachment to things and towards inequality expressed through material symbols. On the other hand, the idea of increasing material well-being was immanent to the socialist system. In general, the ideology legitimised consumption and was aimed at promoting both abundance and a post-materialistic attitude, namely, indifference to material possessions.

The retail trade in the 'first,' official economy functioned according to the state plans rather than to customers' demand. The Soviet consumer market can be called a 'seller's market' with the sales worker, who had access to the goods, being the dominant person in the hierarchy when compared to the consumer. This market produced a culture of selling where the consumer was the one who had to make an effort in order to get the goods. As a result, the culture of selling was characterised by sales workers' lack of attention to their customers, boorishness and a lack of friendliness. However, consumers had their own weapon against the sales worker and could complain. Through such complaints their agency was expressed. Shopping in a socialist consumer culture was not seen in terms of a leisure pursuit, although pleasure could come with obtained goods.

Commodities were officially valued for their use rather than for symbolic reasons, which affected the aesthetics of commodities and the ways of exhibiting and advertising them. The window displays were utilitarian and were supposed to inform and educate a customer about new goods rather than to seduce them. Advertising had the didactic purpose of publicising and elevating the regime's achievements, and also of informing consumers about novelties and how to properly use them. Nevertheless, many of the marketing strategies which were applied by retailers were similar to the ones used in market-driven consumer cultures. The difference was in the interpretations that in Soviet consumer culture were related to state policy.

Despite being a self-proclaimed classless society and disregarding the symbolic value of things, consumption became a means of producing sociocultural distinctions. It distinguished people of different classes, genders, generations, subcultures, etc. The differences were reflected in privileged access to particular stores, in commodities serving as signs of differences and in practices of consumption. The evolution of the class structure was reflected in individualisation and the rise of the role of consumption in identity formation.

Due to the difficult access to commodities and their characteristics, DIY practices were important coping strategies and ways of satisfying the wants and desires of Soviet consumers. These practices, aimed at prolonging the lifecycle of things, also served to express agency and as ways of adjusting the material environment of the Soviet society to consumers' desires and fantasies. Therefore, Soviet consumer culture was formed not only by the state, 'from above'; ordinary consumers were also active agents in constructing it 'from below'.

In sum, Soviet consumption is yet to be put in a global context in consumer culture studies. The potential could have various comparisons, between consumer culture in market and non-market economies or between post-socialist countries and in different historical periods, for instance, in socialist and post-socialist Russia. Some topical areas still have gaps, for instance, the consumption of food and its regulation or the evolution of retail formats in the second half of the twentieth century. Phenomena such as DIY-culture and its relation to today's practices of sustainable consumption have been gaining academic attention recently. Sensorial and technological elements of the socialist consumer culture are also topical areas of current research.

ACKNOWLEDGEMENTS

I would like to thank Olga Kravets who encouraged me to write this chapter and historian Anna Ivanova for her insightful comments.

REFERENCES

Bartlett, D. (2005) 'Let Them Wear Beige: The Petit-Bourgeois World of Official Socialist Dress', *Fashion Theory*, 8(2): 127–164.

Bartlett, D. (2006) 'In Russia, At Last and Forever: The First Seven Years of Russian Vogue', *Fashion Theory*, 10(1-2): 175–204.

Bartlett, D. (2010) *FashionEast: The Spectre that Haunted Socialism*. Cambridge, MA: Massachusetts Institute of Technology.

Bogdanova, E. (2015) 'The Soviet Consumer – More than Just a Soviet Man', in T. Vihavainen and E. Bogdanova (eds) *Communism and Consumerism: The Soviet Alternative to the Affluent Society*, Leiden and Boston: Brill, pp. 113–138.

Boym, S. (1994) *Common Places: Mythologies of Everyday Life in Russia*. Cambridge, MA: Harvard University Press.

Buchli, V. (2000) An Archeology of Socialism (Materializing Culture). Oxford: Berg Publishers.

Chapman, A. (2013a) 'Trofeinost' and the Phantasmagoria of Everyday Consumption in Late Soviet Culture', *Studies in Slavic Cultures*, XI(May): 24–49.

Chapman, A. (2013b) 'Queuetopia: Second-World Modernity and the Soviet Culture of Allocation'. PhD Dissertation. University of Pittsburg.

Chernyshova, N. (2013) *Soviet Consumer Culture in the Brezhnev Era*. New York and London: Routledge.

Cox, R. (2006) 'NEP Without Nepmen! Soviet Advertising and the Transition to Socialism', in C. Kiaer and E. Naiman (eds) *Everyday Life in Early Soviet Russia.* Bloomington: Indiana University Press, pp. 119–152.

Crowley, D. and Reid, S. (2010) 'Introduction: Pleasures in Socialism?', in D. Crowley and S. Reid (eds) *Pleasures in Socialism*. Evanston, IL: Northwestern University Press, pp. 3–52.

Davies, R.W. (2010) 'The Economic History of the Soviet Union Reconsidered', *Kritika: Explorations in Russian and Eurasian History*, 11(1): 145–159.

Degot', E. (2005) Ot tovara k tovarishchu. K estetike nerynochnogo predmeta, *Logos*, 5(50): 201–210.

Dunham, V.S. (1979) *In Stalin's Time: Middle-class Values in Soviet Fiction.* Cambridge: Cambridge University Press.

Fitzpatrick, S. (1999) Everyday Stalinism. Ordinary Life in Extraordinary Times: Soviet Russia in the 1930s. New York and Oxford: Oxford University Press.

Geertz, C. (1973) 'Thick Description: Toward an Interpretive Theory of Culture', in C. Geertz (ed.) *The Interpretation of Cultures*. Basic Books. Retrieved from: http://philpapers.org/archive/GEETTD.pdf

Gerasimova, E. and Chuikina, S. (2009) 'Repair Society', *Russian Studies in History*, 48(1): 58–74.

Golubev, A. (2016) 'Desirable Things of Ogoniok: The Material Face of a Soviet Illustrated Magazine from Stalin to Brezhnev', *The Soviet and Post-Soviet Review*, 43(2): 152–181.

Golubev, A. and Smolyak, O. (2013) 'Making Selves through Making Things: Soviet Do-It-Yourself Culture and Practices of Late Soviet Subjectivation', *Cahiers du monde russe*, 54(3–4): 517–541.

Gorsuch, A.E. (2011) *All This is Your World: Soviet Tourism at Home and Abroad After Stalin*. Oxford: Oxford University Press.

Gradskova, Y. (2007) 'Soviet People with Female Bodies. Performing Beauty and Maternity in Soviet Russia in the mid-1930–1960s', PhD manuscript, Stockholm University. Retrieved from: http://su.diva-portal.org/smash/get/diva2:197398/FULLTEXT01

Gradskova, Y. (2011) 'Femininity and Beauty Practices in Soviet Russia in 1950–1960s', in *Nordic Fashion Studies*. Stockholm: Axi Books, pp. 3–18.

Gronow, J. (1997) *The Sociology of Taste*. London, New York: Routledge.

Gronow, J. (2003) Caviar with Champagne: Common Luxury and the Ideals of Good Life in Stalin's Russia. Oxford, New York: Berg.

Gurova, O. (2006) 'Ideology of Consumption in the Soviet Union: From Asceticism to Legitimating of Consumer Goods', *Anthropology of East Europe Review*, 24(2): 91–102.

Gurova, O. (2008) Sovetskoe nizhnee bel'e: mezhdu ideologiei i povsednevnosti'iu. Moskva: Novoe literaturnoe obozrenie.

Gurova, O. (2009) 'The Life Span of Things in Soviet Society: Notes on the Sociology of Underwear', *Russian Social Science Review*, 50(4): 49–60.

Gurova, O. (2014) 'Institutionalization of the Sociology of Consumption in Russia', *Economic Sociology (Ekonomicheskaya Sotsiologiia)*, 15(4): 76–106.

Gurova, O. (2015) Fashion and the Consumer Revolution in Contemporary Russia. London and New York: Routledge.

Hessler, J. (2004) *A Social History of Soviet Trade: Trade Policy, Retail Practices, and Consumption*, 1917–1953. Princeton: Princeton University Press.

Hilton, M.L. (2012) *Selling to the Masses: Retailing in Russia, 1880–1930*. Pittsburgh: University of Pittsburgh Press.

Ivanova, A. (2013) 'Shopping in Beriozka: Consumer Society in the Soviet Union', *Studies in Contemporary History*, 10(2): 243–263.

Ivanova, A. (2017) *Magaziny 'Beriozka': paradoksy potrebleniia v pozdnem SSSR*. Moskva: Novoe literaturnoe obozrenie.

Karababa, E. and Ger, G. (2011) 'Early Modern Ottoman Coffeehouse Culture and the Formation of the Consumer Subject', *Journal of Consumer Research*, 37(5): 737–760.

Kelly, C. (2000) 'Creating a Consumer: Advertising and Commercialization', in C. Kelly and D. Shepherd (eds) *Russian Cultural Studies: An Introduction*. Oxford: Oxford University Press, pp. 223–246.

Kharkhordin, O. (1999) *The Collective and the Individual in Russia*. Berkeley: California University Press.

Kopytoff, I. (2005) 'The Cultural Biography of Things: Commoditization as Process', in A. Appadurai (ed.) *The Social Life of Things: Commodities in Cultural Perspective*. Cambridge: Cambridge University Press, pp. 64–94.

Kornai, J. (1992) *The Socialist System: The Political Economy of Communism*. Princeton, NJ: Princeton University Press.

Kravets, O. (2013) 'On Things and Comrades', *Ephemera*, 13(2): 421–436.

Kravets, O. and Sandikçi, O. (2013) 'Marketing for Socialism: Soviet Cosmetics in the 1930s', *Business History Review*, 87(3): 461–487.

Lebina, N. (1999) Povsednevnaia zhizn' sovetskogo goroda: normy i anomalii. 1920–1930-e gody. Sankt-Peterburg : Letnii sad.

Lebina, N. (2009) 'Plus the Chemicalization of the Entire Wardrobe', *Russian Studies in History*, 48(1): 33–45.

Lebina, N. (2014) *Muzhchina i zhenshchina: telo, moda, kul'tura.* Moskva: Novoe literaturnoe obozrenie.

Ledeneva, A. (1998) *Russia's Economy of Favours: Blat, Networking and Informal Exchange*. Cambridge: Cambridge University Press.

Lovell, S. (2003) *Summerfolk: A History of the Dacha, 1710–2000*. Ithaca, NY: Cornell University Press.

Lury, C. (2011[1996]) *Consumer Culture*. Cambridge: Polity Press.

Matthews, M. (1986) Poverty in the Soviet Union. The Life-styles of the Underprivileged in Recent Years. Cambridge University Press.

Merkel, I. (2006) 'From Stigma to Cult: Changing Meanings in East German Consumer Culture', in F. Trentmann (ed.) *The Making of the Consumer: Knowledge, Power and Identity in the Modern World*. Oxford, New York: Berg, pp. 249–270.

Miller, B.G. (2013) 'Between Creation and Crisis: Soviet Masculinities, Consumption, and Bodies after Stalin', PhD dissertation, Michigan State University.

Orlova, G. (2009) 'Apologia for a Strange Thing', *Russian Studies in History*, 48(1): 75–88.

Osokina, E. (2001) Our Daily Bread: Socialist Distribution and the Art of Survival. Armonk, NY, London, UK: M.E. Sharpe.

Oushakine, S.A. (2014) '"Against the Cult of Things": On Soviet Productivism, Storage Economy, and Commodities with No Destination', *The Russian Review*, 73: 198–236.

Paretskaya, A. (2010) 'The Soviet Communist Party and the Other Spirit of Capitalism', *Sociological Theory*, 28(4): 377–401.

Pilkington, H. (1994) Russia's Youth and Its Culture: A Nation's Constructors Reconstructed. London and New York: Routledge.

Randall, A.E. (2008) *The Soviet Dream World of Retail Trade and Consumption in the 1930s*. Hampshire: Palgrave Macmillan.

Reid, S. (2002) 'Cold War in the Kitchen: Gender and De-Stalinization of Consumer Taste in the Soviet Union under Khrushchev', *Slavic Review*, 61(2): 211–252.

Reid, S. (2009) 'Consumption and Everyday Culture After Stalin', *Russian Studies in History*, 48(1): 3–9.

Risch, W. (2005) '"Soviet Flower Children": Hippies and the Youth Counter-Culture in 1970s L'viv', *Journal of Contemporary History*, 40(3): 565–584.

Sassatelli, R. (2007) *Consumer Culture: History, Theory and Politics*. London: Sage.

Shevchenko, O. (2002) "In Case of Fire Emergency": Consumption, Security and the Meaning of Durables in a Transforming Society', *Journal of Consumer Culture,* 2(2): 147–170.

Siegelbaum, L.H. (2008) *Cars for Comrades: The Life of the Soviet Automobile*. Ithaca, NY: Cornell University Press.

Slater, D. (1997) *Consumer Culture and Modernity.* Cambridge: Polity Press.

Smolyak, O. (2014) '"Working for Yourself": Recourse Theft at a Factory in the Late Soviet Era', *Laboratorium*, 6(2): 21–57.

Stites, R. (1992) *Russian Popular Culture: Entertainment and Society since 1900*. Cambridge: Cambridge University Press.

Tikhomirova, A. (2007) 'Sovetskoe v postsovetskom: razmyshleniia o gibridnosti sovremennoi rossiiskoi kul'tury potrebleniia odezhdy', *Neprikosnovennyi zapas*, 4(54). Retrieved from: http://magazines.russ.ru/nz/2007/54/ti10.html

Tikhomirova, A. (2010) 'Soviet Women and Fur Consumption in the Brezhnev Era', in D. Crowley and S. Reid (eds) *Pleasures in Socialism*. Evanston, Illinois: Northwestern University Press, pp. 283–210.

Tolstikova, N. (2007) 'Early Soviet Advertising: "We Have to Extract all the Stinking Bourgeois Elements"', *Journalism History*, 33(1): 42–50.

Tsipursky, G. (2013) 'Living "America" in the Soviet Union: The Cultural Practices of "Westernized" Soviet Youth', in E.-M. Stolberg (ed.) *The Soviet Union and the United States: Rivals of the Twentieth Century*. New York: Peter Lang, pp. 139–164.

Vainshtein, O. (1996) 'Female Fashion, Soviet Style: Bodies of Ideology', in H. Goscilo and B. Holmgren (eds) *Russia Women Culture*. Bloomington: Indiana University Press, pp. 64–93.

Vasilyeva, Z. (2012) 'Do-it-Yourself Practices: Technical Knowledge in Late Soviet and Post-Soviet Russia', *Tsantsa. Review de la Societe Suisse d'Ethnologie*, 17. Retrieved from: http://www.tsantsa.ch/de/archiv/tsantsa/inhalt-17-2012/inhalt-17-2012/18-laufende-forschungen/165-do-it-yourself-practices.html

Verdery, K. (1996) *What Was Socialism, and What Comes Next?* Princeton: Princeton University Press.

Vihavainen, T. and Bogdanova, E. (eds) (2015) *Communism and Consumerism: The Soviet Alternative to the Affluent Society*. Leiden, Boston: Brill.

Volkov, V. (2000) 'The Concept of Kul'turnost': Notes on the Stalinist Civilizing Process', in S. Fitzpatrick (ed.) *Stalinism: New Directions*. New York: Routledge, pp. 210–230.

Widdis, E. (2009) 'Sew Yourself Soviet: The Pleasures of Textile in the Machine Age', in M. Balina and E. Dobrenko (eds) *Petrified Utopia: Happiness Soviet Style*. London: Anthem Press, pp. 115–132.

Yurchak, A. (2008) *Everything Was Forever Until It Was No More: The Last Soviet Generation*. Princeton. Oxford: Princeton University Press.

Zakharova, L. (2010) 'Dior in Moscow: A Taste for Luxury in Soviet Fashion Under Khrushchev', in D. Crowley and S. Reid (eds) *Pleasures in Socialism*. Evanston, IL: Northwestern University Press, pp. 95–120.

Zakharova, L. (2013) 'Soviet Fashion in the 1950s–1960s: Regimentation, Western Influences, and Consumption Strategies', in D. Kozlov and E. Gilburd (eds) *The Thaw: Soviet Society and Culture during the 1950s and 1960s*. Toronto: University of Toronto Press, pp. 402–435.

8

New Urbanism, Post-nationalism and Consumerist Modernity in India

Sanjay Srivastava

INTRODUCTION

This chapter seeks to explore the making of contemporary consumer cultures in India through exploring new forms of urbanism and the changing nature of relationships between the state, citizens and capital that characterize contemporary urban developments. It suggests that the reformulation of relationships between the state, citizens and private capital, in turn, fuels the rise of new consumer cultures through normalizing it as self-making. Scholars of India have argued that the relationship between the people and the state has been fundamental to providing insights into post-colonial Indian subjectivity (Fuller and Bénéï 2000; Gupta 1998). This chapter points to an uncoupling of this relationship, and suggests that new urban developments allow us to see how the 'the constant reference made to the state as a single, cohesive apparatus' (Gupta 2012: 33) is undone, thereby leading to an understanding of the relationship between structural change and individual desires.[1]

Within European foundational theories of the state, and subsequently in post-colonial contexts, the state has been imagined as the space and the process that has banished lawlessness and wilderness through – as Max Weber famously put it – gaining the 'monopoly of the legitimate use of physical force in the enforcement of its order' (quoted in Das and Poole 2004: 7). The general neglect of the state in social science disciplines beyond political science has, Fuller and Harriss (2000) suggest, 'contributed to the tendency in scholarship on the state to reproduce the Weberian argument that formal legal rationality eclipses substantive cultural factors, so that all modern states are substantially the same' (Fuller and Harriss 2000: 2). However, as Fuller and Harriss go on to suggest, the state is nowhere as bounded as is imagined and is open to historical influences that transform it as well as the society that exists beyond it. With regard to the present discussion, after India gained independence from colonial rule in 1947, there was significant support for instituting a centralized planning regime with overwhelming emphasis on industrial production and the need to curb consumerist activities in the interest of 'nation-building'.

I have outlined these perspectives on the state as not only do they have considerable currency in India-related scholarship but also provide the background to the discussion of this chapter. In the sections that follow, I introduce two specific concepts – 'post-nationalism' and 'moral consumption' – that, I suggest, illuminate crucial contexts of new forms of urbanism in India as well as changes in the form of the state, which, in turn, have led to a consumerist turn in Indian society. My focus is on the privately developed DLF City – built by the Delhi Land and Finance company – located in the district of Gurgaon that borders Delhi. Gurgaon is in the state of Haryana and is located immediately south of the national capital. Gurgaon, along with Delhi, is part of an area referred to as the National Capital Region (NCR; population approximately 22 million).[2] According to one report, the areas falling under the recently (2008) constituted Municipal Corporation of Gurgaon (that includes DLF City as well as several other privately developed residential enclaves) contained around 1.2 million persons. However, residents' groups (known locally as Residents' Welfare Associations or RWAs) dispute this estimate, claiming the true figure to be closer to 2 million. The RWAs suggested that the actual figure had been suppressed so that the Corporation did not have to make provision for the actual number of residents (Ahuja 2010: 4; for a detailed discussion of RWAs and urban politics, see Kamath and Vijayabaskar 2009).

POST-NATIONALISM

In this section, I provide a discussion of the first of the two concepts I wish to employ as connecting threads between the different ethnographic contexts, viz., post-nationalism. Through this term, I seek to focus upon the changing nature of the relationship between citizens and the state in order to present the relationship as a complex site of new attitudes towards consumption. The discussion implicitly argues that a fuller understanding of consumerist activity in the Indian context must concurrently engage with its sites and processes of production.

The term post-national does *not* mean to imply that the nation-state is insignificant as a context of analysis, or that we now live in a 'post-patriotic' age where the most significant units of analysis are certain 'postnational social formations' (Appadurai 1993: 411) – such as Non-Government Organizations (NGOs) – that putatively problematize nationalist and statist perspectives. Further, my deployment is also different from another recent usage. Here, it is posited as 'a distinct ethico-political horizon and a position of critique' and a concept 'that can be instantiated by suspending the idea of the nation as a prior theoretical-political horizon, and thinking through its impossibility, even while located uncomfortably within its bounds' (de Alwis et al. 2009: 35). Post-nationalism, in my usage, is the articulation of the nationalist emotion with the robust desires engendered through *new practices of consumerism and their associated cultures of privatization and individuation.* A fruitful way of approaching the topic – and providing concrete illustrative examples – is through a brief exploration of the contemporary politics of urban spaces in Delhi.

In 1999, soon after being elected to office, Delhi's erstwhile Chief Minister, Sheila Dikshit, 'called for an active participation of Residents Welfare Associations in governance'. The rationale for this was the 'failure' of 'civic agencies' to carry out their normal tasks. The Chief Minister's Secretary noted that the call to actively involve RWAs in urban governance heralded a new era, marking as it did 'the first step towards a responsive management of the city' (Ojha 1999). Positing a distinction between the state and the community, the Secretary further noted that the 'failure' of 'civic agencies' meant that 'it's really time for the community to be given direct control of managing the affairs of the city' (ibid.). Subsequently, the government decided to 'empower' RWAs to 'take certain decisions on their own'. It was proposed that RWAs be given control over the management of resources such as parks, community halls, parking places, sanitation facilities and local roads. A more direct relationship between the state and RWAs was also mooted through the idea of joint surveys of 'encroached' land – that is, land that had been 'illegally' occupied, usually by slum-dwellers – with the possibility that all illegal structures would 'then be demolished in a non-discriminatory manner'. Finally, it was proposed that RWAs be allowed to impose fines on government agencies which failed to carry out their assigned tasks.

In 2005, the Delhi state government announced that it would raise the electricity tariff by 10 per cent. The Delhi Residents Welfare Association Joint Front (RWAJF) was formed in the same year in order to protest against the measure. The Front consisted of 195 separate member RWAs from around the city. The increase in power rates for domestic consumers was the second one since the state-owned electricity body was 'unbundled' in June 2002 as part of power sector 'reforms'. As a result, three privately owned companies secured contracts for electricity distribution (Sethi 2005: 4).[3]

There was vigorous protest over the price rise and, in addition to the RWAJF, NGOs such as People's Action, and another group known as Campaign Against Power Tariff Hike (CAPTH) joined the campaign. Individual RWAs asked their members to refuse payment of the extra amount, while RWAJF lobbied the government, and organized city-wide protests. The protests gained wide coverage in both the print and electronic media, and, echoing Gandhian anti-colonial strategies, the organizers were reported to have deployed 'the ideas of "civil disobedience" and "people's power"' (Sethi 2005: 5). Indeed, the parallels sought to be drawn between the Gandhian anti-colonial moment and the present times were even more explicit with the Convener of the RWAJF referring to the protests as 'non-violent *Satyagraha*' (Sirari 2006: 5). 'Satyagrah', made up of two words 'satya' (truth) and 'agrah' (insistence), was used by Mahatma Gandhi to refer to non-violent resistance in his struggle against colonial rule. Eventually, the Delhi government backed down and the price rise was shelved. According to Sanjay Kaul, President of the People's Action NGO, the success of the protest heralded the making of a '*middle-class* revolution' (ibid., emphasis added). Kaul is one of many who had re-discovered and deployed anti-colonial vocabulary on behalf of the 'people' at a time when the colonial era itself has become part of the sphere of mass consumption. In the wake of the 2011 anti-corruption movement led by social worker Anna Hazare, yoga guru Swami Ramdev invoked 'Gandhi in calling for a "*satyagrah* against corruption"' (Copeman and Ikegame 2012: 318).

The circulation of the ideas of 'civil disobedience', 'Satyagrah' and 'revolution', and the consolidation of the notion of a 'people' contesting the state occur in a context that might be called post-national. By this, I mean a situation where the original moral frisson of these terms – provided by anti-colonial sentiment – no longer holds. Indeed, in an era of post-Nehruvian economic liberalization characterized by consumerist modernity (Fernandes 2006; Mazzarella 2003; Osella and Osella 2009), the moral universe of the anti-colonial struggle is no longer part of popular public discourse. In fact, what might be called 'colonial ambience' is the stuff of popular marketing strategies. So, the Spencer's department store in DLF City outlines its history through a series of billboard-sized sepia photographs placed at the entrance (see Srivastava 2012). The photographs – of fashionable European women shopping for fine goods at Spencer's stores – are from the colonial period and represent an efflorescence of colonial chic in the Indian public sphere. Other contiguous sites include the five-star Imperial Hotel in central Delhi liberally decorated with the 'Delhi Durbar' series of photographs (consisting of images from a 1911 ceremony held in Delhi to commemorate the coronation of King George V), and themed restaurants such as 'Days of the Raj' and 'Sola Topee', also in Delhi.

Within this new context, the earlier emphases on the ethics of 'saving' and delayed gratification for the 'national good' (Fernandes 2006; Roy 2007) – that were indispensable ideological accompaniments to 'civil disobedience' and 'satyagrah' and also sought to foreground the significance of production of industrial goods and capacities that characterized the Nehruvian era – do not find any resonance in contemporary popular discourses on the role of the state. As I have noted above, the term 'post-national' does *not* mean to imply that the nation-state is insignificant as a context of analysis. But rather, it refers to the new ways in which the nation-state relates to citizens, the contexts within which it relates to different fractions of citizens, and the manner in which it relates to capital.

In light of the above, and to preempt an aspect of my discussion, there appears to be in train a process of rethinking the state (Kamat 2004) such that it is increasingly imagined as a 'friend' of the *middle-classes*. The post-colonial state in India has most significantly been imagined as a benefactor of the poor, with 'development' as its most significant policy focus. Indeed, the 'development' focus of the state has been a defining feature of perceptions of post-coloniality itself (Chatterjee 1993; Gupta 1998). As Akhil Gupta (1998) points out, 'development became the chief "reason of state" in independent India' (Gupta 1998: 107). Investment in 'heavy industry' was, further, seen to be an important aspect of postcolonial development (Roy 2007) and this, in turn, led to a perception of the state as pro-industrialisation and anti-consumption. RWA activity such as that discussed above has become a site for the reformulation of these historically well entrenched notions of the state and its relationships with different class fractions. These neighborhood and city-level activities unfold in tandem with the broad national thrust towards 'de-regulating' the economy (Derné 2008; Guha 2009), including a shrinking public sector and easy loans for consumer purchases. It is this that I refer to as characteristic of post-nationalism, Which, in turn, forms the grounds for the consolidation of new cultures of consumerism.

One of the most significant ways in which the post-national moment resonates within the politics of urban space concerns the repositioning of the language of anti-colonial nationalism from the national sphere to the suburban one. This, in turn, also indexes the move from the idea of the 'national' family to the nuclear (gated) one, and, the translation of the notion of nationalist solidarity to (middle-)class solidarity. Recent scholarship (Baviskar and Ray 2011; Heiman, Freeman and Leichty 2012; Upadhya 2008) has fruitfully outlined the connection between the growth of 'new middle-classes' in the non-Western world and the consolidation of cultures of consumerism. The discussion of this chapter builds upon these works.

CREATING DLF CITY: STATE CONTROL TO CONSUMERIST UTOPIA

The 3500-acre DLF City has been developed by the Delhi Land and Finance (DLF) corporation, India's largest real estate company. It is located south of Delhi, immediately across the border, in the Gurgaon district of the state of Haryana. Beginning in the mid-1980s, the City was constructed by the DLF corporation and is regarded in both scholarly (Dupont 2005; King 2004) as well as popular writing (Jain 2001) as a significant site for the making of contemporary cultures of trans-national urbanism in India.

The Delhi Land Finance company was established in 1946 by Chaudhury Raghvendra Singh, a civil servant and landowner belonging to the agricultural caste of Jats (his caste affiliation was, as I point out below, important in the context of DLF's business success). Until the mid-1950s, DLF had a significant presence in the private real estate market in Delhi. The key aspect of its business strategy was its ability to both surmount as well as manipulate the extraordinary layers of land and 'planning' regulations instituted by the colonial state (see, for example, Hoshagrahar 2007; Legg 2007). The background to this lay in the control the state exercised over vast tracts of the so-called *Nazul* lands, viz., 'the Delhi Crown lands' (*Gazetteer of Rural Delhi* 1987) that the colonial government claimed as its own through representing itself as the legitimate successor to the displaced Mughal empire. Given the state's monopoly over land ownership, private interests in the real estate business such as DLF had two ways of acquiring property for their commercial activities: buying from large land-holders (*Zamindars*) whose properties escaped the Nazul regulations, or acquiring lands falling under the Nazul areas through negotiation with the Delhi Improvement Trust (DIT) that was established in 1937 (DIT Administrative Report 1941; see also Legg 2007). 'Slum clearance' was the Trust's main objective. This was formulated through 'adjustments' to 'European, liberal, welfare policies to the colonial context' (Legg 2007: 191).

By 1949, DLF had developed some of the earliest residential localities in Delhi such as Krishna Nagar in East Delhi (Srivastava 2015). The social imaginary that DLF sought to conjure for its localities was one animated by a curious mixture of American and British stylistic references. Figure 8.1 shows a DLF advertisement from 1955 for some of its key projects in Delhi. Here, in a city still pock-marked by the scars of the post-Partition trauma related to the creation of India and Pakistan

Figure 8.1 DLF Advertisement, 1955

Source: Delhi State Archives, Delhi

(1947) and regulated by the dicta of the DIT Building Manual, is a vision of joyful cartoonish intensity. A man-about-town preens near a fountain in North-West Delhi, an insouciant young couple goes boating in North Delhi, a Hollywood starlet-like figure prepares to descend into a swimming-pool in West Delhi, an 'Oxford' Don welcomes a school-boy in South Delhi, and a prosperous elderly couple surveys manicured domains in Central-South Delhi. It is a fantasy of post-partition Utopia wrenched from the ascetic reaches of the Five-Year Plan state, and distant from the messianic – 'slum-clearing' – gaze of the Delhi Improvement Trust. There is striking continuity of aspirational themes between mid-twentieth-century advertisements such as these, and the ones for twenty-first century gated residential communities that show images of 'modern' men and women jogging on private tracks, swimming in private pools, and enjoying privatized educational facilities. Real estate developments in India have been a prime site for the making of the citizen-consumer and the current phase of middle-class 'activism', in the shape of Resident's Welfare Associations (RWAs), also owes much to urban spatial transformations initiated by companies such as DLF, which gained ground in the wake of economic liberalization policies put in train by the Congress party through its New Industrial Policy in 1991 (see, for example, Dutta 2004; Sengupta 2008).

The *soi-disant* dreams of an alternative spatial modernity – marked by swimming pools and buxom beauties, lakes and carefree couples, 'flower bedecked' roads and their patrician crowds – came to end, however, in 1957. For, following a highly critical report of an inquiry into the functioning of the DIT published in 1951, the post-colonial state promulgated The Delhi (Control of Building Operations) Ordinance of 1955, leading to the establishment of the Delhi Development Provisional Authority. The Provisional Authority was, in turn, succeeded by the Delhi Development Authority (DDA) in 1957.[4] The new Authority not only inherited the monopolistic ownership of land enjoyed by its predecessor, but also extended it. This meant that even those limited avenues of land acquisition open to private developers were now closed off. Even 'while the DDA was in the process of preparing a Master Plan for the city, the government announced a freeze on all vacant undeveloped land within the urbanizable limits' (Dasappa Kacker 2005: 72). And, 'Establishing itself as the sole agency legally authorized to develop and dispose of land, the State left little, or no role for the private land developer' (Dasappa Kacker 2005: 72).

After the curtailment of its real estate business, the DLF corporation undertook a series of other unsuccessful commercial ventures. From the early 1980s, however, it re-focused attention to land and, under a new generation of family leadership (the founder's son-in-law, K.P. Singh), the company began to acquire land in Gurgaon in the bordering state of Haryana. Singh convinced village landlords to sell their tracts at low rates, invoking a shared caste identity and appealing to them as caste-brethren. After some initial uncertainty, DLF's townships, gated communities and office complexes proved an unprecedented success. The corporation managed to combine corporatist ambition with state patronage and communal bonds, and peasant cultural economy paid rich dividends, while by the mid-1980s, DLF had acquired some 3500 acres of land in Gurgaon – much of it on credit, with promises to pay later – and was ready to transform the rural hinterland into, as its publicity later proclaimed, the 'Millennium City'.

Fields of green have, within the space of some three decades, turned into spaces of global commerce and local habitation fueled by changes in the economy since the mid-1990s. One of the most significant of these – spurred by new urbanism and constituting a fundamental stimulant to consumerist activity – has been the rapid expansion of the retail banking sector and the relative ease of obtaining home loans. Aggressive market forays by both state-owned and new private entrants (including foreign banks) sought to target 'young and highly educated professionals who began their careers through the 1980s, [but] could not afford to own their own homes' (Khanna 2007: 107).

DLF City is famous for its shopping malls and gated residential communities. The different sections or 'phases' – there are currently five – of DLF City are located in 'sectors' designated by the state-run Haryana Urban Development Authority (HUDA). Phases I, II and III mainly consist of independent houses built on plots purchased from DLF, and semi-detached bungalows built and sold by it. In Phase III, the 'White Town Houses' are grouped around narrow streets with mock-Victorian street lighting, whereas in other areas the design of the independent houses has been borrowed from the wildest reaches of imaginations made joyous at the thought of owning a house of one's own. Near Silver Oaks Apartments (the first gated condominium built by DLF) in Phase I, there is a large house built in a neo-Gothic style which is quite near another with a façade of a traditional Indian mansion, the *Haveli*. Nearby, just beyond DLF Phase IV, there is an art gallery – whose exhibitions come from the private collection of an industrialist – that is housed in a startling (and recently finished) building that is designed like a massive rusting monolith, its exterior clad in metal and interiors fashioned to give an 'industrial' feel. Almost opposite this building is an under-construction hotel in red and pink sandstone that is a combination of Doric columns and 'Indo-Saracenic' balconies and cupolas. Next to the art gallery is a building that houses the offices of the white goods manufacturer, Whirlpool, with a glass frontage that is a cross between a space ship and a see-through washing machine.

Traffic in the locality flows along several main ('sector') roads and their tributaries, part of the infrastructure that has been constructed through a scheme of 'private-public partnership', an arrangement that finds increasing favor in the making of public spaces in the wake of a broader proliferation of discourses of choice that are significant aspects of consumer culture.[5] Beyond DLF City, there are other significant areas of private real estate developments in Gurgaon which also consist primarily of gated residential enclaves. These carry names such as Nirvana Country, Aspen Greens, Birch Court, the Close, Nile Apartments (based on an 'Egyptian' theme) and The Mansionz (bungalows in 'French style). In DLF City itself there are gated communities with names such as Hamilton Court, Birmingham Apartments and Windsor Court.

SPACES OF CONSUMERISM

Gated communities such as those in Gurgaon are being constructed across 300 Indian cities and such topographical transformations are accompanied by broader discursive shifts regarding family life, state, nation and citizenship (see Landman and Schönteich (2002) for South Africa, Pow (2007) for China, and Geniş (2007) for Turkey). That is to say, the spatial transformations that characterize new urbanism are also contexts of discourses about a new self. In this case, ideas of the entrepreneurial self (Gooptu 2013) – ensconced within spaces made by entrepreneurial urbanism – help to consolidate attitudes towards consumerism as self-making. In this context, gated communities in India have also created a specific relationship between gender, consumerism, domesticity and 'the morality of the market' (Rudnyckyj and

Osella 2017). I will here discuss some specific aspects that address my attempts to outline why post-nationalism and moral consumption (the latter outlined in the next section) are useful in thinking about new urbanism in India and, in turn, about relationships between consumerism, the home and the world.

Spaces and consumerism might be examined through contrasting the mammoth urban transformations currently underway in the contexts described above with another similar experiment during mid-twentieth century, viz., the construction of 'steel towns' by the post-colonial state. A comparison between contemporary – private – spatial transformations and mid-twentieth-century state-sponsored ones points to significant shifts in the imagination that conjures the 'ideal' citizen and 'his' (sic) relationship to the state. It also tells us something about the changing nature of thinking on consumerism and self-making.

From the late 1950s, the Indian state undertook the construction of a number of industrial townships in different – usually economically underdeveloped – areas of the country that were intended to be 'exemplary national spaces of the new India' (Roy 2007: 134). Located within the larger framework of centralized economic development (most significantly manifested through the Russian-inspired Five Year Plans for economic development), the townships were the state's attempts at *post-colonial* modernity where the modern citizen would work and live in an environment that 'proclaimed the birth of the sovereign nation' (Roy 2007: 138). Hence, 'apart from innovations in urban design' (Roy 2007: 143), the thinking behind steel towns also addressed itself to the possibilities of engineering *new* 'forms of subjectivities, practices, and social relations' (Roy 2007: 143) that would distinguish these settlements from the 'backwardness' of their immediate localities, as well as the 'stasis' afflicting national life: they were to be the spatialized models of a new national culture. The townships of Rourkela (Orissa state), Bhilai (Madhya Pradesh), Durgapur (West Bengal) and Bokaro (Bihar) thus came into being. In subsequent years, as Roy also points out, steel towns did not live up to the promise of sovereign modernity that was imposed upon them, but that is another story. Of greater relevance here are the unfolding narratives of citizenship, the state and capital that link them to the contemporary spatial transformations of a similar – or greater – magnitude. However, while both steel towns and contemporary gated communities might be located within the discursive promises of a 'new India', there are significant differences in the nature of the new in each instance. These differences also tells us something about the shifting relationship between national and global cultural and political economies, and the changing senses of being Indian. They also point to the distinction I wish to posit between the 'post-colonial' and the 'post-national'.

Most significant is the post-colonial nationalist project of producing modern citizens within steel towns related to external spaces – such as town planning, streetscape and design of shopping spaces – through which residents were expected to pass. Surrounded by well delineated areas for industrial activity, 'shops, schools, parks, and entertainment centres' (Roy 2007: 142), the citizen was to absorb the spatial geometry, transforming it into a personal discipline across a number of areas of social life such as democratic engagement, secular belief and industrial work practice. The belief that spaces mold human characteristics has a relatively well established history in the annals of Indian modernity (see, for example, Srivastava 1998).

Figure 8.2 Advertisement for a gated residential enclave

Source: Times of India, 20 September, 2011

Discourses of transformation surrounding contemporary gated communities, on the other hand, shift the focus to internal spaces. So, gated communities are presented as effecting transformations that significantly relate to *domestic* (kitchens, dining areas, bedrooms, etc.) aspects of urban living. Intimate spaces are more directly addressed, locating, as it were, the domestic sphere as the indispensable grounds for the making of a global Indian modernity (Figure 8.2 shows a representative advertisement for a gated enclave in Gurgaon). The internal life of the household is one that is populated by goods and commodities and it is these that are imagined to determine contemporary subjectivity. So, whereas steel towns established relationships between the individual and the nation-state through seeking to locate the former within the symbolic and concrete infrastructure of the latter, gated enclaves produce relationships between individuals and commodities. In this way, the public exhibition of intimate spaces indexes an era where contemporary dreams of modernity are inextricably linked to cultures of consumerism. Hence, gated enclaves posit a model of *post-national* citizenship that constitutes a particular gloss on the relationship between the state and its citizens against the backdrop of transnational consumerist modernity. The movement from post-colonial to post-national projects of citizenship also posits the journey from the 'citizen-worker' (Roy 2007) to the consumer-citizen (Fernandes 2006), just as it does from the spaces of national identity to those of suburban and domestic ones.

Further, unlike steel towns, it is no longer Indian and foreign *nation-states* which contribute to spatial transformations that are the putative sites of revolutions in personality and culture.[6] Rather, it is the relationship between the state, citizens and various forms of capital – national and global – that is seen to be fundamental to the task of re-making national life.

CREATING A PEOPLE: MORAL CONSUMPTION

The emergence of the domestic sphere as the site of a new national (or, rather, in terms of this discussion, post-national) identity relates, as implied above, to newer models of family life. This derives significant impetus from narratives of consumerism and the 'social life of things' (Appadurai 1988). What is the family 'type' that is being imagined through the focus upon domestic spaces as the new crucibles of national identity? Sociologist Patricia's Uberoi's (2008) discussion of Indian 'bridal magazines' provides a useful entry into this topic. The magazines Uberoi takes up for discussion were mostly launched in the mid-1990s and address an imagined high-income consumer, not unlike occupants of an up-market gated community. The following quote from an editorial in the inaugural (1997) issue of the *Bride and Home* magazine captures the social terrain that bridal magazines inhabit, and also allows us, via Uberoi's discussion, to think about the discourses of domesticity in a new context of consumer culture:

> Arranging a wedding in India [the editorial says] has traditionally been a family affair, and so it should remain; but it is to offer choice that *Bride and Home* steps in and gives young couples a freedom to partake in the most important decision of their lives: marriage. (Uberoi 2008: 239)

Bridal magazines such as *Bride and Home*, Uberoi says, seek to address young women through the consumerist trope of 'choice' in a social context 'where descent, succession and inheritance are in the male line; post-marital residence is "patrivirilocal" … and authority resides with the senior males of the family or lineage' (Uberoi 2008: 245). And yet, within all this is the idea that the 'modern' form of marriage and domesticity – a modernity defined through an association with goods and services (including those of 'marriage planners') – is a key moment in the making of modern Indian identity. How then to address the tension between older (and very real) structures of power and the apparent promise of consumerism-led liberation? Here, Uberoi suggests, the domestic sphere becomes a site of 'adjustment' to changes on a broader scale: it is a place 'of the consolidation of this new, cosmopolitan culture of Indian kinship and marriage, which is self-consciously both "modern" and "ethnic"' (2008: 245). Applying this insight to the present discussion, we might say that contemporary domestic-nationalism conjures a family type based around a 'couple' whose modernity is based around its 'freedom' to make choices about the goods it might consume rather than, say, 'spousal choice' (Uberoi 2008: 241). That is, the emerging politics of domesticity – one that gathers around the spaces of the gated community as well as ideas of intimacy and marriage conjured by *Bride and Home* – consists of reformulations and reinstitutions of older structures of power in a new era of post-national consumerist modernity.

This is the appropriate point in the discussion to introduce the second concept I wish to utilize in order to understand new urbanism in India, viz., moral consumption. I will also gesture at the relationship between moral consumption and post-nationalism within this context. The making of moral consumption (and a 'moral middle class') is, as I have argued elsewhere a context 'where the active participation in consumerism is accompanied by an anxiety about it and its relationship to 'Indianness' (Srivastava 2011: 381). Moral consumption, in my usage, refers to the context in which consumerist activity is accompanied by explicit and implicit discourses of the possibility of exercising control over it. This is very different from viewing it as a threat to established ways of life (van Wessel 2004). Hence, recent contexts of consumerism indicate that the long-standing Indian cultural discourses of the sacrificing and nurturing mother that actively proscribe 'indulgent' consumption (see, for example, Donner 2011) can be encompassed *within* acts of consumerism by women. I will provide two examples to illustrate my argument. The first of these concerns the Akshardham Temple (AT) complex in Delhi. The Temple complex was opened in 2005 and is in the nature of a religious theme park. The complex is owned by the Hindu Swaminarayan sect, founded in the late eighteenth century. The sect has a global following and has become, as Dwyer (2004) points out, 'the dominant form of trans national Gujarati Hinduism' (2004: 181). Many of the design principles within the complex are based on North American theme parks such as Disneyland and the Hollywood-inspired Universal Studios site (Brosius 2010; Srivastava 2011). Unlike many other public spaces in India, women make up a very substantial portion of visitors to the AT complex. Women visitors to the complex move seamlessly between playing consumers and devoutly religious persons precisely because the same space provides opportunities for both consumerism and religiosity (Srivastava 2011). That is to say, the (masculine) anxiety over female consumerism – signifying a form of autonomy – are 'assuaged' through a process of *moral consumption* whereby women take part in hyper-consumerism *and are also* able to withdraw to the realms of religiosity. And, though each realm is interpenetrative, each is imagined as separate. Hence:

> The making of a moral middle class, one that has control over the processes of consumption, and hence modernity, is, in fact, located in the processes of (surplus) consumption itself. For it is only through consumption that one can demonstrate *mastery* over it. So, one consumes a wide variety of products of contemporary capitalism — IMAX cinema, the Disneyfied boat ride, Akshardham baseball caps — in combination with 'spiritual' goods such as religion and nationalism. What differentiates the moral middle class from others is its *capacity* to take part in these *diverse* forms of consumption, whereas a more 'de-racinated' (or 'Westernized') middle class might only be able to consume the products of capitalism. (Srivastava 2011: 381, original emphases)

For my second example of moral consumption in the context of contemporary urbanism, I return to the gated communities of Gurgaon. Within gated communities – where the 'street' is not the street, and, for precisely that reason, is a site of intense middle-class activity – women can be both the guardian of tradition *and* take part in the sexualized presentations of the self, rather than having to choose between the two, as feminist scholarship describes the choices forced upon women (Phadke 2007). So, while on the occasion of the Hindu festival of *Karva-Chauth*, women dressed in elaborate traditional clothing pray for their husbands' welfare, within a few hours of having performed the ritual they can also be found pacing the condominium grounds on their exercise rounds in skin-hugging clothing. And, unlike the constraints placed on women at public celebrations of *Holi* (the festival of splashing colored water; see Cohen (1995) on the gendered nature of *Holi*), at the Bacardi-sponsored *Holi* celebrations at one of the gated communities, men *and* women dance together to Bollywood songs on an open-air stage. Consumerism here is the grounds for the making of a moral middle class within which women perceive that they are not 'determined' by modernity, but are able to take part in it and return home to 'tradition' when required. Post-national consumerism provides the grounds for the making of moral consumption: for one must take vigorous part in consumerism in order to display one's ability to withdraw from it. One must display modernity to remain traditional. The relationship between post-nationalism, moral consumption and the new urban spaces of gated communities also speaks to the long history of anxiety about the public woman through the question: how can the public woman belong both to the world as well as the home?

POST-NATIONALISM AND ITS CITIZENS

In the discussion above, I have gestured at the relationship between the cultural and political economies of contemporary capitalism and urbanism that, in the Indian case, have specific spatial dimensions. There are two other aspects to the post-national moment that can be illustrated through examples of the politics of urban spaces. The first concerns the accumulating discourse on 'village India'. The 'imperial construct' of 'village India' (Inden 1992) has found a new life through contemporary consumer culture. Through a number of contexts, the Indian village has become a significant site of the urban middle-class imagination. So, discourses of leisure, aesthetics, spirituality, health, and housing – among others – draw upon romanticized images of 'village India'; there are purpose-built 'ethnic villages' to experience 'authentic' rural food and entertainment (Nayar 2006), 'living museums' to watch 'tribals' producing handicrafts (Greenough 1995), clothing designed to reflect rural exuberance, and gated enclaves that promise rural idyll (Dupont 2005). The earlier colonial and anthropological preoccupation with 'village India' has, more recently, been transformed into newer enterprises of the middle-class imagination. A significant consequence of the middle-class idealization of the 'rural' manifests in the hostility towards 'debased' villagers: the urban working classes and slum-dwellers who do not fulfill their vocation as material for the urban imagination. The slum-dwellers are, in this sense, 'improper' and 'inauthentic' villagers, out of place, threats to civic life, and hence, not deserving of sympathy. Hence, the slum is not so much 'the reinvented "compassionate" village' (as Ashis Nandy (2001) suggests), as the site of an urban anger at the dismantling of its rural imaginary that is embedded within consumerist modernity.

Second, there is in train a process whereby capital actively produces its own citizens – consumer-citizens – such that the notion of separate and autonomous spheres of the state, citizens and capital becomes untenable. What we are left with, in fact, is a simulacrum (Baudrillard 1988) of separate spheres. Despite official regulations, many of the privately developed localities in Gurgaon have not been handed over to the Municipal Corporation of Gurgaon and many aspects of their functioning continue to be in the hands of the companies that built them. This is a context for the relationship between citizens (in the shape of RWAs), the state and private capital – DLF.

In 1986, some residents of DLF City combined to form the Qutub Enclave RWA (QERWA). One of its most consistent demands has been that the DLF corporation hand over its townships to the government. As per the Haryana Development and Regulation of Urban Areas Act 1975, a real estate company must transfer a privately developed locality to the government within five years of its establishment. QERWA mounted considerable agitation over this issue. It filed court cases, petitioned the government and even put up candidates – without success – in state assembly elections. In the early 2000s, another RWA – known as the DLF City RWA – appeared on the scene. This is an umbrella body which claims affiliation from many individual RWAs in DLF City. An office holder of the Qutub RWA (the older body) described the situation to me as follows:

> DLF did not want to hand over its townships to the government and the government is not interested either: for as long as DLF has control it can arbitrarily continue to use the land within its areas as it pleases by changing original planning agreements. So, it can build a commercial building on a plot that was earlier indicated on planning documents as a community center or a medical dispensary. The government does not wish to change anything because of the massive amounts of under the table money that it gets from private developers. If these localities were to be handed over to the Municipal Corporation of Gurgaon, it would be more difficult to make money. It's easier to make money from the private sector.

The DLF City RWA was, in fact, created by the DLF corporation to counter what it perceived to be an association of residents (the Qutub Enclave RWA) that was hostile to its interests. In particular, the company was concerned at QERWA's demand that the company hand over the township to be administered by the Haryana state government. The DLF-sponsored RWA has a comfortable air-conditioned office in the same building as many of DLF's corporate offices in Phase 1 of DLF City. A Qutub RWA office holder told me that in the early 2000s DLF initiated moves that led the Haryana government to appoint an administrator to oversee its affairs but that the RWA currently lies dormant. The DLF-sponsored association, on the other hand, appears to be flourishing. It is headed by a retired corporate executive and primarily acts (as the head told me) 'as a bridge between DLF and the residents of DLF City'. The DLF corporation has, in this way, reconfigured the relationship between the state and the market in order to produce a non-state version of the civic sphere which, simultaneously, grows out of the collaboration with the state; it has created its own citizens' group – and a private citizenry – through sponsoring the DLF City RWA. This too is an aspect of post-national urbanism where the idea and the body of the active citizen is produced not through political processes and debates over rights and responsibilities, but through a relationship between the state, the corporate sector and urban real estate markets; the consumer-citizen, once again.

CONCLUSION

The processes of new urbanism in India – as exemplified by the privately developed DLF City – provide a fruitful entry towards an understanding of changing relations between the state, citizens and private capital. The broader context of this, as I have suggested throughout, is the consolidation of new cultures of consumerism. I will conclude through some ethnographic vignettes that suggest that spaces within DLF

City are increasingly sought to be represented as goods that require careful 'brand management' in order to maintain their 'value'. That is to say, this concluding section seeks to reinforce the connections between the making of new urbanism and commodity cultures.

When the DLF corporation began to purchase land in Gurgaon, it did not have sufficient funds to pay for the purchases, its commercial activities since the late 1950s not having generated much revenue. The land purchases came to fruition through two processes, both of which can be grouped under the rubric of kinship capitalism. DLF head K.P. Singh's own caste background was, as I have suggested above, crucial to his negotiations with the agricultural castes who owned land in Gurgaon. In particular, he set about establishing kin-like connections with landowners through taking part in various aspects of rural life, including attendance at weddings and a number of other life-cycle rituals (Radhakrishnan Swami 2005).[7]

This is how a farmer – now real estate dealer – from the nearby village of Nathupur (now part of DLF Phase 3) recently described the situation to me:

> DLF bought the smaller plots of land on cash terms and larger plots on credit. They were very considerate: if our cattle was electrocuted, DLF paid compensation. Now the younger generation of DLF owners is not like that.

The company bought a great deal of land on credit, an aspect that was facilitated by the fact that K.P. Singh was able to invoke a sense of bucolic trust between caste-brethren into his dealings with the landowning farmers. There was another aspect: Singh also managed to convince the villagers to trust him with the money that was paid for the land they sold. It created a financial arrangement [known as 'chit-fund' in India] that offered a slightly higher rate than local banks, and villagers were encouraged to deposit their money with the company itself. Further, when confronted with fragmented land-holdings [a common scenario in rural India], the company consolidated title through direct negotiations with the various claimants. This paved the way for legal sale of the land to the company without any direct state involvement. The state was, however, part of the process in other ways. For, soon after the company began to acquire agricultural land, it lobbied various levels of government and succeeded in changing land-use regulations so that such land could be put towards urban use.

In recent times, the state has tried to exert in its 'stateness' through the formation of the Municipal Corporation of Gurgaon (MCG) in 2008 and this aspect forms the final rung of this story on the relationship between the state, citizens and private capital in a time of post-nationalism and consumerist modernity. It also gestures towards the symbolic and actual production of land itself as a commodity.

Of the 357 square kilometers that constitutes the Gurgaon district, about 156 square kilometers have been handed over to the Municipal Corporation of Gurgaon (MCG). However, in many of these areas, MCG is not able to levy any house taxes as, through a confusing and complicated arrangement, private developers have not handed over ownership of their localities to the state. Here, companies such as DLF levy a 'maintenance' charge upon residents of 'their' areas. A few years ago, the MCG tried to levy a house tax in the localities where residents pay the maintenance charges to private developers. However, as one resident put it, 'we refused to pay it as we are already paying maintenance charges to the builder, so why should we pay another tax to the MCG?' So, currently, MCG is not able to levy charges in areas that have the potential to generate the largest amount of residential and commercial taxes. An official of the DLF City RWA (which is sponsored by the DLF corporation) informed me that residents do not want the MCG to 'take over' the private townships as there was far greater trust in the administrative abilities of the private sector than the state.[8] And, he said, DLF has an interest in looking after its older localities since it is building new townships and wants to maintain 'brand equity', not wanting its existing product to be sullied through poor state administration. That is why, he added, DLF will continue to carefully tend to its already-constructed townships rather than risk shoddy state care; new urbanism institutionalizes ideas of consumerist modernity through naturalizing the idea of space itself as a commodity whose brand value requires nurture and protection.

To conclude, in the preceding discussion, I have pointed to a certain operation upon urban spaces of startling new mechanisms of hybrid administration, commerce and consumer cultures. What I have tried to outline are specific ways in which changing relationships between the categories we call 'the state', 'capital' and 'the people' are significant in the making of new contexts of urbanism in India. And, finally, I have suggested that operations upon urban spaces understood via post-nationalism and moral consumption tell us something about both the public life of the new city and the lives of its residents as consumer-citizens.

Notes

1 Sections of this chapter borrow from the discussion in Entangled Urbanism. Slum, Gated Community and Shopping Mall in Delhi and Gurgaon (2015).

2 In addition to Delhi, the National Capital Region consists of parts of the states of Haryana, Uttar Pradesh and Rajasthan. The National Capital Region was formed under the National Capital Region Board Act of 1985. The Board was established with the aim of encouraging and overseeing a variety of planning and economic development objectives.

3 For a more benign view of privatization, see Kanbur (2007).

4 The inquiry was constituted under the chairmanship of the leading industrialist G.D. Birla and the report came to be known as the Birla Report. It concluded, in blunt terms, that 'the story of the Trust is the story of failure' (Birla Report 1951: 7); that its record of slum-clearance had been 'meagre' (Birla Report 1951: 3), the Town Expansion Schemes had merely resulted in the 'freezing' rather than 'development' of considerable land areas (ibid.), it had commissioned neither a 'civic survey' nor a 'Master Plan', and, its strategy of selling land to the highest bidder had only exacerbated the 'housing problem' (ibid.: 4).

5 India currently ranks second after China in the number of PPP projects being undertaken (Planning Commission of India 2013).

6 The governments of the erstwhile USSR, Germany and the United Kingdom were significant contributors to steel-making technologies in these towns.

7 Singh notes in his 2011 autobiography that 'The acquisition of land was meticulously done over a period of time, taking every farmer or landowner into confidence. ... I myself came from a rural background so I knew their realities. We spent weeks and months on building a relationship with farmers whose land we wanted to buy' (Singh 2011: 99). 'It also helped', Singh points out, 'that my parents-in-law belonged to Haryana and were a leading family in the state' (ibid.: 101).

8 The Haryana state government had passed an order in February 2016 for the MCG to 'take-over' several of the privately developed localities. However, as of August 2017, the process is still ongoing, with no certainty about the schedule.

REFERENCES

Ahuja, Sanjeev K. (2010) '11.53 Lakh Population: The Numbers Lie, Say Residents', *Hindustan Times*, 10 August 2010, p. 4.

Annual Administration Report of the Delhi Province for 1937–38 (1939). Delhi: Manager of Publications.

Appadurai, Arjun (1988) *The Social Life of Things: Commodities in Cultural Perspective*. Cambridge: University of Cambridge Press.

Appadurai, Arjun (1993) 'Patriotism and its Futures', *Public Culture*, 5(3): 411–429.

Baviskar, Amita and Raka Ray (eds) (2011) *Elite and Everyman: The Cultural Politics of the Indian Middle Classes*. Delhi: Routledge.

Baudrillard, Jean (1988) 'Simulacra and Simulations', in M. Poster (ed.) *Selected Writings*. Stanford: Stanford University Press.

Birla Committee Report [DIT Enquiry Report] (1951) *Report of the Delhi Improvement Trust Enquiry Committee, Volume 1*. New Delhi: Manager, Government of India Press.

Brosius, Christiane (2010) India's Middle Class: New Forms of Urban Leisure, Prosperity and Consumption. Delhi: Routledge.

Chatterjee, Partha (1993) *The Nation and its Fragments: Colonial and Postcolonial Histories*. Princeton: Princeton University Press.

Cohen, Lawrence (1995) 'Holi in Banaras and the *Mahaland* of Modernity', *GLQ: A Journal of Lesbian and Gay Studies*, 2(4): 399–424.

Copeman, Jacob and Aya Ikegame (2012) 'Guru Logics', *HAA: Journal of Ethnographic Theory*, 2(1): 289–336.

Das, Veena and Deborah Poole (2004) 'State and Its Margins: Comparative Ethnographies', in V. Das and D. Poole (eds) *Anthropology in the Margins of the State*. New Delhi: Oxford University Press, pp. 3–33.

Dasappa Kacker, Suneetha (2005) 'The DDA and the Idea of Delhi', in Romi Khosla (ed.) *The Idea of Delhi*. Mumbai: Marg.

de Alwis, M., S. Deshpande, P. Jeganathan, M. John, N. Menon, A. Nigam and S.A. Zaidi (2009) 'The Postnational Condition', *Economic and Political Weekly*, XLIV(10): 35.

Derné, Steve (2008) *Globalization on the Ground: New Media and the Transformation of Culture, Class, and Gender in India*. Delhi: Sage.

DIT (Delhi Improvement Trust) (1941) New Delhi: Delhi Improvement Trust.

Donner, Henrike (2011) 'Gendered Work, Domestic Work and Perfect Families: New Regimes of Gender and Food in Bengali Middle-Class Lifestyles', in H. Donner (ed.) *Being Middle Class: A Way of Life*. Abingdon, UK: Routledge, pp. 47–72.

Dupont, Véronique (2005) 'The Idea of a New Chic Delhi Through Publicity Hype', in Romi Khosla (ed.) *The Idea of Delhi*. Mumbai: Marg, pp. 78–93.

Dutta, D. (2004) 'Effects of Globalisation on Employment and Poverty in Dualistic Economies: The Case of India', in C. Tisdell and R. Sen (eds), *Economic Globalisation: Social Conflicts, Labour and Environmental Issues*. Cheltenham, UK: Edward Elgar, pp. 167–185.

Dwyer, Rachel (2004) 'The Swaminarayan Movement', in K.A. Jacosen and P. Pratap Kumar (eds) *South Asians in the Diaspora: Histories and Traditions*. Leiden: Brill Publishers, pp. 180–199.

Fernandes, Leela (2006) *India's New Middle Class: Democratic Politics in an Era of Economic Reform*. Minneapolis: University of Minnesota Press.

Fuller, C.J. and Véronique Bénéï (2000) (eds) *The Everyday State and Society in Modern India*. New Delhi: Social Science Press.

Fuller, C.J. and John Harriss (2000) 'For an Anthropology of the Modern Indian State', in C.J. Fuller and Véronique Bénéï (2000) (eds) *The Everyday State and Society in Modern India*. New Delhi: Social Science Press, pp. 1–30.

Gazetteer of Rural Delhi (1987) Delhi: Delhi Administration.
Geniş, Şerife (2007) 'Producing Elite Localities: The Rise of Gated Communities in Istanbul', *Urban Studies*, 44(4): 771–798.
Gooptu, Nandini (2013) *Enterprise Culture in Neoliberal India: Studies in Youth, Class, Work and Media*. London and New York: Routledge.
Greenough, Paul (1995) 'Nation, Economy, and Tradition Displayed: The Indian Crafts Museum, New Delhi', in Carol Breckenridge (ed.) *Consuming Modernity: Public Culture in a South Asian World*. Minneapolis: University of Minnesota Press.
Guha, Atulan (2009) 'Labour Market Flexibility: An Empirical Inquiry into Neoliberal Propositions', *Economic and Political Weekly*, XLIV(19): 45–52.
Gupta, Akhil (1998) *Postcolonial Development: Agriculture in the Making of Modern India*. Durham: Duke University Press.
Gupta, Akhil (2012) *Red Tape: Bureaucracy, Structural Violence, and Poverty in India*. New Delhi: Orient Blackswan.
Heiman, Rachel, Carla Freeman and Mark Leichty (eds) (2012) *The Global Middle Classes. Theorizing through Ethnography*. Santa Fe: School of Advanced Research Press.
Hoshagrahar, Jyoti (2007) 'Negotiated Modernity: Symbolic Terrains of Housing in New Delhi', in Peter Scriver and Vikramaditya Prakash (eds) *Colonial Modernities. Building, Dwelling and Architecture in British India and Ceylon*. London and New York: Routledge, pp. 219–240.
Hume Report (Report on the Relief of Congestion in Delhi), Volume I (1936). Simla: Government of India Press.
Inden, Ronald (1992) *Imagining India*. Oxford: Blackwell Publishing.
Jain, Madhu (2001) 'Tyrannies at Work', *Seminar*, 'First City? A Symposium on Remembering Delhi' 515 (July).
Kamat, Sangeeta (2004) 'The Privatization of Public Interest: Theorizing NGO Discourse in a Neoliberal Era', *Review of International Political Economy*, 11(1): 155–176.
Kamath, Lalitha and M. Vijayabaskar (2009) 'Limits and Possibilities of Middle Class Associations as Urban Collective Actors', *Economic and Political Weekly*, XLIV(26–27): 368–376.
Kanbur, Ravi, *Development Disagreement and Water Privatization: Bridging the Divide*, 2007, http://www.arts.cornell.edu/poverty/kanbur/WaterPrivatization.pdf (accessed 18 January 2011).
Khanna, Tarun (2007) *Billions of Entrepreneurs: How China and India are Reshaping their Futures*. Boston, MA: Harvard Business Press.
King, Anthony (2004) *Spaces of Global Cultures: Architecture, Urbanism, Identity*. London: Routledge.
Landman, Karina and Martin Schönteich (2002) 'Urban Fortresses: Gated Communities as a Reaction to Crime', *African Security Review*, 1(4): 73–85.
Legg, Stephen (2007) *Spaces of Colonialism: Delhi's Urban Governmentalities*. Oxford: Blackwell.
Liechty, Mark, Carla Freeman and Rachel Heiman (eds) *The Global Middle Classes: Theorizing through Ethnography*. Santa Fe: School of Advanced Research Press.
Mazzarella, William (2003) *Shoveling Smoke: Advertising and Globalization in Contemporary India*. Durham: Duke University Press.
Nandy, Ashis (2001) *An Ambiguous Journey to the City: The Village and Other Odd Ruins of the Self in the Indian Imagination*. New Delhi: Oxford University Press.
Nayar, Pramod K. (2006) *Reading Culture: Theory, Praxis, Politics*. New Delhi: Sage.
Ojha, Abhilasha (1999) 'RWAs Will Soon Have Direct Control Over Sanitation and Community Halls', *Indian Express*, 12 January, www.indianexpress.com/res/ple/ie/daily/19991201 (accessed 11 December 2011).

Osella, Filippo and Caroline Osella (2009) 'Muslim Entrepreneurs in Public Life between India and the Gulf: Making Good and Doing Good', *Journal of the Royal Anthropological Institute*, 15(s 1): S202–S221.

Phadke, Shilpa (2007) 'Dangerous Liaisons: Women and Men, Risk and Reputation in Mumbai', *Economic and Political Weekly*, 42(17): 1510–1518.

Planning Commission of India (2013) Draft Approach Paper for the Twelfth Five Year Plan, 2012–2017. New Delhi: Sage.

Pow, Choon-Piew (2007) 'Securing the "Civilized" Enclaves: Gated Communities and the Moral Geographies of Exclusion in (Post-)Socialist Shanghai', *Urban Studies*, 44(8): 1539–1558.

Radhakrishnan Swami, Meenakshi (2005) 'Building on a Dream', *Business Standard*, March 22.

Roy, Srirupa (2007) *Beyond Belief: India and the Politics of Postcolonial Nationalism*. Durham and London: Duke University Press.

Rudnyckyj, Daromir and Filippo Osella (2017) *Religion and the Morality of the Market*. Cambridge: Cambridge University Press.

Sengupta, Mitu (2008) 'How the State Changed its Mind: Power, Politics and the Origins of India's Market Reforms', *Economic and Political Weekly*, 43(21): 35–42.

Sethi, Aman (2005) 'The Price of Reforms', *Frontline*, 22(19): 5–6.

Singh, K.P. (2011) *Whatever the Odds: The Incredible Story Behind DLF* (with Ramesh Menn and Raman Swamy). New Delhi: Harper Collins.

Sirari, Tanvi (2006) *Civil Uprisings in Contemporary India*. Centre for Civil Society Working Paper No. 161. Delhi: Centre for Civil Society.

Srivastava, Sanjay (1998) *Constructing Post-colonial India: National Character and the Doon School*. London: Routledge.

Srivastava, Sanjay (2011) 'Urban Spaces, Disney-divinity and Moral Middle Classes in Delhi', in Amita Baviskar and Raka Ray (eds) *Elite and Everyman: The Cultural Politics of the Indian Middle Classes*. Delhi: Routledge.

Srivastava, Sanjay (2012) 'National Identity, Kitchens and Bedrooms: Gated Communities and New Narratives of Space in India', in Mark Liechty, Carla Freeman and Rachel Heiman (eds) *The Global Middle Classes: Theorizing through Ethnography*. Santa Fe: School of Advanced Research Press, pp. 57–84.

Srivastava, Sanjay (2015) *Entangled Urbanism. Slum, Gated Community and Shopping Mall in Delhi and Gurgaon*. Delhi: Oxford University Press.

Taussig, Michael (1997) *The Magic of the State*. New York: Routledge.

Uberoi, Patricia (2008) 'Aspirational Weddings: The Bridal Magazine and the Canons of "Decent Marriage"', in C. Jaffrelot and P. van der Veer (eds) *Patterns of Middle Class Consumption in India and China*. New Delhi: Sage, pp. 230–262.

Upadhya, Carol (2008) 'Rewriting the Code. Software Professionals and the Reconstitution of Indian Middle Class Identity', in C. Jaffrelot and P. van der Veer (eds) *Patterns of Middle Class Consumption in India and China*. New Delhi: Sage, pp. 55–87.

van Wessel, Margit (2004) 'Talking about Consumption: How an Indian Middle-Class Dissociates from Middle-class Life', *Cultural Dynamics*, 16(1): 93–116.

Consumption and Consumer Rights in Contemporary China

Erika Kuever

INTRODUCTION

A visit to a Chinese market or department store reveals at a glance the scale and depth of the social and economic changes that have taken place in China over the last three decades. Little more than a generation ago food and personal necessities were distributed by one's work unit and the few shops that existed carried a limited inventory of goods which could only be obtained through one's employer or personal connections. Today, Beijing's many private markets and department stores are full of seemingly endless quantities of everything imaginable. Small greengrocers jockey for space with international chain stores, fast food franchises, and luxury shopping malls in crowded retail clusters, while millions of consumers shop online with their home computers or smartphones. Advertisements co-exist with big-character slogans and propaganda about civility and national pride, but outnumber them vastly. Stroll down a street, open a magazine, ride a bus, turn on a television, and advertisements are inescapable, persistently hailing Chinese citizens as individuals who can create and enrich their lives with their purchasing power. These advertisements hold out the promise of endless choice in meeting any desire, so long as these desires can be safely contained within the realm of the market.

Chinese consumers are the largest market for Chinese-produced goods, including the fakes and counterfeits, unsafe toys, and tainted foodstuffs that have also entered numerous overseas markets, but according to Communist Party policymakers they still aren't consuming enough. For the party-state, China's 'new consumers' are ideal citizens, vital for economic growth and social stability and unlikely sources of political dissent (Croll, 2006; McKinsey, 2013). Attending to the economic, ideological and social changes that have occurred in China over the last several decades also means understanding the transformation in the relationship of citizens to their government that underlie these tectonic shifts. When the state ceased to be the locus of the Chinese economy, ceding the job of feeding, clothing, and housing citizens to the market, it ushered in an exciting, but often dangerous new world of goods. Recent product scandals have added to the many anxieties Chinese citizens face daily: polluted air, unsafe schools, and insecure futures (Notar, 2006; see also Beck, 1992). While outright protest, though occasionally successful, is risky, most ordinary citizens lack the resources to stand up for their labor rights or achieve justice for wrongful incarcerations. In the area of consumer welfare, however, individual citizens have specific and elaborated legal rights and an enormous network of institutions ostensibly devoted to advocacy.[1] As of the 1990 passage of the Consumer Protection Law, Chinese consumers are also, argues Rofel, 'the subjects with the most elaborate rights' (2007, p. 145). If these laws and institutions give Chinese citizens the tools to seek redress in an uncertain and often dangerous market, why do so few use them?[2]

This chapter focuses on the state-sponsored dissemination of consumer rights propaganda and its public reception against the backdrop of the glorification and vilification of consumerism in Chinese popular culture while advancing the debate on political activism in a consumer culture. For adherents of the Frankfurt School (Adorno, 1991), consumption is politically anesthetizing, and consumerism neutralizes desires for political freedom and social engagement by transforming them into individual desires. The phenomenon of consumer activism poses a direct challenge to these claims. As Bevir and Trentmann (2007) have argued, consumption can also be a tool for seeking representation and justice, shaping civil society, and enhancing civic life. This chapter argues that laws and institutions provide a safe language for citizens to express grievances, but also shape the articulation of culpability, in this case successfully producing neoliberal citizens who see protecting their consumer rights as their own responsibility. I address the role of the Chinese party-state in promoting domestic consumption through the construction of a consumer welfare apparatus which simultaneously provides legal tools to aggrieved consumers and produces neoliberal subjects tasked with safely provisioning themselves in a complex and sometimes dangerous marketplace. The chapter provides an overview of consumer rights in China that both updates earlier work (Davis, 2006; Hooper, 2005, 2000; Palmer, 2006; Read, 2008; Rofel, 2007) and provides an ethnographic perspective gleaned from long-term fieldwork. I argue that the consumer welfare apparatus, far from empowering citizens to take market and state actors to task, operates to produce subjects who no longer expect the state, or the 'Maoist social contract' to protect them (see Lee, 2007).

China is unique among modern nation-states: an authoritarian regime with a flourishing consumer culture. The country is also unique for having a consumer welfare apparatus spearheaded by the state itself – elsewhere in Asia the impetus for consumer protection has come primarily from independent citizens' groups (Garon and Mclachlan, 2006). As a state that has used rhetoric on consumer welfare as a means of promoting increased domestic spending, China can be productively compared to the United States, where President Kennedy called in 1962 for a Consumers' Bill of Rights, marking the era of what Cohen (2004) calls the 'purchaser as citizen'. Finally, the case of China draws our attention to an aspect of consumption often overlooked in the literature: the regulatory and legal scaffolding designed by the state to make the market safer. Obtaining safe, reliable, quality goods in complex economies requires functional legal and regulatory systems, making ordinary consumption political insofar as it occurs in a state-structured context against which expectations form. A good that has traveled through legitimate channels is implicitly stamped with state approval. The issue of 'killer commodities' (Singer and Baer, 2009) illustrates this. When goods obtained through the market cause harm, loss, or even death, it is not only the manufacturer or seller that is implicated, but also the regulatory channels through which the product traveled.

CONTEXT AND METHODOLOGY

Two historical facts frame this argument. The first is the dramatic transformation in the relationship between citizens and the state that began in the 1980s in the wake of Deng Xiaoping's 'reform and opening' policy. Goods are now obtained not through membership in the state but on the basis of citizens' consumer power. China's 'consumer revolution' (Croll, 2006) has dramatically altered ideas about gender, ethnicity, age, and class, and transformed vertical patron-client relationships between agents of the state and ordinary citizens into horizontal relationships between transactors (Davis, 2000). The ascendance of the market as distributive regime has restructured Chinese society. Where rights and access to livelihood were once guaranteed by the state, opportunities are now shaped by individuals' market power. The second is that despite being the origin and site of many product scandals, China has a large and highly developed consumer welfare system, including a 1993 Consumer Protection Law revised in 2013 (Jourdan, 2013), the nationwide China Consumers' Association, founded in 1984, and consumer media that covers television, newspapers, and periodicals. Palmer (2006) has estimated that more than 3,000,000 people nationwide are employed in the consumer welfare apparatus.

Studies that have engaged with the topic of consumer rights (Gao, 1991; Hooper, 2000; King and Gao, 1991; Palmer, 2006), have typically assumed these rights to be inherently empowering and to define a specific relationship between citizens and the state. Scholars with a narrower focus on the deployment of consumer rights in specific situations have come to more measured conclusions, finding that rights present opportunities for citizen action and empowerment, but at local levels state agents may restrict consumer activism (Davis, 2006; Read, 2003). Others have described the emergence of a new 'citizen-consumer' (Davis, 2006; Keane, 2007) in terms of a 'desiring subject' (Farquhar, 2002; Rofel, 2007) who relates to her world through the market rather than the state (Ong, 2006).

Given the prevalence of product scandals, 'authenticity anxiety' (Notar, 2006) and serious concerns about food safety among citizens (Gerth, 2010; Veeck et al., 2010; Yan, 2012), it is first puzzling to see how poorly regarded and rarely used these institutions are, but an investigation of the discourse surrounding consumer welfare offers an explanation. I argue here that the state-sponsored consumer welfare system acts as a domestic 'development' initiative that expands state power and extends the reach of the state into the lives of its citizens (Ferguson, 1990). Consumer institutions serve the interests of the party-state by defining consumers as legal subjects and assigning them responsibility for their own safety in the market. Even when these institutions fail to achieve their stated goals, as they often do, they succeed in legitimating and expanding state power (see Fuller and Bénéï, 2012). Like the interventions of development institutions Ferguson describes in Lesotho, Chinese party-state interventions in consumer welfare may 'fail' on their own terms, but produce other, desired, effects that include 'the expansion and entrenchment of bureaucratic state power, side by side with the projection of a representation of economic and social life which denies "politics" and, to the extent that it is successful, suspends its effects' (1990, p. xv). Chinese consumers may deride the usability or efficiency of state institutions, but their functionality is partly beside the point.

The data presented here come from 16 consecutive months of ethnographic research in urban China from 2010 to 2011. The research explored the connection of consumer rights to Chinese conceptions of citizenship and was the first empirical investigation into the lived experience of urban Chinese consumers as subjects of a specific legal and regulatory market system. It included more than 40 semi-structured interviews with lawyers, activists, and employees of consumer institutions, visits to markets and consumer association offices, surveys of consumer media, six focus groups organized by age cohort and representing citizens from various economic, educational, and regional backgrounds, hundreds of informal conversations with taxi drivers, fellow train passengers, shop owners, and many more, and 11 months of participant observation in a project organized around the concept of 'consumer confidence' (*xiaofei fangxin*). Although it implies that consumers ought to feel calm, safe, and protected, the idea of *fangxin* actually tasks consumers with maintaining constant vigilance in market transactions. According to media, official propaganda, and institutional actors, consumer confidence comes from taking proper precautions, making educated decisions, and being aware of any potential problems. As I was told myself when attempting to make a complaint at an office of the Consumers' Association, the law cannot protect you if you do not consume appropriately.[3] This discourse works to produce modern subjects tasked with the national project of increased consumption but discouraged from making claims on the state. The good citizen is a good consumer, a subject motivated by desire: for objects, for advancement, for self-expression; but he is not a political actor.

CONSUMPTION AND CONSUMER CULTURE IN CHINA

From a nation characterized by shared poverty China has rapidly become a country of enormous economic inequality and political privilege. Government spending on massive infrastructural projects such as the Three Gorges Dam and transcontinental high-speed railways have been a huge boost to the economy, but have also helped concentrate wealth in the upper echelons (Pew, 2012). In the most recent estimate China's Gini index was 46.9, making it the 28th most unequal economy out of 145 surveyed (CIA, 2017). China's economic system is officially called 'socialism with Chinese characteristics', while scholars sometimes refer to the present era as 'postsocialism'. Yan provides an insightful definition, describing postsocialism as 'an unstable process in which the emerging hegemony of capitalism in China must deal with living socialist legacies, claims, and structures of feeling that surround the current relations of production and sociality' (2008, p. 13). An ideological transition from socialist values to consumerist ideals has been achieved through government propaganda, globalizing processes, and advertising, which has celebrated consumer values 'in the guise of promoting socialist construction' reconfiguring and naturalizing China's transformation to a consumer society (Zhao and Belk, 2008, p. 240). Yet there remain tensions between socialist legacies of thrift and the national drive to increase domestic consumption (Croll, 2006). Saving is eminently rational in an environment without a comprehensive social safety net, but this practice is decried as backwards and even unpatriotic by state and business leaders. The owner of a chain of grocery stores stated this transparently at a banquet hosted by the consumer confidence project, announcing to the table 'only when the Chinese people change their habits of holding on to money and saving to care for the elderly can profits from consumption be realized in full', an assertion to which the assembled guests responded with a toast.

In the socialist era consumption was limited by the narrow variety and small quantity of consumer goods as well as by its negative political connotations. Assertions of status and self-expression were present to a limited degree, but tolerated only if they advertised one's 'redness' (Schrift, 2001). Socialism leveled inequalities in wealth and property but maintained divisions between cities and the countryside and created new political hierarchies. Party officials and those connected to them enjoyed higher standards of living and access to goods like bicycles and watches difficult for ordinary citizens to obtain (Chan et al., 2009). With 'reform and opening', the economic reforms and increased international communication and exchange initiated by Deng Xiaoping, came new products, new ways of transacting, and eventually new identities. By the second decade of the reform era, the 'individualized economic actor', whether entrepreneur or consumer, had become the dominant cultural representation in electronic and print media (Keane, 2001). In one study of the party organ *People's Daily*, between the years 1995 and 2002 consumers were represented more frequently than either workers or university students (Davis, 2006).

Although it has come to define life in societies around the world, consumer culture is still often seen as the culture of the modern West, inseparable from the 'values, practices and institutions which define western modernity, such as choice, individualism, and market relations' (Slater, 1997, p. 8). In a society with an established consumer culture, 'core social practices and cultural values, ideas, aspirations, and identities are defined and oriented in relation to consumption rather than to other social dimensions such as work or citizenship, religious cosmology or military role' (Slater, 1997, p. 24). Although the word 'consumer' (*xiaofeizhe*), the director of one Consumers' Association office reminded me on our first meeting, is a new term in Chinese, consumption has a long history in China. In the vibrant markets of the Imperial era, commoditization and branding flourished: the practice of using 'merchant marks' on goods appeared as early as the Song Dynasty (960–1269) and was widespread by the seventeenth century (Hamilton and Lai, 1989). Hamilton and Lai have called this period 'consumerism without capitalism'. For contemporary Chinese, consumer goods constitute a vital part of personal and social identity, marking them off as belonging to particular income levels and interest groups and providing tools to both experience and express their status and their place in the world (Croll, 2006; Gerth, 2010; Rofel, 2007). As one young woman told me, 'We [young Chinese] don't go to church, we go shopping'. Evidence of the centrality of consumption to contemporary life in China can be found in the dominance of advertisements in public and private places as well as in their representation in popular culture and entertainment.

While advertising celebrates consumption unreservedly, many citizens are ambivalent about the progress of consumer culture. I spoke with older Chinese concerned that powerful consumer desires are corroding the bonds of family central to Chinese sociability, younger Chinese who felt there was an ideological vacuum in China that could not be filled by wealth and consumer goods, and parents of young children who worried about the safety of food and the health of the environment. Chinese citizens are proud of their nation's economic growth and technological progress, but few are wholly uncritical of the new consumerism. While individuals have various attitudes, their shared references often come from popular entertainment and from stories and characters that act as lightning rods for criticism and discussion. These also provide the signposts by which particular discursive positions mark their territory. In 2010, for instance, a contestant on a Chinese dating show announced she would rather 'cry in the back of a BMW than smile on the back of a motorbike', leading to widespread denouncements of female 'gold-diggers'.

CONSUMPTION IN POPULAR CULTURE

Popular entertainment depicts the consumerist world in which urban Chinese live, albeit fantastic versions of most citizens' realities. Some characters ache with desire for products they will never be able to afford, others orient their values and goals towards accumulating components of 'the good life'. Attitudes towards consumerism vary from celebratory, to cautious, to profoundly cynical. All have a moral component. The 2010 romantic comedy *Go Lala Go!* follows the titular character from an entry-level position through several promotions, bracketing her life with split screens showing her new income and rank, and humorously depicting the pressures of professional and personal life that culminate in costly shopping sprees. In *Go Lala Go!*, originally a popular book of the same name, consumer desires are celebrated for feeding the hunger of a young woman to get ahead and as harmless therapy for the stress of her career, though unequal in the end to her more profound desires for love and security. In the television series *Narrow Dwellings*, a controversial hit in Spring 2010, one of the female protagonists is lured away from her boyfriend and their carefree but low-income life of window shopping and the occasional ice cream splurge by a wealthy and corrupt bureaucrat who buys her the objects she desires but could never afford, while at the same time her older sister scrimps and saves in order to buy a home for her family in Shanghai. In *Narrow Dwellings* some desires are dangerous and some divine: the desire of one protagonist for home ownership is valorized while the slippery slope of wanting more than one can afford is portrayed as a path to immorality and misery. In this context consumerist desires are shown as personally and socially corrosive, threatening familial harmony and closely linked with immorality and corruption, in opposition to the playful and hedonistic role that shopping plays in *Go Lala Go*.

The protagonist of the best-selling book *Leave Me Alone: A Novel of Chengdu*, in contrast, describes the superficiality and shallowness of contemporary life, invoking Christmas in particular as holding out absurd and empty promises of happiness and fulfillment. He describes the scene around the holiday, not officially observed in China but still an occasion for leisure, shopping, and entertainment in urban areas: 'The Chengdu streets throbbed with excitement. Unscrupulous businessmen flew God's banner while thrusting evil money into their pockets. The shops were endlessly discounting, the restaurants endlessly delivering ... Completely insane. There were people everywhere ... Never mind what their family resources were, they were spending like crazy' (Murong, 2009, p. 299). *Leave Me Alone* turns a profoundly cynical eye on the whole enterprise, describing the absurdity, chaos, and anti-social behavior found in temples of consumption everywhere and exposing the emptiness of consumerism as a palliative for the ills of contemporary life. Similar criticisms have been directed at films like *Go Lala Go*, and most recently towards the movie series *Tiny Times*, also based on a wildly popular book series, which features unabashedly materialistic young characters spouting lines like 'Economy class kills me!' (Melvin, 2013).

THE CONSUMER WELFARE SYSTEM

The Chinese party-state has made no secret of its desire to see a sustained increase in domestic consumption, making it a pillar of every five-year plan since 2001 (CIA, 2017; Croll, 2006). Discouraging personal saving and increasing spending is seen as a way to stabilize economic growth and protect the economy from outside shocks such as the 2008 financial crisis (McKinsey and Company, 2013). There are multiple elements to this strategy, among them the introduction of health insurance and social security, the creation of so-called 'golden weeks' to promote tourism and shopping, and directed economic stimulus packages. Given the notorious secrecy and inaccessibility of the Chinese party-state and its agents, it is impossible to prove that a desire to increase consumption was the motivation for the development and expansion of the consumer welfare apparatus, but it is clear from the evidence that it was not, as is officially claimed, to help consumers uphold their rights. Furthermore, in recent years the consumer welfare system has been weaponized: used to charge foreign companies such as Apple, Starbucks, and Samsung with discriminating against Chinese consumers or even violating their rights (Jourdan, 2013), thus clearing the way for their domestic competitors. In the wake of the 2008 melamine-tainted milk and infant formula scandal, which led to six infant deaths and 300,000 victims in total (Ingelfinger, 2008), and followed a similar infant formula scandal in 2005, Chinese consumers have become even more concerned about the provenance and quality of goods.

Despite the appearance of government support for the exercise of consumer rights, the current framework poses significant practical obstacles that deter aggrieved consumers from seeking resolutions through institutional channels. Activism has also been 'severely limited' by weak courts, the difficulty of litigation, and local power holders determined to protect their interests (Davis, 2006). The consumer welfare apparatus is designed not to serve consumers but to serve the party-state's need for continued economic growth and social stability as well as to collect information and perform services for the state (Kuever, 2013). Only party-state propagandists publicly claim the consumer welfare system was established with the primary goal of protecting and empowering consumers. Scholars argue the system was intended to strengthen the state: to make it more modern and 'developed' and to have the practical effects of increasing consumption, alleviating consumer anxiety, raising the quality of domestic goods, and enhancing social stability by providing an outlet for grievances (Davis, 2006; Hooper, 2000, 2005; Palmer, 2006). Policymakers influenced by Euro-American models of national development believe that stable economic growth requires predictability and transparency that can only come from legalization and institutional development. Establishing and enforcing laws, however, threatens powerful private and party-state interests. Tensions between authoritarianism and legalization produce friction: leaders want laws to apply broadly but they also want to be able to make exceptions. Local party-state actors, furthermore, have little incentive to enforce laws that stand in the way of capital accumulation.

While the establishment of these rights has been part of the party-state's strategy for increasing consumer spending, Communist Party leaders remain wary of their potential fallout: the empowerment of consumer-citizens (Davis, 2006). In her study of homeowners' exercise of their consumer rights, Davis finds the Chinese party-state 'deeply implicated in – if not comfortable with – consumer politics', using the language of rights to encourage self-governance but treating claimants who challenge official interests with hostility (2006, p. 295). The party-state has backed itself into a corner, and has 'so thoroughly valorized free markets and consumers as essential agents in the national project of modernization that it can neither easily refute the validity of consumer autonomy nor maintain a firewall between the rights of Chinese consumers and the civic rights of citizens' (Davis, 2006, p. 299). Rights and institutions are used tactically, and often in creative and surprising ways, by consumer activists, but rarely by ordinary consumers (Brandstädter, 2008; Kuever, 2013). Highly placed actors allow so-called 'fake-fighters' (*dajia*) to publicize fake or faulty products – after all this allows local interests to avoid being implicated in crackdowns – but they act swiftly to suppress any activism calling for political action. At the same time, they forbid the formation of independent consumer groups. Taking insight from Ferguson (1990), we can see that even failed enterprises are 'successful' insofar as they develop consumer subjectivities and specify party-state institutions as the only possible channels for resolution. Instead of empowering consumers to make claims that require action by the party-state, the institutional and discursive framework of the consumer welfare apparatus is used to shift responsibility for safe provisioning to the consumer. This is largely achieved through the dissemination of messages which depoliticize consumer welfare and produce neoliberal subjectivities through consumer media and state propaganda.

CONSUMER RIGHTS PROPAGANDA AND ITS DISSEMINATION

While usage of the institutions of the consumer welfare apparatus is quite low, awareness is extremely high. Consumer protection institutions, like the party-state more broadly, have successfully promoted the widespread recognition of certain key terms – particularly numbers – that relate to consumer protection, but they have not created a population invested in the ideas they symbolize. Every one of the hundreds of Chinese citizens I spoke to about consumer rights recognized the terms 315 and 12315 if I mentioned them and most offered them independently, almost unconsciously, when they heard about my research. The number 12315 refers to the national consumer hotline, established in 1999. It builds on recognition of 315, which stands for March 15th, International Consumer Rights Day.[4] A few other terms recurred in focus groups and casual conversation: the Consumer Protection Law and the year it came into effect, the 'three guarantees' (return, exchange, and repair), and the Consumers' Association, but awareness of these institutions rarely indicated a deeper familiarity or understanding of them, only the knowledge that they were associated with the area of consumer rights. The high level of recognition for 315 as shorthand for consumer rights is driven by the enormous attention given to consumer issues every year during the week of March 15. Local newspapers feature stories on consumer issues and consumer law, there are special features on the nightly news, and online news aggregators highlight relevant stories. The Consumers' Association even sponsors events such as the public destruction of large quantities of counterfeit goods. While few pay active attention to these stories and events, the pervasiveness of 315-related media, billboards, and advertisements is nearly impossible to ignore. Many focus group participants said their own consumer awareness was heightened during this period and noted that it was the only time of year when merchants made a show of their own commitment, offering special deals or running advertisements that proclaimed their respect for consumer rights.

POPULAR MEDIA AND PUBLIC PROPAGANDA ON CONSUMER WELFARE

The English term propaganda (*xuanchuan*) is neutral in Chinese, merely connoting a means by which official information is spread. Thus participants in my focus groups acknowledged the role of consumer welfare propaganda in educating them about consumer rights, and many, especially older citizens, were grateful for the information it provided, even if they didn't always trust its source. A few examples, from television shows to public billboards, will illustrate where and how consumers encounter these messages as well as their typical content; specialized consumer media will be addressed in the section following.

A popular daytime television format in China is a talk show in which a host and a few invited guests discuss a particular topic, typically in a light and playful manner. One episode of the long-running show *On Your Side* (*shenbian*) was devoted to consumer disputes, and featured several re-enactments of real-life cases: a woman who was not permitted to return a purse she had decided she didn't like; a man who accidentally broke a café coffee mug and was told he would have to pay 45 dollars to replace it; and a dispute with interior designers.[5] The host and her guests discussed each case in turn, commenting on who was at fault, how common such cases were, how the individuals involved sought recourse, and whether they obtained it. At the end of the show they spoke more broadly about tactics that aggrieved consumers could employ and how to avoid such problems in the first place. Although one of the guests was affiliated with the Consumers' Association, even he chimed in to agree with the host that the process of making an official complaint was time-consuming and difficult and not usually worth the effort, insisting that the best option was to negotiate independently with merchants, precisely how the disputes featured were resolved on the show.

Anecdotal evidence suggests the annual televised 315 evening gala sponsored by the Consumers' Association attracts the greatest audience of any of these events. In 2009, the gala covered stories on topics ranging from faulty flat screen televisions to the use of dangerous chemicals in the production of the single-use chopsticks provided by many restaurants. The chopstick story concluded with a call for consumers to be aware of the potential dangers of ingesting the chemicals used by some manufacturers and to either demand a restaurant provide them with washable chopsticks or bring their own. In fact the story was raised the following week by the head of the consumer welfare project that hosted my research. He mentioned the segment at lunch, noting that we shouldn't use such chopsticks anymore, but when he asked for plastic chopsticks the manager insisted they had none. This anecdote illustrates the limited utility of the stories profiled in the gala, which educated consumers on some of the very real risks they faced in the marketplace, but also burdened them with the responsibility for protecting themselves. There was no discursive space for talking about regulations that would ban these chopsticks or improved inspections that would ensure their safe production; instead consumers were tasked with the responsibility of going out of their way to make safe choices. The gala functioned to depoliticize violations of consumers' rights by disembedding them from structures of social and political inequality and re-framing them as matters of practical action.

In the weeks following the 315 gala, clips from the show were re-played frequently on the televisions installed on every public bus. The televisions also broadcast segments which could only be described as market education, covering topics such as where to go for wedding photographs or how to furnish your home. These segments occasionally offered suggestions on how to make good buys and avoid scams or poor quality goods, but they never broached the topic of what to do after the fact to deal with a dispute, nor did they mention consumer rights directly. The tone of the broadcasts was benevolent, the implication being that these state-produced segments were educating passengers on how to be modern citizens and consumers. Posters about consumer welfare were sometimes mounted in bus shelters or subway tunnels, but more frequent were signs in public places from the local Consumers' Association advertising the 12315 hotline and/or advising consumers to avoid scams. One large sign adjacent to the entrance to Qinhuangdao, where the Great Wall meets the Pacific Ocean, seemed particularly out of place. Although there were a few vendors hawking souvenirs or selling drinks and snacks it was hardly a shopping area. The impact, if any, was to assert the presence of the local authorities in protecting consumers, but what did they need protecting from? There were no fake drugs or tainted milk powder for sale in the area, only cheap trinkets and processed foods. Whether or not anyone paid attention to the poster was less important than their self-recognition as the subjects for whom the messages were intended.

Posters in retail spaces such as pedestrian markets are not uncommon, but are usually inconspicuous, almost always taking the form of all-text re-prints of the consumer law, and easily lost in the dense sea of more eye-catching advertisements, announcements, and posted rules that surround them. Some malls also post signs notifying consumers of their rights but these rarely provide more than something the vast majority of urban consumers are already familiar with, the number for the consumer hotline. Large well-established markets such as the electronics mega-market Hailong in the Haidian district of Beijing have their own in-house branches of the Consumers' Association, but they are typically difficult to find and ill-equipped to help. When I tried to locate complaint offices or find persons responsible for handling disputes in these spaces, from grocery stores to malls, I found that channels for seeking redress were few. Exceptions were to be found in certain private spaces like retail stores, especially foreign-owned chains, which frequently have specialized departments and personnel to deal with complaints and process exchanges and returns.

CONSUMER MEDIA

Specialized consumer media is familiar to many but reaches a limited audience. The media discussed here is all state-sponsored, either through China Central Television (CCTV) or by the Consumers' Association. Consumer issues are also covered by some online and print newspapers and in blogs, with articles falling into one of two categories: reports of product recalls or coverage of the small group of consumer activists known as fake-fighters. It is impossible to estimate the audience for these articles, but focus group participants showed little interest in such stories and a journalist who took part in one group claimed there was little audience for consumer-oriented media, excepting large scandals, which the media was always restricted from covering fully. One of CCTV's most popular programs, *Topics in Focus* (*jiaodian fangtan*), was frequently offered by focus group participants as an example of the power of media and 'public supervision' to tackle injustice and even affect policy. According to the online encyclopedia published by the search engine Baidu the show receives an average of 2,300 tips or complaints from citizens every day, on issues as varied as toll roads, pollution, health care, and consumer grievances, and chooses a handful to investigate and discuss (Baike, n.d.). The show's popularity with citizens is recognized as a source of legitimacy by party leaders, many of whom have visited the set (Miao, 2011). This can be contrasted with the only television show focused solely on consumer issues, *Consumer Advocate* (*xiaofei zhuzhang*), a show well known among individuals professionally involved with consumer welfare, but not familiar to many of my other interlocutors. Airing every weeknight, *Consumer Advocate* covers a range of topics related to consumption. One episode focused entirely on a ring of criminals who stole from a large clothing market in a Southern Chinese city and the police sting that shut it down. The only 'advocacy' in this particular episode was the host's closing warning for consumers to keep their money and belongings safe when shopping or in public places, a call for self-protection similar to those messages directed at consumers from other official sources.

A more typical episode investigated the connection between consuming crayfish and developing a disease that causes the breakdown of muscle tissue. The topic was introduced with footage of a hospital where 19 patients were being treated, moving to the Nanjing press conference where the news was announced, and finally to an empty crayfish restaurant that had lost 90% of its business since the news broke. The body of the show was spent tracing the source of the crayfish the sick patients had eaten and exploring possible ways the disease could have been transmitted. A scientist had the final word: explaining that crayfish remain poorly understood, he announced scientists have 'a difficult challenge' ahead. While the episode appeared to present a thorough investigation of the crayfish scare, its emphasis was on depicting the capacity of local government and relevant departments to deal with the issue and on the ability of science to solve the mystery. Consumers had no role in this except as individuals engaged in a market economy and as victims of unexplainable ailments.

The two periodicals exclusively devoted to consumer issues enjoy only a tiny fraction of television's audience. Neither the daily newspaper *China Consumer News* (*Zhongguo xiaofeizhe bao*) nor the monthly magazine *Chinese Consumer* (*Zhongguo xiaofeizhe*) are available at newsstands – they can only be obtained through subscription or read online. The consumer magazine claims a circulation of 300,000, with institutional subscribers like branches of the CCA (China Consumers' Association) far outnumbering individual subscribers. I was told by an editor that circulation for the newspaper was slightly higher. Both are sponsored and supervised to some degree by the Consumers' Association and both accept limited advertising. *China Consumer News* has reporters stationed across the country and cooperates regularly with the Association, receiving assistance and sharing information. The paper features some general news but focuses on consumer issues, carrying weekly and bi-weekly sections on automobiles, home appliances, food and health, and finance. Advertisements often run in the sections to which their products belong and many make special reference to their concern for consumer well-being.

Like most Chinese official media, *China Consumer News* puts a positive spin on the stories it covers and focuses on progress rather than problems. Instead of calling attention to the 5% of instant noodles that fail to meet the national standard, a headline in the food and health section proclaims that 95% are up to snuff. Stories often feature evidence of China's social, scientific, and economic development, celebrating high-tech food safety systems or announcing that China's rate of trademark registration is the world's highest. One article about a mobile inspection station, 'High tech "escort" for Olympics food safety', appeared during the 2008 Summer Olympics, at a time when information about melamine-tainted milk was still being suppressed. Depicting a scientist tinkering with state-of-the-art equipment inside one of these stations, the article embodied the message that consumer safety is primarily a technical issue, while the very day it ran a matter of pure politics was causing illness and death among consumers of milk and infant formula.

Compared to the newspaper, the magazine *Chinese Consumer* contains more practical information: product comparisons, stories on scandals and frauds, reports on real estate or medical litigation, even a monthly comic that shows victimized consumers' arming themselves with legal knowledge to stand up to retailers. The magazine also publishes soft or propagandistic pieces: a profile of a retired CCA leader turned calligraphist, a feature on stylish wallpapers, and a column where a consumer realizes that retailers can be cheated and disrespected too. I interviewed an editor for the newspaper and talked to several reporters for the magazine, and was impressed by their sophisticated understanding of consumer issues. One even told me she had known for years that something like the melamine scandal was bound to happen eventually because of the way cattle ownership and milk production worked in the dairy land of Inner Mongolia, a place she had visited several times. She notified the authorities of her concerns, but it would have been impossible to publish such a story in any official organ. Official censorship means that consumer media is effectively barred from circulating precisely the kinds of stories that consumers concerned about their safety and welfare would be interested in reading. In conversation with Mr Lu, a long-time employee of the CCA who wrote critiques of the consumer welfare system under an online pseudonym I asked why the CCA didn't try to increase readership by making media easier to obtain. Mr Lu told me this was the wrong question to ask – it wasn't because consumers couldn't obtain the magazine and newspaper that they didn't read them but because they saw them as 'the government talking to itself' and thus irrelevant to their lives.

RECEPTION OF CONSUMER RIGHTS PROPAGANDA AND MEDIA

These examples from television, retail and public spaces, and print media all have very similar messages. While hailing or naming citizens as consumers they also call on these individuals to take responsibility for themselves in the market: the onus is on them to obtain information, to buy safely, and to seek redress by negotiating with the seller or attaining resolution through the proper channels. Their message to consumers is that safe consumption is a matter of making the right choices and developing the right technology rather than the result of a well-regulated market. Focus group participants universally acknowledged the importance of the media, many providing examples of situations where media exposure or threats of it brought results, but their attitudes and expectations varied. They also remarked on the political limitations faced by the media, one pointing out that any scandal that involved the government or monopoly industries like telecommunications or oil would never be truthfully reported. Some said if they encountered a consumer rights violation they would contact a journalist before seeking help from a consumer institution. Participants were also suspicious that both private and governmental bodies accepted money for favorable reviews, or could be bribed to not make a negative report. Because consumer-oriented media is particularly subject to the suspicion of profit-seeking, it is unlikely that a privately run publication will emerge to replace official sources. In the absence of trustworthy, independent sources speaking for or to consumers, state-sponsored media is likely to retain control over the discourse of consumer welfare and rights. Schelling's analogy for official media is appropriate here: 'The participants of a square dance may all be thoroughly dissatisfied with the particular dances being called, but as long as the caller has the microphone, nobody can dance anything else' (in Shirk, 2011, pp. 6–7).

More prosaically, many individuals simply found consumer media boring or irrelevant. As a middle-aged shopkeeper remarked, '[media] need to be a bit entertaining, nowadays people are too tired', the accountant next to her nodding and adding 'no one pays attention'. This seemed to be the case with the television show *Consumer Advocate*, which was lauded by several of the fake-fighters I interviewed, but dismissed by focus group participants as well as my office mates in the consumer confidence project. In discussions focused specifically on consumer media, participants admitted that while they might glance at certain articles while doing research on a planned purchase they would never follow these periodicals regularly, primarily because most of the news was not relevant to them. These comments echoed those of a Chinese fake-fighter whose blog posts on corruption scandals had as many as twenty thousand readers while his posts on fakes garnered at most one to two thousand. He explained this in a framework that loosely invoked citizenship, but divorced it from the realm of consumption. Government scandals, he told me, involved every Chinese person, but product scandals only touched those who had purchased or planned to purchase that particular good. In other words one is always a citizen, but only a consumer of specific things and at specific times.

DISCUSSION: SUBJECTIFICATION AND THE CHINESE CONSUMER-CITIZEN

Propaganda from official consumer welfare institutions speaks little, if at all, to the practical challenges faced by Chinese consumers. In conversations, focus groups, and interviews, consumers expressed their wish for stronger regulation, improved information on and routes to dispute resolution, strengthened law enforcement, and new laws that would punish sellers of dangerous or substandard goods. When asked what an ideal system for the protection of consumer rights would look like, participants in several groups suggested replacing the panoply of consumer-oriented institutions with a simple phone number that could be relied upon for practical advice and assistance in pursuing resolutions. These suggestions were met with nods and vocal support by other participants, some of whom had unsuccessfully tried to use official channels in the past. Soured on the institutional route they later sought resolutions on their own or simply accepted the loss. When focus groups participants discussed consumer institutions the most common refrain was the need for information that was practical and usable. Tired of unrealistic claims and vague promises, they said organizations should publish stories about how individual consumers had resolved disputes, thereby slowly gaining the trust of consumers.

Individuals in my focus groups overwhelming agreed that the only way to make the marketplace safer was for laws and regulations to be improved and enforced. But they also nearly all believed that it was their responsibility to make the right, informed, choices. When we asked the groups whose responsibility it was to protect their consumer rights, roughly 90% said it was their own. The notable exception was in the focus groups of senior consumers, half of whom believed it was the government's responsibility to ensure their safety and welfare. For older citizens, a residue of the Maoist moral contract remains (Lee, 2007; see also Rofel, 1999), but young and middle-aged consumers do not trust their well-being to the party-state. When safety and quality were of the utmost importance, as in purchasing baby formula or medicine, these respondents strongly preferred large, established, and trustworthy retailers, believing that *they* would exercise quality control and take responsibility for problems in order to protect their reputations. When it was possible, they sourced goods destined for the markets of wealthy 'developed' nations such as Britain, Japan, Australia, or the United States (see Kuever, 2014).

The word subject, as Foucault famously explains, has two meanings: 'subject to someone else by control and dependence, and tied to his own identity by a conscience of self-knowledge. Both meanings suggest a form of power which subjugates and makes subject to' (1982, p. 212). Modes of subjectification are historical products and may coexist with outright repression (Foucault, 1995). Socialist subjects were interpellated as 'liberated' citizens of a new nation who had thrown off their oppressors and become protagonists of their own destinies (see Hinton, 1966). By the second decade of the reform era, the discourse of the socialist labor regime had little resonance with younger workers whose self-identity was connected to the capitalist discourse of social mobility, modernity, and self-transformation (Lee, 1998; Rofel, 1999).

Anagnost (1997) has argued that Chinese subject positions are 'overdetermined', ordered by a system that defines structurally appropriate acts grounded in reciprocal obligations, duties, and norms, limiting the potential for political agency. The discourse of *suzhi* (roughly translated as 'personal quality'), for instance, may appear to offer opportunities for social mobility and personal improvement but only if individuals are willing to define themselves in terms of their market value (Yan, 2008). *Suzhi* is a 'key political-cultural-economic operator' in the discourse of development, a standard by which incommensurable individuals can be measured, compared, or ranked (Yan, 2008). Subjects who recognize themselves as lacking *suzhi* relative to the general population are driven to socioeconomic striving and self-development (Anagnost, 2004). The national project of 'development' functions in much the same way, driving the Chinese people to strive so their nation can 'catch up' with the West. As Keane argues, 'The new moral order in China is one in which people are encouraged to be economically productive and self-reliant' (2007, p. 14).[6] The concept that a 'low quality' population holds the nation back not only absolves the state of responsibility for social investment but creates a space for intervention.

Consumer-citizenship transcends the dichotomy traditionally made between citizens, whose rights, responsibilities, and practices constitute membership in a state, and consumers, asocial agents who pursue their own desires through anonymous transactions (Clarke, 2007). Keane attributes the 're-emergence of the citizen concept' in China to the need to deal with the 'new social compact' of the market economy (2001, p. 1). Speaking of post-socialist societies more generally, we can expand Verdery's observation of citizenship to consumer-citizenship – it 'bounds in two ways: it distinguishes belongers from the excluded, and it ties the former to the state as the guarantor of their rights, thus incorporating them as subjects' (1998, p. 293). Those considered full members of the modern Chinese nation are those with the capacity and the knowledge to consume in a way that will develop the economy. Those farmers, migrants, pensioners, and low-wage workers who were full socialist subjects have little claim on the state under this new social compact (Zhang, 2006). Chinese citizens who seek self-transformation through the accumulation of goods are neoliberal subjects whose needs are defined as well as satisfied by the market.

Neoliberalism, the ideological face of global capitalism, prescribes the extension of economic rationality to all areas of life, insisting the market distributes public resources better than the state (Ong, 2006) and that the profitability of social entities, from citizens to cities, defines their value (see Zhang, 2006). Globally, neoliberalism has been associated with shrinking states and expanding markets, but in the Chinese context neoliberal governance centers on producing citizens who bring value to the state. The neoliberal subject, according to Ong, is 'not a citizen with claims on the state but a self-enterprising citizen-subject who is obligated to become an "entrepreneur of himself or herself"' (2006, p. 14). Subjects of what Zhang and Ong (2008) call 'governing at a distance' develop capacities of self-governance, self-improvement, and self-expression. The development of consumer subjectivity is an important part of this transformation. Rofel describes the neoliberal depiction of human nature as self-actualization, a model with 'the desiring subject as its core: the individual who operates through sexual, material, and affective self-interest' (2007, p. 3). Unlike the heavily politicized socialist subject, the desiring subject is apolitical, except when it comes to the right to the best product at the lowest price. For the consumers in my study, however, product scandals and other issues are overtly political because they are shaped by citizens' expectations of their government. Chinese attitudes towards consumer rights are linked to broad social dissatisfaction over inequalities in wealth and power, government corruption, and institutional mismanagement. Citizens may believe, for instance, that cronyism between private business and local government are behind sales of counterfeit drugs or expired foods, but if political challenges are framed as consumer issues their political power is muffled. Grievances channeled through party-state institutions, furthermore, cannot implicate the state.

CONCLUSION: CONSUMER WELFARE AND 'DEVELOPMENT'

The consumer welfare apparatus is designed to place responsibility for safety and well-being with consumers, rather than the state, and this framing has been successfully internalized by the middle-class urban consumers the party-state sees as a vital part of a secure future for the nation as well as for the ruling Communist Party. A decrease in savings and increase in consumption also promises to move China out of the 'backwards' (*luohou*) state where it spent most of the twentieth century – the result of the 'unfair treaties' between China and the West. Many citizens see the current challenges of the marketplace, included tainted food, copyright infringement, and uneducated consumers, as a natural part of China's current stage of development – a stage many developed countries passed through long ago. This framing justifies the fervent pace of economic and technological progress in China, even with the associated social and environmental costs, and fits with the narrative that the party-state has used to justify, among other things, their only recently reversed refusal to sign up to global climate change agreements.

The idea that China is merely at one point of an established developmental trajectory also accords with the party-state's practice of instituting such trappings of the 'developed' states as law and civic institutions. But when the consumer welfare apparatus is understood as an idea and practice of 'development' it becomes an 'anti-politics machine' (Ferguson, 1990) that expands state power while defining consumer protection as technical rather than political. The promise of development thus has a broadly suppressive effect on consumer activism. The insistence that China is still in the midst of 'developing' (*zai fazhan zhong*) explains the problems of today as the mere growing pains of industrialization. Development acts as a justifying ideology, a 'mode of regulation' that renders the current 'mode of accumulation' more tolerable (Boyer and Saillard, 2002). According to the 'lofty telos of development' (Yan, 2008, p. 3), the inequality, injustice, pollution, and unrest of the present are temporary and a small price to pay for a brighter future, a future that promises to be populated by confident consumer-citizens.

Notes

1 Taking a legal route can also be risky when the case is sensitive or well-known. One recent example was the seven-year sentence for subverting state power given to Zhou Shifeng, the former head of a Beijing law firm who represented victims of the 2008 melamine-tainted milk scandal, among others (Mai and Gan, 2016).
2 I base this assessment on both statistics (see for instance CCA, 2010) and my own observations and surveys of consumers.
3 In this case, consuming appropriately meant that I should have made a record of the business registration number of a foot massage business that suddenly moved, leaving me unable to use the remaining credit on my pre-paid card.
4 This connection of a series of numbers to a particular date or movement has many contemporary analogs. For example, 3.8, International Women's Day, is not only shorthand for women's rights but also a slang term for a difficult woman; 6.4, the date of the massacre at Tiananmen Square is synonymous with the movement that preceded it.
5 These re-enactments belonged to a popular genre featuring legal disputes presented then discussed by a panel of experts providing commentary and advice. Such shows rarely feature consumer disputes but typically focus on civil issues such as car accidents or real estate contracts.
6 This illustrates Gramsci's observation that state 'ethics' function 'to raise the great mass of the population to a particular cultural and moral level, a level (or type) which corresponds to the needs of the productive forces for development and hence to the interests of the ruling classes' (1971, p. 258).

REFERENCES

Adorno, T.W. (1991). The Culture Industry: Selected Essays on Mass Culture. New York: Routledge.

Anagnost, A. (1997). National Past-times: Narrative, Representation, and Power in Modern China. Durham, NC: Duke University Press.

Anagnost, A. (2004). The corporeal politics of quality (*suzhi*). *Public Culture*, 16(2), 189–208.

Baike (n.d.). Jiaodian fangtan [Topics in Focus]. Retrieved from http://baike.baidu.com/view/43125.htm#sub43125

Beck, U. (1992). Risk Society: Towards a New Modernity. London: Sage.

Bevir, M. and Trentmann, F. (2007). Introduction: Consumption and citizenship in the new governance. In M. Bevir and F. Trentmann (eds) *Governance, Consumers and Citizens*, London: Palgrave Macmillan, pp. 1–22.

Bosco, J. (2014). The problem of greed in economic anthropology: Sumptuary laws and new consumerism in China. *Economic Anthropology*, 1(1), 167–185.

Boyer, R. and Saillard, Y. (2002). Régulation *Theory: The State of the Art*, C. Shread (Trans.). London: Routledge.

Brandtstädter, S. (2008). Fakes, fraud, value-anxiety, and the politics of sincerity. In K. Sykes (ed.) *Ethnographies of Moral Reasoning*. New York: Palgrave Macmillan, pp. 139–160.

CCA [China Consumers' Association] (2010). Er ling yi ling nian di yi jidu quan guo xiaoxie zuzhi shouli tousu qingkuang fenxi [Analysis of consumer complaints handled by the China consumers' association for the first quarter of 2010]. Retrieved from http://www.saic.gov.cn/zwgk/tjzl/zxtjzl/xxzx/201006/t20100609_89031.html

Chan, A., Madsen, R. and Unger, J. (2009). *Chen Village: Revolution to Globalization*. Berkeley, CA: University of California Press.

CIA [Central Intelligence Agency] (2017, January 12). *The World Factbook: China*. Retrieved from https://www.cia.gov/library/publications/the-world-factbook/geos/ch.html

Clarke, J. (2007). It's Not Like Shopping: Citizens, Consumers, and the Reform of Public Services. In M. Bevir and F. Trentmann (eds) *Governance, Consumers, and Citizens*. New York: Palgrave Macmillan, pp. 97–118.

Cohen, L. (2004). A consumers' republic: The politics of mass consumption in postwar America. *Journal of Consumer Research*, 31(1), 236–239.

Croll, E. (2006). China's New Consumers: Social Development and Domestic Demand. London: Routledge.

Davis, D.S. (2000). Introduction. In D.S. Davis (ed.) *The Consumer Revolution in Urban China*. Berkeley: University of California Press, pp. 1–24.

Davis, D.S. (2006). Urban Chinese homeowners as citizen-consumers. In S. Garon and P. Maclachlan (eds) *The Ambivalent Consumer: Questioning Consumption in East Asia and the West*. Ithaca: Cornell University Press, pp. 281–300.

Farquhar, J. (2002). Appetites: Food and Sex in Post-Socialist China. Durham: Duke University Press.

Ferguson, J. (1990). The Anti-Politics Machine: Development, Depoliticization and Bureaucratic Power in Lesotho. Cambridge, UK: Cambridge University Press.

Foucault, M. (1982). The subject and power. *Critical Inquiry*, 8(4), 777–795.

Foucault, M. (1995). Discipline and Punish: The Birth of the Prison. New York: Vintage.

Fuller, C.J. and Bénéï, V. (eds) (2012). *The Everyday State and Society in Modern India*. New Delhi: Social Science Press.

Gao, T. (1991). Chinese consumer protection philosophy. *Journal of Consumer Policy*, 14(3): 337–350.

Garon, S. and Maclachlan, P.L. (eds) (2006). *The Ambivalent Consumer: Questioning Consumption in East Asia and the West*. Ithaca: Cornell University Press.

Gerth, K. (2010). *As China Goes, So Goes the World*. New York: Hill and Wang.

Gramsci, A. (1971). State and civil society. In Q. Hoare and G.N. Smith (eds) *Selections from the Prison Notebooks*. New York: International Publishers, pp. 206–276.

Hamilton, G.G. and Lai, C.-K. (1989). Consumerism without capitalism: Consumption and brand names in late Imperial China. In H.J. Rutz and B.S. Orlove (eds) *The Social Economy of Consumption*. Lanham: University Press of America, pp. 253–279.

Hinton, W. (1966). Fanshen: A Documentary of Revolution in a Chinese Village. New York: Vintage Books.

Hooper, B. (2000). Consumer voices: Asserting rights in post-Mao China. *China Information*, 14(2), 92–128.

Hooper, B. (2005). *The Consumer Citizen in Contemporary China*. Centre for East and South-East Asian Studies, Lund University, Sweden.

Ingelfinger, J.R. (2008). Melamine and the global implications of food contamination. *New England Journal of Medicine*, 359(26), 2745–2748.

Jourdan, A. (2013, October 25). China overhauls consumer protection laws. Retrieved from http://www.reuters.com/article/us-china-consumer-law-idUSBRE99O05E20131025

Keane, M. (2001). Redefining Chinese citizenship. *Economy and Society*, 30(1), 1–17.

Keane, M. (2007). Chinese citizenship in globalization. In W. Hudson and S. Slaughter (eds) *Globalization and Citizenship: The Transnational Challenge*. London: Routledge, pp. 43–51.

King, D.B. and Tong, G. (1991). Consumer Protection in China: Translations, Developments, and Recommendations. Littleton: Fred B. Rothman & Co.

Kuever, E. (2013). In today's China, you don't starve, you're poisoned: Consumer welfare and citizenship in urban China. Unpublished doctoral dissertation, Indiana University, Bloomington, USA.

Kuever, E. (2014). Mapping the real and the false: Globalization and the brand in contemporary China. In J.W. Schouten, D.M. Martin and R. Belk (eds) *Research in Consumer Behavior*, vol. 16. Bradford UK: Emerald Publishing, pp. 173–189.

Lee, C.K. (1998). *Gender and the South China Miracle*. Berkeley: University of California Press.

Lee, C.K. (2007). Against the Law: Labor Protests in China's Rustbelt and Sunbelt. Berkeley: University of California Press.

Lin, Y.J. (2011). Fake Stuff: China and the Rise of Counterfeit Goods. New York: Routledge.

Mai, J. and Gan, N. (2016, August 14). Head of Beijing law firms gets seven years and crackdown on rights activists continues. Retrieved from http://www.scmp.com/news/china/policies-politics/article/1999111/beijing-law-firm-director-jailed-seven-years-sweeping

McKinsey and Company (2013). McKinsey quarterly: China's next chapter, number 3. Retrieved from http://www.mckinsey.com/quarterly/overview/digital-newsstand/2013-issue-3-mckinsey-quarterly.

Melvin, S. (2013, September 3). A film-fueled culture clash over values in China. Retrieved from http://www.nytimes.com/2013/09/04/movies/in-tiny-times-movies-material-girls-have-a-nation-tsking.html

Miao, D. (2011). Between propaganda and commercials: Chinese television today. In S. Shirk (ed.) Changing Media, Changing China. New York: Oxford University Press, pp. 91–114.

Murong, X. (2009). *Leave Me Alone: A Novel of Chengdu*. Hong Kong: Make-Do Publishing.

Notar, B.E. (2006). Authenticity anxiety and counterfeit confidence: Outsourcing souvenirs, changing money, and narrating value in reform-era China. *Modern China*, 32(1), 64–98.

Ong, A. (2006). Neoliberalism as Exception: Mutations in Citizenship and Sovereignty. Durham, NC: Duke University Press.
Palmer, M. (2006). The emergence of consumer rights: Legal protection of the consumer in the PRC. In K. Latham (ed.) *Consuming China: Approaches to Cultural Change in Contemporary China*. London: Routledge, pp. 56–81.
Pew Research Center (2012, October 16). Growing concerns in China about inequality, corruption. Retrieved from http://www.pewglobal.org/2012/10/16/growing-concerns-in-china-about-inequality-corruption/
Read, B.L. (2003). Democratizing the Neighborhood? New Private Housing and Home-Owner Self-Organization in urban China. *The China Journal*, 49, 31–59.
Read, B.L. (2008). Property rights and homeowner activism in new neighborhoods. In L. Zhang and A. Ong (eds) *Privatizing China: Socialism from Afar*. Ithaca: Cornell University Press, pp. 41–56.
Rofel, L. (1999). Other Modernities: Gendered Yearnings in China under Socialism. Berkeley: University of California Press.
Rofel, L. (2007). Desiring China: Experiments in Neoliberalism, Sexuality, and Public Culture. Durham, NC: Duke University Press.
Schrift, M. (2001). Biography of a Chairman Mao Badge: The Creation and Mass Consumption of a Personality Cult. New Jersey: Rutgers University Press.
Shirk, S.L. (2011). Changing media, changing China. In S.L. Shirk (ed.) *Changing Media, Changing China*. New York: Oxford University Press, pp. 1–37.
Singer, M. and Baer, H. (2009). *Killer Commodities*. Lanham: Altamira Press.
Slater, D. (1997). *Consumer Culture and Modernity*. Oxford: Polity Press.
Veeck, A., Yu, H. and Burns, A.C. (2010). Consumer risks and new food systems in urban China. *Journal of Macromarketing*, 30(3), 222–237.
Verdery, K. (1998). Transnationalism, nationalism, citizenship, and property: Eastern Europe since 1989. *American Ethnologist*, 25(2), 291–306.
Yan, H. (2008). New Masters, New Servants: Migration, Development, and Women Workers in China. Durham: Duke University Press.
Yan, Y. (2012). Food safety and social risk in contemporary China. *The Journal of Asian Studies*, 71(3), 705–729.
Zhang, L. (2006). Strangers in the City: Reconfigurations of Space, Power, and Social Networks within China's Floating Population. Stanford: Stanford University Press.
Zhang, L. and Ong, A. (eds) (2008). *Privatizing China: Socialism from Afar*. Ithaca: Cornell University Press.
Zhao, X. and Belk, R.W. (2008). Politicizing consumer culture: Advertising's appropriation of political ideology in China's social transition. *Journal of Consumer Research*, 35(2), 231–244.

10

Spaces of (Consumer) Resistance

Vera Hoelscher and Andreas Chatzidakis

INTRODUCTION

Following the 'spatial turn' in social sciences (e.g. Warf and Arias 2009), anthropologists, geographers and consumer researchers increasingly recognise that the spaces and places of consumption are more than just a background canvas to everyday activity. Rather, they are, first and foremost, social products; they emplace, materialise and (often) naturalise particular consumer logics and practices that are inherently ideological. This applies as much for online spaces as it does for physical ones. For example, the online realm plays an increasingly important role in these power structures by means of our utilisation of them to navigate cityscapes, participate in working life, and research our consumption choices. It therefore forms an inseparable layer to the shared physical spaces of urban environments and needs to be considered alongside them (Graham et al. 2012). This is particularly relevant with respect to research exploring how digital spaces are used for the propagation of citizen resistance, such as the work of Manuel Castells (2012).

The main thesis of this chapter is that both physical and digital spaces shape, and are shaped by, modes of production and consumption. Accordingly, we aim to familiarize the reader with key conceptual arguments about consumer spaces and the movements of resistance within them; and to empirically illustrate them using examples such as alternative currencies (North 2014), time banking (Seyfang 2004), and voluntary simplicity (Moraes et al. 2010).

REBEL CITIES, REBEL SPACES

> Our cities are what and where we consume. In essence, the city is in fact nothing more than a space for consumption in which we apparently express ourselves as citizens of a consumer

> society. Consumption lies at the ideological core of the contemporary city and, as such, consumption spaces lie at the very heart of what it means to be a citizen of the society in which we live. (Miles 2010: 1)

In trying to understand why consumption has become so central to the depiction of modern cities, we may consider by what factors their quality is perceived and measured. Tied up with the need for cities to attract lucrative investments, capable human resources, as well as an incoming stream of tourists (Massey 2007), cities have established themselves as brands (Kavaratzis 2004). The public space is crucial for developing this with the help of cultural offerings such as art galleries, concerts, and museums. Yet, cityscapes are becoming increasingly dominated by corporate interests such as through the sponsorship of art initiatives and public events, and thus compromise on citizens' rights to utilise them for non-commercial purposes (Evans 2015). Simultaneous to the developments of the wider city, public spaces are forming part of this branded experience. The brand equity that is subsequently formed is not only reflective of factors such as living standards and cultural scene diversity but also the range of property developments and commercial chains.

As illustrated in Miles's quote above, cities are thus being reshaped as the shared spaces within which we consume, publicly display our choices and therefore assert our status and lifestyle. The city space itself has become instrumentalised to the degree that different urban quarters not only carry distinct socio-economic connotations, but also shape our sense of self and identity (Mort 1988). For many of us, the city has thus become emblematic of contemporary consumer culture. Within these shared urban spaces, identities and social events are mediated by the choice of what to wear, where to eat, how to live. While this all-persuasive argument of consumerisation can be seen as rendering citizens into lemmings of commercialisation, it also attributes an immense power to them; a power that Miller (1995: 10) describes as being 'repressive as well as enabling to those who wield it'. Diverging from prevalent consumption strategies is not only a challenge, but also carries the risk of social ousting. Yet, opportunities for the rejection of mainstream consumer culture are offered in various spaces of collective consumer action.

Harvey (2012: xvii) explains how spaces of resistance form 'in a moment of "irruption", when disparate heterotopic groups suddenly see ... the possibilities of collective action to create something radically different'. By engaging in collective action, a group acts 'in pursuit of members' perceived shared interests' (Scott and Marshall 2009: 96). Referring to newly-forming groups of individuals, who may come from a wealth of different backgrounds, Harvey suggests that these can be united by their desire to change the status quo. Championing collective action as a source of resistance to the dictatorship of mainstream consumption, Harvey therewith presents the case for coming together in shared space to engage in the creation of radical alternatives.

One theorisation of alternative forms of economic creation is found in Ostrom's (1990) study of the tragedy of the commons. Researching how collective action could be employed to better allocate finite resources, she proposes that communally owned resources, such as fresh water, are depleted if there is no common agreement in place as to how they are shared. Drawing on game theory, she theorises that without an agreement each party is better off using as much of the resource as possible for itself with a disregard to how that fares for other parties involved. When, however, rules are implemented on the basis of collective action, Ostrom's research suggests there are significantly higher chances of success, compared, for instance, to forms of governance such as private management or government policy.

The ideology of collective action is also central in Gibson-Graham's (1996) spaces of resistance to neoliberalism. Being engaged in action research projects around the globe that work together with 'community researchers of local economic practices and organizations', the joint authors Gibson-Graham consider the importance of transforming oneself in the process of discovering alternative lifestyles (Gibson-Graham 1996 xiv). Aiming to point out the shortcomings of conduct that blocks the 'transformative ambitions' held within culture, they describe the 'familiar understandings of capitalism as a naturally dominant form of economy, or as an entire system of economy, coextensive with the social space'. Desiring to create an alternative movement themselves, the authors Gibson-Graham (1996 ix) 'have been engaged in a collaborative project that seems guaranteed to occupy us for the rest of our lives, long or short as those might be' with their goal being 'to create or reveal landscapes of economic difference'.

Connecting this back to their work *The End of Capitalism As We Know It* (1996), Gibson-Graham propound that it is community work that can uncover forms of alternative economic interaction that are hidden in capitalist systems. Volunteering, caring for loved ones and traditional trading already present a largely unseen sector of non-financial value creation. Accordingly, Williams (2005) reminds us that the economic literature largely ignores daily transactions that do not happen on a monetary basis. Whilst not directly contributing to GDP in terms of a conventional perspective on economics, they are alternative forms of value creation that comprise a significant part of the everyday lives of a great number of people. Such occupations may include unpaid housework, childcare, and charity work among others (Hall 2011; Leyshon, Lee and Williams 2003). Highlighted are both the breadth and scope of care work and the variety of alternative economics that otherwise go unnoticed in conventional accounts of the (capitalist) economy (Leyshon et al. 2003; Gibson-Graham 1996).

Anchoring our knowledge of capitalism in urban space, Harvey (2005) considers the inherently uneven geographies of our cities, whose interpretation so crucially depends on our position within them. This view of shared space rests on the work of Lefebvre, who centrally positions embodiment in his understanding of space. Rejecting the modern philosophy of his contemporaries, who abstract space into a concept far removed from the body and its physicality, Lefebvre argues that it is modes of production – requiring both the human body and nature as well as tools and social practices – that establish an essential connection between thought, practice and nature (Lefebvre 1974; Simonsen 2005). As Harvey argues in *Social Justice and the City* (1973), it is this positionality of the individual that determines our perception and representation of spaces. In a similar vein, Soja (1989) argues that our life stories carry the geography of 'milieu, immediate locales, provocative emplacements which affect thought and action' (1989: 14). Hence, our biographies are intricately tied up both with those individuals that we interact with and the space(s) within which we form social networks and encounters.

Further stressing the importance of history for our knowledge of space, Soja comments that 'an already made geography sets the stage, while the wilful making of history dictates the action and defines the story line' (1989: 14). Accordingly, Massey's (2005) *For Space* elevates our understanding of shared spaces into a more inclusive concept. Lending a new angle to the debate of positionality within shared space, her writings oppose a simplistic account of space dominated by those ruling it by matters of ownership and policy making. Instead, she offers us a vision of understanding space as a meeting up of histories. Herewith space transcends the idea of a Cartesian coordinate system of mutually exclusive points. Historic dimensions are introduced to recognise the importance of the biographies of the individuals participating in a shared space as well as the histories of the objects in space and its overall architecture.

Rather more allegorically, the issue of positionality within space is also addressed by Holloway (2010) to account for how resistance can arise in an enclosed space shared by the citizens of the world: Over time, as ever more resources are depleted by a few to the detriment of all others, the increasing discomfort is visualised by the walls of the space drawing closer. This imaginary room, occupied by representatives of the different strata of a global society, exemplifies how the common resources of our shared space are nearing their end. As this goes on, cracks are forming in the walls. Although some of the inhabitants of the room are still seated comfortably, others are not anymore. This results in a shifting about of people trying to escape the walls that are increasingly posing a claustrophobic threat. Throughout this commotion, some of these citizens realise the cracks forming in the foundation are not only a threat but also an opportunity. Reaching out their hands, they press their fingertips into them to apply more and more pressure with the aim of breaking down the metaphoric walls of capitalism.

RECONFIGURING CONSUMPTIONSCAPES

Spaces of resistance connect themes such as food sovereignty, sustainability, and the building of alternative communities. Exemplifying Holloway's capitalist cracks and Gibson-Graham's call to collective action, the Zapatistas of Chiapas, Mexico, are one such movement that has long recognised the inherent injustices of capitalism. Being discontent with the unfair disownment of their land caused by a trading treaty between Mexico and North America, Zapatista farmers created an army of liberal Marxists to fight back for their land (Gibson-Graham 1996; Holloway 2010). Continuing until today, the movement has succeeded in making their cause known around the globe.

Another example of cracking capitalism is found in the numerous urban gardens that provide a path to food sovereignty in the face of an economic climate that sees citizens in financial hardship. Contrasting with the term 'food security', which describes 'the availability at all times of adequate world food supplies of basic foodstuffs to sustain a steady expansion of food consumption and to offset fluctuations in production and prices' (United Nations 1974), 'food sovereignty' is a counter-call for 'peoples' rights to shape and craft food policy' (Patel 2009: 664). A prominent example is given in Altieri et al.'s (1999) study of the emergence of the urban gardening culture of Cuba after the collapse of the socialist bloc. While gardening for the purpose of growing food was previously looked down on as only for the poor, economic disposition introduced edible plants to available urban spaces.

Urban gardening as a form of creating food sovereignty is also addressed in further studies by Lyons et al. (2013), Dixon (2011), and Walter (2012). Common in these accounts are the stories of citizens willing to create a counter-point to capitalist modes of food production. Lyons et al. (2013) in particular address the ways in which urban food movements empower citizens to renegotiate how urban spaces are used. Their findings suggest that citizens who actively participate in these urban movements challenge dominant modes of thinking about the distinction between public and private spaces and aim to counter bureaucratic adversity through practising the principles of permaculture. This form of gardening, founded by Mollison and Holmgren (1978), propagates low-impact gardening through design that creates balanced eco-systems.

Goodman and Goodman (2009) highlight the sustainability of producing local food, including savings on the emissions caused by transportation and the provision of food that is not affected by commercial pesticide use. For this reason, food sovereignty is also central in the Transition Town movement (Sage 2014). Having been born out of the design principles of Permaculture, Rob Hopkins, the founder of the Transition Network, intended for it to be a way of putting local food growing into the context of a global network of local communities aiming to reduce oil dependency. Owing to this emphasis on the community, Aiken (2015) argues that the Transition Network strongly refers to place, which is also evident in their link between naming Transition Towns after location, such as Transition Town Totnes or Transition Kentish Town.

Fortifying the link between local food production and perceptions of shared space, Selfa and Qazi (2005) focus on the role of scale in the creation of local food networks. They discuss the increased sustainability of local food networks as well as the creation of economic infrastructures for alternative consumption. Resting on the work of Jarosz (2000), Selfa and Qazi (2005: 452) suggest, 'for such local movements to flourish and to provide a real alternative, agri-food networks must build and rely upon social relations that are embedded in a particular place'. They thereby allude to the difference in scale between space and place: whilst space is essential for growing the idea of a network, the concept of place highlights the importance of social connections for these networks grown in space to flourish. Interestingly, Selfa and Qazi's (2005) research highlights that 'local' does not hold the same meaning for urban versus rural consumers. While for 'some food network actors across rural and urban locales, local food systems are defined by social relationships that may or may not be geographically proximate, … for others, local food systems are defined by a politically constructed boundary like a county or a bioregion' (Selfa and Qazi 2005: 462).

Similar to alternative food networks, 'local exchange trading schemes' (LETS) rely on spatial networks to operate. Economic benefits are aimed to remain within a local region through profit redistribution to small, local and independent businesses.

The strength of this concept is also its weakness: Although printed alternative currencies such as the 'Manchester "bobbins", Canterbury "tales" and Bath "olivers"' (North 2014: 249) arguably keep financial means within the local region, participant levels are often too low to make it a viable concept. As one of North's (2014: 249) research participants puts it, 'it would take a massive growth in the number of LETS systems and in the capacity of LETS systems to allow everyone in this city to live off LETS'.

Many of the above studies often highlight the importance of shared space and placial embeddedness in fostering a sense of collectivity and community. For instance, various participants in Kingsley and Townsend's (2006) study on urban gardening appreciated their connection to the community as a means of integrating in their local neighbourhood and creating social contacts. For some, these were the only social contacts they had formed outside their families. Drawing on similar observations, Firth et al.'s (2011) study on community gardening in Nottingham emphasises the need for a distinction between communities of place and communities of interest. While the first reside within the shared locale of the community garden itself, the latter are geographically independent of it. Communities of interest can support concepts or activities asynchronously via digital activities such as social media engagement and email distribution lists. These showings of support can be supplemented by occasional meetings in shared physical space.

Other groups and initiatives aim at renegotiating rather than altogether rejecting existing modes and patterns of consumption. For instance, Moraes et al.'s (2008: 273) exploration of New Consumption Communities (NCCs) shows how eco-village inhabitants were proactively interested in entering 'entrepreneurial positive discourses, practices and choices'. Rather than rejecting the idea of profitable monetary exchanges, these inhabitants saw potential in sustainable and fair business models. Far from the stereotype of an eco-village representing 'radical resistance to prevailing ideologies of consumer society', they were motivated to create viable economic alternatives (Moraes et al. 2008: 273). Chatzidakis et al.'s (2012) empirical study about the anarchist Athenian neighbourhood of Excharcheia further suggests that sharing space is indeed a crucial, yet overlooked, factor in the understanding of how forms of radical consumption evolve. As spaces of resistance, the marketplaces, public parks and cafés of Excharcheia create a shared environment within which radical ideas can be communicated, ultimately cultivating alternative subjectivities.

Many of the movements depicted in the above empirical studies continuously try to expand and scale up through reaching out to a network of potential participants and activists. One such example is the global action research projects of Gibson-Graham. Striving to establish more socio-environmentally just and resilient societies, Gibson-Graham and Roelvink's (2009) Community Economy project spanned across Australia, the USA, the Philippines and Europe with a view to rethinking current economic practices. Their research indicates that co-operative initiatives that re-invest profits back into their localities can have various positive effects for those involved, from providing employment and social links to the community to developing more effective administrative and recreational infrastructures.

EXPLORING DIGITAL LAYERS

> At the most basic level, the Internet is a way of transmitting bits of information from one computer to another. The architecture of the Internet provides for ways of addressing the information that is sent, so that it can be split up into packets, sent out across the network and recombined by the recipient. All kinds of information are in theory equal: bits are transmitted in the same way whether they represent text, audio, images, or video. The meaning of the bits comes from the patterns which they make, from the software which is used to interpret them, and of course from the users who send and receive them. Hine (2000: 2)

Parallel to offline spaces, shared online spaces create forums in which power structures and modes of consumerism are re-articulated and re-established. Within the vastness of digital space, platforms are launched that underpin our social, political, and geographical comfort zones. News sources, social media, the blogosphere and merchants' websites are intricately networked via digital marketing technologies in order to retarget us and reinforce previously expressed behaviours (Zuckerman 2013). This imposes a structure within our shared digital spaces that serves to mark boundaries of subjective security and reel citizens into expected consumption patterns. In this process, public spaces often become branded spaces as our experiences within them are mediated by search engines, social media check-ins and review platforms.

Yet, within and across these digital boundaries there are spaces in which the status quo can be challenged. Digital technologies allow for the creation of shared, anonymous spaces and the fast – and potentially viral – distribution of digital imagery. Shared online spaces can thus become incubators for consumer resistance and facilitate the scaling up of offline movements. This presupposes a strong intersection between the offline and the online; between digitally meeting up in private bedrooms and physically coming together in public squares (Castells 2012).

This intersection is particularly prevalent in urban spaces: Geospatial Information Systems combine with strong mobile Internet to form a digital layer to shared physical space. This digital layer facilitates our navigation of cityscapes, helps us decide on meeting points and allows us to review the physical sites and services that are digitally embedded within them (Zook and Graham 2007). Consequently, physical and digital spaces become increasingly interlinked with one another. They interdependently influence our behaviours within them, the ways in which we publicly express ourselves, and not least how we consume. The intersection of the physical and digital realms is instrumental to modern mobility, logistics, and the pace of contemporary consumption, as it is reliant on technological inventions and digital infrastructure. 'Mobility is central to what it is to be human', writes Cresswell (2006: 1) and therewith underlines one of the most crucial aspects of the urban lives of hyper-connected individuals. He refers to this as 'the effective shrinking of the globe by ever-increasing mobility at speed enabled by innovations in transportation and communications technology' (Cresswell 2006: 4).

As the speed of our travel and communication increases, so does the complexity of their context. Due to the fast trajectories of travellers, messages as well as consumer goods and services, culture 'no longer sits in places, but is hybrid, dynamic – more about routes than roots' (Cresswell 2006: 2). It becomes an ever-evolving and fragmented picture compounded by the travel paths of these individuals and what they choose to consume. Hine's quote above demonstrates how the meaning of digital messages is both created by the sender as well as unpacked by the recipient, and therewith creates a multi-dimensional meaning far beyond the bits of information it comprises. These shared digital spaces can be understood as a meeting up of histories akin to Massey's understanding of the offline world; the trails travelled by the bits and bytes can be considered as enablers and/or additional layers of the physical movements of goods and, most importantly, of people.

Considering these individuals and their digital pathways makes it easier for us to grasp that thoughts and emotions are 'shaped by the social context in which they develop including in virtual or technological contexts' (King-O'Riain 2014: 131). While shared online spaces might be anonymous to a degree, interactions within them are capable of creating distinct environments of their own. These environments, as previously established through the work of Zuckerman (2013), are constitutive of the cognitions, emotions, and behaviours expressed within them.

This demonstrates the multiplicity of digital spaces at which we arrive when considering the digital layer of urban environments alongside the mobility of the participants within them. Klein (2003) writes about this multiplicity of ideas prevalent within activism as one of the main criticisms against counter-consumerism movements: ideas of what it is that needs to be changed can often not be subsumed under one coherent strategy and therewith suffer from a disparity of philosophies. This disparity is also recognised by Harvey, who writes that it can be 'disparate heterotopic groups' that come together to see the possibilities of creating 'something radically different' Harvey (2012: xvii). The result of this, as Klein (2003) describes it, is often a multitude of activist facets and opinions. After such a meeting or demonstration, which can encompass lively discussions and the forming of new discourses in shared physical space, often only a website in shared digital space remains.

This occupation of online spaces, however, can serve to digitally scale up on consumer activism, especially when potential participants do not share physical space on a regular basis (Surin 2010). As sharing digital space makes asynchronous communication possible, we can juxtapose the idea of fast-paced mobility as discussed by Cresswell with the concept of collective action as put forth by Harvey and Holloway. Castells (2012) speaks about this as going on a blind date with other activists whom one might have only digitally met from the comfort of one's own bedroom, and then physically meeting them in the public spaces of the city. This has the potential to connect people from disparate, heterogeneous groups – or even individuals – bringing them together as part of a movement.

It is of increasing relevance that these shared digital spaces may surpass the idea of being a mere digital forum to log in to. Shared digital space, aside from enticing citizens to occupy the Tahir Squares or Wall Streets of this world (Castells 2012), can also become *place*, a destination in its own right for people to travel to and become part of (Rheingold 1994). These places have the potential to form a digital, collective memory; not only of the actions taken together in shared physical space, but also as an exchange platform that constantly undergoes transformation. Hence, we can see cyberspace as an opportunity to become more closely connected (Cresswell 2002; Rheingold 1994).

Simultaneously, we must not forget that these layers of code are typically not open for manipulation by their users. Of course, access to Information and Communication Technologies is the most basic hurdle, which prevents many citizens from being able to participate in the online public sphere. Going further than this, many citizens will also not feel confident enough to participate in discussions as they might not feel well-informed about the issues at stake. Furthermore, and this is crucial, the codes that our digital communications are embedded in are most often actively designed to prevent users taking part in their creation. Most users will lack the knowledge of computer programming skills. Instead, these spaces are hosted by companies that are aiming to make money out of them and will therefore design them accordingly (Graham et al. 2012). Some of the shared digital spaces may have consumer resistance at their core, yet their bedrock will still be commercial servers. True occupancy of digital spaces must thus not only attract those left outside of cyberspace but also seek to educate them in terms of writing and modifying codes.

DIGITAL REBELLIONS

The course of consumer resistance does not necessarily start online and then move into shared physical space. Time banking illustrates how a movement can utilise the Internet for implementing social change that seeks to challenge capitalist modes of consumption. The principle of time banking suggests that citizens can engage in exchanges that do not have to be valued by monetary means, but can be traded for other services. This system works to enable equivalent exchanges through a point system which is logged into an online database. This could include, for instance, exchanging gardening for Spanish lessons. Participants receive credit points which they can trade in for services of their choice. This alternative economic system, according to (Jonas 2010: 15), addresses the fact that 'often the labour performed in capitalism carries no equivalent remuneration in the form of payment; nor are certain forms of work and enterprise always valued in a moral and legal sense'. Therefore, Jonas argues, goods and services produced through the means of capitalistic practice acquire a higher value than the labour that went into them, ultimately generating profits for land and capital owners. In contrast, within time banks labour is performed in a non-exploitative fashion with the result of finding a sort of equivalence in time value. Further, Seyfang (2004) argues that time banking can give its participants the opportunity to develop vital skills that are beneficial to personal development as well as job searching, such as 'confidence-building' and 'forging social networks' (Seyfang 2004: 62). Rather than just presenting economic value to the individual, time banking goes beyond that by offering members tangible social benefits. In either case, the role of digital space is critical here, as time banking cannot be as effectively implemented on the basis of physical infrastructures alone.

More than just connecting members of a movement digitally and providing online platforms and infrastructures, digital spaces enable individuals to become part of digital networks and create social ties that can transfuse into their everyday lives (Petróczi et al. 2007). Regardless of whether users meet one another in the reality of a shared physical space, digital social ties can support them throughout their day-to-day struggles as well as their collective joys. These digital social ties are often found in social networks that are grouped around a particular interest.

Based on findings from a netnographic study, Seraj (2012) also explores the importance of social relationships in online networks. Her research shows that the success of an online platform is strongly determined by its ability to not only provide high quality content, but also the degree to which a platform enables interactivity between users and governs the culture of the community through monitoring the tone and ambience of its forums. When these factors work successfully together, Seraj (2012: 213) argues, online platforms create a high 'perceived value of online community' that will sustain its website traffic for a longer period of time. Seraj's work therefore indicates the importance of curating online spaces in order for them to fulfil their intended community functions.

Considering the backdrop of research findings purported by Seraj (2012) and Petróczi et al. (2007), the question remains as to what the qualitative differences between social interactions in shared physical versus shared digital space are. Rheingold (1994), one of the pioneers of digital communities, documented the first real-life meeting of his online parenting group. While members had previously only used the digital space to extensively exchange parenting tips from their remote locations in the USA, this physical encounter introduced faces to the previously disembodied discourse. Thanks to their in-depth exchanges in times when children were ill and lonely parents found solace through the digital support of others, they had established deep, meaningful connections in this shared online space. These relationships were now transferred offline during their first joint picnic in a park. Though many of them might not have developed friendships on the same deep level had they met in real life, the community continued to meet annually for a picnic in the park and watch each other's children grow up.

In addition to this, Nip's (2004) study is a rare exploration of the qualitative differences between the offline and online spaces of a community. Focusing on the digital bulletin board of a queer women's group in Hong Kong, Nip found that the online spaces employed considerably different discourses and messages from those commonly used offline. Remarkably, a number of individuals in the qualitative part of her study were reported to feel a strong sense of belonging to the online space of the 'Queen Sisters' network despite not having frequented any of its offline spaces.

Kleine (2005) addresses similar issues in her empirical study on e-commerce as a new form of outlet for the Fair Trade products of gepa, the largest German Fair Trade brand. In posing the question as to whether the Internet can provide new potential for a marginal product that had thus far only been sold in a select few outlets frequently located in the vicinity of churches, Kleine argues that the possibility of making Fair Trade purchases online was favoured by some individuals who did not want contact with sales representatives of the so-called 'One World' shops. Meanwhile, for other consumers it was the social contact that made brick and mortar shopping more enticing. Therefore, one key difference, according to Kleine, is the possibility and desirability of social interaction in physical space.

Beyond social encounters (and lack thereof), one can further consider the multi-sensorialiti(es) of physical and digital places. Phenomenological experiences based on smell and touch, for instance, are (for now) impossible in the online realm and yet these are essential to processes of emplacement and displacement alike (e.g. Casey 1993). Furthermore, questions of agency translate differently in online realms where there is little opportunity to alter, reconfigure and subvert space. Beyond moving to less commoditised online spaces (e.g. encrypted ones), more politically inclined consumer-citizens may choose to minimise their engagement with the online realm altogether (e.g. avoiding Facebook, twitter) and yet others may attempt to subvert them through intensively employing and exploiting their communicative power (Hoelscher 2017).

CONCLUSION

Current consumer research is considerably more advanced in terms of understanding space as both the context and object of (anti)consumption activity (Chatzidakis, McEachern and Warnaby 2017). Accordingly, geographical and spatial concepts such as space, place and scale are commonplace across various studies examining the importance of spatial dimensions and the ideological nature of various consumptionscapes and servicescapes such as flagship stores (Kozinets et al. 2004), theme parks (O'Guinn and Belk 1989), and festival shopping malls (Maclaran and Brown 2005). Concurrently, triadic understandings, advanced by the likes of Henri Lefebvre, Ed Soja, Tim Creswell and David Harvey, are increasingly applied in a variety of consumption contexts, from guerilla parks (Chatzidakis et al. 2012) and eco-villages (Vicdan and Hong 2017) to graffiti art (Visconti et al. 2010). Common in such analyses is the insistence in moving beyond the physical and seemingly neutral space, to acknowledge more experiential, phenomenological and ideological dimensions (Low 2016). In addition, there is increasing emphasis on the multi-sensoriality of consumerscapes, foregrounding senses such as sound and smell (Canniford, Riach and Hill 2017); and increased interest in the intersection of temporal with spatial factors (Chatzidakis et al. 2017).

Despite the theoretical sophistication in current spatialisations of consumer culture there is still little in the way of understanding the digital realms, the possibilities of resistance and perhaps more importantly, the intersection of the physical with the digital. Accordingly, this chapter has attempted to sketch a state-of-the-art overview of the key concepts that underpin our current understandings of online and offline realms. In moving forward, we suggest that future research examines the continual (and often conflictual) intersection of physical with digital spaces. As these spaces increasingly inform and reflect one another, so should our understanding of them.

REFERENCES

Aiken, G.T., 2015. (Local-) community for global challenges: Carbon conversations, transition towns and governmental elisions. *Local Environment*, 20(7), pp. 764–781.

Altieri, M. et al., 1999. The greening of the 'barrios': Urban agriculture for food security in Cuba. *Agriculture and Human Values*, 16(2), pp. 131–140.

Bakhtin, M.M., 1968. *Rabelais and His World*. Cambridge, MA: MIT Press.
Canniford, R., Riach, K. and Hill, T. 2017. Nosenography: How smell constitutes meaning, identity and temporal experience in spatial assemblages, *Marketing Theory*, forthcoming
Casey, E.S., 1993. *Getting Back into Place: Toward a Renewed Understanding of the Place-world*. Bloomington: Indiana University Press.
Castells, M., 2012. *Networks of Outrage and Hope: Social Movements in the Internet Age*. New York: Wiley.
Chatzidakis, A., Maclaran, P. and Bradshaw, A., 2012. Heterotopian space and the utopics of ethical and green consumption. *Journal of Marketing Management*, 28(4–4), pp. 494–515.
Chatzidakis, A., McEachern, M. and Warnaby, G., 2017. Consumption *in* and *of* space and place: Introduction to the Special Issue, *Marketing Theory*, forthcoming.
Cresswell, T., 2002. Introduction: Theorizing place. In G. Verstraete and T. Cresswell, eds, *Mobilizing Place, Placing Mobility: The Politics of Presentation in a Globalized World*. Amsterdam: Rodopi, pp. 11–32.
Cresswell, T., 2006. *On the Move: Mobility in the Modern Western World*. Milton-Park: Taylor & Francis.
Dixon, J., 2011. Diverse food economies, multivariant capitalism, and the community dynamic shaping contemporary food systems. *Community Development Journal*, 46(suppl_1), pp. i20–i35.
Evans, M., 2015. *Artwash: Big Oil and the Arts*. London: Pluto Press.
Firth, C., Maye, D. and Pearson, D., 2011. Developing 'community' in community gardens. *Local Environment*, 16(6), pp. 555–568.
Gibson-Graham, J.K., 1996. *The End of Capitalism (As We Knew It): A Feminist Critique of Political Economy*. Minneapolis: University of Minnesota Press.
Gibson-Graham, J.K. and Roelvink, G., 2009. Social innovation for community economies. In D. MacCallum et al., eds, *Social Innovation and Territorial Development*. Farnham, UK: Ashgate, pp. 25–37.
Goodman, D. and Goodman, M.K., 2009. Food networks, alternative. In R. Kitchin and N. Thrift, eds, *International Encyclopedia of Human Geography*. Cambridge: Elsevier, pp. 208–220.
Graham, M., Zook, M. and Boulton, A., 2012. Augmented reality in urban places: Contested content and the duplicity of code. *Transactions of the Institute of British Geographers*, 38(3), pp. 1–16.
Hall, S.M., 2011. Exploring the 'ethical everyday': An ethnography of the ethics of family consumption. *Geoforum*, 42(6), pp. 627–637.
Harvey, D., 1973. *Social Justice and the City*. Georgia: University of Georgia Press.
Harvey, D., 2005. *Spaces of Neoliberalization: Towards a Theory of Uneven Geographical Development*. Heidelberg: Franz Steiner Verlag.
Harvey, D., 2012. *Rebel Cities: From the Right to the City to the Urban Revolution*. London: Verso.
Hine, C., 2000. *Virtual Ethnography*. London: Sage.
Hoelscher, V. (2017). Online and offline spaces of consumer resistance. Unpublished Dissertation.
Holloway, J., 2010. *Crack Capitalism*. New York: Pluto Press.
Jarosz, L., 2007. The city in the country: Growing alternative food networks in Metropolitan areas. *Journal of Rural Studies*, 24(3), pp. 231–244.
Jonas, A., 2010. Alternative'this', alternative'that': Interrogating alterity and diversity. In D. Fuller, A. Jonas and R. Lee, eds, *Interrogating Alterity: Alternative Economic and Political Spaces*. London: Routledge, pp. 3–27.

Kavaratzis, M., 2004. From city marketing to city branding: Towards a theoretical framework for developing. *Place Branding*, 1(1), pp. 58–73.

King-O'Riain, R.C., 2014. Transconnective space, emotions, and Skype: The transnational emotional practices of mixed international couples of the Republic of Ireland. In T. Benski and E. Fisher, eds, *Internet and Emotions*. New York: Routledge, pp. 131–143.

Kingsley, J. and Townsend, M., 2006. 'Dig in' to social capital: Community gardens as mechanisms for growing urban social connectedness. *Urban Policy and Research*, 24(January), pp. 525–537.

Klein, N., 2003. Welcome to the net generation. In A. Roddick, ed., *Take It Personally: How Globalisation Affects you and Powerful Ways to Challenge It*. London: Element, pp. 20–26.

Kleine, D., 2005. *Surfen in Birkenstocks? Das Potenzial des Internets für den Fairen Handel*. München: oekom verlag.

Kozinets, R.V., Sherry Jr, J.F., Storm, D., Duhachek, A., Nuttavuthisit, K. and DeBerry-Spence, B., 2004. Ludic agency and retail spectacle. *Journal of Consumer Research*, 31(December), 658–672.

Lefebvre, H., 1974. *The Production of Space*. Oxford: Blackwell Publishing.

Leyshon, A., Lee, R. and Williams, C.C., eds, 2003. *Alternative Economic Spaces*. New York: Sage.

Low, S., 2016. *Spatializing Culture: The Ethnography of Space and Place*. New York: Routledge

Lyons, K. et al., 2013. Food in the city: Urban food movements and the (re)- imagining of urban spaces. *Australian Planner*, 50(2), pp. 157–163.

Maclaran, P. and Brown, S., 2005. The center cannot hold: Consuming the utopian marketplace. *Journal of Consumer Research*, 32(2), pp. 311–323.

Massey, D., 2007. *World City*. Cambridge: Polity Press.

Massey, D.B., 2005. *For Space*. London: Sage.

Miles, S., 2010. *Spaces for Consumption: Pleasure and Placelessness in the Post-Industrial City*. London: Sage.

Miller, D., 1995. Introduction: Anthropology, modernity and consumption. In D. Miller, ed., *Worlds Apart: Modernity Through the Prism of the Local*. London: Routledge, pp. 1–22.

Mollison, B. and Holmgren, D., 1978. *Permaculture One*. Morebank, NSW Australia: Transworld Publications.

Moraes, C., Szimigin, I. and Carrigan, M., 2008. Consumer resistance, coherent inconsistencies, and new consumption communities. In *1st International Conference on Consumption and Consumer Resistance*. Available at: http://conference2008resistance.e-monsite.com/

Moraes, C., Szmigin, I. and Carrigan, M., 2010. Living production-engaged alternatives: An examination of new consumption communities. *Consumption Markets & Culture*, 13(3), pp. 273–298.

Mort, F., 1988. Boys own? Masculinity, style and popular culture. In R. Chapman and J. Rutherford, eds, *Male Order: Unwrapping Masculinity*. London: Lawrence and Wishart, pp. 193–225.

Nip, J., 2004. The Relationship between Online and Offline Communities: The Case of the Queer Sisters. *Media, Culture & Society*, 26(3), pp. 409–428.

North, P., 2014. Ten square miles surrounded by reality? Materialising alternative economies using local currencies. *Antipode*, 46(1), pp. 246–265.

O'Guinn, T.C. and Belk, R.W., 1989. Heaven on earth: Consumption at Heritage Village, USA. *Journal of Consumer Research*, 16(2), pp. 227–238.

Ostrom, E., 1990. *Governing the Commons*. Cambridge: Cambridge University Press.

Patel, R., 2009. Food sovereignty. *Journal of Peasant Studies*, 36(3), pp. 663–706.

Petróczi, A., Nepusz, T. and Bazsó, F., 2007. Measuring tie-strength in virtual social networks. *Connections*, 27(2), pp. 39–52.

Rheingold, H., 1994. *The Virtual Community: Homesteading on the Electronic Frontier*. Cambridge: MIT Press.

Sage, C., 2014. The transition movement and food sovereignty: From local resilience to global engagement in food system transformation. *Journal of Consumer Culture*, 14(2), pp. 254–275.

Scott, J. and Marshall, G., 2009. Collective action. In *A Dictionary of Sociology*. Oxford: Oxford University Press.

Selfa, T. and Qazi, J., 2005. Place, taste, or face-to-face? Understanding producer–consumer networks in 'local' food systems in Washington State. *Agriculture and Human Values*, 22, pp. 451–464.

Seraj, M., 2012. We create, we connect, we respect, therefore we are: Intellectual, social, and cultural value in online communities. *Journal of Interactive Marketing*, 26(4), pp. 209–222. Available at: http://dx.doi.org/10.1016/j.intmar.2012.03.002

Seyfang, G., 2004. Time banks: Rewarding community self-help in the inner city? *Community Development Journal*, 39(1), pp. 62–71.

Simonsen, K., 2005. Bodies, sensations, space and time: The contribution from Henri Lefebvre. *Geografiska Annaler*, 87B(1), pp.1–14.

Soja, E.W., 1989. *Postmodern Geographies: The Reassertion of Space in Critical Social Theory*. London: Verso.

Surin, J.A., 2010. Occupying the internet: Responding to the shifting power balance. *The Round Table*, 99(407), pp. 195–209.

United Nations, 1974. *Report of the World Food Conference*. Rome: UN.

Vicdan, H. and Hong, S., 2017. Enrollment of space into the network of sustainability, *Marketing Theory*, forthcoming

Visconti, L.M., Sherry, J.F., Borghini, S. and Anderson, L., 2010. Street art, sweet art? Reclaiming the 'public' in public place. *Journal of Consumer Research*, 37(3), 511–529.

Walter, P., 2012. Theorising community gardens as pedagogical sites in the food movement. *Environmental Education Research*, 19(4), pp. 521–539.

Warf, B. and Arias, S., eds, 2009. *The Spatial Turn: Interdisciplinary Perspectives.*, London: Routledge.

Williams, C.C., 2005. *A Commodified World? Mapping the Limits of Capitalism*. London: Zed Books Ltd.

Zook, M. and Graham, M., 2007. Mapping DigiPlace: geocoded Internet data and the representation of place. *Environment and Planning B: Planning and Design*, 34(3), pp. 466–482.

Zuckerman, E., 2013. *Rewire: Digital Cosmopolitans in the Age of Connection*. New York: W. W. Norton & Company Ltd.

PART III

Consumer Culture Studies in Marketing

Consumer Culture Theory: A Front-row Seat at the Sidelines

Linda L. Price

In pursuit of knowledge, every day something is acquired. In pursuit of wisdom, every day something is dropped (Lao Tzu, cited in Weick 2006, p. 1727)

INTRODUCTION

Long ago I lived in Pittsburgh and went to Pirates' baseball games typically sitting somewhere between 3rd base and home plate. I was new to the game. My prior experience included occasionally watching a World Series baseball game on television with my dad. Consequently, I was trying to make sense of both what was happening on the field and what was happening in the stands around me. I spent as much time watching 'regulars' record stats as I spent watching pitchers put out players (and at this particular point in time it was a pitchers' game in Pittsburgh). I soaked it all up, stooping to the symbolic consumption of hotdogs (pretty much in opposition to everything I believe in), and vigorously embracing the seventh inning stretch, when the score was typically 1–0 if we were winning. I'm sure I could have willingly spent a lifetime watching those games and still never felt like an insider, like someone who knew what was happening and could dissect the meaning of the practices, rituals and game, the way Douglas Holt did as a baseball spectator in Chicago's Wrigley Field (Holt 1995). I feel a bit the same way as I reflect on consumer culture theory and how it came to be a term wantonly used to signal belongingness to an academic tribe or the 'other' – the mysterious essence and properties of people labeled that way – those people who do 'weird science' (Brown and Schau 2008).

The rise of neoliberal ideology that bifurcated consumption and production has deep roots. However, some scholars posit a consequential rise of neoliberalism at the beginning of the 1980s that fundamentally altered 'the meaning and significance of consumption, markets and marketing' (Fitchett, Patsiaouras and Davies 2014, 498). In fact, during the 1980s, we saw many scholarly communities arguably linked to this neoliberal surge assemble into 'fields'. Some intersect closely with consumer culture theory such as the rise of the sociology of consumption, concurrent with the cultural turn, globalization and the ubiquitous rise of consumer culture (Featherstone 1991; Sassatelli 2007; Warde 2015). Around this same time, theories of consumption took on increased attention and weight in anthropology (cf., Appadurai 1988; Douglas and Isherwood 1978; Miller 1987). In fact, in a provocative critique of the concept of 'consumption', Graeber (2011), citing Arnould and Thompson (2005), describes the 'synthetic discipline', called 'consumer culture theory' as emerging from 'the increasing number of anthropologists,' working in business schools and the corporate world (2011, p. 491). Other vibrant examples, such as the growth of services marketing (Berry and Parasuraman 1993) and strategic management (Hambrick and Chen 2008) may share fewer intellectual roots or market problems, but nonetheless as intellectual social movements share many structural similarities (Coskuner-Balli 2013).

Emerging fields always entail the contention that existing academic fields have overlooked or are inadequate to address important problems. However, some do so without the repudiation or claim of incorrectness of any existing fields. Such was the case for services marketing and strategic management. Others have more contentious beginnings that confront firmly held ontological beliefs about how the world works. Arguably, such was the case for consumer culture theory (Anderson 1986; Hunt 1990; Sherry 1991; Zaltman 1983). Regardless, using criteria that define academic '"fields" as "reputational work organizations" that are granted the right to evaluate members and some permanence in the academic establishment' (Hambrick and Chen 2008, p. 32; Whitley 1984), consumer culture theory has become an academic community with differentiation, increased legitimacy in established journals and adjacent established fields, and a mobilization of like-minded scholars in various forums (Coskuner-Balli 2013; Hambrick and Chen 2008; MacInnis and Folkes 2010; Merton 1973). As with any story of origin, there are multiple narratives about how consumer culture theory took root and came into existence (cf. Belk 2014; Bode and Østergaard 2013; Cova, Maclaran and Bradshaw 2013; Levy 2003; Tadajewski 2006). When I agreed to write this chapter I was shocked to afterward learn about the already numerous telling and retelling of the origins of CCT – obviously I fell asleep at the ballgame!

In the face of many stories, my own story is of a seat on a sideline – just like all those mysterious baseball games I attended, enjoyed and never quite understood – equally bewildered by the players and the fans. Like those baseball games I watched, it is also told as an American story and doesn't include the numerous consequential European and other scholars who have different, important stories (Askegaard and Scott 2013).

With my brief, partial story, I hope to underscore four things about origin myths: (1) we privilege intentional actions over luck, chance and circumstance; (2) we privilege a few core actors over many significant peripheral actors; (3) we dwell on our gains and ignore, hide or forget our losses; and (4) even as context is our game, we are remarkably unconscious of the water we swim in (Tucker 1974). I use 'we' intentionally. I'm remarkably proud of any small role I have played in the 'we' that is CCT.

At the same time I aspire more for our remarkable and resilient consumer culture theory community, and I aspire more for the broader consumer research and marketing community that sits at the portal between today and a sustainable, fruitful tomorrow.

As many excellent chapters in this volume portend, we are at a fundamental inflection point where the world is not just rapidly changing, but 'is being dramatically reshaped' in many realms all at once (Friedman 2016, p. 28). Whether in the introduction of Airbnb (Miles, this volume); or the flexible, rapidly changing collaborative networks that 'present different forms of interaction and exchange in the same setting' (Cova and Dalli, this volume; Scaraboto 2015); or recent challenges to how we define and understand gift-giving when 'green (currency) goes with everything' and I can print your branded gift with my 3-D Printer (Otnes, this volume; Rindfleisch and O'Hern 2015), we are entering a new world where what we knew before 2007 is increasingly obsolete (Freidman 2016).

In what follows I begin with my own version of how consumer researchers moved: from an abstract consumer to investigating a feeling, thinking doing person; embracing multiple ontologies; and recognizing a consumer culture theory academic sub-discipline category. I hope to stress the idiosyncratic character of all these narratives, of which there are now many. I then return to four modest points I wish to make as we enter the next decade of our organizational history: how luck, chance and circumstances aid in becoming; the key role of peripheral actors; imagining what is missing, hidden, absent in our growing assemblage; and perhaps being more cognizant of the water we swim in. All of these points have been made by others before, but at this critical inflection point are perhaps worth repeating.

FROM ABSTRACT CONSUMER TO A FEELING, THINKING, DOING PERSON

To be clear, I felt like I was there when 'we' took baby steps to resist an approach to consumer behavior that was remarkably detached from any actual person (only sometimes a consumer) experiencing any actual thing in any real social, cultural world (Tucker 1974). I remember being taken aback by experiments that in the name of 'control' took out everything people use in their lives to make decisions (including brand names), and struck by the way it seemed that men sat in offices and imagined how 'people' made bread purchases without actually ever asking about, observing, or participating in their wives' purchase of bread, much less my mother's purposeful, warming and methodical process of making bread instead of buying it – which I identified not as consumption but as 'doing family' (Epp and Price 2008; Moisio, Arnould and Price 2004; Price 2015). I use these gender terms deliberately because it was mostly men imagining mostly women (Fischer and Bristor 1994).

Imagine how excited I was when people (still mostly men) started to do something different? For example, I was delighted as a PhD student to uncover Jim Bettman's research. For his operations research dissertation in 1969 he followed his wife and a couple of her friends around a grocery store for a couple of months with a kind of clunky audio methodology and a brilliant insight that he might learn something from examining an actual person buying bread and the myriad process of things she considered that weren't on anyone's radar. As Kassarjian later noted, 'Bettman was attempting to record and model the behavior of real consumers in real grocery stores long before any of us had heard the term naturalistic inquiry' (1993, p. 6). I was there *on the sidelines* when C.W. Park looked at how couples muddle through the home-buying process without specific decision attributes and weights to find something that 'feels like home', and admitted in a footnote to losing some of the data, which never once detracted from the integrity of what we knew to be the story (Park 1982).

I was there when Beth Hirschman presented her own fraught, emotional efforts to select childcare for her precious children (1987), reverberated decades later in Epp and Velagaleti (2014) as they considered parent outsourcing options and constraints. I was with Beth again when she took us to a place of fantasy and fun (Holbrook and Hirschman 1982), and again when she went into the dark depths of addiction (Hirschman 1992). In 1981 I was handed Melanie Wallendorf's dissertation as a guide for how to write one, even though I was steeped at that time in Kahneman and Tversky (1975) – an intellectual love affair I would never recover from, but can make sense of as a life-long pursuit of how and why contexts matter (Price, Arnould and Moisio 2006).

I was there when the consumer odyssey pulled into town to learn about consumers' complex and nuanced relationships to possessions (Belk, Wallendorf and Sherry 1989) and again when it became an MSI (Marketing Science Institute) 'movie,' that also involved endorsement by an established, legitimized market-facing organization. I was there when John Sherry introduced us to consumer gift giving (1983), took us to market (1990) and pushed us to imagine the limits of how we express and articulate the world around us (Sherry and Schouten 2002). So, I was there as disembodied consumers became living, breathing, exotic, mundane, always surprising instances of individual and collective actors in a complex, dynamic, social, cultural world. *On the sidelines*, I was there.

FROM ONE ONTOLOGY TO MANY

I vividly recall when chairs were thrown across an AMA Winter conference room as a rigid, sterile form of positivism faced down an encroaching relativism perceived as nihilistic in tone and purpose – and there was much truth in these descriptions on both sides. From the rear view mirror, reasonable and gracious people, taken to their intellectual limits, occupied both sides of the conflict and over time moved toward reconciliation and engagement – perhaps not as quickly or effectively as some of us hoped. I remember as Laura Anderson and Julie Ozanne gave us a path forward, a way to recognize, structure and perhaps reconcile differences (Hudson and Ozanne 1988). I held hands with fellow Pittsburgh faculty and PhD students as we watched Jerry Zaltman *nervously* encourage ACR members to pay attention to hidden and 'taken for granted' everyday events at his ACR Presidential address (Zaltman 1983). A decade later this lesson would be reinforced by Eric Arnould as we watched young girls from an alternative high school braid each other's hair after 'shampooing' in a desert river in the early morning of a rafting trip (Arnould and Price 1993).

I remember when Richard Lutz became editor of JCR, from 1988 to 1990, and made consequential acceptance and rejection decisions that would change the course of history for publications in consumer research (see also, Lutz 1989). There were earlier precedents, but arguably this is an important moment when consumer culture theory took on legitimacy and weight. There was no going back, and from that point forward lovely, weird, quirky but consequential papers that focused on consumers in context were part of the JCR landscape. For example, publication of the consumer odyssey happened on Rich Lutz's watch. For the record, his watch involved rejecting my 'trait-based' work on consumer use innovativeness in favor of work that was more cultural, social, embedded and dynamic. It's not quite as stark as that, but the meaning was clear, we were headed somewhere new, somewhere not visited before – we were going for a moon shot. Ambivalent at the time, I'm now grateful for Rich Lutz's conviction and fortitude.

I was there when two outlaws took us into heretical territory, arguing that the foundations of our neoliberal myths were shaken (Firat and Venkatesh 1995). We organized in opposition to the conventions of consumption (Heretical Consumer Researchers), not as a yes, but a no – a conversation of resistance (Penaloza and Price 1993). Years later, I was there with David Mick, Connie Pechmann and others as we sought to carve out a transformative role for consumer research, not around methodology, but with deep regard to circumstances and context (Mick 2006; Mick et al. 2012).

THE NAMING OF CONSUMER CULTURE THEORY

I was *on the sidelines* when two JCR AEs were asked to summarize what we had learned from that 'other category' that they were AEs for. In contrast with other AEs invited to do the same in their already defined spaces, these two AEs decided to write something. Further, they coined a term that has been undeniably consequential – they judiciously gathered up what had appeared in JCR in their 'other category' over the past 20 years and themed and then strategically labeled it Consumer Culture Theory (Arnould and Thompson 2005). I was often in 'the other room' as they debated how to position a new consumer research field around what had appeared in the *Journal of Consumer Research* and assigned to that weird 'other' space. I watched as this term was met with reverence and disdain, and as, regardless of polemics, it gathered weight, community and territory. Later, I was part of the inaugural board of a newborn association that came together and called itself the Consumer Culture Theory Consortium, and I even hosted a CCT conference. So, on the sidelines, I was there when CCT became a category.

FOUR MODEST LESSONS FROM MY JOURNEY

As I reflect on how things have subsequently unfolded, I remember lessons from long ago. What you derive in a factor analysis (or a literature review) is always dependent on what you put into it – the items used to measure a construct will consequentially come to define that construct – the face validity of those items as measures of the construct must always be questioned (Nunnally and Bernstein 1994). This may seem unbelievably obvious to some, but as many others have also noted, it's consequential in how CCT came to include and exclude what it did and the subsequent themes and development of the field. The CCT field was not defined on what could or ought to be (prospectively), but instead what was and had been (retroactively). It was not organized around problems we need to solve, as was the case for TCR. CCT was also not defined consensually, by surveying scholars in the amorphous sub-discipline (Nag, Hambrick and Chen 2007). I'm not suggesting that these would be better or more legitimate ways to build a new academic field, only that they would likely be different.

The AEs charged with the task were and remain 'well aware of the risks of rigidifying and dogmatizing a research tradition that is engendered in the institutionalization and branding processes' (Askegaard 2014, p. 508). Nonetheless, they valiantly undertook an initiative to gather the troops and give future purpose while theming, per their delegated mission, around what had been done before in the *Journal of Consumer Research*. Moreover they gave due consideration to how to make it legitimate and palatable for an outside audience – how to appear theoretical not context driven. How could those in the sub-discipline of consumer culture theory appear as trained natives in basic social fields such as anthropology and sociology, rather than loosely equipped adventurers, or worse still marauders on a foreign planet? These factors were foundational in acceptance of the label and the equivocal, but significant legitimacy that followed. Legitimacy building is a key factor in the success of a new academic discipline and without it is unlikely to grow and thrive (Hambrick and Chen 2008; Merton 1973). Metaphorically, the article and themes became a container that held some things in and kept other things out, and like all containers, 'can inhibit or expand imagination's boundaries' (Zaltman 2016, p. 109).

LUCK, CHANCE AND CIRCUMSTANCE

When I contemplate how I ended up on the sidelines at the birth of consumer culture theory as a legitimate sub-discipline, it seems altogether improbable. It seems as random as that brief period of my life when I went to Pirates' baseball games. For example, my beloved dissertation advisor Rajendra Srivastava does strategy research using quantitative methods – nothing remotely close to CCT. I was lucky to join marketing when Beth Hirschman was bringing her babies to conferences, and Linda Golden (the first woman professor I ever met) was on the marketing faculty at UT Austin. It was a lucky chance to early on be surrounded by imaginative and curious people defined less by what they knew and more by what they didn't *yet* know. It was a lucky chance that I serendipitously tripped over phenomena that left me with burning questions that forced me to learn new tools to answer them. I was lucky to early on meet people such as Tom Tucker (who was already problematizing the bifurcation of production and consumption) and Jerry Zaltman (2000) who encouraged everyone around him to take a hike into the real lives of people and organizations and into disciplines as far-ranging as possible. Jerry Zaltman is still encouraging us to enter into a 'new age of imagination' (Zaltman 2016), against a backdrop of what many scholars describe as an 'age of fragmentation', fragmentation not around specialized attention to a problem such as curing cancer (or studying the cancer patient's journey), but around methods and turf (Coulter 2016).

When a narrative foregrounds chance, luck and circumstance, taking credit for unfolding successes is much harder, and actors' intentions are blurred into relational capacities, networks and flows, often at odds with intentions (Frank 2016). Moreover, we can see how positional concerns may interrupt or displace collective welfare. Robert Frank developed arguments over decades and several books about how positional concerns that serve the individual can decrease everyone's welfare – he draws on vivid examples from the animal kingdom, noting for example that while the size of an individual elk's horns gives him a position of privilege, when all elks' horns get larger as a result, the species suffers in myriad ways. He compellingly demonstrates that people too fall victim to these sub-optimal collective outcomes. For example, he illustrates how positional concerns fuel luxury fever for contemporary consumer societies in ways that hurt all of us (Frank 2010).

Many important rewards depend on relative position, so it is not surprising that people, animals and organizations find it hard to resist scrambling for it (Frank 2016). But these scrambles come with collective costs. As an academic sub-discipline, it behooves us to be attentive to luck, chance and circumstances and how these forces include and exclude certain human and non-human actors. We should also ask whether and how positional concerns might be influencing what we study and who we study with. Are we chasing a new theory as a tool of knowledge to solve an important problem, or as something as impressive as a Rolex watch to flaunt in academic circles?

THE KEY ROLE OF PERIPHERAL ACTORS

Perhaps my own improbable journey makes me attentive to the peripheral actors that participated in breathing life into this new academic field. I could have named many more peripheral actors than I have space for in this chapter (see also Askegaard and Scott 2013). If peripheral players have been highly consequential in helping our ideas flourish, then as consumer culture theorists, we want to insure that our newly filled container is porous and flexible, that we can take things out and put things in – that we have room for something and someone else – that we understand the value of territorializing, but also morphogenic, de-territorializing processes (Bajde 2013; Deleuze 1994; Price and Epp 2015). In an age of acceleration, when everything is changing fast, we may feel loss and anxiety that leads us to close down the container (walled away) rather than reaching for how to create a stronger, larger floor (Friedman 2016).

Acknowledging the myriad roles of peripheral actors, including where we were educated, whom we met early on, how the departments we live in are structured, and so on, can perhaps make us more sensitive to the arbitrary, fluid and consequential character of our assemblages – and to how easy it is for actors and relations to slip into and out of our networks and lines of flight. Or, how easy it is for an assemblage to fall apart (Parmentier and Fischer 2015). We must be careful to hold on to the essence of our community, without reifying an existing set of actors and their structural relations (Harman 2013). Are we sometimes so tightly territorialized around our long-ago published ideas, or our version of a theory or construct, that there's no room for anyone else to breathe new life into them? Are we sometimes so attached to ideas about what belongs or doesn't in our community that we become irrelevant to the outside world that is shifting before our eyes? Have we closed the door on strangers who could invite us to think differently?

IMAGINING WHAT IS MISSING, HIDDEN, ABSENT

According to Jerry Zaltman, 'Imagination is a special instance of thought. It is a process of thinking about something that is missing. Like all thought, its dynamics are shaped by the subject it is about' (2016, p. 99). In a book (and a TED talk), historian Noah Harari (2014) explains that imagination (by which he means the ability to create and believe fictional stories) explains why humans dominate planet earth. Our imaginations give us the collective capacity to cooperate both flexibly and in large numbers. In other work, I talk about how important it is to consider not just the material and expressive, but also the *imaginative* relational capacities of actors (Epp, Schau and Price 2014; Price 2012; Price and Epp 2015). Whereas, other species describe reality, we collectively imagine things – and it turns out that relational capacity is highly consequential. In his subsequent book Noah Harari imagines what that might mean for our future (2016).

Several scholars have drawn attention to what CCT could become or has failed to become as a result of what happened and what happens next. Just like mine, these are all fictional stories. Perhaps none is as playfully poignant as the narrative outlined by Bode and Østergaard (2013) as a cautionary tale for balancing radical and pragmatic voices to ensure a sustainable, dynamic future life for CCT. All of these narratives are imaginings of what is missing, hidden or absent. Have we lost our macro-focus (Cova, Maclaran and Bradshaw 2013)? Where is our attention to the marginalized, the disenfranchised, and the powerless (Askegaard and Scott 2013)? These imaginings are a vital collective capacity that we must empower and privilege whether they seem to emanate from actors within or outside our current assemblage.

As I noted earlier, for whatever may have 'gone missing' as we became a category, one thing we gained is institutional legitimacy. CCT can posture for position and more easily contend for its share of institutional turf. It turns out that because of my lucky and improbable life, I was less attentive to issues of legitimacy than others. In some ways legitimacy seeking was hidden from me because of privilege. I wasn't aspiring to be accepted or respected by some mother discipline, although I had a more or less voracious appetite for all of them. Hence, I was content to be a loosely equipped adventurer on a foreign planet – although I decline the label 'marauder'. I'm not saying legitimacy doesn't matter, clearly it does. Legitimacy especially feels important when people feel it is questioned or at risk. But it is perhaps still worth asking not only what we gain from disciplinary legitimacy, but also what we lose.

Other scholars have argued that our 'quest for respect', whether from economics, psychology, sociology, anthropology or something else prevents us from engaging in organic theorizing that might be more fruitful in addressing the intractable problems we face (Kohli 2017). We face perplexing and intractable problems – problems that are fundamentally reshaping how we do theory, research and live our lives. The accelerating speed of innovations, including new ideas is far outpacing the capacities of people and our structures to adapt and absorb them (Friedman 2016, p. 31). As Eric 'Astro' Teller, CEO of Google's X research and development lab described it to Thomas Friedman, we turn over technology platforms 'in five, to seven years, but it takes ten to fifteen years to adapt to it' (2016, p. 32). In other forums I have talked about how big, fast, deep data is rapidly changing how we theorize and do research (Nielsen 2012; Price 2015b). Arguably, collaborative science makes traditional sources of legitimacy as well as disciplinary boundaries more ambiguous and less relevant. Computer scientists identify medical cures, and non-scientists discover galaxies and stars. Everywhere there is a sweeping democratization of science, with both positive and negative implications for all of us.

As CCT researchers we need to think about how to bring our appreciation for context, social lives and culture to uncover insights from varied, new and hybrid forms of data, analyzed in old, new and hybrid ways (Horst and Miller 2013; Kozinets 2015). For example, what insights might we uncover from looking at dynamic flows of cell phone usage before and after a Tsunami, that other social scientists might not (Gordon 2007)? The pace of technological change should provoke us to consider expanding our data collection and analysis tools in myriad ways. Insights for action in this accelerated, hyper-connected world will be ever more needed (Friedman 2016; Taleb 2012). Moreover, as others have argued, there are many things that big data doesn't do particularly well, including understanding the social, cultural world.

As we contemplate what we have gained from becoming a 'separate' academic sub-discipline, with our own forums and distinct voice, it is worth considering whether there are important things that are now missing, currently hidden, or absent from our view? By imagining some of those absences, can we strengthen our value to external and internal actors alike?

THE WATER WE SWIM IN

Over the years I have become a 'consumer researcher' – it was never something I set out to do, and I'm ambivalent about the label – although I love the associations and people I'm linked to. I noticed perplexing things around me and then studied them in search of personal answers without intending to study consumer behavior. I was encouraged and enabled to define all of it as consumer behavior (cf., Belk 1987). And, it has been a grand adventure (Price 2014)! Until recently, I didn't worry about the way it seemed that people had become *only* consumers, and brands and consumption had become the polluted water we swim in. I had this nagging feeling that as we study friendships, families, communities and experiences, it is important to distinguish between what is commercial and what is not – even as these things are inextricably intertwined (Price 2015a; Price and Arnould 1999; Thomas, Price and Schau 2013). However, far more thoughtful people drove me to consider the need to interrogate consumption more profoundly (Graeber 2011; Vargo and Lusch 2011; Wilk 2004). Although Bob Lusch continued to grapple with how to avoid the term, he felt consumer connoted something 'rather passive, final connotations of a "target" with a primary activity of using stuff up, rather than creating and contributing' (Vargo and Lusch 2011, p. 181). As Doukas writes in response to Graeber's (2011) provocative essay, 'Relegated to the sphere of consumption, social life appears as the pursuit of products, its life-giving creativity all but forgotten. In this ideological regime social life itself … can appear as "a gift granted us by the captains of industry"' (Graeber et al. (2011, p. 503). Wilk (2004) problematizes consumption as fire, destruction, waste and using things up, especially eating things up.

Other scholars question whether we can escape markets and brands, and give us troubling answers (Holt 2002; Kozinets 2002). Nonetheless, from 'people engaging in a complex community organized around forms of (relatively unalienated) production', to people using up water, fossil fuels and creating destruction and waste there is a continuum of 'consumption' worthy of more investigation (Bauman 2013; Graeber 2011, p. 500). This becomes ever more important as lines between consumption and production become increasingly blurred. This also becomes more important because the inflection point of 2007 'has blown apart the basic workplace that we have known since the Industrial Revolution blew away the guild-based workplace' (Friedman 2016, p. 238). How we understand work and consumption are going away. In fact, 'work' as we know it may be going away. As culture theorists who also operate with attention to market phenomena we are perfectly situated to investigate this evolving reality, but to do so we must attend to the water we swim in. Howard S. Becker (2008) in defense of his work on outsiders noted that he never intended for it to be an overarching theory, but meant only to focus attention on the way 'labeling places the actor in circumstances which make it harder for him to continue the normal routines of everyday life and thus provoke him to "abnormal" actions' (p. 179). Becker is a quintessential example of a social scientist always trying to climb out of the water, to understand what is on the other side of a taken for granted reality – the other side of a label. Karl Weick (2006) also warns us to use our categories wisely. Everyday categories serve us well, they help us register what is happening in our world and what it means for us, but we must be careful that categories serve us and not the other way around. As Weick eloquently describes: 'organization is talked into existence when portions of smoke-like conversation are preserved in crystal-like texts that are then articulated by agents speaking on behalf of an emerging collectivity' (2006, p. 1725). We should be grateful for and vigilant about our categories because these categories are the water we swim in.

CONCLUSION

> The after-the-fact, ex post, life-trailing nature of consciousness generally – occurrence first, formulation later on – appears in anthropology as a continual effort to devise systems of discourse that can keep up, more or less, with what, perhaps, is going on. (Geertz 1995, p. 19)

When I first read Clifford Geertz's book *After the Fact* it perfectly captured my non-anthropological life – I was constantly dropping in on a parade that had been going on while I was somehow away and trying to figure out what happened in the interim. I began this chapter with my own version of how consumer researchers moved from an abstract consumer to embrace a feeling, thinking doing person; began to embrace multiple ontologies; and established consumer culture theory as a category and legitimate sub-discipline. It is a story filled with chance omissions and commissions that have to do with my own dropping in and out of an ongoing parade.

I next described what I think might be four modest take-away lessons from this long journey to legitimacy. First, we must attend to the luck, chance and circumstances of our becoming an academic sub-discipline, and further recognize the collective risks of jockeying for relative position or taking credit for individual successes. As part of that, we must look for who was left out and disadvantaged by circumstance, *without placing intentionality or blame on other actors*.

Second, we must recognize and value the vital impact of peripheral actors in becoming a sub-discipline. People such as Jim Bettman, C.W. Park, Richard Lutz, many people I haven't mentioned, and my own dissertation advisor Rajendra Srivastava, only look like outsiders because of a special spin on our origin tale. Many others, unmentioned provoked us on our course. For my own part, I read Maurice Godelier (1973) and Arlie Hochschild (1979) accidentally as a PhD student, and they have been subtly influencing my course of thinking to the present day. And this caution is prospective, encouraging us to make sure we are welcoming and inviting of differences and disruption.

Third, labels and legitimacy have consequences. We should be highly attentive to what we gained (which was substantial), but also reflexive of what was hidden, missing, or absent from the process of containing and territorializing us. We must empower the vital collective imaginings of absences within and outside our community. Perhaps because snapchat is not a second skin, I'm attentive to how the world around me is changing – I teach from textbooks that seem like ancient scrolls – distant from the world we live in. We must be wary of what we are missing because we live in our labels.

Fourth, and relatedly, it is time to call into question whether consumer and consumption is the full scope and interest of our sub-discipline. Perhaps we should more attentively study the full continuum of how markets and people interact without neglecting the relatively un-alienated and creative production of people and social systems, as well as the repression and omission from market systems that thrives amidst all our reported predominance of branding and market activity. Moreover, I could be entirely wrong, but possibly marketing, as we know it, is going away. If so, we should be prepared to cast aside our labels, and embark on sojourns as imaginative, loosely equipped adventurers (not marauders) on the increasingly foreign planet earth.

REFERENCES

Anderson, P.F., 1986. On method in consumer research: a critical relativist perspective. *Journal of Consumer Research*, *13*(2), pp. 155–173.

Appadurai, A., 1988. *The Social Life of Things: Commodities in Cultural Perspective*. Cambridge: Cambridge University Press.

Arnould, E.J. and Price, L.L., 1993. River magic: Extraordinary experience and the extended service encounter. *Journal of Consumer Research*, *20*(1), pp. 24–45.

Arnould, E.J. and Thompson, C.J., 2005. Consumer culture theory (CCT): Twenty years of research. *Journal of consumer Research*, *31*(4), pp. 868–882.

Askegaard, S., 2014. Consumer Culture Theory–Neo-liberalism's 'useful idiots'?. *Marketing Theory*, *14*(4), pp. 507–511.

Askegaard, S. and Scott, L., 2013. Consumer culture theory: The ironies of history. *Marketing Theory*, *13*(2), pp. 139–147.

Bajde, D., 2013. Consumer culture theory (re)visits actor-network theory: Flattening consumption studies. *Marketing Theory*, *13*(2), pp. 227–242.

Bauman, Z., 2013. *Wasted Lives: Modernity and its Outcasts*. Chichester: John Wiley & Sons.

Becker, H.S., 2008. *Outsiders*. New York: Simon and Schuster.

Belk, R.W., 1987. ACR presidential address: Happy thought. *NA-Advances in Consumer Research Volume 14*.

Belk, R., 2014. The labors of the Odysseans and the legacy of the Odyssey. *Journal of Historical Research in Marketing*, *6*(3), pp. 379–404.

Belk, R.W., Wallendorf, M. and Sherry, J.F., 1989. The sacred and the profane in consumer behavior: Theodicy on the odyssey. *Journal of Consumer Research*, *16*(1), pp. 1–38.

Berry, L.L. and Parasuraman, A., 1993. Building a new academic field – The case of services marketing. *Journal of Retailing*, *69*(1), pp. 13–60.

Bode, M. and Østergaard, P., 2013. 'The wild and wacky worlds of consumer oddballs': Analyzing the manifestary context of consumer culture theory. *Marketing Theory*, *13*(2), pp.175–192.

Brown, S. and Schau, H.J., 2008. Writing Russell Belk: Excess all areas. *Marketing Theory*, *8*(2), pp. 143–165.

Chalmers Thomas, T., Price, L.L. and Schau, H.J., 2012. When differences unite: Resource dependence in heterogeneous consumption communities. *Journal of Consumer Research*, *39*(5), pp. 1010–1033.

Coskuner-Balli, G., 2013. Market practices of legitimization: Insights from consumer culture theory. *Marketing Theory*, *13*(2), pp. 193–211.

Coulter, R.A., 2016. From fragmentation to imagination: Moving to marketing's next era. *AMS Review*, *6*(3–4), pp. 132–141.

Cova, B., Maclaran, P. and Bradshaw, A., 2013. Rethinking consumer culture theory from the postmodern to the communist horizon. *Marketing Theory*, *13*(2), pp. 213–225.

Deleuze, G., 1994. *Difference and Repetition*. New York: Columbia University Press.

Douglas, M. and Isherwood, B., 1978. *The World of Goods*. Allen Lane, London, UK.

Epp, A.M. and Price, L.L., 2008. Family identity: A framework of identity interplay in consumption practices. *Journal of Consumer Research*, *35*(1), pp. 50–70.

Epp, A.M., Schau, H.J. and Price, L.L., 2014. The role of brands and mediating technologies in assembling long-distance family practices. *Journal of Marketing*, *78*(3), pp. 81–101.

Epp, A.M. and Velagaleti, S.R., 2014. Outsourcing parenthood? How families manage care assemblages using paid commercial services. *Journal of Consumer Research*, *41*(4), pp. 911–935.

Featherstone, M., 1991. *Consumer Culture and Postmodernism* (Vol. 6). London: Sage.

Firat, A.F. and Venkatesh, A., 1995. Liberatory postmodernism and the reenchantment of consumption. *Journal of Consumer Research*, *22*(3), pp. 239–267.

Fischer, E. and Bristor, J., 1994. A feminist poststructuralist analysis of the rhetoric of marketing relationships. *International Journal of Research in Marketing*, *11*(4), pp. 317–331.

Fitchett, J.A., Patsiaouras, G. and Davies, A., 2014. Myth and ideology in consumer culture theory. *Marketing Theory*, *14*(4), pp. 495–506.

Frank, R.H., 2010. *Luxury Fever: Weighing the Cost of Excess*. Princeton, NJ: Princeton University Press.

Frank, R.H., 2016. *Success and Luck: Good Fortune and the Myth of Meritocracy*. Princeton, NJ: Princeton University Press.

Friedman, T.L., 2016. *Thank You for Being Late: An Optimist's Guide to Thriving in the Age of Accelerations*. New York: Farrar, Straus and Giroux.

Geertz, C., 1996. *After the Fact* (Vol. 5). Cambridge, MA: Harvard University Press.

Godelier, M., 1973. *Rationality and Irrationality in Economics*.

Gordon, J., 2007. The mobile phone and the public sphere: Mobile phone usage in three critical situations. *Convergence*, *13*(3), pp. 307–319.

Graeber, D., Cluley, R., Harvie, D., Doukas, D., Girke, F., Hornborg, A., Stearns, P.N., Sutton, D. and Graeber, D., 2011. Consumption. *Current Anthropology*, *52*(4), pp. 489–511.

Hambrick, D.C. and Chen, M.J., 2008. New academic fields as admittance-seeking social movements: The case of strategic management. *Academy of Management Review*, *33*(1), pp. 32–54.

Harari, Y.N., 2014. *Sapiens: A Brief History of Humankind*. London: Random House.

Harari, Y.N., 2016. *Homo Deus: A Brief History of Tomorrow*. London: Random House.

Harman, G., 2013. An outline of object-oriented philosophy. *Science Progress*, *96*(2), pp. 187–199.

Hirschman, E.C., 1987. Adoption of an incredibly complex innovation: Propositions from a humanistic vantage point. In *NA-Advances in Consumer Research Volume 14*.

Hirschman, E.C., 1992. The consciousness of addiction: Toward a general theory of compulsive consumption. *Journal of Consumer Research*, *19*(2), pp. 155–179.

Hochschild, A.R., 1979. Emotion work, feeling rules, and social structure. *American Journal of Sociology*, *85*(3), pp. 551–575.

Holbrook, M.B. and Hirschman, E.C., 1982. The experiential aspects of consumption: Consumer fantasies, feelings, and fun. *Journal of Consumer Research*, *9*(2), pp. 132–140.

Holt, D.B., 1995. How consumers consume: A typology of consumption practices. *Journal of Consumer Research*, *22*(1), pp. 1–16.

Holt, D.B., 2002. Why do brands cause trouble? A dialectical theory of consumer culture and branding. *Journal of Consumer Research*, *29*(1), pp. 70–90.

Horst, H.A. and Miller, D. eds, 2013. *Digital Anthropology*. London: A&C Black.

Hudson, L.A. and Ozanne, J.L., 1988. Alternative ways of seeking knowledge in consumer research. *Journal of Consumer Research*, *14*(4), pp. 508–521.

Hunt, S.D., 1990. Truth in marketing theory and research. *The Journal of Marketing*, *54*(3), pp. 1–15.

Kassarjian, H.H., 1993. Presentation of the fellow award in consumer behavior to James R. Bettman. In *NA-Advances in consumer research*, 20 Provo, UT: Association for Consumer Research, p. 6.

Kohli, A., 2017. AMA distinguished educators' address. *Winter AMA*. Orlando, FL.

Kozinets, R.V., 2002. Can consumers escape the market? Emancipatory illuminations from Burning Man. *Journal of Consumer Research*, *29*(1), pp. 20–38.

Kozinets, R.V., 2015. *Netnography*. Chichester: John Wiley & Sons, Inc.
Levy, S.J., 2003. Roots of marketing and consumer research at the University of Chicago. *Consumption Markets & Culture*, *6*(2), pp. 99–110.
Lutz, R.J., 1989. Presidential address. Positivism, naturalism and pluralism in consumer research: Paradigms in paradise. *NA-Advances in Consumer Research Volume 16*.
MacInnis, D.J. and Folkes, V.S., 2010. The disciplinary status of consumer behavior: A sociology of science perspective on key controversies. *Journal of Consumer Research*, *36*(6), pp. 899–914.
Merton, R.K., 1973. *The Sociology of Science: Theoretical and Empirical Investigations*. Chicago: University of Chicago Press.
Mick, D.G., 2006. Meaning and mattering through transformative consumer research. *Advances in Consumer Research*, *33*(1), pp. 1–4.
Mick, D.G., Pettigrew, S., Pechmann, C.C. and Ozanne, J.L. eds, 2012. *Transformative Consumer Research for Personal and Collective Well-being*. New York: Routledge.
Miller, D., 1987. *Material Culture and Mass Consumption*. New York: Basil Blackwell Inc.
Moisio, R., Arnould, E.J. and Price, L.L., 2004. Between mothers and markets: Constructing family identity through homemade food. *Journal of Consumer Culture*, *4*(3), pp. 361–384.
Nag, R., Hambrick, D.C. and Chen, M.J., 2007. What is strategic management, really? Inductive derivation of a consensus definition of the field. *Strategic Management Journal*, *28*(9), pp. 935–955.
Nielsen, M., 2012. *Reinventing Discovery: The New Era of Networked Science*. Princeton, NJ: Princeton University Press.
Nunnally, J.C. and Bernstein, I., 1994. *Psychometric Theory*, New York, NY: McGraw-Hill.
Park, C.W., 1982. Joint decisions in home purchasing: A muddling-through process. *Journal of Consumer Research*, *9*(2), pp. 151–162.
Parmentier, M.A. and Fischer, E., 2015. Things fall apart: The dynamics of brand audience dissipation. *Journal of Consumer Research*, *41*(5), pp. 1228–1251.
Penaloza, L. and Price, L.L., 1993. Consumer resistance: A conceptual overview. *NA-Advances in Consumer Research Volume 20*.
Price, L.L., 2012. Materiality and identity, in A.A. Ruvio and R.W. Belk (eds) *The Routledge Companion to Identity and Consumption*. Abingdon: Routledge, pp. 302–312.
Price, L.L., 2014. ACR Presidential Address. Obliquity, wonderment and the grand adventure of doing consumer research. In *NA-Advances in Consumer Research, Volume 22*. Duluth: Association for Consumer Research, pp. 1–5.
Price, L.L., 2015a. Loyalty and brands in consumers' assembled lives. In S. Fournier, M. Breazeale and J. Avery (eds) *Strong Brands, Strong Relationships*. New York: Routledge Press, pp. 13–27.
Price, L.L., 2015b. The role of theory in a big, deep, fast data driven world. Plenary talk, *Asia Pacific ACR*, Hong Kong, China.
Price, L.L. and Epp, A.M., 2015. The heterogeneous and open-ended project of assembling family. In R. Canniford and D. Bajde (eds) *Assembling Consumption: Researching Actors, Networks and Markets*. Abingdon: Routledge, pp. 59–76.
Price, L.L. and Arnould, E.J., 1999. Commercial friendships: service provider-client relationships in context. *The Journal of Marketing*, pp. 38–56.
Price, L.L. Arnould, E.J. and Moisio, R., 2006. Making contexts matter: Selecting research contexts for theoretical insights. In R.W. Belk (ed) *Handbook of Qualitative Research Methods in Marketing*. Cheltenham: Edward Elgar, pp. 106–125.
Rindfleisch, A. and O'Hern, M., 2015. Brand remixing: 3D printing the Nokia case. In D. J. Macinnis and C. W. Park (eds) *Brand Meaning Management*. UK: Emerald Group Publishing Limited. pp. 53–81.

Sassatelli, R., 2007. *Consumer Culture: History, Theory and Politics*. London: Sage.

Scaraboto, D., 2015. Selling, sharing, and everything in between: The hybrid economies of collaborative networks. *Journal of Consumer Research*, *42*(1), pp. 152–176.

Sherry, J.F., 1983. Gift giving in anthropological perspective. *Journal of Consumer Research*, *10*(2), pp. 157–168.

Sherry, J.F., 1990. A sociocultural analysis of a Midwestern American flea market. *Journal of Consumer Research*, *17*(1), pp. 13–30.

Sherry Jr, J.F., 1991. Postmodern alternatives: The interpretive turn in consumer research. In T. Robertson and H. Karsarjian (eds) *Handbook of Consumer Research*. Englewood Cliffs, NJ: Prentice Hall, pp. 548–591.

Sherry, J.F. and Schouten, J.W., 2002. A role for poetry in consumer research. *Journal of Consumer Research*, *29*(2), pp. 218–234.

Tadajewski, M., 2006. Remembering motivation research: Toward an alternative genealogy of interpretive consumer research. *Marketing Theory*, 6(4), pp. 429–466.

Taleb, N.N., 2012. *Antifragile: How to Live in a World We Don't Understand* (Vol. 3). London: Allen Lane.

Tucker, W.T., 1974. Future directions in marketing theory. *The Journal of Marketing*, *38*(2), pp. 30–35.

Tversky, A. and Kahneman, D., 1975. Judgment under uncertainty: Heuristics and biases. In D. Wendt and C. Vlek (eds) *Utility, Probability, and Human Decision Making*. Springer Netherlands, pp. 141–162.

Tversky, A. and Kahneman, D., 1975. Judgment under uncertainty: Heuristics and biases. In *Utility, probability, and human decision making* (pp. 141–162). Springer Netherlands.

Vargo, S.L. and Lusch, R.F., 2011. It's all B2B ... and beyond: Toward a systems perspective of the market. *Industrial Marketing Management*, *40*(2), pp. 181–187.

Warde, A., 2015. The sociology of consumption: Its recent development. *Annual Review of Sociology*, *41*, pp. 117–134.

Weick, K.E., 2006. Faith, evidence, and action: Better guesses in an unknowable world. *Organization Studies*, *27*(11), pp. 1723–1736.

Whitley, R., 1984. *The Social and Intellectual Organization of the Sciences*. Oxford: Oxford University Press.

Wilk, R., 2004. Questionable assumptions about sustainable consumption. In L.A. Reisch and I Røpke (eds) *The Ecological Economics of Consumption*. Cheltenham: Edward Elgar, pp. 17–22.

Zaltman, G., 1983. Presidential address. In *NA-Advances in Consumer Research*, *Volume 10*, Ann Arbor, MI: Association for Consumer Research, pp. 1–5.

Zaltman, G., 2000. Consumer researchers: take a hike!. *Journal of Consumer Research*, *26*(4), pp. 423–428.

Zaltman, G., 2016. Marketing's forthcoming age of imagination. *AMS Review*, 6(3–4), pp. 99–115.

12

Consumer Identity Projects

Gretchen Larsen and Maurice Patterson

> In late capitalism, consumption is the arena where personal and group identities are fought over, contested, precariously put together and licked into shape. The Western consumer readily transfigures into an identity seeker. Whether choosing goods, exploring them, buying them, displaying them, disfiguring them or giving them away, consumers are, above all, frequently presented as thirsting for identity and using commodities to quench this thirst. (Gabriel and Lang 2006: 79)

INTRODUCTION

The use of goods in the service of identity projects is widely acknowledged as a central concern within contemporary consumer culture (Arnould and Thompson 2005; Belk 1988; Bocock 1993). Indeed, it has become something of a truism within studies of consumers to suggest that consumption is the core arena within which personal and collective identities are constructed, performed and contested. It must be recognized, however, that such a suggestion may also be an effect of the theoretical and analytical focus within the field of research on consumer culture (Shankar et al. 2009) in combination with a hermeneutic research approach that 'focuses on the symbolic meanings and processes by which individuals construct a coherent sense of self-identity (i.e. a life narrative)' (Thompson 1996: 389).

To sustain and fuel the consumer demand underpinning economic growth, the market encourages and lionizes individualization and individuality (Jafari and Goulding 2008), qualities made manifest through freedom of choice, the 'core value and emblem' (Gabriel and Lang 2006) of contemporary consumer culture. Through choice, *consumers* are able to pursue fulfillment, autonomy and freedom (Bauman 1988) and, ultimately, endeavor to 'become' (Giddens 1991). In this regard, consumers have long been understood as identity-seekers (Arnould and Thompson 2005; Gabriel and Lang 2006). As a result, the *identity project* takes center stage in depictions of contemporary consumption and under these circumstances all consumer choices impact upon identity and come to represent it to the outside world (Miles 1999).

Fundamentally, the notion of the identity project suggests that people are actively concerned about the creation, enhancement, transformation and maintenance of a sense of identity (Bardhi et al. 2012; Belk 1988). Consumption is argued to perform a vital service in this regard by anchoring and buttressing identity (Bardhi et al. 2012; McCracken 1986), facilitating on-going negotiations across time (Syrjälä 2016) that bolster past lives and pre-empt future opportunities for self-making (Epp and Price 2008; Hill 1991). Further, the cultural imperative to work upon identity has become inescapable, demanding symbolic work of consumers at unprecedented levels such that they process 'an ever-expanding supply of fashions, cultural texts, tourist experiences, cuisines, mass cultural icons, and the like' (Holt 2002: 87). This cultural imperative is underscored by the waning influence of long-established social categories such as class, gender and occupation (Bocock 1993) and by the dilemmas of the self (Giddens 1991) that include 'fragmentation, powerlessness, uncertainty and a struggle against commodification' (Elliott and Wattanasuwan 1998: 131).

Identity work, then, necessitates the shrewd deployment of products and brands, their meanings, and the discourses surrounding them, such that a person is seen to be consuming the right *stuff* in the right ways (Belk et al. 1989; Bengtsson et al. 2005; Cronin et al. 2014; Elliott and Wattanasuwan 1998; Gabriel and Lang 2006; Lury 1996; McCracken 1990). What is more, this negotiation of identity is influenced not only by embracing particular kinds of consumption but also by efforts to resist, abandon and avoid particular consumption artifacts, patterns and meanings (Hogg et al. 2009; Thompson and Haytko 1997; Wattanasuwan 2005). Moreover, achieving distinction and difference through these means relies increasingly on an ability to individuate and re-elaborate the material and symbolic offerings of the market (Arnould and Thompson 2005; Holt 1998).

Meanwhile, and despite the urge towards individuality, we continue to deploy consumption to help us connect to collective identities; that is, we also pursue sameness in either its objective or subjective forms (Brubaker and Cooper 2000). As Elliott and Wattanasuwan (1998) contend, identity work is not only directed inward in respect of the self-symbolism of consumption, it is also directed outward in the urge towards collective identities through social symbolism because 'even sovereign identities require the interpretive support of others to give them ballast' (Holt 2002: 83). These collective identities have been variously referred to as subcultures of consumption (Kozinets 2001; Schouten and McAlexander 1995), consumer tribes (Cova 1997; Cova et al. 2007; Goulding et al. 2009; Goulding, Shankar and Canniford 2013) and brand communities (McAlexander et al. 2002; Muñiz and O'Guinn 2001; Schau et al. 2009).

The declining influence of traditional cultural institutions (McAlexander et al. 2014), the devolution of responsibility to the individual, and the sheer volume of choices open to consumers have conspired to make identity projects ever more complex (Seregina and Schouten 2017). Further compounding matters are a marketing culture that actively promotes a veritable production line of potential, though increasingly unstable identity positions from which to choose (Goulding et al. 2002; Kellner 1992). Part of such complexity includes the multiplicity of identities that consumers are called upon to negotiate. According to Carrington et al. (2015), consumers may deal with such multiplicity by embracing it (Firat and Venkatesh 1995; Goulding et al. 2009), managing it by pursuing a coherent identity narrative (Murray 2002; Thompson 1996; Thompson and Haytko 1997), or by deploying a range of coping strategies (Ahuvia 2005; Schau and Gilly 2003).

We continue the discussion of consumer identity projects in this chapter by first outlining a number of perspectives on identity in consumer culture. Next we take up the nature of consumer identity projects as drawing from the internal-external dialectic of identification (Jenkins 2014), and trace the outline of their emancipatory potential. Following consideration of the very real limits imposed on at least some consumers in terms of their ability to engage in identity play, we begin a process of rethinking the connections between consumption and identity against the backdrop of processes of stigmatization.

PERSPECTIVES ON IDENTITY IN CONSUMER CULTURE

The notion of identity is ubiquitous and pervasive, applying to all living creatures including humans, as well as to things and substances. As such, identity is a concept that many of us feel we intuitively understand – it is, at its most basic, 'the human capacity – rooted in language – to know who's who (and hence what's what). This involves knowing who we are, knowing who others are, them knowing who we are, us knowing who they think we are and so on' (Jenkins 2014: 6). Given the importance of identity projects in consumer culture, and thus in contemporary life, it would be easy to assume that identity is a fundamentally modern concern. In fact, research and theory development on identity has a long history both within studies of consumption (Arnould and Thompson 2005; Joy and Li 2012) and across the broader social sciences. This broad foundation has led, inevitably, to a multitude of definitions and conceptualizations, a full summary of which is beyond the scope of this chapter. It remains important, however, to position the identity project amongst the various perspectives on identity within consumer culture research. Specifically, two further perspectives can be observed (see Gabriel and Lang 2006), both of which are rooted in different ontological positions: ascribed identity and achieved/acquired identity. The prevalence of each perspective across the history of consumer research broadly aligns with the development of the discipline from its psychological origins to a more recent understanding embedded in cultural perspectives (Arnould and Thompson 2005, 2007; Holbrook 1995).

Ascribed identity is an outcome of family lineage and a function of social roles defined by the contingencies of birth (Jenkins 2014) and is therefore unitary, stable and solid (Kellner 1992). It is a fairly essentialist position in that one is born, for example, a woman, a prince, a member of a particular class and/or religion, and that defines one's place in the world and provides an orientation to social life. The duality of the criteria for identifying a thing or person – similarity and difference – is evident in this perspective. These criteria derive from the Latin root of the term *identity* – late Latin *identitas* from *idem* same (*Oxford Dictionary of English*) and which stands for sameness, continuity and distinctiveness (Gabriel and Lang 2006). Thus ascribed identity simultaneously specifies with whom a person is the same and from whom they are different, and it is fixed. As noted by Gabriel and Lang (2006: 80):

> no matter what transformations are undertaken by the individual, his or her identity cannot change. Nor is identity a matter of choice, will or desire; identity is the outcome of family lineage. In this case, confusion over identity, amounts to confusion over parenthood – i.e. this is confusion over facts and not meanings.

From the point of view of an advanced industrialized society, it would be all too easy to write this perspective off as historical and anachronistic. However, there are millions of people globally who do not live in such conditions, and for whom ascribed identities are still of utmost centrality (Shankar et al. 2009). For example, Üstüner and Holt (2007: 46) investigate the identities of poor migrant women living in a Turkish squatter and find that 'women's identities constructed within this milieu – as brides, wives, and mothers – were relatively stable, rarely understood reflexively as identities, and never questioned ... The concept of identity project was not applicable'.

The second main perspective on identity in consumer culture, is captured in the notion of achieved/acquired identity, which is a subjective, changing identity achieved with the aid of others throughout the life course (Jenkins 2014). Embedded in the disciplines of psychology and sociology, achieved/acquired identity revises the qualities of ascribed identity and introduces new features (Gabriel and Lang 2006). Through his work with traumatized World War II soldiers who had lost their sense of self, the psychologist Erikson recognized that identity is not something ascribed or fixed, but rather is achieved through interaction with others. Subsequently, the *identity crisis* is a normal stage of ego development in late adolescence and early adulthood from which the ideal and happiest outcome is the achievement of an integrated coherent identity in which the individual is conscious of both their similarity and difference (Erikson 1950/1995). The sociological perspective highlights that achieved/acquired identity is forged in the social sphere and temporally located: a sense of past, present and future infuses achieved/acquired identity. Jenkins (2014) argues that identity, then, is not so much a fixed possession as it is a social process in which the individual and the social are inextricably related. Here, identity is subjective, coherent, sometimes precarious and the result of psychological and social work (Gabriel and Lang 2006). The importance of material objects in the process of identification is key, as encapsulated in the significant body of consumer research arising from Belk's (1988) seminal work on the extended self.

Jenkins (2014) notes that, in reality, the difference between perspectives on identity (ascribed, achieved/acquired, and worked upon identity projects), is not clear-cut but is more likely to be a matter of emphasis. While the consumer identity project (detailed in the next section) is the prevalent perspective in consumer culture research (Arnould and Thompson 2005), it is important to acknowledge that these perspectives are not easily disentangled theoretically or in lived experience. For example, a person's gender identity is complex and complicated. Biological sex (determined by physical features such as external genitalia and internal reproductive structures) is ascribed at birth, and therefore used to identify a person as male or female. But this ascribed identity also intersects with that person's internal sense of gender across a diversity of binary and non-binary positions; their outward expressions and presentations of gender; society's norms and expectations surrounding gender roles; as well as other social roles. Gender identity can thus be understood simultaneously as ascribed, achieved/acquired and as an on-going project, all of which intersect in a multitude of ways with the market and consumer culture (e.g. Hein and O'Donohoe 2014; Thompson and Üstüner 2015).

CONSUMER IDENTITY PROJECTS

Contemporary consumer society has emerged as part of a historical process that has led to advanced, capitalist political-economies, which are dominated by the logic of economic growth and characterized by mass markets and cultural attitudes that ensure that rising incomes are used to purchase an ever-growing output of market offerings (e.g. Chatzidakis et al. 2014). Economic forces push towards commodification; where undifferentiated goods are produced *en masse* at minimal cost. Meanwhile, no (figurative or actual) stone is left unturned as the market penetrates every conceivable aspect of our lives, from nature (Castree 2003; Duffy 2008; Igoe 2010), to culture (Ritzer and Liska 1997; Shepherd 2002; Tzanelli 2008), and even to those aspects connected to commercial intimacy, for example human tissue and organs, corpses, babies, human eggs, surrogacy and sexuality (Fennel 2009; Goulding, Saren and Lindridge 2013; Laufer-Ukeles 2013).

Set against the backdrop of this commodification of life (Bauman 2007; Kellner 1983), consumer identity projects incorporate the productive dimensions of marketplace consumption, mobilized in the service of identity narratives and involving the creative negotiation of cultural contradictions (Arnould and Thompson 2007; Thompson 2014; Thompson and Haytko 1997). Identity work, then, is portrayed as a reflexive (Giddens 1991), continuous (Cherrier and Murray 2007; Elliott 2004), interminable (Gabriel and Lang 2006) symbolic project (Mikkonen et al. 2011; Thompson 1996). Its purpose is to produce a coherent narrative of the self from marketplace resources that connects the past, present and future (Ahuvia 2005; Marion and Nairn 2011; Mikkonen et al. 2011). In this way, identity may be considered 'as ideology cognized through the individual engagement with discourse, made manifest in a personal narrative constructed and reconstructed across the life course and scripted in and through social interaction and social practice' (Hammack 2008: 2).

The identity project is reflexive and continuous in the sense that the narrative is always being revised as early chapters are rewritten 'so that the activity of writing becomes itself part of the story' (Gabriel and Lang 2006: 83). Of course, the constant revision and fluctuation of identity in these ways also suggests that such projects can be troubled and sometimes characterized by ambivalence (Kozinets 2001; Michael 2015), compensation (Rucker and Galinsky 2008; Woodruffe 1997), contradictions (Carrington et al. 2015; Luedicke et al. 2010), complexity (Harrison and Thomas 2013; Holt and Thompson 2004) and dysfunction (Lastovicka and Sirianni 2011; Reith and Dobbie 2012). Further, in charting the life stories of individuals, identity projects may involve loss (Üstüner and Holt 2007), movement (Ruvio and Belk 2013; Schau et al. 2009) and experimentation with identities over the life course, but particularly during major life transitions (Schau et al. 2009) or *turning points* (Syrjälä 2016). Indeed, identity work has no end and may even continue after death as identities enacted during a person's lifetime are renegotiated post-mortem during consumption-laden funeral rites (Bonsu and Belk 2003).

In all of this the consumption and dispossession (Cherrier and Murray 2007; Türe 2014), of goods, services, ideas and experiences, or even disgust towards them (Morales and Wu 2013), are treated as productive forces because 'the marketplace has become a preeminent source of mythic and symbolic resources through which people, including those who lack resources to participate in the market as full-fledged consumers, construct narratives of identity' (Arnould and Thompson 2005: 871). For their part, marketers have worked tirelessly to connect their offerings to the idea of unique selfhood (Grainge 2000). Epp and Price (2008) detail how the meanings associated with consumption objects, activities and patterns may connect us to a sense of the past (Belk 1991; Brown et al. 2003; Goulding 2001), facilitate identity transition (Hogg et al. 2004; Schouten 1991; VOICE 2010), and generally signal multiple aspects of identity going forward. And yet, while consumption meanings are generally considered to be central to this entire project (Elliott 1997; Holt 1995; Levy 1959; McCracken 1986), Gabriel and Lang (2006) suggest that some consumption objects may rely less on meanings than they do on powerful, if temporary, images. Moreover, recent research (e.g. Bardhi et al. 2012) contends that in an era of liquid modernity (Bauman 2000) some people, such as global nomads, may reject the symbolic, identity-relevant aspects of consumption in favor of a more practical, detached and flexible logic.

Such movements bring to light dialectical tensions between the agency of individual consumers to play with or resist marketplace meanings, and the power of structural processes to colonize such creative experimentation and to dominate meanings (Holt 2002; Kozinets et al. 2004; Murray 2002; see Handelman and Fischer, Chapter 15 this volume). While the pursuit of identity is considered to be the main goal of consumers (Thompson 2014), and the realization of distinction is apparently achieved through the ability to manipulate and play with market-based meanings (Holt 1998), marketplace discourses are nonetheless discourses of power that work to direct consumers' choices and decisions, and, ultimately, guide identities down particular avenues (Thompson 2004). The specter of structure and agency in this regard has long dogged work on consumer culture (Askegaard and Linnet 2011). It may be that we are naturally inclined to favor agentic representations because 'a sharp focus on culture's potentialities is naturally understood as the appropriate course' (Hays 1994: 60) and, in a manner similar to Cultural Studies, consumer research becomes a field of analysis set up to track down resistances (Bennett 1998). Thus, in studying identity projects we need to be mindful of the degree to which individual consumers can forge their own path or are constrained by the discourses of the consumption system. Peñaloza (2001) and Holt and Thompson (2004) underline the importance of considering how marketplace discourses are at one and the same time enabling and constraining, both facilitating consumers' abilities to play with identity while also circumscribing them, entertaining consumers while inculcating them, so that:

'commercial myth making can ... function as an ideological process that merges entertainment, education and indoctrination' (Thompson and Tian 2008: 596). For Parmentier and Fischer (2011) this culture-producing role of marketers is particularly relevant to the work of cultural intermediaries who straddle the production/consumption divide and who may feel more constrained, therefore, by marketplace discourses. The same is true of institutional insiders who may wish to push through institutional change but who are trapped by the fact that they have internalized the myths, discourses and values of the industry (Scaraboto and Fischer 2013). In the end, the outcomes of these negotiations between individual goals and the opportunities afforded by the marketplace may include hegemonic, counter-hegemonic, and hybrid identities (Kates 2002; Üstüner and Holt 2007).

In an effort to deepen our understanding of consumer identity projects in consumer culture, we now explore underlying junctures in the literature. The first of which is the relationship between the individual and the collective.

THE INTERNAL-EXTERNAL DIALECTIC OF IDENTIFICATION

Historically research on identity in consumption has taken the individual as the focal unit of analysis and theorization (Hirschman 1981; Shankar et al. 2009). This is primarily due to the origins of consumer research in psychology (Elliott 2004; Holbrook 1995), the corresponding focus on achieved/acquired identity (Gabriel and Lang 2006), and the emphasis in advanced capitalist markets on the individual and difference (Jafari and Goulding 2008). Much of this literature uses the term *self* (e.g. Belk 1988; Grubb and Grathwohl 1967; Sirgy 1982), which Jenkins (2014: 51) argues is a parallel concept to identity: 'the self [is] an individual's reflexive sense of her or his own particular identity, constituted *vis à vis* others in terms of similarity and difference, without which she or he wouldn't know who they are and hence wouldn't be able to act'. However, a consumer culture perspective on identity aligns with cultural studies and sociology (Arnould and Thompson 2005, 2007) and requires a shift in focus from the individual to the interactions between individuals, the collective, and the socio-cultural context. Jenkins (2014) describes identity as a meta-concept that makes sense both individually and collectively, and which is therefore significant for debates about the individual-collective relationship: 'it brings together C. Wright Mills's public issues and private troubles and makes sense of each in terms of the other' (Jenkins 2014: 17). He describes this as the internal-external dialectic of identification: where the development of individual identity and the determination of collective social identity are inseparable. Identity work is thus embedded in social practice (Elliott and Wattanasuwan 1998).

Research on consumer culture has specifically sought to 'address the dynamic relationship between consumer actions, the marketplace and cultural meanings' (Arnould and Thompson 2005: 868), and thus elucidates the internal-external dialectic of identification as it plays out in the context of markets and consumption. Consumer identity projects are realized through social interaction and validation (Shankar et al. 2009). For example, individual identity projects in the consumption space of a rave are oriented towards the Other and are largely dependent on group approval and acceptance (Goulding et al. 2002). In the world of fashion, consumer identity is consistently defined in perceived contrast to others and interpreted through metonymic use of fashion imagery (Thompson and Haytko 1997). The identity positions available are, along with rules and tastes, produced and reproduced collaboratively by its members (Parmentier and Fischer 2011), and hence personal identity in fashion 'does not reflect a stable set of essential features but is negotiated in a dynamic field of social relations' (Thompson and Haytko 1997: 21). Collective identities, such as that of the family, are also co-constructed in social action through shared interactions among relational bundles within the family and communicative practices such as the symbolic consumption of marketplace resources (Epp and Price 2008).

Moving beyond a focus on the construction of identity, Askegaard and Linnet (2011: 396) argue that if research on consumer identity projects seeks to elucidate consumer culture (and thus the external side of the dialectic), then 'it should acknowledge the cultural, historical and societal conditions that make this identity and the means of attaining it attractive and legitimate in the first place'. Once such condition is that of morality, which reflects a collective's standards or principles regarding *proper* conduct. Luedicke et al. (2010) study adversarial consumer narratives relating to the Hummer brand and show that consumers' moralistic identity work begins with a cultural myth of the moral protagonist, which transforms their ideological beliefs into dramatic narratives of identity. The literature on market-based collectives, such as brand communities and subcultures of consumption, underlines how consumer identity projects are socially, historically and culturally constituted and bound (see Cova and Dali, Chapter 14 this volume). Brand communities and subcultures of consumption are distinguished from subcultures by their embeddedness within the market and consumption practices (Muñiz and O'Guinn 2001; Schouten and McAlexander 1995). However, while subcultures were once viewed as cells of resistance against dominant orders such as the mass market, 'today, sub-cultural activity is recognized as important for the construction and expression of identity ... As such, this activity involves acts of consumption' (Goulding et al. 2002: 263). It is widely accepted that such collectives, both market-based and counter-cultural, provide influential meanings and practices that structure consumers' identities, actions and relationships (Hebdige 1979; Kozinets 2001; Schouten and McAlexander 1995). Inevitably, this raises issues of structure and agency once more, and so this becomes the next juncture in the literature on consumer identity projects to be explored.

EMANCIPATORY POTENTIAL

The notion of choice lies at the very center of the consumer identity project:

> Each of the small decisions a person makes every day – what to wear, what to eat, how to conduct himself at work, whom to meet later in the evening – contribute to such routines. All such choices (as well as larger and more consequential ones) are decisions not only about how to act but who to be. (Giddens 1991: 81)

For Giddens (1991) and many others (e.g. Arnould and Thompson 2005; Elliott and Wattanasuwan 1998; Gabriel and Lang 2006), contemporary individuals perpetually pursue, create, enhance, transform and maintain their identities through the continuous making of choices, many of which are consumption choices. Naturally, an interesting question emerges here about how much choice consumers really have. Warde (1994) notes that the reality of choice lies at the very center of debates about the sociology of consumption. As noted earlier in this chapter, discussions about the nature of symbolic resources used in consumer identity projects bring to light dialectical tensions between the agency of individual consumers to play with (Holt 1998) and choose from among marketplace offerings, and the structural power of the market and its agents in shaping and directing those choices (Thompson 2004).

Drawing on Libertarian principles of distributive justice, *choice* has become enshrined as the key consumer right (Consumers International 2009) and, thus, it underpins most government policies and legislation that shape markets (Larsen and Lawson 2013). As choice also lies at the very heart of democracy, locating it as the central value of markets ideologically positions them as tools of democracy (Turner, 1995) and routes to citizen (consumer) empowerment and emancipation (Barnes and Prior 1995; Firat and Dholakia 2016; Trentmann 2016). Given the conflation of consumer choice, democracy and empowerment in contemporary consumer societies, it is perhaps not entirely surprising that the consumer identity project is often framed as both emancipatory and agentic (see Schwartzkopf, Chapter 25 this volume).

The agentic and emancipatory view of consumer identity projects is rooted in the work of Firat and Venkatesh (1995) on liberatory postmodernism in consumption. The postmodern sensibility helps break down traditional social categories, such as ethnicity and religion, and paves the way for the fragmentation of culture and society and the emergence of multiple, heterogeneous, pluralistic and individualistic discourses and subjectivities. Firat and Venkatesh (1995) view this fragmentation as a potentially liberating force, freeing the consumer from conformity, offering them the opportunity for creativity in the use of commodities and market-mediated meanings in identity projects (e.g. Holt 2002; Marion and Nairn 2011), and allowing them the latitude to establish their own social ties, communities, social groups and cultures (Ulusoy 2016). While this freedom is not without challenge, obligation and consequence (McAlexander et al. 2014), contexts such as the rave provide opportunities to play with different identities through consumption, and are 'part of what might be termed the trend towards compartmentalized lifestyles whereby one identity (the responsible worker) is shed and another adopted' (Goulding et al. 2002: 263). This kind of fragmented consumption, where the same consumer can show multiple preferences towards the same product category, is not bound only to extraordinary experiences, but is also illustrated in the diversity of practices surrounding such mundane consumption as weekday dinners (Holttinen 2014).

A key critique of the emancipatory potential of the postmodern consumer identity project challenges the assumption of full and unfettered freedom of choice, and argues that consumers' choices, and thus their identity projects, are at least in part structured in and through the market. Taken to the extreme, the structural perspective would argue that choice is an illusion, which acts as a mechanism of control in the service of capital (Gabriel and Lang 2006). However, as argued by Hays (1994: 59), 'when social theorists use structure and agency as contrast terms (agency is what structure is not, and vice versa), they neglect the interconnected nature of the two'. Structuring influences such as narratives of socialization (Shankar et al. 2009) and cultural ideologies (Coulter et al. 2003) have most certainly been identified, but the acknowledgement of at least a small amount of agency is necessary as it reflects a foundational element of the consumer identity project as reflexive (Giddens 1991), continuous (Cherrier and Murray 2007; Elliott 2004) and symbolic (Mikkonen et al. 2011; Thompson 1996.

Arnould and Thompson (2007: 10) argue that a consumer culture approach to consumer identity projects discards what they call the 'stale polemic' between agency and structure, and rather interrogates a 'more complex and ambivalent dynamic in which consumers exert agency and pursue identity goals through a dialogue (both practical and narrative) with the cultural frames imposed by dominant ideologies'. They cite a number of studies in support of their claim: Askegaard et al. (2005); Belk et al. (2003); Crockett and Wallendorf (2004); Holt (2002); Kozinets (2002); Peñaloza (2001); Thompson (2004); to which we would also add more recent publications such as Karababa and Ger (2011); Luedicke et al. (2010); Parmentier and Fischer (2011); Sandikci and Ger (2010); and Ulusoy (2016). However, Askegaard and Linnet (2011: 396) argue that while the consumer culture approach has bought socio-cultural context to consumer research, we still need to go further and provide accounts of the 'context of contexts: societal class divisions, historical and global processes, cultural values and norms' in order to situate consumption beyond the subjectivity of the agent and to better understand the underlying ideological forces producing such subjectivities.

THE LIMITS OF IDENTITY PLAY

In engaging with identity projects consumers are driven by a call to compulsory individuality (Skeggs and Loveday 2012) and an ideology of reflexivity, self-discipline, enterprise and improvement (Allen 2014). The narration of identity reverberates with the constant pressure to make the right decisions because, while the story may ultimately be rewritten, failure to meet with normalized ideals is indicative of the inadequacy of the self and its consumption (Slater 1997). Further, individuals must be enterprising in their efforts, embracing instability and uncertainty, for 'enterprising qualities – such as self-reliance, personal responsibility, boldness and a willingness to take risks in the pursuit of goals – are regarded as human virtues and promoted as such' (Du Gay 1996: 56). The goals for all of these efforts are aspirational (Allen 2014) as individuals are called upon to lift themselves up by their bootstraps and better themselves (Askegaard et al. 2002; Joy and Venkatesh 1994). In these ways consumers are summoned to focus their energies upon their identities, to be successful in those endeavors, and to make the fruits of their labor public.

At a fundamental level such identity work requires individuals to mobilize a set of resources including those that are economic, social, cultural and symbolic (Skeggs 2004). Subsequently, and in light of the commodification of everyday life, identities can be ascribed exchange-value (Bauman 2007) and function as capital (Bourdieu 1984), which may be subsequently converted to other forms of capital. However, this exchange-value of identities is circumscribed and only operates effectively within particular social fields (Skeggs 2004) and when carried by particular individuals (Allen 2014).

The notion that everybody wants to, or can, engage with identity projects in this way largely ignores class distinctions and the relative access to resources (Skeggs 2014; Smith Maguire and Stanway 2008). 'It is significant that assumptions proliferate about how individuals have equal access to the cultural resources for self-making, as if the self can be entirely divorced from the conditions that make it possible' (Skeggs 2004: 75). Moreover, the signaling of valuable identities to others requires that individuals have the ability to engage effectively with aesthetic performance and public display (Francombe-Webb and Silk 2016) and that others will read those performances in the way in which they were intended (Allen 2014; Patterson and Schroeder 2010; Skeggs 2005). Finally, for those who lack the necessary resources to narrate their identities through consumption, for those who are excluded and for whom such identity work is out of reach, resistance may be possible in the rejection of the neoliberal agenda and in protest against the system, environmental degradation, and such like (Skeggs 2014).

CONCLUSION: RETHINKING CONSUMER IDENTITY PROJECTS

Identity projects are market-mediated, and thus, when investing in the singularity of the self, consumers are fed a mass-marketed, pre-packaged, commodified form of difference (Halnon 2005). What we see, then, is that individualism and commodification are not dichotomous, but operate in dialectical tension where changes in one stimulate changes in the other (Campbell 2005). A major outcome of such contradictions is that, in the matter of identity, consumers operate under tremendous strain as they seek to negotiate both personalized and commodified experiences (Thompson and Haytko 1997). Indeed, individuals are always in danger of getting it wrong (Smith Maguire and Stanway 2008) precisely because identity projects have become a matter of individual choice. While excessive choice produces its own anxieties (Schwartz 2005), making the 'wrong' choices results in individuals suffering the further injustice of having their efforts read back onto them 'as an individualized moral fault, a pathology, a problem of bad-choice, bad culture, a failure to be enterprising or to be reflexive' (Skeggs 2004: 91); that is, they are stigmatized. While we acknowledge that most of the literature on identity projects is positive in the sense of charting the myriad ways consumers forge identities for themselves, we are interested in this section of the chapter in teasing out a more nuanced characterization by working with the question of what happens when identity projects go wrong.

In addressing stigma, consumer researchers have relied heavily on Goffman's (1963: 3) exposition of it as 'an attribute that is deeply discrediting', where, on the basis of perceived 'difference' or 'deviance', the bearer is reduced 'from a whole and usual person to a tainted, discounted one'. According to Parker and Aggleton (2003), the emphasis placed by Goffman on stigma as a discrediting attribute has seen it treated subsequently as though it were a relatively static characteristic. Further, the focus on the bearer's possession of an 'undesirable difference' has promoted highly individualized analyses. In contrast, in their recent coverage of stigma Sandikci and Ger (2013) urge consumer research to move beyond the socio-cognitive perspective concentrated on individuals, and to recognize stigmatization as a socially embedded process in which both difference and sameness represent important poles in the negotiation of identity. Nowhere are these twin forces of difference and sameness more visible than in the contemporary conditions of production and consumption where the macro level context of commodification and marketization (e.g. Adorno 1991; Attali 1984) intersects with micro-level, everyday consumption logics and practices, at the center of which lies the identity project (Arnould and Thompson 2005).

Recent analyses have evidenced how consumers might respond under these pressures. For example, Thompson and Haytko (1997) point towards a narrative strategy of decommodification, exemplified in the combination of different brands, and that allows consumers of mass-market fashion to carve out a space for uniqueness and personal agency. Harju and Huovinen (2015) identify a range of practices designed to negotiate sameness and difference that they position as similarity-seeking and diversity-asserting tactics. Similarity-seeking essentially amounts to the pursuit of a visible collective difference as a means of establishing social recognition or political legitimization (Thompson 2014). Diversity-asserting, on the other hand, seeks primarily to embrace difference through processes of destigmatization. Sandikci and Ger (2010), in their study of Islamic veiling in urban Turkey, identify how women personalize and aestheticize their veils in an effort to render a stigmatized practice fashionable. Similarly, Scaraboto and Fischer (2013) highlight the work of fatshionistas in appealing to institutional logics, publicizing desirable institutional innovations, and aligning themselves with powerful institutional actors in order to gain inclusion. Of course, not all of these practices are restricted to narrative production for, as Thompson and Üstüner (2015: 260) suggest, 'resistant practices are enacted in interpersonal and institutional spheres and can potentially cross the proverbial edge, placing one at tangible risk of social censure'.

While stigma has historically been associated with difference, oftentimes the pursuit of *cool* is 'structured by a restless quest for non-conformity' (Heath and Potter 2004: 191). We argue for consideration of the *stigma of conformity* that may be associated with too close an adherence to social norms as made manifest in popular culture and fashion in an increasingly market-mediated world. The *stigma of conformity* suggests a reverse movement to the one described earlier on destigmatization, a movement where the fashionable and commodified becomes stigmatized. The *stigma of conformity* is attached to that which is impersonal, superficial, the same. Lack of authenticity is a major factor in the attribution of such a stigmatized status, and individuals strive to get 'closer to the self' and reject commodified styles, establishing 'the imagined mainstream, as a straw man against whom one can set oneself off as more authentic' (Michael 2015: 178). Because authenticity is in the eye of the beholder, the attribution of stigma is also determined according to individual rather than social norms. Individual norms are multiple, varied and fluid, and they coagulate around notions of personal, as opposed to commodified meanings, determinations of authenticity and aesthetic judgments. Stigmatizers can, therefore, be people who also carry the potentially stigmatizing attribute, but in what they believe to be a more authentic or legitimate form. Thus, stigma can originate both within and outside the stigmatized group.

The outcome is a range of micro-level consumption practices that effectively operate as traditional stigma management strategies. For Arsel and Thompson (2011: 803), hipsters use the demythologizing practices of aesthetic discrimination, symbolic demarcation, and proclaiming consumer sovereignty to 'insulate the field of indie consumption from the stigmatizing encroachments of the hipster myth and, in so doing, protect their field-dependent capital from cultural devaluation'. Mikkonen et al. (2011) bear witness to the use of cynical discursive strategies and cynical identity projects for both therapeutic and political purposes in distancing the self from normalized Christmas consumption. Relatedly, Larsen et al. (2014) evidence a type of displaced abjection (Stallybrass and White 1986) whereby those stigmatized by their association with tattoos can turn what little power they have against those even lower than them, those with commodified tattoos.

The emergence and development of the *stigma of conformity* warrants further discussion in order to gain a fuller understanding of its nature, character and scope and how it challenges current theories of consumption, such as consumer resistance. It carries the potential to provide insight into the interplay between macro-level movements such as commodification and micro-level consumer practices.

REFERENCES

Adorno, Theodor (1991) *The Culture Industry: Selected Essays on Mass Culture*, London and New York: Routledge.

Ahuvia, Aaron (2005) 'Beyond the Extended Self: Loved Objects and Consumers' Identity Narratives', *Journal of Consumer Research*, 32(1), 171–184.

Allen, Kim (2014) 'Blair's Children: Young Women as "Aspirational Subjects" in the Psychic Landscape of Class', *The Sociological Review*, 62(4), 760–779.

Arnould, Eric and Craig Thompson (2005) 'Consumer Culture Theory (CCT): Twenty Years of Research', *Journal of Consumer Research*, 31(4), 868–882.

Arnould, Eric and Craig Thompson (2007) 'Consumer Culture Theory (and We Really Mean Theoretics): Dilemmas and Opportunities Posed by an Academic Branding Strategy', in Russell Belk and John Sherry (eds) *Consumer Culture Theory*, Vol. 11 of Research in Consumer Behavior, Oxford, UK: Elsevier, 3–22.

Arsel, Zeynep and Craig Thompson (2011) 'Demythologizing Consumption Practices: How Consumers Protect their Field-Dependent Identity Investments from Devaluing Marketplace Myths', *Journal of Consumer Research*, 37(5), 791–806.

Askegaard, Søren and Jeppe Trolle Linnet (2011) 'Towards an Epistemology of Consumer Culture Theory: Phenomenology and the Context of Context', *Marketing Theory*, 11(4), 381–404.

Askegaard, Søren, Eric Arnould and Dannie Kjeldgaard (2005) 'Post-assimilationist Ethnic Consumer Research: Qualifications and Extensions', *Journal of Consumer Research*, 31(1), 160–171.

Askegaard, Søren, Martine Cardel Gertsen and Roy Langer (2002) 'The Body Consumed: Reflexivity and Cosmetic Surgery', *Psychology & Marketing*, 19(10), 793–812.

Attali, Jacques (1985) *Noise: The Political Economy of Music*, Minneapolis: University of Minnesota Press.
Bardhi, Fleura, Giana Eckhardt and Eric Arnould (2012) 'Liquid Relationship to Possessions', *Journal of Consumer Research*, 39(3), 510–529.
Barnes, Marian and David Prior (1995) 'Spoilt for Choice: How Consumerism Can Disempower Public Service Users', *Public Money and Management*, 15(3), 53–57.
Bauman, Zygmunt (1988) *Freedom*, Milton Keynes, UK: Open University Press.
Bauman, Zygmunt (2000) *Liquid Modernity*, Cambridge, UK: Polity.
Bauman, Zygmunt (2007) *Consuming Life*, Cambridge, UK: Polity.
Belk, Russell (1988) 'Possessions and the Extended Self', *Journal of Consumer Research*, 15(2), 139–168.
Belk, Russell (1991) 'Possessions and the Sense of Past', in Russell Belk (ed.) *Highways and Buyways: Naturalistic Research from the Consumer Behavior Odyssey*, Provo, UT: Association for Consumer Research, 114–130.
Belk, Russell, Guliz Ger and Søren Askegaard (2003) 'The Fire of Desire: A Multi-site Inquiry into Consumer Passion', *Journal of Consumer Research*, 30(3), 326–352.
Belk, Russell, Melanie Wallendorf and John F. Sherry, Jr. (1989) 'The Sacred and the Profane in Consumer Behavior: Theodicy on the Odyssey', *Journal of Consumer Research*, 16(1), 1–38.
Bengtsson, Anders, Jacob Ostberg and Dannie Kjeldgaard (2005) 'Prisoners in Paradise: Subcultural Resistance to the Marketisation of Tattooing', *Consumption Markets & Culture*, 8(3), 261–274.
Bennett, Tony (1998) *Culture: A Reformer's Science*, London, UK: Sage.
Bjerrisgaard, Sofie Møller, Dannie Kjeldgaard and Anders Bengtsson (2013) 'Consumer–brand Assemblages in Advertising: An Analysis of Skin, Identity, and Tattoos in Ads', *Consumption Markets & Culture*, 16(3), 223–239.
Bocock, Robert (1993) *Consumption*, London, UK: Routledge.
Bonsu, Samuel and Russell Belk (2003) 'Do Not Go Cheaply into That Good Night: Death-Ritual Consumption in Asante, Ghana', *Journal of Consumer Research*, 30(1), 41–55.
Bourdieu, Pierre (1984) *Distinction: A Social Critique of the Judgment of Taste*, Cambridge, MA: Harvard University Press.
Brown, Stephen, Robert Kozinets and John Sherry (2003) 'Teaching Old Brands New Tricks: Retro Branding and the Revival of Brand Meaning', *Journal of Marketing*, 67(3), 19–33.
Brubaker, Rogers and Frederick Cooper (2000) 'Beyond Identity', *Theory and Society*, 29(1), 1–47.
Campbell, Colin (2005) 'The Craft Consumer Culture: Craft and Consumption in a Postmodern Society', *Journal of Consumer Culture*, 5(1), 23–42.
Carrington, Michal, Ben Neville and Robin Canniford (2015) 'Unmanageable Multiplicity: Consumer Transformation Towards Moral Self Coherence', *European Journal of Marketing*, 49(7/8), 1300–1325.
Castree, Noel (2003) 'Commodifying What Nature?', *Progress in Human Geography*, 27(3), 273–297.
Chatzidakis, Andreas, Gretchen Larsen and Simon Bishop (2014) 'Farewell to Consumerism: Countervailing Logics of Growth in Consumption', *Ephemera*, 14(4), 753–764.
Cherrier, Hélène and Jeff Murray (2007) 'Reflexive Dispossession and the Self: Constructing a Processual Theory of Identity', *Consumption Markets & Culture*, 10(1), 1–29.

Consumers International (2009) 'How Are Consumer Rights Defined? World Consumer Day: History and Purpose', http://www.consumersinternational.org

Coulter, Robin A., Linda Price and Lawrence Feick (2003) 'Rethinking the Origins and Involvement and Brand Commitment: Insights from Postsocialist Central Europe', *Journal of Consumer Research*, 30(2), 151–169.

Cova, Bernard (1997) 'Community and Consumption: Towards a Definition of the "Linking Value" of Products or Services', *European Journal of Marketing*, 31(3/4), 297–316.

Cova, Bernard, Robert Kozinets and Avi Shankar (eds) (2007) *Consumer Tribes*, Oxford, UK: Butterworth-Heinemann.

Crockett, David and Melanie Wallendorf (2004) 'The Role of Normative Political Ideology in Consumer Behavior', *Journal of Consumer Research*, 31(3), 511–528.

Cronin, James, Mary McCarthy and Alan Collins (2014) 'Covert Distinction: How Hipsters Practice Food-based Resistance Strategies in the Production of Identity', *Consumption Markets & Culture*, 17(1), 2–28.

Duffy, Rosaleen (2008) 'Neoliberalizing Nature: Global Networks and Ecotourism Development in Madagascar', *Journal of Sustainable Tourism*, 16(3), 327–344.

Du Gay, Paul (1996) *Consumption and Identity at Work*, London, UK: Sage.

Elliott, Richard (1997) 'Existential Consumption and Irrational Desire', *European Journal of Marketing*, 31(3/4), 285–296.

Elliott, Richard (2004) 'Consumption as a Symbolic Vocabulary for the Construction of Identity', in Karin Ekström and Helene Brembeck (eds) *Elusive Consumption*, Oxford, UK, Berg, 129–140.

Elliott, Richard and Kritsadarat Wattanasuwan (1998) 'Brands as Symbolic Resources for the Construction of Identity', *International Journal of Advertising*, 17(2), 131–144.

Epp, Amber and Linda Price (2008) 'Family Identity: A Framework of Identity Interplay in Consumption Practices', *Journal of Consumer Research*, 35(1), 50–70.

Erikson, Eric (1950/1995) *Childhood and Society*, London, UK: Vintage.

Fennell, Lee Anne (2009) 'Adjusting Alienability', *Harvard Law Review*, 122(5), 1403–1465.

Firat, A. Fuat and Nikhilesh Dholakia (2016) 'From Consumer to Construer: Travels in Human Subjectivity', *Journal of Consumer Culture*, published online before print, January 15, 2016.

Firat, A. Fuat and Alladi Venkatesh (1995) 'Liberatory Postmodernism and the Re-enchantment of Consumption', *Journal of Consumer Research*, 22(3), 239–267.

Francombe-Webb, Jessica and Michael Silk (2016) 'Young Girls' Embodied Experiences of Femininity and Social Class', *Sociology*, 50(4), 652–672.

Gabriel, Yiannis and Tim Lang (2006) *The Unmanageable Consumer: Contemporary Consumption and its Fragmentation*, London, UK: Sage.

Giddens, Anthony (1991) *Modernity and Self-Identity: Self and Society in the Late Modern Age*. Cambridge, UK: Polity Press.

Goffman, Erving (1963) Stigma: Notes on the Management of a Spoiled Identity, New York: Simon & Schuster.

Goulding, Christina (2001) 'Romancing the Past: Heritage Visiting and the Nostalgic Consumer', *Psychology & Marketing*, 18(6), 565–592.

Goulding, Christina, Michael Saren and Andrew Lindridge (2013) 'Reading the Body at von Hagen's Body Worlds', *Annals of Tourism Research*, 40, 306–330.

Goulding, Christina, Avi Shankar and Robin Canniford (2013) 'Learning to be Tribal: Facilitating the Formation of Consumer Tribes', *European Journal of Marketing*, 47(5/6), 813–832.

Goulding, Christina, Avi Shankar and Richard Elliott (2002) 'Working Weeks, Rave Weekends: Identity Fragmentation and the Emergence of New Communities', *Consumption Markets & Culture*, 5(4), 261–284.

Goulding, Christina, Avi Shankar, Richard Elliott and Robin Canniford (2009) 'The Marketplace Management of Illicit Pleasure', *Journal of Consumer Research*, 35(5), 759–771.

Grainge, Paul (2000) 'Advertising the Archive: Nostalgia and the (Post)national Imaginary', *American Studies*, 41(2/3), 137–157.

Grubb, Edward and Harrison Grathwohl (1967) 'Consumer Self-Concept, Symbolism and Market Behavior: A Theoretical Approach', *Journal of Marketing*, 31(4): 22–27.

Halnon, Karen Bettez (2005) 'Alienation Incorporated: "F*** the Mainstream Music" in the Mainstream', *Current Sociology*, 53(3), 441–464.

Hammack, Phillip (2008) 'Narrative and the Cultural Psychology of Identity', *Personality and Social Psychology Review*, 12(3), 222–247.

Harju, Anu and Annamari Huovinen (2015) 'Fashionably Voluptuous: Normative Femininity and Resistant Performative Tactics in Fatshion Blogs', *Journal of Marketing Management*, 31(15–16), 1602–1625.

Harrison, Robert and Kevin Thomas (2013) 'Negotiating Cultural Ambiguity: A Phenomenological Study of Multiracial Identity and Consumption', in Russell Belk, Linda Price and Lisa Peñaloza (eds) *Research in Consumer Behavior: Consumer Culture Theory, 15*, Bingley, UK: Emerald Publishing, 41–56.

Hays, Sharon (1994) 'Structure and Agency and the Sticky Problem of Culture', *Sociological Theory*, 12(1), 57–72.

Heath, Joseph and Andrew Potter (2004) *Nation of Rebels: Why Counterculture Became Consumer Culture,* New York: Harper Collins.

Hebdige, Dick (1979) *Subculture: The Meaning of Style*. New York: Methuen.

Hein, Wendy and Stephanie O'Donohoe (2014) 'Practicing Gender: The Role of Banter in Young Men's Improvisations of Masculine Consumer Identities', *Journal of Marketing Management*, 30(13–14), 1293–1319.

Hill, Ronald Paul (1991) 'Homeless Women, Special Possessions, and the Meaning of "Home": An Ethnographic Case Study', *Journal of Consumer Research*, 18(3), 298–310.

Hirschman, Elizabeth (1981) 'Comprehending Symbolic Consumption: Three Theoretical Issues', in Elizabeth Hirschman and Morris Holbrook (eds) *SV – Symbolic Consumer Behavior*, New York: Association for Consumer Research, 4–6.

Hogg, Margaret, Emma Banister and Christopher Stephenson (2009) 'Mapping Symbolic (Anti-) Consumption', *Journal of Business Research*, 62(2), 148–159.

Hogg, Margaret, Carolyn Folkman Curasi and Pauline Maclaran (2004) 'The (Re-) Configuration of Production and Consumption in Empty Nest Households/Families', *Consumption Markets & Culture*, 7(3), 239–259.

Holbrook, Morris (1995) *Consumer Research: Introspective Essays on the Study of Consumption*. Thousand Oaks, CA: Sage.

Holt, Douglas (1995) 'How Consumers Consume: A Typology of Consumption Practices', *Journal of Consumer Research*, 22(1), 1–16.

Holt, Douglas (1998) 'Does Cultural Capital Structure American Consumption?', *Journal of Consumer Research*, 25(1), 1–25.

Holt, Douglas (2002) 'Why Do Brands Cause Trouble? A Dialectical Theory of Consumer Culture and Branding', *Journal of Consumer Research*, 29(1), 70–90.

Holt, Douglas and Craig Thompson (2004) 'Man-of-action Heroes: The Pursuit of Heroic Masculinity in Everyday Consumption', *Journal of Consumer Research*, 31(2), 425–440.

Holttinen, Heli (2014) 'How Practices Inform the Materialization of Cultural Ideals in Mundane Consumption', *Consumption Markets & Culture*, 17(6), 573–594.

Igoe, Jim (2010) 'The Spectacle of Nature in the Global Economy of Appearances: Anthropological Engagements with the Spectacular Mediations of Transnational Conservation', *Critique of Anthropology*, 30(4), 375–397.

Jafari, Aliakbar and Christina Goulding (2008) 'We Are Not Terrorists! UK-based Iranians, Consumption Practices and the Torn Self', *Consumption Markets & Culture*, 11(2), 73–91.

Jenkins, Richard (2014) *Social Identity*, 4th edition. Oxford, UK: Routledge.

Joy, Annamma and Eric Li (2012) 'Studying Consumption Behavior Through Multiple Lenses: An Overview of Consumer Culture Theory', *Journal of Business Anthropology*, 1(1), 141–173.

Joy, Annamma and Alladi Venkatesh (1994) 'Postmodernism, Feminism, and the Body: The Visible and the Invisible in Consumer Research', *International Journal of Research in Marketing*, 11, 333–357.

Karababa, Eminegül and Güliz Ger (2011) 'Early Modern Ottoman Coffeehouse Culture and the Formation of the Consumer Subject', *Journal of Consumer Research*, 37(5), 737–760.

Kates, Steven (2002) 'The Protean Quality of Subcultural Consumption: An Ethnographic Account of Gay Consumers', *Journal of Consumer Research*, 29(3), 383–399.

Kellner, Douglas (1983) 'Critical Theory, Commodities and the Consumer Society', *Theory, Culture & Society*, 1(3), 66–83.

Kellner, Douglas (1992) 'Popular Culture and the Construction of Postmodern Identities', in Scott Lash and Jonathan Friedman (eds) *Modernity and Identity*, Oxford, UK: Blackwell, 141–177.

Kozinets, Robert (2001) 'Utopian Enterprise: Articulating the Meanings of Star Trek's Culture of Consumption', *Journal of Consumer Research*, 28(1), 67–88.

Kozinets, Robert (2002) 'Can Consumers Escape the Market? Emancipatory Illuminations from Burning Man', *Journal of Consumer Research*, 29(1), 20–38.

Kozinets, Robert, John Sherry, Diana Storm, Adam Duhachek, Krittinee Nuttavuthisit and Benét DeBerry-Spence (2004) 'Ludic Agency and Retail Spectacle', *Journal of Consumer Research*, 31(3), 658–672.

Larsen, Gretchen and Rob Lawson (2013) 'Consumer Rights: An Assessment of Justice', *Journal of Business Ethics*, 112(3), 515–528.

Larsen, Gretchen, Maurice Patterson and Lucy Markham (2014) 'A Deviant Art: Tattoo-Related Stigma in an Era of Commodification', *Psychology & Marketing*, 31(8), 670–681.

Lastovicka, John and Nancy Sirianni (2011) 'Truly, Madly, Deeply: Consumers in the Throes of Material Possession Love', *Journal of Consumer Research*, 38(2), 323–342.

Laufer-Ukeles, Pamela (2013) 'Mothering for Money: Regulating Commercial Intimacy', *Indiana Law Journal*, 88(4), 1223–1279.

Levy, Sidney (1959) 'Symbols for Sale', *Harvard Business Review*, 37(4), 117–124.

Luedicke, Marius, Craig Thompson and Markus Giesler (2010) 'Consumer Identity Work as Moral Protagonism: How Myth and Ideology Animate a Brand-mediated Moral Conflict', *Journal of Consumer Research*, 36(6), 1016–1032.

Lury, Celia (1996) *Consumer Culture*, Cambridge, UK: Polity Press.

McAlexander, James, Beth Dufault, Diane Martin and John Schouten (2014) 'The Marketisation of Religion: Field, Capital, and Consumer Identity', *Journal of Consumer Research*, 41(3), 858–875.

McAlexander, James, John Schouten and Harold Koenig (2002) 'Building Brand Community', *Journal of Marketing*, 66(1), 38–54.

McCracken, Grant (1986) 'Culture and Consumption: A Theoretical Account of the Structure and Movement of the Cultural Meaning of Consumer Goods', *Journal of Consumer Research*, 13(1), 71–84.

McCracken, Grant (1990) Culture and Consumption: New Approaches to the Symbolic Character of Consumer Goods and Activities, Bloomington, IN: Indiana University Press.

Marion, Gilles and Agnes Nairn (2011) '"We Make the Shoes, You Make the Story", Teenage Girls' Experiences of Fashion: Bricolage, Tactics and Narrative Identity', *Consumption Markets & Culture*, 14(1), 29–56.

Michael, Janna (2015) 'It's Really Not Hip to be a Hipster: Negotiating Trends and Authenticity in the Cultural Field', *Journal of Consumer Culture*, 15(2), 163–182.

Mikkonen, Ilona, Johanna Moisander and A. Fuat Firat (2011) 'Cynical Identity Projects as Consumer Resistance: The Scrooge as a Social Critic?', *Consumption Markets & Culture*, 14(1), 99–116.

Miles, Steven (1999) 'A Pluralistic Seduction? Post-modern Consumer Research at the Crossroads', *Consumption Markets & Culture*, 3(2), 145–163.

Morales, Andrea and Eugenia Wu (2013) 'Disgust and Identity', in Ayalla Ruvio and Russell Belk (eds) *The Routledge Companion to Identity and Consumption*, Abingdon, UK: Routledge, 72–79.

Muñiz, Albert and Thomas O'Guinn (2001) 'Brand Community', *Journal of Consumer Research*, 27(4), 412–432.

Murray, Jeff (2002) 'The Politics of Consumption: A Re-inquiry on Thompson and Haytko's (1997) "Speaking of Fashion"', *Journal of Consumer Research*, 29(3), 427–440.

Parker, Richard and Peter Aggleton (2003) 'HIV and AIDS-related Stigma and Discrimination: A Conceptual Framework and Implications for Action', *Social Science & Medicine*, 57(1), 13–24.

Parmentier, Marie-Agnès and Eileen Fischer (2011) 'You Can't Always Get What You Want: Unsustainable Identity Projects in the Fashion System', *Consumption Markets & Culture*, 14(1), 7–27.

Patterson, Maurice and Jonathan Schroeder (2010) 'Borderlines: Skin, Tattoos and Consumer Culture Theory', *Marketing Theory*, 10(3), 253–267.

Peñaloza, Lisa (2001) 'Consuming the American West: Animating Cultural Meaning and Memory at a Stock Show and Rodeo', *Journal of Consumer Research*, 28(3), 369–398.

Reith, Gerda and Fiona Dobbie (2012) 'Lost in the Game: Narratives of Addiction and Identity in Recovery from Problem Gambling', *Addiction Research & Theory*, 20(6), 511–521.

Ritzer, George and Allan Liska (1997) 'McDisneyization and Post Tourism', in Chris Rojek and John Urry (eds) *Touring Cultures: Transformations of Travel and Theory*, London: Routledge, 96–109.

Rucker, Derek and Adam Galinsky (2008) 'Desire to Acquire: Powerlessness and Compensatory Consumption', *Journal of Consumer Research*, 35(2), 257–267.

Ruvio, Ayalla and Russell Belk (2013) 'Conflicting Selves and the Role of Possessions', in Ayalla Ruvio and Russell Belk (eds) *The Routledge Companion to Identity and Consumption*, Abingdon, UK: Routledge, 141–148.

Sandikci, Özlem and Güliz Ger (2010) 'Veiling in Style: How Does a Stigmatized Practice Become Fashionable?', *Journal of Consumer Research*, 37(1), 15–36.

Sandikci, Özlem and Güliz Ger (2013) 'Stigma, Identity and Consumption', in Ayalla Ruvio and Russell Belk (eds) *The Routledge Companion to Identity and Consumption*, Abingdon, UK: Routledge, 111–118.

Scaraboto, Daiane and Eileen Fischer (2013) 'Frustrated Fatshionistas: An Institutional Theory Perspective on Consumer Quests for Greater Choice in Mainstream Markets', *Journal of Consumer Research*, 39(6), 1234–1257.
Schau, Hope Jensen and Mary Gilly (2003) 'We Are What We Post? Self-Presentation in Personal Web Space,' *Journal of Consumer Research*, 30(3), 385–404.
Schau, Hope Jensen, Mary Gilly and Mary Wolfinbarger (2009) 'Consumer Identity Renaissance: The Resurgence of Identity-inspired Consumption in Retirement', *Journal of Consumer Research*, 36(2), 255–276.
Schau, Hope Jensen, Albert Muñiz and Eric Arnould (2009) 'How Brand Community Practices Create Value', *Journal of Marketing*, 73(5), 30–51.
Schouten, John (1991) 'Selves in Transition: Symbolic Consumption in Personal Rites of Passage and Identity Reconstruction', *Journal of Consumer Research*, 17(4), 412–425.
Schouten, John and James McAlexander (1995) 'Subcultures of Consumption: An Ethnography of the New Bikers', *Journal of Consumer Research*, 22(1), 43–61.
Schwartz, Barry (2005) *The Paradox of Choice: Why Less is More*, New York: Harper Collins.
Seregina, Anastasia and John Schouten (2017) 'Resolving Identity Ambiguity through Transcending Fandom', *Consumption Markets & Culture*, 20(2), 107–130.
Shankar, Avi, Richard Elliott and James Fitchett (2009) 'Identity, Consumption and Narratives of Socialization', *Marketing Theory*, 9(1), 75–94.
Shepherd, Robert (2002) 'Commodification, Culture and Tourism', *Tourist Studies*, 2(2), 183–201.
Sirgy, M. Joseph (1982) 'Self-Concept in Consumer Behavior: A Critical Review', *Journal of Consumer Research*, 9(3), 287–300.
Skeggs, Beverley (2004) 'Exchange, Value and Effect: Bourdieu and the Self', in Lisa Adkins and Beverley Skeggs (eds) *Feminism after Bourdieu*, Oxford: Blackwell, 75–95.
Skeggs, Beverley (2005) 'The Making of Class and Gender through Visualizing Moral Subject Formation', *Sociology*, 39(5): 965–982.
Skeggs, Beverley (2014) 'Values Beyond Value? Is Anything Beyond the Logic of Capital?', *The British Journal of Sociology*, 65(1), 1–20.
Skeggs, Beverley and Vik Loveday (2012) 'Struggles for Value: Value Practices, Injustice, Judgment, Affect and the Idea of Class', *The British Journal of Sociology*, 63(3), 472–490.
Slater, Don (1997) *Consumer Culture and Modernity*, Cambridge, UK: Polity Press.
Smith Maguire, Jennifer and Kim Stanway (2008) 'Looking Good: Consumption and the Problems of Self-production', *European Journal of Cultural Studies*, 11(1), 63–81.
Stallybrass, Peter and Allon White (1986) *The Politics and Poetics of Transgression*, Ithaca, NY: Cornell University Press.
Syrjälä, Henna (2016) 'Turning Point of Transformation: Consumer Communities, Identity Projects and Becoming a Serious Dog Hobbyist', *Journal of Business Research*, 69(1), 177–190.
Thompson, Craig (1996) 'Caring Consumers: Gendered Consumption Meanings and the Juggling Lifestyle', *Journal of Consumer Research*, 22(4), 388–407.
Thompson, Craig (2004) 'Marketplace Mythology and Discourses of Power', *Journal of Consumer Research*, 31(1), 162–180.
Thompson, Craig (2014) 'The Politics of Consumer Identity Work', *Journal of Consumer Research*, 40(5), iii–vii.

Thompson, Craig and Diana Haytko (1997) 'Speaking of Fashion: Consumers' Uses of Fashion Discourses and the Appropriation of Countervailing Cultural Meanings', *Journal of Consumer Research*, 24(1), 15–42.

Thompson, Craig and Kelly Tian (2008) 'Reconstructing the South: How Commercial Myths Compete for Identity Value through the Ideological Shaping of Popular Memories and Countermemories', *Journal of Consumer Research*, 34(5), 595–613.

Thompson, Craig and Tuba Üstüner (2015) 'Women Skating on the Edge: Marketplace Performances as Ideological Edgework', *Journal of Consumer Research*, 42(2), 235–265.

Trentmann, Frank (2016) *Empire of Things: How We Became a World of Consumers, from the Fifteenth Century to the Twenty-first*, London: Allen Lane.

Türe, Meltem (2014) 'Value-in-disposition: Exploring How Consumers Derive Value from Disposition of Possessions', *Marketing Theory*, 14(1), 53–72.

Turner, James S. (1995) 'The Consumer Interest in the 1990s and Beyond', *The Journal of Consumer Affairs*, 29(2), 310–327.

Tzanelli, Rodanthi (2008) 'Cultural Imitations and the Commodification of Culture: Sign Industries as Makers of the Public Sphere', *The Global Studies Journal*, 1(3), 1–10.

Ulusoy, Emre (2016) 'Subcultural Escapades via Music Consumption: Identity Transformations and Extraordinary Experiences in Dionysian Music Subcultures', *Journal of Business Research*, 69(1), 244–254.

Üstüner, Tuba and Douglas Holt (2007) 'Dominated Consumer Acculturation: The Social Construction of Poor Migrant Women's Consumer Identity Projects in a Turkish Squatter', *Journal of Consumer Research*, 34(1), 41–56.

VOICE (2010) 'Buying into Motherhood? Problematic Consumption and Ambivalence in Transitional Phases', *Consumption Markets & Culture*, 13(4), 373–397.

Warde, Alan (1994) 'Consumption, Identity-Formation and Uncertainty', *Sociology*, 28(4), 877–898.

Wattanasuwan, Kritsadarat (2005) 'The Self and Symbolic Consumption', *Journal of the American Academy of Business*, 6(1), 179–184.

Woodruffe, Helen (1997) 'Compensatory Consumption: Why Women Go Shopping When They're Fed Up and Other Stories', *Marketing Intelligence & Planning*, 15(7), 325–334.

Re-presenting, Reinvigorating and Reconciling: Gift-giving Research within and beyond the CCT Paradigm

Cele C. Otnes

INTRODUCTION

If there is ever an award bestowed within consumer research for Most Interdisciplinary Topic, gift giving (the term most frequently used to describe the broad set of behaviors associated with gift exchange) will certainly be a strong contender. Most scholars in our discipline trace the origins of interest in the topic to work by anthropologists engaged in prolonged cultural immersions in the early twentieth century. They then typically discuss research in sociology and psychology that emerges a few decades later – with Gouldner's (1960) paper on the norm of reciprocity almost always cited as a pivotal theoretical contribution. Also robust, but absent from our field, is scholarship in the humanities that probes gift giving in myriad textual forms such as histories, plays, poems, and fictional or non-fictional accounts (Osteen, 2002). As powerful interpersonal, social, and cultural mechanisms of communication and competition, Mauss's (1920/1925) 'big three' exchange behaviors of giving, receiving, and reciprocating are compelling, confounding, confusing, and often contradictory. Nevertheless, those very characteristics explain why gift giving remains fascinating to such a wide swath of scholars.

Gift-giving scholarship makes its first appearance in the consumer behavior canon in the early 1970s. Prior to captaining the Consumer Behavior Odyssey (Belk, 1991) Russell Belk published the first gift-giving paper in the *Journal of Consumer Research*, leveraging the social-psychological theoretical template of balance theory to explore the importance of shared valences between givers, recipients, and gifts (Belk, 1976). After Sherry's (1983) anthropologically-anchored theoretical model appeared in the journal, consumer research in gift giving began in earnest, with the topic maintaining a steady presence within discipline-based conferences and journals ever since.

Much of the topical output within consumer behavior occurred during the last decades of the twentieth century. But as I write this chapter a little over fifteen years into the new millennium, a convergence of forces has seen the study of gift giving branch out (or, some might argue, break off) into myriad interesting directions. The most specific consequence of this fermentation and fragmentation that this chapter explores is that research on gift giving both within consumer behavior in general and CCT scholarship in particular reflects a broader, but perhaps over-diluted, conceptualization of the phenomenon.

Furthermore, most recent research explores gift giving on either the meso or macro levels, focusing on the giving, receipt, and reciprocity that occurs within and between groups connected by loose and/or vulnerable ties, between strangers, and on the communal level. In consequence, the pendulum has swung away – perhaps too far away? – from understanding gift-giving behavior within family and kinship networks. Even as he urges gift-giving researchers to radiate outward from intimate social circles as their locus of interest, Marcoux (2009, p. 681) observes, 'the family is at the heart of the gift economy'. Consider too that Christmas gifts generated $630 billion in revenue in the US alone in 2015 (cited in Weinberger, 2016), with people giving most of these goods, services, and experiences to family members, friends and close associates.

Moreover, in the almost two decades since CCT researchers have eschewed the study of interpersonal gift-exchange practices, fundamental changes on the macro- and meso-levels have directly impacted expectations and enactments of gift giving that (most often) occur on the interpersonal or 'micro' level. For example, Webley et al. (1983) offer compelling evidence that recipients often perceive money as a sub-par gift, and as impersonal and unable to convey relational sentiment. Recent scholarship discussing the acceptability of money still cites Webley et al.'s paper as a definitive source on the topic (e.g., Belk, 2010). However, it appeared over thirty years ago, before entrenched and often contradictory macro factors may have propelled money to the status of a much-desired gift. These include: a skyrocketing global market for luxury goods (made even more challenging to acquire during a prolonged global economic downturn), the dissolution of the manufacturing economy and its relatively highly paid labor force, and college-loan burdens that saddle a generation of millennials who may never achieve their parents' standard of living. As a result, discourses about money as a gift now seem to lean toward the old American adage that 'green goes with everything' (reflecting the color of our currency). Rather than eschew monetary gifts, etiquette experts and even consumer watchdog organizations often now offer advice about how *best* to give money for various occasions (e.g., Braverman, 2016).

Thus, I argue it is time for CCT scholars to reconsider their disinterest in interpersonal gift giving by drawing on what current CCT research on the topic does best – namely, taking into account factors that can shape dyadic and small-network exchange that stem from the broader sociocultural environment. Furthermore, several other robust streams of scholarship where gift giving receives attention warp and weave within the broader domain of consumer research. As I observe below, these could be invaluable in reinvigorating the study of gift giving by CCT scholars.

I structure this chapter as follows. First, I discuss six research streams that currently influence the definition and scope of gift-giving research in consumer behavior. These are: (1) the sociocultural focus on gift giving; (2) experimental approaches to gift giving; (3) charitable donating vs gift giving; (4) giving vs sharing; (5) gift-giving research in the marketplace; and (6) gift-giving and the digital economy. Given the goals and scope of this volume, I devote most of the review to the first topic. Next, drawing upon the review of these streams, I offer a research agenda for CCT (and other) gift-giving scholars I hope can reconcile and reinvigorate research on the topic. I frame this agenda by offering my own gift-giving experiences to emphasize the real-world aspects of questions that deserve attention.

GIFT-GIVING RESEARCH STREAMS IN CONSUMER BEHAVIOR

Reflecting the robustness of gift-giving research across disciplines, in the twenty-first-century consumer researchers working within both the psychological and CCT paradigms began to embrace a diversity of approaches, contexts, and topics pertaining to the subject (but not really a variety of theoretical approaches – a concern I revisit later). Specifically, after the 1990s, when interpersonal gift-exchange behavior occupied center stage (e.g., Otnes et al., 1993; most contributors to Otnes and Beltramini, 1996), six distinct currents emerged within consumer behavior with intersections to gift scholarship. These exerted simultaneous but independent influences on the discipline – my diplomatic way of observing that authors within one camp often do not acknowledge, or reflect knowledge of, work in the others. Taken as a whole, however, consumer researchers have definitely broadened, but also blurred, the fundamental definition and disciplinary domain of gift giving.

Emergence of the Sociocultural Focus

Belk et al.'s (1989) impactful delineation of sacred versus profane consumption prompted myriad scholars to produce theoretically stimulating and rigorous research exploring linkages between culture and consumption in ritual contexts (e.g., Bonsu and Belk, 2003; Kozinets, 2002; Wallendorf and Arnould, 1991). The discussion of commonalities and challenges of similar work representative of the CCT paradigm (Arnould and Thompson, 2005) also established a set of expectations that future scholars would delve deeply into cultural norms, practices, and discourses that shape and mold consumer behavior. Ironically, twentieth-century researchers in our field consistently pay homage to the foundational anthropological work on gift exchange (e.g., Levi-Strauss, 1969/1949; Malinowski, 2002/1922; Mauss, 1990/1925), while typically omitting a cultural perspective from their own empirical enterprises. In that respect, the CCT paradigm exerts a profound impact on gift-giving research, one I believe is best demonstrated by discussing papers published since 2000 in the top journals that publish work on consumer research.

Before doing so, I wish to make an important distinction between gift-giving scholarship that is not 'CCT', but relies on the qualitative research techniques ubiquitously associated with that paradigm, and gift-giving research that actually 'is CCT'. I distinguish these approaches by the attention each devotes to the sociocultural elements that shape gift giving. For example, studies published in and since the 1990s focus on self-gifts (e.g., Mick and DeMoss, 1990) and/or giving and receiving between family, friends, and intimate others (Bradford, 2009; Curasi et al., 2004; Price et al., 2000; Lowrey et al., 2004; Wooten, 2000). However, they do not truly explore how sociocultural factors inform giving, receiving, or reciprocating. Rather, they hone in on internal, interpersonal, or even micro-social-psychological aspects, such as the emotions givers or recipients experience (e.g., Price et al., 2000; Wooten, 2000), or how givers engage with intimate others to assist with gift purchasing (Lowrey et al., 2004). Two exceptions are Belk and Coon (1993), who theorize an agapic model of gift giving and compare it to other culturally-rooted models, and Otnes et al. (1993), who leverage Merton's social role theory to understand what motivates givers to perceive people as easy or difficult gift recipients.

Given this observation, it may seem paradoxical that I select as the first twenty-first-century publication that truly embraces the 'CCT approach' (albeit five years before the acronym appears) Annamma Joy's (2001) exploration of interpersonal gift-exchange practices in Hong Kong. However, it clearly explicates how broader cultural norms such as face and filial piety influence gift exchange on the micro level. Furthermore, it demonstrates how gift giving within those intimate circles in turn helps people acquire, restore, or lose face within their broader sociocultural milieux. Joy also explores how consumers' understandings of those norms vary across givers and recipients, depending on their stage in the life cycle. In other words, her focus on gift giving in a non-Western cultural context is *not* what makes her work sociocultural in focus. In fact, scholars have explored gift-giving practices in different cultures for decades (e.g., Green and Alden, 1988; Kimura and Belk, 2005). Rather, it is Joy's interpretation of gifting as a phenomenon truly entrenched within and reflective of deep-seated cultural norms that makes her work a CCT-oriented exemplar.

Another significant aspect of Joy's work is that she argues for the inapplicability of Gouldner's Western-rooted (and thus theoretically dominant) norm of reciprocity as an enabling mechanism to explain gift giving in Hong Kong. She demonstrates how the norm is irrelevant within hierarchical, collective, and often competitive cultures, where implicit rules governing the manifestation of core cultural constructs such as face and filial piety may in fact mandate *non*-reciprocal behavior. For example, parents in Hong Kong do not buy gifts for children, and incur no loss of face for this inaction; however, children must give to parents. In this cultural context, the norm of filial piety trumps expectations of reciprocity, and children learn that parental sacrifices for the family are themselves gifts that offspring must repay.

Kozinets (2002), in exploring how consumers leverage the Burning Man festival to escape the strictures of a consumer society, is the next to affix a cultural (or in this case, a countercultural) lens to the study of gift giving. Like Joy, he also challenges the stalwart norm of reciprocity, first by discussing the historical evolution of gifting practices at Burning Man (e.g., the transition from participants bartering supplies for worthless trinkets during the early years, to their more recent creations of status-laden, competitive gifts that deflect and reflect marketplace influences, even in a venue ostensibly eschewing commercialism). He observes that in their attempt to escape the real-world gift economy, Burning Man participants follow several key tenets. First, the most valued gifts to the community (the primary gift-exchange level) are those that are manifest as public art and entertainment. Second, broadening Gouldner's conceptualization, Kozinets avers that recipients of communal-level gifts may reciprocate in myriad tangible and intangible ways. However, the more commercially-charged offerings often must undergo a process of transformation, so any rhetorical meanings that the marketplace intends and embeds are removed and reinterpreted.

Third, Kozinets observes that the calculi governing reciprocity within dyads or families (e.g., setting a price limit for gifts, givers practicing 'equipollience' by spending the same amount on recipients of equal status; Lowrey et al., 1996) are meaningless in a context that valorizes creativity and effort as core communal-gift elements. In short, reciprocity is much more difficult to ascertain among Burning Man participants than among celebrants of traditional holidays, where participants may obey more transparent rules, and even negotiate these themselves.

Criticizing the dominance of research exploring dyadic gift exchange within consumer research, Giesler (2006) remarks that the overabundance of research exploring that unit of analysis has essentially restrained gift giving research in a 'conceptual straightjacket' (p. 289). He explores gifting practices within the context of the burgeoning social-network industry – specifically, the norms and practices governing music file sharing though Napster. He argues that this sharing system is actually a networked community of givers that leverages some of the standard aspects of other gifting relationships; for example, reciprocity, rituals, and symbols, while illuminating and enabling the moral aspects of community participation. Yet, as I will discuss later, a close reading of this paper reveals the dominance of a vocabulary pertaining not necessarily to gifting behavior, but to sharing.

In a very different context, and with the goal of expanding the notion of what forms gifts can take, Marcoux (2009) explores the benefits and downsides of people expecting and offering time and effort within the context of moving from one residence to another. Like Belk (1989) who unpacks the historical roots of Christmas gift giving, and Weinberger and Wallendorf (2012) who explain the roots of gifting practices at Mardi Gras, Marcoux recounts the sociocultural history of moving in Montreal, both for residents whose lives are disrupted by the activity, and for those who assist in relocation. He argues that the pervasiveness and frequency of moving means people understand it as an entrenched cultural practice – one requiring gifts of time, effort, and participation by friends and family before, during, and after the actual move. Marcoux thus expands the definition of gift giving to include kinetic and embodied practices, and unpacks how these forms pose additional physical, emotional, and temporal challenges within dyads and intimate networks. Furthermore, he contextualizes this discussion by highlighting the sociocultural discourses that contribute to moving being a taken-for-granted practice in Montreal.

Weinberger and Wallendorf's (2012) study of communal gifting practices during the first Mardi Gras celebration in New Orleans after Hurricane Katrina also clearly falls into the 'CCT camp' of gift-giving research, for numerous reasons. In the same vein as Kozinets, Giesler, and Marcoux, the authors focus on communal-level giving – framing citizens' staging of Mardi Gras as a gift to the city. Moreover, the event involves both highly visible tangible gifts (e.g., the beads that krewe members toss to parade attendees) and, as in Marcoux, those of time, money, physical effort, and emotion. Second, the authors argue that this manifestation of communal giving is embedded within the moral vs the market gift economy, as participation in the first post-Katrina Mardi Gras is motivated by a desire to assist the city in both moving past its crisis and demonstrating resilience. This moral role contrasts starkly with the intent of pre-Katrina Mardi Gras celebrations as full-out commercial, tourist-drawing enterprises.

Scaraboto's (2015) discussion of gift giving on the sociocultural level also shares an interest in the macro versions of the behavior. Importantly, her work explores how gifting practices are situated within a 'hybrid economy', one that features the co-existence and collaboration of market and non-market forms of exchange, such as gift-giving, sharing, and morally-motivated types of exchange behavior. As such, she demonstrates how cultural factors shape various types of exchange, and how gifting is just one of many practices that helps networked-community members fulfill their reciprocal social, emotional and economic obligations. Thus, Scaraboto situates gift giving within a nexus of other exchange practices, reminds us that these practices may be more or less salient within communities at given times, and explicates how consumer collaboration helps determine the roles these often-competing forms of exchange can fulfill within a networked community.

Like Weinberger and Wallendorf's exploration of communal giving in a city experiencing crisis, Klein et al. (2015) explore how people might strategically leverage gift offerings in contexts typified by extreme stress, where surviving is uncertain. In analyzing books and memoirs books about life in concentration camps by Holocaust survivors, the authors leverage Oyserman's (2009) framework of Identity-Based Motivation to explain why people were (or were not) generous in giving food and other vital items to help other prisoners survive. They introduce the construct of 'anticipated reckoning' – or people's perceptions that their actions in one context will influence the makeup of their future selves and lives – as motivating prisoners to take risks and give to others in an environment where doing so could lead to their own death. The paper also explains the gift practices between actual or pseudo-family members by exploring the impact between such sociological phenomena as the power imbalances between prisoners and guards, as well as broader cultural factors such as how Judaic principles informed people's behavior.

Summarizing the contribution of these papers, it is evident that they situate gift giving within a broader nexus of exchange and cultural practices. Nevertheless, they still focus on how gifting and receiving are enacted within dyads or intimate groups. Furthermore, they expand their assumptions about what gifts can actually entail, extending their analysis beyond mere tangible items to include kinetic activities or effortful enactments. Clearly, the publication of these papers in the premiere journals in our field signals that the gatekeepers of gift-giving scholarship agree (or at least wish to open up for debate) such a definitional expansion.

Nevertheless, what is often lacking in this work (and in much of my own, to be honest) is actual advancement in theorization on gift giving. Have we focused too much on challenging the definitions and scope of gift giving, and too little on understanding the interplay between micro, meso and macro factors to determine how gift-giving practices emerge, maintain their resilience, and (possibly, but not always) die? I revisit this issue at the end of the chapter.

'Discovery' of Gift Giving by Experimentalists

Popular-media discourses on gift giving, especially during the holiday seasons entrenched in Western and Eastern cultures, often draw attention to the heightened levels of psychological stress and ambivalence that gift buying and giving can elicit. Thus, it is surprising that until recently, consumer psychologists have kept gift giving at arm's length. In fact, it is only in the past decade that a critical mass of consumer psychologists has begun to recognize that gift-giving contexts and behavior can serve as useful springboards from which to understand fundamental psychological phenomena. Space restraints preclude me from fully explicating the template of theories that undergird these studies. However, I think it is important to offer a brief summary of constructs and theories that experimentalists apply when studying gift giving. These include: (1) understanding how children manage their display of negative emotions when receiving undesirable gifts (Kieras et al., 2005); (2) how the mindsets givers form when engaging in gift exchange shape the types of gifts they select (Baskin et al., 2014); (3) how the number of recipients on a giver's shopping list influences the types of gifts selected (Steffel and Le Bouef, 2014); and (4) how aspects of identity, such as perceived identity threat and relational signaling between giver and recipient, can influence gift selection (Ward and Broniarczyk, 2011, 2016). Most recently, researchers delve into whether givers and recipients in 'ambiguous' relationships (e.g., where partners are unclear in terms of who feels more affinity toward the other) differ in the timing of reciprocal gift offerings (Park and Kim, 2017).

Furthermore, consumer psychologists are adept at leveraging stalwart 'enabling theories' – or established theoretical frameworks from marketing, psychology and other disciplines – when exploring aspects of gift exchange. Both Helion and Gilovich (2014) and Reinholtz et al. (2015) explore how mental accounting (Thaler, 1985) explains recipients' redemption behavior of a popular pillar of contemporary gift giving – the gift card. Using lab experiments and actual retail data, Helion and Gilovich find people apparently assign 'the monetary value of a gift card to a hedonic mental account and spend it accordingly' (2014, p. 386). Furthermore, receiving a retailer-specific gift card may lead recipients to indicate increased preferences for that retail brand in the future (Reinholtz et al., 2015; see also Sherry's [1996] introspective account of how redeeming a gift card altered his buying behavior).

My goals in providing this admittedly truncated tour of the experimental work that focuses on gift giving within consumer behavior is twofold. First, I merely wish to demonstrate that a topic once seemingly perceived as 'qualitative' now draws the attention of prominent consumer psychologists as well. More importantly, however, these scholars often are exemplary at leveraging robust enabling theories to probe aspects of gifting behavior – a scholarly practice absent from much qualitative and/or CCT research on gift giving. Yet CCT scholars are not novices at successfully leveraging enabling theories, as recent work incorporating assemblage theory, practice theory, and institutional theory attests (e.g., Canniford and Shankar, 2013; Scaraboto and Fischer, 2013; Schau et al., 2009). It therefore might be wise if CCT/qualitative gift-giving scholars might be wise to emulate the approach of their consumer-psychologist colleagues, and consider the applicability of enabling theories to gift-giving research as means of explicating and enriching their findings. Yet Belk's point in his keynote speech at the 2017 CCT conference is that generating grounded theory is a vital goal in the field as well, and gift-giving scholarship certainly would benefit from a renewed quest for robust grounded theoretical interpretations.

Charitable Donating vs Gift Giving

The Transformative Consumer Research (TCR) paradigm attracts scholars interested in a plethora of topics, and who employ a variety of methodological approaches within our field (Mick et al., 2012). One consequence is an upsurge of interest in various forms of pro-social behavior, including the popular topic of charitable donating. Indeed, consumer psychologists plumbed this activity before turning their attention to consumer-to-consumer gift giving. The types of dependent variables observable in studies of charitable donating typically pertain to level and type of donation intentions, or to the actual donation levels of money over other resources, such as time and effort (e.g., Lichtenstein et al., 2004; Winterich et al., 2009).

In contrast, I could find no studies within major consumer research journals where qualitative or CCT scholars explore charitable donating. However, one niche journal, the *International Journal of Nonprofit and Voluntary Sector Marketing*, includes qualitative studies on topics such as consumers' patronage of charity brands, and on other types of donating such as volunteer behavior – albeit not that recently (Hibbert and Home, 1997; Tapp, 1996).

Understanding the motivations for, and mediators and moderators that influence, charitable donating is no doubt a worthy endeavor, especially as income disparities become increasingly dramatic between the haves and the have-nots, and as the marketing discipline seeks to understand how the skills and talents of those it trains can contribute to socially conscious and just outcomes. But one question still looms large – are charitable donating and gift giving 'related'? That is, are they different versions of gift giving, or different types of behaviors entirely? In fact, the titles of many articles seem to indicate that the boundaries between the two are for all practical purposes nonexistent. Article searches yield the words 'gift giving' in works that focus on charitable donating, rather than the occasion-oriented types of exchange typically associated with the term. Fischer et al. (1996) attempt to de-muddy the definitional waters, arguing that gift giving is distinct from charitable donating because donating represents a transfer, but not an exchange, of desired assets. For example, charitable donating can occur when no relationship exists between donor and recipient, and when there is no expectation of reciprocity. Furthermore, requests for donations typically emanate from potential recipients, or from entities acting on their behalf.

Recently, however, Domen Bajde, a CCT scholar, argues forcefully that charitable donating is, in fact, a form of gift giving, because it enables both parties in the exchange to participate in 'imagined communities' linked by emotional and other affiliative ties (2009). Echoing his like-minded colleagues who push back on the dominance of a focus on dyadic exchange, Bajde argues that focusing on charitable giving will enable us to understand other motivations such as humanitarian giving, because 'the imagined community of humanity becomes an entity that can receive gifts' (2009, p. 70). Importantly in this conceptual article, he leaves many questions for future scholars to address, such as the nature of imagined communities, and how their members actually perceive distinctions between gift giving and charitable donating.

Sharing vs Giving

Once again demonstrating his prowess for pioneering important constructs in consumer research, Belk (2010) presents his conceptual argument for regarding sharing as a core consumption-laden behavior that deserves attention by scholars. One of the key aspects of this publication is his discussion of the similarities and differences between sharing and giving. He draws distinctions between the two constructs by offering prototypes of each, which he believes places their differences in high relief. He avers that two appropriate prototypes for sharing are 'mothering and the pooling of allocations within the ideal family' (2010, p. 717), because these conceptualizations are absent of expectations of reciprocity, represent joint ownership, and are often practiced on the communal level.

In contrast, Belk offers as the prototype for gift giving his own metaphor of the 'perfect gift', with its characteristics of sacrifice, intention to please the recipient, a luxury good (an element I revisit in my research agenda), and eliciting surprise and delight. He acknowledges that both giving and sharing can bind the parties involved in an intimate way, and basically argues that the main difference between the two is that 'whereas the gift imposes an obligation of reciprocity, sharing does not' (2010, p. 718). He also observes that several scholars interchange the use of giving and sharing in their research. I noted above that although Giesler's work portends to discuss networked giving, his own discussion makes as much of a case for the behavior as a case study of sharing. Belk's seminal piece on sharing does feature a table where he delineates what he sees are the dimensions and differences between giving, sharing, and commodity exchange. Although I agree with many of his differentiating dimensions between giving and sharing, I respectfully would argue that the 'perfect gift' metaphor is not always an accurate prototype for giving. In their work, Belk and Coon (1993) present three different models that can govern gift giving – namely, economic exchange, social exchange, and (their contribution in the article) – agapic giving. I would argue that the 'perfect gift' prototype fits that category – and that sometimes, the other gift-exchange models are salient. In other words, we do not always seek a perfect gift to fulfill our social-network obligations – sometimes we just want to get it over with, and select a cheese basket. What I think Belk (2010) reveals is that the distinction between giving and sharing should remain open for future debate.

Gift Giving (Buying) in the Marketplace

Weinberger (2016) explores how the types and sources of gifts people offer at holidays and special occasions evolved in America, chronicling the transition from homemade items to goods and services increasingly obtained from the commercial sphere. She notes that 'a confluence of social, cultural, and market conditions in the early 1800s laid the groundwork for the commercialization of gift giving … The marketplace is now the main source for … gifts [with] retailers central to the cultivation of this acceptance' (n.p.). In fact, consumer gift-buying behavior is so vital to the health of many stakeholders in the retail, tourist, and experience industries that many depend on revenues from gift sales for survival.

In 1989, John Sherry and Mary Ann McGrath published what remains one of the most detailed ethnographies pertaining to gift buying in the field. It foreshadowed and stimulated a core aspect of their personal research agendas – specifically, understanding the reflexive relationship between consumers' reliance on marketplace experiences and their conceptualizations and creations of domestic ritual occasions. In this chapter, the authors each immersed themselves in the ethnographic study of one gift store for an entire month before, during and after the Christmas season. Meticulously crafting thick descriptions of the atmospherics, activities, and customer/salespeople interactions in these stores, they then offer several research propositions to propel the study of gift buying and selling. With respect to the salience of the gift store during the holiday season, one conclusion they offer is that the retail store itself (and not just special wrapping and preparations of a potential gift object) helps transform what consumers might perceive as ordinary commodities into gifts. Specifically, retail stores can 'alter and disrupt mundane perceptions and assumptions by enriching stimulation … the experience of the stores … is [itself] a gift … from proprietor to prospect' (1989, p. 161).

The authors follow this work with marketplace-related gift research focused on consumers' perceptions and retail-related activities when returning gifts. Leveraging Sidney Levy's deep knowledge of the human psyche, they rely on projective and other techniques to study actual and fantasized gift-return scenarios, which reveal how consumers' marketplace experiences contribute to the 'dark side' of gift giving (Sherry et al., 1992, 1993).

Although gift-buying activities associated with Christmas dominate the early literature (e.g., Fischer and Arnold, 1990; Laroche et al., 2000; Otnes et al., 1993), recently scholars have begun to explore marketplace activities associated with wedding gifting as well. Bradford and Sherry (2013) delve deeply into this topic. In particular, exploring the retail institution of the bridal registry provides a lens into the previously neglected topic of branded goods as gifts. In addition, exploring registries from the perspective of givers (or 'donors' – the term Sherry favors) and recipients illuminates how registries reduces the anxiety for both givers who wish to select a socially appropriate gift, and for recipients learning how to make decisions as a couple.

Furthermore, this work spotlights how both retailers and brands help 'serve as brokers in consumer-to-consumer relationships as [couples] perform their roles in view of the ritual audience [e.g., givers] within the arena provided by the retailer and the registry it houses' (2013, p. 164).

Thus, gift-giving research in the twenty-first century fully recognizes the importance of incorporating not just the enactment of actual gift exchange, but also how consumers rely on the marketplace when selecting gifts. Of course, the dominant new frontier of gift buying is now the consumer's computer or smartphone; recent estimates place these devices as the sites for over half of all gift shopping in the US (Allen, 2015). This topic is the newest, and last, stream of research I will discuss.

Gift Giving and the Digital Economy

Even as computer-mediated marketplace behavior represents an unprecedented paradigm shift in the ways consumers shop, how retail marketplaces and social-media communications facilitate or hinder consumer gift buying and giving is sorely underexplored. Because of space constraints and the lack of any robust empirical stream, I discuss just one conceptual article that addresses this issue. Belk (2013) extends his original conceptualization of possessions as extensions of the self to include social-media enactments, experiences, and expressions. In highlighting the key areas of research pertaining to the digital extended self, he calls attention to gift giving – an interest that should not surprise anyone familiar with his career, or even reading this chapter (see also Otnes, 2014). Belk first highlights five key ways the digital world has transformed entities pertaining to the extended self (including dematerialization, re-embodiment through such phenomena as avatars and consumer co-construction of entities and experiences). Next, he argues that the digital world also contributes new and impermanent gift forms, such as compliments on social-media posts, text messages, and tags on photos. He observes that the digital arena reveals the manifestation of 'various motivations [for] digital gift giving, ranging from reciprocity-seeking, ingratiation, and status-seeking to altruism and love' (Belk, 2013, p. 492). Certainly, old-school gift (and identity) scholars might find Belk's assertion pertaining to these new forms of gifts to be controversial. However, the important issue here is that Belk urges scholars to explore how the digital world reconfigures (and perhaps even razes) the definitions and delineations of gift giving rooted in a pre-digital landscape.

GIVING TO THE FIELD: REINVIGORATING AND RECONCILING THE SCOPE OF GIFT-EXCHANGE RESEARCH

About ten years ago, I submitted a paper on gift giving to a conference. A reviewer returned this one-sentence critique: 'the last thing consumer research needs is another paper on gift giving'. I hope this chapter negates any notion that the topic is stagnant and no longer of value to the discipline. New configurations of kinship groups, new marketplace opportunities, and of course, the dominance (hegemony?)

of social media continue to exert influence and reshape general cultural norms and practices, as well as those that govern (or lead to resistance to [Weinberger, 2015]) gift giving. Furthermore, if the review above demonstrates anything, it is that several often distinct groups of scholars would no doubt benefit greatly from a joint effort or event in which to share their different perspectives on the topic.

Framed by gift episodes from my own experience, in this section I offer a research agenda that seeks to connect some of the findings and foci from the six research streams discussed above. I do so hoping to reconcile some of the seemingly disparate and disconnected strains that continually tug at the definition and domain of gift giving within consumer research, and to stimulate research that recognizes the value of integrating micro, meso, and macro approaches. If research in gift giving is to move beyond its siloed approach and become truly intra-disciplinary, it is important to consider more holistic approaches to understanding the antecedents, processes, and consequences of the behavior.

Understanding Impactful Gifts

Cycling back to Sherry's (1983) seminal gift-giving framework, the Reformulation phase – where gifts exert an impact on a recipient's future life, and on relational outcomes within a dyad or intimate network – remains the least understood. Researchers plumb the short-term relational effects of gift exchange in dyads (Ruth et al., 1999) – but what do we know of the positive or negative long-term impact of gifts? For example, when interacting with intimate others, givers (and especially family members, provided the relationships are healthy!) often devote a great deal of time and energy mulling over what gifts can make the most difference to their loved ones. When we consider the gifts that have made the most difference in our lives, what are they? Are they gifts of money that recipients then convert into investments of social, cultural, or educational capital (Bradford, 2009)? Do millennials – especially those living in the 'age of entitlement' (Twenge and Campbell, 2009) even perceive such offerings as tuition payments at elite institutions, trips abroad, or years of dance lessons as gifts? How do people living in countries such as those in the Nordic region who enjoy macro-level entitlements such as free college, healthcare, and retirement pensions, perceive these entitlements? Are they cultural-level gifts? If so, how do these citizens reciprocate (if at all)? Furthermore, how do their perspectives on such entitlements shape the types of goods, services, and experiences exchanged at the micro-level?

In short, what do we understand about the nature and impact of truly impactful gifts in our lives? Popular accounts of gifting behavior typically focus on the 'hot' items for different gift occasions – with some even stimulating violence as givers fight over scarce goods (e.g., Fitzpatrick, 2015). However, I seriously doubt that recipients would ultimately deem even a scuffle-inducing 'Tickle Me Elmo' doll as life changing – so which gifts (if any) can and do contribute to our transformations of self in our social networks and broader communities, in positive and negative ways?

For example, in America it used be quite common for many middle- and upper-class students to receive cars when graduating from high school or college, and research discusses the transformational outcomes of these items (e.g., Otnes et al., 2014). When I moved to Austin in 1982 for graduate school, my parents gifted me their 'beater' – a

1976 Chevy Nova, which enabled me to take a job across town as a copywriter, and to foster social relationships with my co-workers and the Austin advertising community in general. However, millennials are more reluctant to accept the inherent burdens of driving and car ownership. So which gifts now symbolize the passage to adulthood in contemporary culture? Scholars across the six research streams I discuss above could work together and explore this topic, and enable a truly deep understanding of how impactful gifts emanate from and transcend the micro, meso, and macro levels.

Revisiting Gift Traditions

This chapter affirms that the overwhelming balance of gift-giving activity still occurs within intimate dyadic and family groups. Like many people, my history as a gift giver began in childhood, and is replete with gift-giving traditions enjoyed with friends and family members. These range from the relatively tame – for example, always giving my mother-in-law a jigsaw puzzle for Christmas – to the greatly-anticipated and often hilarious (for years, Sharon Shavitt and I tried to one-up each other in our selection of tacky-souvenir gifts). My own research with Tina Lowrey and Julie Ruth found us reviewing countless instances of gift traditions. Given the potential importance of such repetitive and entrenched behavior to social networks and to marketers, it is worth exploring how such traditions get started, what causes them to remain stalwart, and what contributes to their demise (after alligator back-scratchers and light-up Rosetta Stone pins, Sharon and I somehow implicitly agreed to switch to kitschy food souvenirs). Again, researchers could inform explorations of this topic at a cultural level as well. Work in the tourism field avers that Japanese consumers seem sociologically mandated to buy souvenirs for friends and family members (e.g., Park, 2000). Furthermore, recent experimental research reveals that traditions during family rituals can enhance consumers' happiness with these occasions (Sezer et al., 2016) – integrating findings from the now-robust stream of happiness research in the area of ritual studies, when most of the previous emotions explored in that space focus on ambivalence and anxiety (e.g., Otnes et al., 1997; Wooten, 2000).

What is Gift Giving, Anyway?

If my review of the literature demonstrates anything, it is that the meaning(s) of gift giving, and the characteristics distinguishing it from related behaviors such as sharing and charitable donating, remain murky. I do not advocate becoming bogged down in definitional diatribe. However, it may be time to take a good, hard look at what may or may not constitute gift giving, gift buying, and even gift making (e.g., how people respond to items produced with 3-D printers; Rindfleisch and O'Hern, 2015) – recognizing that what constitutes a gift is an historically and culturally situated judgment. When I ask my husband what he wants for Christmas every year, inevitably he tells me, 'a hug'. Although he always finds more than that under the tree, where do these gifts of the self fall on the continuum of value for recipients? Other scholarship examines gifts from the body (e.g., blood, organs, embryos; Healy,

2010). Revisiting the notion of impactful gifts, deciding to become a donor in the most literal sense may be the most crucial of all offerings for the potential recipient. Perhaps rather than bogging down in devising 'the' definition of gift giving, it would be better to consider what aspects of giving, sharing, or donating each of the tangible and intangible forms convey. Scaraboto's explication of the theoretical landscape that explains the relative contribution of various types of exchange behavior within a networked community is an excellent example in this regard.

Gift Giving and Strategic Marketing Decisions

It is now a truism that many consumers across the globe are captivated by luxury brands, although readers of extant gift-giving research would be forgiven if they came away thinking such goods are not popular gift options. Indeed, my search for literature on this topic yielded literally no study focusing on luxury goods as gifts. Consider, however, that luxury goods seem to fulfill a number of key roles in terms of status signaling, from both the social-competitive and the evolutionary-psychology perspectives (e.g., Nelissen and Meijers, 2011). Luxury goods might also seem to satisfy the criteria Belk (1996) identifies as central to the 'perfect gift'. One Christmas, I opened what I thought was a white leather clasp purse from my mother, only to realize it was a high-end jewelry case containing a strand of genuine pearls (a contemporary strand, with the pearls about an inch apart, but still!). I remember immediately thinking how different – and amazing – this gift was, compared to the many from her I had regarded as 'so not me' (and often 'so her') over the years. Clearly, the cultural discourses surrounding luxury goods are tempting and trenchant – but how does this fascination translate into the experience of giving, receiving and reciprocating them (or not being able to)?

With regard to another marketplace trend, the rise of gift cards, with annual sales in the US alone topping $130 billion ('2015 gift card sales …', 2015), is also a phenomenon worthy of attention, not only among their givers and recipients, but also at the social-network and cultural levels. Indeed, an entire industry now exists to support people unloading undesired gift cards at discounts to website brokers (e.g., www.raise.com). Culturally, what do gift cards really mean – e.g., do they signal a cultural malaise with holiday shopping, a realization that people are basically greedy and (again) entitled, wanting what they want – and don't really like others to select items for them? Recent experimental studies broach the topic – but here, researchers rather than study participants select the variables they deem salient. Surely, such a ubiquitous phenomenon could (and probably should) be the focus of deep qualitative study.

Theorizing Gift Giving

Given the abundance of scholars who approach the topic of gift-giving from different angles, I believe the most important question they could explore (preferably by crossing/transgressing into each other's terrains) is: (How) has our theorization of gift-giving improved – and how can scholars deepen it in the future? Extant work reflects approaches ranging from: (1) experiments that leverage enabling theories; (2) a few qualitative/CCT studies that do the same; and (3) dominating the qualitative paradigm, grounded-theoretical empirical studies. Some scholars – Belk in particular – consistently strive to expand the construct of gift giving. He now includes the gifting practices associated with hospitality behavior (Sobh et al., 2013), as well as the aforementioned digital 'presents' of communication and feedback.

To deepen the level of theorization, I offer three routes for gift-giving scholars. First, they can follow the precedent of their experimental colleagues, and consider exploring the salience of robust consumer-psychological theories through historical and sociocultural lenses (and methods that enable their application). As an example, Klein et al. (2015) ponder how to interpret gift-giving practices among Holocaust prisoners, through the enabling lens of Oyserman's identity-based motivation theory. It enables us to both explain the significance of gift-giving incidents within concentration camps, but also to make sense of survivors' discussions of how these gifts informed the prisoners' selves as they wrote their memoirs later in life. Furthermore, a robust theory such as the horizontal/vertical individualism-collectivism stream that Sharon Shavitt, Carlos Torelli and other scholars plumb would certainly seem to enrich cross-cultural research on gift giving (Shavitt et al., 2006; Torelli and Shavitt, 2010).

Second, scholars could also consider new work by anthropologists who are revisiting and reinterpreting the seminal research on gift giving conducted in the early twentieth century within the context of contemporary societies. Several recent book-length treatments (Godbout, 1998; Godelier, 1996; Rupp, 2003; Sykes, 2005) challenge these core theoretical pillars – which consumer scholars often (re)cite without reconsidering their relevance to contemporary gifting practices. For example, Sykes (2005) discusses how scholars can revisit Mauss's conceptualization of the gift as a 'total social fact' to help scholars compare the meaning of gift giving across cultures. In other words, because the concept is 'profoundly a sociological, and not a philosophical concept … it is best discussed in ethnographic examples' (2005, p. 63) and thus, can re-energize the study of comparative exchange practices, to determine whether, to what extent, and how the core constructs of reciprocity, obligation, and competitive giving, as well as sacrifice still manifest within various cultural contexts.

Third, reflecting on the current value placed upon understanding process-approaches to consumption, especially in the CCT domain (e.g., Giesler and Thompson, 2016), gift scholars certainly could pay more attention to the ways gift giving and gift buying unfold. Although my colleagues and I can speak to the difficulty of conducting longitudinal research on gift behavior (Lowrey et al., 2004), I believe we also successfully demonstrated how over time, entrenched exchange histories with specific dyadic partners exert power to shape people's perceptions of (in)appropriate gifts. In truth, however, most gift-giving research is essentially devoid of process, and even that study extrapolates"longitudinal" explanation from retrospective accounts.

Gift Giving and Consumer Welfare

As noted, disparate groups of scholars across the discipline pursue research on gift giving and charitable donating. However, the Transformative Consumer Research paradigm could serve as a common bridge across these camps, given that they all traverse consumer-welfare issues (e.g., the stress and responsibilities of participating in gift buying and giving; the burdens of offering various resources when making charitable donations). Furthermore, the TCR agenda also prompts deep questions about gift giving that pertain to social injustice and underprivileged consumers' inability to meet their social demands. Simply addressing how the poor negotiate the gift economy is a compelling question. Research indicates that for highly visible sociocultural rituals such as weddings and funerals, lower-income consumers often spend a higher percentage of their income than those in the middle or upper class (Otnes and Pleck, 2003). Yet (perhaps paternalistic, but definitely critical) questions abound as to the 'rationality' of these decisions, given the struggle for most of these families to engender a daily existence. Fundamentally, considering the costs people might incur if they choose to forego their social obligations strikes at issues related to the ability to maintain face, and to preserve dignity and pride.

CONCLUSION

I began this chapter a few weeks prior to Christmas 2016, and ended it in the second week of January, 2017 – an appropriate time of the year to ponder the state of gift-giving research. My foray through sales flyers and Facebook ads for 'perfect gifts', and my memorable dash through the Dallas Cowboys airport store on Christmas Eve reminded me of the blessings and burdens of entrenchment in a gift economy. As both life in a consumer culture and the literature discussed above attest, gift giving is still a 'total social fact,' at least in terms of its existence, but perhaps not exactly manifest in form and function as Mauss describes it.

A few days after Thanksgiving, I received an envelope in my newspaper from our paper-route provider. Chockablock with printed family photos that identified his wife and kids by name, it featured the helpful instructions: 'For Christmas tips: tape to the door – just leave the lights on so I can see it!' A few days before our Christmas travels, I dutifully taped a tip to the door in the envelope, with the lights on, as 'suggested'. This example alone could serve as the foundation for a study of compliance in gift giving – in all of its explicit and implicit glory. But whatever future gift-giving topic appeals, I hope this chapter proves enlightening, and encourages a cornucopia of studies that see CCT scholars, TCR scholars, experimentalists, retail-strategy scholars and others working together to re-energize and re-theorize this fascinating topic. What a gift to the field such an effort could be!

REFERENCES

2015 gift card sales to reach new peak of $130 billion, 2015. *PR Newswire.* Retrieved from http://www.prnewswire.com/news-releases/2015-gift-card-sales-to-reach-new-peak-of-130-billion-300189615.html

Adloff, F., 2006. Beyond interests and norms: Toward a theory of gift-giving and reciprocity in modern societies. *Constellations*, *13*(3), pp. 407–427.

Allen, K.G., 2015. Retailers in for a very digital holiday season, according to NRF survey. Retrieved from https://nrf.com/media/press-releases/retailers-very-digital-holiday-season-according-nrf-survey

Arnould, E.J. and Thompson, C.J., 2005. Consumer culture theory (CCT): Twenty years of research. *Journal of consumer research*, *31*(4), pp. 868–882.

Bajde, D., 2009. Rethinking the social and cultural dimensions of charitable giving. *Consumption markets & culture*, *12*(1), pp. 65–84.

Bardhi, F. and Eckhardt, G.M., 2012. Access-based consumption: The case of car sharing. *Journal of consumer research*, *39*(4), pp. 881–898.

Baskin, E., Wakslak, C.J., Trope, Y. and Novemsky, N., 2014. Why feasibility matters more to gift receivers than to givers: A construal-level approach to gift giving. *Journal of consumer research*, *41*(1), pp. 169–182.

Belk, R.W., 1976. It's the thought that counts: A signed digraph analysis of gift-giving. *Journal of consumer research*, *3*(3), pp. 155–162.

Belk, R.W., 1989. Materialism and the modern U.S. Christmas. In E. Hirschman, ed., *Interpretive Consumer Research*, Provo: Association for Consumer Research, pp. 136–147.

Belk, R.W., ed., 1991. *Highways and Buyways: Naturalistic Research from the Consumer Behavior Odyssey*, Provo, UT: Association for Consumer Research.

Belk, R.W., 2004. Possessions, self, and the sacred. In A. Griffin and C. Otnes, ed., *The Sixteenth Paul D. Converse Symposium*, Chicago: American Marketing Association, pp. 46–66.

Belk, R.W., 1996. The perfect gift. In C. Otnes and R. Beltramini, eds, *Gift-giving: A Research Anthology*, Bowling Green, KY: Popular Press, pp. 59–84.

Belk, R.W., 2010. Sharing. *Journal of consumer research*, *36*(5), pp. 715–734.

Belk, R.W., 2013. Extended self in a digital world. *Journal of consumer research*, *40*(3), pp. 477–500.

Belk, R.W. and Coon, G.S., 1993. Gift giving as agapic love: An alternative to the exchange paradigm based on dating experiences. *Journal of consumer research*, *20*(3), pp. 393–417.

Belk, R.W., Wallendorf, M. and Sherry Jr, J.F., 1989. The sacred and profane within consumer research: Theodicy on the Odyssey. *Journal of consumer research*, *16*(1), pp. 1–38.

Bonsu, S.K. and Belk, R.W., 2003. Do not go cheaply into that good night: Death-ritual consumption in Asante, Ghana. *Journal of consumer research*, *30*(1), pp. 41–55.

Bradford, T.W., 2009. Intergenerationally gifted asset dispositions. *Journal of consumer research*, *36*(1), pp. 93–111.

Bradford, T.W. and Sherry, J.F., 2013. Orchestrating rituals through retailers: An examination of gift registry. *Journal of retailing*, *89*(2), pp. 158–175.

Braverman, B., 2016. How to give large money gifts for the holidays. *Consumer reports*. Retrieved from http://www.consumerreports.org/taxes/how-to-give-large-money-gifts/

Canniford, R. and Shankar, A., 2013. Purifying practices: How consumers assemble romantic experiences of nature. *Journal of consumer research*, *39*(5), pp. 1051–1069.

Curasi, C.F., Price, L.L. and Arnould, E.J., 2004. How individuals' cherished possessions become families' inalienable wealth. *Journal of consumer research*, *31*(3), pp. 609–622.

Fischer, E. and Arnold, S.J., 1990. More than a labor of love: Gender roles and Christmas gift shopping. *Journal of consumer research*, *17*(3), pp. 333–345.

Fischer, E., Gainer, B. and Arnold, S.J., 1996. Gift giving and charitable donating: How (dis)similar are they? In C. Otnes and R. Beltramini, eds, *Gift-Giving: A Research Anthology*, Bowling Green, KY: Popular Press, pp. 175–194.

Fitzpatrick, M., 2015. Black Friday through the years: Toys that made parents lose their damn minds. *Fusion*, retrieved from http://fusion.net/story/234679/black-friday-hottest-holiday-toys-fads/

Giesler, M., 2006. Consumer gift systems. *Journal of consumer research*, *33*(2), pp. 283–290.

Giesler, M. and Thompson, C.J., 2016. Process theorization in cultural consumer research. *Journal of consumer research*, *43*(4), pp. 497–508.

Godbout, J.T., 1998. *The World of the Gift*, trans. D. Winkler, Montreal: McGill Queen's University Press.

Godelier, M., 1996. *The Enigma of the Gift*, trans. N. Scott, Chicago: University of Chicago Press.

Gouldner, A.W., 1960. The norm of reciprocity: A preliminary statement. *American sociological review*, *25*(2), pp. 161–178.

Green, R.T. and Alden, D.L., 1988. Functional equivalence in cross-cultural consumer behavior: Gift giving in Japan and the United States. *Psychology & marketing*, *5*(2), pp. 155–168.

Healy, K., 2010. *Last Best Gifts: Altruism and the Market for Human Blood and Organs*, Chicago: University of Chicago Press.

Helion, C. and Gilovich, T., 2014. Gift cards and mental accounting: Green-lighting hedonic spending. *Journal of behavioral decision making*, *27*(4), 386–393.

Hibbert, S.A. and Home, S., 1997. Donation dilemmas: A consumer behavior perspective. *International journal of nonprofit and voluntary sector marketing*, *2*(3), pp. 261–274.

Joy, A., 2001. Gift giving in Hong Kong and the continuum of social ties. *Journal of consumer research*, *28*(2), pp. 239–256.

Kieras, J.E., Tobin, R.M., Graziano, W.G. and Rothbart, M.K., 2005. You can't always get what you want: Effortful control and children's responses to undesirable gifts. *Psychological science*, 26(5), 391–396.

Kimura, J. and Belk, R.W., 2005. Christmas in Japan: Globalization versus localization. *Consumption markets & culture*, *8*(3), pp. 325–338.

Klein, J.G., Lowrey, T.M. and Otnes, C.C., 2015. Identity-based motivations and anticipated reckoning: Contributions to gift-giving theory from an identity-stripping context. *Journal of consumer psychology*, *25*(3), pp. 431–448.

Kozinets, R.V., 2002. Can consumers escape the market? Emancipatory illuminations from Burning Man. *Journal of consumer research*, *29*(1), pp. 20–38.

Laroche, M., Saad, G., Kim, C. and Browne, E., 2000. A cross-cultural study of in-store information search strategies for a Christmas gift. *Journal of business research*, *49*(2), pp. 113–126.

Levi-Strauss, C., 1969/1949. *The Elementary Structures of Kinship.* Boston: Beacon.

Lichtenstein, D.R., Drumwright, M.E. and Braig, B.M., 2004. The effect of corporate social responsibility on customer donations to corporate-supported nonprofits. *Journal of marketing*, *68*(4), pp. 16–32.

Long, H., 2015. Americans will spend over $130 on 'self-gifting', November 26, 2015, retrieved from: http://money.cnn.com/2015/11/26/news/economy/black-friday-self-gifting/

Lowrey, T.M., Otnes, C. and Robbins, K., 1996. Values influencing Christmas gift giving: An interpretive study. In C. Otnes and R. Beltramini, eds, *Gift-giving: A research anthology*, Bowling Green, KY: Popular Press, pp. 37–56.

Lowrey, T.M., Otnes, C.C. and Ruth, J.A., 2004. Social influences on dyadic giving over time: a taxonomy from the giver's perspective. *Journal of consumer research*, *30*(4), pp. 547–558.

Malinowski, B., 2002/1922. *Argonauts of the Western Pacific*, London: Routledge.

Marcoux, J.S., 2009. Escaping the gift economy. *Journal of consumer research*, *36*(4), pp. 671–685.

Mauss, M., 1990/1925. *The Gift*. London: Cohen and West.

Mick, D.G. and DeMoss, M., 1990. Self-gifts: phenomenological insights from four contexts. *Journal of consumer research*, *17*(3), pp. 322–332.

Mick, D.G., Pettigrew, S., Pechmann, C.C. and Ozanne, J.L., eds, 2012. *Transformative Consumer Research for Personal and Collective Well-Being*, London: Routledge.

Nelissen, R.M. and Meijers, M.H., 2011. Social benefits of luxury brands as costly signals of wealth and status. *Evolution and human behavior*, *32*(5), pp. 343–355.

Osteen, M., ed., 2002. *The Question of the Gift: Essays across Disciplines*. London: Routledge.

Otnes, C., ed., 2014. *Legends in Consumer Behavior: Russell Belk: Gift-giving, Sharing, and Consumption Holidays (v.7)*, Thousand Oaks, CA: Sage.

Otnes, C. and Beltramini, R., eds, 1996. *Gift Giving: A Research Anthology*, Bowling Green, KY: Popular Press.

Otnes, C. and Pleck, E., 2003. *Cinderella Dreams: The Allure of the Lavish Wedding*. Berkeley: University of California Press.

Otnes, C., Lowrey, T.M. and Kim, Y.C., 1993. Gift selection for easy and difficult recipients: A social roles interpretation. *Journal of consumer research*, *20*(2), pp. 229–244.

Otnes, C., Lowrey, T.M. and Shrum, L.J., 1997. Toward an understanding of consumer ambivalence. *Journal of consumer research*, *24*(1), pp. 80–93.

Otnes, C., Ruth, J.A. and Crosby, E.M., 2014. Product-agency benefits: Consumer perspectives and strategic implications. *European journal of marketing*, *48*(5/6), pp. 878– 898.

Oyserman, D., 2009. Identity-based motivation and consumer behavior. *Journal of consumer psychology*, *19*(3), pp. 276–279.

Park, M.K., 2000. Social and cultural factors influencing tourists' souvenir-purchasing behavior: A comparative study on Japanese 'Omiyage' and Korean 'Sunmul'. *Journal of travel & tourism marketing*, *9*(1–2), pp. 81–91.

Park, P.S. and Kim, Y.H., 2017. Reciprocation under status ambiguity: How dominance motives and spread of status value shape gift exchange. *Social networks*, *48*, pp. 142–156.

Parmentier, M.A. and Fischer, E., 2015. Things fall apart: The dynamics of brand audience dissipation. *Journal of consumer research*, *41*(5), pp. 1228–1251.

Price, L.L., Arnould, E.J. and Curasi, C.F., 2000. Older consumers' disposition of special possessions. *Journal of consumer research*, *27*(2), pp. 179–201.

Reinholtz, N., Bartels, D.M. and Parker, J.R., 2015. On the mental accounting of restricted-use funds: How gift cards change what people purchase. *Journal of consumer research*, *42*(4), 596–614.

Rindfleisch, A. and O'Hern, M., 2015. Brand remixing: 3D printing the Nokia case. *Brand meaning management*, 12, pp. 53–81.

Rupp, K., 2003. *Gift-Giving in Japan*, Stanford, CA: Stanford University Press.

Ruth, J.A., Otnes, C.C. and Brunel, F.F., 1999. Gift receipt and the reformulation of interpersonal relationships. *Journal of consumer research*, *25*(4), pp. 385–402.

Scaraboto, D., 2015. Selling, sharing, and everything in between: The hybrid economies of collaborative networks. *Journal of consumer research*, *42*(1), pp. 152–176.

Scaraboto, D. and Fischer, E., 2013. Frustrated fatshionistas: An institutional theory perspective on consumer quests for greater choice in mainstream markets. *Journal of consumer research*, *39*(6), pp. 1234–1257.

Schau, H.J., Muñiz Jr, A.M. and Arnould, E.J., 2009. How brand community practices create value. *Journal of marketing*, *73*(5), pp. 30–51.

Sezer, O., Norton, M.I., Gino, F. and Vohs, K.D., 2016. Family rituals improve the holidays. *Journal of the association for consumer research* *1*(4), pp. 509–526.

Shavitt, S., Lalwani, A.K., Zhang, J. and Torelli, C.J., 2006. The horizontal/vertical distinction in cross-cultural consumer research. *Journal of consumer psychology*, *16*(4), pp. 325–342.

Sherry Jr, J.F., 1983. Gift giving in anthropological perspective. *Journal of consumer research*, *10*(2), pp. 157–168.

Sherry Jr, J.F., 1996. Reflections on giftware and giftcare: Whither consumer research? In C. Otnes and R. Beltramini, eds, *Gift Giving: A Research Anthology*, Bowling Green, KY, pp. 217–227.

Sherry Jr, J.F. and McGrath, M.A., 1989. Unpacking the holiday presence: A comparative ethnography of two gift stores. In E. Hirschman, ed., *Interpretive Consumer Research*, Provo, UT: Assn. for Consumer Research, pp. 148–167.

Sherry Jr, J.F., McGrath, M.A. and Levy, S.J., 1992. The disposition of the gift and many unhappy returns. *Journal of retailing*, *68*(1), pp. 40–65.

Sherry Jr, J.F., McGrath, M.A. and Levy, S.J., 1993. The dark side of the gift. *Journal of business research*, *28*(3), pp. 225–244.

Sobh, R., Belk, R.W. and Wilson, J.A., 2013. Islamic Arab hospitality and multiculturalism. *Marketing theory*, *13*(4), 442–463.

Steffel, M. and Le Boeuf, R.A., 2014. Overindividuation in gift giving: shopping for multiple recipients leads givers to choose unique but less preferred gifts. *Journal of consumer research*, *40*(6), pp. 1167–1180.

Sykes, K. 2005., *Arguing with Anthropology*. London: Routledge.

Tapp, A., 1996. Charity brands: A qualitative study of current practice. *International journal of nonprofit and voluntary sector marketing*, *1*(4), pp. 327–336.

Thaler, R., 1985. Mental accounting and consumer choice. *Marketing science*, *4*(3), pp. 199–214.

Torelli, C.J. and Shavitt, S., 2010. Culture and concepts of power. *Journal of personality and social psychology*, *99*(4), pp. 703–723.

Twenge, J.M. and Campbell, W.K., 2009. *The Narcissism Epidemic: Living in the Age of Entitlement*. New York: Simon and Schuster.

Wallendorf, M. and Arnould, E.J., 1991. 'We gather together': consumption rituals of Thanksgiving Day. *Journal of consumer research*, *18*(1), pp. 13–31.

Ward, M.K. and Broniarczyk, S.M., 2011. It's not me, it's you: how gift giving creates giver identity threat as a function of social closeness. *Journal of consumer research*, *38*(1), pp. 164–181.

Ward, M.K. and Broniarczyk, S.M., 2016. Ask and you shall (not) receive: close friends prioritize relational signaling over recipient preferences in their gift choices. *Journal of marketing research*, 53(6), pp. 1001–1018.

Webley, P., Lea, S.E. and Portalska, R., 1983. The unacceptability of money as a gift. *Journal of economic psychology*, *4*(3), pp. 223–238.

Weinberger, M.F., 2015. Dominant consumption rituals and intragroup boundary work: How non-celebrants manage conflicting relational and identity goals. *Journal of consumer research*, *42*(3), pp. 378–400.

Weinberger, M.F., 2016. Gifts: Intertwining market and moral economies and the rise of store bought gifts, *Consumption markets & culture*, *20*(3), 245–257, retrieved from http://www.tandfonline.com/doi/full/10.1080/10253866.2016.1231748

Weinberger, M.F. and Wallendorf, M., 2012. Intracommunity gifting at the intersection of contemporary moral and market economies. *Journal of consumer research*, *39*(1), pp. 74–92.

Winterich, K.P., Mittal, V. and Ross, W.T., 2009. Donation behavior toward in-groups and out-groups: The role of gender and moral identity. *Journal of consumer research*, *36*(2), pp. 199–214.

Wooten, D.B., 2000. Qualitative steps toward an expanded model of anxiety in gift-giving. *Journal of consumer research*, *27*(1), pp. 84–95.

14

Prosumption Tribes: How Consumers Collectively Rework Brands, Products, Services and Markets

Bernard Cova and Daniele Dalli

INTRODUCTION

This chapter deals with two important assumptions of consumer behaviour theories that are rooted in cognitive psychology and economics. The first is methodological individualism: the unit of observation is the individual consumer. The second is related to the nature of consumption activities: the consumer is seen as using (destroying) the utility created by companies and channelled through products and services.

Interpretive researchers (Beckmann and Elliott, 2000) have challenged these two assumptions as follows:

- Consumption is a collective phenomenon: groups just as individuals are capable of agency and, as such, they can be considered as the unit of analysis of the consumption process. Consumers are embedded in networks of social relations that are enacted through their behaviours and that – at the same time – assume their own agencies (Cova, 1997; Schouten and McAlexander, 1995). As such, these collectives are intermediaries between individuals and institutions (markets, companies, public agencies, other consumption collectives, etc.)
- Consumption is a constructive activity in which consumers actively add value to products and services (Aubert-Gamet, 1997; Firat and Shultz, 1997). Consumers work and re-work companies' offerings from the material point of view (e.g. customisation). They also add immaterial value through cultural and social interactions in which goods, services and brands are enriched through comments, reviews and discourses. In addition, consumers construct the social network in which and through which these offerings are actually channelled: without social networks the market alone – as we actually know it from the economic perspective – should not effectively work.

Interpretive scholars developed these ideas thanks to their strong theoretical orientation towards the cultural dimension of consumption (Arnould and Thompson, 2005, 2015): starting from sociological and anthropological premises, theoretical and empirical research drove the attention of scholars towards the **collective** and **constructive** dimensions of consumption. These streams of research grew up separately even if there are articles and scholars that tried to bridge them together (Schau et al., 2009); this chapter will provide a further contribution in this direction.

We first describe how the tribal phenomenon is growing in today's consumer culture and highlight similarities and differences between consumer tribes, subcultures of consumption, brand communities and brand publics. Then, we focus on communal practices and productive activities of consumer tribes and highlight how these lead companies to promote and capture consumers' value creation. Finally, we discuss how the prosumption tribe phenomenon challenges the boundaries between market and work and the roles played by economic agents (e.g., companies, tribes, consumers) and how this requires rethinking the related and established theories.

THE RISE OF TRIBES: FROM BRAND COMMUNITIES TO BRAND PUBLICS

Marketplace cultures and co-consuming groups stand on the forefront of interpretive consumer research (Cova et al., 2007) and form one of the four key realms of consumer culture research (Arnould and Thompson, 2005).

For the past two decades, and inspired in part by the application of the tribal theories of French sociologist Michel Maffesoli (1996), a new understanding of consumer collectives has emerged within consumer research and marketing theory. This approach rejects an atomistic, overly individualistic, information processing view of consumers as individuals who are sealed off and separated from their experiential worlds. Rather, a variety of studies, from both a North American anthropological tradition (Arnould and Price, 1993; Kozinets, 2001; Schouten and McAlexander, 1995) and a European micro-sociological tradition (Cova and Cova, 2002; Goulding et al., 2002), have ascertained that human life is essentially social. Social life is a rich, complex, kaleidoscopic mixture of affective and cultural relations. Scholars in this tradition refuse to analyse market-based phenomena through the imposition of abstract modernist structures (class, age, gender, etc.) in favour of what might be termed a bottom-up postmodern sociology (Maffesoli, 1996). In this view, the building blocks of human life are not to be found in abstract categories applied to the analysis of social life, but in the multiplicity of groupings that we all participate in, knowingly or not, through the course of our everyday lives. 'There is a shift from the individual with a stable identity, exercising a function in contractual groups, to the person playing different roles in *affectual* tribes' (Maffesoli, 2000, p. xvii). Through *re-tribalisation*, society therefore appears more and more like a network of societal micro-groups in which individuals entertain strong emotional bonds, experiences and common passions.

These tribes are fundamental to our experience of life in general. They differ from traditional tribes in an anthropological sense in one important way; we belong to many little tribes at the same time and we are not exclusively tied to one single tribe. From this perspective the consumption of cultural resources circulated through markets (goods, brands, leisure experiences, etc.) are not the *sine qua non* of contemporary life. Rather, they are means to facilitate meaningful social relationships (Cova, 1997). The 'links' (social relationships) are more important than the things (products, services, and brands).

These social, proximate groupings have an important effect on consumers' behaviour. The collective dimension of consumption is growing in importance due to various factors: consumers interact and communicate through identification and interaction with other consumers, as individuals and as groups. This holds on the direct, face-to-face level, but also through the medium of the Internet and related resources. More and more resources are available for consumers through which they can actually take part in the *re-tribalisation* of society (Maffesoli, 1996). The digital dimension of tribalisation is very important as individuals are given the opportunity to participate in tribes largely beyond their physical or local presence. Consumers all over the world are able to connect and contribute to events, campaigns, and discourses in general through digital technologies and social networks. Individual consumers from different contexts get in touch over the web and feel united and committed to each other under the umbrella of their common interest: products, services, brands, and experiences. The notion of the consumer has changed a lot recently, thanks to the digital drive and the resulting opportunities for social interaction (Belk, 2013). As a result, tribes and collectives assume an even greater role and the (digital) discursive domain becomes central for the process of consumers' acculturation to and participation in tribes.

In the wake of this interest for collective experiences, different labels in consumer research and marketing theory have been introduced to describe divergent – and sometimes overlapping – forms of co-consuming groups (Goulding et al., 2013):

- *Consumer tribe:* for a fluid group of people who share ephemeral experiences based on a particular product, service, brand or consumption activity (Cova et al., 2007);
- *Subculture of consumption:* for a group of people who share temporary ritualised experiences and commitment to a particular product, brand, or consumption activity (Schouten and McAlexander, 1995);
- *Brand community:* for a group of people who share rituals and ways of thinking and traditions, as well as a sense of moral responsibility towards other members, and religious zeal towards a focal brand (Muñiz and O'Guinn, 2001).

The similarities between brand communities, subcultures of consumption and consumer tribes are greater than their differences. They are all led by the return of community feeling that characterises contemporary tribalisation (Maffesoli, 1996). However, this categorisation allows researchers to differentiate between collective experiences according to three main traits: (1) the strength of the ties that bind people (from strong to fluid); (2) the type of interaction (from long-established rituals to ephemeral experiences); and (3) the object of their shared passion (a product, service, brand, or consumption activity).

Consumer tribes (Cova et al., 2007) are naturally occurring groups where tribe members identify with one another (or alternatively they can be 'activated' and encouraged to be linked together by social media or marketing activities); they have shared experiences and emotions; and they are capable of engaging in collective, though ephemeral, social action – that is, as members of the tribe consumers can 'do' things that they would not be able to do as non-members. A consumer tribe could form around any leisure-based activity, interest, hobby, or passion. 'If you are passionate about surfing, traveling, a TV show, snowboarding, running, reading books, a band or singer, knitting, fine wine, a film-star, music, international politics, fossil-hunting, or fishing, the rise of social media via the internet means that you can search for and find other likeminded devotees and voilà you will have the basis of a tribe' (Cova and Shankar, 2012, p. 180).

A subculture of consumption reunites individuals sharing the same original culture, or which otherwise deviates compared to a dominant culture. It is 'a distinctive subgroup of society that self-selects on the basis of a shared commitment to a particular product class, brand, or consumption activity' (Schouten and McAlexander, 1995, p. 43). Kozinets (2001) sees it as a group of devoted consumers socially constructing reality outside of the dominant system. In all cases, from Harley-Davidson to Star Trek for example, there exist offline (e.g., face to face) and online (e.g., Internet) intermediary groupings which are informally linked to one another to form constellations:

> the constellation of meanings and practices that characterise a consumption subculture are not uniquely grounded in a particular set of socioeconomic circumstances. Instead, members of a consumption subculture can inhabit diverse social positions. Their primarily affiliative tie is a shared avocational interest (such as skydiving or biking) and its attendant consumption experiences. (Thompson and Troester, 2002, p. 553)

A brand community is a co-consuming group of people that have a common interest in a specific brand and create a parallel social universe (subculture) abounding with its own myths, values, rituals, vocabulary and hierarchy (Muñiz and O'Guinn, 2001; Pongsakornrungsilp and Schroeder, 2011). On a sociological level, brand communities herald new forms of collectives emerging in contemporary society: rather than communities creating symbols, they form around symbols (Luedicke et al., 2010; Stratton and Northcote, 2016). On a managerial level, brand communities are described as the perfect locus of value co-creation (Schau et al., 2009). Brand co-creation (Ind et al., 2013) and consumer-generated branded content (Muñiz and Schau, 2011) are among the most significant aspects of this value co-creation process (Galvagno and Dalli, 2014).

Past research on these co-consuming groups has been recently criticised and redressed in several ways.

- First, some researchers contend (O'Reilly, 2012) that consumer culture scholars' view on tribes is only loosely 'inspired' by Maffesoli's theory and that a stronger theoretical connection with his 1996 piece is needed. One major drawback is that Maffesoli in his 1996 book describes tribes in different ways, such as a 'communion of saints' (p. 73); 'electronic mail, sexual networks, various solidarities including sporting and musical gatherings' (p. 73); 'youth groups, affinity associations, small-scale industrial enterprises' (p. 75); and 'small community group[s]' (p. 94) (O'Reilly, 2012, p. 343), and these are not always consistent with the 'reduced' use of the term made in consumer research. Moreover, Maffesoli's recent work emphasises what he calls the 'three defining traits of tribalism' (Maffesoli, 2010, p. 85): (1) prevalence of the (local) territory;

(2) sharing of taste; and (3) come back of the face of the ever-present child. Again, this does not seem to be all encapsulated in the definition of consumer tribes (Cova et al., 2007) and thus requires further reinvestigation.

- Second, other researchers (Thomas et al., 2013) argue that past research has emphasised the homogeneity of co-consuming groups, privileging the shared experiences of community members over their differences. However, they claim that heterogeneity is often at play in consumer collectives and that research must acknowledge it. On one side, heterogeneity is necessary for the development of strong and successful tribes. As Fournier and Lee (2009) maintain, inside the community different roles and profiles are necessary in order to give different people with different orientations and goals the opportunity to participate. Moreover, within the same community there are different ways in which members provide support for the co-creation of value: different goals and personal characteristics lead members towards various exchange regimes within the same community (Corciolani and Dalli, 2014; Scaraboto, 2015). On the other side, heterogeneity often incites tensions and conflict that represent a constitutive dimension of collectives (Husemann et al., 2015): conflicts arise between members or factions as well as between members and companies (Thomas et al., 2013).
- Third, Arvidsson and Caliandro (2015) argue that a category of co-consuming group is missing, what they label 'brand publics'. A brand public is an organised media-space kept together by a continuity of mediation practices. Brand publics result from an aggregation of a large number of isolated expressions that have a common focus. Contrary to brand communities, they do not build on sustained forms of interaction or any consistent collective identity (Arvidsson and Caliandro, 2015) although they actually affect community formation and development, as well as individual consumers' identity projects. The concept of brand publics emerged through an empirical study about the Louis Vuitton brand and it is characterised by its orientation towards the society (or the crowd) as a whole, its connective nature, its focus on publicity value and its reliance on interpassivity, a concept coined by Slavoj Žižek (1997) to describe the participation of individuals in the general socio-cultural discourse. On the contrary, the brand community concept is oriented towards the community (or the tribe), it shows a collective nature and focuses on linking value and interactivity, that is individual members actively interact with each other and with the focus of their interest (brand, company, etc.). More generally, brand communities are still attached to the idea that individuals and groups are the main units of analysis and as such they constitute the locus of management and control of brands and their social networks. Brand publics are more oriented towards communication and discourse: the unit of analysis here is the medium and the flow of communication within it and therefore management is oriented towards this fluid dimension: social media, social networks, and the like.

Following the introduction of the 'brand public' concept, Zwick and Bradshaw (2016) argue that the central object at stake in CCT research, the brand community, barely actually exists. According to these authors, the community concept therefore is employed as an ideological tool for maintaining social and behavioural commitment behind an imagined practice of sort, and they ponder why such ideologies are necessary, and what they allow the marketer to do. Zwick and Bradshaw (2016) build on Kozinets (2010, p. 2), who reports that 'there are at least 100 million, and perhaps as many as a billion people around the world who participate in online communities as a regular, ongoing part of their social experience', and on Arvidsson (2013, p. 371), who points out that from a sociological perspective user aggregations such as the 'now defunct Geocities web space with its "more than three million members" are not to be understood as communities, at least not in anything that resembles the significance that that term has originally held in social theory (not to speak of

Facebook or YouTube that are most definitely not communities)'. Despite all the talk about communities – especially marketing scholars' and professionals' favourite version of such a community, the brand community – Zwick and Bradshaw (2016) contend that they remain difficult to locate as social formations characterised by dense webs of interpersonal interactions and durable attachments to a shared territory or identity as understood in sociology. The non-enduring character of virtual communal engagement and social communication reduces engagement to pure participation and resembles an energetic but ultimately short-lived and meaningless flash mob rather than a collective of engaged subjectivities. Online communities – when defined as a social formation of sustained and meaningful interpersonal interaction – are then hard to find.

In sum, the new concept of brand publics helps in bridging the gap between the hard, physical, interpersonal, and social character of consumption communities, however defined, and the fluid, digital, and communicative or conversational nature of consumers' collectives. This is not a sort of juxtaposition between old and new forms of engagement, but rather the necessary integration of two parallel dimensions of consumption processes. Consumers participate in both the social and the discursive processes and contribute to the development of communities and publics (Canniford and Shankar, 2013; Parmentier and Fischer, 2015).

PROSUMPTION AND VALUE CREATING TRIBES

Since the 1990s, the consumer research literature has identified blurred boundaries between consumption and production (Firat and Venkatesh, 1995). Consumers are no longer the final link in the production chain, the one in which value is actually deployed and *destroyed*; on the contrary, they actually create value and this activity lies at the very heart of the consumption process. Consumer researchers thus acknowledge a productive role for consumers (Arnould and Thompson, 2005), who engage in a wealth of productive actions, such as generating new product ideas, providing leads through word of mouth, defining the brand's meaning and staging experiences for other customers. Recent examples of this research are McQuarrie et al. (2013), Hartmann and Ostberg (2013), Brosius et al. (2013), Martin and Schouten (2014), Moisio et al. (2004, 2013), Peters et al. (2012), and Press and Arnould (2011), to name a few.

This literature soon converged towards the concept of prosumption, originally developed by Toffler (1980), according to which production and consumption are not separable from each other (Cova and Cova, 2012; Ritzer, 2014). By moving between production and consumption, consumers engage in prosumption, such that they produce at least part of what they consume (Ritzer and Jurgenson, 2010). Prosumption activity also has increased in recent decades, as an effect of social changes (Ritzer et al., 2012) enhanced by the emergence of the Internet with its platforms and resources. The overall idea that emerges from this literature is that consumers participate in the physical and cultural construction of their consumption objects (Keat et al., 1994): often implicitly, the assumption behind these theorisations is that consumer engagement in production is a necessary, if not essential, condition for a satisfactory consumption experience.

In addition, prosumption relates to research initiated by sociologists (Dujarier, 2008) suggesting that 'work' offers the best description of consumer activity. That is, customers are systematic workers or quasi-employees (Rieder and Voß, 2010). Yet working consumers also differ from prosumers, who are *selectively* involved with enterprises. Furthermore, though the notion of consumer work has not been broached directly in the consumer literature, a few studies build on the sociology of work to investigate the existence of working consumers (Cova and Dalli, 2009) and the effects of putting consumers to work (Zwick et al., 2008), then link these themes to collaborative marketing approaches (Beckett and Nayak, 2008).

In Table 14.1 we try to identify a list, though not exhaustive, of the approaches in which the active role of the consumer has been acknowledged. We acknowledge the metaphor (the face) mobilised by researchers to connect the consumer to a certain kind of activity.

First of all as a partner (lead user) in the new product development process, the consumer is responsible and active in the idea generation activity (Franke et al., 2006). Secondly, sometimes he/she acts as a partial employee when, in the service business, he/she is involved in the production and delivery of the appropriate set of activities and resources surrounding the core service he/she asks for (Manolis et al., 2001).

Building on previous user innovation literature and services marketing research, service dominant logic (Vargo and Lusch, 2004) sees the consumer as a resource integrator who combine personal resources with those offered by the company to co-create value for both parties. In interpretive research studies (Arnould and Thompson, 2005), the consumer is seen as a cultural producer in the sense that he/she adds or alters meaning and cultural reference to market offerings (Firat and Venkatesh, 1995; Ritson and Elliott, 1999). In the sociology of work perspective (Dujarier, 2008), consumers are put to work as they contribute with unpaid material, cognitive, and affective labour to value creation which – finally – turns out to be appropriated by companies. Finally, in the sociology of consumption approach (Ritzer and Jurgenson, 2010), consumers are prosumers as the production and consumption activities collapse into one unitary activity that actually redefines the consumption as such: prosumers do not work as well as they do not merely consume. They manipulate

Table 14.1 On the road to prosumption in the academic literature

Fields	*User innovation*	*Services marketing*	*Service-dominant logic*	*Consumer culture theory*	*Sociology of work*	*Sociology of consumption*
Foundations	Von Hippel, 1986	Gummesson 1991	Vargo and Lusch 2004	Arnould and Thompson 2005	Dujarier 2008	Ritzer and Jurgenson 2010
Consumer 'face'	Lead user	Partial employee	Resource integrator	Cultural producer	Working consumer	Prosumer
Consumer activity	Generation of ideas	Co-production of services	Co-creation of value	Production of meanings	Production of immaterial work	Prosumption of activities

market offerings in such a way that these resources increase their use value, that is, the very objective of prosumption. This value cannot be appropriated as it is subjective and idiosyncratic, but it can be shared and imitated by other consumers or employed by companies.

During the last two decades, a number of studies in consumption research questioned the separation between production and consumption and assessed the active role of consumers in the creation of value (Firat and Venkatesh, 1995). Following these developments in interpretive consumer research, marketing and management scholars theorised the 'co-creation of value' as a process in which consumers collaborate with companies in the production of value (Prahalad and Ramaswamy, 2004; Vargo and Lusch, 2004). From the theoretical perspective (Galvagno and Dalli, 2014), it is useful to keep these approaches separate, as the first (consumers create) does not necessarily end up in the second (consumers co-create): first, not all of the value created by consumers is actually or necessarily introduced into products and services and hence traded on the market, and, second, sometimes consumers criticise, delegitimise, and destroy products' and brands' value, that is they do not improve the value of goods, but they act for the opposite (Luedicke et al., 2010).

Brand Community Value Co-creation Practices

Until this point, we have been discussing prosumption as an individual construct: the individual consumer is the subject of prosumption and value co-creation. As we have been discussing in the preceding section, consumers participate in consumption communities within which they create value through communal practices and collective activities (Schau et al., 2009). Most of the research about consumer collectives value creation is about brand communities: brand success increasingly relies on the presence of a community of active, loyal fans (Muñiz and O'Guinn, 2001). Brand communities provide sites for various value-creating practices. Members of brand communities create extensive brand content through their interactions. Schau et al. (2009) use social practice theory to indicate the process of value co-creation within brand communities. They identify four key categories of practices within brand communities:

- *social networking* (welcoming, empathising, governing). Brand supporters create, enhance, and sustain ties among brand community members;
- *impression management* (evangelising, justifying). Brand community members direct their attention outside the community trying to create favourable impressions of the brand;
- *community management* (staking, milestoning, badging, documenting). Brand community members perform activities that reinforce members' escalating engagement with the brand community;
- *product use* (grooming, customising, (de-)commoditising). These practices are specifically related to improved or enhanced use of the focal brand.

The contribution of this research about brand communities and consumers' collectives in general is about the identification of 'practices', that is coded, routinary micro-activities actually performed by a variety of subjects within the community that bring value to the community itself, to the public, and ultimately to the brand. They are channelled through the individuals that participate in the community and the relationships between them, but also between members and non-members. Some of these practices move beyond extant relationships and go outside the community in order to bridge the gap between it and the rest of the society. Practices are value drivers and managed accordingly.

In the last decade, branding phenomena have been accelerated by the rising power of brand communities (Cova et al., 2007), backed by development of the Internet and social media. An important dimension of value creating practices is the digital one, based on Internet resources and tools. Prosumption tribes such as brand communities produce 'brand surfeits'. According to Nakassis (2013), 'surfeits' are generated around the brand by social media practices such as discussion forums, blogs, social platforms and video, photo and news-sharing sites. Brand surfeits are material forms and immaterial social meanings that exceed and transgress a brand's authority and intelligibility (Muñiz and Schau, 2011). Material surfeits can be knockoffs, fakes, brand-inspired goods, overruns, defective goods, etc. Immaterial surfeits emerge from engagement with the brand in the form of resignifications, parodies, hijacks, etc. In linking 'counterfeits' with novel and often unpredictable social meanings that emerge through moments of brand consumption, Nakassis (2013, p. 123) argues that 'the brand is troubled by the surfeit of social meaning that is constantly produced by idiosyncratic and contextualized experiences of consumer engagement with brand forms (authorized or otherwise)'. The phenomenon of brand surfeiting is particularly at play when a brand community of enthusiasts is prepared to generate brand surfeits that transgress the marketer's brand definition.

As a form of workshop, a brand community enables consumers to nurture and protect their favourite brands. In particular, brand communities often unleash consumers' desire to contribute to the culture, myths or histories of the brands they love (Pongsakornrungsilp and Schroeder, 2011). Brand community members thus are skilful, proficient and prolific in their creation of brand content, even when collaborating with relatively unknown others for no compensation. For example, thousands of novels written by Harry Potter devotees appear on the web. In response, companies actively encourage consumer engagement with brand content in brandscapes. Doing so requires managers to relinquish considerable control of brand meanings and create brand-oriented spaces for consumers to congregate and discuss the brand. Thus, various people come to share in the brand and engage in brand-relevant work (Spicer, 2010). An increasing variety of instruments is available to brand supporters to enhance their ability to contribute to community and brand success.

The managerial relevance of brand co-creation has given rise to collaborative approaches whereby marketing is evolving into participatory conversations around the brand and its community to co-create branded content (Berthon et al., 2008; Muñiz and Schau, 2011). Notable examples of brand communities facilitating collaborative marketing include Dell with its initiative *Idea Storm: Where Your Ideas Reign*, Starbucks with *My Starbucks Ideas*, and Barilla with *Il Mulino che Vorrei (The Windmill I Dream About)*. Collaborative approaches go beyond lead users collaborating with companies on new product development (Sawhney et al., 2005): these involve not only lead users but any creative consumers who are willing to collaborate;

they do not only concern new products but a host of different tasks related to the brand, its products, its services, its communication, and so forth. LEGO is a notable case of a company that has manifested this capacity to work with its brand community members to innovate and enrich the brand (Antorini et al., 2012).

Brand Public Value Co-creation and Beyond

Although most of the research about prosumption tribes' value creation is about brand communities, recent works have already gone beyond to investigate any type of value creative co-consuming groups. Marketing thinkers have reconceptualised the participatory web for marketing purposes and coined popular buzz terms like 'crowdsourcing', 'prosumption', 'mass collaboration', 'peer production' and 'user generation'. These diverse terms share an emphasis on what is often referred to as the social nature of the web. Here the message to fellow marketers has been generally consistent: the Internet has evolved into a participatory medium instituted by masses of self-directed autonomous actors that use their tremendous creative intellect to communicate in new ways, develop new ideas, and generally make and do interesting and innovative things (see Cova and Dalli, 2009; Hong and Chen, 2013; Ritzer and Juergenson, 2010, for analytical synopses of the recent streams of research into working consumers and co-creators). And, as critically reviewed by Arvidsson (2006) and Cova and Dalli (2009), marketing professionals recognised that much could be gained from stimulating and channelling these resources into the spirit of marketing (Zwick and Bradshaw, 2016).

Research highlights the active role of consumers' communities in the creation of value on the web with or without relation to a company or a brand (Mathwick et al., 2008). Consumers' communities first generate an affective value. Consumers produce and use communal relationships and create feelings of ease, well-being, satisfaction, excitement, and passion that permeate their joint activities. Second, they generate a cultural value. Consumers are responsible for selecting ideas, symbols, codes, texts, linguistic figures, and images that are then put into their activities. These voluntary contributions of consumers' communities rely on motivations intrinsic to humanity. They can exist inside co-consuming groups which create value for the tribe and destruct value for the company, or create value without the existence of a company.

Once limited to the realm of service activities, knowledge of C-to-C encounters has become paramount for marketing following the rise of social networks and the tribal approach to consumption. Helping behaviours form the vast majority of prosumption tribes' activities. By studying the specific '*la repasse*' (French slang) phenomenon that occurs when an individual hands over their ticket to someone else, Fuschillo and Cova (2015) detail how a brand public formed around a transportation organisation can at the same time destroy value for the organisation and generate value for the collective. Handing over used but still valid tickets for public transport is common practice in the city of Marseilles. It generally involves someone approaching a stranger, holding a ticket in her/his hand and suggesting (verbally or otherwise, i.e., using gestures) that the latter take the ticket the giver has just used but which is still valid for a useful period of time. The interaction is very rapid and generally involves few explanations, often nothing more than '*It's still good for...*'. The potential recipient may or may not take this free ticket. Albeit prohibited by the RTM (*Régie des Transports de Marseille*) such a practice appears not as an isolated act but an act belonging to a wider and collectively self-organised system of helping. Nothing is written; however, many of the users of the services under consideration know about and accept the code of conduct established. This behavioural code is not obligatory or coercive. Quite the contrary, a person's desire to apply the rules of this code is viewed as fundamental to making the interaction possible. Fuschillo and Cova (2015) define this collective practice as a micro-subversion of the marketplace with the aim of maintaining a minimal level of citizenship. It is an immoral act for the sake of helping the greater good. Indeed handing over used tickets breaks rules dictated by the organisations in charge of a municipality's public transport, and thus destroys value for the organisation, but at the same time it creates value for the tribe.

Collaborative consumption is a way to co-create value without the business involved. Instead of buying and owning things, consumers get access to shared goods and just pay for the experience of temporarily accessing them (Bardhi and Eckhardt, 2012). It exists for a variety of categories of goods and services as diverse as P2P lending, crowd funding, shared Wi-Fi, community supported agriculture, skill barter banks, car repair, child care, and catering (Belk, 2014). The investigation of a shared game such as geocaching (Scaraboto, 2015) provides an extreme case of this collective value creation. The game of geocaching works this way: using a GPS or Google Earth, geocachers set out in search of mysterious 'treasures' buried in geocaches by other geocachers, throughout the globe. Typically, a geocache is a small water- and weatherproof container harbouring a logbook and one or more valueless objects – nothing dangerous or illegal. Before setting out on their expedition geocachers look up the caches available in a given area on geocaching websites like geocaching.com. Once the cache has been found, geocachers come back from their expedition and share their discoveries on a geocaching website together with stories and photographs of their experience. Driven by the imaginations of players, the game is developed and structured into multiple versions which foster the development of geocaching sub-communities associated with each new game variant. It is a kind of collective project associated with the web, where a spirit of 'doing it together' and 'passing it along' holds sway. The practices of geocaching appear to generate value for this prosumption tribe, without businesses or other commercial actors wresting exclusive control of such value away to the detriment of the tribe.

Where Does the Value Slip?

Rewarding consumers for participating in collaborative programmes is a theme that has been studied, and a key argument is that consumer participation is intrinsically rewarding. For example, Antorini et al. (2012, p. 77) investigated the LEGO collaborative programme and suggested that 'the intrinsic rewards associated with designing and building products are frequently more motivating than financial rewards.

Recognising this, Lego has tended to pay outside collaborators with a combination of experience, access and Lego products'. Indeed, intrinsically motivated consumers consider their contribution to a collaborative programme as a meaningful and valued activity for its own sake. Moreover, monetary rewards can have a detrimental effect and may erode collectively oriented participation in a co-consuming group (Wittke and Hanekop, 2011). Social recognition is instead acknowledged as having a positive individual and collective effect (Pongsakornrungsilp and Schroeder, 2011) both in non-profit and for-profit organisations. This is the case of a community organised around a non-profit project such as Wikipedia that is 'created and constantly revised and updated with input from large numbers of unpaid prosumers' (Ritzer et al., 2012, p. 390). This is also the case of the brand community of Tough Mudder, a premier obstacle course series in the world, where the company proposes that enthusiasts join its volunteer programme and these volunteers are given a significant amount of responsibility and a variety of roles (they help register participants and spectators and manage the flow of start groups).

One key question is how 'value created by one source or at one level of analysis may be captured at another – a process we call "value slippage"' (Lepak et al., 2007, p. 181)? Indeed, brand transformation practices can benefit the company owning the brand, the brand community or any other stakeholder. There is no strong indication that this potential value can necessarily be 'captured' (Bowman and Ambrosini, 2000) by the company owning the brand; it may spill over to other operators including brand community members. 'Consumers are able to 'capture' some value from companies and share this, thus developing linking value at the expense of the market, as in peer-to-peer networks' (Cova and Dalli, 2009, p. 485). Consumers may also manufacture and sell their own productions 'by harvesting the digital virtual "raw materials" available' (Denegri-Knott and Molesworth, 2010, p. 123) in games and other fictions (for an example, see Kozinets's fanfictions based on Star Trek, 2007) and thus become sellers. The firm that owns the brand may or may not be able to capture or retain the value in the long term. Indeed, 'in some cases, organizations that create new value will lose or have to share this value with other stakeholders, such as employees, competitors, or society' (Lepak et al., 2007, p. 187). Although value slippage provides opportunities to increase brand value, there is no assurance that the company owning the brand will obtain the benefits.

CONSUMER TRIBES BETWEEN MARKETS AND HIERARCHIES: NEW PERSPECTIVES

Prosumption tribes challenge the boundaries between demand and supply, between capital and labour, and they put into question the roles usually attributed to economic agents by traditional economic and management literature. Companies have to deal with tribes when deciding branding and marketing strategies. Some tribes became powerful enough to subvert market structures and impose new competitive standards. Individual consumers add value to products and services through relationships, practices, and discourses.

Moreover, some aspects of tribal consumption challenge the very role of the market as one of the institutions that contribute to social and cultural development (Arnould and Thompson, 2015). A new stream of studies witnesses the active role of consumers and tribes in actually opening up new markets (Giesler, 2012; Martin and Schouten, 2013). As such, consumer tribes stimulate scholars in rethinking related and established theories. Recent research helps us to draft some directions on the way prosumption tribes challenge our thinking and oblige us to rethink some of our concepts beyond exploitation and towards recirculation.

Beyond Exploitation

Ritzer (2014, p. 20) argues that Marxian theorists position prosumers as:

> ... suffering from false consciousness and that, in fact, they are deluding themselves in thinking they are not being exploited. However, it is also possible that they are not exploited in a classic Marxian sense and that the concept needs to be revised to take into account the new realities. It is also possible that an entirely new concept is needed.

Cova et al. (2015a, 2015b) provide a useful basis for going beyond exploitation with their ethnography of the Alfa Romeo/Alfisti (Alfa brand enthusiasts) collaborative programme. The Italian automaker Alfa Romeo Automobiles S.p.A. was founded on 24 June 1910 in Milan and has been part of the Fiat Group since 1986. In Italian, the owner of an Alfa Romeo is referred to as an 'Alfista', which becomes 'Alfisti' in the plural. A kind of cult has developed around this company and its brand, with many models serving as cultural icons. There are many thriving Alfa Romeo owners clubs across the world. A survey carried out by the company in 2008 concluded that 20% of the clubs had more than 2000 members; 30% had between 500 and 2000 members; and 50% had fewer than 500 members. These clubs are usually very active around the Alfa brand. For instance 95% organise rallies focusing on old and new Alfa Romeo models, with 62% organising more than five rallies a year. Starting in June 2008, Alfa Romeo's Management team decided to embark on a collaboration project with Alfisti. In June 2009 – exactly one year before the Centennial anniversary in June 2010 – Alfa Romeo's Management announced the launch of the Alfisti.com online platform, portrayed as 'a veritable workshop, somewhere you [Alfisti] can drop in, exchange ideas and work together on two very important projects: the future Alfisti community and celebrating the Alfa Romeo centenary' (the Alfa Romeo Director's online address on 24 June 2009). Some 6,700 signed up and joined the online platform which was open for one year. The website consisted of (1) a blog where Alfa Romeo asked questions and received responses from Alfisti on specific themes and (2) a forum allowing thematic discussion of a more open nature. Cova et al.'s one year study (2015a, 2015b) of the Alfisti.com project builds on previous critical research to suggest that consumers within such collaborative marketing programmes can be considered volunteers contributing social and emotional skills. Exploitation and emancipation are intertwined in a process where consumers compromise with a company but also with themselves and their own values.

Cova et al. (2015b) define brand volunteers as brand enthusiasts who are committed to providing unpaid work for the exclusive benefit of the brand. Under certain conditions, consumers form an unpaid workforce that is relatively committed to volunteering for a for-profit company. They produce this unpaid work in a specific prosocial context, namely, a brand community. The sense of moral obligation, a key characteristic of a brand community (Muñiz and O'Guinn, 2001), forms the basis of brand volunteer prosocial behaviour. When invited to volunteer, these consumers volunteer for the brand community and not for the company, i.e., they are not consumers working for a company such as 'working consumers' (Cova and Dalli, 2009; Zwick et al., 2008); they volunteer for the brand that is the symbol of their 'we-ness' and their community. Cova et al. (2015b) introduce the notion of compromise to resolve the conflict between theories that see value co-creation processes as a form of exploitation of consumers (Cova and Dalli, 2009) and theories that perceive such processes as consumer emancipation (Arnould, 2007) which is at play in the interpretation of the Alfa Romeo/Alfisti collaboration.

Value co-creation has spurred debates amongst marketing researchers (see *Marketing Theory* 2006, 2011 and 2012 special issues). The intensity of these debates 'demonstrates how much is at stake – conceptually and politically – when the roles of consumer and producer become blurred' (Cova et al., 2011, p. 231).

On the one hand, some researchers, such as Arnould (2007, p. 192), seem convinced that the typical consumer has shifted from being passive to active and creative: 'Whether one chooses protagonist, consum'actor, prosumer or some other neologism of choice, the point of these awkward verbal gestures is that the co-creative producer of genuine, political, less commercial experiences is far removed from the passive mass market consumer of the post-war consumerist boom'. Researchers holding this and similar views laud consumer involvement in branding and production since it empowers consumers to create their own lives and contribute positively to companies.

On the other hand, other researchers see value co-creation practices as a way of shaping and disciplining consumers through marketing discourses (Shankar et al., 2006; Zwick et al., 2008). Zwick and Cayla (2011, p. 8) argue that, through these discourses, consumers are urged 'to engage in proactive destabilization and permanent requalification of themselves', and Cova and Cova (2012) question the liberating claims associated with value co-creation. From this perspective, following the advice of some sociologists (Dujarier, 2014), it is suggested that 'work' offers the best description of consumer activity under the regime of value co-creation, and that consumers can be conceived as 'working consumers' (Cova and Dalli, 2009; Rieder and Voß, 2010). As such, they run the risk of being exploited by companies that could benefit from their unpaid contribution.

The notion of compromise answers Ritzer's (2014) call for theory development. Interpreting these brand volunteers as engaging in compromise makes more sense than interpreting them as being exploited or emancipated. Consumers who make compromises do not have a naïve or romantic view of their involvement in value co-creation processes, as sometimes stated (Shankar et al., 2006). Aware that they are being manipulated, they freely choose the extent of their 'dupery' and involve themselves to maximise individual and collective enjoyment.

Towards Recirculation

In a recent book, Arsel (2015) introduces the notion of commodity 'recirculation'. She sees recirculation as one of the domains in which communities and relational networks create and transfer value. Recirculation takes the form of exchanges between individuals who act as members (even if part-time or occasional) of communities whose purpose is that of facilitating such exchanges: swap events, barter platforms, sharing communities, etc. The empirical analysis by Arsel (2015) is conducted in the context of a community of cosmetics swappers, but it applies to other cases as well in the general domain of recycling and barter communities. In these settings, used objects acquire a new existence through the exchanges that occur between individuals: new (use) value is provided to the object by the mere fact that it is passed along by one person to another. In some cases barters occur, but in other cases (Freecycle) there is no need to compensate the giver who benefits from clearing their house, saving money from displacement or transport services, and accrues some cultural value deriving from the awareness that the object is not trashed, but provides further value for someone else.

In the case of barter communities, for instance, individual actors are embedded in a network of relations in which they often exchange with the same counterparts: these conditions can be regarded from the perspective of assemblage and actor-network theories, as evidenced by Arsel (2015). Barter exchanges in these communities stand as series of steps in a trajectory of interactions in which the identity, values, and personality of actors actually change the nature of the exchange. Moving from a market (spot) exchange towards a social exchange relationship, collectivistic attitudes and behaviours emerge and compete with individualistic ones. Barter is one of the forms of market exchange: individuals negotiating and assessing respective offerings with the aim of extracting the highest value from a single transaction. When located in a community setting, and given specific circumstances, these transactions appear different and mutuality and inclusion emerge: individuals participate in a process in which personal, economic and short-term objectives, which are typical of market transactions, turn out to be collective, social and long term. One of the outcomes of this process is that the bartered items are often considered as collective endowments that pass along between members who hence share rather than exchange them (Dalli and Fortezza, 2016).

These communities are *institutional* substitutes or complementary agencies that operate within, together, or even against traditional markets (Albinsson and Perera, 2012). If we consider the Freecycle example, objects received through Freecycle act as competitors to market offerings, but – at the same time – they are complementary to them. In fact, those who get the object for free and not through the market could be willing to buy something new by using the amount of money they saved. Moreover, it could be the case that owning a new (second hand) good could stimulate a new consumption activity that could then promote new purchases in complementary markets. In given conditions, traditional markets turn into recirculation markets, as in the case of Amazon and other e-commerce platforms selling used items together with new ones, something that depends also on the competitive pressure coming from Freecycle and similar models. Guillard and Roux (2014) effectively describe the institutional conflict between different logics of exchange: the dominant, mainstream market exchange logic vs. the niche, marginal, though sustainable, logic of gleaners and disposers.

Moreover, recirculation markets offer a growing variety of opportunities to community members to exchange and share their items: these opportunities go far beyond the archetypal market exchange. As evidenced by Scaraboto (2015) and Corciolani and Dalli (2014), collaborative networks present different forms of interaction and exchange in the same setting, and members choose the preferred form according to personal characteristics and contingent conditions. In the case of Bookcrossing (Corciolani and Dalli, 2014), for instance, books are exchanged following at least four distinct practices:

- *into the wild:* the book is made available for other people in a public space;
- *official Bookcrossing zone:* books are left in a specific and formally identified place, usually in a library, club, etc;
- *meet up:* books are exchanged between people participating in an ad hoc meeting;
- *bookring:* the owner sends the book to someone who reads it and then sends it to another one, and so on until the last one sends the book back to the owner.

These practices present traits that belong to different exchange regimes: in some cases the gift dimension seems dominant, as in the first two cases. In the case of meet-up exchanges, the market exchange dimension emerges as actual negotiation and barter-like processes are at play. And, finally, the bookring practice appears to be a form of collective borrowing, very close to a sharing practice in which the exclusive property of a member is made available to others for a given period of time.

These networks are flexible, they change very rapidly, and they are able to satisfy a wide range of necessities in institutional terms. It is in this sense that Scaraboto (2015) speaks of 'hybrid economies' in which market and non-market practices interact and in which individuals are given the possibility to choose or even actually develop the preferred personal, even on a contingent base, form of exchange. Recirculation markets and collaborative networks demonstrate that the value-creating activities of consumers' communities strongly interact with traditional market exchange systems and – in given conditions – they can act as agents of change. Economic actors that operate in traditional market exchange economies are actually influenced by these 'new' institutions and adapt accordingly.

CONCLUSION

By advancing the notion of the 'prosumption tribe', this chapter goes beyond the traditional perspective on consumer culture as the intensification of consumerism to depict it as a hybrid realm where consuming and producing mesh to put into question the roles usually attributed to societal and economic agents. Prosumption tribes are at play in very different hybrid practices, such as helping, recirculation, surfeiting, or volunteering – to name a few – which are shaping the future of consumer culture from a collective point of view.

REFERENCES

Albinsson, P.A., & Perera, B.Y. (2012). Alternative marketplaces in the 21st century: Building community through sharing events. *Journal of Consumer Behaviour*, *11*(4), 303–315.

Antorini, Y.M., Muñiz Jr, A.M., & Askildsen, T. (2012). Collaborating with customer communities: Lessons from the LEGO Group, *MIT Sloan Management Review*, *53*(3), 73–79.

Arnould, E.J. (2007). Consuming experience. Retrospects and prospects. In A. Carù, & B. Cova (Eds), *Consuming Experience* (pp. 185–194), Oxon, Routledge.

Arnould, E.J., & Price, L.L. (1993). River magic: Extraordinary experience and the extended service encounter. *Journal of Consumer Research*, *20*(1), 24–45.

Arnould, E.J., & Thompson, C.J. (2005). Consumer culture theory (CCT): Twenty years of research. *Journal of Consumer Research*, *31*(4), 868–882.

Arnould, E.J., & Thompson, C.J. (2015). Introduction: Consumer culture theory: Ten years gone (and beyond). In A.E. Thyroff, J.B. Murray, & R.W. Belk (Eds), *Consumer Culture Theory, Research in Consumer Behaviour* (Volume 17, pp. 1–21). London, Emerald.

Arsel, Z. (2015). Assembling markets and value. In R. Canniford & D. Bajde (Eds), *Assembling Consumption: Researching Actors, Networks and Markets* (pp. 32–41). London, Routledge.

Arvidsson, A. (2006). *Brands: Meaning and Value in Media Culture*. London, Routledge.

Arvidsson, A. (2013). The potential of consumer publics. *Ephemera: Theory and Politics in Organization*, *13*(2), 367–391.

Arvidsson, A., & Caliandro, A. (2015). Brand public. *Journal of Consumer Research*, *42*(5), 727–748.

Aubert-Gamet, V. (1997). Twisting servicescapes: Diversion of the physical environment in a re-appropriation process, *International Journal of Service Industry Management*, *8*(1), 26–41.

Bardhi, F., & Eckhardt, G.M. (2012). Access-based consumption: The case of car sharing. *Journal of Consumer Research*, *39*(4), 881–898.

Beckett, A., & Nayak, A. (2008). The reflexive consumer. *Marketing Theory*, *8*(3), 299–317.

Beckmann, S., & Elliott, R. (Eds) (2000). *Interpretive Consumer Research*. Copenhagen, Copenhagen Business School Press.

Belk, R.W. (2013). Extended self in a digital world. *Journal of Consumer Research*, *40*(3), 477–500.

Belk, R.W. (2014). You are what you can access: Sharing and collaborative consumption online. *Journal of Business Research*, *67*(8), 1595–1600.

Berthon, P., Pitt, L., & Campbell, C. (2008). Ad lib: When customers create the ad. *California Management Review*, *50*(4), 6–30.

Bowman, C., & Ambrosini, V. (2000). Value creation versus value capture: towards a coherent definition of value in strategy. *British Journal of Management*, *11*(1), 1–15.

Brosius, N., Fernandez, K.V., & Cherrier, H. (2013). Reacquiring consumer waste: Treasure in our trash? *Journal of Public Policy & Marketing*, *32*(2), 286–301.

Canniford, R., & Shankar, A. (2013). Purifying practices: How consumers assemble romantic experiences of nature. *Journal of Consumer Research*, *39*(5), 1051–1069.

Corciolani, M., & Dalli, D. (2014). Gift-giving, sharing and commodity exchange at Bookcrossing.com: new insights from a qualitative analysis. *Management Decision*, *52*(4), 755–776.

Cova, B. (1997). Community and consumption: Towards a definition of the 'linking value' of product or services. *European Journal of Marketing*, *31*(3/4), 297–316.

Cova, B., & Cova, V. (2002). Tribal marketing: The tribalisation of society and its impact on the conduct of marketing. *European Journal of Marketing*, *36*(5/6), 595–620.

Cova, B., & Cova, V. (2012). On the road to prosumption: Marketing discourse and the development of consumer competencies. *Consumption, Markets and Culture*, *15*(2), 149–168.

Cova, B., & Dalli, D. (2009). Working consumers: The next step in marketing theory? *Marketing Theory*, *9*(3), 315–339.

Cova, B., Dalli, D., & Zwick, D. (2011). Critical perspectives on consumers' role as 'producers': Broadening the debate on value co-creation in marketing processes. *Marketing Theory*, *11*(3), 231–241.

Cova, B., Kozinets, R., & Shankar, A. (2007). *Consumer Tribes*. London, Routledge.

Cova, B., Pace, S., & Skålén, P. (2015a). Marketing with working consumers: The case of a carmaker and its brand community. *Organization*, *22*(5), 682–701.

Cova, B., Pace, S., & Skålén, P. (2015b). Brand volunteering: Value co-creation with unpaid consumers. *Marketing Theory*, *15*(4), 465–485.

Cova, B., & Shankar, A. (2012). Tribal marketing. In L. Penaloza, N. Toulouse, & L.M. Visconti (Eds), *Marketing Management: A Cultural Perspective* (pp. 178–193). London, Routledge.

Dalli, D., & Fortezza, F. (2016). From ownership to sharing, through barter communities. In L. Petruzzellis & R. Winer (Eds), *Rediscovering the Essentiality of Marketing* (pp. 103–109). London, Springer.

Denegri-Knott, J., & Molesworth, M. (2010). Concepts and practices of digital virtual consumption. *Consumption, Markets and Culture*, *13*(2), 109–132.

Dujarier, M.A. (2008). *Le travail du consommateur: De Mac Do à eBay: comment nous coproduisons ce que nous achetons*. Paris, La Découverte.

Dujarier, M.A. (2014). The three sociological types of consumer work. *Journal of Consumer Culture*, *16*(2), 555–571.

Firat, A.F., & Shultz, C.J. (1997). From segmentation to fragmentation: Markets and marketing strategy in the postmodern era. *European Journal of Marketing*, *31*(3/4), 183–207.

Firat, A.F., & Venkatesh, A. (1995). Liberatory postmodernism and the reenchantment of consumption. *Journal of Consumer Research*, *22*(3), 239–267.

Fournier, S., & Lee, L. (2009). Getting brand communities right. *Harvard Business Review*, *87*(4), 105–111.

Franke, N., von Hippel, E., & Schreier, M. (2006). Finding commercially attractive user innovations: A test of lead-user theory. *Journal of Product Innovation Management*, *23*(4), 301–315.

Fuschillo, G., & Cova, B. (2015). Subverting the market to help other consumers: The 'la repasse' phenomenon. *Journal of Consumer Behaviour*, *14*(4), 261–269.

Galvagno, M., & Dalli, D. (2014). Theory of value co-creation: A systematic literature review. *Managing Service Quality*, *24*(6), 643–683.

Giesler, M. (2012). How doppelganger brand images influence the market creation process: Longitudinal insights from the rise of Botox cosmetic. *Journal of Marketing*, *76*(6), 55–68.

Goulding, C., Shankar, A., & Elliott, R. (2002). Working weeks, rave weekends: Identity fragmentation and the emergence of new communities. *Consumption Markets and Culture*, *5*(4), 261–284.

Goulding, C., Shankar, A., & Canniford, R. (2013). Learning to be tribal: facilitating the formation of consumer tribes. *European Journal of Marketing*, *47*(5/6), 813–832.
Guillard, V., & Roux, D. (2014). Macromarketing issues on the sidewalk: How 'gleaners' and 'disposers' (re)create a sustainable economy. *Journal of Macromarketing*, *34*(3), 291–312.
Gummesson, E. (1991). Marketing-orientation revisited: the crucial role of the part-time marketer. *European Journal of Marketing*, *25*(2), 60–75.
Hartmann, B.J., & Ostberg, J. (2013). Authenticating by re-enchantment: The discursive making of craft production. *Journal of Marketing Management*, *29*(7–8), 882–911.
Hong, R., & Chen, V.H. (2013). Becoming an ideal co-creator: Web materiality and intensive laboring practices in game modding. *New Media & Society*, *16*(2), 290–305.
Husemann, K.C., Ladstaetter, F., & Luedicke, M.K. (2015). Conflict culture and conflict management in consumption communities. *Psychology & Marketing*, *32*(3), 265–284.
Ind, N., Iglesias, O., & Schultz, M. (2013). Building brands together. *California Management Review*, *55*(3), 5–26.
Keat, R., Whiteley, N., & Abercrombie, N. (1994). *The Authority of the Consumer*. London, Taylor & Francis.
Kozinets, R.V. (2001). Utopian enterprise: Articulating the meanings of Star Trek's culture of consumption. *Journal of Consumer Research*, *28*(1), 67–88.
Kozinets, R.V. (2007). Inno-tribes: Star Trek as wikimedia. In B. Cova, R. Kozinets, & A. Shankar (Eds), *Consumer Tribes* (pp. 194–211). London, Routledge.
Kozinets, R.V. (2010). *Netnography: Doing Ethnographic Research Online*. London, Sage.
Lepak, D.P., Smith, K.G., & Taylor, M.S. (2007). Value creation and value capture: A multilevel perspective. *Academy of Management Review*, *32*(1), 180–194.
Luedicke, M.K., Thompson, C.J., & Giesler, M. (2010). Consumer identity work as moral protagonism: How myth and ideology animate a brand-mediated moral conflict. *Journal of Consumer Research*, *36*(6), 1016–1032.
Maffesoli, M. (1996). *The Time of the Tribes*, London, Sage.
Maffesoli, M. (2000). Trouver les mots. In *Le temps des tribus. Le déclin de l'individualisme dans les sociétés postmodernes* (Foreword to the 3rd Edition). Paris, La Table Ronde.
Maffesoli, M. (2010). *Le réenchantement du monde*. Paris, Editions de la Table Ronde.
Manolis, C., Meamber, L.A., Winsor, R.D., & Brooks, C.M. (2001). Partial employees and consumers: A postmodern, meta-theoretical perspective for services marketing, *Marketing Theory*, *1*(2): 225–243.
Marketing Theory (2006). Special issue: The Service-dominant Logic of Marketing: Insights from The Otago Forum.
Marketing Theory (2011). Special issue: Critical Perspectives on Co-Creation.
Marketing Theory (2012). Special issue: Enhancing the Status of Consumer Research in Non-Western Contexts.
Martin, D.M., & Schouten, J.W. (2014). Consumption-driven market emergence. *Journal of Consumer Research*, *40*(5), 855–870.
Mathwick, C., Wiertz, C., & De Ruyter, K. (2008). Social capital production in a virtual P3 community. *Journal of Consumer Research*, *34*(6), 832–849.
McQuarrie, E.F., Miller, J., & Phillips, B.J. (2013). The megaphone effect: Taste and audience in fashion blogging. *Journal of Consumer Research*, *40*(1), 136–158.
Moisio, R., Arnould, E.J., & Price, L.L. (2004). Between mothers and markets: Constructing family identity through homemade food. *Journal of Consumer Culture*, *4*(3), 361–384.

Moisio, R., Arnould, E.J., & Gentry, J.W. (2013). Productive consumption in the class-mediated construction of domestic masculinity: Do-it-yourself (DIY) home improvement in men's identity work. *Journal of Consumer Research*, *40*(2), 298–316.

Muñiz Jr, A.M., & O'Guinn, T.C. (2001). Brand community. *Journal of Consumer Research*, *27*(4), 412–432.

Muñiz Jr, A.M., & Schau, H.J. (2011). How to inspire value-laden collaborative consumer-generated content. *Business Horizons*, *54*(3), 209–217.

Nakassis, C.V. (2013). Brands and their surfeits. *Cultural Anthropology*, *28*(1), 111–126.

O'Reilly, D. (2012). Maffesoli and consumer tribes developing the theoretical links. *Marketing Theory*, *12*(3), 341–347.

Parmentier, M.A., & Fischer, E. (2015). Things fall apart: The dynamics of brand audience dissipation. *Journal of Consumer Research*, *41*(5), 1228–1251.

Peters, C., Bodkin, C.D., & Fitzgerald, S. (2012). Toward an understanding of meaning creation via the collective co-production process. *Journal of Consumer Behaviour*, *11*(2), 124–135.

Pongsakornrungsilp, S., & Schroeder, J.E. (2011). Understanding value co-creation in a co-consuming brand community. *Marketing Theory*, *11*(3), 303–324.

Prahalad, C.K., & Ramaswamy, V. (2004). *The Future of Competition*. Boston, Harvard Business School Press.

Press, M., & Arnould, E.J. (2011). How does organizational identification form? A consumer behaviour perspective. *Journal of Consumer Research*, *38*(4), 650–666.

Rieder, K., & Voß, G.G. (2010). The working customer – an emerging new type of consumer. *Psychology of Everyday Activity*, *3*(2), 2–10.

Ritson, M. & Elliott, R. (1999). The social uses of advertising: An ethnographic study of adolescent advertising audiences. *Journal of Consumer Research*, *26*(3), 260–277.

Ritzer, G. (2014). Prosumption: Evolution, revolution, or eternal return of the same? *Journal of Consumer Culture*, *14*(3), 3–24.

Ritzer, G., & Jurgenson, N. (2010). Production, consumption, prosumption. The nature of capitalism in the age of the digital 'prosumer'. *Journal of Consumer Culture*, *10*(1), 13–36.

Ritzer, G., Dean, P., & Jurgenson, N. (2012). The coming of age of the prosumer. *American Behavioral Scientist*, *56*(4), 379–398.

Sawhney, M., Verona, G., & Prandelli, E. (2005). Collaborating to create: The Internet as a platform for customer engagement in product innovation. *Journal of Interactive Marketing*, *19*(4), 4–17.

Scaraboto, D. (2015). Selling, sharing, and everything in between: The hybrid economies of collaborative networks. *Journal of Consumer Research*, *42*(1), 152–176.

Schau, H.J., Muñiz Jr, A.M., & Arnould, E.J. (2009). How brand community practices create value. *Journal of Marketing*, *73*(5), 30–51.

Schouten, J.W., & McAlexander, J.H. (1995). Subcultures of consumption: An ethnography of the new bikers. *Journal of Consumer Research*, *22*(1), 43–61.

Shankar, A., Cherrier, H., & Canniford, R. (2006). Consumer empowerment: A Foucauldian interpretation. *European Journal of Marketing*, *40*(9/10), 1013–1030.

Spicer, A. (2010). Book review: Branded life: A review of key works on brands. *Organization Studies*, *31*(12), 1735–1740.

Stratton, G., & Northcote, J. (2016). When totems beget clans: The brand symbol as the defining marker of brand communities. *Journal of Consumer Culture*, *16*(2): 493–509.

Thomas, T.C., Price, L.L., & Schau, H.J. (2013). When differences unite: Resource dependence in heterogeneous consumption communities. *Journal of Consumer Research*, *39*(5), 1010–1033.

Thompson, C.J., & Troester, M. (2002). Consumer value systems in the age of postmodern fragmentation: The case of the natural health microculture. *Journal of Consumer Research*, *28*(4), 550–571.

Vargo, S.L., & Lusch, R.F. (2004). Evolving to a new dominant logic for marketing. *Journal of Marketing*, *68*(1), 1–17.

Von Hippel, E. (1986). Lead users: a source of novel product concepts. *Management Science*, *32*(7), 791–805.

Wittke, V., & Hanekop, H. (2011). *New Forms of Collaborative Innovation and Production on the Internet*. Göttingen, Universitätsverlag Göttingen.

Žižek, S. (1997), *The Plague of Fantasies*. London, Verso.

Zwick, D., Bonsu, S.K., & Darmody, A. (2008). Putting consumers to work: 'Co-creation' and new marketing govern-mentality. *Journal of Consumer Culture*, *8*(2), 163–196.

Zwick, D., & Bradshaw, A. (2016). Biopolitical marketing and social media brand communities. *Theory, Culture & Society*, *33*(5), 91–115.

Zwick, D., & Cayla, J. (2011). Inside marketing: Practices, ideologies, devices. In D. Zwick, & J. Cayla (Eds), *Inside Marketing* (pp. 3–19), Oxford, Oxford University Press.

15

Contesting Understandings of Contestation: Rethinking Perspectives on Activism

Jay Handelman and Eileen Fischer

INTRODUCTION

Social science scholars have long been interested in how and why people contest systems of authority such as firms, industries, or governments that they believe are imposing economic, social, and cultural harm on society (e.g. McCarthy and Zald 1977; Soule 2012; Weber, Heinze, and De Soucey 2008). In this chapter, we review prior consumer culture research on activism and suggest that it is premised on a series of assumptions or taken-for-granted understandings that may be creating blind spots in past work and opportunities for future research. The purpose of this chapter is threefold. First, we aim to present an integrative framework that serves to compare and contrast prior research on consumer activism. Second, we highlight the assumptions upon which our understanding of activism is built in order to consider their validity and identify gaps in our understanding. Third, based on these gaps, we present a series of ideas to stimulate future research on activism.

We commence this undertaking by reviewing major perspectives on activism that have informed the thinking of consumer culture scholars. We draw on these perspectives to derive a simple framework that enables us to compare and contrast prior research papers and to examine some of the shared underlying assumptions or understandings. This framework consists of three questions.

1 What actors matter?
2 What is being mobilized?
3 What is being achieved?

THEORETICAL PERSPECTIVES ON ACTIVISM

Activism is regarded as a movement comprised of loosely organized social actors who share a common set of beliefs and goals around contesting some system of authority such as firms, industries, or governments that the activists believe are imposing economic, social, and/or cultural harm on society (Den Hond and De Bakker 2007; McCarthy and Zald 1977; Soule 2012; Weber, Heinze, and De Soucey 2008). In a consumer context, activism is regarded as the decentralized but collective grassroots efforts by activist consumers to contest the actions of marketers and their organizations, as well as to more broadly mobilize a change in the cultural frames that guide consumption behavior (Glickman 2009; Kozinets and Handelman 2004; Murray and Ozanne 1991). Our understanding of activism in general, and consumer activism in particular, is rooted in the work of McCarthy and Zald (1977) and their resource mobilization theory (RMT). According to RMT, in order to achieve their desired social change, coalitions of social actors must aggregate resources, including money, participants, skills, and/or influential allies (McCarthy and Zald 1977). This view of activism brings into view three core questions that come to serve as the framework upon which we draw for our investigation.

What Actors Matter?

Activism is most typically regarded as involving two dichotomous groups of social actors: activists who are pushing for change to the existing social order and powerful social actors such as corporations and governments who work to defend their positions. Activists are presented as moral protagonists who challenge the instrumental, often economic-based, interests of the powerful societal antagonists.

The activist as protagonist

Early work typically regarded activists as rational actors in that a weighing of 'costs and rewards explains individual and organizational involvement' by activists (McCarthy and Zald 1977, p. 216). Citizens who see themselves as victims of an existing dominant social order will engage in activism if they believe the benefits of activist involvement and the potential for social change outweigh the costs of living under the current social order. This early work on activism typically regarded the activist as aggrieved by direct, tangible conditions such as the case of workers pushing for the right to form a union to counter punishing working conditions imposed by uncaring, profit-driven employers.

More recent investigations have loosened this strictly rational view of the activist by documenting the rise in the latter part of the twentieth century of New Social Movements (NSMs). NSMs involve activists who do not appear to tangibly suffer from the current social order, or to directly benefit from the desired social change (Buechler 1993). NSM theory emerged to explain a type of activism born in a post-industrialized society where increasingly powerful global corporations were seen to be intruding on democratic freedoms, individual self-determination, and environmental well-being (Buechler 1993). In reaction to what is regarded as an intrusion of corporate economic interests in modern society, activists work to counter this trend by advancing an alternative social paradigm based on human and environmental rights, individual freedom and self-determination (Buechler 1993). Instead of a 'rational' calculation of costs and benefits, NSM activists advance a moral point of view in that 'they were not working for the interests of their members, but for those of humanity and nature' (Salter 2003, p. 127). The infamous 'Battle in Seattle' protests in 1999 targeting the World Trade Organization's negotiations to expand global trade stands as an early illustration of the anti-corporate, anti-globalization nature of NSMs.

The marketer/corporation as antagonist

Consistent with Habermas (1991), the RMT and NSM perspectives on activism portray the sanctity of the public sphere of society as constantly under threat from the instrumental agenda of powerful, authoritative social actors, such as political elites and corporations, who seek to restrict the ability of citizens to engage in critical reflection to protect moral values (Salter 2003). This leads to the efforts by activists to 'patrol the borders between the system (the instrumental agenda of political elite and corporations) and the lifeworld (the moral convictions that bind citizens together in the public sphere), protecting civil society from encroachments by the system' (Salter 2003, p. 126). Therefore, marketers and their corporations are portrayed as belonging to 'the system' in which selfish, economic, instrumental agendas drive behavior. As such, marketers are seen to engage in a strategic, self-serving assessment of the power of the activists to threaten the organization's position in the marketplace. Marketers thus arrive at a rationally determined assessment of the costs and benefits of addressing the specific demands of the activists (Maignan and Ferrell 2004; Polonsky and Scott 2005).

What Is Being Mobilized?

Activists who share a common set of grievances work to mobilize resources such as money, participants, skills, and influential allies in support of their cause (McCarthy and Zald 1977). Early work on activism tended to focus on these tangible resources. However, later work began to identify less tangible constructs. Collective action frames is one example of this shift.

Participants are said to be bound together and motivated by 'collective action frames' whereby a coalition of activists come to share a common view of the world (Benford and Snow 2000; Buechler 1993; Salter 2003). RMT drew attention to specific social classes of people who share a set of grievances about day-to-day life, such as workers in a given organization. The NSM perspective broadened this to include people across class structures who share in a collective identity based on a shared ideology of a better world (Buechler 1993). Melucci (1996) argued that it is this collective identity that explains why a person would engage in activism even though his/her own economic and social situation allows for a comfortable life. It is a shared definition of the way the world should be, a shared sense of right versus wrong, that mobilizes people to contribute their time, money, skills, and passion towards the activists' efforts (Ayers 2003).

Through collective action frames, activists 'negotiate a shared understanding of some problematic condition, make attributions of blame, and urge others to act' (Benford and Snow 2000, p. 615). It is consistent with Goffman's (1974) theory of frames to argue that socially constructed collective frames enable activists to arrive at a shared interpretation of events that is simplified and condensed, providing an action-oriented set of beliefs that both inspire and legitimate activist endeavors (Benford and Snow 2000). These collective action frames, also referred to as 'injustice frames' (Gamson 1992), provide activists with a perspective on a problem accompanied with a cause-effect account of who is to blame, the corresponding effects on society, and what is to be done to change the situation. They also animate a collective identity (Ayers 2003; Benford and Snow 2000; Gamson 1992; Salter 2003).

What Is Being Achieved?

Activist work is typically regarded as goal driven behavior aimed at altering existing social arrangements in order to protect or restore the moral order of society as defined by citizens within the public sphere (Habermas 1991; Salter 2003). Activists engage in a series of tactics that are meant to trigger the desired social change. Trigger events are described as 'transient perturbations whose occurrences are difficult to foresee and whose impacts ... are disruptive and potentially inimical' (Meyer 1982, 515); they are ideologically imbued cultural occurrences that are often manufactured by activists, designed to bring to life the purported immorality of the opposition and the morality of the proponents. Trigger events hold the potential to serve as catalysts, sparking engagement by galvanizing support for protest. Such events can be critical for precipitating social change (Hoffman 1999; Meyer 1982). For example, trigger events can help to alter a firm's image by increasing public perception that a firm's practices are leading to societal harm (Vasi and King 2012). The publication in 1962 of Rachel Carson's 'Silent Spring' served as a trigger event that crystalized perceptions of the environmental harm being committed by the chemical industry, setting in motion a series of institutional changes that affected the whole industry (Hoffman 1999).

EMPIRICAL CONSUMER CULTURE RESEARCH ON ACTIVISM

The previous section provides a review of the conceptual origins of the contemporary work on consumer activism. This review has allowed us to develop a framework against which to compare and contrast recent empirical work on activism and consumer culture. In this section, we review the recent empirical work to see how it resonates with the dominant theoretical tradition in activism as presented in the previous section.

We identified papers to include in our review by using the following criteria:

- The paper has empirical data.
- The paper was published in one of the four main journals featuring consumer culture research: *Consumption Markets & Culture*, *Journal of Consumer Culture*, *Journal of Consumer Research*, and *Marketing Theory*.
- The paper was published from 2000 onwards.

Table 15.1 provides a summary of the empirical articles that we used for our review. Our review involved analyzing this body of work against the framework of the three core questions that characterizes the conceptual origins of activism. We now discuss the themes that emerged from our review of this empirical work.

Table 15.1 Empirical articles on consumer activism

Article	*What actors matter and how*	*What is being mobilized*	*What is being achieved*
Aspara, J., Aula, H-M., Tienari, J., & Tikkanen, H. (2014). Struggles in organizational attempts to adopt new branding logics: The case of a marketizing university. *Consumption Markets & Culture*, 17(6), 522–552	An organization (Aalto University) attempting to make branding and other changes and to move from a non-market to a market logic; the government that backed and funded the initiative; Stakeholders including faculty ('suppliers') and students ('customers')	Defiant, public resistance, e.g. satirical ad parodies; Newspaper coverage; Public discussion in the broader university community in Finland	Shifts over time in stakeholders who had power, significant modifications and adjustments to rebranding; Internal struggles between those for and against the rebranding and re-organization
Cronin, J.M., McCarthy, M.B., & Collins, A.M. (2014). Covert distinction: How hipsters practice food-based resistance strategies in the production of identity. *Consumption Markets & Culture*, 17(1), 2–28	Hipster community of consumption in opposition to mainstream consumption	Mundane daily consumption of food as resistance strategies, such as vegetarian choices, the choice and avoidance of various brands of food, and the decommodification of brands	Covert community performances that entrench the identity of the hipster community as counter to the mainstream, while making it difficult for the mainstream to co-opt the hipster identity
Giesler, M. (2008). Conflict and compromise: Drama in marketplace evolution. *Journal of Consumer Research*, 34(6), 739–753	Consumers who admonish greater fidelity to social utilitarian ideals versus anonymous music industry that admonishes greater fidelity to ideals of possessive individualism	Through narrative and performance, countervailing ideals of social utilitarian and possessive individualism are blended	Evolution of a market through various stages of ideological instability, with corresponding market structure arrangements
Gopaldas, A. (2014). Marketplace sentiments. *Journal of Consumer Research*, 41(4), 995–1014	Consumers who share their expressions about the marketplace; Corporations as villains	Activist expressions by way of magazines, videos, websites	Marketplace sentiments that include, among other things, contempt for corporations who are identified as villains
Hollenbeck, C.R. & G.M. Zinkhan (2010). Anti-brand communities, negotiation of brand meaning, and the learning process: The case of Wal-Mart. *Consumption Markets & Culture*, 13(3), 325–345	Consumers who are members of an anti-brand community (anti-Walmart) and who learn to 'negotiate' a brand's meaning; Negotiating a brand's meaning is defined as interpreting experiences and perceptions of brands; Also PRO-brand (i.e. pro-Walmart) people who target rallies by anti-Walmarters and thus 'fuel the other groups' cause	Anti-Walmart sentiment and (presumably) knowledge	Collective learning, oppositional consciousness
Humphreys, A. & Thompson, C.J. (2014). Branding disaster: Reestablishing trust through the ideological containment of systemic risk anxieties. *Journal of Consumer Research*, 41(4), 877–910	Mainstream media (WSJ, NYT, USA Today) contains anxieties related to industrial accidents which might otherwise result in increased anti-industry activism; Brands (BP in particular) as portrayed in the media	Nothing is mobilized because 'ideological containment' prevents any sustained anti-industry sentiment or behavior from being mobilized	Preservation of 'consumer culture status quo' in terms of ongoing or resurgent trust in expert systems and unchanged consumer risk perceptions

Izberk-Belgin, E. (2012). Infidel brands: Unveiling alternative meanings of global brands at the nexus of globalization, consumer culture, and Islamism. *Journal of Consumer Research*, 39(4), 663–687	Marginalized, low-income Turkish consumers; Global brands from market societies	Religious ideology that upholds social equality, morality, and justice	Consumer 'jihad' that protests the social crisis posed by modernity and globalization
Kozinets, R.V. (2002). Can consumers escape the market? Emancipatory illuminations from Burning Man. *Journal of Consumer Research*, 29(1), 20–38	Burning Man participants who distance themselves from the marketplace; Anonymous marketplace actors, such as consumers and companies, who practice market logics	Social logics that distance Burning Man participants from market logics by way of temporary practices of alternative exchange	Temporary community where divergent social logics can be expressed (in contrast to market logics)
Kozinets, R.V. & Handelman, J.M. (2004). Adversaries of consumption: Consumer movements, activism, and ideology. *Journal of Consumer Research*, 31(3), 691–704	Anti-advertising, anti-Nike, and anti-GE food activists; Mainstream consumers as passive dupes who become the targets of the activists	Information, by way of parodies, boycotts, and other activist material. The information connects corporate greed and misdeeds to the end-consumer's behavior	Awakening consumers to how they have been blind to corporate misdeeds
Kucuk, U. (2015). A semiotic analysis of consumer-generated antibranding. *Marketing Theory*, 15(2), 243–264	Digital anti-branders (activists); Brands (targets); Visually literate consumers	Semiotic value creation in the form of anti-brand images that demonize, criminalize, and dehumanize brands	Consumer decoding and rejection of company's intended brand semiotics
Mikkonen, I. & Bajde, D. (2013). Happy Festivus! Parody as playful consumer resistance. *Consumption Markets and Culture*, 16(4), 311–337	Consumers who resist dominant consumption discourses and marketplace ideologies	Consumer resistors engage in 'parodic resistance' by mobilizing parodies of the mainstream, marketplace dominated beliefs of Christmas. In this case, the parody of 'Festivus' is mobilized, which is a grand narrative of 'meaningful nothingness'	The Festivus celebration is presented as a viable means of circumventing the oppressiveness of Christmas whereby the higher goals and meanings of Christmas are erased (by way of the achievement of a holiday of 'nothingness')
Moraes, C., Szmigin, I., & Marylyn Carrigan, M. (2010). Living production-engaged alternatives: An examination of new consumption communities. *Consumption Markets & Culture*, 13(3), 273–298	'New Consumption Communities' defined as production engaged consumers who question market practices deemed inadequate or unfair	Concerns about systemic risks such as the perceived disconnect between producer and consumer, environmental degradation, lack of respect for diversity and spiritual values, lack of cooperation and some degree of self-sufficiency, as well as a lack of educational and personal development	Entrepreneurial reconnections with production. These communities are more interested in pro-entrepreneurial discourses, practices and choices than in acting against consumer culture or markets
Murray, D.C. (2015). Notes to self: The visual culture of selfies in the age of social media. *Consumption Markets Culture*, 18(6), 490–516	Post-feminist female bloggers	By way of the 'selfie', 'feminist aesthetics' are being mobilized. This aesthetic portrays sexually provocative self-portraits that are accompanied with meanings of impassioned defiance against unhealthy body standards perpetuated by mainstream media	Defiance against mainstream media portrayals of impossible-to-achieve female body images; female empowerment by women who take control of how their bodies and sexuality are portrayed

(continued)

Table 15.1 Empirical articles on consumer activism (Continued)

Article	*What actors matter and how*	*What is being mobilized*	*What is being achieved*
Page, A. (2014). 'How many slaves work for you?' Race, new media, and neoliberal consumer activism. *Journal of Consumer Culture*, October, 1–16	Neoliberal consumer activists – ethical consumers concerned with social, economic, and environmental conditions	Political brand cultures that urge consumers to see themselves as activists in relation to consumption practices. The ethical consumer citizen	Unwittingly, a culture of consumption is achieved whereby the consumer is responsible and the producer is left off the hook. Consumption obscures alternative forms of resistance
Portwood-Stacer, L. (2012). Anti-consumption as tactical resistance: Anarchists, subculture, and activist strategy. *Journal of Consumer Culture*, 12(1), 87–105	Participants in anti-consumption movements as self-identified anarchists	Lifestyle orientation – anti-consumption as both abstinence from consumption and a form of consumption that signifies opposition to consumption	Habitualized anti-consumption practices that provide material alternatives (to mainstream) social conditions
Sandikci, Ö. & Ger, G. (2010). Veiling in style: How does a stigmatized practice become fashionable? *Journal of Consumer Research*, 37(1), 15–36	Members of a distinguishable subgroup that see themselves as marginalized by religion. Small, local businesses play a role working with this marginalized group	A reaction against mainstream fashion brands that celebrate secularism, in favour of fashionable tessetur alternatives that destigmatize expressions of non-secularism	A 'reveiling movement' that helped to destigmatize non-secular dress practices
Scaraboto, D. & Fischer, E. (2013). Frustrated fatshionistas: An institutional theory perspective on consumer quests for greater choice in mainstream markets. *Journal of Consumer Research*, 39(6), 1234–1257	Marginalized consumers who are deemed not legitimate by mainstream marketers; Mainstream marketers; Institutional entrepreneurs	Institutional logics from adjacent fields; Institutionalized practices	Legitimacy for a marginalized group of consumers; Market structures that give this marginalized group access to the mainstream marketplace
Thompson, C.J. (2004). Marketplace mythology and discourses of power. *Journal of Consumer Research*, 31(1), 162–180	Anti-brand activists against corporate power – countervailing forces	Discourses of resistance that draw from cultural models of environmental sustainability, human rights, etc.	Shifting power relationships between activists and corporations based on mythic contrasts of good vs evil
Thompson, C.J. & Arsel, Z. (2004). 'The Starbucks brandscape and consumers' (anticorporate) experiences of glocalization. *Journal of Consumer Research*, 3(4), 631–642	Consumers who form politicized anti-corporate, anti-globalization identifications; Global brands that structure consumers' experiences of glocalization	Refusal to patronize a global brand that contributes to driving out local brands; active opposition to further incursions of the global brand; Patronizing communal spaces and exchange systems that offer an alternative to the profit-driven commodity logic of corporate capitalism	The 'hegemonic brandscape' that is partially created by a company like Starbucks continuously includes a 'nexus of oppositional brand meanings' largely beyond the company's control
Varman, R. & Belk, R.W. (2009). Nationalism and ideology in an anticonsumption movement. *Journal of Consumer Research*, 36(4), 686–700	Marginalized, dislocated people (due to globalization) in Mehdiganj, India, versus Western branded goods	Re-enactment of nationalist ideology of Swadeshi in which indigenous goods are preferred over imported substitutes; Boycott against global brands (Coca-Cola in this case)	Sacrifice, purity, morality through boycott of global (outside) corporations; Countering the sinful creation of products made by machines from the outside

Thematic Summary: What Actors Matter?

Our review of empirical papers in the consumer culture tradition that have examined activism, broadly defined, unsurprisingly reveals that the single most common type of actor that has been assumed to matter as a protagonist is a consumer of some kind. In some cases, the consumer is very broadly defined, for example as a 'mainstream' consumer (Kozinets and Handelman 2004), an individual who experiences marketplace sentiments (Gopaldas 2014) or a visually literate consumer (Kucuk 2015). More often, studies have focused on members of a distinguishable subgroup, such as customers of a particular organization (Aspara, Aula, Tienari, and Tikkanen 2014; Hollenbeck and Zinkhan 2010); opponents of a particular brand (Thompson and Arsel 2004); hipsters (Cronin, McCarthy, and Collins 2014); participants in 'Festivus' (Mikkonen and Bajde 2013) or 'Burning Man' (Kozinets 2002); female bloggers (Murray 2015); people marginalized by dislocation (Varman and Belk 2009), religion (Izberk-Bilgin 2012; Sandikci and Ger 2010), or body size (Scaraboto and Fischer 2013); or members of alternative consumption communities (Moraes, Szmigin and Carrigan 2010; Portwood-Stacer 2012).

In most studies we looked at, a second category of actors is also assumed to matter: the 'opponent' or antagonist against whom activism is directed. In some cases, the opponent is a particular organization or brand such as Aalto University (Aspara, Aual, Tienari and Tikkanen 2014); Walmart (Hollenbeck and Zinkhan 2010); British Petroleum (Humphreys and Thompson 2014); Nike and GE (Kozinets and Handelman, 2004); Coca-Cola (Varman and Belk 2009) or Starbucks (Thompson and Arsel 2004). In other cases, the opponent identified is a broader set of brands or firms, such as Western brands (Izberk-Bilgin 2012), mainstream fashion brands (Sandikci and Ger 2010; Scaraboto and Fischer 2013), or the recorded music industry (Giesler 2008). In a few cases, the opponent is a relatively diffuse one, such as 'the market' or market logics (Cronin, McCarthy, and Collins 2014; Kozinets 2002; Mikkonen and Bajde 2013; Portwood-Stacer 2012); mainstream media that idealizes unhealthy body images (Murray 2015); or corporate producers who pollute, exploit, or offer ethically or environmentally questionable products (e.g. Gopaldas 2014; Kucuk 2015). It is worth noting, however, that while nearly all consumer culture works on activism acknowledge the opponent that is resisted, only two studies in the set we examined (Aspara, Aula, Tienari, and Tikkanen 2014; Humphreys and Thompson 2014) devoted much analytic attention to the actions of opponents that matter in a context where activism is nascent.

A few papers delineated a third category of actor relevant to resistance: we will refer to them as 'lead activists'. We single out lead activists from those who participate in activism because of their proactive role in issue framing. Notable examples of papers that highlight lead activisits are Kozinets and Handelman (2004), who saw quite different roles for leaders and mainstream consumers in social movements against consumption; Kucuk (2015), who discussed 'digital anti-branders' as actors who inspired visually literature consumers to resist specific brands; Scaraboto and Fischer (2013), who noted how 'institutional entrepreneurs' helped inspire 'Fatshionistas' in the plus sized fashion market; and Thompson (2004) who noted the unique role of anti-brand activists as bringing important issues (such as that of genetically modified food) to the attention of consumers.

Further, a handful of papers identified other categories of actors that mattered in the context under investigation. For example, Humphries and Thompson (2014) examine how the media serves as an actor that helps to preserve the 'consumer status quo' in the BP oil spill context where activism against the status quo might have been anticipated. Conversely, Sandikci and Ger (2010) highlight the role that small business (as opposed to mainstream brands) played in helping religious consumers resist the secularization of dress that mainstream Turkish culture supported. Hollenbeck and Zinkhan (2010) and Aspara, Aula, Tienari, and Tikkanen (2014) both analyze the roles employees of an organization may play in activist movements. And a paper by Page (2014) singled out for examination the role that an intermediary organization, slaveryfootprint.org, did (and did not) play in helping fuel effective consumer activism. Among the categories of actors to which little or no attention was paid were governments and nongovernmental organizations, both of which might be expected to play meaningful roles in some contexts where consumer activism occurs or might arise.

Thematic Summary: What Is Being Mobilized

The articles that we reviewed reveal a range in what is mobilized by social actors to achieve their various objectives. We see them as forming a continuum of sorts, with tangible actions and artefacts anchoring one end of the continuum and intangible resources the other end.

Tangible actions and artefacts

The tangible action most readily associated with traditional views of activism is the boycott (Glickman 2009) in which activists mobilize the actions of consumers to withhold their purchases from target firms. When consumers withhold their purchases, it is believed that the target company will experience financial harm, thus motivating the target firm to correct its actions (Kozinets and Handelman 2004).

Beyond tangible actions against targeted companies, Cronin, McCarthy, and Collins (2014) examined mundane, day-to-day tangible consumer actions that stood in opposition to mainstream consumption in general. Their study examined the mobilization of daily food consumption choices, such as choosing vegetarian options, amongst self-identified members of the 'hipster' community. Similar to a boycott, these mundane, day-to-day actions are tangible in nature. However, no specific companies were the target of these mobilized consumer practices (Cronin et al. 2014). Instead, a broader community identity served as the target of these tangible consumer efforts.

Our review of the literature also shows certain kinds of tangible artefacts that came to be mobilized for various collective interests. For example, Kucuk (2015) examined the mobilization of anti-brand images by activists. These tangible images served to demonize, criminalize, and dehumanize the target brands (Kucuk 2015). In Murray's (2015) study of post-feminist bloggers, the tangible artefact mobilized was sexually provocative self-images that were infused with feminist aesthetics. Similarly, Scaraboto and Fischer (2013) also noted the creation and mobilization of images – pictures of plus sized consumers who created fashion-forward photos of themselves.

In the study by Mikkonen and Bajde (2013), the tangible artefact being mobilized was parodies of mainstream marketplace beliefs.

Intangible resources

The majority of the articles we reviewed focused on activists who were working to change the way other social actors viewed the world around them. While these efforts did involve tangible actions, the focus of the activist effort was to mobilize a change in the broader logics, ideals, ideologies, knowledge structures, and orientations that come to shape societal practices. These resources are considered 'intangible' in that there is a lack of physicality associated with the resource being mobilized (unlike a boycott, for instance, in which physical consumption practices are being mobilized to achieve a desired goal).

At the most intangible end of the continuum, we find the mobilization of ideology. Izberk-Bilgin (2012) noted how marginalized, low-income Turkish consumers worked to mobilize a religious ideology that upholds social equality, morality, and justice. And Varman and Belk (2009) observed marginalized and dislocated people re-enacting a nationalist ideology that celebrates indigenous goods over imported substitutes. While both of these articles discuss tangible actions that activists take, the focus of what is being mobilized is a highly intangible ideology. The commonality in these articles is that the activists work to mobilize a previously marginalized societal ideology that aligns with their own marginalized position in society. However, the mobilization of this marginalized ideology was not an end in itself, but rather a way of moving towards a broader goal (as we will discuss in the next section).

Other intangible resources that are mobilized include various types of logics, such as social logics that counter market logics (Kozinets 2002), and institutional logics (Scaraboto and Fischer 2013) which help to de-marginalize a particular group of consumers. As with those that focus on ideology, these studies reveal various tangible actions taken by activist consumers, but the engagement of these tangible actions is used to mobilize broader societal logics. Similar to logics, Giesler (2008) identifies the mobilization of societal ideals that celebrate social inclusion and well-being (as opposed to individual or commercial interests). Thompson (2004) focuses on the discourses of resistance put forward by anti-brand activists. These discourses gain a cultural presence as they draw from cultural models of environmental sustainability, human rights, and other prevalent cultural frames.

Other intangible resources include the mobilization of activists' negative sentiments about the marketplace (Gopaldas 2014), lifestyle orientations favoring anti-consumption practices (Portwood-Stacer 2012), and a neoliberal political culture that fosters the ethical consumer citizen (Page 2014). As with ideology and logics, the mobilization of these negative sentiments, lifestyle orientations, and a particular type of political culture all serve to legitimate an otherwise marginalized view of the way society should work.

Thematic Summary: What Is Being Achieved?

A number of the papers in the set we reviewed were not explicit about what had been achieved through the activist efforts they investigated. In part, this may be due to the fact that outcomes of activism were not central to the authors' research questions. Alternatively, it may be because outcomes were assumed. Another possibility is that outcomes were of interest, but had yet to materialize during the span of time under investigation.

In those cases where studies did document or speculate on the achievements of activist efforts, a common outcome is that the status quo remains intact. Kozinets (2002) concludes that despite the fact that Burning Man participants managed reasonably successfully to forge a gift-based economy, it was only within a small enclave and for a short time; he (famously) asserts that consumers cannot escape 'the market'. Scaraboto and Fischer (2013) indicate that despite the mobilization of Fatshionistas to encourage mainstream marketers to offer them stylish clothing options, there was little evidence of any significant or permanent improvement in the plus size fashion on offer from major brands as a result of their activism. And Humphreys and Thompson (2014) document that, even when consumers might be expected to protest en masse against the practices of corporations that have caused disasters, brand-centric disaster myths promulgated by media coverage serve to reestablish consumers' trust while also insulating corporations and governmental institutions from systematic critiques.

In other cases, some amount of change does occur. Specifically, when resistance efforts are targeted at particular brands, those brands develop a 'doppelganger'. Thompson, Rindfleisch and Arsel (2006) define doppelganger brands as 'a family of disparaging images and meanings about a brand that circulate throughout popular culture'; they identified this phenomenon through their study of consumers' anti-corporate responses to Starbucks (Thompson and Arsel 2004). In like fashion, a consumer 'jihad' against certain global and local brands precipitated disparaging images of those brands as 'infidels' among the Turkish consumers studied by Izberk-Bilgin (2012). And Coca-Cola developed negative images in India as a result of the boycott against it waged by marginalized individuals re-enacting the nationalist ideology of Swadeshi (Varman and Belk 2009). Even Christmas can be said to have developed something of a doppelganger brand image through the playful parodies mounted by Festivus celebrants (Mikkonen and Bajde 2013).

In a few cases where more system-level changes were sought, it appears that resistance efforts did precipitate some kinds of market-level effects. For example, Sandilkci and Ger show that the 'reveiling movement' in Turkey was successfully able to destigmatize the practice of veiling and to precipitate the emergence of a market for fashionable tessetur. And Giesler (2008) documents that downloaders attempting to resist paying for recorded music ultimately did precipitate evolution in the music marketplace, though their efforts did not result in the kinds of outcomes they had originally envisioned. Thompson (2004) notes that discourses of resistance can bring about shifting power relations between anti-brand activists and corporations premised on mythic contrasts of good versus evil. Interestingly, in cases where resistance is effective, opportunities appear to arise for entrepreneurial actors to take advantage of market dynamics precipitated by consumer activists.

Observations

After reflecting on the corpus of work reviewed, we discerned three types of tacit assumptions that seem to have been relatively pervasive in research on activism in the consumer culture literature. We do not mean these observations as criticisms, and we acknowledge that they hold true to varying degrees for the papers reviewed. However, we believe that drawing attention to unrecognized assumptions can be valuable in helping us move forward in new directions for research on activism.

A first type of assumption we infer concerns the actors who matter. Based on the readings we reviewed, one might infer that only a small set of actors matter in activism, and that consumers are of most importance. Across the papers we examined, actors other than consumers are rarely examined systematically, and when the set is broadened, it includes only one or two other categories of actors. Moreover, the literature tends to assume that the key actors in 'opposing' groups are relatively homogeneous within groups and readily distinguished from one another.

In broad brush strokes, portrayals of the key categories of actors can be summarized as follows. Consumers are, not surprisingly given the discipline we work in, front and center. Typically, they are portrayed as seeking opportunities for empowerment in order to counter the constraining forces against them. At times, consumers are presented as being unaware of the conditions of their domination (cf. Kozinets and Handelman 2004) and as insufficiently sensitized to the negative impact of the hegemonic consumption culture within which they are immersed. In these cases, activists as a category of actor play an important role in raising important issues that would otherwise remain unexamined. Countering the consumers and activists are powerful corporations and their global brands, whose actions subjugate consumers in the hegemony of the marketplace. As noted by Thompson (2004), dichotomizing these stakeholders leads to a 'good versus evil' assessment whereby consumers and activists are revered as uniformly morally righteous, and corporations or the brands they market are reviled as unmitigated villains.

A second type of assumption concerns the outcomes of activism. The papers as a whole seem to devote more analytic attention to actors and their actions than to the range of consequences that activism may precipitate. The tacit assumption here might be that the desired and desirable outcomes, as well as the likely outcomes, are self-evident. And even when the end results of activism are captured in the empirical work we examined, they tend to be conveyed in relatively simplified ways: when consumer activists are successful, they are able to achieve alternative community, cultural, and market arrangements. These arrangements are sometimes temporary (Kozinets 2002), and sometimes more permanent (e.g. Sandikci and Ger 2010). Their broader implications for the social system in which they are situated, and the recursive or ripple effects they might generate, are generally not focal in analytic efforts.

A third, related, type of assumption concerns the distinction between activism and the socio-historic context in which it occurs. Although it is doubtless an oversimplification, there is an extent to which prior research in this genre assumes activism itself can be analytically separated from the broader institutional setting in which it is occurring, so that possible ways in which activism might be shaped by the contextual milieu in which it occurs are rarely systematically assessed. Put differently, we might paraphrase Askegaard and Linnet (2011, p. 381) to observe that the 'systemic and structuring influences of market and social systems that is not necessarily felt or experienced by consumers in their daily lives, and therefore not necessarily discursively expressed' may often not be in analytic view in research on activism.

We now articulate research opportunities that might arise from considering each of these three types of assumptions or taken-for-granted tendencies.

OPPORTUNITIES FOR FUTURE RESEARCH ON CONSUMER ACTIVISM

Opportunity 1

Future research can do more to challenge the presumed homogeneity of the various stakeholder groups. Are all social actors in a given stakeholder category alike? And is any given category well understood as 'good' in relation to another that is 'evil'? As noted by Aspara, Aula, Tienari, and Tikkanen (2014), organizations have employees whose attitudes and actions may deviate significantly from the official corporate position. And consumers themselves often differ greatly from one another, whether because of roles they hold, their relative social status, their motives, or their tastes and affinities. Adding a further complication to this, Luedicke, Thompson, and Giesler (2010) note that social actors work to construct opponents as a way to present the morality of their own positions. Taken together these observations highlight that categories of social actors are likely to be heterogeneous, and that our understanding of activism will be advanced if we are open to exploring within-category heterogeneity and also possibly between-category commonalities.

Opportunity 2

Future research can examine a greater range of categories of actors. Consumers, activists and corporations are entangled in complex socio-cultural systems. The interpenetration of media, government, special interest groups, and of entrepreneurial and political actors inevitably must work to shape perspectives and the actions that constitute activism in any given case under investigation. The study of the BP oil spill disaster by Humphreys and Thompson (2014) highlights the crucial role played by the media in de-escalating potential activism. Beyond the consumer culture literature, in their study of the rise of the market for grass-fed meat and dairy products, Weber et al. (2008) found that a coalition of previously unaffiliated categories of actors including animal breeding experts, environmentalists, and food critics came together to share a set of cultural frames about the harms of industrial agriculture. The nature of these cultural frames arose as a result of this particular constellation of groups of actors which ultimately allowed for the corresponding consumer support for the new market of grass-fed meat products. Together these studies are suggestive of the range of roles that diverse social actors can play in instances of activism, or potential activism. In light of the growing body of work that draws attention to object agency (e.g. Canniford and Shankar 2013; Epp and Price 2010; Parmentier and Fischer 2015), activist researchers might find value in considering how entities other than human actors have agency in cases of activism.

Opportunity 3

Future research can purposefully examine consumer activism from a processual perspective. The complexity of the social actors combined with the plethora of actions, artefacts and resources being mobilized raises fascinating questions about the processes of activism. A couple of articles that we examined did take processual perspectives with fruitful results. Specifically, Humphreys and Thompson (2014) found that as media and corporate actors became increasingly engaged in narrating the story surrounding the BP oil spill, potentially destabilizing societal implications were contained by a process involving disaster myths and the corresponding framing of public discourses. In contrast, Giesler (2008) developed a dialectical process model in which a breach in normative cultural practices leads to a crisis, followed by redress, and then reintegration as new mainstream practices emerge. These studies begin to capture the dynamic societal processes unleashed by activism.

We believe that embracing a processual perspective in general will encourage researchers to explore the complexity of activism more fully, and that it may be particularly fruitful for researchers interested in activism to familiarize themselves with the burgeoning process literature on how paradoxes are navigated (e.g. Farjoun, Ansell, and Boin 2015; Hargrave and Van de Ven 2016; Jay 2013). Paradox occurs when two mutually contradictory yet interdependent elements coexist and must both be dealt with by actors striving to achieve goals in that context (Lewis 2000); we believe this to be a common feature in many cases of activism, yet one that is insufficiently theorized in the extant literature.

Opportunity 4

Future research can examine consumer activism as an element of the fabric of broader societal institutions, including the social institution of the marketplace. If activism entails the mobilization of the very beliefs and ideologies that animate social institutions, then the ongoing evolution of these ideologies will logically trigger the ongoing evolution of the corresponding social institutions. By focusing attention on activism as an essential fabric of social institutions, we come to see these institutions not as stable entities punctuated by periodic change, but rather as spaces of constant evolution. Again, a processual perspective will help with research that examines the triggers and trajectories of activism over time within a given context.

Opportunity 5

As another related option, future research can examine the unintended and unforeseen system-level consequences that arise as a result of activism. Given the multiple categories of actors relevant in any given case of activism, and the systemic contextual embeddedness of their actions, the triggered outcomes of activism may be more wide-ranging than is often considered. For example, in their examination of the activism in the late 1800s that led to the prohibition of alcohol in the United States,

Hiatt, Sine, and Tolbert (2009) found that activists were able to change society's norms and beliefs about drinking alcohol by framing new behaviors as 'acceptable' – such as making the abstinence from drinking acceptable behavior in social situations. At the same time, activists framed new cause and effect relationships that linked particular social problems (such as violence in the home and unemployment) with alcohol consumption. These collective action frames helped mobilize changes in consumer drinking habits and the enactment by governments of more restrictive laws regulating the distribution and consumption of alcohol. These changes adversely affected the brewing industry, and had the unintended consequence of fostering a new market for soft drink manufacturers such as Coca-Cola and Pepsi (Hiatt et al. 2009). Similarly, Giesler (2008) found that once the 'war' on downloading music played itself out, unintended opportunities for other market players (such as iTunes) arose.

CONCLUSION

Our review of the empirical work examining activism in the consumer culture literature has revealed both its breadth and some of its tendencies toward unduly limiting underlying assumptions. By opening up these assumptions for examination, we have identified five opportunities that could potentially be productive for future scholarship on activism. Of course, the opportunities we identify are by no means exhaustive. We hope, however, that they will help to inspire a new, even richer, wave of research on consumer activism.

REFERENCES

Askegaard, S. & Linnet, J.T. (2011). Towards an epistemology of consumer culture theory: Phenomenology and the context of context. *Marketing Theory*, 11(4), 381–404.

Aspara, J., Aula, H-M., Tienari, J., & Tikkanen, H. (2014). Struggles in organizational attempts to adopt new branding logics: The case of a marketizing university. *Consumption Markets & Culture*, 17(6), 522–552.

Ayers, M.D. (2003). Comparing Collective Identity in Online and Offline Feminist Activists. In *Cyberactivism: Online Activism in Theory and Practice*, M. McCaughey and M.D. Ayers (Eds). New York: Routledge.

Benford, R.D. & Snow, D.A. (2000). Framing processes and social movements: An overview and assessment. *Annual Review of Sociology*, 26, 611–639.

Buechler, S.M. (1993). Beyond resource mobilization? Emerging trends in social movement theory. In *Social Movements: Perspectives and Issues*, S.M. Buechler and F.K. Cylke (Eds). Mountain View, CA: Mayfield Publishing Company, 193–210.

Canniford, R. & Shankar, A. (2013). Purifying practices: How consumers assemble romantic experiences of nature. *Journal of Consumer Research*, 39(5), 1051–1069.

Cronin, J.M., McCarthy, M.B., & Collins, A.M. (2014). Covert distinction: How hipsters practice food-based resistance strategies in the production of identity. *Consumption Markets & Culture*, 17(1), 2–28.

Den Hond, F. & De Bakker, F.G.A. (2007). Ideologically motivated activism: How activist groups influence corporate social change activities. *Academy of Management Review*, 32(3), 901–924.

Epp, A.M. & Price, L.L. (2010). The storied life of singularized objects: Forces of agency and network transformation. *Journal of Consumer Research*, 36(5), 820–837.

Farjoun, M., Ansell, C., & Boin, A. (2015). Pragmatism in organization studies: Meeting the challenges of a dynamic and complex world. *Organization Science*, 26(November–December), 1787–1804.

Gamson, W.A. (1992). *Talking Politics*. New York: Cambridge University Press.

Giesler, M. (2008). Conflict and compromise: Drama in marketplace evolution. *Journal of Consumer Research*, 34(6), 739–753.

Glickman, L.B. (2009). *Buying Power: A History of Consumer Activism in America*. Chicago: University of Chicago Press.

Goffman, E. (1974). *Frame Analysis: An Essay on the Organization of Experience*. Boston: Northeastern University Press.

Gopaldas, A. (2014). Marketplace sentiments. *Journal of Consumer Research*, 41(4), 995–1014.

Habermas, J. (1991). *The Structural Transformation of the Public Sphere: An Inquiry into a Category of Bourgeois Society*. Cambridge, MA: The MIT Press.

Hargrave, T. & Van de Ven, A. (2016). Integrating dialectical and paradox perspectives on managing contradictions in organizations. *Organizational Studies*, 38(3–4), 1–21.

Hiatt, S.R., Sine, W., & Tolbert, P. (2009). From Pabst to Pepsi: The deinstitutionalization of social practices and the emergence of entrepreneurial opportunities. *Administrative Science Quarterly*, 54(4), 635–667.

Hoffman, A.J. (1999). Institutional evolution and change: Environmentalism and the U.S. chemical industry. *Academy of Management Journal*, 42(4), 351–371.

Hollenbeck, C.R. & Zinkhan, G.M. (2010). Anti-brand communities, negotiation of brand meaning, and the learning process: The case of Wal-Mart. *Consumption Markets & Culture*, 13(3), 325–345.

Humphreys, A. & Thompson, C.J. (2014). Branding disaster: Reestablishing trust through the ideological containment of systemic risk anxieties. *Journal of Consumer Research*, 41(4), 877–910.

Izberk-Bilgin, E. (2012). Infidel brands: Unveiling alternative meanings of global brands at the nexus of globalization, consumer culture, and Islamism. *Journal of Consumer Research*, 39(4), 663–687.

Jay, J. (2013). Navigating paradox as a mechanism of change and innovation in hybrid organizations. *Academy of Management Journal*, 56(1), 137–159.

Kozinets, R.V. (2002). Can consumers escape the market? Emancipatory illuminations from Burning Man. *Journal of Consumer* Research, 29(1), 20–38.

Kozinets, R.V. & Handelman, J.M. (2004). Adversaries of consumption: Consumer movements, activism, and ideology. *Journal of Consumer Research*, 31(3), 691–704.

Kucuk, U. (2015). A semiotic analysis of consumer-generated antibranding. *Marketing Theory* 15(2), 243–264.

Lewis, M. (2000). Exploring paradox: Toward a more comprehensive guide. *Academy of Management Review*, 25(4), 760–776.

Luedicke, M.K., Thompson, C.J., & Giesler, M. (2010). Consumer identity work as moral protagonism: How myth and ideology animate a brand-mediated moral conflict. *Journal of Consumer Research*, 36(6), 1016–1032.

Maignan, I. & Ferrell, O.C. (2004). Corporate social responsibility and marketing: An integrative framework. *Journal of the Academy of Marketing Science*, 32(1), 3–19.

McCarthy, J.D. & Zald, M.N. (1977). Resource mobilization and social movements: A partial theory. *American Journal of Sociology*, 82(6), 1212–1241.

Melucci, A. (1996). *Challenging Codes: Collective Action in the Information Age.* Cambridge, UK: Cambridge University Press.

Meyer, A.D. (1982). Adapting to environmental jolts. *Administrative Science Quarterly*, 27(4), 515–537.

Mikkonen, I. & Bajde, D. (2013). Happy Festivus! Parody as playful consumer resistance. *Consumption Markets and Culture*, 16(4), 311–337.

Moraes, C., Szmigin, I., & Marylyn Carrigan, M. (2010). Living production-engaged alternatives: An examination of new consumption communities. *Consumption Markets & Culture*, 13(3), 273–298.

Murray, D.C. (2015). Notes to self: The visual culture of selfies in the age of social media. *Consumption Markets Culture*, 18(6), 490–516.

Murray, J.B. & Ozanne, J.L. (1991). The critical imagination: Emancipatory interests in consumer research. *Journal of Consumer Research*, 18(2), 129–144.

Page, A. (2014). 'How many slaves work for you?' Race, new media, and neoliberal consumer activism. *Journal of Consumer Culture*, October, 1–16.

Parmentier, M.-A. & Fischer, E. (2015). Things fall apart: The dynamics of brand audience dissipation. *Journal of Consumer Research*, 41(5), 1228–1251.

Polonsky, M.J. & Scott, D. (2005). An empirical examination of the stakeholder strategy matrix. *European Journal of Marketing*, 39(9/10), 1199–1215.

Portwood-Stacer, L. (2012). Anti-consumption as tactical resistance: Anarchists, subculture, and activist strategy. *Journal of Consumer Culture*, 12(1), 87–105.

Sandikci, Ö. & Ger, G. (2010). Veiling in style: How does a stigmatized practice become fashionable? *Journal of Consumer Research*, 37(1), 15–36.

Salter, L. (2003). Democracy, new social movements and the internet: A Habermasian analysis. In *Cyberactivism: Online Activism in Theory and Practice*, M. McCaughey & M.D. Ayers (Eds). New York: Routledge.

Scaraboto, D. & Fischer, E. (2013). Frustrated fatshionistas: An institutional theory perspective on consumer quests for greater choice in mainstream markets. *Journal of Consumer Research*, 39(6), 1234–1257.

Soule, S.A. (2012). Social movements and markets, industries, and firms. *Organization Studies*, 33(12), 1715–1733.

Thompson, C.J. (2004). Marketplace mythology and discourses of power. *Journal of Consumer Research*, 31(1), 162–180.

Thompson, C.J. & Arsel, Z. (2004). 'The Starbucks brandscape and consumers' (anticorporate) experiences of glocalization. *Journal of Consumer Research*, 3(4), 631–642.

Thompson, C.J., Rindfleisch, A., & Arsel, Z. (2006). Emotional branding and the strategic value of the doppelgänger brand image. *Journal of Marketing*, 70(1), 50–65.

Varman, R. & Belk, R.W. (2009). Nationalism and ideology in an anticonsumption movement. *Journal of Consumer Research*, 36(4), 686–700.

Vasi, I.B. & King, B. (2012). Social movements, risk perceptions, and economic outcomes: The effect of primary and secondary stakeholder activism on firms' perceived environmental risk and financial performance. *American Sociological Review*, 77(4), 1–24.

Weber, K., Heinze, K.L., & DeSoucey, M. (2008). 'Forage for thought: Mobilizing codes in the movement for grass-fed meat and dairy products. *Administrative Science Quarterly*, 53(3), 529–567.

PART IV

Consumer Culture in Media and Cultural Studies

16

Consumer Culture and the Media

Mehita Iqani

INTRODUCTION

Two inescapable features of contemporary society are the wide availability of media texts and technologies, and the organisation of life around various forms of market exchange. It is arguably impossible to understand or analyse the human condition in almost any context, be it at the local, national or global scales, without engaging to some extent with either the media or consumer culture (Iqani, 2012a). This chapter takes this claim as a starting point. Based thereon, its intention is to present to the reader a number of propositions about important ways in which media systems and cultures of consumption are inextricably linked. The overarching claim of this chapter is that it is impossible to study one without the other, and that any attempt to research some facet of consumer culture requires a consideration of the media, and any attempt to research some facet of the media requires a consideration of consumer culture. The chapter is organised in three sections. The first sketches out some of the political-economic links between consumer culture and the media. The second considers the same question from the perspective of discourse and aesthetics. The third and final section explores how the links between consumer culture and media are inscribed by global histories and contemporary international relations.

MEDIA ECONOMIES AND NEOLIBERAL CULTURE

Arguably, media technologies, texts and practices are deeply intertwined with neoliberal economics and power structures. This section examines some of the key global political-economic issues that link media and consumer culture.

The Mainstream Media Economics Model

Perhaps the most obvious connection between consumer culture and the media is the well-established fact that the majority of mainstream media forms (and platforms) are objects produced by corporations motivated by profit, and intended for exchange in one form or another on the open market. The various television programmes, books, films, newspapers, magazines, and website articles that are purchased by consumers around the world are produced by huge companies, sometimes multinationals, who invest significant resources into packaging information and producing entertainment for global audiences (Jin & Winseck, 2012). Despite the commonplace nature of peer-to-peer sharing and online pirating of copyrighted material, the dominant structure of legally sanctioned media consumption remains a relationship of market exchange. Audiences are consumers in the extent to which they literally buy media commodities (Doyle, 2013). Whether it is over the counter of the corner store, in the queue at the supermarket, or through an online transaction, money changes hands and very often the goods that are bought and sold are informational: MP3s, magazines, concert tickets, a subscription to a news service, a download of an academic article. Simply put, the global economy is to a significant extent comprised of activities related to the production, distribution and consumption of media (Hafez, 2013; Rantanen, 2005; Robertson, 1992). A large portion of the media landscape therefore is comprised of material produced by corporate actors in the service of neoliberal economic goals: profit and the expansion of markets at almost any cost. Although not exclusively, the success of many media productions is judged on the basis of sales: box office numbers, viewership and circulation figures, bestseller lists, and so on. This underlines the commodity status of many media objects.

In addition to this crude economic aspect to global consumer media is another, only slightly more complex layer to the economic links between media and cultures of consumption. Notwithstanding the huge importance of public service broadcasters, very few national broadcasters are entirely publically funded like the UK's BBC. Most broadcasters, publications and web platforms rely on the sale of advertising to fund their operations. This is a classic insight into the operations of media economics (Alexander, Owers, Carveth, Hollifield, & Greco, 2003; Doyle, 2013; Picard, 2003). Most media companies – those in the business of producing informational or entertainment content for direct sale to audiences – are rarely able to cover their costs merely through the sales of the commodities they produce. What they do profit from – and handsomely – is the sale of their audiences' attention to advertisers. The inclusion of advertising means that an entire 'world of goods' (Iqani, 2012a, p. 103) is marketed through media commodities. This tight relationship between, say, the washing powder and vacuum cleaners advertised during commercial breaks and the wildly popular soap operas and telenovelas that captivate audiences during prime time, is an important characteristic of both media and consumer economies (Lavin, 1995). The process of selling space to advertisers is effectively a commodification of audiences. As such, even viewers who do not directly pay for access to their favourite media content pay for it indirectly through the conversion of their attention into value in the form of the income that the platforms earn from advertisers. In the context of social media platforms, this form of value creation has been theorised as an exploitation of the creative labour of users (Banks & Humphreys, 2008; Fuchs & Sevignani, 2013). In the post-analogue economy, it is not only the attention of media users but also their creative power and interactive engagement that are converted into value and profit by media corporations.

As well as being commodities with use and exchange value in their own right, and serving as channels and platforms for the communication of other commodities, media platforms and companies are also commodities in another sense. They are brands: informational commodities linked to specific products or services, which communicate certain values and invite certain relationships from the public (Aronczyk & Powers, 2010; Arvidsson, 2005; Lury, 2004). But brands do not only serve to make products and services recognisable, they also accrue value and thereby become valuable assets in their own right. The biggest and most successful media companies and products (think, Fox, Google, CNN) also have highly valuable brands, which are likewise traded in national and global processes of accumulation, merger, and acquisition.

As this brief summary articulates, there are important structural issues at play when considering the links between consumer culture and the media. These are best examined within the framework of the political economy of media, both global and national, and can also be explored through critical studies of media economics and branding.

The Commodification of Communication?

An important cultural question that comes up when surveying the landscape of consumer media economics, is the extent to which various forms of communication have become commoditised by mere virtue of their existence within a neoliberal context. It is uncontroversial to outline how various mainstream, commercial media forms and platforms are consumerist in the sense in which they are organised around forms of market exchange. What may be considered more contentious, however, is the claim that the rise of consumer culture and the growing influence of profit-oriented worldviews in contemporary society has fundamentally altered the process of communication – all human communication – itself.

From a psycho-social perspective, the ability to communicate in complex ways is what defines the human condition (Craig, 1999; Hardt, 2008; Schiller, 1996). Arguably, we strive for understanding of ourselves and those close to us, and have only communication as a means to achieve that. The same can be said for intercultural and collective, more distant, forms of communication, which again have been idealised as – perhaps the only – vehicle available to build bridges, cross boundaries, and achieve something akin to a global humanist understanding (McLuhan, 2001). Throughout history, the emergence of new technologies, from papyrus, to ink and paper, to the printing press, to satellite networks and Bluetooth, have allowed individuals to share their ideas, thoughts, and emotions with others, both dialogically and through mass dissemination (Peters, 2012). Historical studies of various media forms at times romanticise the new possibilities for the expansion of enlightenment, cross-cultural understanding, even democracy, along with the rise of each new communication technology and network (Hofmeyr, 2013; Peters, 2012; Schiller, 1996). Yet, considered within the strictures of a profit-oriented global media economy, does the innately transformative and liberating potential of communication become tainted (Deetz, 1992)?

To some extent, the answer is yes. If the large majority of communicative forms are being produced by powerful actors in charge of communicative infrastructures and resources, mainly in the service of profit, it stands to reason that those motivations will shape the products that are made available and circulated. Some argue that this has profound implications for democracy (McChesney, 2015). Ongoing critical analyses of the mis- or under-representation of oppressed and marginalised groups in mainstream media is just one outcome of that particular political economy of media. However, some have argued that the rise of new technologies, especially digital platforms, has heralded a new liberating age of the democratisation of human expression (McLuhan, 2001). Instead of powerful corporations controlling the majority of outputs of mass communication, skewing it towards groups that already have economic power and cultural dominance, Internet culture has allowed for a democratisation of expression (Carpentier, Dahlgren, & Pasquali, 2013; Hackett & Zhao, 2005). Anyone can make their own television or radio show in the form of webcasts and podcasts, anyone can publish their writing on blogs and personal websites, and anyone can produce and share their own imagery through mobile-phone platforms such as Instagram.

Of course, these new possibilities create a more democratic media landscape than that once controlled completely by media conglomerations. Yet, the tsunami of self-expression that has been unleashed by the rise of new technologies, broadened (though not yet universal) Internet access, and interactive platforms must also be viewed through the lens of 'conditional freedom' (Chouliaraki, 2008, p. 846). Ordinary citizens who make their own media – be it through a sophisticated blog or YouTube channel or simply a Facebook status update – all function within the formats and confines determined by global media companies. As such, it could be argued that many forms of inter-personal communication are now – more than ever – at best influenced and at worst regulated by commercial media power. Others argue that various forms of personal communication facilitated by social media platforms have become yoked into processes of self-branding (Dijck, 2013). Taking the logic of the exploitation of labour by capital into a critique of the operation of power within social media, it is argued that neoliberalism has extended beyond the management of the self, into the production of the self as a commodity itself and the extraction of value therefrom. The 'labour' that social media users do both produces value for the platform within which they socialise, and also forces them into a style of self-promotion and branding that mirrors other forms of commoditisation.

Linked to these concerns about the commodification of identity and human interaction, are arguments that various spheres of communication have become increasingly influenced by commercial values and aesthetics. Alongside claims that society in general has become celebritised (Driessens, 2017), some argue that politics has become celebritised (Drake & Higgins, 2006): we see politicians increasingly behaving like celebrities in the public realm, just as we see more celebrities entering politics (this is the case not only in the US where Ronald Reagan and Donald Trump are well-known former entertainers, but also in other locations, such as the Ukraine, where former boxing champion Vitali Klitschko is now a heavyweight political player). Evidence shows that political communication has been increasingly infiltrated by methods formerly favoured by product-pushers: candidates and parties are 'branded', policies are 'sold' by being dressed up as attractive titbits, voters and citizens are increasingly treated like customers. All the while, public services and goods like clean water, education, and social services are privatised, branded, and sold to consumers rather than provided to citizens. Even humanitarianism – that set of ethics most closely connected to a cosmopolitan ethic and imaginary, perhaps a last hope for idealists who dream of a world in which more privileged human beings take care of those who suffer – has become overtaken to some extent by practices of branding, appeals to individual egos, celebrity appropriation and the music industry (Chouliaraki, 2013; Richey, 2015; Vestergaard, 2008).

From all of these perspectives, it is not only Culture but also Communication that has been industrialised and integrated into the 'social factory' (Prodnik, 2012). No media or communication form can escape the influence of neoliberal power. This summary has not intended to suggest that human actors have no agency, but to emphasise how those forms of agency are inherently shaped and constrained by the operations of the media political-economy.

MEDIATING CONSUMPTION: THE POLITICS OF AESTHETICS AND DISCOURSE

With some key perspectives thus mapped out on the structural dynamics to do with the overlap of media and consumer economics, it is now necessary to turn our attention to more cultural and aesthetic dimensions. As I have argued in detail elsewhere, with a focus on the case study of the magazine cover genre, consumption is provoked and shaped by media discourse (Iqani, 2012a). Consumer cultures, including invitations to specific forms of self-regard and orientations towards material lifestyles and commodities, are consistently sold on the open market through a wide variety of media forms.

The Discursive Construction of Consumer Culture

The discursive perspective on mediated culture is by now well established in media studies scholarship (Macdonald, 2003; Matheson, 2005). Discourse analysts argue that social reality is constructed through regimes of communication and knowledge that are strongly influenced – although not absolutely determined by – relationships of power (Hook, 2005). From this standpoint, consumer culture is a product of the intersections of power, knowledge, and communicative technologies (Iqani, 2012a, 2016). The production of consumer culture through discourse arguably happens to a very large extent in media content and form. The messages, objects, lifestyles, identities, and practices that are made visible in media intersect in order to promote certain ideas over others, to the extent that they extend into hegemonic narratives that become widely accepted as natural. This is at once the power of discourse and an example of the operations of power through discourse. To extend this discussion into an empirical direction, it is worth considering some examples. Three will be briefly addressed: the discursive construction of commodity culture, celebrity, and gendered consumer practices. These are indicative – and widely researched – areas in which media discourses play a significant role in the social construction of consumer culture.

As well as being commodities themselves, media also function as powerful conduits for the promotion of other commodities. Both directly and explicitly, through advertising and product placement, as well as indirectly and implicitly through the promotion of general ideas about commodity-centred lifestyles, the world of media and the world of commodities are tightly intertwined. Through ever evolving genres and narrative forms, human relationships with various manufactured items are constantly reiterated and discursively constructed.

Commodity culture has been theorised as an iteration of material culture (Haug, 1987). Although human societies have always been partly produced through the production and exchange of objects (Appadurai, 1988), the material dimension to human relations was exaggerated by the industrial revolution and the rise of modern and post-modern capitalism. As production technologies became more industrialised and efficient, mass manufacture saw the transformation of the object into the commodity: something produced purely for the purposes of exchange at a rate of profit (Appadurai, 2012). Much critical writing has focused on the commodity as evidence of the alienation of the worker's labour, the chasm between use and exchange values, and also a symbol for a capitalist system driven by greed to overproduction and built-in obsolescence (Marx, 1867). But also worth theorising is the extent to which the commodity is inherently bound up in systems of communication and aesthetics. Commodities, as well as being three-dimensional objects with functions and uses, are also signs in their own right (Baudrillard, 1998; Haug, 1987). By virtue of their design, packaging and display in retail spaces, commodities can also be theorised as media forms: sites on which messages and ideas are transcribed through various communicative technologies (Iqani, 2011, 2013). As well as this inherently semiotic nature, commodities are again mediated through their discussion and presentation in media forms, including advertising, product reviews, the curating of 'must-have' items in magazine editorials, and through sophisticated forms of sponsorship and product placement in films, television shows and computer games, for example. This adds up to the mediation of a world of goods through media forms that, in tandem with the inherently mediated condition of commodities themselves, suggests that we also need to consider theories of mediation and the hyperreal alongside those of the material (Iqani, 2012a, p. 37) when defining and studying commodity culture.

Another empirical orientation point for considering the importance of media in the discursive construction of consumer culture is the celebrity. In perhaps even more explicit ways, the celebrity is a construct of media culture. The very notion of fame – of being widely recognised and visible – is produced through media exposure (Evans & Hesmondhalgh, 2005; Rojek, 2001; Turner, 2010). Indeed, since the turn of the twenty-first century with the rise of reality television and social media, more and more celebrities are produced directly through their appearance in media. Celebrities are a crucial part of consumer culture: not only are they extreme examples of how subjectivities are commoditised and turned into brands, but they link their identities and images with a wide range of consumer products (Iqani, 2012a, 2016). By directly participating in the marketisation of various commodities, celebrities profit themselves through the hefty payments they receive to be associated with other brands, and also explicitly validate a view of the world in which manufactured goods and brands are centre stage. Media are central to the discursive construction of celebrity, which in turn is central to the mediation of consumer-oriented lifestyles.

Another important empirical avenue for considering the discursive construction of consumer culture is gender, specifically femininity. Heteronormative and patriarchal notions of the feminine are a constant theme in the representative work of media as well as in 'everyday' ideas about consumption (Gill, 2007a; McRobbie, 1997, 2004). Important work has been done by feminist scholars to show how consumption was historically framed as a feminine pursuit. The emergence of new retail geographies and feminine media forms are directly linked to the idea of consumption – particularly in service of managing the domestic environment – as a feminine pursuit (Ballaster, 1991; Ferguson, 1983; Ohmann, 1996). Women were relegated to the realms of the domestic, private, and consumption, while men were privileged to enjoy the worlds of production, labour, and politics. Although consumption has become more 'democratised' in that men are increasingly being addressed as consumers, contemporary feminist scholars continue to reveal how gender is constructed in particular ways in consumer media. In the current, 'postfeminist' moment, women are increasingly invited by media discourses to present themselves as empowered through consumption and beauty practices (Gill, 2007b, 2008; McRobbie, 2004). In particular, the discourse of sexiness has become central both to media and consumer cultures. Women are invited to produce and present themselves as sexy, as a mode of achieving empowerment and influence in contemporary society. Sexiness has become one of the most important items in a catalogue of sales techniques (Iqani, 2012b; Schroeder & McDonagh, 2005), it is increasingly common to see women's bodies and sexualities being objectified in the service of selling commodities as banal as fish fingers, soft drinks, and car insurance. The gendered dimension to mediated consumer culture deserves to receive on-going critical attention.

Consumer Aesthetics and Multimodality

As well as the many important questions that arise when considering the ways in which communication and power intersect in discourse in order to construct consumer culture, it is also important to consider the place of aesthetics in the intersection of consumer culture and the media. Arguably, contemporary media culture is more visual than ever (Kress & Van Leeuwen, 2006; Schroeder, 2002). Popular culture and public space – especially in cities – is saturated with images and visual forms of communication. Media texts are also inherently – and increasingly – visual. Even the most textual of media texts, which do not necessarily include visual components, are carefully designed using typography, layout tools and text placement and as such become visual in their own right. Arguably the power of the image has never been stronger: entertainment websites curate image galleries of the most banal topics (cue the infamous internet obsession with domestic cats), viewers on opposite sides of the world gaze in horror at photo-journalism collections featuring devastation caused by natural disasters, and consumers scroll absently through streams and streams of hash-tagged photos on Instagram. What this re-loaded, interactive visuality means for consumer culture is an important question for future conceptual work.

Multimodality has been highlighted as a key framing device for the analysis of contemporary communication forms (Jewitt, 2009; Kress, 2013; Kress & Van Leeuwen, 2001) and it is arguably also the case for the study of consumer culture. In addition to the question of the power of the visual – and its role in contemporary consumer culture – is the question of other modalities of communication and how they play into the formation and promotion of cultures of consumption. Most explicit, perhaps, is the question of space. A significant sub-field of cultural geography has examined the spatial characteristics of the retail landscape. Studies have presented ethnographies of branded retail spaces, from the high street to the mall, in order to gain deeper insight into practices of consumption (Brottman, 1997; Penaloza, 1998; Sherry et al., 2001). Work has also been done that highlights the communicative aspects of spatial arrangement, linking in with visual forms of communication (Iqani, 2011). As geographers and architects have long argued, spatial design carries meaning. How do various spaces of consumption – from street-side traders to glossy high-end malls – produce consumer culture as well as facilitate various forms of consumption?

Along with the modality of space, other modes of communication are arguably central to consumer media forms. The study of colour, and the ways in which certain hues and shades are deployed in the service of specific ideological perspectives, is important (Kress & Van Leeuwen, 2002). For example, the ways in which pink has been gendered as feminine is indicative of the communicative power that colour holds (Koller, 2008), and the ways in which that power is very effectively harnessed by those who produce marketing communications. Arguably, contemporary mediation takes place in hyperreal (Baudrillard, 1983) full colour, and as such it will be increasingly important to understand the role that colour plays both in consumer culture and in the everyday forms of mediation that saturate public space and shared human experiences. Another under-studied modality is texture. Specific materials carry specific meanings: for example the message communicated by a smooth, glazed ceramic cup will be very different to that of a raw baked clay mug, a shift of silk means something very different to a swatch of linen. How texture is harnessed into various forms of consumerist mediation is an important area of ongoing aesthetic analysis. In my own work on glossiness and smoothness, I have argued that these two textures in particular hold a special cachet in the toolbox of consumerist communication (Iqani, 2012a, 2012b). These textures work to communicate the virginal, untouched qualities of brand new commodities, which is one of the affective mechanisms used to make those objects desirable. The textures of smoothness and glossiness are also deployed in representations of women in popular culture, in such a way as to make rhetorical links between the object world and hyper-femininity. As just one example of the communicative power of texture, more research needs to be done on a whole variety of textural modalities, in order to understand their specific aesthetic and discursive functions, and how they contribute to the aestheticisation of consumer culture more broadly.

THE GLOBAL POLITICS OF MEDIATED CONSUMER CULTURE

Thus far, this chapter has sketched out key concerns in the political-economic and discursive-aesthetic dimensions to the overlap between media and consumer cultures. It is now necessary to explore some historical and global dimensions to these themes. Arguably, both consumer and media cultures are inherently global (Iqani, 2016). Tightly linked as they are, it is perhaps stating the obvious that both commodities and media texts cross borders and flow across cultures, to and from both North and South, East and West. But the inherent globalisation – of both media and consumption – deserves closer discussion. This is offered in two sweeps: the first considers the links between colonialism, developmentalism and mediated consumer culture; the second the politics of globalised commodity cultures.

As I have argued elsewhere, contemporary studies of consumer culture are lacking in the attention paid to the global South (Iqani, 2016). To a certain extent, consumption has been theorised as an inherently Western set of practices, to which the non-Western world is increasingly demanding access. In order to properly contextualise the contemporary landscape of consumer culture, it is necessary to acknowledge the role that histories of colonialism played in producing the contemporary global political-economy of consumption (Sinclair & Pertierra, 2012, p. 5). Colonialism was not simply an ideological and military system, it was also an acutely economic enterprise that aimed at producing new markets for the glut of commodities newly produced by the industrial revolution (Duignan & Gann, 1975). Although most of the post-colonial world is half a century beyond the shackles of imperialism, traces of the colonial economy remain. These are visible not only in a global economy in which the West remains powerful despite the rise of new BRICS economies (Armijo, 2007; Lo & Hiscock, 2014), but also in the enduring forms of racism and sexism that are evidenced in many mainstream media spaces. White supremacist capitalist patriarchies (hooks, 2014) continue to wield a huge amount of power both in consumer economies and global media. As such, critical race, feminist and queer theories remain central to the project of examining the operations of consumer culture and media, which simply cannot be divorced from their histories.

Although there are many aspects to the consideration of the links between colonial histories and contemporary consumer cultures (Burke, 1996; Magubane, 2004; McClintock, 2013), what is worth highlighting for the purposes of this chapter, is the question of aspiration (Iqani, 2016). For decades, consumer culture has profited from selling the idea of a better life: a fitter, slimmer body, a more beautiful home, more holidays to exciting places, a more harmonious family, and so on. Traces of colonial mentalities and power structures are often visible in these different symbolic tyrannies. The media genre that most explicitly capitalises on aspiration is advertising – but arguably the ethics of aspiration filter through to every moment of consumerist mediation. Aspiration can be summed up as the hopes for, or promises of, a better life. These hopes exist at both the macro and micro scales; at the level of entire nations and regions, and at the level of individuals and their families (Cavalcanti, 2007). It is an innately human value to imagine a better tomorrow, to hope for and work towards access to more resources than one currently has: this is almost certainly true for most of the world's population, which is forced to share only a tiny percentage of the world's income. It is no surprise, therefore, that appeals to aspiration form a central theme in consumerist mediation.

There is, however, another angle to thinking about aspiration. Development theory suggests that there is an under-developed world, and a developed world, and that it is preferable for the former to evolve towards the state of the latter (Beer, 2000). This perspective takes for granted that industrialised modernity is the only possible version of successful statehood, and that in turn the types of consumer societies produced by neoliberal economics are the only possible versions of successful societies. A trickle-down effect of these ideas would be that the only possible model of a successful citizen is one that is fully enrolled in practices of consumption (Canclini, 2001; Couldry, 2004; Couldry, Livingstone, & Markham, 2007). This raises important questions about the extent to which consumption is a right to which people should be able to demand access, or merely a luxury that is, although consistently mediated through a wide variety of messages, attainable only by a small crust of the world's population. An important question that scholars of consumer culture and the media should be asking is which narratives of consumption and consumer culture are prioritised in media in different parts of the world. To what extent is consumption linked in with developmentalist policies, politics, and intergovernmental initiatives? How do practices of consumption manifest in dreams of a better life and aspirations for brighter futures? It is precisely this latter question that brings up important questions about the distribution of the resources and opportunities attendant on consumer culture.

New developments in global media and consumer culture raise questions about the extent to which cultural imperialism remains a useful theoretical framework. The argument that Western power is extending its reach through the export of media and cultural products (Golding & Harris, 1996; Tomlinson, 2001) might need reconsidering, at least in the extent to which other cultures are increasingly participating in the global economy. As well as this, it is necessary to rethink classic manipulationist views on consumption, which see it as part of a system of false consciousness (Adorno & Horkheimer, 1944; Marcuse, 1964). Without doubt, all human beings on this planet deserve to have some share in the many material comforts that only a small minority are currently enjoying. As leading scholars have argued, mediation is a sociological concept that allows for a conceptualisation of how media production and consumption processes coalesce in texts and technologies (Chouliaraki, 2006; Silverstone, 2005). If we accept the proposition that consumer culture is inherently mediated in a number of ways, then it follows that important questions about the global distribution of resources and consumption opportunities are also questions about mediation.

The world of commodities and the variety of human practices linked to cultures of consumption are important defining features of contemporary consumer culture. As both material and hyperreal structures, commodities are central to media cultures as well as the global neoliberal political-economy. Brands and branded items cross borders in different ways, the former through global trade, the latter through the global media (Lash & Lury, 2007). Arguably, there is a global division of labour currently manifesting in the global consumer economy: on the one hand is the hard, physical labour of 'sweatshops' and production lines in the factories of the global South; on the other is the creative and informational labour of workers in the global North, who produce the advertisements and communications strategies of the brands attached to the goods manufactured in special economic zones elsewhere (Iqani, 2016, p. 30). Contemporary consumer culture also sees interesting divisions in markets: Western brands are increasingly aiming to increase their market share in 'new' Southern markets, while some massive corporations from the global South, such as China's Alibaba, are increasingly attempting to make inroads into Western markets. From the perspectives of both global mediation and the global consumer economy, important questions about representation, discourse and mediation arise: how resources – both material and mediated – distributed on a global scale, are shaped by history as well as shifting political and economic relations within and across borders.

CONCLUSION

This chapter has sketched out a number of key concerns that emerge when considering the links between consumer culture and the media. It has accounted for big questions that arise from a political-economic perspective: namely, the operations of corporate actors and governments in relation to global media production and markets. It has also sketched out key issues in relation to cultural and aesthetic questions that arise when studying consumer media: namely, the importance of discourse and multimodality as framing concepts. Finally, a number of key issues related to the global politics of mediated consumer culture were outlined. In summary, it can be argued that neither media systems nor consumer culture can be understood in isolation from one another. This is true at local, national and global levels. In order to continue to develop nuanced and complex accounts of consumer culture, media culture, and consumerist mediation – accounts which are necessary in order to gain deeper insight into the operations of the global neoliberal economy and the many forms of culture attendant thereto – scholars should continue to build interdisciplinary approaches that pay attention to political, economic, and aesthetic factors.

REFERENCES

Adorno, T., & Horkheimer, M. (1944). The culture industry: Enlightenment as mass deception. In *Dialectic of Enlightenment*. New York: Continuum.

Alexander, A., Owers, J.E., Carveth, R., Hollifield, C.A., & Greco, A.N. (2003). *Media Economics: Theory and Practice*. Routledge.

Appadurai, A. (1988). *The Social Life of Things: Commodities in Cultural Perspective*. Cambridge University Press.

Appadurai, A. (2012). Commodities and the politics of value. In S. Pearce (Ed.), *Interpreting Objects and Collections* (pp. 76–91). London: Routledge.

Armijo, L.E. (2007). The BRICS countries (Brazil, Russia, India, and China) as analytical category: Mirage or insight? *Asian Perspective*, *31*(4), 7–42.

Aronczyk, M., & Powers, D. (2010). *Blowing Up the Brand: Critical Perspectives on Promotional Culture*. Peter Lang.

Arvidsson, A. (2005). Brands: A critical perspective. *Journal of Consumer Culture*, *5*(2), 235–258.

Ballaster, R. (1991). *Women's Worlds: Ideology, Femininity [sic] and the Woman's Magazine*. Macmillan Education.

Banks, J., & Humphreys, S. (2008). The labour of user co-creators: Emergent social network markets? *Convergence: The International Journal of Research into New Media Technologies*, *14*(4), 401–418.

Baudrillard, J. (1983). *Simulations*. Semiotext(e), Inc.

Baudrillard, J. (1998). *The Consumer Society: Myths and Structures*. London: Sage.

Beer, F.D. (2000). *Introduction to Development Studies*. Oxford University Press.

Brottman, M. (1997). 'The last stop of desire': Covent Garden and the spatial text of consumerism. *Consumption, Markets and Culture*, *1*(1), 45–79.

Burke, T. (1996). *Lifebuoy Men, Lux Women: Commodification, Consumption, and Cleanliness in Modern Zimbabwe*. Durham: Duke University Press Books.

Canclini, N.G. (2001). *Consumers and Citizens: Globalization and Multicultural Conflicts*. University of Minnesota Press.

Carpentier, N., Dahlgren, P., & Pasquali, F. (2013). Waves of media democratization: A brief history of contemporary participatory practices in the media sphere. *Convergence: The International Journal of Research into New Media Technologies*, *19*(3), 287–294.

Cavalcanti, J.G. (2007). Development versus enjoyment of life: A post-development critique of the developmentalist worldview. *Development in Practice*, *17*(1), 85–92.

Chouliaraki, L. (2006). Towards an analytics of mediation. *Critical Discourse Studies*, *3*(2), 153–178.

Chouliaraki, L. (2008). The media as moral education: Mediation and action. *Media, Culture & Society*, *30*(6), 831–852.

Chouliaraki, L. (2013). *The Ironic Spectator: Solidarity in the Age of Post-Humanitarianism*. John Wiley & Sons.

Couldry, N. (2004). The productive 'consumer' and the dispersed 'citizen'. *International Journal of Cultural Studies*, *7*(1), 21–32.

Couldry, N., Livingstone, S., & Markham, T. (2007). *Media Consumption and Public Engagement: Beyond the Presumption of Attention*. Palgrave Macmillan.

Craig, R.T. (1999). Communication theory as a field. *Communication Theory*, *9*(2), 119–161.

Deetz, S. (1992). *Democracy in an Age of Corporate Colonization: Developments in Communication and the Politics of Everyday Life*. SUNY Press.

Dijck, J. van (2013). 'You have one identity': Performing the self on Facebook and LinkedIn. *Media, Culture & Society*, *35*(2), 199–215. https://doi.org/10.1177/0163443712468605

Doyle, G. (2013). *Understanding Media Economics*. Sage.

Drake, P., & Higgins, M. (2006). 'I'm a celebrity, get me into politics': The political celebrity and the celebrity politician. In S. Holmes & S. Redmond (Eds), *Framing Celebrity: New Directions in Celebrity Culture* (pp. 87–100). London: Routledge.

Driessens, O. (2017). The celebritization of society and culture: Understanding the structural dynamics of celebrity culture. *International Journal of Cultural Studies*, *7*(1), 46–71.

Duignan, P., & Gann, L.H. (1975). *Colonialism in Africa 1870–1960*. CUP Archive.

Evans, J., & Hesmondhalgh, D. (2005). *Understanding Media: Inside Celebrity*. McGraw-Hill Education.

Ferguson, M. (1983). *Forever Feminine: Women's Magazines and the Cult of Femininity*. Heinemann.

Fuchs, C., & Sevignani, S. (2013). What is digital labour? What is digital work? What's their difference? And why do these questions matter for understanding social media? *tripleC: Communication, Capitalism & Critique. Open Access Journal for a Global Sustainable Information Society*, *11*(2), 237–293.

Gill, R. (2007a). *Gender and the Media*. Polity.

Gill, R. (2007b). Postfeminist media culture: Elements of a sensibility. *European Journal of Cultural Studies*, *10*(2), 147–166.

Gill, R. (2008). Culture and subjectivity in neoliberal and postfeminist times. *Subjectivity*, *25*(1), 432–445.

Golding, P., & Harris, P. (1996). *Beyond Cultural Imperialism: Globalization, Communication and the New International Order*. Sage.

Hackett, R.A., & Zhao, Y. (2005). *Democratizing Global Media: One World, Many Struggles*. Rowman & Littlefield Publishers.

Hafez, K. (2013). *The Myth of Media Globalization*. John Wiley & Sons.

Hardt, H. (2008). *Critical Communication Studies: Essays on Communication, History and Theory in America*. Routledge.

Haug, W.F. (1987). *Commodity Aesthetics, Ideology & Culture*. International General.

Hofmeyr, I. (2013). *Gandhi's Printing Press*. Harvard University Press.

Hook, D. (2005). Genealogy, discourse, 'effective history': Foucault and the work of critique. *Qualitative Research in Psychology*, *2*(1), 3–31.

hooks, bell (2014). *Talking Back: Thinking Feminist, Thinking Black*. Taylor & Francis.

Iqani, M. (2011). Reading the newsstand: The signifiers of placelessness in London magazine retail sites. *Space and Culture*, *14*(4), 431–447.

Iqani, M. (2012a). *Consumer Culture and the Media: Magazines in the Public Eye*. Palgrave Macmillan.

Iqani, M. (2012b). Smooth bodywork: The role of texture in images of cars and women on consumer magazine covers. *Social Semiotics*, *22*(3), 311–331.

Iqani, M. (2013). Just looking? Choice and constraint in practices of visual consumption at magazine newsstands. *Consumption Markets & Culture*, *16*(4), 338–355.

Iqani, M. (2016). *Consumption, Media and the Global South: Aspiration Contested*. London: Palgrave Macmillan.

Jewitt, C. (2009). *The Routledge Handbook of Multimodal Analysis*. Routledge Chapman & Hall.

Jin, D.Y., & Winseck, D. (Eds). (2012). *The Political Economies of Media: The Transformation of the Global Media Industries*. London and New York: Bloomsbury Academic.

Koller, V. (2008). 'Not just a colour': Pink as a gender and sexuality marker in visual communication. *Visual Communication*, *7*(4), 395–423.

Kress, G. (2013). *Multimodality: A Social Semiotic Approach to Contemporary Communication*. Routledge.
Kress, G., & Van Leeuwen, T. (2001). *Multimodal Discourse*. Bloomsbury Academic.
Kress, G., & Van Leeuwen, T. (2002). Colour as a semiotic mode: Notes for a grammar of colour. *Visual Communication*, *1*(3), 343–368.
Kress, G., & Van Leeuwen, T. (2006). *Reading Images: The Grammar of Visual Design*. Routledge.
Lash, S., & Lury, C. (2007). *Global Culture Industry: The Mediation of Things*. Wiley.
Lavin, M. (1995). Creating Consumers in the 1930s: Irna Phillips and the Radio Soap Opera. *Journal of Consumer Research*, *22*(1), 75–89.
Lo, V.I., & Hiscock, M. (2014). *The Rise of the BRICS in the Global Political Economy: Changing Paradigms?* Edward Elgar Publishing.
Lury, C. (2004). *Brands: The Logos of the Global Economy*. Routledge.
Macdonald, M. (2003). *Exploring Media Discourse*. Arnold.
Magubane, Z. (2004). *Bringing the Empire Home: Race, Class, and Gender in Britain and Colonial South Africa*. University of Chicago Press.
Marcuse, H. (1964). *One-Dimensional Man: Studies in the Ideology of Advanced Industrial Society*. Routledge.
Marx, K. (1867). The fetishism of commodities and the secret thereof. In O.Z. Cruz & R. Guins (Eds), *Popular Culture: A Reader*. Sage.
Matheson, D. (2005). *Media Discourses*. McGraw-Hill International.
McChesney, R.W. (2015). *Rich Media, Poor Democracy: Communication Politics in Dubious Times*. The New Press.
McClintock, A. (2013). *Imperial Leather: Race, Gender, and Sexuality in the Colonial Contest*. Routledge.
McLuhan, M. (2001). *Understanding Media: The Extensions of Man*. Routledge.
McRobbie, A. (1997). Bridging the gap: Feminism, fashion and consumption. *Feminist Review*, *55*, 73–89.
McRobbie, A. (2004). Post-feminism and popular culture. *Feminist Media Studies*, *4*(3), 255–264.
Ohmann, R.M. (1996). *Selling Culture: Magazines, Markets, and Class at the Turn of the Century*. Verso.
Penaloza, L. (1998). Just doing it: A visual ethnographic study of spectacular consumption behavior at Nike Town. *Consumption Markets & Culture*, *2*(4), 337–400.
Peters, J.D. (2012). *Speaking into the Air: A History of the Idea of Communication*. University of Chicago Press.
Picard, R.G. (2003). The economics of the daily newspaper industry. In A. Alexander, J.E. Owers, R. Carveth, C.A. Hollifield, & A.N. Greco (Eds), *Media Economics: Theory and Practice* (pp. 109–126). Routledge.
Prodnik, J. (2012). A note on the ongoing processes of commodification: From the audience commodity to the social factory. *tripleC: Communication, Capitalism & Critique. Open Access Journal for a Global Sustainable Information Society*, *10*(2), 274–301.
Rantanen, T. (2005). *The Media and Globalization*. Sage.
Richey, L.A. (2015). *Celebrity Humanitarianism and North-South Relations: Politics, Place and Power*. Routledge.
Robertson, P.R. (1992). *Globalization: Social Theory and Global Culture*. Sage.
Rojek, C. (2001). *Celebrity*. Reaktion Books.
Schiller, D. (1996). *Theorizing Communication: A History*. Oxford University Press.
Schroeder, J.E. (2002). *Visual Consumption*. Routledge.

Schroeder, J.E., & McDonagh, P. (2005). The logic of pornography in digital camera promotion. In T. Reichert & J. Lambiase (Eds), *Sex in Consumer Society* (pp. 219–244). Routledge.

Sherry, J.F., Kozinets, R.V., Storm, D., Duhachek, A., Nuttavuthisit, K., & DeBerry-Spence, B. (2001). Being in the zone: Staging retail theater at ESPN Zone Chicago. *Journal of Contemporary Ethnography*, *30*(4), 465–510.

Silverstone, R. (2005). The sociology of mediation and communication. In C. Calhoun, C. Rojek, & B. Turner (Eds), *The Sage Handbook of Sociology* (pp. 188–207). Sage.

Sinclair, J., & Pertierra, A.C. (2012). *Consumer Culture in Latin America*. Palgrave Macmillan.

Tomlinson, J. (2001). *Cultural Imperialism: A Critical Introduction*. A&C Black.

Turner, G. (2010). Approaching celebrity studies. *Celebrity Studies*, *1*(1), 11–20.

Vestergaard, A. (2008). Humanitarian branding and the media: The case of Amnesty International. *Journal of Language and Politics*, *7*(3), 471–493.

17

Body Projects: Fashion, Aesthetic Modifications and Stylized Selves

Rossella Ghigi and Roberta Sassatelli

INTRODUCTION

Consumer capitalist societies have been described as inviting individuals to joyfully take responsibility for their bodies and to invest in body maintenance and enhancement in order to perform culturally appropriate self-presentation. The body is said to become the 'visible carrier of the self' in contemporary 'consumer culture' (Featherstone, 1982), the finest consumer object subject to endless triumphant, commercially mediated 'rediscovery' (Baudrillard, 1998). Fitness culture, for example, has been described as the epitome of such a trend in consumer capitalism, spreading all over the global West (Sassatelli, 2015). All in all, a variety of products and services indeed give evidence to the increasing process of performative, aestheticized rationalization of the body, whereby individualization is coupled with standardization, self-surveillance with spectacularization, discipline with hedonism (Sassatelli, 2012). Via commercial aestheticization, especially the surface of our bodies is endlessly celebrated or stigmatized as iconic representation of selves. In this chapter, we will focus on three arenas of body surface modification techniques which, as opposed to physical activity, are relatively instantaneous: fashion, body art and cosmetic surgery. Differently placed on the body modification spectrum in terms of physical risks, permanence and invasiveness, fashion, body art and cosmetic surgery allow us to reflect on the dominant cultural framing of bodies and selves in contemporary consumer culture, putting the structuration of consumers' experience of embodied subjectivity under a critical lens.

BODY PROJECTS AND CONSUMER CAPITALISM

In the last decades, sociologists have conceived the body as a key element in the everyday construction of one's identity (Frank, 1991; Turner, 1996). In an age of increasing individualization and privatization of risks (Bauman, 1992; Beck, 1992), not only has the body been conceived as an ever-perfectible matter, but also a responsibility of the self. The responsibility of the individual for his/her state of health and appearance (Featherstone, 1982), the growing importance of first impressions in celebrity and visual culture, information technology and new forms of work (Elliott, 2008), the joyous duty to maintain one's own body as useful, docile and fit (Sassatelli, 1999, 2010) and the spreading of a variety of body modification subcultures (Pitts, 2003) are only a few of the many factors that have been put forward to support this argument. According to many authors, the body can become a project that is to be 'accomplished' as part of the construction of self-identity (Shilling, 2013).

The concept of a 'body as project' or 'body project' draws upon Anthony Giddens's (1991) argument about the reflexive self in high modernity, an age of anxiety dominated by ontological insecurity. This existential condition is broadly due to the increasing inability of the grand narratives of religion and politics to counter people's uncertainties and the dismantling of Fordist organization of work and its institutions. Facing anxiety, other authors had claimed, the individual puts his/her attention inward, and the physical body represents an ultimate site of control, an arena where the sense of self can be achieved through individual planning (Lasch, 1979). What characterizes Giddens's argument is that reflexive self-fashioning becomes a process of identity construction. Self-identity is not a sum of distinctive traits possessed by the individual, 'it is the self as reflexively understood by the person in terms of her or his biography' (Giddens, 1991, 53). This reflexivity extends to the body, as it is part of an action system:

> The body is less and less an extrinsic given functioning outside the internally referential systems of modernity, but becomes itself reflexively mobilised. What might appear as a wholesale movement towards the narcissistic cultivation of bodily appearance is in fact an expression of a concern lying much deeper actively to 'construct' and control the body. Here there is an integral connection between bodily development and lifestyle – manifest, for example, in the pursuit of specific bodily regimes. (ibid., 7)

In other words, not only have we become responsible for the design of our own bodies, but how far our body and its appearance can be carried on in ways that are consistent with our biographical narrative is fundamental vis-à-vis feelings of ontological security.

According to such theories, such individual projectuality is expressed mainly through consumption: the surface and the interior of the body are open more than ever to reconstruction or re-incorporation through products and services available in the market (Hancock et al., 2000). Consumer capitalism offers a pre-selection of choices which work through the enticement of promotional culture and its imaginary, commercial institutions and their capacity to construct meaningful paths for self and body transformation. Such an approach implies a critical stance, as we cannot simply choose, as consumers, *any* body (and *any* self) we want. If for liberalism choice is just freedom, choice is here a continuous burden to be taken with a smile: it is somehow compulsory (see Schwarzkopf, Chapter 25 this volume). We are forced into it not so much by the drive of the capitalist economy, but by the absence of a stable social and cultural order in a post-traditional society. We have 'no choice, but to choose' – writes Giddens (1991, 81). For Beck (1992, 131) '[l]iberalism presupposed a coherent identity, yet identity seems to be precisely the main problem of modern existence and is itself something to be chosen'; the self as performed through the body is thus a 'project'. Of course, together with choice comes self-responsibility, and risk-perception changes accordingly: now risks are in the region of anomy, linked to the incapacity to perform convincingly a body that fits. As Giddens observes (1991, 80), late modernity confronts the individual with a complex diversity of choices which is 'non-foundational', produces anxiety and offers 'little help as to which options should be selected'. Circularly, the solution to such risk and anxiety found in contemporary society is, for Bauman (1992, 200), 'technical': consumer culture solves the problem of the durable and coherent self-presentation by treating all problems as solvable through specific commodities. Each of them may be highly functional to a precise task, but they still have to be arranged in a coherent, credible whole, meaningful and revealing of the self. Body projects are attempts to construct and maintain a coherent and feasible sense of self-identity through the consumption of goods and services addressed to the body, particularly the body's surface.

All in all, performing an adequate body image, both in terms of surface appearance and demeanor, becomes of the essence. In consumer capitalism, the body has become, in Bourdieu's (1984) terms, a source of symbolic capital, less because of what the body is able to *do* than because of how it *looks* and *feels*. It is not only a matter of increased quantity of goods and services, or of their availability in mass market and global distribution to vaster ranges of the population, but of meaning attached to body work: efforts to transform it are now understood by a growing number of individuals as part of a biographical project, where messages about self-identity are transmitted and distinction from others can be marked (Shilling, 2013).

The body is thus no longer conceived as a fixed essence; the ultimate target is to pull any physical modification off from natural physiological processes and to draw it uniquely upon the individual's willingness and taste. Self-identity is now derived not so much from work and production, as from consumption (Sassatelli, 2012): we do not simply consume according to what we are, but we become what we consume. This is intrinsically related to the current structuring of the economy, based on information technologies, global production and the imperatives of adaptability. According to Martin (1994) the mantra of flexibility now includes everyone's personality, body and organization, not only job market. The body thus becomes plastic, a sort of lifestyle accessory, a matter to be shaped and 'stylized'.

The notion of body projects has been widely used by sociologists, but it has also been criticized as it can overemphasize the individual's capacity for bodily self-narration and self-creation. In general, it has been noted that access to cultural resources for identity construction is not equally available to people in consumer society, but is influenced by gender, age, socio-economic position, education, race and ethnicity. As Bordo argued as early as in 1993, the idea of endless possibilities of the plasticity of the body is an ideology that effaces material and social inequalities, and the historical conditions of its construction. To put it in her own words, cultural imagery, advertising discourses and practices addressed to bodily appearance modification contribute altogether to 'a construction of life as plastic possibility and weightless choice, undetermined by history, social location, or even individual biography' (ibid., 250–251). Even if practices and imagery surrounding body projects in consumer culture are presented as individual enterprises, they nonetheless produce and reproduce economic inequalities and power relations.

Individuals are differently located in aesthetic, social and economic hierarchies and they have unequal access to the material possibilities to cultivate the body as a means of self-expression. As Boltanski (1971) noted, for example, one's orientation to the body is influenced by class position and has a feedback effect on class as well. For example, if we consider the health market, we can see that there are very different attitudes to the body and its state of health which correspond to different forms of health service consumption. The middle classes tend to operate around the idea that they can and must control their body and their state of health, and thus they generally have more medical check-ups with the result that they effectively have a longer life-span. Instead, the working class tend to adopt a fatalist attitude, not worrying about small illnesses or discomforts, and they only reluctantly visit the doctor in cases of emergency, with the result that their life-span is shorter, and they are more prone to invalidating disease, therefore almost enacting their fatalistic prophecy at its worst (Boltanski, 1971). More broadly, by considering the features of different occupational groups' somatic culture as the product of the objective conditions they retranslate in the cultural order, Boltanski showed not only the variability in the daily consumption of body-related practices, but also the different rhetoric supporting them. As one rises in the social hierarchy, the level of education increases and correspondingly the importance of manual labor decreases for the benefit of intellectual work; the body becomes more and more the site of a growing number of consumption practices that allow one to be distinguished from people of lower classes, who have a more instrumental approach to the body. Boltanski's findings would suggest that the notion of body projects could apply only for individuals from higher social class and who are highly educated, as their body maintenance and enhancement practices can be conceived within a larger reflexive process of producing a sense of self through consumption. A few years later, Bourdieu considered these dynamics as part of distinction practices and bodily class habitus (1984).

More recently, the notion of 'body projects' has been used by empirical investigations on self enhancement and bodily transformation as the focus of embodiment in a consumer lifestyle, from bodybuilding to fitness, from piercing to cosmetic surgery (Davis, 1995; DeMello, 2000; Sanders, 1989; Sassatelli, 2010; Sweetman, 1999). Other research accounts for reflexivity as based on the capacity to achieve an outside perspective on oneself, a process which generates a sense of being distinct from the qualities identified with the self when assuming an external perspective – the standpoint of 'other's eye'. To the extent that bodies are thereby conceived as moral, aesthetic, sensuous and active, body projects are reflexive projects (Crossley, 2001; Entwistle, 2000; Sweetman, 1999; Wacquant, 1995, 2004).

Working on one's own body through diet and exercise is then a matter of lifestyle: shaping materiality is part of the aestheticization of everyday life.

But body modifications can be very different from one another, in terms of duration, invasiveness, safety, social meanings, spread, painfulness and expenditure. Crossley (2005) suggests, for example, looking at practices of body modification and body maintenance separately, as they imply sets of practices with different meaning, purpose and accessibility. According to Crossley, Giddens's account of the body project as a need for social agents to construct coherent self-narratives in an increasingly de-traditionalized and risk-aware environment is more suitable to particular body modification such as exercise or diet, but not all. Can daily and widespread practices, he asks, such as tooth-brushing and washing, and marginal ones, such as scarification and multiple piercing, be explained in the same way? In a study based on survey data, he takes into account a diverse range of practices altogether while remaining sensitive to their specificities. By analyzing clusters of reflexive body practices belonging to a common lifestyle, habitus or self-narrative, he suggests that a whole range of body maintenance practices, such as norms of hygiene, are 'normal' in both the statistical sense that most agents practice them and in the sense that they reflect pervasive moral norms. They are integral to the construction of a self, but not in the 'choice' and narrative-based sense suggested by Giddens with his idea of 'body projects', since they are too widely practiced and done as a matter of course in daily life to reflect anything distinctive about the self. In this case, the practices oriented to maintaining rather than modifying the body (as they reproduce sameness through time with a temporal structure which is more repetitive than transitional) are less amenable to be placed under the body project definition. Other clusters of body practices are better accounted for by notions of choice and active self-identity construction; statistically deviant ones, in particular, from bodybuilding to extreme body art, are more accountable as related to agent's choices and reflexive biographical narratives.

The distinction between immediate body modifications (such as fashion, body art and cosmetic surgery), and time-demanding body transformations (such as diet, bodybuilding or fitness exercise) could represent a further framework for analysis, as 'instant self-reinvention fits in perfectly with the flexibility, flow and flux that mark society today' (Elliott, 2008, 19). Following both these approaches, in this chapter we will then focus on these three arenas of instant surface non-routinized body modifications: fashion, cosmetic surgery, and body art. These practices are good examples of the way individual experience of embodied subjectivity can be structured by consumption and canalized in a reflexive practice of autobiographical narration. Fashion is historically associated with the emergence of consumer culture, as it played a crucial role in the very beginning of consumer society; it is the most widespread and transversal along different dimensions of social differentiation (such as gender, social class, age and race). At the same time, it is one of the most volatile, less risky and less invasive body surface modification practices, and it can be the object of a consumption choice in everyday life. Cosmetic surgery and body art are less statistically 'normal', as they are rarer, more intrusive, permanent (or semi-permanent), more expensive and risky. Nonetheless, they are increasingly relevant among wider strata of the population, potentially more subversive and experimental, and extremely revealing of the politics of body appearance in contemporary consumer culture.

FASHION

In the classical treatment of fashion much emphasis has been placed on its role in the diffusion of commodities in the genesis of consumer capitalism. Historically, the emulative mechanism which goes under the name of 'trickle-down' and has been attributed both to Veblen and to Simmel is key just like the role of class distinction: the last trends spread from higher to lower social groups and this promotes the consequent attempt of the former to search for distinctive and novel items of status, initiating a consumption spiral. Fashion thus appears as a key structural mechanism for the spreading of consumer culture (Aspers and Godart, 2013). While fashion may be considered a broad social mechanism, to be applied to any commodity, material or cultural as it may be, the majority of the literature has considered it in relation to clothing. In such a guise, and in high modernity in particular, fashion directly concerns the construction of reflexive body projects. Indeed, in fashioning our bodies appropriately we 'learn to feel at home in them' (Entwistle, 2000, 7). Thus, fashion is both a superficial and an intimate experience, which allows for the surface of our bodies to appear convincing, appropriate both to others and to ourselves.

Before the advent of modernity, the so-called sumptuary laws prescribed which colors, styles and materials could be used by people of different social positions, at least in public, so that it was in fact forbidden by law to dress 'above' your station. Basing one's body project on clothes and appearance was not at stake at the time, at least for the vast majority of the population, and fashion, in clothing and elsewhere, was the precinct of the nobility. These laws were slowly abolished, and with the division of labor, social mobility and the monetary economy which have come to characterize consumer capitalism, everyone – provided they have sufficient money – has the right to *choose* and buy whatever good they please on the market to fashion their bodies. In this situation, the merry-go-round of fashion enticed people to choose the latest fad as an act of self-determination and social participation. Fashion in clothing thus becomes an important practice to construct an individual project on one's own body, perhaps the first one. It becomes a moment of self-narration, presentation and indeed performance where individual identity and character – including originality, authenticity and all the attributes of the high modern subject – can and must be expressed.

In terms borrowed from Simmel (1971 [1904]), we may say that especially clothing, and ceremonial non-ordinary consumption along with it, has come to be socially regulated by fashion mechanisms, thus reflecting and facilitating the divergent tendencies of consumer capitalism: standardization, diversification, individualization and change. Extending to larger and lower social strata, fashion becomes a disciplining mechanism with ambivalent outcomes: it allows consumers to feel a sense of belonging to a particular group, whilst at the same time distinguishing themselves; it allows for individual body stylization, but provides the toolkit for its expression, it provides anchorage to others, but one which is by definition temporary and ever-changing. This stresses the subject's need to govern fashion, to keep up to date, to fashion him or herself in ways which are both new and personal. All in all, as Arjun Appadurai (1986, 32) wrote in a celebrated essay '[m]odern consumers are the victims of the velocity of fashion as surely as primitive consumers [or 'traditional' ones] are the victims of the stability of sumptuary law' which selectively forbids the use and possession of numerous non-essential goods according to status, gender, age, etc.

While clearly a superficial, external item, fashionable clothing is not necessarily conspicuous. Both in past and in contemporary societies we do find that especially among the elites, fashion works through the subtleties of understatement and sober sophistication. Both historically and in contemporary societies, the display of austerity has been the best way to make oneself visible, sobriety has been used as a highly elaborated way of presenting oneself, and demonstrative consumption occurs through the subtlest understatement or even staged carelessness – just think of the black severity of Dutch merchants in the sixteenth century or of the late 1990s minimal chic of Italian fashion such as Armani or Prada (Steele, 2003). And, note that surface is still, possibly more, central as a category to define the kind of body project which is accomplished by fashion in such cases: it is the game of conspicuous invisibility that clothes are playing.

Modern consumers express and narrate themselves through clothing, and have to display a remarkable capacity to reflect on how they do present their bodies through fashion. This may be quite risky and it often requires the capacity to make choices which are – and must be – increasingly interpreted as personal and original. In doing so, consumers face the fashion industry, a complex set of institutions where consumption, production, distribution and representation intersect (Crane, 2000; Kawamura, 2004) and which is devoted to influencing consumers' choices. Herbert Blumer (1969) was amongst the first authors to underline the importance of the fashion industry and its mediating role in the mechanism of the trickling down of novelties from higher to lower social strata. According to Blumer, a style becomes fashion not when the privileged groups wear it, but when it corresponds to the 'incipient taste of the fashion consuming public'. A 'wish to be in fashion, to be abreast of what has good standing, to express new tastes which are emerging in a changing world' (ibid., 281) is important in contemporary societies, and it precisely matches the diffusion among larger social strata of reflexive fashion projects that go beyond class and stress individuality. The privileged classes can influence the direction of taste but they cannot control it; furthermore, what is fashionable is also the product of selective choices made by what Pierre Bourdieu called 'cultural intermediaries' – from stylists to fashion journalists and up to stockists and shop-keepers (Bourdieu and Delsaut, 1975). Cool-hunting among marginal social groupings is also crucial. Thus, fashion not only trickles down from the higher social groups to the lower social strata, it also trickles up. Contemporary consumer capitalism provides plenty of such examples. Weak social groups, far from adopting purely imitative strategies, tend to develop fashions which can be considered genuine and original. Even the so-called 'street-styles' often end up being adopted far outside these social circles (Polhemus, 1994). This was the case with punk styles and the piercing that the first punks adopted with clearly transgressive intents, using everyday objects (safety-pins for instance) and transforming them into decorations which appeared unattractive to those outside the group (Hebdige, 1979). More broadly, consumers from all venues contribute to the ongoing negotiation of the fashion code, responding both to the fashion industry and to wider cultural circumstances. Lise Skov's (2005) research on the return of the fur coat shows, for example, that the renewed fashion for furs in recent years has been the result of combined changes in production, distribution and consumption, partly in response to animal welfare protests. Changes in the production of furs (from wild to farmed) and in their marketing (increased use of promotional techniques), in the manufacture of fur garments (from craft to ready-to-wear) and their distribution (from specialized shops to fashion boutiques), and in consumers' outlook (a new generation of women exploring new images of femininity) have contributed to re-position the fur coat. Now furs may be coded as a young, sexy and rebellious fashion statement for the assertive woman in her thirties as opposed to a life investment for the middle-aged, middle-class traditional woman.

If Bourdieu himself (1984) considered the role of clothing as a way through which, in fashioning their bodies, elites secure their positions of power, increased cultural de-classification, globalization and the dominance of pop fashion leaders has made gender more relevant in the literature (Crane, 2000; Entwistle, 2000; Tseëlon, 1995; Wilson, 1985). Indeed, classical sociologists such as Simmel and Veblen were very aware of this. For Simmel fashion was 'the valve through which a woman's craving for some measure of conspicuousness and individual prominence finds vent, when its satisfaction is denied her in other fields' (Simmel, 1971 [1904, 309]). For Veblen (1899) women of the upper middle classes became a 'subsidiary leisure class', whose delicate office was the performance of 'vicarious' leisure and consumption, especially around their bodies, in the name of the household and his male head. It is no coincidence that one of the rhetorical critiques used to stigmatize consumer society associated fashion with the feminine, intended as superficiality and effeminacy, using this to denounce the risks run by traditionally masculine civic virtues. Yet, as modernity proceeds, fashion stresses different forms of femininity and masculinity.

Indeed, fashion specifies the peculiarity and social specificity of the subject that adopts it. So, when at the end of the nineteenth century women often from the suffrage movement started to wear Bloomers, they used them both to ride bicycles and to make a statement about their right to full citizenship. They were exploring new ways of being feminine while not wanting to be men; they rather used the fashioned body to signal their being women entitled to certain liberties (Finnegan, 1999). Much later, especially in the last three decades of the twentieth century, working women have used male dress codes to appropriate those expressive qualities normally attributed to men and to become accepted as competent work colleagues. This has required a complex negotiation of male and female connotations: the selective adoption of male codes which convey authoritative images at work, so-called *power dressing*, has been a way in which women have eased their access to professional environments maintaining some femininity but also restricting sexual connotations. The structured jacket in somber colors is thus combined with skirts and high-heels, creating an unstable hybrid between masculine connotations (authority/detachedness) and feminine ones (sexuality/emotiveness) which women are sometimes able to work in their favor, but which force them to be constantly more self-aware than their male colleagues (Entwistle, 2000). As Tseëlon (1995) points out, the 'paradox of modesty' in the Western ideology of femininity asks women not to give the wrong sexual signals with their dress, but at the same time not to be fully desexualized: the woman is constructed as seduction, and is punished for it.

Clothes have ambivalent potential for gender: they disguise or enhance sensuality, they de-sexualize parts of the body or re-sexualize ordinary items such as jeans (Sassatelli, 2011). The ambivalence of fashion for women has been a feature of scholarly research in the last few decades. Spending time in preparing oneself, in choosing the right dress among the plethora of styles which are available for women, may be a way to distract women from where real business takes place, yet, conversely, it may also provide specific forms of pleasure and self-identification. Susan Bordo (1993) for example has notably been wary of the role of fashion for women, maintaining that at work women mix male dress with female accessories to recall their decorative role and to appear as less dangerous in the career market. Elisabeth Wilson in her celebrated *Adorned in Dreams* (1985), more clearly embraces ambivalence by considering that dress can also be a source of rebellion and a catalyst, as we have seen, for reformist groups, including feminists (see also Evans and Thornton, 1989; Nava, 1991). However, feminist research insists that the burden of the body is heavier on women: new forms of sexism are seen as bourgeoning when young women claim their commoditized, eroticized bodies as capital to gain the favors of otherwise powerful men. (These attitudes may be seen as a populist, post-feminist reaction to what feminist scholar Sandra Bartky (1990) called the 'fashion-beauty complex', suggesting that production, marketing, retail and information companies work together to regulate feminine identity). Thus, pressure to conform to gender ideals goes beyond just advertisements. Department stores, for example, are spatially segregated by gender, clearly defining which items should be purchased for men and for women. For Bartky, the fact that it is women who suffer and spend more time, effort and thought in conforming to body ideals that are ever more elusive suggests that they support the fashion-beauty complex and ensure the financial success of the beauty industry (Peiss, 1998). Aesthetic labour is performed not only by consumers but also by workers, along gender lines, in the fashion industry (Mears, 2014).

All in all, fashion and dressing practices appear as a terrain of gender negotiation (Woodward, 2007), and this is true also for men. Some studies, including those by Frank Mort (1996) and Sean Nixon (1996), have shown that traditional masculine identity is constantly engaged and challenged by 'superfluous' and 'frivolous' commodities, by shopping as entertainment and by visual codes that cross genders. Indeed, the model of the 'female' 'glossy' magazine, covering consumption, health and beauty, which had a key role in linking femininity with luxury consumption, has now been extended to the male public, as the success of magazines like 'Men's Health' demonstrates. Heterosexuality is privileged and largely expected within many consumer spheres, but lesbian, gay and bisexual sexualities are also increasingly influential in the commercialization process of fashion items as well as other commodities, as well as influenced by it (Chasin, 2000). 'Metrosexual' became a new buzzword over a decade ago, describing urban, fashion-conscious men who are not afraid to express an interest in fashion or beauty, areas typically thought of as the preserve of women and gay men. Still, the multiplicity of gender coding, and even the cultural valorizing of queer identities in fashion magazines, advertising and popular culture does not translate into equality of choice. For example, while there is a proliferation of cultural imagery of sexuality and femininity and while women can now choose among a variety of styles from which to perform their version of these, the burden faced is one of 'having it all', whereby having it all, a good career, good sex and a nice family, becomes an imperative rather than an option and requires the capacity to continuously re-position oneself against gender coding (McRobbie, 2004).

There is evidence, thus, that binary gender coding is still dominant. Even when we consider fairly casual, ordinary and apparently unisex fashion items such as jeans, sexualization along dichotomous lines is very evident. Empirical research shows that jeans are indeed a heavily sexualized item, often deemed the 'sexiest of all' especially for women. These dynamics are quite heavily gendered: jeans minimize defects and stress appreciated body parts, but men are more concerned with expressing bulk and strength, while women with concealment and containment. Women's concern with concealment is turned upside down once a woman feels her favorite jeans have helped her to achieve the appropriate curvy slenderness and she willingly deploys them as a seduction device. In a move which grants women agency only within the terms of an eroticized male gaze, the successful deployment of seduction is the ultimate guarantee that an appropriately feminine figure in jeans has been achieved. Femininity itself is revealed as the ability to create a sexualized image that draws the gaze to one's own body (Sassatelli, 2011a). Holliday (2001) on her part shows that the careful use of clothing and fashion items to shape quite differentiated and context-specific body projects in a variety of situations is a feature of the *queer self*, whose reflexivity about self-presentation appears to be comparatively high. Other dimensions such as aging also greatly influence how reflexivity, body projects, clothing and fashionable items are intertwined. As Twigg (2007) suggests, the effacement of the aging body through an effacement of one's own participation in fashion is now counteracted by new ways of aging which put at a premium continuous body maintenance and even the sexualization of the aging body. The same can be said of ways of clothing that may appear unattractive to the Western eye. The phenomenon of Islamic fashion (Gökariksel and McLarney, 2010) where brands such as Dolce and Gabbana get along with religious prescription as to what to cover of a woman's body and make it into a fashion statement with powerful sexual innuendos has become widely debated both within and without the fashion system, in the global West and beyond.

COSMETIC SURGERY

At the beginning of the twentieth century, in Western societies, an emerging branch of medicine began to spread in public discourse, especially in periodic magazines addressed to middle- and upper-class women: cosmetic surgery. This term commonly refers to a set of procedures aimed at beautifying the appearance of a healthy body. Differently from reconstructive surgery, it is not implicated in repairing the functionality of body parts and correcting defects due to birth disorders, trauma, burns, or disease, but its aim is to enhance the aesthetic features according to cultural standards.

As Haiken (1997) and Sullivan (2001) highlight, cosmetic surgery was one of the first medical disciplines to be advertised and commercialized. Throughout the twentieth century, plastic surgeons worked quite aggressively to enter aesthetic surgical interventions into common imagery and beauty practices with strong reliance on advertisements and the popular press. Their success was built on cultural changes that occurred at the turn of the century in urban, industrialized Western societies. First came the emergence of a beauty business and cosmetic industry, with its cultural imagery of modern femininity, sustained by the growing belief that individuality was a purchasable style. In the rising consumer context, consumption and body discipline became meaningful ways to perform identity. The use of cosmetics, as with other beauty facilities, gradually became the salient marker of new social identities. A commercial culture of 'you-tooism' democratized beauty, suggesting that it could be achieved by all women, if only they used the correct products and services. Workplace or leisure activities were presented as occasions where young women could perform their femininity through manufactured beauty and succeed (Peiss, 1998). The second development was the amelioration of surgical procedures – the introduction of successful techniques of anesthesia and disinfection, and other technical innovations that allowed the broadening of what constituted a medical problem in the domain of appearance (Ghigi, 2009). The third factor was the growing importance of the management of first impressions in anonymous contexts (such as the metropolis and in the job market) and the idea that happiness can be reached through the modification of the body (Gilman, 1999). The spread of psychological accounts like Adler's 'inferiority complex' in the first decades of the century gave further legitimacy to cosmetic surgery (Haiken, 1997). Many pioneers of the beautifying scalpel opened their offices in major cities in the US and Europe, and a widespread market of qualified but also non-medical practitioners flourished alongside each other.

As for fashion, cosmetic surgery is then somehow coeval with the emergence of consumer capitalism and reflects its divergent tendencies: standardization, diversification, individualization and change. Even if it was initially performed by elites (especially upper-class women and wealthy racial minorities), it was advertised upon the same material supports, developed in similar urban contexts and targeted at similar strata of the population as fashion. It developed in Europe and the United States, especially among people desiring both to be 'physically' integrated into the country by standardizing their facial characteristics (Gilman, 1999) and to invest in their 'physical capital' in an increasingly competitive context of labor and personal relations (Davis, 1995). Moreover, it can be interpreted both as the result of aggressive marketing by cosmetic surgeons and as a way for the ascending middle class to respond to uncertainty in high social mobility societies. In some ways, cosmetic surgery is extremely revealing of the notion of body projects in consumer culture, as it implies a reflexive narration of the self in a context of 'image obsessed consumerism' (Fraser, 2003; Sullivan, 2001) and a 'somatic society', a society where 'major political and personal problems are both problematized within the body and expressed through it' (Turner, 1996, 7).

Today, cosmetic surgery represents an impressive global market. Several billion dollars are spent every year on aesthetic procedures all over the world. Surgical procedures account for about half of the total expenditures, but non-surgical and mini-invasive procedures (such as injections of botulinum toxin and hyaluronic acid, microdermabrasion, chemical peels, etc.) are increasingly relevant. The most popular procedures in US are liposuction, breast augmentation, tummy tucks, eyelid surgery, breast lifts and rhinoplasty (ASAPS, 2016), and the list is not very different if we take into account global statistics. The United States, Brazil, Japan, South Korea and Mexico are the countries where most of these procedures are performed worldwide, at an ever-growing rate in the last decades (ISAPS, 2014).

The sociological literature explains this growth by taking into account various elements, ranging from the new global economy and its work vulnerabilities (leading people to endlessly reinvent and remake themselves in order to improve their life prospects), to technological advancements, the medicalization of everyday life, the development of a tertiary labor market, a bi-dimensional image-obsessed society, and the globalization of beauty standards (Blum, 2003; Elliott, 2008; Fraser, 2003). Undoubtedly, this rise works on an old legacy. The quest for white skin and Caucasian racial features has existed for centuries in the global South. In the countries colonized by Europe or particularly influenced by the US, 'whiteness' was presented as an ideal of beauty and modernity (Gilman, 1999; Hunter, 2005), but today it is increasingly hegemonic and mass-marketed around the globe. Skin bleaching and cosmetic surgery are on the rise, particularly among educated, urban women, throughout Africa, Asia and Latin America. As Hunter notes (2011), the current merging of new technologies with old colonial ideologies has created a context where consumers can purchase 'racial capital' through skin-bleaching creams or cosmetic surgeries:

> [I]mages of white beauty do not simply rely on white women with blonde hair and light eyes to sell products. Images of white beauty sell much more than beauty ideals or fashions for women around the globe. Taken as a whole, images of white beauty sell an entire lifestyle imbued with racial meaning. (p. 144)

Interestingly, this notion of lifestyle makes whiteness, modernity, sophistication, beauty, power, and wealth converge.

Whatever its driving force, cosmetic surgery has always had middle-aged women as the main target of its campaigns and today 90 percent of the clientele are still female. Due to this strongly gendered feature, feminist accounts form the majority of the sociological explanations. They generally mix a critical account of the way the larger social and cultural context informs the choice to undergo a surgical procedure with curiosity about what cosmetic surgery means to individuals (Heyes and Jones, 2009, 7). However, it is possible to divide them roughly into three approaches.

The first and most important speculations on cosmetic surgery were made by radical feminist theorists. The main accounts in the 1990s interpreted it within the paradigm of male domination and female subordination: cosmetic surgery is a dangerous and coercive device of patriarchal control, leading women to conform to standardized ideals of youth and beauty and become objects for the male gaze and male sexual desire. In contemporary consumer culture, a pro-knife culture convinces women that surgical enhancement is a concrete option for psychological survival in a world hostile to ugly, obese and aged women (Blum, 2003; Bordo, 1993; Jacobson, 2000). In the most drastic scenario, the result would be a subject dependent on her false-consciousness and inducted needs (Bartky, 1990; Jeffreys, 2005; Morgan, 1991). This approach can be defined as the prospect of 'false consciousness': women, who are a dominated group, can only use as such their dominants' cognitive schemas; thinking they embark on beauty treatments for themselves, but in fact they do so for male desire. They think to personalize their bodies by keeping fit, by using make-up or by making changes, but in fact they normalize their bodies by adapting them to the canons defined by others. The consequence is that a female face and body, if not treated, are defective, and this imagery reinforces the lack of confidence and self-esteem among women. One of the most popular texts of this approach is *The Beauty Myth* (1990). The author, Naomi Wolf, argues that beauty is a strategic weapon expressly designed to divert women into an internal competition, thus preventing their socio-economic progress, their union, their sense of solidarity and their political consciousness. From this perspective, cosmetic surgery represents one of the most extreme outcomes of a cultural and social system pressuring women to conform to demeaning and disempowering ideas of femininity.

The second approach, on the contrary, conceives of cosmetic surgery and beauty enhancement techniques in general as effective ways to invest in one's own aesthetic capital, thus empowering individuals (and women, in particular) in their personal interactions and relationships. Research on the benefits of being beautiful conducted in evolutionary and social psychology generally show a concordance of aesthetic judgments and the importance of beauty in many dimensions of social life (Amadieu, 2002). Although the power of beauty is normally denied, and parents, teachers, recruiters refuse to recognize the impact of the appearance of a child, a student or candidate on their evaluations and decisions, much research based on questionnaires and judgments pictures show a tendency to discriminate against ugly faces (Maisonneuve and Bruchon-Schweitzer, 1999). Comparative and historical studies on the success of beautiful individuals in their schooling, in love affairs, friendship relations and work also show that aesthetic capital generates other forms of resources, mainly major self-confidence (even if cosmetic surgery patients are more likely than others to have dysmorphic syndromes and lower rates of body satisfaction). In this light, cosmetic surgery is no different from any act of consumption aimed at body enhancement. This approach is very critical toward the former, since it sees women as 'cultural dopes' (Davis, 1995), as sponges that uncritically absorb media messages, which means to double discriminate against them. The highly-debated essay by Catherine Hakim (2010) on erotic capital can be understood in this second perspective. By introducing it next to the other forms of capital studied by Bourdieu (economic, social, cultural and symbolic), Hakim defines erotic capital in several dimensions, including beauty. The positive effects of the use of this capital are observed in all areas of social life, but women are the most supplied with it and can enjoy it more in exchange for the economic capital of men. Following this approach, it is entirely rational for them to invest their time and energy in increasing it with the scalpel, a fortiori in contemporary society where erotic capital has become more important than ever. Some scholars have also presented cosmetic surgery as a potential strategy for bodily expression and a site for staging new identities (Balsamo, 1992).

As the 'agency vs structure' debate seems to lead to a theoretical impasse in studies of cosmetic surgery, a number of researchers have turned to new empirical approaches, paying more attention to the way the meanings of surgery are produced by multiple actors and forces, on one hand, and to its 'discursive framing', on the other (for an account of the debates see Gimlin, 2012; Sanchez Taylor, 2012). More specifically, empirical investigations explore situated processes of negotiating the 'necessity' of the procedures through observations of doctor–patient face-to-face encounters (Jordan, 2004; Mirivel, 2007) and individuals' reflexive accounts, analyzing how language and experiences of cosmetic surgery mutually constitute one another (Adams, 2010; Atkinson, 2008; Gill et al., 2005; Gimlin, 2001, 2012; Holliday and Cairnie, 2007). A third approach to cosmetic surgery has then come to light. Scholars have considered elective surgery as a matter of choice, but under conditions of constraint (Davis, 1995; Gillespie, 1996). The research falling into this framework can be connected to other accounts giving voice to beauty practitioners in consumer culture (as research on beauty salons or gyms customers, beauty magazine readers, participants in beauty contests, etc.; see Gimlin, 2001; Sassatelli, 1999, 2010). The major result of this perspective is to disentangle the different dimensions of the relationship between beauty and power, especially in terms of the effect on individual actors and on social groups. As Gagné and McGaughey (2002) observe, cosmetic procedures can be disempowering for women as a group, contributing to the stigmatization and medicalization of ugliness (Ghigi, 2009) and the representation of femininity as a sort of commodity. At the same time, at the individual level, this experience may well be rewarding and enjoyable, and represent a useful tool to develop one's self-esteem and position in social interactions. As Blum observes (2003, 51), 'beauty culture can be simultaneously coercive and liberating'. One of the first examples of analysis adopting this mixed perspective is Kathy Davis's much-quoted research on patients in the Netherlands (Davis, 1995): while recognizing cosmetic surgery as an expression of the most dangerous culture of Western beauty, Davis does not relegate interviewees to a role of passive sponges of aesthetic standards. Allowing them to tell their stories, she shows how they are plunged into conflicting tensions: they maintain a critical consciousness of powerful normalizing beauty standards while claiming the individual right to feel 'normal'. As both patients and consumers, women work hard to reconnect their new, modified body to themselves and to recognize it as 'their own' body, as pointed out by Davis (1995) and Gimlin (2001). The need to justify their decision allows patients to bring their experience into a new reflexive narration of themselves, involving their embodied subjectivity and their personal account of desires, emotions and values.

More recently, a number of studies have broadened all these approaches. In analyzing medical literature, feminist accounts, regulatory discourse and women's magazines, Fraser highlights distinct patterns in linguistic repertoires producing specific subjectivities available to consumers (2003). Other research takes into account men resorting to cosmetic surgery, offering new perspectives of the gendered meanings of this practice. As men are more and more involved in beauty enhancement practices, it has been suggested, the traditional definition of masculinity as 'unconcern for the body' should be abandoned. The juxtaposition of products with images of power and performance, combined with the high visibility and commodification of the male body, puts pressures on men to transform their body into an integral element of their male identity (Holliday and Cairnie, 2007; Ricciardelli et al., 2010; Rohlinger, 2002). But permanent surface body modifications such as cosmetic surgery could entail a more radical deviation from the meanings of traditional hegemonic masculinity than other goods and services aimed at modifying physical appearance. Having a surgical procedure requires performing a number of practices normally coded as autonomy-taking (and consequently stigmatized for men in a culture that celebrates self-determination and power as proper masculine qualities), and entails admitting to being so unsatisfied with one's physical appearance as to be willing to face risks and pain in order to improve it. In other words, having hair implants or eye bags removed could call masculinity into question more so than the purchase of perfume, a suit or a moisturizing cream. By highlighting similar contradictions, feminist accounts of cosmetic surgery emphasize that cosmetic surgery is still not supposed to improve masculinity the way it improves femininity (Atkinson, 2008; Davis, 2003). Male cosmetic surgery patients are forced more than women to justify their behavior, and this could entail a deeper reflexive process. In a research based on interviews with young British men, Gill, Henwood and McLean (2005) explore how body projects through a set of body modification practices (including working out in a gym, tattooing, piercing and cosmetic surgery) can fit into normative masculinity performances. As the authors note, in discussing the appearance of their bodies, the interviewees 'talked less about muscle and flesh and skin than about their own selves located within particular social, cultural and moral universes. For them, the body was a key vehicle for establishing a sense of individuality and for claiming a place in contemporary society' (p. 57). Interestingly, despite tenacious notions of appropriate masculine behavior in relation to the body being regulated and policed by normative injunctions (specifically, not to be vain, not to become obsessive and not to 'let themselves go'), the men interviewed repeatedly emphasized their independence and freedom of choices according to what the authors define a 'grammar of individualism'. In this case, cosmetic surgery proves to fit better into the definition of a 'body project' precisely for those people, as men, for whom it is more problematic, forcing them to insert their choice as consumers into a reflexive and justificatory account of themselves as embodied subjects.

Research has also focused on cosmetic procedures performed among marginalized and minority groups. Don Kulick, for example, investigates why Brazilian transgendered prostitutes inject industrial liquid silicone into their bodies, reporting that they do it not because they feel themselves to be 'women', but because they want to be more 'feminine' (1997). In a study of Asian American women in the San Francisco Bay Area who received plastic surgery, ethnographer Eugenia Kaw finds that patients undergo plastic surgery in order to 'escape persisting racial prejudice that correlates their stereotyped genetic physical features ("small, slanty" eyes and a "flat" nose) with negative behavioral characteristics, such as passivity, dullness, and a lack of sociability' (1993, 75). Interestingly, by superposing the imagery of 'modernity' with the idea of 'activity' and with Western society, these patients fully interiorize a racial ideology which associates Asiatic natural features with dullness, passivity and lack of emotion, thus they want to look more 'alert' by embodying Caucasian features (for a critical interpretation of this analysis, see Heyes and Jones [2009]). Askegaard and colleagues (2002) explore Scandinavian women's accounts of the motivation and emotions they experienced when they underwent cosmetic surgery. Resting their analysis on Giddens's body project framework, these authors observe that in patients' rhetoric of choice, cosmetic surgery fully participated in their reflexive construction of self-identity, self-determination and self-esteem.

In general, as it involves an effort to intercede in and transform the body, cosmetic surgery virtually epitomizes the contemporary body project (Gimlin, 2006): patients accept its costs and physical risks just because they are deeply invested in their physical appearance. Moreover, research shows that people who have cosmetic surgery do so in part because they believe that the surgically altered body will better represent characteristics (such as youthfulness, femininity or health) that are central to their identity (Davis, 1995; Gimlin, 2001).

BODY ART

Surface body modification practices are acts of social and cultural body marking through mutilations, decoration, modelling or addition. They are forms of symbolic body shaping common to all human societies (see Larsen and Patterson, Chapter 12 this volume). In contemporary consumer societies, some of them are related to daily practices of body maintenance (from make-up to hair dying, but also single earlobe piercing for women) and are very standardized and widespread in the population, requiring minimum reflexivity. Crossley (2005) notes that, in this case, body modification is rarely verbalized in terms of 'choice' or 'project'. More radical, permanent and intrusive practices aimed at modifying bodily appearance, instead, fit better into the notion of 'body projects', as far as they ask for justification within one's autobiographical narration. Body art is one of them.

This term commonly indicates a variety of practices, including tattooing, body piercing, scarification, branding and permanent cosmetics, all of which have been considered deviant behavior in Western societies at a certain point of their history. Similarly to fashion and cosmetic surgery, nowadays body art is strictly linked to consumer capitalism. Differently from them, although, it has a more fluctuating history of social and legal acceptance, it is less widely tolerated in its most radical forms, and it is more explicitly concerned with the cultural politics of the body and reflexive experiences of embodiment – by social researchers who investigate it as well as by people who are committed to it as consumers or professionals.

Tattoos and piercing are the most widespread forms of body art in Western societies. As DeMello (2000) and Inckle (2008) suggest, there's evidence that tattoos were practiced from ancient times all over the world. They made their official entry into Europe at the end of the eighteenth century, developed among seafarers, craftsmen, criminals and slaves, and had a fluctuating acceptance since then. Some people in Britain and continental Europe showed a certain fascination for this 'exotic' practice, but the majority, along with the dominant values of colonizers, regarded it with hostility as a savage tradition. Gradually, convicts began to mark their bodies themselves with tattoos, thus identifying with the marks of a previously compulsory stigma. In the late nineteenth century, thanks to the emergence of consumer capitalism and the introduction of technological developments which improved the precision of tattooing equipment, tattoos was used by members of the US and European upper classes willing to signal their worldliness and good taste for art (Inckle, 2008, 485). At this time the first professional body art studios opened in major cities, such as London and New York. But, at the beginning of the twentieth century, the status of body art once again slightly decreased; tattooing was reframed as the hallmark of working-class men or internees in penal institutions who used Westernized, patriotic body inscriptions as class-specific, masculine status symbols. It was not until the mid-twentieth century onward that body art began a slow, patchy consumerist resurgence, as it rose in popularity among dissident youth subcultures in Europe and the United States. As Sanders (1989) notes, from that moment body art was established as a deviant practice in the public mind as it represented the mark of disaffection from society.

The first subcultures embracing tattoos as membership symbol were bikers, who developed an extensive countercultural system based on hypermasculinity, and hippies in the late 1960s (DeMello, 2000). But the most notable case was punks, who choose not only tattoos but also pierced their noses, ears and cheeks with everyday objects, such as safety-pins. They had clearly transgressive intents, transforming ordinary items into decorations which appeared unattractive to those outside the group (Hebdige, 1979). Their creativity was expressive of the social contradictions of Britain at the time, since it dramatized joblessness, poverty and changing moral standards through bodily bricolage.

Gradually, other subcultures adopted tattooing and piercing as marks of their particular status, from heavy-metal followers to skinheads, but also rock stars. Neo-tribal and eroticized forms of body piercing, which had been used for decades by gay men, along with scarification, branding and corsetry, spread in popularity within gay and lesbian SM communities in the late 1980s and 1990s. As Pitts (2003) emphasizes, many critical subcultures such as modern primitives and the queer movement (LGBT and also BDSM practitioners) have now incorporated radical forms of body art into their identities to express their rejection of contemporary Western values, including individualism and ecologically destructive aspects of consumer capitalism, in favor of symbols of small-scale societies and tribal spirituality. More generally, current extreme body modification movements can be conceived as an outgrowth of punk culture and feminist, gay liberation and New Age movements. Altogether, these resistant cultures had in common the idea that the body is politics, as it is the primary site of social control and regulation, but also an arena on which one can stage alternative, empowering identities (Wojcik, 1995, quoted in Pitts, 2003).

Nevertheless, many scholars agree that body art's rebellious potential was weakened by the commercialization and commodification of styles typical of consumer capitalism. As a matter of fact, from the late 1980s onward, discrete forms of body art have been included in mainstream visual culture and, today, body art has become a mass-consumer phenomenon and a multi-billion-dollar industry. According to DeMello (2000), one US citizen in every five has some form of body art. Even if it has been documented across all age groups, now the highest rates of tattoos and body piercing are among young adults. Official statistics are unavailable, and quite a bit of research has been devoted to estimating the incidence of body art over the population. Resting upon a national probability sample of US people aged 18 to 50, for instance, Laumann and Derick (2006) report 24% people having tattoos and 14% having body piercings; tattooing is equally common in both sexes, but body piercing is more common among women. Many studies are conducted by surveying college students and indicate that at least one in every four students has some form of body art. Just to mention one of them, Mayers and colleagues (2002) report of a prevalence of body piercing among half of the university students in New York, and that of tattooing in one in four people. Interestingly, sporty boys were more likely to be tattooed than non-athletes. The authors repeated the survey five years later (Mayers and Chiffriller, 2008), reporting no significative changes. Studies on high school pupils are rarer, but show an increasing rate of acceptance and interest among younger generations. A recent survey conducted in the north of Italy on more than four thousand students aged 11 to18 years reported about 15 percent of the sample being tattooed (Cegolon et al., 2010). The great majority of studies on teens' body art is conducted by psychologists and pediatrics with the purpose of estimating the statistical association of body art with risk-taking practices such as alcohol abuse or unhealthy conducts, or with psychological problems. Biolcati Ghigi, Mameli and Passini (2017), for instance, show that body dissatisfaction, internalization of media messages and pressure to conform to aesthetic ideals influence adolescents' attitudes toward tattoos and piercing.

Piercing and tattooing have thus become a widespread and even normal way of marking the body, emerging from marginality and even becoming chic. Adopted by famous people within the music industry as well as the world of sport and high fashion, made more elegant with the addition of jewels conventionally thought of as elegant, spread by piercing studios that are increasingly fashionable and which also conform to sanitary regulations, they have lost part of their transgressive character and have become, at least in some forms, a widespread, normal practice amongst youth of all social classes (Le Breton, 2002). The rapid growth of tattooing and piercing among mainstream youth cultures is undoubtedly linked to the attraction of marginal body practices among suburban adolescents in search of elements of (supposed) authenticity alternative to dominant values. As Davis points out (1992), the anti-fashion affront of these rebellious youth subcultures have much more in common with middle-class taste than with ethnic minority and marginal groups. Their styles smack 'more of subversion from within than opposition from without' (p. 184): from counterculture anti-fashion to mainstream middle-class fashion it is but a short step. But the widespread popularity of body art is also the result of its explicit promotion by the music industry and media visual culture, as well as practitioners' marketing and expanded networks (Atkinson, 2004). In *Bodies of Inscription*, DeMello (2000) explains how elite body art professionals, magazine editors and leaders of body art consumers have de-emphasized the working-class roots of tattooing in order to make it more attractive for the US middle-classes. Her analysis of community publications, tattoo conventions, articles in popular magazines and interviews with tattooed people and their artists show how professionals have promoted an exotic, primitive flavor in tattooing art through an emphasis on non-Western symbols, such as Celtic, tribal and Japanese images. This shift encountered middle-class taste celebrating surface body modification as spiritual, poetic and self-empowering. Commercialization and commodification of body art subsequently emerged in its global dimensions. Siorat (2006), for instance, highlights the reintroduction of tattooing in French Polynesia since the 1980s, noting that tattooing subsequently became a lucrative aspect of the tourist trade.

However, commercialization is an ambiguous process that forces body artists to reconsider the meaning of their work. As a result of their history as symbols of deviant subculture, tattooing and piercing have not been fully included into mainstream service professions for a long time; this enabled the tightening of body artists networks and specific regulation procedures. As body art became part of mainstream consumer culture from the late 1990s, tattooists and piercing artists had to change the definition of their work and community. As Maroto (2011) shows, most tattoos and piercing providers consider their practice as part of an 'art world': a social world defined by art, consisting of all people whose activities are necessary to the production of those works which are defined, by in-group members and perhaps others, as art (Becker, 1982). Their identification as artists comes into collision with commercialization. Consumers once shared specific subcultures, styles and a sense of belonging, while what is now a vast and varied clientele does not identify as a community. When confronted with the increasing size and popularity of their service, professional body artists struggle to maintain control over their job by resorting to formal and informal strategies, from standardization to social networking, although avoiding too strict regulation that they consider incompatible with an artistic field.

In her work on elite tattoo collectors and tattooists, Irwin (2003) explains how these people see tattoos as an art form and enjoy collecting artwork on bodies. Elite tattoo collectors are 'a subset of heavily tattooed individuals who desire the best art available' (p. 29), get inspired and craft the concept, while tattoo artists execute the already constructed ideas. Both achieve fame and popularity through the public display of the body work. Interestingly, Irwin reports how they protect non-tattooed areas from public sight because of the embarrassment they would feel in exposing patches of plain skin, as it would remind them of the unfinished, unbalanced nature of their body suits.

All in all, contemporary non-radical forms of tattooing and piercing seem to be no different from various fads that characterized different young generations over the course of the twentieth century. Nevertheless, some authors (Randall and Polhemus, 1996) find that current trends express a new desire for continuity, community and a commitment to contrast fragmentation and anonymity. This interpretation is confirmed by some qualitative narrative-based and ethnographic works. By analyzing how body modifiers welcome the painful aspects of body art, for instance, Sweetman (1999) and Le Breton (2002) point out that the bleeding, the pain and the healing of the body generates the need for self-attention and heightens the sense of reflexivity. People who thus perform body art experience subjectivity 'to the full' and produce new modes of embodiment by defying normative aesthetics and pushing tolerable sufferance to its limits. Pitts (2003) describes the world of extreme body art from the viewpoint of cyberpunks, radical queers, leather dykes and modern primitives. She notes that their consideration of the body as a limitless frontier of invention and self-stylization reflects, consciously or not, the social and political locations of individual bodies in the larger social power relations.

Indeed, common to many accounts of elective body modification is the experience of taking control over one's body, of marking identity, of contrasting the body natural and the tyranny of habitus. But current commercialization casts doubts on it always working this way. Turner (1999) distinguishes the social framing of body art in traditional societies from postmodern ones, arguing that traditional tribalism, with its hot commitments and thick solidarities, produced obligatory markings inscribed in rituals which led to the stability of the in-group against outsiders, because 'they were set within a shared culture of collective meanings' (p. 39). In postmodern society, in contrast, the meaning and motivations behind tattoos become individualistic representations of self-expression. Body art is now 'optional, decorative, impermanent and narcissistic' (p. 42). In consumer society, body marks are playful, superficial, narcissistic attempts to address the alienation of postmodernity.

With a different approach, Sweetman (1999) also posits sharp distinctions between contemporary and traditional societies. Tattoos and body piercing are attractive for many people because they are permanent and irreversible. In this sense, they should be considered differently from other superficial, transitory forms of consumption. They are attempts to fix and anchor the self by permanently marking the body. Tattoos, in particular, can assist in the construction of a coherent personal narrative being related to particular events or periods of life. As one interviewee told Sweetman, 'tattooing has a lot to do with memory' because the tattoo itself 'will always remind you of the time you had it done' (p. 69). Of course permanence and visibility can vary, but if the integrity, healthiness and attractiveness of the body are praised in consumer culture, the disregard and violation of the body through cutting, scarification or branding then suggest a challenge to the dominant ideology. According to this approach, body art contrasts with more ephemeral forms of body surface modification, since its lack of easy reversibility would be indicative of the rejection of the consumer capitalist ideology praising social mobility and endless change. Similarly, Atkinson (2003), with an ethnographic work on tattoo enthusiasts, explores how they negotiate and celebrate their 'difference' as it relates to the social stigma attached to body art, and suggests that they use their bodies as cultural canvases to protest social constraints.

In any case, even most passionate commentators of body art as a tool of self-expression disagree with the idea that consumers are totally free to invent the self through body modification. As Featherstone (1991) and Pitts (2003) note, for instance, body projects themselves are historically produced and can be read only within a social system of organization and meaning. Capitalism provides one such system, and the way embodied selves are encouraged to be self-transforming are informed by consumer culture. Notions of individual self-awareness in contemporary body art projects derive from the self-help and pop psychology movement of the 1960s and 1970s, and the transformation of tattoos into meaningful, intellectual and exotic marks is linked to commodification and middle-class dynamics of distinction (DeMello, 2000).

All in all, body art has generated a great debate among scholars, similarly to cosmetic surgery. In some cases, it has been argued that it represents another form of denigration of the body or a society-driven pathologization; in some other cases, it has been read as a challenge to conventional beauty ideals, often resulting in a shocking look with a subversive potential (Pitts, 2003). Again, studies based on personal accounts of people with some form of body art encourage more blurred and nuanced conclusions. Instead of revealing personality disorders or psychopathological conditions, these analyses show that body art should be understood as part of a process of the expression and reception of meanings through consumption within a postmodern cultural context. Authors tend to agree that it can reveal striving for identity, protest and cultural defiance, while also accepting that it has become part of the 'supermarket of style' (Polhemus, 1994). As Sweetman puts it, even in its pop and fashioned versions, body marking contributes to a coherent and viable sense of self-identity through the attention it drives to the body (1999, 53). Accordingly, body art can be included among those practices that are fed by (and, in turn, feed) body reflexivity and the proliferation of embodied, consistent narratives of the self.

CONCLUSION

As suggested, high modernity has produced an unprecedented 'individualization' of the body, in which meanings are privatized and the body becomes a bearer of symbolic value. Coupled with consumer capitalism, we get a particular dualistic situation whereby the self becomes responsible for his or her body by drawing on commercial services. Given the relevance of performative rationalization and visual culture, it is especially the body as a surface which has been invested by consumer culture with the power to modify, enhance or maintain one's own physical endowment towards projects capable of constructing and presenting an adequate identity for oneself, and for other people and institutional tasks. In this chapter, we have looked at three different areas where body projects are increasingly teased out by consumer culture: fashion, plastic surgery and body art. They have largely been researched as useful terrains to grasp commercially mediated body projects and show how research on body modifications intersects with consumer culture. Still, there are a number of practices and examples that we could have chosen to show the way commoditization and consumer culture goes well beyond a sharp distinction between surface and depth of bodies. To be sure, practices such as physical activity or meditation are very often predicated on the idea that what is deep (muscle, soul) needs to be engaged directly by the self, in order to obtain real body changes even at the surface level. More than this, we may say that our bodies as depth are implicated in consumer culture. Indeed, it is as profundity, that our bodies are portrayed as the site of feeling and taste, likes and dislikes. Commercially-mediated managing techniques are put at work to produce a reflexive widening of consumers' capacity to feel and want in what are considered culturally appropriate ways.

Reinterpreting what Arlie R. Hochschild has shown (2012), projects related to our emotions are becoming fundamental. Our capacity to outsource paid care work for our family or find a new partner on an online platform with the help of a consultant and still retain, in both cases, a feeling of authenticity, commitment and intimacy are now among the new commodity frontiers for embodied projectuality. Managing emotions, with appropriate 'emotion work', working reflexively on oneself, the way one communicates through one's body (voice, eyes, demeanor) is becoming central for the middle-class consumer, as it were, indeed, for the upper classes. The commodity frontier is thus expanding through the increased reflexive commercialization of services that allow more and more consumers to cultivate their capacities to feel and taste, including commodities as diverse as personal life coaching services and wine tasting courses. Thus, what we may call the soul boundary is probably also the frontier for future research. Commercialized services which try to bypass the body/mind dualism, which address emotions and even the soul, are clearly amongst the most promising frontiers for the commercial spirit. The increasing supply of customized and 'fully aesthetic' bodily experiences (from resort packages combining cosmetic surgery and a beach holiday to Botox parties, from organic ink tattoos to Spas with holistic treatments) may well testify to this. In consumer capitalist democracies we are obliged to be the source of value (as consumers for the market, as citizens for the state), increasingly drawing on our capacity to feel and want (Sassatelli, 2007). So, we must want in appropriate ways. We must make a difference, somehow, in a world which is increasingly based on the logic of commutability promoted by the cash nexus: everything has a price, but price is not why we buy. Mature markets need (well-managed) feelings to facilitate exchange relations, but they need (well-managed) desires to make exchange meaningful in the first place. Future research will certainly have to spin around our reflexive need to manage emotions through the body, and manage the body through deep emotion work.

REFERENCES

Adams, J. (2010) 'Motivational narratives and assessments of the body after cosmetic surgery', *Qualitative Health Research*, 20(6): 755–767.

Amadieu, J. (2002) *Le poids des apparences*, Paris: Odile Jacob.

Appadurai, A. (1986) 'Introduction: commodities and the politics of value', in A. Appadurai (ed.) *The Social Life of Things. Commodities in Cultural Perspectives*, Cambridge: Cambridge University Press.

ASAPS (2016) *Statistics 2015*, http://www.surgery.org/media/statistics (last retrieved: Sept 2016).

Askegaard, S., Cardel Gertsen, M. and Langer, R. (2002) 'The body consumed: Reflexivity and cosmetic surgery', *Psychology and Marketing*, 19(10): 793–812.

Aspers, P. and Godart, F. (2013). Sociology of fashion: Order and change. *Annual Review of Sociology*, 39: 171–192.

Atkinson, M. (2003) *Tattooed*, Toronto: University of Toronto Press.

Atkinson, M. (2004) 'Tattooing and civilizing processes: Body modification as self-control', *Canadian Review of* Sociology, 41(2): 125–146.

Atkinson, M. (2008) 'Exploring male femininity in the "crisis": Men and cosmetic surgery', *Body & Society*, 14: 67–87.

Balsamo, A. (1992) 'On the cutting edge: Cosmetic surgery and the technological production of the Gendered Body', *Camera Obscura*, 10(1): 206–237.

Bartky, S. (1990) *Femininity and Domination*. London: Routledge.

Baudrillard, J. (1998) *The Consumer Society: Myths and Structures*. London: Sage.

Bauman, Z. (1992) *Intimations of Post-modernity*. London: Routledge.

Beck, U. (1992) *Risk Society: Towards a New Modernity*. London: Sage.

Becker, H. (1982) *Art Worlds*. Berkeley: University of California Press.

Biolcati, R., Ghigi, R., Mameli, C. and Passini, S. (2017) 'What can I do with my body? Boys and girls facing body dissatisfaction', *International Journal of Adolescence and Youth*, 22(3): 283–295. DOI: 10.1080/02673843.2016.1167748

Blum, V. (2003) *Flesh Wounds*. Berkeley: University of California Press.

Blumer, H. (1969) 'Fashion: From class differentiation to collective selection', *Sociological Quarterly*, 10(3): 275–291.

Boltanski, L. (1971) *Les usages sociaux du corps*, *Annales*, 26(1): 205–233.
Bordo, S. (1993) *Unbearable Weight*, Berkeley: University of California Press.
Bourdieu, P. (1984 [1979]) *Distinction: A Social Critique of the Judgement of Taste*. London: Routledge.
Bourdieu, P. and Delsaut, Y. (1975) 'Le couturier et sa griffe: contribution à une théorie de la magie', *Actes de la Recherche en Sciences Sociales*, 1(1): 7–35.
Cegolon, L. et al. (2010) 'Body art in 4,277 Italian secondary school adolescents: Prevalence and associations with personal and family characteristics', *Family Medicine*, 42(4): 273–279.
Chasin, A. (2000), *Selling Out*. New York: St. Martin's Press.
Crane, D. (2000) *Fashion and its Social Agenda: Class, Gender and Identity in Clothing*. Chicago: University of Chicago Press.
Crossley, N. (2001) *The Social Body: Habit, Identity and Desire*. London: Sage.
Crossley, N. (2005) 'Mapping reflexive body techniques: On body modification and maintenance', *Body Society*, 11(1): 1–35.
Davis, F. (1992) *Fashion, Culture, and Identity*. Chicago: University of Chicago Press.
Davis, K. (1995) *Reshaping the Female Body*. New York: Routledge.
Davis, K. (2003) *Dubious Equalities and Embodied Differences*. Lanham: Rowman & Littlefield.
DeMello, M. (2000) *Bodies of Inscription*. Durham: Duke University Press.
Elliott, A. (2008) *Making the Cut*. London: Reaktion.
Entwistle, J. (2000) *The Fashioned Body*. Cambridge: Polity.
Evans, C. and Thornton, M. (1989) *Women and Fashion*. London: Quartet Books.
Featherstone, M. (1982) 'The body in consumer culture', *Theory, Culture & Society*, 1(2): 18–33.
Featherstone, M. (1991) *Consumer Culture and Postmodernism*, London: Sage.
Finnegan, M. (1999) *Selling Suffrage: Consumer Culture and Votes for Women*. New York: Columbia University Press.
Frank, A. (1991) 'For a sociology of the body: An analytic review', in M. Featherstone, M. Hepworth and B. Turner (eds) *The Body: Social Process and Cultural Theory*, pp. 36–102. London: Sage.
Fraser, S. (2003) *Cosmetic Surgery, Gender and Culture*. New York: Palgrave Macmillan.
Gagné, P. and McGaughey, D. (2002) 'Designing women: Cultural hegemony and the exercise of power among women who have undergone elective mammoplasty', *Gender & Society*, 16(6): 814–838.
Ghigi, R. (2009) 'The medicalization of ugliness', *Salute e Società*, 2: 67–77.
Giddens, A. (1991) *Modernity and Self-identity*. Cambridge: Polity Press.
Gill, R., Henwood, K. and McLean, C. (2005) 'Body projects and the regulation of normative masculinity', *Body & Society*, 11(1): 37–62.
Gillespie, R. (1996) 'Women, the body and brand extension in medicine: Cosmetic surgery and the paradox of choice', *Women & Health*, 24(4): 69–85.
Gilman, S. (1999) *Making the Body Beautiful*. Princeton, NJ: Princeton University Press.
Gimlin, D. (2001) *Body Work*. Berkeley: University of California Press.
Gimlin, D. (2006) 'The Absent Body Project: Cosmetic Surgery as a Response to Bodily Dys-appearance', *Sociology*, 40(4): 699–716.
Gimlin, D. (2012) *Cosmetic Surgery Narratives*. New York: Palgrave Macmillan.
Gökariksel, B. and McLarney, E. (2010) 'Muslim women, consumer capitalism, and the Islamic culture industry', *Journal of Middle East Women's Studies*, 6(3): 1–18.
Haiken, E. (1997) *Venus Envy*. Baltimore: Johns Hopkins University Press.
Hakim, C. (2010) 'Erotic capital', *European Sociological Review*, 26(5): 499–518.

Hancock, P. et al. (2000) *The Body, Culture and Society*. Buckingham: Open University Press.
Hebdige, D. (1979) *Subculture: The Meaning of Style*. London: Methuen.
Heyes, C.J. and Jones, M. (2009) *Cosmetic Surgery: A Feminist Primer*. Farnham, Surrey and Burlington, VT: Ashgate Publishing.
Hirsch, P. (1972) 'Processing fads and fashions: An organization-set analysis of cultural industry systems', *American Journal of Sociology*, 77(4): 639–659.
Holliday, R. (2001) Fashioning the queer self, in J. Entwistle & E. Wilson (eds) *Body dressing*, pp. 215–231. Oxford: Berg.
Holliday, R. and Cairnie, A. (2007) 'Man made plastic: Investigating men's consumption of aesthetic surgery', *Journal of Consumer Culture*, 7(1): 57–78.
Hoschschild, A.R. (2012) *The Outsourced Self*. New York: Metropolitan Books.
Hunter, M. (2005) *Race, Gender, and the Politics of Skin Tone*. New York: Routledge.
Hunter, M. (2011) 'Buying racial capital: Skin-bleaching and cosmetic surgery in a globalized world', *The Journal of Pan African Studies*, 4(4): 142–164.
Inckle, K. (2008) 'Tattoos', in V. Pitts (ed.) *Cultural Encyclopedia of the Body*. Westport, CT: Greenwood Press.
Irwin, K. (2003) 'Saints and sinners: Elite tattoo collectors and tattooists as positive and negative deviants', *Sociological Spectrum*, 23(1): 27–57.
ISAPS (2014) *Global Statistics*, http://www.isaps.org/news/isaps-global-statistics (last retrieved: Sept 2016).
Jacobson, N. (2000) *Cleavage*. New Brunswick, NJ: Rutgers.
Jeffreys, S. (2005) *Beauty and Misogyny*. London: Routledge.
Jordan, J. (2004) 'The rhetorical limits of the "plastic body"', *Quarterly Journal of Speech*, 90(3): 327–358.
Kaw, E. (1993) 'Medicalization of racial features: Asian American women and cosmetic surgery', *Medical Anthropology Quarterly*, 7(1): 74–89.
Kawamura, Y. (2004) *Fashion-ology*. Oxford: Berg.
Kulick, D. (1997) 'The gender of Brazilian transgendered prostitutes', *American Anthropologist*, 99(3): 574–585.
Lasch, C. (1979) *The Culture of Narcissism*. New York: Norton.
Laumann, A. and Derick, A. (2006) 'Tattoos and body piercings in the United States: A national data set', *Journal of the American Academy of Dermatology*, 55(3): 413–421.
Le Breton, D. (2002) *Signes d'identité. Tatouages, piercings et autres marques corporelles*. Paris: Métailié.
Maisonneuve, J. and Bruchon-Schweitzer, M. (1999) *Le corps et la beauté*. Paris: PUF.
Maroto, M. (2011) 'Professionalizing body art a marginalized occupational group's use of informal and formal strategies of control', *Work and Occupations*, 38(1): 101–138.
Martin, E. (1994) *Flexible Bodies: Tracking Immunity in American Culture from the Days of Polio to the Age of AIDS*. Boston: Beacon Press.
Mayers, L.B. and Chiffriller, S.H. (2008) 'Body art (body piercing and tattooing) among undergraduate university students: "then and now"', *Journal of Adolescent Health*, 42(2): 201–203.
Mayers, L.B., Judelson, D.A., Moriarty, B.W. and Rundell, K.W. (2002) 'Prevalence of body art (body piercing and tattooing) in university undergraduates and incidence of medical complications', *Mayo Clinic Proceedings*, 77(1): 29–34.
McRobbie, A. (2004) 'Postfeminism and popular culture', *Feminist Media Studies*, 4(3): 255–264.
Mears, A. (2014). Aesthetic labor for the sociologies of work, gender, and beauty. Sociology Compass, 8: 1330–1343.

Mirivel, J.C. (2007) 'Managing poor surgical candidacy: Communication problems for plastic surgeons', *Discourse & Communication*, 1(3): 309–336.

Morgan, K.P. (1991) 'Women and the knife: Cosmetic surgery and the colonization of women's bodies', *Hypatia*, 6(3): 25–53.

Mort, F. (1996) *Cultures of Consumption: Masculinities and Social Space in Late Twentieth-Century Britain*. London: Routledge.

Nava, M. (1991) *Changing Cultures: Feminism, Youth and Consumerism*. London: Sage.

Nixon, S. (1996) *Hard Looks: Masculinities, Spectatorship and Contemporary Consumption*, London: University College London Press.

Peiss, K.L. (1998) *Hope in a Jar: The Making of America's Beauty Culture*. New York: Metropolitan Books.

Pitts, V. (2003) *In the Flesh*. New York: Palgrave Macmillan.

Polhemus, T. (1994) *Streetstyle: From Sidewalks to Catwalks*. London: Thames and Hudson.

Randall, H. and Polhemus, T. (1996) *The Customized Body*. New York: Serpent's Tail.

Ricciardelli, R., Clow, K.A. and White, P. (2010) 'Investigating hegemonic masculinity: Portrayals of masculinity in men's lifestyle magazines', *Sex Roles*, 63(1): 64–78.

Rohlinger, D. (2002) 'Eroticizing men: Cultural influences on advertising and male objectification', *Sex Roles*, 46(3): 61–74.

Sanchez Taylor, J. (2012) 'Fake breasts and power: Gender, class and cosmetic surgery', *Women's Studies International Forum*, 35(6): 458–466.

Sanders, C. (1989) *Customizing the Body*. Philadelphia: Temple University Press.

Sassatelli, R. (1999) 'Interaction order and beyond: A field analysis of body culture within fitness gyms', *Body and Society*, 5(2–3): 227–248.

Sassatelli, R. (2007) *Consumer Culture: History, Theory and Politics*. London: Sage.

Sassatelli, R. (2010) *Fitness Culture: Gyms and the Commercialisation of Discipline and Fun*. Basingstoke: Palgrave.

Sassatelli, R. (2011a) 'Indigo bodies: Fashion, mirror work and sexual identity in Milan', in D. Miller and S. Woodward (eds) *Global Denim*, pp. 72–95. Oxford: Berg.

Sassatelli, R. (2011b) 'Consumer Identities', in A. Elliott (ed.) Handbook of Identity Studies, Routledge, London, pp. 236–253.

Sassatelli, R. (2012) 'Self and body', in F. Trentmann (ed.) *Handbook of the History of Consumption*, pp. 633–652. Oxford: Oxford University Press.

Sassatelli, R. (2015) 'Healthy cities and instrumental leisure', *Modern Italy*, 20(3): 237–250.

Shilling, C. (2013) *The Body and Social Theory*, 3rd edition. London: Sage.

Simmel, G. (1971 [1904]) 'Fashion', in G. Simmel, *On Individuality and Social Forms*, pp. 294–323. Chicago: Chicago University Press.

Siorat, C. (2006) 'The art of pain', *Fashion Theory*, 10(3): 367–380.

Skov, L. (2005) 'The return of the fur coat: A commodity chain perspective', *Current Sociology*, 53(1): 9–32.

Steele, V. (2003) *Fashion, Italian Style*. New Haven: Yale University Press.

Sullivan, D.A. (2001) *Cosmetic Surgery*. New Brunswick: Rutgers University Press.

Sweetman, P. (1999) 'Anchoring the (postmodern) self? Body modification, fashion and identity', *Body & Society*, 5(2–3): 51–76.

Tseëlon, E. (1995) *The Masque of Femininity*. London: Sage.

Turner, B.S. (1996) *The Body and Society*, 2nd edition. London: Sage.

Turner, B.S. (1999) 'The possibility of primitiveness. Towards a sociology of body marks in cool societies', *Body and Society*, 5(2–3): 39–50.

Twigg, J. (2009) 'Clothing, Identity and the Embodiment of Age', in J. Powell and T. Gilbert (eds) *Aging and Identity: A Postmodern Dialogue*, pp. 93–104. New York: Nova Science Publishers.
Veblen, T. (1899) *The Theory of the Leisure Class*, London: MacMillan.
Waquant, L. (1995) 'Why men desire muscles?', *Body and Society*, 1(1): 163–179.
Wacquant, L. (2004) *Body and Soul*. Chicago: Chicago University Press.
Wilson, E. (1985) *Adorned in Dreams: Fashion and Modernity*. London: Virago.
Wojcik, D. (1995) *Punk and Neo-Tribal Body Art*. Jackson: University Press of Mississippi.
Wolf, N. (1990) *The Beauty Myth*. New York: Chatto & Windus.
Woodward, S. (2007) *Why Women Wear What They Wear*. Oxford: Berg.

Who Takes the First Bite? A Critical Overview of Gender Representations in Food Advertising

Daniela Pirani, Benedetta Cappellini
and Vicki Harman

INTRODUCTION: BLAME IT ON EVE – LITERATURE, GENDER REPRESENTATIONS AND FOOD ADVERTISING

Advertising is a powerful device that helps to shape our understanding of contemporary consumer culture, provides information about social identities and acts as an important reference point for our own consumption practices. Furthermore, advertisements are 'socio-political artefacts' capable of revealing hegemonic powers (Borgerson & Schroeder, 2002: 571). The broader consideration that informs this study is that representations are powerful, but equally of importance is the way that scholars talk and write about them. Thus, when considering how gender is represented in advertising it is important not only to focus on what kind of gender representations are available, but also on how they are studied and reported. As such, representations in advertising are sources of information, imagination and leisure whose meanings simplify and reinforce certain identities, influencing present and future thinking of the self and the Other in terms of gender, class and cultures (Borgerson & Schroeder, 2002). Arguably, gender in advertising is often presented as natural and 'common sense' rather than offering contested representations suitable for a reflective understanding of diversities. Nevertheless, these representations are imbued with value (Alcof, 1999 in Borgerson & Schroeder, 2002) since bodies, roles, practices, collectives and spaces often reflect and enact stereotypes and stigmas. One key role of interpretivist consumer research is to consider advertising and its reception among consumers. The question shaping our analysis is then: What is revealed, and what is left unsaid, through academic scholarship about representations of gender in food advertising?

To answer this question, this chapter critically reviews how interpretive consumer research scholars have considered gender representations in food advertising and personal branding. We provide a broad reading of the literature about the gendered representations of food practices in advertising, highlighting what is known, what is unknown and what appears to have been ignored thus far. Our aims consist of providing 'a reflexive exploration of our own practices of representation' (Woolgar, 1988: 98) via a categorization of the existing literature. By considering the scholarship on such gender representations in food advertising, our perspective is one-step removed from the advertisements themselves, but is nonetheless still revealing of social processes and potential biases and blind-spots.

We begin by engaging in an overview of the main theoretical concepts adopted in the relevant literature on food advertising and practices and we proceed by mapping the existing scholarship. We do this by highlighting the use of a set of gender characters mainly divided into male and female roles in which the family roles of mother (the Domestic Juggler) and father (the Breadwinner/the Nurturing Father) are dominant. Other female characters have been also individuated including the Yummy Goddess and the Hedonic Vamp. Male characters including the Domestic Divo and the Wild Bachelor have been identified. Our analysis highlights how academic representations reflect the distorted mirror of advertising, highlighting some of the power relations entailed in each character.

Our discussion seeks to advance academic understanding of gender representations, inviting scholars to account for those elements that make them possible. The first element that we focus on is the context, which has a crucial role in determining how gendered roles are re-constructed. In particular, we consider the role of collectives – such as family – in conditioning the gender identity displayed. The second element is the one of practices, understood as the actions, attitudes and displays that mark and distinguish certain gendered performances. Finally, we attempt to detect the gaze implied in certain representations, and to highlight how the gaze concurs with the construction of the gender characters here articulated. We argue that the gaze is always present, although often not fully unpacked, not only in the media representations but also in the academic scholarship.

AN APPETITE FOR GENDER

Gender studies have developed substantially in the last century, bringing discussions that used to belong to feminist circles into marketing debates (Scott, 1986). Different theoretical strands have developed around the definition of gender, but the work of West and Zimmermann (1987) and Butler (1990) has been particularly influential in marketing studies.

West and Zimmermann (1987) have confuted the assumption that gender is imposed on us by nature as a consequence of our biological sex. Instead, they claim gender is a way of accounting in the social sphere for individual sex-related categories. Sex-category markers (a beard, nail polish, etc.) are not enough, *per se*, to be socially accountable for one's gender: they need interaction. West and Zimmermann (1987) coined the notion of 'doing gender' to highlight the activity people engage in to manage their gendered enactment according to the sex category they adopt and display. Sex and sex-categories are not causally connected but interrelated through the way individuals enact them in their ways of doing gender. West and Zimmerman highlight the role of individual agency in enacting specific ways of doing gender without undermining the fact that gendered categories and roles are more the result of a social co-constructed negotiation than the outcome of individual qualities. A more critical point of view on the role of individual agency is offered by Butler (1990), arguing that there is not a pre-existing gendered identity, but that this emerges only via performativity. However, Butler (1990) argues that not all gendered performativities are possible: those in which sex and gender are not aligned are considered illegitimate and not tolerated. As a result, our performativity tends to replicate the 'correct' way of 'doing' gender, but while we do it, we not only follow a social script, we create our own gendered script, conditioned by our bodies and idiosyncratic pleasures and conditions. Since Western society is based on the privilege of heterosexual arrangements, femininity and masculinity are the only categorisations socially accepted, and any other gender expression tends to be sanctioned (Butler, 1990). Being both empty labels that constitute themselves in dialectical terms, rather than as entities per se, a thick web of practices and signs is essential to fully pass as a man or a woman in mundane social interactions.

Given that gender emerges from practices, food practices become particularly relevant as they re-produce gendered scripts multiple times a day, on a range of social dimensions spanning from domesticity to public conviviality. Furthermore, the symbolic value of food sustains some of these practices. The strongest symbol of hegemonic masculinity in food is red meat. The association of hegemonic masculinity with meat motivated scholars such as Adams (1990) to think about vegetarianism as a form of resistance to patriarchy. In fact, red meat symbolically evokes a traditional manhood that is tightly bonded with sexual drive and domination (Adams, 1990; Cudworth, 2008; Irvine, 2015; Potts & Parry, 2010; Sobal, 2005). Eating red meat with a voracious appetite means to eat like a man (Buerkle, 2009; Newcombe, McCarthy, Cronin & McCarthy, 2012).When men associate themselves with vegetables, as in the case of vegetarians, they are labelled by discourses usually attributed to femininity, such as compassion, weakness and emotionality (Irvine, 2015). On the contrary, women are associated with vegetables and sweets, reproducing their role as saints or sinners (Calamita, 2014). Vegetables are coded as feminine because they are positioned as being in direct opposition to meat. Associated with purity and asexuality, they own the qualities that have been historically associated with angelical figures, such as the angel of the hearth. Sweets are prominently considered to be female, as they are related to the world of pleasure, childhood and sometimes associated with a subordinate position compared to 'proper food' (James, 1990; Lupton, 1996; Mintz, 1985). Eating sweets is a form of weakness that reflects women's role as sinful transgressors (Stevens & Maclaran, 2008). Women's sweet tooth comes out as a double temptation: on one hand it corrupts men's will power (Parasecoli, 2005), on the other it creates expectations regarding women's choices. Women not only are more likely to define themselves as chocolate or sweets consumers, but they are also more likely to feel judged while indulging in them (Belk & Costa, 1998; Stevens & Maclaran, 2008).

SETTING THE TABLE, SETTING THE RULES

The vast majority of consumer studies looking at domestic food practices took inspiration from concepts of doing gender and performativity, showing how laying the table, shopping, cooking and dealing with leftovers are enactments of gendered scripts in which specific performances are done depending on the roles individuals occupy within the family. For instance, when food is a matter of care for others, it is seen as a women's duty (Cairns et al., 2010; Newcombe et al., 2012) and more specifically a duty of motherhood (De Vault, 1991). Domestic labour is often considered primarily to be a women's domain (ibid.), even when both partners are working (Miller, 2012), and the recurring self-sacrifice and responsibility for everyday chores is internalized as a woman's job (Cappellini & Parsons, 2012; Sassatelli et al., 2015). The domestic, emotional and material burden is sustained because it contributes to women's gender identification and recognition: being the caretaker in the kitchen and in the pantry is a synonym for being the woman in the house (Carrington, 2013). Furthermore, women's 'labour of love' has implications for the collective identity of the family, as maternal labour in the kitchen has been seen by women themselves as helping the household to get together, physically and symbolically (Moisio et al., 2004). While homemade food serves as a metonym for a 'happy' family (ibid.), in practical terms it is also perceived not only as a devotional act but also as a frustrating duty that someone has to do (Sassatelli et al., 2015). That someone ends up being a woman most of the time, because women's time is thought to be more elastic and suitable to cope with family needs, and the emotional work involved is almost never counted (ibid.; Cappellini et al., 2014).

If the discourse of female self-sacrifice dominates the practice of feeding the family, recently, women have gained more legitimization in cooking for pleasure and gaining expertise in this area (Cairns et al., 2010). This personal enjoyment, which conflicts with the role of devotional caretaker, has been usually reserved for men. In fact, husbands and partners tend to cook in a limited, peripheral way (Swenson, 2009), choosing special occasions when they can display their skills to others (Cairns et al., 2010). When faced with everyday cooking, men adopt adjusting strategies, including using sexual jokes, to restore their normative masculinity (Deutsch, 2005). However, such gendered scripts around food and masculinity are not static, and young single men have been found to engage with cooking and to distance themselves from the stereotypical bachelor behaviour of the man who doesn't care about food (Sellaeg & Chapman, 2008). Some men *do* cook for caring purposes, and claim to be satisfied not because of the hedonic and self-assuring performance but because of the nurturing feeling, drawing elements of self-identification from traditional culinary femininity (Szabo, 2013). Furthermore, some fathers and male partners have embraced cooking and practices around food as their way of contributing to the division of domestic labour without the risk of emasculation (Neuman, Gottzén & Fjellström, 2017).

THE BITTER TASTE OF COMMERCIALS

Advertising belongs to reality as much as the practices just listed do, but as a powerful and ideological device it shapes our visual landscape (Schroeder & Borgerson, 1998), contributing to our sense-making of the world and confining our imagination under the rules of its commercial purpose (Schroeder, 2002). As mentioned in the introduction, the way gender is depicted in advertising is never neutral, but it represents an intervention in our world. When it comes to gender roles, advertising replicates and magnifies social inequalities, normative behaviours and related moral sanctioning. Food advertising is particularly interesting in this respect, as it often displays extreme gender polarization (Calamita, 2014).

A milestone in the study of gender is the visual analysis conducted by Erving Goffman (1979), a study now dated in terms of the sources used but still relevant for its methodological contributions. Goffman analysed the gender displays in advertising, and how they set a hierarchy among characters. He noted that when a man deals with a woman or a subordinate man, he enacts the same strategies adopted within the child–parent relationship: mitigation of distance, coercion and hostility. These visual codes detail women's subordination in a vast array of ways. For example, when the scene is set in a kitchen or living room being cleaned, men are represented as 'engaged in no contributing role at all' or as 'candidly unreal [so] the competency image of real masculinities could be preserved' (Goffman, 1979: 36). The feminine touch, whether it is hetero-directed or concerns the woman's own body, never grasps or firmly holds objects. Women's hands are caressing, barely touching, making sense of their own body as something delicate and fragile. These ritualized expressions are advertisers' inventions which have been perpetuated over time, however they are connected symbolically to everyday life situations. Thus, a campaign glimpsed from a magazine can make sense to us without more detailed information, allowing us to assess whether the representation matches our lived experience. Because of the symbolic associations attached, food can contribute to generating gendered meanings within advertising, even when not relevant for the story told.

A final remark over gender images should address the role of the Other in constructing certain identities. If in practice gender identities are done – and undone – through recognition by others (Butler, 2004), the same is true for gender representations. These representations often already include a certain gaze, or the eyes of the Other legitimizing and co-constructing the gendered image. As with any other visual material, advertising images have a 'way of looking' inscribed within them that is already gendered (Mulvey, 2009) and that allocates the power between the gazer and the gazed. The gaze reproduces gender possibilities and expected sexualities, by putting the observer in a position of power in relation to the person observed: 'to gaze implies more than to look at – it signifies a psychological relationship of power and sexuality in which the gazer dominates the object of the gaze' (Schroeder & Zwick, 2004: 30). Because of the 'lack of reciprocity between the gaze and the gazed-upon' (Morgan, 2011: 93), the gaze usually is turned to women, represented as passive objects against self-assertive males. The voyeurism of the male gaze embedded in female representation has recently been re-conceptualised, opening up power arrangements that have the potential to overcome the antagonism between men as the bearer of the look and women as passive recipient of that gaze. Scholars have studied women who are practitioners themselves of a fetish gaze (Rose, 2012), men gazing over men (Patterson & Elliott, 2002), queer gazes and gazes that belong to non-hetero-sexist possibilities (Schroeder & Zwick, 2004). One example is the lesbian gaze implied in fashion advertising targeted at women, where women cultivate the fantasy of being at the centre of other women's desiring looks (Lewis, 1997).

FROM THE DOMESTIC DIVO TO THE HEDONIC CONSUMER: MAPPING GENDER REPRESENTATIONS

The map of gender characters here presented – and summarized in Table 18.1 – points out salient points identifiable within scholarship focusing on gender portrayals in food advertising. As such, our analysis and the table deriving from it does not look directly at the complexity of the advertising industry, but at the mediated look of scholarship on the advertising representations of gender and food. The review is based on 12 articles of interpretive marketing and consumer research that discuss gender representation in food advertising broadcast in Western countries. The articles have been selected among the papers and proceedings published since 2000 – with two exceptions – in *Association of Consumer Research* (North American and European), *Journal of Marketing Management*, *Journal of Advertising*, *Journal of Advertising Research*, *Marketing Theory*, *Journal of Consumer Research* and *Consumption Markets & Culture*. The selection was based on a specific interest in gender categorization in food advertising, but it also includes articles on personal

Table 18.1 Gender types in food advertising

	Women	*Practices*	*Men*	*Practices*
Family	*Domestic Juggler*	Devoted and Nurturing. Food is a metaphor for familial love. She never eats Feeder (Fischer, 2000) Supermom (Robinson & Hunter, 2008)	*Breadwinner/ Nurturing Father*	Evolving role, from useless to engaged. Food is not always emotional engagement Evolving fathers (Marshall & Davis, 2014) Useless fathers (Gentry & Harrison, 2010)
Collective	*Yummy Goddess*	Seductive and Domestic. Food is her personal fulfilment and passion. She entertains the audience Dramatisation of domesticity (Hewer & Brownlie, 2009) Staging the glamour (Stevens, Cappellini & Smith, 2015)	*Domestic Divo*	A chef in the kitchen. Food is expertise. He advises and instructs the audience Blurring work and leisure (Brownlie & Hewer, 2007) Domestic Divo (Swenson, 2009)
Alone	*Hedonic Vamp*	Sexualised and Indulgent. Food is 'naughty but nice'. She undergoes a voyeuristic scrutiny Carnal femininity (Stevens & Maclaran, 2008) Sexual pleasure (Coleman, 2007) Madonna/Medusa (Brown, Stevens, Maclaran, 1999) Couple: temptress (Fischer, 2000)	*Wild Bachelor*	Careless and Intentional Food is a personal quest for pleasure. He doesn't compromise The Budweiser guy (Hirschman, 2016) Couple: Narcissistic male gaze (Schroeder & Zwick, 2004)

brands, such as Nigella Lawson and Jamie Oliver, given the intertextual reference between the world of entertainment media and advertising. Relevant articles from other disciplines have also been used to support the discussion.

The analysis considered three aspects related to the gender observed: collectives, practices and gaze. With the term collectives we identified if the main character of the advertisement was part of a group and what kind of group that was. The term practices refers to the actions and attitudes that scholars isolate in relation to gender. The gaze refers to the 'inscribed look' identified in the advertisements. Collectives, practices and gaze account for the relational nature of gender entailed in interaction as well as in the legitimisation granted by the other's look. As such, we believe that these three aspects should also be considered in any visual analysis aimed at identifying gender roles. The collectives we observed are three: the family, the character alone and in 'company' (which means the direct or suggested presence of other subjects in the picture). We identified six characters, here labelled according to their most prominent features. When portrayed with a family, women are *Domestic Jugglers*, when alone *Hedonic Vamp*, but in the kitchen cooking for others they become *Yummy Goddesses*. Men with their families range from *Breadwinners* to *Nurturing Fathers*, when in a kitchen they become *Domestic Divos* and alone they turn into *Wild Bachelors*. These characters are associated with defining practices that distinguish them from one another, such as eating or serving others, or failing to contribute to food-related activities. We suggest the use of the gaze as a further layer of analysis. While collectives can easily be detected in the studies we suggested, the gaze was made explicit only in some of them. As such, the discussion of gaze developed from the categories here presented is a provocative elaboration on the existing literature in order to keep refining the way we write and talk about gender. We now move on to outline each of the identified categories.

The Domestic Juggler

Domestic Juggler refers to a woman represented with her family, busy cooking, feeding the children, and setting the table for others. At the moment of eating, she is never the first to take a bite, as she holds a 'serving role' towards the other members of the family. The term Domestic Juggler has been previously used in relation to women's *juggling* lifestyle, defined as 'time-pressed' and 'emotionally demanding' (Thompson, 1996: 388). From a family perspective, Robinson and Hunter (2008) underline how 'mothers are more likely than fathers to be shown as buying, preparing, or serving food items' (p. 480). In her postmodern analysis, Fischer (2000), addressed how mothers are always judged as feeders of their own family, with this expectation so strong that mothering is implied whenever a caring action is portrayed, even if the other actor is absent.

The Yummy Goddess

Literature on advertising doesn't directly mention the woman who cooks for indistinct others, but in the world of Nigella Lawson, media, advertising and endorsement interlace enough to have the literature about her participating in this analysis. The Yummy Goddess cooks for others, inspired by her own pleasure and passion, reigning over a staged kitchen. Nigella embodies this model as the voluptuous mother who cooks while keeping her erotic charge, embodying glamour and vulnerability at the same time (Stevens, Cappellini, & Smith, 2015). Not only does she appeal to heterosexual male desire, but she owns her own desire – for food. Nigella is a culinary celebrity brand offering enchantment and seduction to both her male and female followers (Hewer & Brownlie, 2013), while making the kitchen spectacular in a new version of 'doing domesticity' (Hewer & Brownlie, 2009). She represents a privileged woman, whose glamour has survived motherhood and whose success is highly individualized.

The Hedonic Vamp

When describing hedonic consumption, Hirschmann and Holbrook (1982) meant 'those facets of consumer behaviour that relate to the multisensory, fantasy and emotive aspects of one's experience with products' (Hirschmann & Holbrook, 1982: 92). They suggested a clear demarcation from rationally driven consumption. Hedonic consumption is not based on 'what consumers know reality is but on what they would love reality to be' (Holbrook & Hirschmann, 1982: 94). This means that consumers engage with projective fantasies, fantasies that contribute to the consumption experience. Building upon hedonic consumption theory, Stevens & Maclaran (2008) have explored chocolate advertising, looking at what kind of femininity is associated with sweets. The authors isolated a femininity associated with body, temptation and (sexual) desire, that they defined as 'carnal'. Carnal femininity oscillates between the erotic, the carnivalesque and the pornographic, and it is linked to products, such as chocolate or body lotions, that promise pleasurable experiences. The consumption of these products is enjoyed as a private moment, even if the privacy is clearly fictional due to the voyeuristic male gaze implied in the advertisements. Portrayed through this gaze, Hedonic Vamps are overwhelmed by the enjoyment of food, as if surprised or seen in a private moment, letting desserts do that 'personal service' (Coleman, 2007: 175) they are advertised for. Thanks to the 'porn codes' (Stevens & Ostberg, 2011) used to represent these female characters, their appreciation for food recalls sexual pleasure, transforming the subject of the advertisement into a sexual object. However, Coleman (2007) points out that 'food is not always a metaphor for sex, but rather sometimes is depicted as being an erotic experience in and of itself' (p. 176). This discourse on female weakness enforces the 'naughty but nice' rhetoric (Stevens & Maclaran, 2008) of chocolate and sweet advertising. As emerging from the analysis of Coleman (2007) and Fisher (2000), the Hedonic Vamp keeps her attitude also when in a romantic couple.

The Breadwinner/Nurturing Father

This category represents men with their family, whose attitude towards domestic chores has evolved significantly since the second half of the last century (Marshall &

Davis, 2014; Stevens & Ostberg, 2011). The breadwinner is often portrayed with no emotional engagement in the domestic sphere in general and even less in the food one in particular (Gentry & Harrison, 2010). Illustrating the persistence of traditional gender roles, scholars have argued that fathers and children are consistently being waited on within television commercials and that 'the father baking cookies is literally 1 in 1000' (Kaufman, 1999: 456). Gradually, things are changing in food advertising; fathers are shown with feelings, as caring partners and as having 'softer' masculinities (Marshall & Davis, 2014). These nurturing fathers, however, embody this caring role with some compromises. Progressive masculinities are portrayed as fit, white and often middle class, the last bastion of dominant masculinity (Marshall & Davis, 2014). Caring 'Splenda daddies' show love and commitment but only outside the kitchen (Robinson & Hunter, 2008).

The Domestic Divo

Men are represented in the kitchen cooking for others, but when they do they tend to be celebrity endorsers or domestic maestros. The kitchen is appropriated by these chefs, who affirm a 'very masculine style of cooking' (Brownlie & Hewer, 2007: 247) that oscillates between male informality and rolled-up sleeves, hard-working masculinity. Marketing overlooks this category in terms of advertising, but Jamie Oliver's visual communication highlights some aspects of men cooking for others. In his media presentation, women are largely left out and the focus is on Jamie's cooking for 'others' or his camaraderie in the kitchen, through which he presents the rhetoric claim that:

> it may be necessary to reclaim this space, to render it inclusive, for the performance of new forms of masculine communion, dependency and intimacy. In this manner the kitchen and its traditional associations with domesticity, sociability, nurturing, nourishment and motherhood is visualised as somewhere masculine men can be at ease. (Brownlie & Hewer, 2007: 241)

The term 'Domestic Divo' was coined by Swenson (2009) to define male celebrities in the kitchen, where chefs are literally borrowed to show off, instruct and sometimes scold everyday women who are seen as lacking skills and ideas on what to cook.

Wild Bachelor

The last male figure is represented by a single man whose appetite cannot be satisfied in the domestic sphere. He is also 'the Budweiser guy', whose presence is largely detected in alcohol ads. These single men enjoy food or beverages as an expression of their own taste, and they have the right as well as the means to pursue their own narcissistic pleasure (Schroeder & Zwick, 2004). The Wild Bachelor is also the man whose appetites, including sensual ones, cannot be satisfied within the domestic environment and kinship. Outside the marketing literature, we find the Bachelor as the protagonist of burger advertising, marked by an untamed hunger for meat, unable to make do with small portions, displaying a primitive virility that needs to break loose from social (and feminine) constrictions (Buerkle, 2009). The self-appreciative gaze embedded in the Wild Bachelor portrays the same self-centred attitude even when the character is in a couple (Schroeder & Zwick, 2004).

DISCUSSION

This review mapped female and male characters emerging in interpretive research in food advertising. These sometimes show a transition within different gender models, in the case of the breadwinner slowly turning into a caring father. The point of this review is not to monitor what happens in the advertising industry but how the existing literature talks about it. Thus, attention should be paid not only to what is said but also to what is silenced. By concealing the conditions that make certain gender representations possible and plausible in advertising, and the context in which such representation take place, scholars run the risk of talking about gender as if it is a de-contextualized category. Another problematic aspect is the silence over the fact that advertising generally portrays white and middle-class characters, whose gender performances are then considered universal. Not only does this omission prevent any focus on the intersectionality among gender, class and ethnicity in emerging social identities, but it also obscures the avenues that the advertising industry is exploring in real life in representing different classes, ethnicities and genders. This consideration brings our attention to the relationship between the literature on advertising, the literature on practices and industry. In fact, we observed that the literature on advertising is mirroring the available scholarship around food and gender practices, even beyond the marketing field. What is missing from academic literature, though, is a closer look at which gender roles are actually used in today's advertising industry, especially those that defy the expected arrangements of gender or kinship. As a result, there is no update on how current adverts are trying to accommodate a plurality of gender identities and relations, from queer individuals to multi-racial families to single parents. We suggest three elements to be considered for an improved methodical analysis of gender performances: the collectives, the practices and the gaze. By applying them to the sample of existing scholarship, we aim to provide further elements on gender portrayals and how effective literature is in accounting for it.

Collectives

In the literature explored, the reproductive family is the ideal, if not the only possible collective to eat together. Collectivities help provide an understanding of the importance of their absence: family meals are the least common type of eating situation in food advertising broadcast to children (Roberts & Pettigrew, 2007). But families are not the only collective possible: friendship, co-housing, couples, co-workers are all collectives where people often consume food but that seems not to be registered in the literature. In particular, friends or housemates eating together, especially among female characters, has not been documented.

When talking about gender, the matter has often been assimilated to a two-sided coin, accounting only for the extreme polarities of the heterosexual spectrum, a spectrum where 'real men' don't cook (Parasecoli, 2005). This absence can be explained by the fact that few advertisements actually target non-normative domesticities and genders. In the articles here observed, gender is often portrayed as an essential quality, obscuring the visual clues and the gestures that define these genders in relation to others. The collective that surrounds the subject emerges as a condition of gender performativity: a woman can eat first only if alone, without a family and under the condition of becoming attractive to someone else. If with her family, a woman has only the model of the Domestic Juggler, who sacrifices her desires to satisfy her loved ones. If alone at home, that same woman can add a seductive twist to her domestic chores and become a Yummy Goddess, staging her passion for the benefit of others. Often well-groomed and put together, regardless their hectic lifestyle, the Domestic Jugglers – and to some extent the Yummy Goddesses – are offered as an ideal version to other women involved in the same multi-tasking effort.

Practices

When defining genders, few scholars take the time to isolate what elements distinguish a certain gender identity. While it is easy to notice how Domestic Jugglers never take the first bite when with their families, little mention is dedicated to any other practice she is recognisable for besides serving and attending to her family. Nevertheless, it would be useful to reinstate Goffman's (1979) dedication to details in visual analysis. This scrupulous account of practices and display would allow commentators to draw chronological comparisons in gender portrayals, but also help to determine what make certain characters so distinguishable. For instance, Gentry and Harrison (2010) describe the 'horse's ass' – the useless father at home – but they do not systematize the practices mentioned, nor account for what he actually does. The focus appears to be more on what he does not do: 'If it is his "turn" to cook meals for the family, they know what to expect, i.e. take-out, delivery, or drive-through (p. 88)'. Still, the articles studied call attention to certain patterns. First, on the micro-level, certain gestures mark the characters. The masculine smirk in front of a burger (Buerkle, 2009) is the same as that which graces the face of the male protagonist in the article by Schroeder and Zwick (2004), and appears equivalent to the expression that George Clooney sports in Nespresso advertising. If analysed on the macro-level, we can see how the same practices can lead to different gender roles across the collectives. A man cooking for his daughter embodies a markedly different masculinity than the chef who instructs an admiring audience. A lady spoon-feeding her man with seductive intentions (Fischer, 2000) appears to have little in common with the woman who feeds her husband by putting a plate on the table. Clearly, reporting the visual clues that substantiate a given practice (such as feeding) would help to better characterize genders.

Gaze

The literature openly acknowledges the gaze only concerning the Hedonic Vamp and the Wild Bachelor, highlighting how the predominantly male gaze positions them in the heteronormative spectrum. The systematic use of gaze in visual analysis can be used to reveal the relations embedded in advertising images. In fact, few of the articles selected mentioned the gaze, this has often been inferred from the articles rather than articulated in them. The focus on gaze is motivated by a feminist agenda that explores what conditions make certain representations possible, and what power relations are presented to the viewer. Instead of gaze, literature tends to focus on the audience, gaze does not overlap with the expected audience nor with the look. The gaze does not overlap with the audience because it is constitutive of the image, not of its interpretation. Keeping the male gaze as an example, Kaplan (1983) claimed that the look is not essentially male, 'but to own and activate the gaze, given our language and the structure of the consciousness, is to be in the "masculine" position' (p. 13). That is why the male gaze can be activated even in female-targeted images, and offered as a pre-determined form of interpretation of the image that the audience is invited to adopt. As such, the gaze can be redeployed by the audience, who might end up resisting this pre-conceived interpretation. Research shows that consumers do not associate with the assumed gaze when faced with a representation that does not mirror their cultural and day-to-day experience of consumption (Borgerson et al., 2006; Stevens et al., 2003).

The regulatory power of the male gaze is clear in romantic portrayals: when in a couple, the characters show the same gender traits of their gender of single – or 'alone' – characters (Fischer, 2000; Schroeder & Zwick, 2004). This could be justified in two ways. The first is that, in the game of seduction, genders are represented before the moment of giving in to the other, and therefore are still single. The second is that the gaze detected is consistently male: she is always a temptress and he is always a predator because they are inscribed in the image by the same power relations and expectations that define the Hedonic Vamp and the Wild Bachelor. However, the male gaze is not the only one present. The Domestic Juggler implies a feminine gaze that confers a normative power to this character: the model offered is already aligned with a social order that prescribes what a good mother should be, and that is enforced by other women's surveillance. Other categories are at the centre of multiple gazes, such as the Yummy Goddess. Because of the entertainment world she belongs to, the Yummy Goddess is tailored for heterosexual desire, but at the same time she is showing her glamour and confidence to women who enact their 'homey self' (Cronin et al., 2014). Along the same lines, the Domestic Divo embodies a male gaze that grants him a 'recognizable masculinity' (Hollows, 2003), but his status as 'unofficial expert' implicitly demands the legitimization of more gazes, such as the 'foodie'.

While some gazes are obvious, others are difficult to detect, as if the image was built upon a strategic ambiguity. An example is the familial gaze, which allows people to read their own family members into the portrayal, but also to identify with family practices more broadly (Morgan, 2011). In light of changes in domesticities, such as the presence of egalitarian ideologies if not practices (Miller, 2012) ambiguity is a way to account for and include different family and gender arrangements without openly representing them (Robinson & Hunter, 2008; Roseneil & Budgeon, 2004; Weeks, 2009). At a time when a family eating together is not speaking to consumers the same way it used to, ambiguity is a transitional strategy that demands no subversion of traditional gender roles. Thus, ambiguous gazes accommodate more inclusive readings of the advertising image. However, keeping an analytical focus on gaze allows us to monitor if and how gender clues are changing, alone or in collectives. An example would be to see how the familial gaze is adapted to a proliferation of different family arrangements, considering that the visual clues for family can be highly subjective (Borgerson et al., 2006).

Finally, we should remember that gazes not only differ according to gender, but also in terms of class, desires, experiences, ethnicity and family roles. For instance, the well-off Yummy Goddess appears to invoke a complicit middle-class gaze. However, not all of the gazes are equally represented. Advertising is a genre of perfection, where flawed or problematic portrayals rarely appear unless normalized and perfected, and where 'some identities are systematically excluded from marketing images, while others are represented in ethically problematic ways' (Schroeder & Borgerson, 2005: 585). Since minorities in terms of class, gender and ethnicity are not only excluded from representation but by implication less likely to be consumers of advertising, it should not be surprising that certain gazes – such as queer ones – are not explicitly considered in the advertising literature.

CONCLUSION

When seeking to understand contemporary consumer culture, the way in which advertising represents social identities and social practices remain important areas to consider. This chapter has focused on what is said and what is left unsaid within scholarship about gender representations in food advertising. Through the identification of gendered characters, we wanted to highlight how gender stereotypes are re-produced via images. However, gender representations are not only about consolidated stereotypes, but also concern the evolving visual clues that are used to signal masculinities or femininities, and specific practices and values attached to different gender roles.

The evolution of visual clues has also brought out a certain ambiguity, justified by the effort of the industry to accommodate consumers' experiences without overturning or expanding the fixed roles of the characters here presented. In other words, ambiguous representations broaden their possible interpretations – therefore appearing more in tune with current gendered debates – while keeping conservative elements.

We argue that analysing the practices that make gender types recognizable and engaging more explicitly with the gaze offers more possibilities for countering stereotyping and blind-spots in the advertising industry as well as in academic debates. At the same time, the invitation to focus on interactions instead of normative structures (family/couple) would allow research to grasp how the advertising industry is adapting to the current changes in food practices and domesticities.

REFERENCES

Adams, C.J. (1990) *The Sexual Politics of Meat: A Feminist-Vegetarian Critical Theory*. New York, Continuum.

Alcoff, L.M. (1999) Towards a phenomenology of racial embodiment. *Radical Philosophy*. 95(May/June): 15–26.

Belk, R. & Costa, J. (1998) 'Chocolate delights: Gender and consumer indulgence', in Eileen Fischer & Daniel L. Wardlow (eds), *Proceedings of the Conference on Gender, Marketing and Consumer Behavior*. San Francisco, Association for Consumer Research. pp. 179–193.

Borgerson, J.L. & Schroeder, J.E. (2002) Ethical issues of global marketing: Avoiding bad faith in visual representation. *European Journal of Marketing*, 36(5/6): 570–594.

Borgerson, J.L., Schroeder, J.E., Blomberg, B. & Thorssén, E. (2006) The gay family in the ad: Consumer responses to non-traditional families in marketing communications. *Journal of Marketing Management*, 22(9–10): 955–978.

Brown, S., Stevens, L. & Maclaran, P. (1999) I can't believe it's not Bakhtin! Literary theory, postmodern advertising, and the gender agenda. *Journal of Advertising*, 28(1): 11–24.

Brownlie, D. & Hewer, P. (2007) Prime beef cuts: Culinary images for thinking 'men'. *Consumption, Markets and Culture*, 10(3): 229–250.

Buerkle, C.W. (2009) Metrosexuality can stuff it: Beef consumption as (heteromasculine) fortification. *Text and Performance Quarterly*, 29(1): 77–93.

Butler, J. (1990) *Gender Trouble: Feminism and The Subversion of Identity*. London, Routledge.

Butler, J. (2004) *Undoing Gender*. New York, Routledge.

Cairns, K., Johnston, J. & Baumann, S. (2010) Caring about food: Doing gender in the foodie kitchen. *Gender and Society*, 24(5): 591–615.

Calamita, F. (2014) Voracious dolls and competent chefs: Negotiating femininities and masculinities in Italian food advertisements of the 1990s–2010s. *Gender/Sexuality/Italy*, 1: 10–13.

Cappellini, B. & Parsons, E. (2012) 'Sharing the meal: Food consumption and family identity', in Russell W. Belk, Søren Askegaars & Linda Scott (eds), *Research in Consumer Behavior. Volume 14*. Bingley: Emerald Group Publishing Limited. pp. 109–128.

Cappellini, B., Marilli, A. & Parsons, E. (2014) The hidden work of coping: Gender and the micro-politics of household consumption in times of austerity. *Journal of Marketing Management*, 30(15–16): 1597–1624.

Carrington, C. (2013) 'Feeding lesbigay families', in Carole Counihan & Penny Van Esterik (eds), *Food and Culture: A Reader*, 3rd edition. New York, Routledge. pp. 187–210.

Coleman, C. (2007) 'Dessert: Heavenly or sinful? Consumption, carnality and spirituality in food advertising', in Stefania Borghini, MaryAnn McGrath & Cele Otnes (eds), *European Advances in Consumer Research*. Duluth, Association for Consumer Research. pp. 245–250.

Cronin, J.M., McCarthy, M.B., Newcombe, M.A. & McCarthy, S.N. (2014) Paradox, performance and food: Managing difference in the construction of femininity. *Consumption Markets & Culture*, 17(4): 367–391.

Cudworth, E. (2008) Most farmers prefer blondes: The dynamic of anthroparchy in animals' becoming meat. *Journal for Critical Animal Studies*, 6(1): 32–45.

Deutsch, J. (2005) 'Please pass the chicken tits': Rethinking men and cooking at an urban firehouse. *Food and Foodways*, 13(1–2): 91–114.

DeVault, M. (1991) *Feeding the Family: The Social Construction of Caring as Gendered Work*. Chicago, University of Chicago Press.

Fischer, E. (2000) 'Consuming contemporaneous discourses: A postmodern analysis of food advertisements targeted toward women', in J. Stephen Hoch & J. Robert Meyer (eds), *Advances in Consumer Research*. Provo, Association for Consumer Research. pp. 288–294.

Gentry, J. & Harrison, R. (2010) Is advertising a barrier to male movement toward gender change? *Marketing Theory*, 10(1): 74–96.

Goffman, E. (1979) *Gender Advertisements*. New York, Harper & Row.

Hewer, P. & Brownlie, D. (2009) 'Culinary culture, gastrobrands and identity myths: "Nigella", an iconic brand in the baking', in Ann McGill & Sharon Shavitt (eds), *Advances in Consumer Research*. Duluth, Association for Consumer Research. pp. 482–487.

Hewer, P. & Brownlie, D. (2013) Spaces of hope, enlivenment and entanglement: Explorations in the spatial logic of celebrity culinary brands. *Journal of Consumer Culture*, 13(1): 46–63.

Hirschman, E.C. & Holbrook, M.B. (1982) Hedonic consumption: Emerging concepts, methods and propositions. *Journal of Marketing*, 46(3): 92–101.

Hirschman, E.C. (2016) *Branding Masculinity: Tracing the Cultural Foundations of Brand Meaning*. London, Routledge.

Hollows, J. (2003) Oliver's twist: Leisure, labour and domestic masculinity in the naked chef. *International Journal of Cultural Studies*, 6(2): 229–248.

Irvine, B. (2015) Vegetarian masculinities: How discourses of normative masculinities are challenged and (re)produced through food consumption. *The New Birmingham Review*, 1(2): 33–63.

James, A. (1990) The good, the bad and the delicious: The role of confectionery in British society. *The Sociological Review*, 38(4): 666–688.

Kaplan, A.E. (1983) *Women and Film: Both Sides of the Camera*. New York, Methuen.

Kaufman, G. (1999) The portrayal of men's family roles in television commercials. *Sex Roles*, 41(5–6): 439–458.

Lewis, R. (1997) Looking good: The lesbian gaze and fashion imagery. *Feminist Review*, 55: 92–109.

Littler, J. (2013) The rise of the 'Yummy Mummy': Popular conservatism and the neoliberal maternal in contemporary British culture. *Communication, Culture & Critique*, 6(2): 227–243.

Lupton, D. (1996) *Food, the Body, and the Self*. London, Sage.

Marshall, D. & Davis, T. (2014) From overt provider to invisible presence: Discursive shifts in advertising portrayals of the father in Good Housekeeping, 1950–2010. *Journal of Marketing Management*, 30(15–16): 1654–1679.

Miller, T. (2012) Balancing caring and paid work in the UK: narrating 'choices' as first-time parents. *International Review of Sociology*, 22(1): 39–52.

Mintz, S.W. (1985) Sweetness and Power: The Place of Sugar in Modern History. New York, Viking.

Moisio, R., Arnould, E.J. & Price, L.L. (2004) Between mothers and markets: Constructing family identity through homemade food. *Journal of Consumer Culture*, 4(3): 361–384.

Morgan, D.H.J. (2011) *Rethinking Family Practices*. Basingstoke, Palgrave Macmillan.

Mulvey, L. (2009) *Visual and Other Pleasures*, 2nd edn. Basingstoke, Palgrave Macmillan.

Neuman, N., Gottzén, L. & Fjellström, C. (2017) Narratives of progress: Cooking and gender equality among Swedish men. *Journal of Gender Studies*, 26(2): 151–163.
Newcombe, M.A., McCarthy, M.B., Cronin, J.M. & McCarthy, S.N. (2012) 'Eat like a man': A social constructionist analysis of the role of food in men's lives. *Appetite*, 59(2): 391–398.
Parasecoli, F. (2005) Feeding hard bodies: Food and masculinities in men's fitness magazines. *Food and Foodways*, 13(1–2): 13–37.
Patterson, M. & Elliott, R. (2002) Negotiating masculinities: Advertising and the inversion of the male gaze. *Consumption, Markets & Culture*, 5(3), 231–249.
Potts, A. & Parry, J. (2010) Vegan sexuality: Challenging heteronormative masculinity through meat-free sex. *Feminism & Psychology*, 20(1): 53–72.
Roberts, M. & Pettigrew, S. (2007) A thematic content analysis of children's food advertising. *International Journal of Advertising*, 26(3): 357–367.
Robinson, B.K. & Hunter, E. (2008) Is mom still doing it all? Reexamining depictions of family work in popular advertising. *Journal of Family Issues*, 29(4): 465–486.
Rose, G. (2012) *Visual Methodologies: An Introduction to Researching with Visual Materials*. London, Sage.
Roseneil, S. & Budgeon, S. (2004) Cultures of intimacy and care beyond 'the family': Personal life and social change in the early 21st century. *Current Sociology*, 52(2): 135–159.
Sassatelli, R., Santoro, M. & Semi, G. (2015) *Fronteggiare la Crisi*. Bologna, Il Mulino.
Schroeder, J.E. & Borgerson, J.L (1998) Marketing images of gender: A visual analysis. *Consumption Markets & Culture,* 2(2): 161–201.
Schroeder, J.E. (2002) *Visual Consumption*. London, Routledge.
Schroeder, J.E. & Borgerson, J.L. (2005) An ethics of representation for international marketing communication. *International Marketing Review*. 22(5): 578–600.
Schroeder, J.E. & Zwick, D. (2004) Mirrors of masculinity: Representation and identity in advertising images. *Consumption Markets & Culture*, 7(1): 21–52.
Scott, J.W. (1986) Gender: A useful category of historical analysis. *The American Historical Review*, 91(5): 1053–1075.
Sellaeg, K. & Chapman, G.E. (2008) Masculinity and food ideals of men who live alone. *Appetite*, 51(1): 120–128.
Sobal, J. (2005) Men, meat, and marriage: Models of masculinity. *Food and Foodways*, 13(1–2): 135–158.
Stevens, L., Cappellini, B. & Smith, G. (2015) Nigellissima: A study of glamour, performativity and embodiment. *Journal of Marketing Management,* 31(5–6): 577–598.
Stevens, L. & Maclaran, P. (2008) 'The carnal feminine: Womanhood, advertising and consumption', in S. Borghini, M.A. McGrath & C. Otnes (eds), *European Advances in Consumer Research*. Duluth, Association for Consumer Research. pp. 169–174.
Stevens, L. & Ostberg, J. (2011) 'Gendered bodies: Representations of femininity and masculinity in advertising practices', in L. Peñaloza, N. Toulouse & L.M. Visconti (eds), *Marketing Management: A Cultural Perspective*. London, Routledge. pp. 392–407.
Stevens, L., Maclaran, P. & Brown, S. (2003) 'Red time is me time': Advertising, ambivalence and women's magazine. *Journal of Advertising*, 32(1): 35–45.
Swenson, R. (2009) Domestic Divo? Televised treatments of masculinity, femininity and food. *Critical Studies in Media Communication*, 26(1): 36–53.
Szabo, M. (2013) Men nurturing through food: Challenging gender dichotomies around domestic cooking. *Journal of Gender Studies*, 23(1): 18–31.
Thompson, C.J. (1996) Caring consumers: Gendered consumption meanings and the juggling lifestyle. *Journal of Consumer Research*, 22(4): 388–407.

Weeks, J. (2009) The remaking of erotic and intimate life. *Política y Sociedad*, 46(1): 13–25.

West, C. & Zimmerman, D. (1987) Doing gender. *Gender and Society,* 1(2): 125–151.

Woolgar, S. (1988) *Knowledge and Reflexivity: New Frontiers in the Sociology of Knowledge*. London, Sage.

19

Biopolitical Marketing and Technologies of Enclosure

Detlev Zwick and Janice Denegri-Knott

INTRODUCTION

Recently, there has been a lot of talk about consumer empowerment through new information and communication technologies. Corporate captains of marketing, Wired Magazine's neolibertarian techno-utopians, marketing consultants of the digital economy and many marketing academics agree that we all have more choices, more information, more entertainment, more transparency, and lower prices thanks to Amazon, Facebook, YouTube, and all the rest. We are liberated from the burdens of material ownership, free to access digital objects and services in ways that satisfy our needs in highly targeted and efficient ways. The empowerment through technology chorus is so loud and cohesive that we generally take the message for granted. And in some limited respect, consumers may feel empowered when shopping on Amazon.com or in the malls with their iPhones on hand. But let us be very clear about the idea of empowerment that is promoted by the cheerleaders of what Jodi Dean (2005) calls communicative capitalism. Real empowerment, so much should be clear, will never be 'granted' to consumers by those in economic (and thus political) power. In the final analysis – and putting aside for a moment the fact that even empowered consumers are still interpellated first and foremost as subjects of consumption – the ideal of the empowered consumer (rational, enlightened, informed, restrained, un-manipulable) is completely antithetical to the needs of capital and the marketing regime within consumer capitalism. Therefore, any call for actual consumer empowerment would automatically be a radical demand and an insurgent claim aimed at undermining and replacing capital's power to dominate the consumer totally. In the end, it is important to recognize that any technology employed by marketing today becomes a technology of enclosure (even if never completely successful), which permits empowerment only in a version sanction by capital. That is why marketing (and capital more generally [see Lazzarato, 2004]) today is biopolitical. It wants to govern life completely while appearing to not govern at all.

In this chapter we argue that new technologies in contemporary marketing management are best thought of as technologies of enclosure. On the one hand, marketing encloses the subject as an individualized and individuated consumer. On the other, marketing aims to enclose (i.e. capture, make proprietary, appropriate) what is common or collectively produced or cherished by individuals as inalienable expressions of personal identity and agency. At the same time that marketing encloses, it operates ideologically, although not in the classical Marxist sense of creating a false consciousness. Rather, the challenge for marketers is to enclose and capture the subject and the common while appearing not to do any of these things. By accepting as non-ideological terms such as choice, identity, fulfillment, empowerment, enrichment, collaboration, creativity and so on, marketers and consumers alike choose to believe, just as anyone sensible would believe, that new techniques and technologies of enclosure are really just good marketing practice aimed at value creation and delivery, not customer domination and exploitation.

We should remember that an atmosphere of distrust has accompanied the development of marketing from the beginning and marketers have long been suspected of being professional manipulators, devising salacious techniques and technologies with which to incite, manipulate and exploit consumer desire and anxiety. As Packard put it fifty years ago, '[T]hese depth manipulators are in their operations beneath the surface of conscious life, starting to acquire a power of persuasion that is becoming a matter of justifiable public scrutiny and concern' (1957, pp. 9–10). More recent popular indictments of marketing include Adam Curtis's documentaries on *The Century of the Self*, Naomi Klein's *No Logo* (2000), and the BBC series *The Men Who Made Us Spend* (presented by Jacques Peretti).

Criticism of marketers is compounded by widespread consumer cynicism regarding the genuineness of marketing messages (see Gabriel and Lang, 1995). Interestingly, the emerging generation of online marketers – typically referred to as digital or social media marketers – see marketing's crisis of legitimacy as directly tied to what it considers the corporate, top-down marketing methods devised in the 1970s and 1980s and designed to discipline and control consumers. For a new generation of tech-savvy marketers, imbued with a solid dose of techno-libertarian ideals of independence and a frontier mentality that rejects top-down authority and bureaucracy in favor of self-organizing systems, radical autonomy and freely collaborative networks, a dramatic shift in mindset was needed in the age of participatory media and Big Data. In a radical turn propagated, for example, by prominent social media marketing experts like Solis (2010) and Stratten (2010), marketing has to be 'un'-done. The term 'un-marketing' rises to prominence in the consulting literature and offers a reframing of marketing that rejects corporate-controlled top-down techniques, and favors horizontal, collaborative and participatory customer engagement (Kutcher in Solis, 2010; Stratten, 2010, 2014). In this context, the idea of online customer communities gains popularity because it provides a fantasy of restructuring marketplace relations according to principles of co-creation, sovereignty, equality and sharing. More recently, what we call Big Data marketing is framed according to similar registers where data magnetizes consumers and marketers to a shared ethos of the 'opt-in' economy (Godin, 1999). Big Data marketers – at least in the version propagated by Google's Hal Varian, for example – pose innocuously enough as personal recommendation and consulting agents for consumers who in return for giving up personal information receive ever more relevant, valuable and desired information, goods and services (Zuboff, 2015). Who would not like such a deal that appears to be based on liberal ideals of good intentions on all sides and the equal distribution of costs and benefits, even as companies manage communities and customer data not on behalf of consumers but on behalf of corporate profit.

In sum, new marketing technologies – from blogs to communities to surveillance-based collaborative filtering and recommender systems – no matter how invasive, ever-present and insidious, have been framed by technology-driven marketers as democratizing and equalizing forces reshaping the contemporary marketplace in favor of the consumer. Customer and brand communities are happy places of collaboration and collective value creation governed by an ethos of mutual respect, sharing and dispersed control. Big Data Marketing, which aspires to intensify consumer surveillance and control (Zuboff, 2015), is often presented as part of the contemporary ethos of collaborative 'in-this-together-ness' and collective support structures between companies and consumers. Marketers are asked to employ Big Data to better understand, assist, support and connect with customers; the technology magnetizing both exchange parties to a fantasy of better products, better choices, better experiences, better prices, better service and generally happier lives. To live in a world where companies strain to innovate and please consumers, all we need to do in return is give companies complete access to our personal information. Such a request makes sense to a generation of marketing professionals and consumers who have grown up with Google, Facebook and Amazon tracking their every move.

In the next section we explore critically new marketing technologies such as online customer communities and Big Data, and possession of digital objects as consumer lock in. We suggest that these technologies are technologies of biopolitical marketing. They aspire to enclose all forms of life for profit. We suggest that marketing innovation is now structured according to the imperative of biopolitical marketing: the making, valorizing and enclosing of all forms and expressions of life.

ONLINE COMMUNITY MARKETING

We should have no illusions about the new marketers of the social media age, what meme hustler Tim O'Reilly (Morozov, 2013) has termed Web 2.0. As these 'un-marketers' replace the disciplinary technologies of marketing with technologies of communitarian self-governance, two-way communication and collaboration, new contradictions emerge characteristic of communicative capitalism. Specifically, even a community of autonomous, creative, collaborative and networked participants must be commercially exploited – this is, after all, still marketing's *raison d'être*. Social media marketers understand this practical challenge of commodifying communicatively structured social relations that do not want to be commodified. Or, to put it another way, marketers must enclose the space where production of reproduction of the common takes place (Cvijanovic, Vercellone and Fumagalli, 2010; Hardt and Negri, 2009). The trick is to privatize without disrupting what Dyer-Witheford (2009) calls the circuit of the common, where collectives or associations of people 'organise shared, common resources including creativity, machinery and resources into productive ensembles that create more commons which in turn provide the basis for new associations'.

Mastering the paradox of on the one hand enabling, and enabling sharing of, human creativity and cognitive production owned by no one, and on the other exploiting the work of the many for the benefit of the few requires the 'correct marketing mind-set'. Internet marketing consultant Tamar Weinberg (2009, pp. 52–53) articulates this tension in unmistakable terms:

> Later, your 'ulterior motive' can be communicated (just as long as you continue giving back to the community and its members look up to you as a respected contributor), but it's more important to establish yourself as a reputable member who wants to give back to the community first. Once you do, you can begin to take, as long as the community is receptive and wants to know more about you as a community participant, but you should always keep giving.

There is something revealing about the frantic back and forth between the double exhortation to keep giving and making sure to 'take'. The new technologies of marketing render give-and-take immediate and necessary. Weinberg understands that marketing must take, but that it must do so without appearing to take (by also giving back). There is no cynicism or element of conscious deception at work when new marketers talk about the riches to be found in the common spaces of the wild Web 2.0. Rather, marketers of the digital age really do believe that when the new commons of communicative capitalism produce creative and cognitive value it belongs to them as much as to anyone else. To extract communicative surplus value from the community, marketers must adopt a 'commun-ist sensibility' (Zwick and Bradshaw, 2016). As actor-cum-social media consultant Ashton Kutcher puts it (Solis, 2010, p. ix):

> The roles are reversing and individuals and brands have the ability to reach and rouse powerful and dedicated communities without ever having to pay for advertising. I'm just part of a bigger movement of empowering the people who care enough to change the world. Social media is socializing causes and purpose and inciting nothing short of a revolution.

At the heart of this utopian conception of communal marketing is the idea of a perfect communion with consumers based on a sincere belief that 'we all want the same thing'. From this vantage point, appropriating for corporate profit the affective, communicative and cognitive work of communities is entirely justified, if not required if marketers are to hold up their end of the bargain and deliver all the good things they promise in return for this appropriation.

A neo-libertarian impulse defines the enthusiasm of Kutcher, Solis and others (see e.g. Rubel in Miller, 2008; Downes and Mui, 2000). Consumer community marketing is imagined as the logical extension of the cyber-utopian project in which horizontality, anti-authority, and bottom-up power facilitate entrepreneurialism, value creation, and innovation. Representative of the neo-libertarian narrative is Kevin Kelly's (2009) enthusiastic announcement of the arrival of a 'global collectivist society', which, he argued, amounts to a 'New Socialism'. This socialism is 'not class warfare. It is not anti-American; indeed digital socialism may be the newest American innovation'. The irony is that the revolutionary socialism envisioned by Kelly propagates both self-organising and entrepreneurial commons and successful privatization of the common.

Within the communal ethos of digital socialism, marketing transforms into the enactment of consensual partnership with consumers who are no longer controlled but invited by the corporation as equals in the joint task of co-creation. Hence, practices that control consumers, or absorb them into centralized, technocratic, and rationalized structures appear crude, abusive and anachronistic. Instead, under conditions of communicative capitalism, marketing must try to enclose the multitude while maintaining the conditions under which the multitude labors cognitively and creatively (see e.g. Fournier and Lee, 2009; Schau, et al., 2009; Weinberg, 2009). For O'Dwyer, this perspective imagines the web as a 'virtual communism'; an 'immaterial space that trades in knowledge and culture, at once free from commercial subjugation and conversely capable of exerting influence on the material substrate of capital' (O'Dwyer, 2013, p. 498).

Hence the communism of Web 2.0, as described by Kleiner and Wyrick (2007), is one where companies retain ownership of content, while opening up a method of content creation. The popular narrative of Web 2.0 as a democratizing force that brings emancipatory empowerment occludes how, as Stallabrass (2012) relates, peer-to-peer systems had previously allowed users to control the frame as well as the content. Therefore, Web 2.0 is an enclosure of a commons and not the other way around. It is in this context that capital wants to harness this commonist ethos in what are in effect privatized spheres (see also Arvidsson and Peitersen, 2013; Beverungen et al., 2013).

The tension that arises from marketers' pursuit of new modes of commodification versus the multitude's productive value that depends on remaining untouched by the institutional logic of marketing becomes acutely visible in the context of participatory media. Social media marketers like Solis and Weinberg warn that the productive anarchy of the crowd is a statement *against* institutions, discipline and commercial enclosure. These authors announce that exciting new online activities such as prosumption, peer collaboration, co-creation and crowd sourcing clearly show that consumers do not need – and likely do not want – marketers in the picture. Enclosure of the commons for the benefit of the firm therefore requires marketing techniques and technologies that recruit consumers into value production in a way that appears voluntary and free. Resolving this contradiction becomes the challenge and, in their search for innovative ways of commodifying the crowd without antagonism, marketers turn towards customer communities.

BIG DATA MARKETING

The customer community is just one example of a technological innovation that is motivated by, consciously or not, resolving this contradiction of marketing under communicative capitalism. Database-driven marketing, or what we call here Big Data marketing, represents another such technology. The challenge of studying Big Data marketing from a cultural and critical theory perspective is to move beyond the immediate urge to focus on the technology's intensification of consumer surveillance and control (e.g. Zuboff, 2015) and instead recognize that Big Data is fundamentally motivated and sustained by its ability to generate and enclose value immanent to consumer life. Thus, while very different in technique and operation, Big Data marketing shares with community marketing that it is a technology of biopolitical marketing.

Business sociologist Shoshana Zuboff (2015) suggests the term surveillance capitalism to describe what she calls the logic of creating, collecting, manipulating and, most importantly, valorizing information. She argues, as indeed others have before (e.g. Arvidsson, 2005; Lury, 2004; Zwick and Denegri-Knott, 2009), that today the goal of many technology companies – in fact, increasingly any company because there is a sense that all companies are becoming technology, or at least information companies – is not to produce products or services based on some identified customer need. Instead, companies aim to build what we could call platforms of co-production where consumers do things they want to do, and for that privilege they either have to pay the platform provider a fee or they have to pay in other ways (micro transaction, eyeballs/data that can be resold, etc.). If the business model is based on information value, the goal is to capture as much information about the users of the platform as possible and then find ways to repackage and commodify this information for a buyer.

The hope is that the greater the amount of data that can be collected and analyzed the more money can be made. This is one reason why data-monitoring technologies are so widespread and continue to spread. Taking Google's chief economist Hal Varian's exposition of Google's business model, Zuboff develops the notion of surveillance (or Google) capitalism. Varian characterizes Google's business vision as founded on four pillars, the first one speaks directly to the idea of Big Data: 'More data extraction and analysis'. Varian explains how most of the data today is generated via computer-mediated interactions and how all our interactions with machines are recorded and logged for possible mining and analysis. In addition, there is the data generated by the Internet of everything. Finally, governments and other noncommercial bureaucratic agencies and groups collect and store data, which is linked to the Internet and can be used for analysis.

Zuboff is correct to point out, as others have before (e.g. Fuchs, 2010, 2012; Juergenson, 2010), that data generation, collection and use is based on asymmetrical power relations. Google owns us and our future a lot more than we own Google and its future (Lanier, 2013). The common response by commentators and analysts such as Zuboff to Google's 'More data extraction and analysis' doctrine is to focus on Google's desire for a totally knowable and known world of people, markets, goods and services and their flows. From this perspective, Big Data becomes a matter of privacy invasion, universal surveillance and neoliberal forms of government. However, from the perspective of biopolitical marketing we recognize that Big Data becomes a technique of capture, appropriation and enclosure. Surveillance capitalism is thus not so much the end of privacy as another expression of marketing's desire to appropriate value from consumers without antagonizing them. The surveillance infrastructure is after all rather passive and the process of marketing based on Big Data not always very obvious or intrusive. However, Big Data desires to not only know reality but shape it. It is this aspect of Big Data marketing that makes it biopolitical and therefore so much more problematic than the analytical registers of privacy and surveillance suggest.

On this point, Zuboff's analysis of surveillance capitalism is instructive because Zuboff sees in the continuous experimental marketing interventions the potential for what she calls reality mining (see also Zwick and Denegri-Knott, 2009). The idea behind reality mining is that with experimentation, researchers, businesses and what she somewhat vaguely calls the technological infrastructure can capture what people do at all times but also alter behavior, then capture again, then alter again and recapture and so on. What is real and what is the outcome of real-time techno-cybernetic manipulation becomes indistinguishable (see also Elmer, 2004). It is through this recursive process that marketing aims to constitute not merely consumer subjects and identities but entire modes of being, or as Lazzarato (2004) puts it, entire worlds of capital-life.

DIGITAL POSSESSIONS AND CONSUMER ENCLOSURE

Marketing technologies of enclosure have morphed into lock-in systems that *both* valorize and operate through consumers' psychic and financial investment in transforming digital objects into personally meaningful possessions. Within these digital enclosures, consumers' own attempts to incorporate homogenous digital commodities into the domain of private possession end up facilitating their own entrapment (Molesworth, Watkins and Denegri-Knott, 2016). This enclosure also has the potential to amputate consumers from their digital possessions in ways that reduce a digital object's social utility and capacity to help develop and express personal identity. This mutation in technologies of enclosure not only diminishes the public domain, as already noted (see Benkler, 2000; Lessig, 1999), but also undermines the liberal ideals legitimizing enclosing technologies themselves (see Denegri-Knott and Tadajewski, 2010, 2016). Both classical libertarianism and neo-libertarianism promote the idea that private goods are closely linked to our individuality in that the sense of control and privacy afforded by them allow us to develop and embody our personality as acts of self-actualization and will (Hegel, 1821 in Gauss, 2012; Demsetz, 1967; Munzer, 1990; Snare, 1972). It follows that it is only fair that those who invest themselves in transforming an object should have ownership rights over it (Demsetz, 1967; Munzer, 1990; Snare, 1972). However, the right to full private property, central to the neo-libertarian project legitimating high-tech companies' rights to benefit from their investments in the digital economies, is denied to consumers. Full property rights are often cited as paramount in conferring objects with an important role in helping people develop a sense of self and establishing and strengthening alliances between them. Hence, technologies of enclosure fence in both public and private domains.

As a project of enclosure, these technologies operate by erecting proprietary walls around what consumers deem as their digital possessions. In doing so, they erode rights safeguarded by private ownership. Outright, total ownership, understood as exclusive rights to use, possess, exploit, manage, profit from and power to exclude, transfer, abandon and destroy (Snare, 1972), it is claimed, is redundant within the context of digital consumption. Digital objects are complex entities that generally include code, software, hardware, Internet infrastructures and end user license agreements (EULAs) in order to be enacted and experienced as targets of consumption activity (Molesworth and Watkins, 2014; Watkins et al., 2016). Digital objects, like our e-books, playlists, social media posts, our Instagram pictures and video game purchases and prizes, in their material lightness are celebrated as both needs-satisfying and needs-liberating. Provided they are readily accessible they are likely candidates for communal sharing (Belk, 2013a, 2013b; Bardhi and Eckhardt, 2012; Bardhi et al., 2012) and short-term access, as well as good exemplars of liquid possessions – malleable and vaporous enough to fulfil consumers' functional and situational needs to suit shifting identity projects (Bardhi et al., 2012) without the obligations and responsibilities associated with ownership (Bardhi et al., 2012; Rifkin, 2000). As Rifkin (2000) notes, in a digitized, hyper-speed network economy, ownership of physical capital 'becomes increasingly marginal', and access a primary source of value for both access providers and their users. Ownership again, is seen by Rifkin (2002) as too cumbersome and slow to keep up with the speed of delivery offered by Internet-enabled platforms; instead of being burdened by ownership it pays to 'be always connected to a steady stream of just in time experiences'.

For these *just in time* experiences 'to pay' consumers need to 'pay' to access their digital objects. Digital objects are in effect rented rather than fully owned, because they require continuous investment of time, money and other resources in order to be accessed. Even pay-per-download digital objects once saved onto a password-protected account, like iTunes or Amazon's Kindle, become entangled with a firm's proprietary system, limiting consumers' ability to transfer accumulated objects to a friend or family member (Denegri-Knott, 2015; Watkins et al., 2016). There are even lingering attachments between firms and consumers in situations where payment is not required. For example, though there is no direct monetary exchange between consumers and Facebook, Wordpress or YouTube, possession can be interrupted; digital objects may become lost or corrupted at any time. And here lies the paradox. Access is marketed as providing exactly what it denies: access. Note for example how subscription-based services like Spotify are marketed on the premise that there are 'No More Limits' (Spotify News, 2014), or Amazon Kindle's 'Bought Once, Read Everywhere' (Wired, 2011) promise. Areas of access themselves are branded as 'my areas'; the music you curate with Spotify as a freemium customer is accessed in a menu entitled 'your music'. Bloggers and vlogers have 'their areas', 'their posts', 'their content'. The language of enclosure is nurturing and reassuring. It is the language of freedom and empowerment. It invites consumers to engage with digital objects as if they were theirs.

Reference to Igor Kopytoff's (1986) influential work on commodity biographies offers a useful entry point to see how digital possessions can operate as technologies of enclosure. Kopytoff's premise is that commodities are defined quantitatively and in relation to other commodities. Their tendency for proliferation is spearheaded by a commoditizing impulse, limited only by what 'the exchange technology permits'

(Kopytoff, 1986, p. 87). On the other hand, singular possessions are defined qualitatively in terms of their relationship to cultural categories and personal histories. In that way, they are driven and defined by cultural and individual requirements to classify, discern and sacralize. In Kopytoff's proposed continuum between sacred, singularized objects and homogenized commodities, moving commodities from their market sphere into the domain of personal possession requires self-investment (Belk et al., 1989; McCracken, 1986; Richins, 1994; Wallendorf and Arnould, 1988). This includes work on meanings that attach an object to another person, time or place (Czikszentmihalyi and Rochberg-Halton, 1981), or work on customizing, cleaning, repairing, displaying to create and maintain the preferential status of a meaningful or sacred possession (Belk et al., 1989).

Digital objects however cannot be transitioned so easily. Like their material equivalents, digital possessions that are experienced as meaningful are so because they have become focal points of psychological attention and investment over time (Denegri-Knott et al., 2012). Consider the time spent curating the perfect Spotify playlist or in winning trophies accumulated in game play. These digital objects have been, in effect, to borrow from Czikszentmihalyi and Rochberg-Halton (1981), cultivated with focused attention and thus become meaningful possessions. Focused attention is expended in harnessing objects to help achieve a goal – for instance in harvesting a character in a video game to help complete missions or in storing them to help protect their sacred status (Belk et al., 1989; Czikszentmihalyi and Rochberg-Halton, 1981; Fournier, 1998; McCracken, 1986; Richins, 1994). This investment produces relationships of attachment, where objects are not defined by their exchangeability to other things only, but rather by their qualitative relationships to personal histories (Belk, 1988) and cultural categories (Kopytoff, 1986).

Yet, in the case of digital objects, they are never too far from their market origins. In fact digital objects come to inhabit multiple positions, both as objects of personal significance and assets for the firms that help create and host them. In this way they are quasi possessions (see Denegri-Knott, 2015) or commodity-possession hybrids. This hybridity is well illustrated in Google's music streaming service, Google Play Music, with the service pitched as a combination of 'your collection and our catalogue' (The Guardian, 2016). As hybrids, singularizing processes are equally commoditizing, inasmuch as they are supported by market exchange. Differently put, commodity-possession hybrids are defined by singularizing action that does not sever links to the market, because that action often enrolls firm resources to cultivate their possession and because the hosting firm arbitrates access. Thus, the more a consumer invests in crafting the perfect playlist on Spotify, the more reluctant she will be to abandon the service. The same applies to social media. Thus, processes of singularization that are meant to strip objects from their commodity status are more market entangling than severing (see Molesworth et al., 2016).

This creates an unusual situation, where possession becomes precarious and unstable. Consumers, having formed attachments to their digital objects continue to be entangled in on-going commercial relationships in ways that reconfigure supposedly inalienable possessions into technologies of enclosure that also happen valorize consumers' investments. If a consumer wants continued access to a favorite playlist or digital object, they will have to either continue to pay or at the very least engage with the hosting firm. In doing this, they help accrue profits for companies hosting their digital possessions. For example, users of social media make significant contributions in enhancing the social utility of the networking sites they use, and therefore also their exchange value. The benefits for Facebook and MMORGs are obvious: consumers are locked into using platforms that host their meaningful digital possessions, and hosting companies benefit financially through monetizing strategies facilitating access, either directly or through the sale of advertising. Consumers may also be subject to further monetising attempts from companies seeking to profit from their attachment to their digital possessions. To illustrate, when Facebook decided to delete photographs synched from users' phones to Facebook to encourage the adoption of their new Moments App, it was consumers' attachment to their accumulated photographs that catapulted the app into the top 100 free Android and iOS apps in the UK, and made it the third most popular free app on iOS (The Guardian, 2016).

Possessions as technologies of enclosure also diminish an object's social utility in ways that reduce consumers' freedom to control their own possessions. Objects that are gifted, lent, shared and bequeathed fulfil important social functions – they can help establish and strengthen bonds of affiliation and reciprocity between people (Douglas and Isherwood, 1979; McCracken, 1986). Because full ownership of rights can be denied by EULAs, the movement of digital objects may be unlikely. Take for instance the limitations on gifting, re-selling and bequeathing imposed on many digital objects, and compare them to the rich biographies of fully owned material consumption objects: Amazon applies its own digital rights management (DRM) to Kindle eBooks, meaning they cannot be accessed via other devices; Apple applies its FairPlay DRM to files that are purchased from the iBookstore, limiting opportunities to share and lend; World of Warcraft's terms and conditions prohibits the selling, or trading or gifting of an account (Blizzard, 2016); iTunes collections cannot be lent, shared or bequeathed. There are no legal second-hand markets for digital goods. In this way digital objects may be described as 'terminal commodities' (Appadurai, 1986).

Similarly, without the sanction of legal ownership, possession is fragile. Only full ownership guarantees exclusive and future use over a possession, and thus the lack of this guarantee limits our sense of freedom and independence. As Rudmin (1988) argues, failure to guarantee future use produces an unstable, precarious possession. Without the guarantees that total legal ownership provides, digital possession is precarious because it is prone to being disrupted or terminated at any time. Such disruptions threaten the very fabric of possession as an anchor for the development of the self and social linking, in that its objectual characteristics are no longer permanence and stability (Molesworth et al., 2016). This also undermines the classical and digital libertarian defense for the need for private ownership to nurture and safeguard our sense of independence and freedom. Instead, marketing systems of enclosure that operate through precarious possession, as we have shown, supplant independence and freedom, with ever-growing dependence and diminution of personal autonomy. Consumers in such systems of enclosure are best described as renters, in that, thinking alongside de Certeau (1984, p. 33), they only have transient rights to operate resources furnished by capitalism without real ownership. This creates a relationship of unbalanced dependency. The ultimate owners and arbitrators are the technologies of enclosure themselves – the firms providing access and hosting digital objects, who collectively produce, returning to de Certeau (1984, p. 40), a 'system too vast to be able to fix them [renters] in one place, too constraining for them [renters] ever to be able to escape'. So here, while opportunities and mechanisms to access and possess digital objects are vast, they also pin down renters to relationships of dependency that are not easily extricated. Consumers as renters cannot escape because having invested their psychological and financial resources in singularizing digital objects into meaningful possessions, the costs of leaving are too high. Renting becomes a means of enclosure, because it is a precarious way of life, defined by uncertainty, dependency and reduced freedom. The idea that everything can be had, but not owned, is disingenuous in that nothing is ever had, only temporarily accessed.

CONCLUSION

Marketing technologies – and more broadly marketing *as* technology – pursue the enclosure of the consumer subject (with Lazzarato [2004], via the production of capital-worlds where specific consumer subjectivities are made possible) and of the commons (via the innovation of capitalist commons [see Zwick and Bradshaw, 2016] that permit the production and exploitation of collective productivity). What makes this marketing project so insidious is that at the same time that marketing (as) technology attempts to enclose, its aspiration appears to be democratic: democratizing access to goods and services via digital possessions and sharing, democratizing innovation and communication via brand communities and democratizing information via Google and Big Data. The democratizing discourse functions here ideologically because it allows marketers to resolve a key contradiction of marketing specific to participatory media: how to continue to control consumers in the age of democratization, empowerment and participation.

Today, even digital possessions are becoming technologies of enclosure. Via the notion of entanglement and renting, we suggest that the digital never provides real ownership and the sort of freedom from power authentic possession can provide. Rather, digital possessions are always precarious and unstable. The possession remains meaningful only for as long as the 'owner' of the possession also is its 'user'. Therefore, ever more entanglement with the object does not create possession and ownership but merely the right to its continuous use. In the age of biopolitical marketing, it is the job of marketers to ensure that this distinction disappears.

Is the insidious assimilation of revolutionary concepts – participation, empowerment, autonomy, democratic determination – not the perfect expression of the cultural logic of capitalism? Instead of pushing the consumer to accept a brand's version of the world, which can only lead to resistance and rejection of the message as the message of capital, the brand provides the context for what is then celebrated as the moment of 'consumer empowerment', when the consumer decides for herself that she really wants the brand and wanted it all along. But we should be very clear that this project of so-called consumer empowerment and consumer sovereignty gets consumers to the same place where they were always already going to be.

Therefore, in the age of biopolitical marketing, analyses of consumer empowerment fail unless they realize the concept's ideological function in marketing practice.

Unlike the corporate persuaders of the twentieth century, digital and social media marketers no longer aspire to command consumers to consume. These new marketers wish to unify marketing, community, conversation and the general work of making a life for oneself. There is no more separation between what the marketer wants and what the consumer wants. This is the credo of biopolitical marketing: in a world of total enclosure of consumers and the commons, marketers and consumers become one. Marketers want what consumers want and vice versa. Everyone is in this together, not on two different sides of an anachronistic struggle but participating on the same side in the making of worlds. The contradictions brought about by the increasing interaction of marketing and technology abound and any comprehensive analysis of marketing technologies in communicative capitalism has to take these contradictions into account.

After all, this symbiosis of marketer and consumer can never really hold. The consumer will always be the 'other' of marketing and the job of marketing can best be described as a process of constant and incessant identification and appropriation of a non-commodified 'other'. This fundamental tension will not go away but the technologies of identification and appropriation are constantly changing. In the era of what Zuboff (2015) calls Surveillance Capitalism, networked commercial reconnaissance has become a totalizing reality. To put it in the language of biopolitical marketing, surveillance capitalism is the latest stage in a continuous dialectic of marketing forever forced to oscillate between a relentless need for more and better 'othering' and a desire to co-create worlds and 'become one' with the other. We suggest that technology-enabled marketing techniques and tools therefore will always be measured against their ability to accomplish these two seemingly opposed tasks. We might be imprisoned but it will feel good.

REFERENCES

Appadurai, A. (1986). Introduction: Commodities and the politics of value. In A. Appadurai (Ed.), *The Social Life of Things: Commodities in Cultural Perspective*, pp. 3–63. Cambridge: Cambridge University Press.

Arvidsson, A. (2005). Brands: A critical perspective. *Journal of Consumer Culture*, *5*(2), pp. 235–258.

Arvidsson, A. and Peitersen, N. (2013). *The Ethical Economy: Rebuilding Value after the Crisis*. New York: Columbia University Press.

Bardhi, F. and Eckhardt, G.M. (2012). Access-based consumption: The case of car sharing. *Journal of Consumer Research*, 39(4), pp. 881–898.

Bardhi, F., Eckhardt, G.M. and Arnould, E. (2012). Liquid relationship to possessions. *Journal of Consumer Research*, 39(3), pp. 510–529.

Belk, R.W. (2013a). Extended self in a digital world. *Journal of Consumer Research*, 40(3), pp. 477–500.

Belk, R.W. (2013b). You are what you can access: Sharing and collaborative consumption online. *Journal of Business Research*, 67(8), pp. 1595–1600.

Belk, R.W., Wallendorf, M. and Sherry Jr., J.F. (1989). The sacred and the profane in consumer behavior: Theodicy on the Odyssey. *Journal of Consumer Research*, 16(1), pp. 1–38.

Belk, R.W. (1988). Possessions and the Extended Self. *Journal of Consumer Research,* 15(2), 139–168.
Benkler, Y. (2000). From consumers to users: Shifting the deeper structures of regulation toward sustainable commons and user access. *Federal Communications Law Journal,* 52(3), pp. 561–579.
Berverungen, A., Murtola, A. and Schwartz, G. (2013). The communism of capital? *Ephemera: Theory & Politics in Organization*, 13(3), 483–495.
Blizzard (2016). World of Warcraft end user licence agreement. Available at: http://us.blizzard.com/en-us/company/legal/wow_eula.html (accessed 26 May 2016).
Cvijanovic, V., Vercellone, C. and Fumagalli, A. (2010). *Cognitive Capitalism and its Reflections in South Eastern Europe*. Frankfurt am Main: Peter Lang.
Czikszentmihalyi, M. and Rochberg-Halton, E. (1981). *The Meaning of Things: Domestic Symbols and the Self.* Cambridge, MA: Cambridge University Press.
de Certeau, M. (1984). *The Practice of Everyday Life*. Los Angeles, CA: University of California Press.
de Certeau, M. (1988). *The Practice of Everyday Life*. Los Angeles, CA: University of California Press.
Dean, J. (2005). Communicative capitalism: Circulation and the foreclosure of politics. *Cultural Politics*, 1(1), pp. 51–74.
Demsetz, H. (1967). Toward a theory of property rights. *The American Economic Review*, 57(2), pp. 347–359.
Denegri-Knott, J. (2015). MP3. *Consumption Markets and Culture*, 18(5), pp. 397–401.
Denegri-Knott, J. and Tadajewski, M. (2010). The emergence of MP3 technology. *Journal of Historical Research in Marketing*, 2(4), pp. 397–425.
Denegri-Knott, J. and Tadajewski, M. (2016). Sanctioning value: The legal system, hyper power and the legitimation of market systems, and the MP3. *Marketing Theory*, pp. 1–22 [published online].
Denegri-Knott, J., Watkins, R. and Wood, J. (2012). Transforming digital virtual goods into meaningful possessions. In M. Molesworth and J. Denegri-Knott (Eds), *Digital Virtual Consumption*, pp. 76–91. Oxford: Routledge.
Douglas, M. and Isherwood, B. (1979). *The World of Goods*. New York: Basic Books.
Downes, L. and Mui, C. (2000). *Unleashing the killer app: Digital strategies for market dominance*. Boston: Harvard Business School Press.
Dyer-Witheford, N. (2009). The circulation of the common. Available at: http://www.globalproject.info/it/in_movimento/Nick-Dyer-Witheford-the-Circulation-of-the-Common/4797 (accessed 2 February 2012).
Elmer, G. (2004). *Profiling Machines: Mapping the Personal Information Economy*. Cambridge, MA: MIT Press.
Fournier, S. (1998). Consumers and their brands: Developing relationship theory in consumer research. *Journal of Consumer Research*, 24(4), pp. 343–373.
Fournier, S. and Lee, L. (2009). Getting Brand Communities Right. *Harvard Business Review* (April), pp. 105–111.
Fuchs, C. (2010). Labor in informational capitalism and on the internet. *The Information Society*, 26(3), pp. 179–196.
Fuchs, C. (2012). Dallas Smythe today – The audience commodity, the digital labour debate, Marxist political economy and critical theory. Porolegomena to a digital labour theory of value. *TripleC*, 10(2), pp. 692–740.
Gabriel, Y., and Lang, T. (1995). *The unmanageable consumer: Contemporary consumption and its fragmentations*. London and Thousand Oaks, CA: Sage.

Gaus, G. (2012). Property and ownership. In D. Estlund (Ed.), *Oxford Handbook of Political Philosophy*, pp. 93–112. Oxford: Oxford University Press.
Godin, S. (1999). *Permission Marketing: Turning Strangers into Friends, and Friends into Customers*. New York: Simon & Schuster.
Hardt, M. and Negri, A. (2009). *Commonwealth*. Cambridge, MA: Belknap Press of Harvard University Press.
Juergenson, N. (2010). The de-McDonaldization of the internet. In G. Ritzer (Ed.), *McDonaldization: The Reader*, pp. 159–170. Thousand Oaks, CA: Pine Forge Press.
Kelly, K. (2009). The New Socialism: Global Collectivist Society Is Coming Online. Available at: http://www.wired.com/culture/culturereviews/magazine/17-06/nep_newsocialism (accessed 23 May 2009).
Kleiner, D. and Wyrick, B. (2007). InfoEnclosure 2.0. *Mute*, 2(4). Available at: http://www.metamute.org/editorial/articles/infoenclosure-2.0 (accessed November 2014).
Kopytoff, I. (1986). The cultural biography of things: commoditization as process. In A. Appadurai (Ed.), *The Social Life of Things Commodities in a Cultural Perspective*, pp. 64–94. Cambridge: Cambridge University Press.
Kutcher, A. (2010). Foreword. In B. Solis, *Engage! The Complete Guide for Brands and Businesses to Build, Cultivate, and Measure Success in the New Web*. Hoboken, NJ: John Wiley. pp. xiii–xiv.
Lanier, J. (2013). *Who Owns the Future?* (first Simon & Schuster hardcover edition). New York: Simon & Schuster.
Lazzarato, M. (2004). From capital-labour to capital-life. *Ephemera: Theory & Politics in Organization*, 4(3), pp. 187–208.
Lessig, L. (1999). *Code and Other Laws of Cyberspace*. New York: Basic Books.
Lury, C. (2004). *Brands: The Logos of the Global Economy*. London: Routledge.
McCracken, G. (1986). Culture and consumption: A theoretical account of the structure and movement of the cultural meaning of consumer goods. *Journal of Consumer Research*, 13(1), pp. 71–84.
Miller, M. (2008). *Online marketing heroes: Interviews with 25 successful online marketing gurus*. Indianapolis, IN: Wiley Pub.
Molesworth, M. and Watkins, R. (2014). Adult videogame consumption as individualised, episodic progress. *Journal of Consumer Culture*, 16(2), pp. 510–530.
Molesworth, M., Watkins, R. and Denegri-Knott, J. (2016). Possession work on hosted digital consumption objects as consumer ensnarement. *Journal of the Association for Consumer Research*, 1(2), pp. 246–261.
Morozov, E. (2013). The Meme Hustler. Available at: https://thebaffler.com/salvos/the-meme-hustler (accessed 31 August 2017).
Munzer, S. (1990). *A Theory of Property*. Cambridge: Cambridge University Press.
O'Dwyer, R. (2013). Spectre of the commons: Spectrum regulation in the communism of capital. *Ephemera: Theory & Politics in Organisation*, 13(3): 497–526.
Packard, V.O. (1957). *The Hidden Persuaders*. New York: Pocket Books.
Richins, M. (1994). Valuing things: The public and private meanings of possessions. *Journal of Consumer Research*, 21(3), pp. 504–521.
Rifkin, J. (2000). *The Age of Access: The New Culture of Hypercapitalism Where all of Life is a Paid for Experience*. New York: Penguin.
Rifkin, J. (2002). The age of access, the new politics of culture vs. commerce, *Ars Electronica*. Available at: http://90.146.8.18/en/archives/festival_archive/festival_catalogs/festival_artikel.asp?iProjectID=11765 (accessed 4 January 2015).
Rudmin, F.W. (1988). Ownership as interpersonal dominance: A history and three studies of the social psychology of property (Unpublished doctoral dissertation). Kingston, ON: Queens University.

Schau, H. J., Muniz Jr., A. M. and Arnould, E. (2009). How Brand Community Practices Create Value. *Journal of Marketing*, 73(5), pp. 30–51.

Snare, F. (1972). The concept of property. *American Philosophical Quarterly*, 9(2), pp. 200–206.

Solis, B. (2010). *Engage! The Complete Guide for Brands and Businesses to Build, Cultivate, and Measure Success in the New Web*. Hoboken, NJ: John Wiley.

Spotify News (2014). No more limits. Available at: https://news.spotify.com/uk/2014/01/15/no-more-time-limits-on-spotify-freeyourmusic/ (accessed 4 January 2015).

Stallabrass, J. (2012). Digital Partisans: on Mute and the Cultural Politics of the Net. *New Left Review, 74*(March–April), pp. 125–139.

Stratten, S. (2010). *Unmarketing: Stop marketing, start engaging*. Hoboken, NJ: John Wiley & Sons.

Stratten, S. (2014). *Unselling: Stop selling, start connecting*. Hoboken, NJ: John Wiley & Sons.

The Guardian (2016). Which is the best music streaming service? Available at: https://www.theguardian.com/technology/2016/feb/16/which-is-the-best-music-streaming-service-spotify-apple-music (accessed 4 June 2016).

Wallendorf, M. and Arnould, E. (1988). 'My favorite things': A cross-cultural inquiry into object attachment, possessiveness, and social linkage'. *Journal of Consumer Research*, 14(4), pp. 531–547.

Watkins, R.D., Denegri-Knott, J. and Molesworth, M. (2016). The relationship between ownership and possession: Observations from the context of digital virtual goods. *Journal of Marketing Management*, 32(1–2), pp. 44–70.

Weinberg, T. (2009). *The new community rules: Marketing on the social web*. Beijing and Sebastopol, CA: O'Reilly.

Wired (2011). Kindle Lending Library Takes a Chance with Borrowing Books. Available at: https://www.wired.com/2011/11/kindle-lending-library/ (accessed 24 June 2015).

Zuboff, S. (2015). Big other: Surveillance capitalism and the prospects of an information civilization. *Journal of Information Technology*, 30(1), pp. 75–89.

Zwick, D. and Bradshaw, A. (2016). Biopolitical marketing and social media brand communities. *Theory, Culture & Society*, 33(5), pp. 91–115.

Zwick, D. and Denegri-Knott, J. (2009). Manufacturing customers: The database as new means of production. *Journal of Consumer Culture*, 9(2), pp. 221–247.

PART V

Material Cultures of Consumption

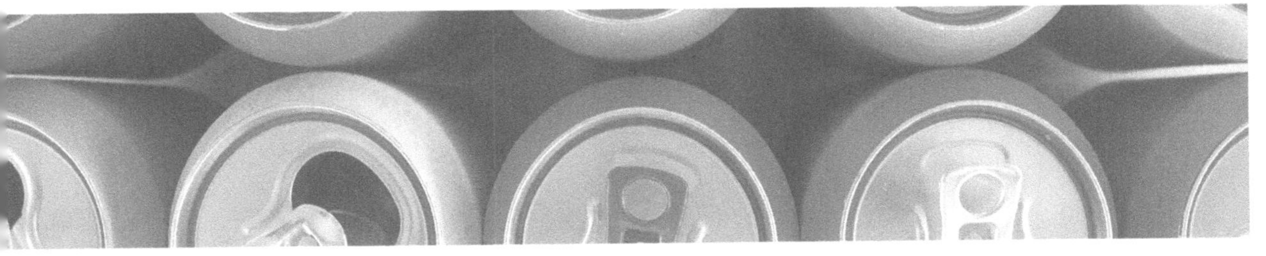

20

The Materiality of Consumer Culture

Paul R. Mullins

INTRODUCTION: IMAGINING THINGS – CONSUMERS, MATERIAL CULTURE, AND MATERIAL DESIRE

It is not at all surprising that consumer scholarship has routinely examined material things as lenses onto marketing and economic structure, dominant ideologies, and a host of dimensions of social and individual subjectivity. Nevertheless, material things often figure in such scholarship as rather shallow symbols, their meanings dispensed by style makers, marketers, and ideologues. Material things paradoxically occupy a central position in consumer scholarship even as concrete material culture, systematic empirical analysis, and the sensory experience of things often remain unexamined.

The concept of materiality is sometimes wielded simply as a clumsy reference to concrete objects and their physical presence. Most materiality scholarship instead champions a more ambitious theorization of things, avoiding dualisms between objects and people, complicating agency, and illuminating the ways things shape human experience and imagination beyond our control and perhaps even our articulation. Materiality underscores the power of things, resisting consumer scholarship that reduces things to hollow receptacles constituted by human interaction. Materiality scholarship fundamentally resists theorizing objects as entities that are distinct from social subjects. Materiality theories instead reject distinctions between human subjects and concrete objects and argue that a breadth of material culture and people constitute a mutual subjectivity. Materiality potentially pushes consumer scholars to more systematically examine the bodily, imagined, and visual experiences of material things and confront how the concrete qualities of things shape material life.

THEORIZING MATERIALITY

Materiality theory acknowledges things' distinctive capacity to charge human experience, placing material things in a pleasant if largely inchoate sensory experience and imagination that consumers often fail to express, rationalize, and understand. Things routinely spark powerful imaginative and bodily experiences that consumers struggle to comprehend and marketers aspire to manage, even as ideologues express their alarm with the sensuous desires unleashed by the material world. Materiality theory focuses on this enormous power of things while ambitiously extending the boundaries of the material. Materiality illuminates how systematic material, ethnographic, and empirical analysis of things' concrete presence can paint consumption as something more complicated than humans' symbolic projection of meaning onto mute objects.

Materiality theories build on a social scientific scholarship of consumption that emerged in the 1980s. Mary Douglas and Baron Isherwood's *The World of Goods* (1979) was perhaps the most influential early volley in the scholarship on consumption, advocating an explicit focus on how consumers shape the meanings of things. Anthropology in particular and social sciences in general had a long record of material culture studies reaching back over a century, but it was dominated by empirical description or vulgar materialism. Douglas and Isherwood signaled a turn to consumption symbolism and a new-found interest in the social, cultural, and historical dimensions of material meaning. *The World of Goods* was foremost a reaction against economic determinism, proposing that economically driven explanations of material desire provided little substantial understanding of how people give meaning to material culture. Douglas and Isherwood cast things as visible manifestations of cultural categories, stressing the symbolic and culturally distinctive dimensions of consumption over rational decision-making and utilitarian demand (cf. Miller, 1995: 274–275). *The World of Goods* championed a perspective on consumer symbolism that rejected facile economically driven notions of consumption simply as commerce, and in her own work Douglas (2001: 262) persistently resisted the assumption that consumers 'are mindless automatons'. Douglas stressed that consumption's 'essential nature is to make sense of things, creatively'; that perspective did not necessarily discount the relationship between things and people or the ways material things shape human life, but it focused on how consumers dynamically assign goods meaning within cultural frameworks.

Among the most ambitious studies of consumption was Pierre Bourdieu's 1979 study *Distinction: A Social Critique of the Judgement of Taste*, which first appeared in English in 1984. Bourdieu marshalled an enormous amount of empirical evidence to examine taste and its relationship to status, which takes shape based on possession of things and qualities that demonstrate cultural capital. *Distinction* argues that aesthetic presentation in public and concrete material consumption patterns reflect deeply instilled class dispositions and maintain divisions between status groups. Bourdieu referred to this as 'habitus,' a classificatory framework of normative meanings instilled in social agents, or the 'conditionings associated with a particular class of conditions of existence' (Bourdieu, 1990: 53). Habitus links structures and practices and tends to reproduce the dispositions associated with a specific social position.

That notion of habitus has subsequently been part of a broad range of scholarship examining consumption. For instance, Daniel Miller (1987: 105) proposed that the effectiveness of such dispositions and order is rooted in seemingly mundane material details. Miller (1987: 103) argued that things 'mediate between subjective and objective worlds', hewing to a culturally specific underlying order while taking aim on the distinction between subjects and objects.

Miller's (1987) *Material Culture and Mass Consumption* was the first of a series of studies he authored outlining a theory of materiality indebted to Bourdieu as well as Hegel. Miller's (2005: 9) theoretical framework revolved around a notion of objectification he takes from Hegel, one that is 'distinct from any theory of representation'. Rather than assume already-existing subjects and objects, Miller (1987: 28–29) instead argues that objectification is a 'relationship within which the subject and object are created' and consumption is 'simultaneously a practice in the world and a form in which we construct our understandings of ourselves in the world' (Miller, 1995: 30; cf. Miller, 2005: 9). Miller championed ethnographic methods to interpret everyday practices and practical engagement with things. That anthropological focus on everyday consciousness, patterned practices, and analysis of everyday material culture aspires to acknowledge human agency. In particular, it aims to reveal what might circumspectly be dubbed resistance (or the negotiation of dominant meanings), arguing that people 'appropriate the objects of consumption to construct moral projects, not necessarily intended by the producers' (Miller, 1995: 30–31).

One thread of this work, borrowing from Bourdieu, championed what Miller refers to as the 'humility of objects'. One of the key insights of Miller's (1987: 96) analysis was his critique of material culture studies that tended 'to perceive objects as being reflective in a relatively passive sense', voicing an uneasiness about the theoretical differentiation between human subjects and material objects and acknowledging that goods are not simply representational symbols with no effect on meaning. Miller (1987: 101) argued that most everyday material things 'play an inconspicuous and normative cultural role', steeped in a 'humility' that does not draw attention to itself even as it provides significant consequence framing socioculturally specific meanings. Miller argued that most things serve as a sort of framing backdrop against which consumers fabricate contextually distinctive meanings. This borrowed from Erving Goffman's (1974) notion of framing, and it is simultaneously indebted to Bourdieu's theory of habitus.

In the midst of the 1980s' 'turn to things', relatively few projects firmly focused on empirical description of artifacts. Among the most empirically rich projects documenting material consumption patterns was William Rathje's 'Garbage Project,' which began to systematically assess household refuse patterns in 1973. Rathje's (1977) initial interest was in simply assessing archaeological epistemology by comparing peoples' perception of their everyday detritus with concrete quantified refuse patterns from household trash and dumps. Ethnographic research and surveys alongside refuse analysis underscored that most people knew very little about their everyday material use and discard patterns. Rathje and Cullen Murphy's *Rubbish! The Archaeology of Garbage* (1992) outlined an applied scholarship that could dissect concrete discard patterns and shape waste management, recycling, and food consumption practices. Rathje championed systematic material analysis methods and densely described empirical data that have often been absent from consumption scholarship, painting the social dimensions of waste and refuse management by focusing on that empirical data rather than ethnographic or documentary evidence. That research obliquely illuminated a chain of everyday material practices resulting in things that secured the mostly unexamined social status of waste.

While a literature on the cultural and ethnographic dimensions of consumption was emerging in the 1980s, historians were simultaneously dissecting the depths of past material consumption. Most of that work was crafted in a relatively traditional historical narrative, focusing on the chronological spread of global mass consumption and defining distinctive local patterns of material consumption since the fifteenth century. Among the earliest of these studies was Neil McKendrick's (1960) research on Josiah Wedgwood's success marketing commonplace ceramics. McKendrick (1960: 410) carefully documented labor organization and its role in the Wedgwood firm's success, acknowledging that Wedgwood was part of a revolution in industrial production. Much of his picture of demand revolved around emulation of the upper classes, with McKendrick (1960: 429) arguing that 'the lower classes' purchased Wedgwood's mass-produced wares 'in imitation of their social superiors'. This picture of consumption explained desire by reference to the structural dimensions of marketing and style, yet McKendrick also examined concrete ceramic style and how consumer desire for specific aesthetics was monitored (if not induced) by Wedgwood. McKendrick's detailed research provided a thorough aesthetic and empirical description of Wedgwood ceramics, but those things loomed as vehicles for style being shrewdly managed by Wedgwood himself. For instance, Wedgwood instructed his factory artists to clothe 'naked figures that were "too warm" for English taste', alluding to his effort to manage consumers' reception of nudity (McKendrick, 1960: 415). Yet McKendrick's analysis did not question why particular things and aesthetics became desirable, instead reducing consumption patterns simply to idiosyncrasies for Wedgwood to manage. Things loomed in McKendrick's analysis as vehicles reflecting the genius who was cleverly orchestrating style and demand.

Warren Susman's (1984) work was part of a historical scholarship that embraced the consequence of seemingly mundane material things and the web of social practices in which they were embedded. Susman in particular highlighted how a very broadly defined world of things shaped Americans' imagination of citizenship in the first half of the twentieth century. Susman explored prosaic dimensions of everyday American life, including how popular films, radio soap operas, and the 1939 New York World's Fair created a 'special community of all Americans (possibly an international community) unthinkable previously' (Susman, 1984: 160). For Susman, society's fundamental values began to be articulated in material consumption and things in the 1930s, something that might be termed a genuine 'consumer culture'. Susman suggested that much of the American embrace of goods and a culture of consumption occurred in mundane things that had escaped scholarly attention, and perhaps even consumers' consciousness as well. Echoing Susman, Jean-Christophe Agnew (1993: 32) suggests that in the second quarter of the twentieth century 'a redefinition of rights and obligations articulated itself in the innocuous language of soft drinks, cars, and household appliances'. For Agnew, the conversation about the rights invested in things and the ways they shape collective subjectivity happened 'privately, imaginatively, and inconspicuously – in short, without discussion'.

An enormously rich historical scholarship of material consumption in the 1980s focused on the broadly defined social and political effects of mass consumption. While this scholarship effectively politicized all things (especially commodities), it devoted little focus to the concrete qualities of material things that distinguished them in everyday life. For instance, Richard Wightman Fox and T.J. Jackson Lears's 1983 edited volume *The Culture of Consumption* assembled a group of scholars who situated the roots of American consumer culture in the 1880s. The contributions to the Fox and Lears collection illuminated the tension between mass cultural producers and everyday consumers and underscored how consumers negotiated dominant ideological meanings. Nevertheless, their assessment of a hegemonic consumer culture gravitated toward a focus on culture producers like advertisers and novelists and posed things as symbolic battlegrounds contesting class and cultural tensions.

This scholarship ambitiously pressed to define the political effects of material consumption and the 'language of goods', assessing how commodities framed social and political imagination. For instance, T.H. Breen's 1993 paper 'Narrative of commercial life: Consumption, ideology, and community on the eve of the American Revolution' proposed that colonial American consumers were part of what he calls an 'empire of goods' (an argument he expanded in his 2004 study *The Marketplace of Revolution*). Breen contended that colonial Americans secured a collective political voice against British control of marketing through non-importation agreements. Non-importation boycotts of British goods were politically galvanizing mass movements that became the voice of a revolution against the crown. Breen is among a host of scholars who have made strong cases for the politicization of consumption itself. Nevertheless, the experience of specific material goods – such as what made British goods desirable as aesthetic, physical, and sensory things – remains somewhat less clearly illuminated.

Possibly one of the richest threads of consumer scholarship champions a moral critique of consumption that tends to distill things to style and casts style as ideological manipulation. For example, Stuart Ewen's 1988 study *All Consuming Images* bemoans the triumph of 'style over substance', a critique of consumer culture that takes aim at advertisers in particular for crafting stylistic artifice from concrete material presence. That critique certainly is not unique to Ewen, echoing the Frankfurt School's criticism of popular culture and sharing some anxieties voiced by observers since the nineteenth, if not the eighteenth, century (cf. Horowitz, 1985). Ewen (1988: 263) examines the commodified thing as a provocative and seductive image that has been divorced from objective materiality, with style posing as a way to comprehend the world that 'addresses deep-seated desires' and 'promises to release people from the subjective condition of their experience'. For Ewen, that alluring promise has disempowering implications because it means 'style – as a form of *information* – discourages thought'. Ewen's analysis of things as stylistic artifice is distinctively dystopian, but it shares a common scholarly focus on things as symbolic vehicles.

Perhaps materiality scholars' fundamental critique of consumption scholarship is that the literature on consumption in particular and material culture in general fixates on the social meaning of consumption and says very little about things. The focus on the meanings of material culture in public social spaces often borrows from

Thorstein Veblen's (1899) landmark analysis of the 'leisure class'. Veblen's analysis of an urban bourgeoisie at the turn of the twentieth century focused on social and material practices associated with status. Veblen (1899: 28) championed a picture of conspicuous consumption among the elite in which 'non-productive' consumption of expensive things and leisure demonstrated their wealth and taste. The leisure class's consumption revolved around ideals that essentially signaled social standing through material style, and Veblen cited a host of examples including lawns, furnishings, and dress. An enormous number of scholars focus on material style in much the same way as a mechanism that has more-or-less accepted public meaning that reflects the negotiation of mainstream ideals, which may encompass their reproduction as well as resistance to them. This approach to things views them as public symbols whose aesthetic visibility marks them out socially and publicly in service to a consumer's social and political interests.

Some theorists have focused their attention on things as vehicles for imaginative desire, shifting focus from dominant social symbolism to individualized experiences of things. For instance, Colin Campbell's *The Romantic Ethic and the Spirit of Modern Consumerism* (1987: 89–90) argues that a 'modern' consumer is motivated less by 'insatiable desire to acquire objects' than a desire to experience in material reality what is otherwise 'enjoyed in imagination'. Campbell suggests that consumer desire emerged in the eighteenth century as an imaginative and pleasurable contemplation preceding possession. Rather than distinguish between a puritanical discipline and a romantic hedonism, Campbell argues that hedonistic material desire is meaningless outside its productive tension with self-discipline; that is, the yearning for things is tempered by a puritanical discipline that suppresses some pleasures and admits others. Campbell concludes that the apparent divide between puritanical discipline and romantic hedonism is not so much a contradiction as it is a productive amalgam that fosters a day-dreaming imagination countered by consumers' self-policing. This tends to view things as vehicles for imagination, and the most desirable things accommodate the richest daydreams. For Campbell (1987: 89), the material features that might ignite desire for a thing tend to revolve around novelty and 'their potential for "dream material"', but the specific attributes that distinguished such imaginative things from other objects are not especially clear in Campbell's study. Campbell is not alone in his argument that imagination is not simply a reflection of marketing manipulation or an ideologically duped escapist fantasy; rather, as Arjun Appadurai (1996: 7) argues, 'imagination is today a staging ground for action'. Appadurai suggests that a collective imagination has emerged in contemporary everyday life in which disparate groups share mass-mediated sensory experiences that can be the grounds for political agency (cf. Appadurai, 1986).

Much of the scholarship on materiality aspires to disrupt unexamined mechanisms of representation and move away from a fixation on the social meaning of things. In an analysis of Derrida's implications for material culture scholarship, Timothy Yates (1990) examined the relationship between material culture and textuality and how material things are narrated in text. Yates (1990: 265–266) hoped to problematize representation, arguing that the 'material artifact is *unwritten*, therefore it is not a sign, therefore it cannot signify'. Yates instead evoked a material world at the boundaries of cognition, imagination, and substance. Material culture, Yates (1990: 266) suggested, has 'no use for the sign, but is rather immediate, undivided, present. It is without utterance, without voice, silent; its testimony, therefore, will always be a silent soliloquy, which is to say that it is heard but it does not sound'. Some scholars share this sense that things reside at the boundaries of articulation, wary of the depth that we can know or express things. Miguel Tamen's *Friends of Interpretable Objects*, for instance, argues that there 'are no interpretable objects or intentional objects, only what counts as an interpretable object or, better, groups of people for whom certain objects count as interpretable' (Tamen, 2001: 3). Tamen examines how people speak *for* the material world, which is fundamentally unresponsive but is made interpretable by what he calls 'friends' like museum curators who 'speak' to things.

Tamen's study examines how the material world enters utterable meaning, an issue likewise examined by Bill Brown's (2001) 'Thing theory'. Brown (2001: 4) argues that 'we look *through* objects (to see what they disclose about history, society, nature, or culture – above all, what they disclose about *us*), but we only catch a glimpse of things'. Like subsequent materiality theories, Brown's focus on things probes the relationship between inanimate objects and human subjects and stresses that things shape the human world. Yet Brown distinguishes between things and objects, with things emerging from objects when those objects do not conform to their intended meanings. When an object's unexamined presence is arrested somehow – a window breaks, a laptop stops operating, a nut falls on your head – it becomes a thing and interrupts the codes and signification that make objects meaningful and allow us to use them as facts (Brown, 2001: 4).

Materiality scholars have taken increasingly ambitious aim on specifically what constitutes the material and moved beyond physical stuff to seemingly substance-less digital things. For instance, Paolo Magaudda (2011) probes the apparent 'dematerialization' of digital music and concludes that the digitization of music in particular (if not broadly defined media in general) has counter-intuitively boosted the prominence of things in peoples' lives. In his ethnographic study of Italian music consumers, Magaudda found that apparently intangible digital media are embedded in an inseparable web of practices involving novel technological objects, seemingly obsolete things (e.g., vinyl records), bodily activities, and ever-emergent media technologies. Magaudda argues that digital things cannot be understood in isolation from an armada of things ranging from ipods to phones to headphones, and they cannot be collectively understood without considering a range of attitudes toward new and archaic technologies alike. While an enormous number of Italians embraced digital music consumption, many Italian music consumers reacted against digital music as 'inauthentic' in its placeless violation of an embodied musical experience represented in practices such as listening to and curating vinyl records. The emergence of digital music has a paradoxical effect of intensifying the prominence of material things, both boosting digital goods' consumption and 're-materializing' things like vinyl records that break from the social and performative activities associated with digital music.

Materiality scholars are ambitious to animate things and illustrate the specific ways they influence, constrain, and liberate imagination and action, sometimes referring to the 'agency' of things to shape particular sorts of action (e.g., Knappett and Malafouris, 2008). In some hands the notion of material agency risks conferring on things a nearly inexpressible if not mystical power, but this scholarship most clearly takes aim on the assumption that agency is simply conscious willful action. Jane Bennett (2010: 6), for instance, has referred to this as 'thing power', which she defines as 'the curious ability of inanimate things to animate, to act, to produce effects dramatic and subtle'. Bennett's perspective is shared by many materiality scholars who take aim on dismantling agency as a uniquely human and largely self-aware instrument of intentionality. Bruno Latour's (1996: 369) collapse of dualisms between subjects and objects leads him to a similarly broad notion of agency (though he avoids the term agency). Rather than reduce the material to objective things acted on by social agents, Latour refers to things as 'actants', a category that includes '*non-human, non-individual* entities'. Actants' collective sway over reality is as consequential as self-conscious human agents, and Latour (1993) champions the notion that scholars study associations of humans and non-humans (Cochoy and Mallard, this volume).

Bennett (2010) underscores that things are 'vital' and always in flux, blurring the distinction between things and humans and instead examining how all entities are composed of ever-dynamic materials. Some materiality research celebrates this perpetual dynamism of things and the material properties of all existence – human bodies, dirt, buildings, and air are all materials with complex ever-changing properties. For example, Tim Ingold (2007) lobbies against the notion of materiality and argues for seeing a world of dynamic materials in which we are all immersed. Rather than draw boundaries between various sorts of material things, Ingold (2007: 7) suggests that humans are immersed within 'an ocean of materials'. Ingold (2007: 35) argues that there are not relationships *between* things as much as there is a host of materials in various states of flux, some appearing to our eye as crystallized things – a phone, the highway off-ramp, a backyard garden – but all immersed in a world of interwoven substances. The only flux in which most commodities appear immersed is their intentionally short use life; when people are finished with manufactured things, they will indeed break down into their constituent ingredients, but they will likely do so in the landfill with their 'vitality' subject only to the rhetorical attention of archaeologists.

Nevertheless, this potentially reads the death rites to any notion of materiality that revolves around the way in which material properties are contextually experienced, defined, and imagined. For many scholars, materiality remains firmly wedded to some distinction between objects and the social contexts in which they assume meanings, even if such meanings are dynamic, idiosyncratic, and more complicated than facile subject/object divides. For instance, Christopher Tilley (2007) counters Ingold's rejection of materiality by arguing that the notion of materiality examines the meanings of things in relation to people and a sociopolitical and historical context. Tilley acknowledges that there is a world of things that have properties that exist outside their human articulation. However, he stresses that materiality research must illuminate why certain sorts of things and material properties become significant to people under particular conditions. Materiality scholars grounded in an anthropological or social scientific tradition typically reject simplistic distinctions between subjects and objects or mind and body, but they tend to lead the chorus advocating nuanced contextual analysis (e.g., Preucel and Meskell, 2004).

Some scholars appear unconvinced that materiality theory articulates the qualities of material things, a critique that may take aim less on materiality than on consumption scholarship. For instance, Bjørnar Olsen (2010) has advocated a picture of things that ambitiously includes a host of physical entities that collectively mediate action. Olsen frames his perspective as a 'defense of things', with that defense coming against conventional pictures of materiality that reduce things to inanimate objects securing their vitality from the social world. In particular, Olsen (2010: 32) argues that consumption scholarship reduces objects to consumable signs. Olsen complains that consumption studies have little to say about how material goods are used and lived with and instead reduces things to possessed commodities. Olsen suggests that consumer research hazards ignoring nearly all of the prosaic material world that is not strictly a commodity and fixates on the 'staged' material world of consumer goods being constantly arranged to represent self. Christopher L. Witmore (2007) and Olsen (Olsen and Witmore, 2015) instead champion an analysis of things that invokes the concept of 'symmetry' (Latour, 2005: 76–77). A focus on the symmetry between various entities in the world revolves around how disparate things constitute the world through myriad entanglements. In a similar vein, Ian Hodder's 2012 study of the 'entanglements' between humans and things argues that relationships between things frame a 'distributive agency'; that is, actions are shaped by reflective human decision-making, the material properties that constrain and animate action, and the mostly unarticulated sensory experience of things. Olsen and Witmore (2015: 191) advocate a picture of things that embraces both the autonomy and connectivity of all people, objects, environments, and stuff in the lived-in world, and all entities in the world are 'thingly' even if they remain different. However, Ingold (2012: 431) rejects such a 'defense' of things seemingly ignored by social scientists, arguing that a symmetrical picture of materiality reduces all things to objects.

It is perhaps not surprising that some of this most novel theory rethinking things and materiality avoids a focus on narrowly defined consumer goods and examines prosaic if not idiosyncratic materiality. For instance, a significant range of interdisciplinary scholars have examined ruins and processes of ruination (e.g., Edensor, 2005; Mah, 2012; Olsen and Pétursdóttir, 2014). Ruins have conventionally been cast as moral lessons for contemporary people, symbols that demonstrate modernity's flaws, state or class arrogance, or the instabilities of even the most stable societies. Ruins have a captivating visual dimension captured in sight as well as photography (Pétursdóttir and Olsen, 2014); there is a compelling bodily engagement for scores of people exploring decaying structures (Bennett, 2011); and there is an ethnographic dimension to the experience of abandoned places (Mah, 2012). Unlike commodities seemingly arrested in style and form, ruins are in an obvious state of decline exposing their historical depth as well as environmental processes of ruination. For example, ruin photographer Matthew Christopher (2012) suggests that photography captures these transformative processes, arguing that 'the photography of ruins is fundamentally about death. … Much in the same way, a host of chemical and biological processes continue in a corpse but it is still no longer considered living'. In that sense, Christopher's ruin images define things as materials in an unsettling state of flux, illuminating material dynamism and casting things as something more complex than objects arrested in form and condition. Dylan Trigg (2009: 94) casts ruins as an embodied experience mediating between the 'destruction of the past, the lapse in time thereafter, and the unexpected persistence of damaged materiality in the present'. Trigg focuses on traumatic ruins, arguing that ruins create the material conditions to articulate the past, but the traumatic ruin secures its power from its material absences rather than from its 'points of presence'.

For consumer scholars, ruins may make a challenging analogy to marketplace goods. While materiality theorists often dissect idiosyncratic material things ranging from ruins to zoos to beaches, consumer research typically revolves around conventional commodities and consumers' experience and transformations of goods. Some of the most sustained analyses of consumer transformations come from subcultural scholarship. Dick Hebdige's 1979 *Subculture: The Meaning of Style* is among the most prominent studies examining the ways transformations of things defied dominant social values. Hebdige's study of punk style was part of the Centre for Contemporary Cultural Studies' (1976) ambitious scholarship of everyday British life, especially postwar working-class youth culture (e.g., Willis, 1977). Those scholars examined a broad range of seemingly mundane material practices to analyze how subcultural collectives negotiated social and material normalization. Hebdige championed a very expansive sense of the material world that included dance, the body, and conventional commodities (e.g., off-the-rack clothes). Hebdige's analysis casts style as the aesthetic surface of alternative values negotiating complex sociohistorical conditions and 'mainstream' or 'parent' culture.

Hebdige distinguished subcultural consumption by its mining of disparate styles reassembled into new assemblages, what is often referred to as bricolage. Hebdige (1979: 102–106) painted bricolage as a 'science of the concrete' in which consumers rearrange material minutia in ways that subvert intended meanings (cf. Hebdige, 1988). He argued that subcultures view things as signs uniting an object and its dominant meaning, and subcultural materialism aspires to unravel unquestioned representational frameworks for normality. Much of Hebdige's material analysis revolved around the ways subcultures upset dominant meanings and create new representational signs: for example, working-class teddy boys transformed the 'ultra-respectable' motor scooter into a 'menacing symbol of group solidarity', and sharpened metal combs 'turned narcissism into an offensive weapon' (Hebdige, 1979: 104). Nevertheless, subcultural things were not simply reduced to representational mechanisms with new meanings. For instance, Hebdige (1979: 105) argued that teddy boys adopted suits, ties, and short hair – the 'conventional insignia of the business world' that evoked efficiency, compliance, and authority – and viewed that ensemble as an '"empty" fetish, objects to be desired, fondled and valued in their own right'. Apparently incompatible subcultural juxtapositions of things secure much of their power simply from disrupting accepted meanings even if they do not pose any especially concrete social representation of meaning.

Subcultures such as Hebdige's punks are often cast as conspicuous consumption collectives that wield material goods to distinguish themselves materially. The ways in which 1970's punks socialized things tended to revolve around class inequality, which is a consistent structural feature of youth subcultural resistance in British studies influenced by the Centre for Contemporary Cultural Studies. Various post-subcultural (Redhead, 1990; Muggleton, 1997, 2000) and neo-tribal (Maffesoli, 1996; Bennett, 1999) theorists have subsequently complicated or rejected the implied dichotomy between mainstream and subculture while championing a picture of exceptionally fluid group boundaries that underscore the sway of individual agency. On the one hand, mainstream social values or the very existence of a 'parent culture' may indeed be heuristic if not ideological, and the neatly defined spectacular subculture painted in research such as Hebdige's study may not capture much of the fluidity of contemporary social collectives. On the other hand, though, the rhetorical notion of a mainstream has a real effect on social imagination and material experience, even if it is a complex reality and the boundaries for group affiliations are exceptionally dynamic.

A significant amount of scholarship interrogating fringe social collectives has explored the fluidity of transgressive subjectivities and the material dimensions of such identity. For instance, in the 1990s the term hipster began to be used to refer to urbanites distinguished by a taste for novelty and discriminating if not unique individual style. Hipsters might constitute a subculture, a neo-tribe, a lifestyle, or a market demographic, depending on how those terms are defined, but the people cast as hipsters share the bricolage and aesthetic spectacle associated with subcultures like punks. Hipsters' material distinctions perhaps most clearly revolve around a notion of authenticity in which personal style expresses an individual taste and creativity that eschews mass cultural conformity (Michael, 2015). Analyzing hipster materialism as a measure of personal taste runs slightly counter to caricatures of it as either mocking parody or insincere irony; that is, hipsters' consumption of 1970s' t-shirts, working-class beer, or mainstream pop music is often reduced to a masquerade that makes fun of the authentic (e.g., working-class culture, concrete historical moments) and evades sincere politics. For instance, hipster fashion in particular mines historical styles, which critics dismiss as pallid mimicry of styles grounded in authentic cultural and historical contexts. The appropriation of styles emptied of their historicity may be what Fredric Jameson (1983) referred to as the 'perpetual present' in which 'all that is left is to imitate dead styles.' Rather than cast hipster materiality as ironic representation or symbolic parody, hipster materiality may signify nothing especially concrete. It may be what Jameson (1983: 114) referred to as pastiche, the 'blank irony' in which there is no assumption of the normality that is being satirically imitated. A fixation on the symbolic and representational dimensions of hipster material assemblages risks ignoring that hipster things may be less about transgression, irony, or parody than idiosyncratic imagination of a creative and individualized self.

While spectacular displays like punk materialism make for a powerful example of style being wielded for public effects, starkly distinct aesthetics grounded in resistance may not capture most everyday materiality. Instead, much of the everyday world may be less about transgressive resistance than idiosyncratic imagination. Contemporary consumer subjectivity may be invested in social fluidity and idiosyncratic sensory experience, which breaks from the conventional perception of consumption as the acquisition of goods that symbolically stake claims to clear subjectivities and individuality. For instance, the material style referred to as 'acting basic' consciously selects for non-descript if not banal aesthetics, and the broader 'normcore' lifestyle implies a desire for social fluidity that is reflected in the anonymity of a stylistic blank slate. A term hatched by the trend forecasting firm K-Hole (2013), normcore departs from the aversion to 'sameness' and the implication that individuality is necessarily expressed in distinct practices, styles, and things. Instead, normcore argues for a 'post-authenticity' subjectivity in which people favor sameness and belonging over exclusivity and reject the premise that 'normality' exists. The suggestion that contemporary people fluidly appropriate disparate activities and things from a host of lifestyles or social collectives resonates with much of the post-subcultural scholarship that focuses on social dynamism and rejects 'mainstream culture'. Normcore selects against the 'trappings of uniqueness'; the implication is that in the early-twenty-first-century world 'people are born individuals and have to find their communities' (K-Hole, 2013: 27). To 'act basic' in this context means that people favor fashion and material things that are not inscribed as uniforms of exclusive social groups. Normcore suggests that the search for material exclusivity is an isolating experience, but normcore argues that there is 'liberation in being nothing special' (K-Hole, 2013: 36).

CONCLUSION: MATERIALITY AS EMBODIED AND IMAGINED EXPERIENCE

Perhaps normcore expresses the aftermath of signification, a moment in which materiality is an experience no longer tied to styles, branding, public display, historical precedent, concrete social symbolism, or even clear articulation. Nevertheless, while materiality theory frames things in an enormously complicated and dynamic ensemble of practices and things, in most thinkers' hands it does not deliver the eulogy for social symbolism, the deterministic power of class and inequality, and the consequence of ethnographic voices. Instead, materiality tempers a fixation on shallow notions of social determinism and probes how consumption might be framed in complex ways that reach beyond market determinism, resistance to dominant values, or stylistic distinction. Materiality underscores that things are part of an imagined and embodied human experience that is profoundly shaped by objects themselves. Consumer scholars committed to understanding the desire for things and the roles of goods in contemporary society can expand their analysis of things by more ambitiously analyzing the breadth of materiality in consumer culture.

REFERENCES

Agnew, J-C. (1993) Coming up for air: Consumer culture in historical perspective. In: Brewer, J. and Porter, R. (eds) *Consumption and the World of Goods*. New York: Routledge, pp. 19–39.

Appadurai, A. (1986) Introduction: commodities and the politics of value. In: Appadurai, A. (ed.) *The Social Life of Things: Commodities in Cultural Perspective*. New York: Cambridge University Press, pp. 3–63.

Appadurai, A. (1996) *Modernity at Large: Cultural Dimensions of Globalization*. Minneapolis: University of Minnesota Press.

Bennett, A. (1999) Subcultures or neo-tribes? Rethinking the relationship between youth, style and musical taste. *Sociology* 33(3): 599–617.

Bennett, J. (2010) *Vibrant Matter: A Political Ecology of Things*. Durham, NC: Duke University Press.

Bennett, L. (2011) Bunkerology – a case study in the theory and practice of urban exploration. *Environment and Planning D: Society and Space* 29(3): 421–434.

Bourdieu, P. (1984) *Distinction: A Social Critique of the Judgment of Taste*. Trans. Richard Nice. Cambridge: Harvard University Press.

Bourdieu, P. (1990) *The Logic of Practice*. Stanford, CA: Stanford University Press.

Breen, T.H. (1993) Narrative of commercial life: Consumption, ideology, and community on the eve of the American Revolution. *William and Mary Quarterly* 50(3): 471–501.

Breen, T.H. (2004) *The Marketplace of Revolution: How Consumer Politics Shaped American Independence*. New York: Oxford University Press.

Brown, B. (2001) Thing theory. *Critical Inquiry* 28(1): 1–22.

Campbell, C. (1987) *The Romantic Ethic and the Spirit of Modern Consumerism*. New York: Basil Blackwell.

Centre for Contemporary Cultural Studies (1976) *Resistance Through Rituals: Youth Subcultures in Post-War Britain*. London, Hutchinson.

Christopher, M. (2012) Confessions of a ruin pornographer, Part III: Dealing with the dead. Available at: http://www.abandonedamerica.us/confessions-of-a-ruin-pornographer (accessed 16 May 2016).

Douglas, M. (2001) Why do people want goods? In: Miller, D. (ed.) *Consumption: Theory and Issues in the Study of Consumption*. London: Routledge, pp. 262–271.

Douglas, M. and Isherwood, B. (1979) *The World of Goods: Towards an Anthropology of Consumption*. London: Basic Books.

Edensor, T. (2005) *Industrial Ruins: Space, Aesthetics and Materiality*. New York: Routledge.

Ewen, S. (1988) *All Consuming Images: The Politics of Style in Contemporary Culture*. New York: Basic Books.

Fox, R.W. and Lears, T.J.J. (eds) (1983) *The Culture of Consumption: Critical Essays in American History, 1880–1980*. New York: Pantheon.

Goffman, E. (1974) *Frame Analysis: An Essay on the Organization of Experience*. Cambridge, MA: Harvard University Press.

Hebdige, D. (1979) *Subculture: The Meaning of Style*. New York: Methuen.

Hebdige, D. (1988) *Hiding in the Light: On Images and Things*. London: Routledge.

Hodder, I. (2012) *Entangled: An Archaeology of the Relationships between Humans and Things*. New York: Wiley-Blackwell.

Horowitz, D. (1985) *The Morality of Spending: Attitudes toward the Consumer Society in America, 1875–1940*. Chicago: Elephant Books.

Ingold, T. (2007) Materials against materiality. *Archaeological Dialogues* 14(1): 1–16.

Ingold, T. (2012) Toward an ecology of materials. *Annual Review of Anthropology* 41: 427–442.

Jameson, F. (1983) Postmodernism and consumer society. In: Foster, H. (ed.) *The Anti-Aesthetic: Essays on Postmodern Culture*. Townsend, WA: Bay Press, pp. 111–125.

K-Hole (2013) Youth mode: A report on freedom. Available at: http://khole.net/issues/youth-mode/ (accessed 23 May 2016).

Knappett, C. and Malafouris, L. (eds) (2008) *Material Agency: Towards a Non-Anthropocentric Approach*. New York: Springer.

Latour, B. (1993) *We Have Never Been Modern*. New York: Harvester Wheatsheaf.

Latour, B. (1996) On actor-network theory: A few clarifications. *Soziale Welt* 47(4): 369–381.

Latour, B. (2005) *Reassembling the Social: An Introduction to Actor-Network-Theory*. Oxford: Oxford University Press.

Maffesoli, M. (1996) *The Time of the Tribes: The Decline of Individualism in Mass Society*. London: Sage.

Magaudda, P. (2011) When materiality 'bites back': Digital music consumption practices in the age of dematerialization. *Journal of Consumer Culture* 11(1): 15–36.
Mah, A. (2012) *Industrial Ruination, Community, and Place: Landscapes and Legacies of Urban Decline*. Toronto: University of Toronto Press.
McKendrick, N. (1960) Josiah Wedgwood: An eighteenth-century entrepreneur in salesmanship and marketing techniques. *The Economic History Review* New Series 12(3): 408–433.
Michael, J. (2015) It's really not hip to be a hipster: Negotiating trends and authenticity in the cultural field. *Journal of Consumer Culture* 15(2): 163–182.
Miller, D. (1987) *Material Culture and Mass Consumption*. New York: Basil Blackwell.
Miller, D. (1995) Consumption Studies as the Transformation of Anthropology. In: Miller, D. (ed.) *Acknowledging Consumption: A Review of New Studies*. New York: Routledge, pp. 264–295.
Miller, D. (2005) Materiality: An introduction. In: Miller, D. (ed.) *Materiality*. Durham, NC: Duke University Press, pp.1–50.
Muggleton, D. (1997) The Post-subculturalist. In: Redhead, S., Wynne, D. and O'Connor, J. (eds) *The Clubcultures Reader: Readings in Popular Cultural Studies*. Malden, MA: Blackwell, pp. 167–185.
Muggleton, D. (2000) *Inside Subculture: The Postmodern Meaning of Style*. Oxford: Berg.
Olsen, B. (2010) *In Defense of Things: Archaeology and the Ontology of Objects*. Lanham, Maryland: Altamira.
Olsen, B. and Pétursdóttir, Þ. (eds) (2014) *Ruin Memories: Materialities, Aesthetics and the Archaeology of the Recent Past*. New York: Routledge.
Olsen, B. and Witmore, C. (2015) Archaeology, Symmetry, and the Ontology of Things: A Response to Critics. *Archaeological Dialogues* 22(2): 187–197.
Pétursdóttir, Þ. and Olsen, B. (2014) Imaging modern decay: The aesthetics of ruin photography. *Journal of Contemporary Archaeology* 1(1): 7–56.
Preucel, R.W. and Meskell, L. (2004) Knowledges. In: Meskell, L. and Preucel, R.W. (eds) *A Companion to Social Archaeology*. New York: Blackwell Publishing, pp. 3–22.
Rathje, W. (1977) In praise of archaeology: Le projet du garbage. In: Ferguson, L. (ed.) *Historical Archaeology and the Importance of Material Things*. Special Issue of *Historical Archaeology* 2: 36–42.
Rathje, W. and Murphy, C. (1992) *Rubbish! The Archaeology of Garbage*. New York: HarperPerennial.
Redhead, S. (1990) *The End-of-the-century Party: Youth and Pop Towards 2000*. Manchester: Manchester University Press.
Susman, W. (1984) *Culture as History: The Transformation of American Society in the Twentieth Century*. New York: Pantheon.
Tamen, M. (2001) *Friends of Interpretable Objects*. Cambridge, MA: Harvard University Press.
Tilley, C. (2007) Materiality in materials. *Archaeological Dialogues* 14(1): 16–20.
Trigg, D. (2009) The place of trauma: Memory, hauntings, and the temporality of ruins. *Memory Studies* 2(1): 87–101.
Veblen, T. (1899) *The Theory of the Leisure Class*. New York: Dover.
Willis, P. (1977) *Learning to Labour: How Working Class Kids Get Working Class Jobs*. New York: Columbia University Press.
Witmore, C.L. (2007) Symmetrical archaeology: Excerpts of a manifesto. *World Archaeology* 39(4): 546–562.
Yates, T. (1990) Jacques Derrida: 'There is nothing outside of the text'. In: Tilley, C. (ed.) *Reading Material Culture*. Cambridge, MA: Basil Blackwell, pp. 206–280.

21

Subject/Object Relations and Consumer Culture

Shona Bettany

INTRODUCTION: THE UBIQUITY OF SUBJECT/OBJECT RELATIONS

It is possible to argue that all work on consumer culture deals explicitly or (more often) implicitly with subject/object relations. This chapter therefore moves between the implicit and explicit to render an understanding of the vista of theoretical underpinnings around subject/object relations and consumer culture. The chapter begins with studies of consumer culture and qualitative and interpretive culturally-oriented consumer research and examines their implicit underpinnings, and the political/ideological assumptions of the nature of subject/object relations that endures even in work that purports to challenge these assumptions, using three exemplar texts to illustrate the arguments made. The chapter then moves outwards into the broader disciplines that concern themselves with consumer culture, to examine the theories of subject/object relations that allow the reader to locate and situate this within its broader intellectual milieu. I conclude with three theoretical areas that directly relate to the subject/object relation that provide fruitful, challenging and insightful theoretical bases with which to deliver research and thought on consumer culture and materiality for the future.

Examining subject/object relations in cultural theory raises two inextricably linked issues. Firstly, in terms of the character of the relation between subject and object, as Hoskins (2006) argues, since Mauss (1925) and Malinowski (1922) cultural theorists have asserted that the lines between persons and things are culturally variable. Secondly, in terms of the hierarchy of the relation between subject and object, as Arnold et al. (2008) assert 'in its valorisation of the world of the mind, Western thought has long defined itself as above the world of things' (Arnold, Shepherd and Gibbs, 2008: 48). That is, different cultures not only assign, or perform, the descriptors 'subject' and 'object' differently, and draw the cultural boundaries between those nomenclatures differently, but, in Western cultural thought at least, they privilege that which is designated subject over that which is designated object. So what?, you might ask. Well, I suppose it depends whether one is designated a subject or an object! How does that happen, though? Taken from the dominant neo-liberal humanist perspective of Western thought, it could be argued in a common-sense way that objects are usually inanimate things and subjects are usually human, so taken from this perspective although 'we' think we know instinctively what is a subject and what is an object, it can still be argued that some things can become more subject-like (for example a prized sports car, an AI gadget, a talisman, a sentimentally valued heirloom, etc.) and some human subjects can become more object-like (for example, a slave or trafficked person, a refugee as seen through the lens of the right-wing media, even a much photographed and desired model or celebrity). Sticking with common sense, we seem to have no problem in developed and rational Western society in imbuing inanimate things with human subject-like qualities, with power, with thought, even with feelings, and, sadly, the corollary to this is that we have no problems, it seems, in objectifying certain other humans, giving them less than subject status, for a variety of functions and purposes. The central construct around which such designations are performed and become obdurate, lasting and eventually common-sense is agency. Subjects have agency, that is, they can 'act', objects, from this common-sense Western perspective, are *acted upon*, and, importantly within this worldview, any subject-like qualities are those that particular human subjects 'act upon' objects, and the meaning of those qualities resides in the minds and meaning systems of the human subjects that possess, experience, know or desire them. Any reader with little or no understanding of the theoretical vista around subject/object relations would read the above and recognise it as a part of the Western cultural understanding that allows us to categorise the sides and shades of this important structural binary.

The Western cultural common-sense understanding of subject/object relations outlined above, is where I start in this chapter, to outline the vista of understanding of subject/object relations in cultural theory relating to consumption. Cultural consumer studies are replete, unremarkably, with considerations of subject/object relations. The dominant underpinning assumption of the subject/object relations, I would argue, is that consumer subjects buy material objects to consume, reject, pay to experience them, or desire them, and it is this relation and all its baggage that continue to dominate the theorising around consumer culture. The consumer subject has agency, and can buy, act on and dispose of a range of non-agentic objects, and this relation and its myriad activities, meanings and experiences provides contextual fodder for the studies of, and underpins the theorising of, consumer culture. It is this set of Western common-sense underpinning assumptions about the subject/object relation, or binary, that this chapter explores, outlines and unpicks in order to deliver a deeper understanding to the reader of the role the subject/object binary plays in consumer culture studies, and what part it might play in the future.

DISCIPLINARY HISTORIES OF SUBJECT/OBJECT RELATIONS

Where I entered the debate about subject/object relations and consumer culture began with an intervention into interpretive, and culturally oriented consumer research with a critique of the handling of subject/object relationships within that paradigm (Bettany, 2007). Having recently completed an interdisciplinary PhD between sociology, feminist science studies and marketing (Bettany, 2005) I was immersed in the world of feminist material-semiotics (Haraway, 1992), actor-network theory (Latour, 1987; Law, 1992), heterogeneous networks (Callon, 1986) and agentic objects (Latour, 1992), and was dismayed to see the discipline of consumer research behind the meta disciplinary curve on the theorising of subject/object relations. The humanist, interpretive roots of the counter positivist movement (Belk, 1988; Hirschman, 1986) dominated a consumer-centric understanding of the subject/object relation (here mainly wrought as the relation between consumers and things); the object fulfils a myriad of functions for the consumer, but the underpinning philosophy of the relation remained as outlined in the Western neoliberal common-sense approach outlined above, that consumers are agentic, and use objects for a range of identity projects, experiences and meanings. This is outlined in the example used to explain the differences between humanism and positivism given by Hirschman in her 1986 paper, as follows;

> A positivist researcher investigating a consumer subculture might envisage the task as one of identifying exogenous background variables (e.g., socioeconomic status, geographic locale, and recency of immigration), which might influence group members' relative social mobility, achievement motivation, and materialism, which in tum may contribute to the group's preferences for certain types of apparel, home furnishings, and leisure activities. Thus a three-stage a priori model would be conceived and the researcher would try to operationalize and measure the several causes and effects composing the model. A humanist researcher investigating the same consumer subculture would work very differently. Because the goal is to understand the phenomenon in its own terms, the humanistic researcher would view the subculture as an amalgam of its members' values, actions, beliefs, motives, traditions, possessions, and aspirations. The researcher is primarily interested in learning the group's construction of reality and, for a marketing research study, how possessions, purchasing, apparel, automobiles, and leisure time activities fit into that reality. (Hirchman, 1986: 240–1)

In this comparative example, it can be seen that humanistic enquiry, like positivistic enquiry, albeit in a very different manner, privileges the human subject, and makes the assumption that the subject of enquiry is the subcultural group's members. How objects are dealt with in this type of analysis is only in terms of how consumption objects fit into those subjects' socially constructed realities. These humanist underpinnings have two main consequences. Firstly, following this history of thought within consumer research, the object in interpretive and culturally-oriented consumer research remains largely essentialised as something which is acted on, a 'thing in itself' that 'groups use' to construct 'practices, identities and meanings – to make collective sense of their environments and to orient their members' experiences and lives' (Arnould and Thompson, 2005: 869). Secondly, this then provides a theoretical rendering of the part the consumption object plays in consumer culture, which is incommensurate with contemporary theories of cultural materiality where theories have been developed which challenge the Cartesian subject/object binary and 'examine the entangled co-production and ontological indeterminacy of subject and object in cultural processes and action' (Bettany, 2007: 42).

The primary researcher explicitly examining subject/object relations within consumer culture, within this historical period in consumer research, and one of the pioneers of the movement away from the dominant positivist paradigm in the consumer research discipline, Russell Belk (1988), developed the theory of the extended self, a thesis that through its examination of possessions and self, developed a theory of subject/object relations in consumer culture that has become one of the most influential and important works in the discipline. Belk's original thesis is that we as humans develop and maintain our sense of self partly through the possessions we own. Belk uses as evidence for this, the harm to sense of self when possessions are lost or stolen, involuntarily dispossessed; the trends of materialism and self-definition in contemporary Western society being more about what one owns than what one does, and self-investment in possessions. Belk outlines special categories of possession that are most commonly incorporated by the human subject into the sense of self, 'collections, money, pets, other people and body parts' (Belk, 1988: 140). The implications of this incorporation of possessions into the self of the consumer are seen here predominantly in terms of defining meaning in life. Given that this watershed paper explicitly focuses on consumer subject/object relations, and was groundbreaking at the time in relation to this issue, the interpretation of the influence of that paper since then (Arnould and Thompson, 2005; explained further by Arnould, as documented in Ladik, Carrillat, and Tadajewski, 2015) is in its contribution to the development of theorising consumer identity projects. In other words, the agential primacy in the subject/object relationship theorising emerging from this hugely influential paper going forward is given most resolutely to the human consuming subject. Given this, it is perhaps unsurprising that it took until nearly thirty years later for papers to emerge that explicitly flipped this agency in order to challenge the common-sense understanding of subject/object relations in consumer culture theory. Given that this was the paradigm-shaping theory in consumer culture studies at the time I was doing my doctorate, in order to discuss a range of subject/object cultural theories I shifted my attention towards feminism, sociology, and science, technology and society studies.

SUBJECT/OBJECT RELATIONS AND CONSUMER RESEARCH: SOME EXEMPLARS

More recently (Bettany, 2016) I revisited the critique in my original work, ten years on, and found that despite the plethora of work drawing on the disciplines and writers spearheading this focus on subject/object relations, the underpinning common-sense Western humanist, neoliberal philosophy of subject/object relations outlined at the beginning of this chapter largely persists in consumer research. As Campbell and McHugh (2016: 101), in the same volume, argue, consumer research is embedded in 'a correlationist view of human beings doing things in the world to inanimate objects to make immaterial effects happen. Where marketing scholarship has taken up the case of materiality interest has lain not in stuff but in our human relation to it'. The result, they posit is that studies of consumption have remained stubbornly about 'humans interacting with humans'. Two key works that have emerged in the interim that explicitly challenge this hegemony of subject/object common-sense relationality are outlined below, and can be used to explore a challenging paradigm to that outlined in the opening sections of this chapter. The first is my follow-up paper from the original critique chapter (Bettany, 2007), 'Figuring companion-species consumption' (Bettany and Daly, 2008). In this article I use actor-network theory and feminist material-semiotics to analyse how pedigree dogs, due to being simultaneously performed as within the categories subject and object, nature and culture, and oscillating between these binaries in complex relationships with a range of heterogeneous actors, co-enable simultaneously conflicting cultures of subjectification and objectification, nature-ing and culture-ing, in international dog exhibition and breeding cultures. Drawing on Haraway's binary collapsing naturecultures trope I develop the idea of naturecultural consumption to explain how dog feeding and grooming practices emerge and are shaped by a drive to make sense of and reconcile the boundary-defying ontology of dogs. The second exemplar text I draw on Epp and Price (2010), whose work draws on Kopytoff's (1986) theory of the cultural biography of things and Daniel Miller's (1987) (see below) work on material culture to explore and theorise the agency of a dining room table in the lives of an extended family. In doing so they use the concept of singularity, where objects are given personal meaning, to explore how singularised objects move in and out of networks, effectively becoming decommodified and recommodified, how the singularised object agency is constrained and enabled by the network within which it is embedded, and ask how the network is affected similarly by the singularised object.

Both Epp and Price (2010) and Bettany and Daly (2008) clearly articulate their theoretical positions as moving on from the consumer identity-work focus of interpretive and culturally-oriented research on subject/object relations which have dominated the subject/object theoretical vista since Belk (1988), as outlined above. Both of these papers are ontologically different from the mainstream in terms of their approach to subject/object relations in consumer culture along three main lines, what is agency? What is/becomes an object/subject? and what is a relation? Although both papers draw on different theories of materiality, the understanding of these questions is very similar, and highly counter-intuitive to the dominant conceptualisations more commonly found in consumer research.

Taking the first of these theories, actor-network theory (ANT) (see Cochoy and Mallard, this volume), which is drawn on in both papers, this school of thought emerged in the 1980s, just prior to the first of Belk's influential works on subject/object relations in consumer culture research. ANT emerged initially from the sociology of science and technology (SST) and science, technology and society (STS) and initially produced beginning studies of laboratories and scientific endeavour (Callon, 1986; Latour, 1987), and quickly extending to research examining socio-technological networks in a wide variety of contexts (Law, 1992; see also Bajde, 2013 for an excellent review). The primary driver of the emergence of ANT was the debates in SST and STS about the agency of technologies, and the dominant heroic stories of the production of science and technology. It can be argued therefore that the basis for the emergence of ANT was a critique of common-sense notions of subject/object relations that had become ossified in scientific and technological stories. The key central questions in SST/STS were around the relationship between people/society/science and technologies and the relationship of the scientist subject and his studied/discovered objects. The fields of STS and SST prior to this were dominated by a dualist argument (somewhat reified and simplified here due to space constraints) between social determinism and technological determinism (see MacKenzie and Wajcman (1999) and Latour (1992) for further reading on this). In social determinism the social (i.e. the human subjects) determined the shape of the technologies and discoveries that emerge, in other words, the needs, wants, desires and cultural mores of a society, and the human subjects involved directly in these areas, determine what science and technology produces and discovers. On the other hand, technological determinism arguments held that technologies and discoveries were not shaped or produced by human subjects like scientists, or by society, but emerge through the logic of heroic discovery, and in their turn shape society (and the activity of scientists and technologists) around them. It is likely that, as most readers would deduce, everyone understood that a more complex combination of the two is going on, and the texts, read in depth, reflect that, but at the time in the early 1980s there was not a theoretical hook to hang an alternative explanation on. ANT then emerged as a hugely successful and influential actor in its own right (see Law, 1999) to provide an alternative to the common-sense and essentialist subject/object dualism inherent in both of these accounts. To unpick that sentence, both accounts see an already pre-existing subject and object (an essentialist idea of what subject and object is – this is taken as common sense). The point of analysis in both is the relationship between the two (the relation between two already pre-existing entities) and the point of difference between them is merely from which way round comes the shaping of technology and society (i.e. where is the majority of the agency coming from). ANT handled subject/object relations and agency in a very different way. As Latour explains:

> Those advocating the actor network approach agree with the social constructivist claim that sociotechnical systems are developed through negotiations between people, institutions, and organizations. But they make the additional interesting argument that artefacts are part of these negotiations as well. (Latour, 1992: 151)

Latour (1992) was at pains to argue for analyses that attended to what he called 'the missing masses', that is, the artefacts and objects that have been long ignored by theorists of social and cultural life. The ontological basis of ANT is material-semiotic (meaning and materiality are entangled and inseparable in analysis), and the research is based on in-depth ethnographic studies of networks of heterogeneous human and non-human actors (Haraway, 1991; Law, 1999), with a flat, symmetrical ontology which implies that all human and non-human participants in an analysis should be treated as equal, active participants. Agency, therefore is a central construct changed from the dominant ideas of agency outlined in the previous sections. Agency, as seen in the Western (particularly individualist neoliberal) cultures, relates to the ability to do reflexive, purposeful, goal-directed activity and is almost exclusively attached to the primary sentient being, namely human subjects (although other non-human animals – like dogs – get somewhat of a look in too). Objects, in this view, are seen as not having agency, and human society becomes a little paranoid and worried when stories emerge around non-human, non-sentient agentic developments (see for example, Belk, 2016). However, Latour (and other ANT theorists) argue that agency should be reconceptualised as an outcome of networks of actors, rather than an impulse or drive of the individual subject. Latour (2000: 192) argues that 'purposeful action and intentionality may not be properties of objects, but they are also not properties of humans either. They are properties of collectives of human and non-humans'. Latour's argument is that agency is linked to how the meaning and materiality of objects, bodies and other entities emerge. Agency is not something that human actors have (and apply) to the material world around them. The material object (and the subject) emerge as effects of the surrounding relations within which they are embedded. That is, meaning and materiality, subject and object, co-emerge and are co-constituted. Meaning and materiality are embedded within complex socio-material assemblages of people, things and ideas (Canniford and Shankar, 2013; see also DeLanda, 2006 for further insights into the assemblage concept). 'ANT seeks to understand how these assemblages become stable or fail to achieve stability (Latour, 2005)' (Bettany, Kerrane and Hogg, 2014: 7). This not only means a change in what is deemed to *have* agency in analyses, but also *in what agency as a concept actually means*. Furthermore, again challenging the subject/object common-sense articulation, in this worldview subjects and objects are not essential things, pre-existing the analysis of their relation, but are also effects of the heterogeneous network, not only in terms of what kind of subject or object they emerge as within the network (remember the idea above that we naïve readers can see as sensible – that objects can carry meanings that make them more subject like, and vice versa) but in terms of the network actually producing them as object or subject *per se*. In both of the example texts I have used, these challenging ideas to the mainstream paradigm understanding of subject/object relations are evident. In Epp and Price's work, the table has agency within the network and the analysis looks at the variable agencies produced by the network that change what might be seen as the essential nature of the table, it is commodified and decommodified, has a singularity that might vary depending on its locations within the network. In Bettany and Daly's work, the deliberate choice (following Haraway, 2003) of an ambiguous subject/object (the dog) is used to understand how the processes of subjectification and objectification within the network result in complex regimes of care, and ontological oscillation of the dog, the human subject, the culture of dog exhibition and a myriad of other human and non-human actors. As documented in Bettany (2016), other works drawing on these symmetrical, processual and emergent approaches to the subject/object relation in consumer research are: Bettany and Kerrane (2011), who use actor-network theory to examine how mass-produced plastic chicken coops are made and remade as important actors within the network of families in the context of the formation and maintenance of identification with a voluntary simplified lifestyle; Giesler (2012), who uses Callonian ANT theory (Callon, 1986) to theorise the market-making processes around doppelganger brand management using the example of Botox; Hui (2012), who examines mobile assemblages of people and bird-watching; Thomas, Price and Schau (2013), who use ANT, in their study of long-distance runners to examine how heterogeneous communities align their interests and achieve cohesion through resource-dependence; Bettany, Kerrane and Hogg (2014), who use ANT to theorise how caring technologies co-configure ambivalently gendered actor-networks within new family settings; Martin and Schouten (2014), who use ANT to theorise how consumers mobilise human and non-human actors to co-constitute products, practices and infrastructures towards new market emergence in the motorcycle industry; Epp,

Schau and Price (2014), who examine how brands and technologies mediate long-distance family relationships; and Parmentier and Fischer (2015), who conceptualise brands as assemblages of heterogeneous components and examine how fans contribute to the destabilisation of a brand's identity. Other writers have produced theoretical/conceptual papers outlining this alternative approach to subject/object relations. Examples here include: rethinking ontologies of consumption as enacted through precarious networks of heterogeneous relations (Bajde, 2013); discussing as taken for granted the concepts of materiality, materialism and agency and connecting consumer research to high-level theorisations of materiality (Borgerson, 2014); outlining the differences between ANT and other consumer theories, taking into account non-human actors (Belk, 2014); illustrating how non-representational theory can augment existing ANT applications in consumer research (Hill, Canniford and Mol, 2014); and, finally, Canniford and Badje's (2016) excellent edited collection of work on the engagement of heterogeneous assemblages with consumer research studies.

Many of the above selection of works, it might be argued (and I include some of my own work in this critique), differ somewhat from the exemplar texts used to delineate in detail the theoretical debate on subject/object relations in consumer research. In them, the reader might find the ghost of humanism and the Western agentic subject (as exemplified in the 'objects as primarily identity formation tools' paradigm critiqued above) are very much present! I argue that this has occurred for two reasons. Firstly, as mentioned before, interpretive and culturally oriented works' roots in the humanistic, semiotic approach to consumer research (e.g. Hirschman, 1986) that was a necessary political response to mainstream positivism continues to make the emphasis on human meaning and action the dominating worldview. Secondly, and perhaps more contentiously, I would argue that due to consumer research being dominated by US journals (particularly JCR and JM) it perhaps unreflexively mirrors the neoliberal political ideology that reflects the political conditions (i.e. the USA) from which it emerges. The neoliberal political worldview sees the human (consumer) subject as free, choosing, and with primary agential power. The neoliberal subject has an individualist purview, with responsibility for the self, and human outcomes are rendered through free, autonomous (consumer) choices made within a competitive market-based political economy (Ball, 2012). Taking this as the starting point for analysis of subject/object relations it then becomes highly problematic to reconfigure consumer agency as made up in the multiplicity of material-semiotic heterogeneous actor networks within which it emerges, much less that objects and non-human others should be dealt with symmetrically in analysis, or that human intentionality needs to be carefully written out of accounts. In reading (particularly US published) accounts drawing on theoretical approaches that challenge the common-sense subject/object relation assumptions of neo-liberalism 'one can read the struggles between the lines … consumers assemble experiences and collectives, managers struggle with brands and markets, consumers make markets using resources' (Bettany, 2016: 192). I recognise these struggles very well from my own encounters with reviewers! Although all of the works ostensibly draw on symmetrical and emergent ontologies in terms of subject/object relations, it might be a worthwhile exercise for the reader new to these debates to try to categorise the empirical works above into those where the Western humanist, agentic consumer subject still stalks the pages, and those where the ontological symmetry and emergent nature of subject and object is, as far as possible, theoretically expressed. Please note though in this exercise, the aim is not to critique the authors but rather to critique the conditions of possibility of the discipline.

SUBJECT/OBJECT RELATIONS: THEORETICAL UNDERPINNINGS

Having written a substantial amount outlining and then challenging the dominant idea about (human/consumer) subjects and the kind of agency implied in our Western understanding of them, using three exemplar texts (Belk, 1988; Bettany and Daly, 2008; Epp and Price, 2010) to draw boundaries between the dominant and challenging theoretical paradigms of subject/object relations in interpretive work within the discipline of consumer research, it is necessary now to dig down into the theoretical vista of objects, things and materiality to further develop the discussion on subject/object relations in consumer culture. The key concepts used to theorise subject/object relations in consumer culture studies have been materiality, objects and affordances. As described above, objects in interpretive qualitative work in consumer research have tended historically to be defined in terms of something that 'groups use' to construct 'practices, identities and meanings – to make collective sense of their environments and to orient their members' experiences and lives' (Arnould and Thompson, 2005: 869), with, as I have argued above, an enduring humanist flavour. However, the wider social sciences around cultural studies handle 'the object' very differently.

One of the primary theorists of materiality in relation to consumer culture is Daniel Miller (1987), who, in the relational ontology tradition, akin to Latourian work cited above, for example, seeks to challenge the subject/object dualism and understand how we consume with and through material objects. He is situated within material culture studies, an interdisciplinary space for research into the ways in which 'artefacts are implicated in the construction, maintenance and transformation of social identities … the investigation of the relationship between people and things irrespective of time and space' (Miller and Tilley, 1996: 5). This relation is seen as an ongoing dialectic rather than dichotomy, as in subject creating object creating subject (Geismar, 2011). Miller's first book directly dealing with this area, *Material Culture and Mass Consumption* (1987), was the start of an ongoing large and prolific publishing career that is international and multi-audience in scope, and recently has fully embraced the new technological vista of society, for example Facebook and social media, in relation to consumption and life (Horst and Miller, 2013). The importance of Miller's work is outlined by Borgerson (2009), where she makes the point that Miller has highlighted the oft-ignored relation between 'consumption-based assumptions and theories of materiality' (Borgerson, 2009: 155) and argues that Miller's position vis-à-vis this relation, as outlined in this early book, drawing on a hybrid rendering of subject/object relations, is that 'consumption is a process by which human beings materialise or objectify values and meanings' and 'resolve conflicts and paradoxes in everyday life'. Objectification is an important concept in Miller's work, where, drawing on Hegel, he shows how value and meaning, for example, pass between people and things in a dialectical relation. Objectification refers to the activity by which human beings fashion themselves in the external world through consumption activities, by which he means 'the diverse appropriations by which consumers turn impersonal, standard commodities into personal, singular possessions. This activity of appropriation is "consumption work"' (Foster, 2011: 44, see also Miller, 1987). Although Miller's work is kaleidoscopic, and one needs to read a range of his work to reflect and understand this, for the purposes of this chapter about subject/object relations and consumer culture, the book I would recommend to early readers on materiality and consumption would be *Stuff* (2010). The aim of *Stuff* is to provide an account of Daniel Miller's personal and research anthology over around thirty years of his ethnographic study of material culture. In terms of theoretical positioning, vis-à-vis the subject/object relation, *Stuff* characterizes much of Miller's work, as it is a pulling together of the different and diverse strands of his work, to give a broad picture of the range of work (and perspectives on material culture) by this author. *Stuff* illustrates Miller's more anthropological, dialogic rendering of the subject/object dualism to ANT, for example, which has tended in some treatments to focus more on the object in the analysis. I would characterize many ANT studies as shading into more of an object-oriented ontology (OOO) than Miller's work, but would also note that for me this flipping of (privileging of) the object in analyses is a necessary political move to counter the primacy of the human subject in analyses (see also Blackhurst, 2015; Campbell and McHugh, 2016). As might be expected from someone situated within anthropology, the context and descriptions in Miller's work are rich and his work is theoretically diverse. As Hart (2010) in his review of *Stuff* argues, *Stuff* typifies Miller's approach throughout his work that 'people not only make things, but things make people, that is, we are unconsciously shaped by the artefacts that surround us'. This illustrates that, in common with ANT, Miller does not begin his analyses with an essentialised notion of what the subject or object of his study is, in contrast to the Western common-sense notions of this as reflected in much of consumer studies, and outlined above, but sees what is the subject and the object as outcomes of relations. It is for this reason he forms an important part of what might be called the oppositional paradigm to the dominant views on subject/object relations, as recounted earlier.

A new entrant into the lexicon of consumer culture studies vis-à-vis subject/object relations is the concept of affordances. This is not a new concept in itself but one that has gradually started creeping into stories of assemblages, socio-techno networks and distributed agency, of the approaches outlined above when applied to consumer culture theorisations. As argued above, socio-material approaches derive from and are mainly utilised to analyse human-technology relations. Technologies are seen as constructed in reciprocal socio-material relations, where it is assumed that technological objects have certain 'affordances' that suggest what potentials they offer in a relation with the user (Akrich and Latour, 1992; Bloomfield et al., 2010; Pfaffenberger, 1992). The idea of affordances, originally from ecological psychology (Gibson, 1979) was developed as a theory to help understand from an interactionist perspective how abilities and constraints in action are based on relational agent situation interactions. Put simply:

> in any interaction involving an agent with some other system, conditions that enable that interaction include some properties of the agent along with some properties of the other system … affordance refers to whatever it is about the environment that contributes to the kind of interaction that occurs. (Greeno, 1994: 338)

It is therefore a theory about object ('environment') agency as defined within a set of relations. Affordance theory migrated to studies of the socio-technical, and here it is argued that they 'are not reducible to their material constitution', that is they are not a list of features, 'but are inextricably bound up with specific, historically situated modes of engagement and ways of life' and that analysis should focus on 'how specific action possibilities emerge' (Bloomfield et al., 2010: 420). In other words, it is a means to understanding the possibilities of what can be done (possible agencies) as a result of the relation between subject and object, what activities and constraints the object/subject relation affords. As Gibson (1979/1986) argues, affordance cuts across the subject/object dichotomy, and he was at pains to dismiss the notion that meaning and opportunities for action of objects are products of the human or animal mind (Withagen et al., 2012). As a means to study the attribution of action possibilities in relation to technologies, affordance theory has been utilised in studies of how disability gets constituted alongside technological artefacts such as computers (Bloomfield et al., 2010); the affordances of play areas for children's physical development (Sandseter, 2009); the consumption of music in a digital age (Nowak, 2016); how poor youths and mobile phone usage objectified the digital divide in Sri Lanka (Wijetunga, 2014); how learners and mobile learning institutions are linked and produce technologies designated as 'for learning' (Wright and Parchoma, 2011); the moral affordances of alternative tourism, through the digital site couchsurfing.com (Molz, 2013); technologies of social media in organisations, with specific regard to the emergence of new organisational communications styles (Treem and Leonardi, 2012); and how new digital technologies and backpackers create new forms of tourism and mobile society (Molz and Paris, 2015). In consumer research, although, as mentioned above, the term affordance/s has started to be mentioned in specific research, it is very early days in terms of developing affordance theory. A search of the *Journal of Consumer Research* (04/01/17) found several very recent articles within this school that mention affordances but do not conceptualise or theorise the term (Dolbec and Fischer, 2015; Figueiredo and Scaraboto, 2016). As mentioned, although the term has crept into the lexicon, it has not been the articulated focus of the work, and has therefore, understandably, not been defined nor conceptualised. One recent paper (Bettany and Kerrane, 2016), within studies of consumer culture, that has addressed this hiatus has used a combination of affordance theory and neutralisation theory to examine the uptake and consumption of a controversial product, the child surveillance tracker. This is an electronic, GPS and often SIM-enabled device that parents buy to track the movement of their children. It has found that the positive and negative affordances rendered between parents, children and the product co-enact and cohere ambivalent parental styles of laissez-faire and over-controlling parenting in the accounts of parents using this technology. The importance of this for thinking about subject/object relations and consumer culture is to take a social-psychological theory, oft used to understand and theorise controversial consumption and how consumers rationalise and justify their use and purchase of them, neutralisation theory – a theory that makes assumptions about the dominant perspective on subject/object relations – and engage it with a theory that assumes the challenging paradigm's perspective on object and subject relations, including the relational agency of the consumer subject and their consumption object. In doing this, new and fresh understandings of how consumers, together with the action possibilities and constraints of their consumption objects, collectively make sense of their consumption in terms of (in this case) parental style. Understanding the often conflicting agencies that emerge from this relation can, we argue, help designers, marketers and policy makers to gain new insights that cannot be found in studies of the human subject/social alone.

A final influence on the theories of subject/object relations I will discuss in cultural studies of culture, consumption and materiality, is feminist material-semiotics, as outlined and promulgated primarily by Donna Haraway. Coming from a feminist perspective, for Haraway, and many other feminist theorists, dualisms (like subject/object) and the way that these are assigned, performed and hierarchised have been a key and enduring political target. This is because in their hierarchies, they often reflect the binary masculine/feminine, so for example, women are culturally reduced to the body (object/nature), and men to the mind (subject/culture). This reflects the masculinist and patriarchal Cartesian underpinnings of much common-sense cultural understanding. Material-semiotics recognises that the material world of things and the semiotic (how meaning is made) are co-constitutive and emergent, and as such akin to the subject/object hybridity of the alternative theories outlined above. In fact, John Law, one of the primary theorists associated with the emergence and success of ANT has argued that it is better to talk about material-semiotics than ANT, as the former 'catches the openness, uncertainty, revisability and diversity of the most interesting work' (Law, 2008: 142). Haraway, being primarily a feminist, has critiqued the ostensibly acritical nature of ANT and asked what difference do such studies make, and as such, using her binary-challenging material-semiotic tropes, like the cyborg and companion species, unpicks worlds that might be otherwise, through challenging taken-for-granted formulations of the way things are. The cyborg (cybernetic organism), her most influential trope, is used to destabilise the subject/object (and concomitantly the human/non-human) binaries to unpick the cultural assumptions about them written into scientific, political, popular and academic accounts and to the detriment of marginalised groups and inequalities. Her later work uses companion species (Haraway, 2003), notably, dogs, as a way to disrupt the subject/object binary. This use of a mundane (pet dog) rather than mythical, futuristic (cyborg) trope is deliberate, and illustrates the hybrid nature of the commonplace. I used this as a theoretical lens in my critique chapter and the example paper given above (Bettany, 2007; Bettany and Daly, 2008), deliberately looking at dog exhibition and breeding cultures, an often denigrated, not-taken-seriously context, to show how nationalities, histories, cultures and worlds are built from the assumptions around these mundane but taken from granted subject/object and nature/culture binaries, and what consumer culture theory can learn from this. Haraway's subject/object hybridity stems from her feminist politics, and can be understood as an intervention in the dominant ideas of purity and the 'truth' of essential binary structures around culture and the systems of knowing of it. Here she draws on the work of anthropologist Mary Douglas (1966) about how the body is 'made up' culturally, and not an essential taken-for-granted, where hybridity and impurity are seen as taboo and liminal, and she uses deliberate tropes of impurity (like the Cyborg) to expose and challenge the binary certainties underpinning much inequality. This positions her work differently to all of the above, although she allies herself with both cultural studies and science studies, within which all are located, what distinguishes her work is that her quest is to produce knowledge of the world that can disrupt structured inequalities and knowledge regimes and unquestioned realities, particularly scientific objectivism, that keep these structured inequalities obdurately commonplace and natural, 'knowledge-power processes that inscribe and materialise the world in some forms rather than others' (Haraway, 1997: 7). To explain further, if subjects and objects are being 'made up' in relations, then there can be the assumption that different orderings or types of those relations can make up different subjects and objects, with different outcomes for the world. What Haraway calls 'the relentless commitment to show the established disorder is not necessary, nor perhaps even real. The world can be otherwise' (Haraway, 1994: 64). Newcomers to Haraway's work on subject/object relations (and other structuring binaries) might begin with the book *Modest Witness* (Haraway, 1997), particularly the way she presents material entities, the foetus, chip, seed, bomb, etc. and unpicks their imploded worlds of meaning and materiality, agency and agencies and her use of them in 'tearing down the Berlin wall between the world of subjects and the world of objects' (Haraway, 1997: 270).

SUBJECT/OBJECT RELATIONS: FUTURE POSSIBILITIES

In terms of future developments for subject/object theorising vis-à-vis consumer culture research, I see great possibilities in particularly affordance theory. This, firstly, is because I think that the concept of affordances allows a softer way in to relational agency for the US-dominated neoliberal sub-discipline of consumer culture theory. The action possibilities idea enables a common-sense (although not strictly ontologically correct) understanding of human choice, that sits more easily with the aforementioned neoliberal political underpinnings. It is for this reason that, I would argue, it has started to emerge within the consumer culture theory lexicon. Secondly, in terms of the broader study of consumer culture I think it also has the promise to engage with and intervene in many sociological and psychological theories of consumer relations with material objects, beyond its current focus on technologies. In the example paper given above, I think that I have shown it can provide an alternative lens to understanding consumer cultures. On the other ontological extreme from humanism lies another future possibility for scholars interested in alternative paradigms of subject/object relations, object-oriented ontology (OOO) (see Campbell and McHugh, 2016 for a review). This approach is not, as far as I know, currently explored in studies of consumer culture, and thus it does not form part of my substantive review. However, OOO, rendered through Lingis (1998) asserts that our worlds are filled with non-human imperatives, to which we respond as objects. Further, and reminiscent of Haraway's imploded nodes of bomb, chip, foetus, gene, within OOO the concept of the hyperobject (Morton, 2013), an object massively distributed in space and time, also provides a fruitful and alternative ontological basis to explore the subject/object relation. It is somewhat of a misnomer to use this here, as OOO views everything as an object, and object/object relations are a focus. Bradshaw and Canniford (2010) (also see Canniford and Bradshaw, 2016) allude to the concept of hyperobjects in terms of how excrement is ubiquitous and thus resistant to disposition, a key concept in consumer research; hyperobjects like bacteria, ozone (or poo) cannot be 'put away' (Campbell and McHugh, 2016: 96) or disposed of. This directs the consumer culture researcher to the object as the centre of analysis in what might be described as a radical anti-humanist stance. The final area recommended for development in studies of consumer culture vis-à-vis the subject/object relation is feminist *material* semiotics. The reason for this selection returns me to my original critical work (Bettany, 2007) and, more particularly, my revisiting of this critique in Bettany (2016). Studies of consumer culture and materiality remain stubbornly acritical, and the interrogation of the rendering of the subject/object relation lies, I suggest, at the heart of a possible revitalised critique. As outlined above, Haraway's material-semiotics exposes the making up and hardening of categories, through binary opposition, where we take for granted 'what fits where'. In one example, in terms of ascription to subject and object, the turn to more language, or semiotically driven understandings of consumer culture, in the face of a new digital world, concepts such as dematerialisation, immateriality and liquid consumption (as discussed in Belk, 2013; Bardhi and Eckhardt, 2012; Bardhi et al., 2012) have emerged. Material-semiotics can be employed within this conceptual universe to unpick and challenge the processes of the subjectification and objectification of human and non-human actors. So, for example, the serially interchangeable, dislocated (i.e. usually migrant), unconnected (i.e. not employed) worker, becomes as much an object within this world as his car, or the smart phone used to summon him by the privileged subject consumer. In this raced, classed (and often gendered) system of liquidised (I chose that word carefully, for this is a violence) bodies, and hyper-subjectified (i.e. with enhanced agency) consumers, a challenger theory that explicitly examines the making and ossification through consumer culture, and its theories, of the subject/object binary and its politics, is invaluable.

CONCLUSION

In conclusion, in this chapter I have attempted to outline the region of discourse around the subject/object relation in consumer culture studies. Firstly, to introduce the reader to this complex field I outlined a common-sense understanding of this relation, the terms of the debate – subject, object and agency – and gave some illustrative examples to explore what many readers might recognise as a commonplace understanding, but one which is quite specific to predominantly Western, neoliberal cultures; that is, that the subject is largely seen as hierarchically superior, with agency, and human, and the object is seen as secondary to, non-agentic, often non-sentient, and non-human. I then outlined my own engagement with the debates around subject/object relations, specifically, my interventions into the field of consumer culture theory, a sub-discipline of consumer behaviour research with a humanistic history that has coloured, and arguably continues the colour, the theorisation around this important structural binary. I then presented three example texts to illustrate the dominant paradigm around subject/object relations in consumer culture theory, and its paradigmatic alternatives. Having done this, I outlined some of the major approaches and theorists that have been drawn upon from the broader social/scientific disciplines to formulate these alternative and successor approaches to subject/object relations. These approaches, although not a definitive list, outline broadly the background ontologies and politics of alternative approaches to guide the reader into a fuller understanding of the differences and similarities of the approaches on offer. These approaches are the ANT school, the work on material culture by Daniel Miller, affordances theory, and feminist material-semiotics. The reason for the choices made, are to offer the reader a cross-section of alternatives to the dominant humanist paradigm, not just in terms of differences ontologically, that is, the differences between how the humanist and ANT approaches see subject and object, but also politically, that is, how all the other approaches differ from feminist material-semiotics in that the politics of the subject/object relation are implicated in the structuring not only of inequalities, but that material-semiotic analyses can be used to expose fragility in seemingly taken-for-granted and obdurate power structures and suggest interventions towards possible different realities.

REFERENCES

Akrich, M. and Latour, B. (1992) 'A summary of a convenient vocabulary for the semiotics of human and nonhuman assemblies'. In W.E. Bijker and J. Law (eds), *Shaping Technology/Building Society: Studies in Sociotechnical Change* (pp. 259–264). Cambridge, MA: The MIT Press.

Arnold, M., Shepherd, C. and Gibbs, M. (2008) 'Remembering things', *The Information Society*, 24(1): 47–53.

Arnould, E.J. and Thompson, C.J. (2005) 'Consumer culture theory (CCT): Twenty years of research', *Journal of Consumer Research*, 31(4): 868–882.

Bajde, D. (2013) 'Consumer culture theory (re)visits actor–network theory: Flattening consumption studies', *Marketing Theory*, 13(2): 227–242.

Ball, S.J. (2012) 'Performativity, commodification and commitment: An I-spy guide to the neoliberal university', *British Journal of Educational Studies*, 60(1): 17–28.

Bardhi, F. and Eckhardt, G.M. (2012) 'Access-based consumption: The case of car sharing', *Journal of Consumer Research*, 39(4): 881–898.

Bardhi, F., Eckhardt, G.M. and Arnould E.J. (2012) 'Liquid Relationship to Possessions', *Journal of Consumer Research*, 39(3): 510–529.

Belk, R.W. (1988) 'Possessions and the extended self', *Journal of Consumer Research*, 15(2): 139–168.

Belk, R.W. (2013) 'Extended self in a digital world', *Journal of Consumer Research*, 40(3): 477–500.

Belk, R.W. (2014) 'You are what you can access: Sharing and collaborative consumption online', *Journal of Business Research*, 67(8): 1595–1600.

Belk, R.W. (2016) 'Extended self in a digital world', *Current Opinion in Psychology*, 10: 50–54.

Bettany, S.M. (2005) *The Making of Marketing Knowledge* (Doctoral dissertation, University of Lancaster).

Bettany, S.M. (2007) 'The material semiotics of consumption or where (and what) are the objects in consumer culture theory?', *Consumer Culture Theory (Research in Consumer Behavior)*, 11: 41–56.

Bettany, S. (2016) 'Where (and what) is the critical in consumer-oriented actor-network theory?' In R. Canniford and D. Bajde (eds), *Assembling Consumption: Researching Actors, Networks and Markets* (pp. 187–197). London: Routledge.

Bettany, S.M. and Daly, R. (2008) 'Figuring companion-species consumption: A multi-site ethnography of the post-canine Afghan hound', *Journal of Business Research*, 61(5): 408–418.

Bettany, S. and Kerrane, B. (2011) 'The (post-human) consumer, the (post-avian) chicken and the (post-object) Eglu: Towards a material-semiotics of anti-consumption', *European Journal of Marketing*, 45(11/12): 1746–1756.

Bettany, S. and Kerrane, B. (2016) 'The socio-materiality of parental style: Negotiating the multiple affordances of parenting and child welfare within the new child surveillance technology market', *European Journal of Marketing*, 50(11): 2041–2066.

Bettany, S.M., Kerrane, B. and Hogg, M.K. (2014) 'The material-semiotics of fatherhood: The co-emergence of technology and contemporary fatherhood', *Journal of Business Research*, 67(7): 1544–1551.

Blackhurst, A. (2015) 'From life writing to thing writing: François Bon's Autobiographie des objets', *French Cultural Studies*, 26(4): 426–438.

Bloomfield, B.P., Latham, Y. and Vurdubakis, T. (2010) 'Bodies, technologies and action possibilities: When is an affordance?' *Sociology*, 44(3): 415–433.

Borgerson, J.L. (2009) 'Materiality and the comfort of things: Drinks, dining and discussion with Daniel Miller', *Consumption, Markets and Culture*, 12(2): 155–170.

Borgerson, J.L. (2014) 'The flickering consumer: New materialities and consumer research'. In R.W. Belk, L. Price and L. Peñaloza (eds), *Consumer Culture Theory (Research in Consumer Behavior, Volume 15)*. Emerald Group Publishing Limited.

Bradshaw, A. and Canniford, R. (2010) 'Excremental theory development', *Journal of Consumer Behaviour*, 9(2): 102–112.

Callon, M. (1986) 'The sociology of an actor-network: The case of the electric vehicle'. In M. Callon, J. Law and A. Rip (eds), *Mapping the Dynamics of Science and Technology*. Houndmills, UK: Palgrave Macmillan.

Campbell, N. and McHugh, G. (2016) 'OOO:Oooh!'. In R. Canniford and D. Bajde (eds), *Assembling Consumption: Researching Actors, Networks and Markets*. London: Sage.

Canniford, R. and Bajde, D. (2016) Assembling Consumption: Researching Actors, Networks and Markets. London: Routledge.

Canniford, R. and Bradshaw, A. (2016) 'Shit happens', *The Practice of the Meal: Food, Families and the Market Place*, 10: 233–244.

Canniford, R. and Shankar, A. (2013) 'Purifying practices: How consumers assemble romantic experiences of nature', *Journal of Consumer Research*, 39(5): 1051–1069.

DeLanda, M. (2006) *A New Philosophy of Society: Assemblage Theory and Social Complexity*. Edinburgh: A&C Black.

Dolbec, P.Y. and Fischer, E. (2015) 'Refashioning a field? Connected consumers and institutional dynamics in markets', *Journal of Consumer Research*, 41(6): 1447–1468.

Douglas, M. (1966) *Purity and Danger*. London: Routledge and Kegan Paul.

Epp, A.M. and Price, L.L. (2010) 'The storied life of singularized objects: Forces of agency and network transformation', *Journal of Consumer Research*, 36(5): 820–837.

Epp, A.M., Schau, H.J., and Price, L.L. (2014) The role of brands and mediating technologies in assembling long-distance family practices. *Journal of Marketing*, 78(3): 81–101.

Figueiredo, B. and Scaraboto, D. (2016) 'The Systemic Creation of Value Through Circulation in Collaborative Consumer Networks', *Journal of Consumer Research*, 43(4): 509–533.

Foster, R.J. (2011) 'The uses of use value: Marketing, value creation, and the exigencies of consumption work'. In D. Zwick and J. Cayla (eds), *Inside Marketing: Practices, Ideologies, Devices* (pp. 42–57). Oxford: Oxford University Press.

Gibson, J.J. (1979/1986) *The Ecological Approach to Visual Perception*. Boston, MA: Houghton Mifflin.

Geismar, H. (2011) '"Material culture studies" and other ways to theorize objects: A primer to a regional debate', *Comparative Studies in Society and History*, 53(01): 210–218.

Giesler, M. (2012) 'How doppelgänger brand images influence the market creation process: Longitudinal insights from the rise of Botox cosmetic', *Journal of Marketing*, 76(6): 55–68.

Greeno, J.G. (1994) 'Gibson's affordances', *Psychological Review*, 101(2): 336–342.

Hansson, N. (2015) '"Mobility-things" and consumption: Conceptualizing differently mobile families on the move with recent purchases in urban space', *Consumption Markets & Culture*, 18(1): 72–91.

Haraway, D.J. (1988) 'Situated knowledges: The science question in feminism and the privilege of partial perspective', *Feminist Studies*, 14(3): 575–599.

Haraway, D.J. (1991) *Simians, Cyborgs, and Women: The Reinvention of Women*. London and New York: Routledge.

Haraway, D.J. (1992) 'The promises of monsters: A regenerative politics for inappropriate/d others'. In L. Grossberg, C. Nelson, P.A. Treichler (eds), *Cultural Studies* (pp. 295–337). New York: Routledge.

Haraway, D.J. (1994) 'A game of cat's cradle: Science studies, feminist theory, cultural studies', *Configurations*, 2(1): 59–71.

Haraway, D.J. (1997) Modest_Witness@Second_Millennium. FemaleMan_Meets_OncoMouse: Feminism and Technoscience. New York: Routledge.

Haraway, D.J. (2003) *The companion species manifesto: Dogs, people, and significant otherness* (Vol. 1). Chicago: Prickly Paradigm Press.

Hart, K. (2010) 'The book review: Stuff by Daniel Miller', Open Anthropology Cooperative Press: http://openanthcoop.net/press/2010/10/14/stuff/

Hill, T., Canniford, R. and Mol, J. (2014) 'Non-representational marketing theory', *Marketing Theory*, 14(4): 377–394.

Hirschman, E.C. (1986) 'Humanistic inquiry in marketing research: Philosophy, method, and criteria', *Journal of Marketing Research*, 23(3): 237–249.

Horst, H.A. and Miller, D. (2013) *Digital Anthropology*. Edinburgh: A&C Black.

Hoskins, J. (2006) 'Agency, Biography and Objects'. In C. Tilley et al. (eds), *Handbook of Material Culture* (pp. 74–84). London: Sage.

Hui, A. (2012) 'Things in motion, things in practices: How mobile practice networks facilitate the travel and use of leisure objects', *Journal of Consumer Culture*, 12(2): 195–215.

Kopytoff, I. (1986) 'The cultural biography of things: Commoditization as process', in A. Appadurai (ed.), *The Social Life of Things: Commodities in Cultural Perspective* (pp. 70–73). Cambridge: CUP.

Ladik, D., Carrillat, F. and Tadajewski, M. (2015) 'Belk's (1988) "Possessions and the Extended Self" Revisited', *Journal of Historical Research in Marketing*, 7(2): 184–207.

Latour, B. (1987) *Science in Action: How to Follow Scientists and Engineers Through Society*. Cambridge, MA: Harvard University Press.

Latour, B. (1988) *The Pasteurisation of France*. Cambridge, MA: Harvard University Press.

Latour, B. (1992) 'Where are the missing masses?' In W.E. Bijker and J. Law (eds), *Shaping Technology/Building Society: Studies in Sociotechnical Change* (pp. 225–258). Cambridge, MA: MIT Press.

Latour, B. (2000) 'When things strike back: A possible contribution of "science studies" to the social sciences', *The British Journal of Sociology*, 51(1): 107–123.

Latour, B. (2005) *Reassembling the Social: An Introduction to Actor-Network-Theory*. Oxford: OUP.

Law, J. (1992) 'Notes on the theory of the actor-network: Ordering, strategy, and heterogeneity', *Systems Practice*, 5(4): 379–393.

Law, J. (1999) 'After ANT: Complexity, Naming and Topology', *The Sociological Review*, 47(S1): 1–14.

Law, J. (2008) 'Actor-network theory and material semiotics'. In B.S. Turner (ed.), *The New Blackwell Companion to Social Theory*, 3rd Edition (pp. 141–158). Oxford: Blackwell.

Lingis, A. (1998) *The Imperative*. Bloomington: Indiana University Press.

MacKenzie, D. and Wajcman, J. (1999) *The Social Shaping of Technology*. Buckingham: Open University Press.

Malinowski, B. (1922/1961) *Argonauts of the Western Pacific*. New York: Dutton.

Martin, D.M. and Schouten, J.W. (2014) 'Consumption-driven market emergence', *Journal of Consumer Research*, 40(5): 855–870.

Mauss, M. (1925/1990) The Gift: Forms and Functions of Exchange in Archaic Societies. New York: Norton.

Miller, D. (1987) *Material Culture and Mass Consumption*. Oxford: Blackwell.

Miller, D. (1998) *Material Cultures: Why Some Things Matter*. Chicago: University of Chicago Press.

Miller, D. (2010) *Stuff*. Cambridge: Polity Press.

Miller, D. and Tilley, C. (1996) Editorial. *Journal of Material Culture*, 1(1): 5–14.

Molz, J.G. (2013) 'Social networking technologies and the moral economy of alternative tourism: The case of couchsurfing.org', *Annals of Tourism Research*, 43: 210–230.

Molz, J.G. and Paris, C.M. (2015) The social affordances of flashpacking: Exploring the mobility nexus of travel and communication. *Mobilities*, 10(2): 173–192.

Morton, T. (2013) *Hyperobjects: Philosophy and ecology after the end of the world*. Minneapolis: University of Minnesota Press.

Nowak, R. (2016) *Consuming Music in the Digital Age: Technologies, Roles and Everyday Life*. London: Palgrave Macmillan.

Parmentier, M.A. and Fischer, E. (2015) 'Things fall apart: The dynamics of brand audience dissipation', *Journal of Consumer Research*, 41(5): 1228–1251.

Pfaffenberger, B. (1992) 'Social anthropology of technology', *Annual Review of Anthropology*, 21(1): 491–516.

Sandseter, E.B.H. (2009) Affordances for risky play in preschool: The importance of features in the play environment. *Early childhood education journal*, 36(5): 439–446.

Thomas, T.C., Price, L.L. and Schau, H.J. (2013) 'When differences unite: Resource dependence in heterogeneous consumption communities', *Journal of Consumer Research*, 39(5): 1010–1033.

Treem, J.W. and Leonardi, P.M. (2013) 'Social media use in organizations: Exploring the affordances of visibility, editability, persistence, and association', *Annals of the International Communication Association*, 36(1): 143–189.

Wijetunga, D. (2014) 'The digital divide objectified in the design: Use of the mobile telephone by underprivileged youth in Sri Lanka', *Journal of Computer-Mediated Communication*, 19(3): 712–726.

Williams-Bradford, T.W. and Sherry, J.F. (2015) 'Domesticating public space through ritual: Tailgating as vestaval', *Journal of Consumer Research*, 42(1): 130–151.

Withagen, R., de Poel, H.J., Araújo, D. and Pepping, G.J. (2012) 'Affordances can invite behavior: Reconsidering the relationship between affordances and agency', *New Ideas in Psychology*, 30(2): 250–258.

Wright, S. and Parchoma, G. (2011) 'Technologies for learning? An actor-network theory critique of "affordances" in research on mobile learning', *Research in Learning Technology*, 19(3): 247–258.

22

Another Consumer Culture Theory. An ANT Look at Consumption, or How 'Market-things' Help 'Cultivate' Consumers

Franck Cochoy and Alexandre Mallard

INTRODUCTION

For more than forty years now, the field of consumer research has experienced an endless controversy about who and what consumers are, how they think and act, and how they should be studied. The main dispute opposes (on the one hand) the views of economists and psychologists, who conceive consumers as rational individual agents, possibly subject to various cognitive biases, and (on the other hand) the theories of other social scientists and marketing analysts, who insist on the importance of situated practices and consumer culture (Arnould and Thompson, 2005). However, both views implicitly agree that consumption rests on consumer behavior and, consequently, that understanding markets amounts to studying consumers and their logic, be they calculative or cognitive schemes for economists and psychologists, brain structures for neuromarketers, or consumer culture for qualitative and interpretive consumer researchers.

But before looking at the consumer, would it not be wise to look at what the consumer looks at? If the consumer points at a package on a shelf, should we not study the package and the packaging profession as well as the consumer? What does 'consumer culture' mean? Until now, consumer culture has been understood as some mental/immaterial ideas, feelings, ideologies, knowledge, and so on. Would it not be helpful to depart from this classic view of culture by referring to what the word means in biology and farming? In other words, is not marketing about 'cultivating' consumers by using different means and devices that play on consumers' dispositions of course, but that also shape and redefine them?

This chapter aims to show that actor-network theory (ANT) helps raise and answer such questions. Since the mid-1980s, actor-network theorists have successfully shown the extent to which non-human entities contribute to reshaping who actors are and what they do. Their approach calls for a renewal of 'consumer research' by broadening and redefining it as 'consumption research'. Indeed, studying consumption has for too long been confused with studying consumers. Of course, consumer research had merit in showing that consumer behavior partly rests on processes that call for the expertise of anthropology, sociology, and psychology (Cova and Cova, 2009). But other works have pointed to the role of market professionals: by using their specialized knowledge to frame and shape economic exchanges, marketing managers, retailers, merchandisers, and logisticians clearly contribute to orienting consumption behavior (Araujo et al., 2010; Cayla and Zwick, 2011; Cochoy and Dubuisson-Quellier, 2013). Finally, other studies have focused on the contribution of 'market-things' (product innovation, merchandising devices, packaging, price tags, and so on) (Cochoy, 2007b, 2008, 2015). Actor-network theory proposes revisiting consumption phenomena at the crossroads of the three perspectives. Indeed, it implies studying market professionals, market devices, and consumers at the same time, without restricting the analysis to one of them. Our purpose is to present an overview of the origins, foundations, and orientations of this approach. We will first present the basic notions of ANT and highlight the 'object-oriented sociology' it proposes. Then, we will show how this approach could enrich the analysis of consumption processes.[1]

ACTOR-NETWORK THEORY: ELEMENTS OF AN 'OBJECT-ORIENTED SOCIOLOGY'

Let us introduce actor-network theory (ANT) and its potential for consumer research. Although no specific genealogy is available, three figures are usually acknowledged behind research stream: Michel Callon, Bruno Latour, and John Law. The early development was fueled by the work of Madeleine Akrich, Antoine Hennion, and their colleagues at the *Centre de Sociologie de l'Innovation*. It was largely developed at the international level in the 1990s, and is nowadays viewed as a theoretical affiliation or as a field to challenge, in disciplines as diverse as science and technology studies (Law and Hassard, 1999), urban planning and geography (Farias and Bender, 2010), organization sciences (Czarniawska and Hernes, 2005), and management and marketing (Araujo et al., 2010). Here, we propose to present two articles written by two of its main founders. The first article, written by Michel Callon, is usually referred to for a particularly clear expression of why and how we should take into account 'non-human' entities in sociological analysis. The second, written by Bruno Latour, offers a striking formulation of what this approach implies for the philosophy of action.

Accounting Symmetrically for the Humans and Non-humans Engaged in Scientific and Technical Innovation

Michel Callon's most famous article, and probably his most useful paper to thinking differently about consumer phenomena, is paradoxically an article to which students of economic sociology or marketing would pay no attention, as it would appear completely anecdotal or irrelevant to them. Indeed, this article is not about a market case, but about a scientific experiment. Specifically, it tells how a group of marine biologists once tried (without success!) to domesticate a Japanese species of scallops in the Bay of Saint-Brieuc, France (Callon, 1986). To achieve this objective, these scientists undertook various operations to enlist their colleagues, some fishermen, and also the scallops themselves in their project. Specifically, they tried to persuade each of the three groups of actors that none of them could reach its own goals (writing articles for the scientists, preserving their activity for fishermen, multiplying themselves for the scallops) without joining the scientists' domestication project. But apart from the exotic character of this story, we must not forget the subtitle of the article, 'a sociology of translation': the case study is primarily an educational tool aimed at building, illustrating, and validating a complete theory. The latter is transposable to any sociological object and particularly, as we shall see, to the analysis of the market.

To understand Callon's approach, we must recall that it was defined as an answer to the shortcomings of traditional sociological theories when applied to scientific activity: even though this activity is about bringing into existence novel non-human entities with original capacities and properties (particles that travel space at the speed of light, chemical molecules that combine with each other, planets that exert gravitation forces, etc.), sociology failed to recognize the authors, arguing that action should remain the inalienable property of human beings and the social groups they form.

Callon's approach to dealing with this situation is based on three fundamental principles: first, he proposes a 'generalized agnosticism', which aims to encourage researchers to question the natural causes as well as the social forces that are supposed to determine the observed phenomena. This first principle is best understood when one refers to the second, the 'principle of generalized symmetry'. Having observed that the fulfillment of a project always combines material and social forces, Callon refuses to decide that the explanatory power of the first should be necessarily weaker than that of the second (generalized agnosticism). He thus asks researchers not to separate the one from the other (generalized symmetry): human and non-human entities take their share in any action, and must thus be treated symmetrically. In other words, for Callon and his colleagues, scientific discoveries and innovations are not the results of pure social processes, but the result of a 'successful alignment' between human and non-human agencies. This last idea is derived from the third and final principle: that of 'free association'. Instead of deciding in advance who (and what) matters and acts, and who (and what) is related to whom or what, Callon recommends instead compiling a list of relevant actors and actions from observations of the network made up of all the elements involved in a given practice. This theory of translation is also a methodology based on the thick description of such a network. To conduct the survey and understand the action, no external sociological knowledge is needed. If a new entity is named and involved in the network, it must be listed, its action should be recorded, and its connections described, whether or not this entity is human.

Translation, in this context, is therefore defined as an operation in which an actor tries to move another one away from its position or original goals in order to bring it, him, or her to a different position or to other objectives. Beyond the specific analytical tools that Callon offers to analyze the translation process, and its sub-parts of 'problematization', 'interessement',[2] 'enrollment', and 'mobilization', what matters is the construction of a narrative in which all the entities involved in the situation are described with the same vocabulary. For instance, no difference in principle is made between the scallops and the human actors (fishermen, other researchers) in the account created to explain how the ones and the others do or do not support the project of marine biologists (all of them 'act', 'resist,' 'cooperate', and so on, although of course differently given their specific nature and characteristics).

This case is easily transferable to consumer issues. Let us replace the scallops with any new good or service and substitute marketing professionals for scientists (on the one hand) and consumers, manufacturers, or service providers for fishermen (on the other): it becomes obvious that marketing objects, as in the case of scallops, is all about interesting the partners who take part in the exchange, detaching goods from their competitors, attracting users, and enlisting a set of allies and resources to mobilize and represent them appropriately. Beyond this analogy, which brings the history of scallops to concerns related to consumption, what matters is the single project of a sociology that gives a strong status to non-human entities – or, in the case that we will address, to market objects and things – or 'market-things'.[3]

A Relational Definition of Action

This reintegration of objects in sociological analysis has a consequence: the need to provide a new definition for the concept of action. This need is echoed repeatedly in the actor-network literature. It is clearly expressed in a text where Bruno Latour addresses the issue of 'interobjectivity' (Latour, 1996). Provocatively, Latour says that the common definition of interaction – a situation in which two physically copresent actors communicate and adapt their behavior based on the behavior of the other – is more appropriate to account for the organization of simian societies than human ones: with apes, indeed, each interaction is a moment when individuals experience and test the hierarchical relationships at stake, and thus replay, enact, and construct the global social order within their particular group (Strum and Latour, 1987). By contrast, with humans, interactions rest on other 'ingredients' that do not exist in ape societies and that the usual definition of interaction ignores: human actions involve material things that play a central role in establishing and stabilizing the social order. What makes the difference between human and ape is less humans' cultural or cognitive skills than humans' ability to inscribe their rules into a set of material objects.

Latour emphasizes that two people who interact engage a series of objects in their relationship that are external to their actual interaction. These objects were forged elsewhere, by others, and for purposes other than the interaction at stake: the clothes that mark their identities, the words they use to communicate, various technical devices that help define the scope of their exchange (walls, windows, doors, communication tools, etc.). Therefore, no human relationship exists without the things that help define its texture, extension, and meaning. But how can we account for the specific contribution of objects in such a context? Latour says that one should depart from three conventional views that social scientists have developed vis-à-vis the commitment of objects in action: objects have been conceived 'as invisible and faithful tools, as the determining superstructure and as a projection screen' (Latour, 1996: 235). In the first case, the object appears as a pure means of action, conveying an intention without adding anything to it. In the second case, the object belongs to a material context that determines social relations and acts autonomously on humans. In the third case, objects are there to reflect the social status of individuals. Although Latour does not explicitly refer to them, it is easy to recognize three classic positions in social sciences: the theories of rational action, in which the objects are part of the resources mobilized to achieve the aims of an action that is decided independently; that of Marxism, for which the degree of technological development of a society is part of the infrastructure that helps determine the elements of the superstructure, like culture, morality, etc.; and that of Durkheimian tradition and all its derivative forms, in which objects are seen essentially as signs conveying the binding force of the social group that acts on each individual. None of these conceptions provides a positive account of the capacity of things to act in social relations, for example in the course of interactions.

Faced with these three conceptions, Latour claims that it is the action itself that must be redefined. In order to do so, he proposes moving away from a conception in which action has an origin, a purpose, and a clearly defined direction, to a 'relational' conception of action, in which the latter stems from the composition of beings with each other. Action is not a property that can be traced in a being or an other. It is a distributed force that emerges from the relationships human beings have with each other. Therefore, the constitutive opposition between the active voice ('I act') and the passive voice ('I am acted upon by') is a false alternative that Latour proposes to replace with another mode of action, the 'make one act'.[4] In order to illustrate this idea, Latour evokes the image of the puppeteer. The game of the puppet cannot be interpreted as a pure and simple enactment of the puppeteer's theatrical intentions. The character's action is of course the result of the puppeteer's will and of the movements of his hands that enact this will. But the character's action is also the expression of the puppet itself, and of what this puppet can transmit with the specific capacity of incarnation and movement embedded in its technical design and aesthetic characteristics. The puppeteer does not control his puppet any more than the puppet controls the puppeteer; however, it is the puppet as well as the puppeteer who makes the couple they form do something ('make one do'). It should be noted that such a conception does not imply a nihilist or anthropomorphic tropism, to ignore all the differences between the protagonists involved in action, and in particular to confuse human and non-human agencies. Beings engaged in action fall within 'differentiated ontologies'; they evidence different properties, and these properties are what make the action possible as a composition of differentiated and distributed capabilities (intelligence, will, beliefs on the human side; force, durability, materiality on the object side, even if humans also have a material dimension with their body, and if objects more and more incorporate cognitive features, especially in the field of electronic devices).

To summarize this conception, we can refer to a very vivid illustration that Latour proposes at the end of his text, in which he adopts the point of view of a shepherd using a wooden barrier to prevent his sheep from escaping while he is asleep. How can we understand the role of the barrier in the interaction between the sheep and the shepherd?

> Who is acting while I am asleep? Me, the carpenters, and the fence. Am I expressed in this fence as if I had actualized outside of myself a competence that I possessed in potential form? Not in the slightest. The fence doesn't look at all like me. It is not an extension of my arms or of my dog. It is completely beyond me. It is an actant in its own right. Did it appear all of a sudden out of objective matter ready to crush my poor fragile, sleepy body with its material constraints? No, I went folding myself into it precisely because it did not have the same durability, duration, plasticity, temporality – in short the same ontology as me. … Are the sheep interacting with me when they bump their muzzles against the rough pine planks? Yes, but they are interacting with a me that is, thanks to the fence, disengaged, delegated, translated and multiplied. … Any time an interaction has temporal and spatial extension, it is because one has shared it with non-humans. (Latour, 1996: 239)

Acting is about making people and things do 'something', and objects play a central role in this process. Let's now see how these precepts can be useful for the analysis of consumption phenomena.

AN ANTHROPOLOGY OF 'MARKET-THINGS'

This introduction to the actor-network theory literature right away suggests a metaphor for grasping how to redefine consumption: it might be a matter of 'cultivating consumers' similar to the process of 'breeding scallops' or 'farming sheep', that is to say, enrolling various non-humans to reconfigure the resources of action in the consumption situation. Yet we need to go beyond this intuitive metaphor and follow Michel Callon, Bruno Latour, and their colleagues to examine how the 'acting things' organize the relationship between goods and their consumers. Among these, the consumer goods come first, and a large part of current research in 'actor-network inspired' market studies is about the manufacture of products in the dynamics of innovation. But other works from the same research stream also explore the contribution of another type of things involved in consumption, namely the 'market-things' that stage the shopping scenes.

Consumption Viewed from the Path of Innovation

The actor-network approach first leads to a study of marketing goods as things, and, to be precise, as things that have been developed by diverse and varied protagonists to be delivered to persons who are highly elusive, 'the consumers'. This approach captures consumption less through the common and regular practices that enact it (shopping, eating, enjoying cultural activities, entertaining oneself, etc.) than through the uncertain encounter between products and their public as it occurs through the innovation process. This opens a question about what consumption owes to the particular history that gave birth to the product. Among the innovation studies conducted within the actor-network school, many cases directly address consumer products, for instance in the fields of nutrition (Méadel and Rabeharisoa, 2001; Teil et al., 2011), cultural products (Hennion, 2015a), communication technologies (Akrich, 1993a; Akrich and Méadel, 2006; Canu and Mallard, 2006; Mallard, 2012; Méadel, 1994), luxury goods (Trébuchet-Breitwiller, 2015), and energy consumption (Akrich, 1993b). But what matters here is the more general approach of research on innovation, regardless of the type of product concerned. Research has particularly underscored the diversity of actors involved in the story that goes from 'the great inventor' who got the idea of the product, to the consumer whose needs and desires it satisfies, as if by magic. The intermediary actors who intervene behind this bilateral fable of marketing felicity and make it workable are marketers, manufacturers, consultants, designers, advertisers, distributors, merchandisers, and so on. It is the specific role of each of these mediators and the nature of the trajectory along which they follow each other that are brought into question.

To understand this trajectory, we must abandon a first image that comes to mind, that of the product passing from hand to hand from conception to consumption, like a rugby ball flies from player to player until the marking of the final try: while the oval ball reaches its destination without being changed at all during the course of the game, the product very often evolves to suit the dynamics of innovation. 'No movement without transformation', says one of the first precepts of Callon's sociology of translation. Innovation thus follows a trajectory in which the product, the entities that make it, and how it acts upon other entities, happen to be continuously reshaped and transformed.[5]

In the same way that the genesis of a good refers to various actors and different transformations, consumption may itself be developed into multiple processes. It can be understood, for example, from the perspective of how the product is sold, or from the perspective of how we actually experience it (the moment of use or consumption, in its strict meaning, of food products, for instance). For certain categories of economic goods, the purchase and consumption of the product overlap and are intertwined (see the consumption of a meal in a restaurant), while for others they are two moments that follow each other linearly (see the 'at home' consumption of a food product purchased in the supermarket). In all cases, the reference to these two processes is necessary when it comes to understanding the consumption phenomenon. In addition, consumption will sometimes be considered in relation to the use of after-sale services or through recycling systems that are now at work in many areas.

What matters here is that consumption appears as a specific stage in the innovation trajectory: on the one hand, it is a moment among others in the path followed by the product, but on the other hand, it is a horizon towards which all the actors involved in the innovation process aim, because it features its success. The actor-network approach brought decisive elements for understanding this back-and-forth dynamic of product shaping between innovation and consumption, notably through Madeleine Akrich's reflections on socio-technical dynamics (1991, 1992, 1993a, 1995).

From the Innovator to the Consumer and Vice Versa: The Product as a Delegate

Two major ideas emerge from this reflection. The first is that 'any innovation decision can be described as a division between what is delegated to [the object] and, within that object, to such component rather than to another, and what can be entrusted to the "environment" (in the broad sense)' (Akrich, 1991: 342). The course of innovation involves so-called 'inscription' processes, in which the innovator seeks to incorporate into the product several elements of its consumption scenario, and other processes in which the same innovator tries to control this scenario in other ways. Inscription consists of delegating to the product (to one of its dimensions or components) a number of actions that it is supposed to perform during the consumption process. As for the 'other processes' just mentioned, they can be many and varied: they may be, for example, the development of related products that will be necessary for consumption, the setting of standards to define the consumption environment, the shaping of the future behavior of consumers through advertising and communication, and so on. The product therefore carries the traces of a number of divisions that show, indirectly, what the actors who participate in the innovation process are trying to include in the object itself and what they have to delegate to other entities.

The second key idea is that inscription does not guarantee that what was considered by the innovator will actually occur. In fact, this delegation of an innovation program conveys uncertain outcomes because what things will do is by nature never entirely predictable. This assertion may seem difficult to understand in contemporary culture in which the ability to produce objects is associated with the idea of a technical mastery of the world. But it becomes clear if we take into account the relational nature of action in the actor-network approach. In this frame, indeed, for humans as well as for objects, action makes sense and is effective only when it is related to the entities with which one acts. Therefore, the product-thing developed in innovation contexts (technical study, simulation, marketing survey, and so on) will certainly produce at least partially unexpected effects when engaged in consumption practices, as these contexts do not have the same composition and the same texture. What the product will 'make its user do' therefore partially escapes what the designer anticipated. Once we accept such a relational conception of action, the realization by the things of what has been delegated to them appears as an open and unpredictable process.

As a whole, this stresses the double nature of the product: it is simultaneously a delegate and a thing, which, from the actor-network perspective, means exactly the contrary of passivity or obedience and points instead to agentivity in the full sense. This explains, in turn, that innovators seek by various means to anticipate the confrontation between the product and its future consumer: the protagonists of innovation spend considerable energy in conducting various studies (surveys, technical tests, lab experiments, focus groups, etc.) to describe what is involved in the consumption scene and what the outcomes could be, so that they can identify the most relevant possible scripts (Boullier, 2002; Grandclément-Chaffy and Gaglio, 2012; Mallard, 2005). We thus understand why market success requires abandoning the traditional innovation diffusion model, which assumes that new products are stable objects supposed to penetrate society thanks to their alleged rationality, but confront the alleged 'social resistance' of the social milieu. But as we have seen, the market success of innovations does not place the *a priori* technical rationality of objects in opposition to the subsequent social and cultural resistance of subjects. On the contrary, it involves a process of successive interactions between subjects and objects. During such interactions, an object has a chance to be adopted if it is continuously 'adapted', reworked, and redefined by taking into account the consumers' expectations and experiences (Akrich et al., 2002a, 2002b).

These two big ideas, the idea of innovation as a selective delegation of consumption scenarios to the product-thing, and the idea of inevitable discrepancies between innovation projects and their realization, are well illustrated by Akrich's (1991, 1992) emblematic case study on the photovoltaic kit. The story concerns the free supply of a photovoltaic generator to rural African populations as part of a development program. The kit aimed, for instance, at powering radios so that children could listen to broadcasted education programs or light lamps so they could review their lessons in the late evening. Viewed from the design offices, the solar kit was simple, efficient, robust, functional, and useful, and its benefits were immensely greater than its costs, since it was provided for free. Yet when put into practice, the object, despite these qualities, was not adopted. Refusing to question the rationality of the object for this failure is to open the door to explanations in terms of social resistance and thus, at best, to face the risk of developing culturalist explanations, and at worst, of relying on latent racist-like prejudices (these people may be culturally averse to technologies; they may not have the necessary skills; and so on). However, conducting a symmetrical study, that is, a study that pays equal attention to the subjects and to the object at stake, helps realizing that the solar kit, even if it was *a priori* perfectly rational and functional from the engineering point of view, was not suitable for the use it was designed for: cattle knocked it down, the wire was too short to be placed on the roof, the object was conceived as a closed entity that was not serviceable by local actors, and so on. The survey conducted by Akrich shows both the truly serious work performed by the innovators, who formulated specific assumptions about the product use and inscribed them into the device, and the strong mismatch between these assumptions and the actual context of use, a mismatch that the kit itself failed to reduce.

The Product as a Collective Composition

We can now see better what 'cultivating the consumer' is all about: it is a matter of going back and forth from product design to consumption, in a very iterative manner, through a series of projections, experiments, simulations, and trials enacting successive in-scription and de-scription processes. Through these dynamics, the consumer is cultivated in the sense that the relationship that binds him/her to the product progresses from fiction and hypothesis to reality. Yet an important question emerges here: What are the implications of the collective nature of the innovation dynamic? We have seen that the actors involved in innovation are diverse. Innovation is certainly a creative ground, but how is order produced in it? How can we understand a product's composition from these different perspectives and from the multiple inscriptions they generate? Should we conclude that each involved actor provides the product with one of its dimensions? For example, the engineer brings the 'technical qualities'; the designer cares for the 'aesthetics'; the marketer defines the 'economic characteristics'; the lawyer sets the 'legal dimensions', etc. The reality, however, is a bit different.

First, following Akrich's reflection, we can assume that each stakeholder tries to delegate actions to the product that are related to his or her specific approach to consumption. Thus, to the extent that she is interested in the product's 'function', the engineer will consider consumption as a situation where a person who previously acquired the product seeks to use it. A marketer, in charge of positioning the product in the realm of the market (within the 'marketing mix'), will see things differently: the stage of consumption she is interested in is the shelf in a store or the website of an Internet retailer, where the price and qualities of the product (its 'promises,' to use a term dear to marketing) have specific meanings in relation to the similar surrounding objects with which it competes. A lawyer involved in innovation will in turn see the product through the lens of the associated property rights, legal procedures, and trade remedies. What each of these actors will 'delegate to the object' and the particular type of 'inscription' he will mobilize for this will be very different in the three cases. However, it is a single object, the 'product-as-a-thing', that these inscriptions will shape in the end. This can give rise to very different configurations depending, on the one hand, on the degree of overlap between the various inscriptions involved and, on the other hand, on how the intervention of the stakeholders is organized along the innovation process.

There is a low degree of overlap between inscriptions when the stakeholders on the innovation path focus on different product components. Composing the product from the different requirements can then be seen as adding features, carried out by different spokespersons. A design engineer will, for example, require that a mobile phone receive a particular microprocessor to improve its performance, while a marketer will focus more on its modern aesthetics so that it can compare positively with competing products at the sales point. The first actor concentrates on the usability of the thing, while the second is interested in its 'sellability'. Here, it is convenient to envisage the product composition as a juxtaposition of two separate inscriptions (the choice of a processor and the shape of the terminal). In practice, however, many features of the product involve several dimensions at once: in our example, it may happen that a processor has a bigger or smaller size depending on its functionalities, and that the choice recommended by the design engineer will make the mobile phone more or less bulky, a dimension that the marketer watches warily. The composition of the product-as-a-thing may entail various trade-offs of that kind and may set in tension the mutual priorities of different requirements. This shows that the inscription dynamics underlying the participation of several players in the innovation may result in complementary but also very often in conflicting logic, leading to negotiation between them.

Thus, organizing the contribution of the different innovation stakeholders is key to keeping a low degree of conflict in the enactment of various delegations to the product-as-a-thing. In modern design processes, the project organization plays a central role: a project can be considered as an organizing device for managing inscription conflicts resulting from the participation of different specialists (Boullier, 2002). Note, however, that for some given innovation patterns, or in some segments of an innovation trajectory, the intervention of the players follows a sequential mode where each specialist is in the situation of accepting, rejecting, or transforming decisions made at the previous stage. The reflection of Barrey et al. (2000) on the relationship between the designer (the professional in charge of defining the features of the product), the packager (the one who defines the packaging), and the merchandiser (the one who physically positions products at the sales point) is very insightful from this perspective: it makes visible the various tensions and compromises at stake in a situation where three categories of marketing professionals, with contrasting definitions of what consumption is, operate on the product in a sequential way, without any framing of these interventions through explicit organizational procedures.

As a whole, this approach tells us that the product cannot be considered as a reservoir of qualities, some of which are technical while others are commercial or legal. It also teaches us that the same product is rather a single entity to which a multiplicity of actors have delegated various purposes. This product-as-a-thing carries the traces of a plurality of inscription processes that cannot be summarized or represented comprehensively in any simple way – if we accept, maybe, a detailed history of all decisions, conflicting or not, made by different actors at different times along the innovation path. Given the difficulty of writing such a history, one may think that the product remains a highly enigmatic entity, and that the various trials it will undergo in the consumption process may reveal only some of the projections to which it was subjected.

These 'Market-things' that Make One Sell: From Packaging to Market Devices

If we had to find a product attribute that could make us think about its embodiment as a thing, and about the exchanges between innovators and consumers it underlies, packaging would certainly be the best candidate. Packaging nowadays appears as a central component of the consumption product, accompanying it from the final stage of design to the moment of customer experience. Indeed, packaging is the envelope that makes it possible for the product to circulate from the factory to the consumer, passing through a series of intermediate loci such as warehouses, stockpiles, wholesale stores, and the shelves of the retail outlet. In the distribution channels, it protects the product, as a more or less fragile thing, from the vicissitudes of travel; in the realm of the consumer's home, it is this component of the product that one will open and get rid of in order to truly access use or consumption – at best, the consumer will cautiously keep the packaging briefly, just for the time she needs to check that the product conforms to her expectations, as the possibility of a refund in case of discontent often requires that the product be returned to the sales point 'in its original packaging'.

This first reflection suggests some specific forms of delegation that the packaging is subjected to from the designers. However, a thorough examination shows that packaging plays an even more pivotal role in the articulation of the factory and the consumer's location as interrelated market stages. It not only protects the product, it also displays various information that decisively contributes to shaping consumer choice. In fact, the implementation of packaging in diverse consumption sectors has changed the whole economy of products (Cochoy, 2004). Indeed, this envelope of cardboard or plastic carries out the task of matching supply (the good) and demand (the consumer) through the representation of the former to the latter: there is no possible contact between the consumer and the product without this mediation, and, contrary to appearances, the contribution of packaging is not neutral in this process.

Take the example of a consumer in a store buying a box with the inscription 'Sweet corn; 150 grams'. Upon opening the box, she gains access to contents, which are consistent with the information written on the container. But the packaging does not do only this; it also deprives the consumer of some information that she could benefit from before the implementation of this written mediation. In doing so, it can also enable her to discover other information. Whereas at the time of a bulk sale, the consumer would have to engage in a physical relationship with an ear of corn and undertake a sensory evaluation, the box prevents her from seeing the content, and from smelling, touching, or tasting it. But the metal and paper screen allows as many additions as subtractions. While it deprives the consumer of any sensory access ('tasting'), it saturates her with informational elements and with assessments delegated to external instruments and devices ('testing'). The customer learns that she is not only in the presence of 150 grams of sweet corn, but it is 'brand X' corn, 'without added sugar', 'low in salt', 'GMO free', etc. This latter information is particularly interesting because it does not match any perceptible quality from a sensory point of view: GMOs are invisible, and their presence is indistinguishable through the senses. Packaging thus endows the consumer with new preferences: without it, he could never feel any inclination or aversion for strange and controversial entities such as GMOs, Omega 3, bisphenol A, etc.

Finally, the packaging is a mediation between the consumer and the product in the strongest sense of the term, to the extent that it impacts all the entities involved. The product is no longer the same, since the generic good of yesteryear can now be differentiated ceaselessly, and can receive new qualities, such as a brand, the absence of GMOs, etc. The packaging also changes the company, which can now, thanks to it, undertake operations of lasting attachment to consumers, cultivate brands, play more on quality than price, etc. Finally, the packaging changes the consumer, who no longer considers the products through her own bodily senses or relatives' recommendations, but shows her able to consider abstract analytical dimensions, such as chemical constituents, symbols, and so on.

Packaging thus offers a striking illustration of the role of things that, as we said above, 'make us do' things in the realm of consumption and, in the present case, of things that 'make the consumer choose'. I do not choose a package, any more than a package chooses me, but the packaging 'makes me choose'. Consumers and objects combine their mutual agency to position action in a particular direction. The case of packaging invites us to further reflect on and explore the role of the diverse artifacts that support commercial distribution. Much research inspired from actor-network theory has tackled this task. Indeed, packaging is not the only device that 'makes one choose' the product: distribution abundantly relies on technology to equip this particular moment of consumption that the act of purchase represents. One can mention the many artifacts – shelves, advertising panels, etc. – that channel customer activity at the sales point (Canu and Mallard, 2006; Grandclément-Chaffy, 2008; Dubuisson-Quellier, 2007), loyalty programs (Araujo and Kjellberg, 2016), barcodes and all the tools that equip the consumer to get market information in the situated context of purchase (Cochoy, 2015), and even shopping trolleys that transform the consumer into a buyer, help multiply her choices, make her forget prices from the shelf up to the checkout desk, increase the scale of operations, and change small businesses into mass distributors (Grandclément, 2006; Cochoy, 2009).

The backdrop of this research is the study of the work of professionals who contribute to shaping commercial spaces. While corporate history has shown the importance of the shift from the invisible hand of the market to the visible hand of managers (Chandler, 1977), economic sociology has clarified this direction by showing how important the special category of 'market professionals' is among these managers (Cochoy and Dubuisson-Quellier, 2013). These actors segment the demand (Strasser, 1989), stage the products (Barrey et al., 2000), frame the purchase scene and the consumers' ability to choose (Mallard, 2007), invent all sorts of devices for 'capturing' them (Cochoy, 2007a; Trompette, 2007), explore the alchemy of their desire (Hennion and Méadel, 1989), and stimulate the proliferation of customer figures (Cova and Cova, 2009; Dubuisson, 1999; Ohl, 2004). This movement has reached such a point that some marketers nowadays propose that to understand the functioning of markets, scholars should focus on their own professional practices instead of studying the consumer's routines and market organization as they have hitherto done (Araujo et al., 2010; Cayla and Zwick, 2011).

All 'artifacts that make us choose' found in the world of distribution can be addressed from the same perspective as that developed for the analysis of products. As technical devices to which market professionals delegate the enactment of certain operations in the commercial area (classifying products in a specific order, highlighting some of them, explaining the possible consumption alternatives, preparing transactions, etc.), these artifacts are a form of embodiment of marketing knowledge, and in this way, they contribute to their performativity (Callon, 1998). But only an analysis of situated market action, for example through an ethnographic approach (Canu and Mallard, 2006; Cochoy, 2007b; Grandclément-Chaffy, 2008) makes it possible to take the full measure of these delegations and their combined contribution to the development of consumer practices.

The Qualifications and Attachments of the Consumer Product

We would like to present a last contribution of the actor-network approach to the study of consumption. It relates to the skills involved in the development of relations between consumers and products. This research invites us to shift from conventional notions of taste or quality, to the concepts of qualification and attachment.

The concept of taste was brought to the fore in sociology by Pierre Bourdieu (1984) through the role this author gives to the 'habitus' in the shaping of cultural and consumption practices: the capacity to differentiate between products takes root in the embodied skills by which actors differ in the social space. This is why consumption is inherently a socially stratified phenomenon according to this theory: products work as anchoring points for social ranking processes. The concept of quality originated in a different analytical tradition that developed in the 1970s in economics: this tradition insists on the idea that the consumer skills involved in the handling of a product do not come only under taste categories but also integrate information regarding its quality (a kind of information that is more or less accessible or available). The economist Georges Akerlof (1970) first demonstrated the possibility of a strategic game on product quality, for example, when a seller hides certain pieces of information at stake in a transaction to his advantage. In the 1980s and 1990s, this line of analysis spread in the school of convention economics (Eymard-Duvernay, 1989) and in sociology (Karpik, 2010). The concept of quality helps to explain how economic coordination can emerge in the absence of information on prices, as in the case of the profession of lawyers studied by Karpik (1999).

The actor-network research stream continued along this perspective and proposed a shift in emphasis away from quality *per se* and towards a focus on the 'qualifying work'. In a now classic article, Michel Callon, Cécile Méadel, and Vololona Rabeharisoa (2002) show that the enactment of market exchange involves less the encounter between the pre-existing supply and demand, than a very fine work aimed at defining, ranking, and positioning objects that can help adjust them. The qualifying work is the engine of this adjustment process. It provides access to the intrinsic qualities of products, but also to the extrinsic qualities that enable positioning them in the market dynamics. This work notably mobilizes operations of attachment and detachment: it is a question both of breaking the routines that organize the consumer's relationship with the current supply (detachment) and of forging a relationship with the new product (attachment). Managing the duality of attachment and detachment proceeds through a series of trials showing diverse modalities of confrontation between the consumer and the product. These trials can neither be reduced to the consumption of signs (as in the logic of taste) nor to the operations of judgment (as in the logic of quality): they refer more generally to a variety of experiences that, among other things, involve bodily performance (Gomart and Hennion, 1999; Hennion, 2007, 2015b). Thus, it is through the recognition of the specific modalities of participation of the product-as-a-thing in the consumption experience that one can account for the logic of attachment.

In this perspective, an emblematic, though particular, figure of the consumer is that of the amateur described by Hennion (2010). It features an actor endowed with reflexive skills supporting a sometimes tenuous but still structured relationship with the product. Reflexive skills are based less on the acquisition of distinctive taste patterns through socialization, or on the formation of a cognitive ability to identify quality, than on a reflective process of becoming open and sensitive to things and on learning how to let them 'make oneself do things': testing different olfactory species in a perfumer's shop (Trébuchet-Breitwiller, 2015), recognizing the singular personality of a *terroir* wine, identifying the special texture of a stringed instrument, feeling the peculiar contact with the cliff wall when climbing with appropriate shoes, all of these practices involve an ability to 'bring about differences' based on an intimate relationship with things. Thus, the character of the amateur appears as an extreme figure of the consumer, one in which the reflexivity in the development of the relationship with the product-as-a-thing is the most visible, and one in which the articulation between tasting and testing is very rich. Note that the skills at stake here do not emerge *ex nihilo* and involve consumer practices that are often developed in the collective arenas of ordinary social situations (family meals, cultural and social activities, etc.). To a certain extent, this conception meets the idea of 'cultivating the consumer' in a traditional Bourdieusian sense: producing abilities to distinguish between things and, consequently, to distinguish between people who are able to show a differentiated relationship with legitimate culture. However, actor-network theory adds to this conception not only the notion of reflexivity in the relationship to things (instead of ignorance and denial in Bourdieu's view), but also, and above all, the idea that the practices at play are not alien to innovation and market professionals: these practices are at least partly implemented by these professionals, and they fuel the qualifying work through which possible attachment between consumers and products are produced (Callon et al., 2002; Dubuisson, 2010; Mallard, 2010, 2012). Cultivating the consumer is a multifaceted process occurring not only in socialization, but also in the dynamics of innovation.

CONCLUSION

What should we look at when a customer points to a can of corn in a store? Paraphrasing Latour's statement – 'it is both the shepherd, the barrier, and the carpenter who herd the sheep' – we could answer that it is the consumer, the packaging, and the marketer who designed this product that should attract our attention: they all 'make us consume'. It is the implications of this type of response that the perspective of actor-network theory invites us to explore. As we can see, it leads us to pay attention to various forms of entanglements of things in consumption trials – the choice of food in a supermarket, the situation of tasting in a friendly circle, the testing of quality in the production phase, the focus groups through which consumption patterns were anticipated, and so on – and explore the complex web of relations between all these trials.

Such a perspective may seem paradoxical, but it should open up new avenues for the study of consumption practices that avoid both the critical theory of the *ex nihilo* creation of consumption needs by the production industries, and the idealized vision of the omnipotence of a consumer inventing the uses and meanings of the products she consumes. There is no doubt that innovation leads to the creation of new consumer needs; for instance, how could we otherwise explain that a product that was completely unknown and almost unimaginable 25 years ago, namely the mobile phone, could enslave so many of its contemporary users? Yet what the actor-network approach underlines here is that such a need creation process required the joint participation of consumers and innovation professionals, through a series of multifaceted, iterative, and interactive processes; through patient 'cultivating' practices that cannot be reduced to the projection of *a priori* managerial or consumer cultures. Conversely, the consumer is certainly an actor endowed with energy and imagination, and is sensitive to political, moral, and aesthetic considerations. But one still has to understand why these skills and attitudes are activated in the relationship with some products and not with others. Here again, it is difficult to reflect on consumption without examining the things that make it possible and without considering the history of all the missions we have entrusted to them.

Historically, the notion of consumer culture was proposed to show that consumption was not only about the domination of the final consumer by cultural industries, and that most mundane consumption practices were culturally creative. If this perspective, later joined and enriched by Consumer Culture Theory (Arnould and Thompson, 2005), indeed rehabilitates ordinary consumption acts, it also faces two risks that are easily visible when looking at consumption from a Bourdieusian perspective. The first risk is the reduction of consumed objects to mere symbolic signs, according to the Durkheimian view of cultural objects; the second risk is the deepening of the divide between consumers and market professionals. What is at stake with a shift from the concept of culture to the notion of cultivation, is the identification of alternative ways to account for these two problems. On the one hand, this shift helps acknowledge the centrality of things and their agentivity as far as the relationship between the consumer and the consumed good is concerned; on the other hand, the same shift helps flatten the asymmetry between consumers and market professionals and shows that consumer cultivation occurs in the networks of innovation as well as in the social arenas of consumption.

Notes

1 This chapter is an adapted and updated version of a former text published in French (Mallard and Cochoy, 2015).

2 'Interessement' should be considered as a coined word (based on the French 'intéressement') rather than as a French word that has been mistakenly left untranslated.

3 *A priori*, the category of 'non-human' addressed by the actor-network theory is very large, as it seeks to welcome things, technical objects, animals (such as scallops), collective beings (for example, a company or an organization), fictional or supernatural beings (gods), etc. The concept has two serious drawbacks: on the one hand, it is defined only negatively, by reference to the category of so-called human beings, which makes it largely indeterminate; on the other hand, it tends to reintroduce a strong dualism where the spirit of the actor-network theory generally seeks to challenge dualistic postures. We can only evoke these drawbacks that have led to important critical debates. Let us simply note that in the approach taken in this chapter, we will focus on 'objects' and 'things,' which specify a set slightly less wide than the 'non-human' in general, although we recognize that this reduction does not escape the two criticisms we just mentioned.

4 This expression aims at translating the French locution '*faire faire*'. The idea that '*faire quelque chose, c'est toujours le faire faire*' well formulates the fact that acting is always based on the redistribution of action between the actor and its delegates. On this precise point, see Latour (1999). The 'make one do' should not be equated with the 'make do', although acting may to some extent be conceived as the achievement of a compromise among the active entities at stake in action.

5 Of course, the transformation is at a maximum during the innovation and production operations, where the object is similar to a hot and malleable 'product', and is more modest during times of marketing and consumption, where the object turns into a cooler and more stable 'good' (Callon et al., 2002), to the point that one might consider supplementing the sociology of translation designed for malleable technical products with a sociology of 'conduction' more appropriate for monitoring the marketization of goods with sharp edges (Cochoy, 2010).

REFERENCES

Akerlof, G.A. 1970. The market for lemons: Qualitative uncertainty and the market mechanism. *Quarterly Journal of Economics* 84(3): 488–500.

Akrich, M. 1991. L'analyse socio-technique. In *La gestion de la recherche*, Vinck, D. (ed.). Bruxelles: De Boeck-Wesmael, 339–353.

Akrich, M. 1992. The de-scription of technical objects. In *Shaping Technology/Building Society: Studies in Sociotechnical Change*, Bijker, W. and Law, J. (eds). Cambridge MA: MIT Press, 205–224.

Akrich, M. 1993a. Les objets techniques et leurs utilisateurs. De la conception à l'action. *Raisons Pratiques* 4, Les objets dans l'action: 35–57.

Akrich, M. 1993b. 'Essay of technosociology: a Gasogene in Costa Rica'. In *Technological Choices: Transformation in Material Cultures since the Neolithic*, Lemonnier, P. (ed.). London: Routledge, 289–337.

Akrich, M. 1995. User representations: Practices, methods and sociology. In *Managing Technology in Society: The Approach of Constructive Technology Assessment*, Rip, A., Misa, T. and Schot, J. (eds). London: Pinter, 167–184.

Akrich, M. and Méadel, C. 2006. Télévision à la carte, un divorce annoncé. *Réseaux* 139: 75–103.

Akrich, M., Callon, M. and Latour, B. 2002a. The key to success in innovation, Part I: The art of interessement. Translated by Adrian Monaghan. *International Journal of Innovation Management* 6(2): 187–206.

Akrich, M., Callon, M. and B. Latour, B. 2002b. The key to success in innovation, Part II: The art of choosing good spokespersons. Translated by Adrian Monaghan. *International Journal of Innovation Management* 6(2): 207–225.

Akrich, M., Callon, M. and Latour, B. 2006. *Sociologie de la traduction*. Paris: Presse des mines.

Araujo, L. and Kjellberg, H. 2016. Enacting novel agencements: The case of frequent flyer schemes in the US airline industry (1981–1991). *Consumption Markets & Culture* 19(1): 92–110.

Araujo, L., Finch, J. and Kjellberg, H. 2010. *Reconnecting Marketing to Markets*. Oxford: Oxford University Press.

Arnould, E.J. and Thompson, C.J. 2005. Consumer Culture Theory (CCT): Twenty years of research. *Journal of Consumer Research* 31(4): 868–882.

Barrey, S., Cochoy, F. and Dubuisson-Quellier, S. 2000. Designer, packager et merchandiser: trois professionnels pour une même scène marchande. *Sociologie du Travail* 42(3): 457–482.

Bloor, D. 1976. *Knowledge and Social Imagery.* Chicago: The University of Chicago Press.

Boullier, D. 2002. Les études d'usages: entre normalisation et rhétorique. *Annales des télécommunications* 57(3–4, mars–avril): 190–210.

Bourdieu, P. 1984. *Distinction: A Social Critique of the Judgement of Taste*. Cambridge, MA: Harvard University Press.

Buzzell, R.D. 1963. Is marketing a science? *Harvard Business Review* 41(January–February): 32–40.

Callon, M. 1986. Some elements for a sociology of translation: Domestication of the scallops and the fishermen of St-Brieuc Bay. In *Power, Action and Belief: A New Sociology of Knowledge?*, Law, J. (ed.). Sociological Review Monograph, London: Routledge and Kegan Paul, 196–223.

Callon, M. 1998. *The Laws of the Markets*. Oxford: Blackwell Publishers.

Callon, M., Méadel, C. and Rabeharisoa, V. 2002. The economy of qualities. *Economy and Society* 31(2): 194–217.
Canu, R. and Mallard, A. 2006. Que fait-on dans la boutique d'un opérateur de télécommunications? Enquête ethnographique sur la mise en référence des biens marchands. *Réseaux* 24(135–136): 161–192.
Cayla, J. and Zwick, D. (eds) 2011. *Inside Marketing*. Oxford: Oxford University Press.
Chandler, A. 1977. The Visible Hand: The Managerial Revolution in American Business. Cambridge, MA: Belknap Press.
Cochoy, F. 2004. Is the modern consumer a Buridan's donkey? Product packaging and consumer choice. In *Elusive Consumption*, Ekström, K. and Brembeck, H. (eds). Oxford and New York: Berg Publisher, 205–227.
Cochoy, F. 2007a. A brief theory of the 'captation' of the public: Understanding the market with Little Red Riding Hood. *Theory, Culture & Society* 24(7–8): 213–233.
Cochoy, F. 2007b. A sociology of market-things: On tending the garden of choices in mass retailing. In *Market Devices, Sociological Review Monographs* 55(777), Callon, M., Muniesa, F. and Millo, Y. (eds). London: Blackwell, 109–129.
Cochoy, F. 2008. 'Calculation, qualculation, calqulation: Shopping cart's arithmetic, equipped cognition and clustered consumers'. *Marketing Theory*, special issue on Markets Forms and Marketing Practices 8(1): 15–44.
Cochoy, F. 2009. Driving a shopping cart from STS to business, and the other way round: On the introduction of shopping carts in American grocery stores (1936–1959). *Organization* 16(1): 31–55.
Cochoy, F. 2010. La sociologie est un sport collectif: petit match avec Michel Callon. In *Débordements. Mélanges offerts à Michel Callon*, Akrich, M., Barthe, Y., Muniesa, F. and Mustar, P. (eds). Paris: Presses des Mines, 69–86.
Cochoy, F. 2015. 'Consumers at work, or curiosity at play? Revisiting the prosumption/value co-creation debate with smartphones and 2D barcodes. *Marketing Theory* 15(2): 133–153.
Cochoy, F. and Dubuisson-Quellier, S. 2013. The sociology of market work. *Economic Sociology, the European Electronic Newsletter* 15(1): 4–11 http://econsoc.mpifg.de/archive/econ_soc_15-1_docm.pdf#page=4
Cova, B. and Cova, V. 2009. Faces of the new consumer: A genesis of consumer governmentality. *Recherche et applications en marketing* 24(3): 81–100.
Czarniawska, B. and Hernes, T. 2005. *Actor-Network Theory and Organizing*. Copenhagen: Liber and Copenhagen School Press.
Dubuisson, S. 1999. Le prestataire, le client et le consommateur. Sociologie d'une relation marchande. *Revue Française de Sociologie* 40(4): 671–688.
Dubuisson-Quellier, S. 2007. The shop as a market space: The commercial qualities of retail architecture. In *Boutiques and Other Retail Spaces*, Vernet, D. and De Wit, L. (eds), Abingdon: Routledge, 16–33.
Dubuisson-Quellier, S. 2010. Product tastes, consumer tastes: The plurality of qualifications in product development and marketing activities. In *Reconnecting Marketing to Markets*, Araujo, L., Finch, J. and Kjellberg, H. (eds). Oxford: Oxford University Press, 74–93.
Eymard-Duvernay, F. 1989. Conventions de qualité et formes de coordination. *Revue Economique* 40(2): 329–359.
Farias, I. and Bender, T. 2010. Urban Assemblages: How Actor-Network Theory Changes Urban Studies. London: Routledge.
Grandclément-Chaffy, C. 2006. Wheeling one's groceries around the store: The invention of the shopping cart, 1936–1953. In *Food Chains: From Farmyard to Shopping Cart*,

Belasco, W. and Horowitz, R. (eds). Philadelphia: University of Pennsylvania Press, 233–252.

Grandclément-Chaffy, C. 2008. *Vendre sans vendeurs: sociologie des dispositifs d'achalandage en supermarché*. Thèse de doctorat de sociologie, Ecole des Mines de Paris.

Grandclément-Chaffy, C. and Gaglio, G. 2011. *Convoking the Consumer in Person: The Focus Group Effect*. In *Inside Marketing: Ideologies, Practices, Devices,* Zwick, D. and Cayla, J. (eds). Oxford: Oxford University Press, 87–114.

Gomart, E. and Hennion, A. 1999. A sociology of attachment: Music amateurs, drug users. In *Actor Network Theory and After*, Hassard, J. and Law, J. (eds). Oxford: Blackwell Publishers, 220–247.

Hennion, A. 2007. Those things that hold us together: Taste and sociology. *Cultural Sociology* 1(1): 97–114.

Hennion, A. 2010. The price of the people: Sociology, performance and reflexivity. In *Cultural Analysis and Bourdieu's Legacy*, Silva, E. and Warde, A. (eds). London, Routledge, 117–127.

Hennion, A. 2015a. The Passion for Music: A Sociology of Mediation. Farnham: Ashgate.

Hennion, A. 2015b. Paying attention: What is tasting wine about. In *Moments of Valuation: Exploring Sites of Dissonance*, Barthoin-Antal, A., Hutter, M. and Stark, D. (eds). Oxford: Oxford University Press, 37–56.

Hennion, A. and Méadel, C. 1989. The artisans of desire: The mediation of advertising between the product and the consumer. *Sociological Theory* 7(2): 191–209.

Karpik, L. 1999. French Lawyers: A Study in Collective Action, 1274 to 1994, Oxford, Clarendon Press.

Karpik, L. 2010. *Valuing the Unique: The Economics of Singularity*. Princeton: Princeton University Press.

Latour, B. 1996. On interobjectivity. *Mind, Culture, and Activity: An International Journal* 3(4): 228–269.

Latour, B. 1999. Factures/fractures: From the concept of network to the concept of attachment. *RES: Anthropology and Aesthetics* 36: 20–32.

Law, J. and Hassard, J. 1999. *Actor Network Theory and After*. Oxford: Blackwell Publishers/The Sociological Review.

Mallard, A., 2005. Following the emergence of unpredictable uses? New stakes and tasks for the social scientific understanding of ICT uses. In *Everyday Innovators: Researching the Role of Users in Shaping ICTs*, Haddon, L., Mante, E., Sapio, B., Kommonen, K., Fortunati, L. and Kant, A. (eds). Dordrecht: Springer, 39–53.

Mallard, A. 2007. Performance testing: Dissection of a consumerist experiment. In *Market Devices*, Callon, M., Millo, Y. and Muniesa, F. (eds). Oxford: Blackwell Publishing, 152–172.

Mallard, A. 2010. De l'usage dans l'échange. Quelques propositions issues de la perspective de l'économie des qualités. In *Débordements. Mélanges offerts à Michel Callon*, Akrich, M., Barthe, Y., Muniesa, F. and Mustar, P. (eds). Paris: Presses de Mines, 303–314.

Mallard, A. 2012. Developing uses, qualifying goods: On the Construction of market exchange for internet access services. *Consumption, Markets and Culture* 15(2): 191–212.

Mallard, A. and Cochoy, F. 2015. 'Quand le consommateur montre les choses du marché ...': Contributions de Bruno Latour, de Michel Callon et de leurs collègues à l'étude de la consommation. In Rémy, É. and Robert-Demontrond, P. (eds), *Regards croisés sur la consommation, Tome 2, Des structures au retour de l'acteur*. Cormelles-le-Royal: EMS éditions, 239–262.

Méadel, C. 1994. Histoire de la radio des années trente. De l'auditeur au sans-filiste. Paris: Economica-Anthropos.

Méadel, C. and Rabeharisoa, V. 2001. Taste as a form of adjustment between food and consumers. In *Technology and the Market: Demand, Users and Innovation*, Coombs, R., Green, K., Richards, A. and Walsh, A. (eds). Cheltenham: Edward Elgar, 234–253.

Ohl, F. 2004. Staging identity through consumption: Exploring the social use of sporting goods. In *Sport, Culture and Advertising: Identities, Commodities and the Politics of Representation*, Jackson, S.J. and Andrews, D.L. (eds). London: Routledge, 241–262.

Peter, P.J. and Olson, J.C. 1983. Is science marketing? *Journal of Marketing* 47(4): 111–125.

Strasser, S. 1989. Satisfaction Guaranteed: The Making of the American Mass Market. New York: Pantheon Books.

Strum, S. and Latour, B. 1987. Redefining the social link: From baboons to humans. *Social Science Information*, 26(4): 783–802.

Teil, G., Barrey, S., Floux, P. and Hennion, A. 2011. *Le vin et l'environnement*. Paris: Presses des Mines.

Trébuchet-Breitwiller, A.-S. 2015. Making things precious: A pragmatist inquiry into the valuation of luxury perfumes. In *Moments of Valuation: Exploring Sites of Dissonance*, Barthoin-Antal, A., Hutter, M. and Stark, D. (eds). Oxford: Oxford University Press, 168–186.

Trompette, P. 2007. Customer channeling arrangements in market organization: Competition dynamics. *Revue Française de Sociologie* 48(5): 3–33.

23

Objects: From Signs to Design

Benoît Heilbrunn

INTRODUCTION

Consumer culture often deals with products, commodities and goods, and seems to have forgotten objects and things. Objects made or modified by humans are clumped together under the term 'artifact'. That word connects two words – art and fact – reflecting its double Latin root. The word art derives from *ars, artis* (skill in joining), and fact derives from *factum* (deed or act) from *facere* (to make or to do), emphasizing the utilitarian meaning already implicit in the word art; thus, skill or knowledge is applied to the making of a thing. The term art refers to objects whose primary initial purpose has been to represent, to memorize, to induce veneration, elevation or contemplation, to provide access to or influence supernatural forces, to delight the eye, or otherwise to affect human thought or behavior through visual means (Prown, 1994, p. 2). Now, what is the exact definition of an object? Etymologically, 'object' (*objectum*) means 'thrown against', something that exists outside of ourselves, that is placed in front of us, and has a material nature (Moles, 1972). Transforming a thing stemming from the natural world (a stone found on the beach) into a cultural artifact makes it an object (a paperweight for instance). At all events, the distinction between subject and object is a relatively recent one. Its premises go back to Roman times (notably the distinction between persona/res), although it has only really developed in what we call modern times. Kopytoff points out the dichotomy that has existed in recent Western thought where there is an analytical separation between people and things, the relationship between the two being thin and instrumentally defined (Kopytoff, 1986). The dissemination of worthless products leads to an impoverishment of sensory experience and a loss of relations with objects. It is for instance possible to consider that at the beginning of the twentieth century, a four-person family would have about 2500 to 3000 objects, including electrical appliances and decorative objects (Branzi, 1988). A person is said to come into daily contact with approximatively 20,000 objects and to own an average of 10,000 objects. As Trentmann reminds us in his *Empire of Things*, 'In Los Angeles, a middle-class garage often no longer houses a car but several hundred boxes of stuff. The United Kingdom in 2013 was home to 6 billion items of clothing, roughly a hundred per adult; a quarter of these never leave the wardrobe' (Trentmann, 2017: 1). An object, insofar as it can become non-transformable, impenetrable, offering us smoothness and an indifferent nudity, is first and foremost something that resists. This relates to the Latin origin of object, which is 'objectum, what stands against and resists (Moles, 1972). Anyhow, an interesting difference is the resistance of objects as theorized by French thinkers (Sartre, Moles, Baudrillard, for instance), versus the kind of the invisibility of things (Miller, 2010), which has more to do with an Anglo-Saxon anchorage. The French intellectual tradition takes for granted the subject/object dichotomy which is constitutive of articulate languages, and this may be an explanation for the importance of the linguistic metaphor to illustrate the system of objects (see Baudrillard, 1968, for instance). To build this idea of invisibility, Miller refers to two important ideas. The first one is derived from Goffman's *Frame Analysis*, in which he argues that much of our behavior is determined by the frames which constitute the context of action. The other is developed by Gombrich in *The Sense of Order*, and relates to the fact that when a frame is appropriate we simply do not see it. Material objects are a setting. They help us to classify our environment by telling us that this is a wedding ring, that is a gun. But things work most effectively when we do not actually look at them, we just accept them (Miller, 2010, p. 50). This is what Miller calls the *humility of things* (Miller, 2010, p. 50). In other words, objects are important not so much because they seem visible and physically constrain or enable, but quite the opposite: 'It is often precisely because we do not see them' (Miller, 2010, p. 50). The less we are aware of them, the more powerfully they can determine our expectations, by setting the scene and ensuring appropriate behavior, without being open to challenge. Things work by being invisible and unremarked upon, a state they achieve by being familiar and taken-for-granted.

SEMANTICIZATION AND THE MEANING OF OBJECTS

Do things mean anything? This important question for anyone interested in material culture was once raised by Roland Barthes in a conference he gave in Venice in 1964 (Barthes, 1988). There are of course several ways of answering this question depending on whether one takes a semiotic, a philosophical or an anthropological perspective. Objects proliferate in our daily lives and they constitute a language. To better grasp what objects mean, it is necessary to accept that to consume is not just the fact of using or destroying an object, but rather a set of signifying practices whereby individuals handle physical and non-physical objects to create meaning. Consumption therefore brings about the transformation of a physical substance into a meaningful substance, so the object must necessarily be transmuted into a name or system of signs to become an object for consumption. This process of semanticization means that one attaches to the physical dimensions that constitute the object (its weight, color, volume, etc.) imaginary dimensions (values, a symbolic universe, a lifestyle, etc.). Semanticization means the possibility for objects to become signs – *conditio sine qua non* of the object of consumption to Baudrillard – and to signify beyond their use-value.

Any object always thus embodies both a denotative message and a connotative message. Denotation refers to the fact that the object conveys information about its functions, what it stands for (semantic function), whereas connotation refers to an aesthetic dimension which conveys a subjective impression and emotion about the product (aesthetic function). Thus the task of the product designer is to understand what are the main expectations (functional and existential) of consumers towards products and to design products accordingly. In other words, the designer's role is to design shapes and to use materials which schematize, strengthen and activate the desired and appropriate dimensions (solidity, resistance) valued by the target customers, given the fact that this functional dimension of the product is always accompanied by an aesthetic message. The main virtue of a semantic of objects is to make known for objects of consumption (like all objects), in addition to their denotative and functional value, a connotative function related to their propensity to signify beyond their strict functional and utilitarian value. As illustrated by Barthes (1993), a bunch of red roses is not merely an aesthetic and olfactory delight, but a cultural symbol of romance and love, whereas the wedding ring is a traditional symbol of romance and love. A symbol means that the relationship between the signifier and the signified is conventional, which means it is a type of contract that ties a community. Therefore, few symbols are universal because they are linked to a given community that shares a specific meaning.

There are for instance different ways to look at a crucifix. For someone living in a country that identifies Christianity as a predominant religion, this object is much more than two pieces of wood, because it carries a symbolic meaning which is a crucial narrative of Christianity (Woodward, 2007, p. 65). A safety pin can be considered an innocuous object linked to a functional purpose which is to temporarily affix clothing when a button or a zip is missing. Yet, within the system of punk style, this object is re-appropriated by being worn outside its normal conventions. Its symbolic potency is precisely linked to a rerouting of the usual and functional meaning and the fact that the object functions as a sign which is worn outside of context. This is a typical example of re-semantization, whereby an object gains a new cultural meaning through the appropriation by a given community and a decontextualization of the object use (Hebdige, 1979; Woodward, 2007). In other words, objects are signs, meaning that they always stand for something else. The material part of any object (the signifier) is always connected to abstract elements (the signified) and this connection between two heterogeneous levels of the object as a sign makes the meaning of the object happen. The meaning may be linked to a social status, a religious affiliation, gender and so forth.

In the semiotic approach, the signifier has no meaning per se, but helps to communicate a signified. An object may only exist in an instrumental and functional relationship with the user; it must necessarily be invested with values that exceed its sole function. Objects have a social life and cannot be solely defined by their sheer technical commodity status because they are immersed within cultural and cognitive processes. They are therefore not inanimate, fixed and stable, they move in and out of various phases. Kopytoff (1986) proposes a processual view of things (and of persons), whereby the status of objects undergoes transformations in category and associated meaning. Objects go through constant commodification-decommodification-recommodification processes, and objects, not just people, have social lives. As we shall see later, the meaning of objects is not only symbolic, as individuals may also project personal and emotional meaning onto these objects (Richins, 1994a, b) beyond the social meaning these objects have encapsulated.

The implicit background of this approach is that the best way to appreciate the role of objects is to consider them as signs and symbols that represent us (Miller, 2010). In other words, there is a language of commodities (Nöth, 1998). The social exchange of goods is essentially a symbolic process which enables people to communicate through the medium of objects. With consumer society, objects lose their material and functional status by their integration into sign systems. That is why consumption is defined by Baudrillard as the organization of material substance into signifying substance: 'to become an object of consumption the object must become a sign' (Baudrillard, 1968, p. 277). Goods have meaning not solely as objects, but also as elements of a vast sign system, through a process of semantization.

Every object is thus imbued with an ideology, that is, a way of seeing the world and therefore, of thinking. As Jean-Marie Floch states:

> a pocket knife always says something about its owner ... I therefore believe it legitimate to imagine that the handle of a knife in fact extends into a certain way of doing things, one that ultimately speaks to a certain way of life or way of being. Approaching the topic this way ... we are trying to identify, if not a culture ... then at least a way of thinking and a particular mode of interaction between self and world.

Hence, the Opinel is a mountain knife that offers a single solution for each function; it is a generalist that seems to say to its users: 'You're on your own'; by contrast, the Swiss Army knife works like a specialist by offering a specific solution for each type of use; it seems more to be saying to its users: 'Serve yourself' (Floch, 2000). Thus consumer goods are not only systems of communication, but are more generally given the function of cultural and ideological *transmission* by significantly changing a meaningful chain of structural elements of the socio-economic environment (belief systems, rules of behavior, rituals, etc.).

In his *Mythologies* (originally published in 1957), Roland Barthes was the first author to consider the symbolic meaning of material culture within advanced consumer societies. He investigates the bourgeois culture by focusing on specific objects. The hypothesis is that objects have a story to tell. The commodity object appears as natural, transparent and just magically 'exists' (Barthes, 1993; Woodward, 2007). Taking inspiration from Saussure, Barthes shows that the structuralist approach has the capacity to unmask and show the linguistic working of the commodity-based ideological system and its underlying myths. But what exactly is a myth? For Barthes it is much more than a physical object, but rather a mode of signification that is attached to objects (Barthes, 1993). Myths add a certain patina to objects, endowing them with special qualities and abilities. Myth equals pure matter plus ideology (Woodward, 2007, p. 69). By analyzing myths, Barthes attempts to uncover the ideological system beyond the bourgeois culture which is shaped by the false promises of consumerist objects. Most ordinary objects dress up reality by giving it a glossy appearance, imitating something natural and transparent, but which is in fact for Barthes false, deceptive and implicitly ideological. Objects do not manifest the everyday commonsense order of things, but rather hide ideological interests which are primarily capitalist interests. That is why for Barthes a myth is a type of speech which acts to mislead or obfuscate, a 'delusion to be exposed' (Culler, 1983, p. 33).

POSSESSIONS AND THE EMBODIMENT OF VALUES

One of the consequence of the semanticization process that characterizes consumer society is that objects have meanings which are cultural, social and personal. The seminal work of Csikszentmihalyi and Rochberg-Halton (1981) is based on the assumptions that objects are symbols that can tell who people are, who they have been and who they wish to become. Some objects are cherished for affording action (a bike), while some others are cherished for contemplation (a sculpture). The dominant paradigm is, that the signified which is conveyed is strongly connected to the personal and social identity of the owner due to a constant self-extension process (Belk, 1988).

Richins (1994b) distinguished between the public meanings of objects (meanings assigned by members of a society at large) which are fashion, status or stigma, and private meanings (what the possession means for an individual). Public meanings result from shared socialization experiences as well as participation in social activities whereas private meanings are more idiosyncratic. The meaning of objects shifts over time, from what one can do with an object to what one has done in the past. That is why as one gets older, objects serve to connect one with the past. There are also gender differences expressed in the meaning of objects when individuals are asked about their cherished possessions, as illustrated by Kamptner (1995), who shows that men tend to report instrumental objects (such as furniture) whereas women tend to rank expressive categories such as visual arts. In terms of meanings of treasured objects, men refer more to enjoyment (mood enhancement such as 'feeling good' or 'escape') and utilitarian resources (getting a job done), whereas women are more interested in the social meaning of objects (objects that tie to another person), followed by the self and enjoyment. The objects young people cherish are the ones that cultivate or encourage action – they are instruments for doing, and require physical manipulation and engagement, such as musical instruments or skateboards, whereas grandparents tend to cherish objects that require mostly mental and emotional engagement, such as photographs.

There are basically two kinds of values associated with objects: utilitarian values and existential values. An object is seen as essentially utilitarian when it is perceived by the user as mainly serving particular functions (electrical goods, furniture, kitchen appliances, etc.). The effectiveness with which objects fulfill these functions plays a large part in their evaluation, and much consumer behavior is directed at searching for information about such effectiveness. The role of design is to convey an impression of effectiveness, solidity, through appropriate features, colors and materials. Objects may also have existential connotations such as emotional value, importance to the individual, etc. The design of products and signs necessarily has to take into consideration the various types of existential values related to the consumption of objects. These might include such values as social values (the product design might indicate that the user belongs to a given social category), emotional values (the product design has to arouse feelings and affective states) and epistemic values (the ability of the product to arouse curiosity and to provide novelty). The latter refers to the necessity for consumers to live new experiences through the use of products, which provides innovative combinations of shape, materials, colors, and so forth. The importance of these existential values is the choice of products and brands, and therefore the way consumers perceive the design of products is also related to hedonic consumption which has become a new paradigm of consumption. Hirschman and Holbrook (1982) have identified the main characteristics of this hedonic consumption process, that is, first, emotional desires prevail over utilitarian motivations in the choice of products and services, and second, consumers may project on to a product a subjective meaning which exceeds by far the real attributes this product may actually possess. The consumption of products does not thus refer any longer to an act of destruction effected by the consumer, but rather to an experience in which priority is given to affective factors.

OBJECTS AND THE CATEGORIZATION PROCESS

The structuralist approach to material objects is based on the idea that there is a small number of fundamental generative cultural schemes within a society that can be combined in different ways (Lévi-Strauss, 1966). This is what Lévi-Strauss calls 'systems of transformations', knowing that the structuralist generative scheme is supposed to be objective and can be observed and analyzed through scientific investigation. Also, objects do not act alone and should not be regarded as entities in isolation. As Lévi-Strauss's structuralism has shown, we should always start from the relationships between elements within a system instead of looking at isolated units (Lévi-Strauss, 1963). Objects achieve definition by relationships of contrast with what they are not, as much as from what they are. That is why structuralism focuses on the relationships between things rather than the things themselves. Lévi-Strauss shows in *The Way of the Masks* (1982) that the masks used by the Indians of the American Northwest Coast were the material equivalent of myths. Like myths, they would undergo inversion, either in their physical attributes or in the symbolic interpretation of their material form, at the boundaries between different tribal groups. Thus the Xwexwe Mask of the Kwakiutl, with its bulging eyes, protruding jaws and tongue, is the inverse transformation of their Dzonk mask, which has sunken eyes, hollow cheeks, and no tongue, but is the same as the mask called Swaihwe of the neighboring Salish. Here, the objects of one society are seen to derive their meanings not only from their relations one with one another, but from the ways in which this system of relations undergoes partial inversion as it crosses the boundaries with neighboring societies (Miller, 1994, p. 401). Similarly, the meaning of British food becomes clear when seen as a systematic inversion of French culinary symbolism. That is what Lévi-Strauss and Barthes did through their analysis of food, fashion, cars and so forth. Cultural objects such as cuisine are linked to preferences that can be decoded as if they were a language. And systems of preference exist through rules of transformation that are characterized by rules of oppositions. For example, cultural forms of gastronomy may be analyzed through a culinary triangle opposing what is cooked, what is boiled and what is raw.

Semiotics, which is the study of signs and meaning, dominated the study of consumer culture in the second part of the twentieth century. Beyond the question of their meaning also lies the power of consumer culture to classify people and things. But how are objects used to classify individuals and groups? Any theory of the object is rooted in a classification issue. Classifications have salience because they allow individuals to make categorizations and demarcations which are important in personal, psychological, social and cultural life. Goods can be markers of culture, social groups or individuals. The first function of goods is to categorize people in a given society (Douglas and Isherwood, 1978). As shown by Durkheim and Mauss, classifications form the basis of daily life and constitute fundamental cultural practices, through the assessment of things as pure or not, good or bad, beautiful or ugly, rich or poor. Such processes allow things in the natural world to be classified within a cultural system and to become cultural artifacts. Through this classification process, things become goods endowed with a meaning which is shared by a community. Such a meaning is called a symbolic meaning (as opposed to a natural meaning which has the characteristics of natural signs, i.e. signs in which (for Charles Sanders Peirce) the signifier is a natural representation of the signified – the smoke is a signal of fire for instance). Things can be considered as natural signs whereas objects exist through shared meaning. In other words, a thing comes from the natural world and becomes an object through a culturalization process that makes it an artifact endowed with meaning.

AESTHETICIZATION AND THE ROMANTICIZATION OF OBJECTS

In 1917, the French artist Marcel Duchamp caused a scandal at a famous exhibition in New York by exhibiting a public urinal, which was to become the very first ready-made object. Duchamp's artistic gesture intended to show that manufactured objects such as bicycle wheels, dustbins or chairs could arbitrarily be promoted as works of art and thus be exhibited in museums and exhibitions, depending on the discretionary power of the artist. This historical artistic posture is very significant as regards the status of the work of art in contemporary society. Duchamp's aim was to question the distinction which had been made since the Renaissance between the craftsman and the artist. This social mythification of the artist responded to a diffuse and collective aspiration which corresponded to the gradual de-Christianization of Western societies that transferred their religious fervor to art. Museums have replaced places of pilgrimage and now represent, for the tourist industry, much more than a cultural alibi: a cultural tribute, a sacred legitimization. Duchamp therefore aimed at a substantial and self-deconstructive activity by promoting standardized objects as artistic. This blurring of genres together with a deconstruction of symbolic hierarchies illustrates the shift of art into industry, thereby leading to a collapse of the boundaries between art and everyday life. The correlated expansion of the role of art within consumer culture led to the famous 'aestheticization' of everyday life promulgated by Featherstone (1991) and others. This movement has been said to be characteristic of the postmodern condition (Lyotard, 1979).

The American philosopher John Dewey had already pointed out the fact that art is not something special but a significant part of everyday experience and that real understanding of life is synonymous with aesthetic enjoyment. The aesthetic dimension has gained importance within the area of mass consumption, which means that visual and sensory aspects have gained increasing importance in terms of consumer preference and choice for many products: clothes, cars, kitchen appliances, etc. The consumer has shifted from *homo economicus* to *homo aestheticus* (Ferry, 1990) in the sense that sensory and aesthetic dimensions have gained much more importance in consumer choice than they used to have. Additionally, our time is based on the concept of reproducibility, which goes together with the concepts of authenticity, authority and originality. The loss of meaning in consumer objects, mainly due to the societal move from craftsmanship to industrialization, raises the question of how to reconcile the necessary standardization of objects, which is intrinsically linked to the consumer society, with the need for objects which are still able to communicate an aesthetic dimension even though they are widely reproduced and copied. Industrialization is linked to the capacity to reproduce identically any object across time and space. As Benjamin remarked, in contemporary society the object has lost the status of originality and of uniqueness.

Benjamin interprets two kinds of art: auratic and mechanical. Traditional art, he argues, possessed an aura of authenticity which surrounded the original – non-mechanically reproducible – work, endowing it with qualities of 'uniqueness', 'distance' and 'otherness'. These auratic qualities of the original, humanly crafted work of art elicited a meditative response from the onlooker which enabled him or her to transcend time and to perceive the beauty of the work of art as a quasi-eternal moment of completion. Benjamin traces this auratic dimension of art back to its magico-cultic origins in primitive history (Kearney, 1994, p. 164). He invokes the theological idea of a collective psyche (animal mundi) which could generate recurring archetypal images and thereby transcend the limits of normal time. He further identifies these auratic images with Goethe's *Urphänomene* (eternal forms that recur through history), Baudelaire's *correspondances* (an aesthetic conflation of spiritual and material meaning) and Leibniz's monads (the idea that each autonomous consciousness somehow precontains the totality of experience within itself in crystallized form) (Kearney, 1994, p. 164). The distinction made by Benjamin between handcrafted and technological art is expressed in two different kinds of experience: 'auratic' *Erfahrung*, or integrated narrative experience, and technological *Erlebnis*, or atomized, fragmented experience. *Erlebnis* exemplifies the loss of the sense of traditional wisdom and communal narrative. Thus, the rise of radio and electronic media spells the death of linear, narrative coherence by promoting a form of dislocated information and simulation which communicates in isolated sensory moments – in a 'shock of novelty', as Benjamin described it – subversive of the auratic qualities of contemplative distance and uniqueness (Kearney, 1994, pp. 164–165). Whereas *Erfahrung* provides an experience of the beautiful in which the ritual value of art appears through an authentic aura of the work of art which depends on its being embedded in the fabric of sacred tradition, the technologically reproduced work demands an immediate accessibility: the social basis of the contemporary decay of the aura rests on two circumstances, both of which are related to the increasing significance of the masses in contemporary life. Namely, the desire of contemporary masses to bring things 'closer' spatially and humanly; and their equally ardent penchant for overcoming the uniqueness of every reality by accepting its reproduction.

THE TRINITY OF THE OBJECT

From a semiotic point of view, an object revolves continuously on two levels: a level called expression or meaning, which refers to its various physical dimensions and a plan; and the level of content or meaning that corresponds to different meanings conveyed by this object. An object is thus, as Saussure said about a sign like a coin whose two sides are inextricably linked, (1) a set of meanings and (2) meanings attached to these different meanings. If these objects hold such an important place in our lives, it is because they occupy a physical space, a symbolic space, a mental space (by filling our minds with changes in direction about choosing, using, storing, rejecting) and a temporal space, as well as a tangle of feelings and emotions. Therefore, marketing is concerned with objects and places that permanently associate a material dimension with an immaterial dimension. We can then understand the three-dimensional levels that apply to all objects (Heilbrunn, 2015):

- A *physical and sensorial* dimension that mostly refers to the consumption good's physical emanations, its tangible and other aspects directly understood by the consumer through his senses (color, effect of the material, product smell, etc.). The focus on the symbolic dimension of objects has somewhat tarnished the study of the proper physical anchoring of the consumer experience. Furthermore, most of the time the physical anchoring of consumption is considered only in its visual dimension, leaving little room for a truly multi-sensory approach. Yet 'individuals are not satisfied with considering, contemplating, examining, desiring, and admiring objects, but must touch, taste, and feel them in constant collaboration of the five senses' (Löfgren, 1996, p. 39).
- A *symbolic* dimension that refers to the good's own ideological dimension, its ability to convey an imaginary dimension and values. The economy of brands resides in part in its willingness to lend competence to the consumer in terms of sensory discrimination skills; even though blind tests prove quite ruthless since they prove that most people are totally unable to tell the difference between unidentified food products. Due to consumption's own semantization phenomenon, food enjoyment is more in the order of textual enjoyment than the strictly sensorial. In other words, the consumer frequently feasts upon the words he is served more than the dishes.
- A *pragmatic* dimension that refers to the clutch of bodily practices that act through the rituals of purchasing and the consumption of consumer goods. Objects presuppose staging and present 'ways of doing things' that are sometimes ritualized. The act of applying perfume can

be broken down into a precise syntax of gestures that enable an appropriation, and even an incorporation of the object. If objects play such an important role in our lives, it is because they occupy a physical space, a symbolic space, a mental space (by filling our minds with dilemmas about choice, utilization, storage and rejection), and a temporal space – as well as a mixture of sensations and emotions. In other words, an object becomes an essential mediator between individuals and their daily environments, helping them to reconsider their surrounding spaces. Objects all summon up practices, rituals and, therefore, a specific type of corporeal experience. Any consumption action (ironing, vacuum cleaning, etc.) can be broken down into a precise syntax of gestures that enable an appropriation and even an incorporation of objects. The sensorial experience with objects is inseparable from a specific corporeal experience. From mother to daughter, household knowhow is perpetuated by imitation and technical learning, until women begin to identify deeply with linen, an attachment materialized through simple gestures whose nature seems self-evident and natural (Verdier, 1990). It remains that the experience of an object evokes, above and beyond any sensorial imprint, a universe of consumption that is emotionalized and socialized (Boutaud, 2004). In short, our relationship to objects always more or less mediates a relationship to someone else.

OBJECTS: FROM SUBSTANCE TO INTERACTIONS

This emotional power of objects becomes even stronger if we consider their resolutely polysensorial nature. However, marketing is culturally primarily a device for the audio-visual sphere and has only recently looked at polysensoriality. The rise of the so-called consumer experience forces marketing to delve deeper into the consumer's sphere of privacy by developing procedures related to touch, taste and smell, as evidenced, for example, by the surge in olfactory logos or even by the development of tactile design. In other words, the challenge for marketing is for distant senses (sight, hearing) to invest in what proximity senses (touch, taste) as well as the olfactory as an intermediate register. Therefore, any object may be considered by following a spectrum ranging from purely instrumental values to sociability and relationship values. In doing so, the object becomes an essential mediator between the individual and his daily environment, and allows the reconfiguration of relationships between individuals: it makes the unpleasant pleasant, it eases tensions, it brings harmony. In this approach it is not neutral but an essential mediator of human relationships, especially in the space of the family home. In addition to the ideal–physical axis that appears crucial to understanding the mechanics of our relationship to objects, we must also consider an axis related to interpersonal relationships. Indeed, a practice of consumption is in essence multi-modal, that is, the consumption of a product is a synaesthetic experience that convenes, beyond the sensory impression, an affective and socialized universe of consumption.

One may then consider several levels of evaluation and valuation of a product, which are, successively (Boutaud, 2004):

- The *substantive* level, related to the valuation of materials (the feel of a fabric, the smell of a fragrance, the elements of sound design).
- The *referential* level, which refers to the various functions of that product: to have fun, to relax, to meet other people, etc.

- The *situational* level, which highlights the product's consumer framework and returns to different metaphors that can recover the experience of this place, is it similar to a garden where we walk, to a highway on which we travel as quickly as possible, a magical place in which one is meant to experience exotic adventures, a playground, an art gallery, etc.?
- The *interactional* level, which focuses on human relationships involved in the act of consumption.

We may also deduce that all sensorial experiences are inseparable from a specific corporeal experience. In short, our relationship to objects always more or less mediates a relationship to someone else. Psychotherapists have long recognized that our love for objects constitutes a replacement for difficult emotional relationships. One interesting example was found by Serge Tisseron (1999), who tells the story of a young man who used to greatly enjoy repairing old sofas. This activity was an extension of what he did as a child to 'repair' his parents, whom he always saw as being broken down and used up. Having failed in this task, he tried to do better with sofas. The choice of this particular piece of furniture was symptomatic of his desires, as a sofa is a lap that people can sit on. Moreover, sofas have arms that can hold you, which is more or less the expectation that any child has of parents. As the young man's therapy sessions progressed, he began to concentrate on renovating the kind of veneer wood that was used to decorate early twentieth-century sofas, discovering how gestures such as sanding, polishing, varnishing and cleaning the wood's 'skin' could help him to unconsciously work through early experiences in which he had been the object of too much hugging from his parents. This had happened because the young man's parents used him to give free rein to their own frustrated needs for closeness and contact. Once their son had grown up, they reacted to their own incestuous desires by adopting attitudes of coldness and distance that the child found all the more difficult to explain because they would occur after periods of excessive intimacy. What the young man was trying to heal through the various facets of his DIY activity were these two traumas, the invasive contact followed by the sudden distancing.

THE LURE OF OBJECTS

The semiotic approach studies objects as signs and postulates that objects always refer to something more than themselves, hence the idea that the sign is intrinsically a lie, which means a proxy for some other social meaning (Eco, 1976). The lie of the object is linked to what McCracken calls displaced meanings (McCracken, 1998). He outlines a gap between the real and ideal in people's everyday life. In consumer society, the pursuit of desirable objects is an important resource for making bridges between the real and the ideal. Dreaming and fantasizing are important because this is the imagined domain in which people come to define and build up their notion of an ideal (McCracken, 1998; Woodward, 2007), and thus to deal with a material world which is associated with abundance and excess. The sociology of consumption proposed by Baudrillard (1996, 1999) is very original in this respect because it is not so much consumer-centered as object-centered. He attempts to conduct an analysis of the architecture of contemporary material culture by looking at the overarching structure of meanings and codes. He is one of the few authors to study objects themselves, regardless of the discourses and practices of actors. Rather than considering consumption as an autonomous phenomenon which fulfills individual needs, he views consumption as a social institution where social forces (class, status, prestige) are measured and played out (Woodward, 2007, p. 74). As they are in a flight from technological structure towards their secondary meaning, which is cultural, objects have a symbolic value rather than a use value or exchange value. Even though objects are theoretically endowed with a pragmatic or utilitarian component, what is more important is their symbolic value. The main function of objects is to mark social status and prestige. This idea is of course not far from the classification property of objects (Douglas and Isherwood, 1979). That is why, according to Baudrillard, objects as signifiers have a significant role to play in reproducing relations of social power. The consumer citizen is therefore someone who plays with signs as an integral part of his/her identity. Hence a process of liberalization in which individuals use objects as signs to reroute their function. Consumption is about weaving objects into a coherent signifying fabric. Baudrillard claims that commodities are bought and displayed as much for their sign-value as their use-value, and that the phenomenon of sign-value has become an essential constituent of the commodity and consumption in the consumer society. For Lukàcs and the Frankfurt School, *reification* – the process whereby human beings become dominated by things and become more thinglike themselves – comes to govern social life. In consumer society, culture and consumption also became homogenized, depriving individuals of the possibility of cultivating individuality and self-determination. That is the reason why consumption is often defined by Baudrillard as a kind of labor, 'an active manipulation of signs', a way of inserting oneself into the consumer society, and working to differentiate oneself from others through the manipulation of the sign-value of objects. Objects participate in the organization of a social order where identities are constructed by the appropriation of images, and codes and models determine how individuals perceive themselves and relate to other people. Social life is governed by the mode of simulation, whereby codes and models determine how goods are consumed and used, politics unfold, culture is produced and consumed, and everyday life is lived. And while for classical social theory modern societies were characterized by differentiation, for Baudrillard, postmodern societies are characterized by dedifferentiation, the 'collapse' of (the power of) distinctions, or *implosion* (Kellner, 2007). Consumer society is therefore a simulacrum in which people are caught up in the play of images, spectacles and simulacra that have less and less relationship with an outside, with an external reality, to such an extent that the very concepts of 'reality' no longer seem to have any meaning. That is why Baudrillard claims that henceforth the masses seek spectacle and not meaning. The consequence of the predominance of sign values over use values and exchange values is that the materiality of commodities disappears.

POACHING AND BRICOLAGE

We owe a debt to Michel de Certeau for coming up with the most acute yet subtle thoughts about how individuals can rightly reclaim the system of consumption. Keeping a distance from this sort of binarity, which shows the origins of something being perverted by mass consumption, means being more interested in the modes of creativity in consumer practices that no system can reduce to silence. De Certeau proposed the idea of internal invention even within everyday life by running through a series of tricks that divert the systems of control. By focusing on the tricks, intelligence, plurality and inventiveness of each individual's modes of appropriation, de Certeau examines the processes of subjugation and individuation as possible ways to enjoy and respond to wants in the interstices, the constant deviations from established standards and accepted codes. Therefore, mass consumption is no longer stigmatized as a source of inauthenticity, but only considered in the light of each individual's authenticity. He leads to the figure of the sphinx consumer '(whose) creations are disseminated within the grid of a televised, urbanistic and commercial production'. The issue is not that of consumption as reception but as production. Hence de Certeau's question: 'The users of the supermarket, the practicants of urban space, the consumers of journalistic stories and legends, what do they create with what they have "absorbed," received and paid for? What are they doing?' (de Certeau, 1998). A streamlined, expansionist, centralized production, one that is dramatic and noisy, must face a completely different type of production, which is called 'consumption', known for its tricks, its breaking down over time, its poaching, its underground character, its tireless murmur, in short, a near invisibility because it is not seen through its own products (which it would prefer) but in the art of using them that is imposed on them.

Thus, de Certeau's re-appropriation refers to poaching and various possible re-uses, that is, a turnaround of constraints established from above against themselves through which individuals try to appropriate time and space by changing the names, by diverting them from their purpose, in short, through tricks. *The Practice of Everyday Life* discusses an attempt to 're-enchant the world' to the extent that de Certeau seeks to bring forth from the banality of everyday life a poetic inventiveness that reveals an inexhaustible power of creativity. A *poïesis,* an active sense of re-creation that lives inside the subjects with the most routine lives (Dosse, 2007, p. 502). Everyday life, in its poetic dimension, makes possible the tricks and tactics for changing the modes of appropriation expected by strategists. It serves to exceed the cut-off postulated between an active-type production and consumption, which is not passive and tends to dissolve under users' continual resistance to following the rules. To speak of an amateur is to talk about consumers who are not familiar with the producers, who become poets in their own lives, trailblazers in the jungles of functionalist rationality. Consumers produce something that appears in the 'wander lines' Deligny spoke about. They map out seemingly senseless 'unspecified trajectories' inconsistent with the built environment, which maps out and prefabricates where they will go. As de Certeau shows, although the prescribed routes should cover them, these crossings remain heterogeneous to systems they infiltrate and places where they cross the tricks of different interests and desires. They circulate, come and go, overflowing and drifting in a forced relief, movements of a frothy sea insinuated among the rocks and mazes of an established order. Thus, 'to live, move, speak, read, go shopping or to cook, these activities seem to match the characteristics of the tricks and surprise tactics: … the art of shooting in someone else's field of the other, the tricks of hunters, maneuverability and polymorphic mobility, exhilarating discoveries, poetic and warlike' (de Certeau, 1998). Whereas, for example, the tactics of the culinary arts organize a network of relationships, poetic bricolage and the re-use of merchant structures.

As de Certeau also found, the form of poaching at play in consumers' tactics induces another form of exchange, that of a gift economy (of dependent opposing *generosities*), an aesthetic of blows (artistic operations) and a tenacity ethic (a thousand ways to reject the order established by law, meaning or fatality). The reconfiguration that allows the deployment of these tactics leads to a style (resistance), an aesthetic of a different type that brings to mind the *potlatch* of Marcel Mauss (1967). By using the market and its standard model in which each individual seeks to maximize his personal gain, de Certeau substitutes another logic, that of a concrete symbolic exchange characterized by a gift and a desire. This is close to the idea of bricolage which proves useful to understand how most people interact with material objects (Lévi-Strauss, 1966). The bricoleur is a kind of tinkerer, who is able to bring multiple creative tools and strategies to bear to solve material problems or create new structures. Using a host of materials lying at various stages of construction or (dis)repair, he continuously responds to the ever-changing requirements of a task, as makeshift materials show themselves to be useful or not, to varying degrees (Lévi-Strauss, 1966; Woodward, 2007, p. 66). Although the medium may be material objects, the bricoleur always works more or less with signs.

OBJECTS AS PARTNERS

The psychoanalyst Donald Winnicott introduced the notion of a transitional object to designate a material object that is imbued with an elective value for an infant and a young child, notably at bedtime (a corner of a blanket or a towel that the child sucks on). The transitional object is halfway between the internal and the external world and specifically presupposes the existence of a transitional space. This idea of a kind of initial indistinction is reminiscent of certain studies of emotions and passions. For example, at the origin of an emotion, there is always a meeting. According to Sartre, 'the emotion is a certain way of apprehending the world', one where 'the subject feeling the emotion and the object of the emotion are united in a synthesis that cannot be dissolved' (Sartre, 1943, p. 37). As indicated by its name, 'e-motion' is not a purely internal state, but more of a movement that brings the subject feeling the emotion out of him/herself, with the subject then being able to express him/herself by modifying his/her relationship to the world. Consciousness projects emotional significations upon the surrounding world and, in return, 'vibrates at its most intimate level, "living" this modification of the world and providing it with consistency through physical reactions that serve as its "substance"' (Sartre, 1943, pp. 50–51). The being that feels the emotion is overwhelmed both internally and externally. Through its emotional power, an object plays an essential mediator's role that makes it possible to express some of its user's character or personality traits via a sort of mechanism based on an incorporation and marginalization of the individual's psychic life. The emotional power of objects raises questions as to where they begin or end. Are objects defined in opposition to 'living substances' or rather by their own functions? Should they be contrasted with humans? Can they occasionally supplement humans or become part of them? Yet to understand the emotional power of an object over a subject, we need to hypothesize the existence of an exchange between subject and object, an idea that the Western mindset particularly dislikes. The same does not hold in other traditions that recognize no such chasm. For example, Chinese thinking is based on a participation of both the body and the human mind in the winds that blow through the cosmos. Poetry specifically affirms the solidarity of the I (*wo*) with things (*wu*), as well as the inseparability between emotions of internal experiences (*ch'ing*) and the 'setting' or the outside world (*ching*). Similarly, in the African tradition, emotion occupies an eminent position, not as the expression of personal feelings, but as an openness to the world. For a black African, a work of art expresses confrontation, an embrace of a subject and an object. Aesthetic emotion supposedly has traces of this kind of distinction, or feels nostalgia for it. The differentiation of this state entails an investment in the object that specifically implies an exchange between the inside and the outside worlds, one based on a mediation of the body that feels something. What we mainly remember here is the continuity of the psychic processes that invest, in one and the same movement, in the body as well as the objects that surround it. But doesn't this psychological continuity mean that we should in fact view objects as if they were our partners?

The positions that our Western cultures attribute de facto to objects exist in relation to a subject. But if we accept that an object entails an experience, would this not be tantamount to hypothesizing the reciprocity, or more precisely, the reversibility of objects? This would intimate that the consumption experientialization paradigm means that objects and brands constitute fully fledged actors in consumers' emotional and daily environments, much like relatives of friends. One significant analysis here is of the relationship that individuals can have with mobile phones: 'we sometimes touch them delicately as we would a dearly beloved friend' (Tisseron, 2000, p. 20). Indeed, if the relational paradigm is to be something other than purely metaphorical, we must accept some symmetry in the exchange between an individual and an object. The wealth of the relationships we entertain with objects stems from their reversible nature, for example from the fact that an object may only be an object yet, at the same time, it is capable of mutating into a true subject partner. Take, for example, something that is 'treated like a face, hence "envisaged" or "given a face" and which in turn faces us and looks at us ...' (Deleuze, 1986). What this means is that a 'face-giving' process exists for objects, and that 'even an object we use (a house, a utensil ... a piece of clothing, etc.) will be given a face. We will say that they are watching me, not because such objects resemble a face, but because they are connected to the abstract machine of face-giving' (Deleuze and Guattari, 1988). Imbued with curative powers, an object becomes much more than an object.

DESIGN AND THE RE-ENCHANTMENT OF EXPERIENCE

The penetration of science and technique into our daily environment has eliminated most technical barriers to the production of objects. New forms and functions can now be used, thus enlarging the field of possibilities and the creative abilities of designers. An increasingly competitive environment has increased the use of new technical and creative possibilities in design. The conjunction of these two factors has led to three major challenges related to the status of objects in contemporary society. First, objects have experienced a crucial disjunction between matter and form. Matter – which is always considered the solid, stable, inert counterpart of ideas – has, thanks to huge technological progress, become pliable and capable of being molded into any possible form (Manzini, 1995, p. 222). New forms and functions are now possible. Design has an essential role in giving meaning to objects, doing so through the shapes, colors and materials of the object. Second, the reproducibility of objects inevitably leads to the fading of meaning of most everyday objects which have become mere commodities and have thus lost their substance (Heilbrunn, 2015). Looking at objects always more or less confronts us with aesthetic issues. Benjamin (1992) was one of the first to show how art objects have lost part of their original meaning and authenticity due to their ever-increasing reproduction and diffusion. The reproduction of art objects goes together with the loss of authenticity, uniqueness and distinctiveness, which considerably reduces their propensity to surprise, fascinate and thus to illuminate.

Design infuses every object in the consumer world and gives form to immaterial processes such as goods, services, etc. In a culture of 'doing', it becomes essential to determine why and for whom things are designed and produced. Giorgio Vasari (1511–74), an Italian painter and architect, author of the famous *Lives of the Painters, Sculptors and Architects*, was one of the first artists to attempt a definition of painting through the concept of design. Drawing (*disegno*), he writes, means the art of outlining figures by means of appropriate curves. In most marketing textbooks the concept of 'design' is either completely ignored, or fallaciously presented as a mere dimension of the product. The meaning of design is nevertheless much more profound. As an English word, 'design', which appeared in 1588 as a modern derivative of the Latin *designare*, means to mark or point out, delineate, contrive. 'Design' also comes from the French *désigner*, to indicate or designate, and can be defined as planning for action or miniature action. In a broad sense, Simon defines design in the following manner: everyone designs who devises a course of action aiming at changing existing situations into preferred ones (Simon, 1969, p. 55). It is interesting to note that the French word 'design' has two antecedents which cast light on its meaning; design is related to both *dessein* (project, invention of a plan of action, constructive forethought) and *dessin* (drawing). Design thus means both to plan out in systematic, usually graphic, form and to create or contrive for a particular effect or purpose.

Design can also be understood as the manipulation of content through form, and vice versa. Even though content is the raw material of design, form is the reorganization of content, in the sense that 'to form' is to fix visual relationships in a given space. Therefore, design is much more than simply to assemble, to order, or even to edit: as Paul Rand states, 'it is to add value and meaning, to illuminate, to clarify, to modify, to dignify, to dramatize, to persuade, and perhaps even to amuse. To design is to transform prose into poetry' (p. 419).

Design activity is part a Promethean activity which consists in the production of both material and immaterial artifacts from which we build our everyday environment

(Manzini, 1995). The designer's role is to make the world habitable in both utilitarian and existential terms. The increasing importance of design for consumers is related to the growing importance in contemporary culture of images, which become a persuasive means of motivating people to express themselves. The social exchange of goods is essentially a symbolic process which enables people to communicate through the medium of objects. With consumer society, objects lose their material and functional status by their integration into sign systems. That is why the designer is a 'modest demiurge … who takes charge of the daily environmental pattern in a hedonistic context where the measure of his action is the quality of life' (Moles, 1972).

REFERENCES

Barthes, R. (1988) 'Sémantique de l'objet', Colloqium at the Cini Foundation in Venice, reproduced in: *The Semiotic Challenge*. Berkeley: University of California Press: 179–190.

Barthes, R. (1993) *Mythologies*. London: Vintage.

Baudrillard, J. (1981) *For a Critique of the Political Economy of the Sign*. St Louis: Telos [1972].

Baudrillard, J. (1996) *The System of Objects*, London: Verso [1968].

Baudrillard, J. (1999) *The Consumer Society: Myths and Structures*. London: Sage [1970].

Belk, R. (1988) 'Possessions and the Extended Self', *The Journal of Consumer Research*, 15(2): 139–168.

Benjamin, W. (1992) 'The Work of Art in the Age of Mechanical Reproduction'. In *Illuminations*. London: Fontana Press: 211–244 [1935].

Boutaud, J.-J. (2004) 'De la difficulté de communiquer un concept polysensoriel, Kenzoki de Kenzo'. In: Boillot, F. and Grasse, M.C. (eds) *Olfaction et patrimoine: quelle transmission?* Aix-en-Provence: Edisud: 79–89.

Branzi, A. (1988) Pomeriggi alla media industria, Milan: Idea Books.

Buchanan, R. and Margolin, V. (eds) (1995) *Discovering Design: Explorations in Design Studies*. Chicago: The University of Chicago Press.

Clarke, A. (1999) *Tupperware: The Promise of Plastic in 1950s America*. Washington: Smithsonian Institution Press.

Crozier, R. (1994) *Manufactured Pleasures: Psychological Responses to Design*. Manchester: Manchester University Press.

Csikszentmihalyi, M. and Rochberg-Halton, E. (1981) *The Meaning of Things: Domestic Symbols and the Self.* Cambridge: Cambridge University Press.

Culler, J. (1983) *Barthes*. London: Fontana.

De Botton, A. (2006) *The Architecture of Happiness: The Secret Art of Furnishing Your Life*. London: Penguin.

de Certeau, Michel (1998) *The Practice of Everyday Life*; Berkeley: University of California Press (1980).

de Certeau Michel et al. (1998) *The Practice of Everyday Life: Vol. 2*, Living and Cooking. Minneapolis: University of Minnesota Press [1994].

Deleuze, G. (1986) *The Movement-Image*. Minneapolis: University of Minnesota Press [1983].

Deleuze, G. and Guattari, F. (1988) *A Thousand Plateaus: Capitalism and Schizophrenia*. Minneapolis: University of Minnesota Press [1980].

Deleuze, G. and Guattari, F. (1983) *Anti-Oedipus: Capitalism and Schizophrenia*. Minneapolis: University of Minnesota Press [1973].

Deligny, F. (2007) *Oeuvres*, Paris: L'Arachnéen.

Dittmar, H. (1992) *The Social Psychology of Material Possessions: To Have Is to Be*. New York: St Martin's Press.

Dosse, F. (2007) *Michel de Certeau. Le marcheur blessé*, Paris: La Découverte.

Douglas, M. and Isherwood, B. (1978) *The World of Goods*. New York: Basic Books.

Douglas M. and Isherwood, B. (1980) *The World of Goods*, London: Routledge.

Eco, U. (1976) *A Theory of Semiotics*. Bloomington: Indiana University Press.

Ferry, L. (1990) *Homo aestheticus*. Paris: Grasset.

Featherstone, M. (1991) *Consumer Culture and Postmodernism*, London: Sage.

Floch, J.-M. (1995) *Identités visuelles*, Paris PUF.

Floch, J.-M. (2001) *Semiotics, Marketing and Communications: Beneath the Signs, the Strategies*. London: Palgrave Macmillan.

Floch, J.-M. (2000) *Visual Identities*. London and New York: Continuum International Publishing Group.

Flusser, V. (2002) *Petite philosophie du design*. Belfort: Circé.

Forty, A. (1986) *Objects of Desire: Design and Society from Wedgwood to IBM*. New York: Pantheon.

Foucault, M. (1970) *The Order of Things*. New York: Random House [1966].

Friedel, R. (1994) 'Some Matters of Substance'. In: Lubar, S. and Kingery, D. (eds) *History from Things: Essays in Material Culture*. Washington: The Smithsonian Institute: 41–50.

Furby, L. (1978) 'Possession in Humans: An Exploratory Study of Its Meaning and Motivation', *Social Behavior and Personality*, 6(1): 49–65.

Gombrich, E. (1979) *The Sense of Order, A Study in the Psychology of Decorative Art*, New York: Cornelle University Press.

Greimas, A.-J. and Courtès, J. (1979) *Semiotics and Language: An Analytical Dictionary*. Bloomington: Indiana University Press.

Hebdige, D. (1979) *Subculture: The Meaning of Style*. London: Methuen & Co.

Heilbrunn, B. (1998) 'In: Search of the Lost Aura: the Object in the Age of Marketing Re-illumination'. In: Brown, S. et al. (eds), *Romancing the Market*. London: Routledge: 187–201.

Heilbrunn, B. (2006) 'The Blandness and Delights of a Daily Object'. In: Carù, A. and Cova, B. (eds) *Consuming Experience*. Abingdon: Routledge: 79–91.

Heilbrunn, B. (2015) *Market Mediations: Semiotic Investigations into Consumers, Objects and Brands*. London: Palgrave Macmillan.

Heskett, J. (2002) *Design: A Very Short Introduction*. Oxford: Oxford University Press.

Hirschman, E. and Holbrook, M. (1982) Hedonic consumption: Emerging concepts, methods and propositions, *Journal of Marketing*, 46(3): 92–101.

Kamptner, L. (1995) 'Treasured Possessions and their Meanings in Adolescent Males and Females', *Adoloescence*, 30(118): 301–318.

Kearney, R. (1994) *Modern Movements in European Philosophy. Phenomenology, Critical Theory, Structuralism*, Second edition, Manchester: Manchester University Press.

Kehret-Ward, T. (1987) 'Combining Products in Use: How the Syntax of Products Use Affects Product Design and Promotion'. In: Umiker-Sebeok, J. (ed.) *Marketing and Semiotics: New Directions in the Study of Signs for Sale*. Berlin: Mouton de Gruyter: 219–238.

Kehret-Ward, T. (1988) 'Using a Semiotic Approach to Study the Consumption of Functionally Related Products', *International Journal of Research in Marketing*, 4(3): 187–200.

Kellner, D. (2007) 'Jean Baudrillard', *The Stanford Encyclopedia of Philosophy* (https://plato.stanford.edu/entries/baudrillard).

Kerney, R. (1994) *Modern Movements in European Philosophy*. Manchester: Manchester University Press, second enlarged edition.

Kirkham, P. (ed.) (1996) *The Gendered Object*. Manchester: Manchester University Press.

Kopytoff, I. (1986) 'The Cultural Biography of Things: Commoditization as Process'. In: Appadurai, A. (ed.) *The Social Life of Things: Commodities in Cultural Perspective*. Cambridge: Cambridge University Press.

Lévi-Strauss, C. (1963) *Structural Anthropology*. New York: Basic Books [1958].

Lévi-Strauss, C. (1966) *The Savage Mind*. Chicago: The University of Chicago Press [1962].

Lévi-Strauss, C. (1982) *The Way of the Masks*. Washington: University of Washington Press [1975].

Levy, S. (1959) 'Symbols for Sale', *Harvard Business Review*, 37(4): 117–124.

Levy, S. (2006) *The Perfect Thing: How the iPod Shuffles Commerce, Culture, and Coolness*. New York: Simon & Schuster.

Löfgren, O. (1996) 'Le retour des objets? L'étude de la culture matérielle dans la culture suédoise', *Ethnologie Française*, *'Culture matérielle et modernité'*, 1(Mars): 38–49.

Lyotard, J.-F. (1997) *The Postmodern Condition: A Report on Knowledge*, Manchester: Manchester University Press [1979].

Mackay, H. (ed.) (1997) *Consumption and Everyday Life*. London: Sage.

Manzini, E. (1995) 'Prometheus of the Everyday: The Ecology of the Artificial and the Designer's Responsibility', *Design Issues*, 9(1): 5–20.

Margolin, V. (ed.) (1989) *Design Discourse: History, Theory, Criticism*. Chicago: The University of Chicago Press.

Margolin, V. and Buchanan, R. (eds) (1995) *The Idea of Design: A Design Issues Reader*. Cambridge, MA: The MIT Press.

Mauss, M. (1967) *The Gift: Forms and Functions of Exchange in Archaic Societies*. New York: Norton.

McCracken, G. (1988) *Culture and Consumption*. Bloomington: Indiana University Press.

Miller, D. (1994) 'Artefacts and the Meaning of Things'. In: T. Ingold (ed.) *Companion Encyclopedia of Anthropology*. Oxon: Routledge: 396–419.

Miller, D. (1995) 'Consumption as the Vanguard of History'. In: D. Miller (ed.), *Acknowledging Consumption. A Review of New Studies,* London. Routledge: 1–57.

Miller, D. (1998) *A Theory of Shopping*. Ithaca: Cornell University Press.

Miller, D. (2010) *Stuff*. Cambridge: Polity.

Moles, A. (1972) *Théorie des objets*. Paris: Editions universitaires.

Nöth, W. (1988) "The language of commodities: ground work for a semiotics of consumer goods", *International Journal of Research in Marketing,* 4, 173–186,

Prown, Jules David (1993) 'The Truth of Material Cutlure: History or Fiction?'. In: Lubar, Steven & Kingery, David (eds) *History From Things. Essays on Material Culture*, Washington: Smithsonian Institution Press, 1–19.

Rand, P. (1993) *Design, Form and Chaos*. New Haven: Yale University Press.

Richins, M.L. (1994a) 'Valuing Things: The Public and Private Meanings of Possessions', *Journal of Consumer Research*, 21(3): 504–521.

Richins, M.L. (1994b) 'Special Possessions and the Expression of Material Values', *Journal of Consumer Research*, 21(3): 522–533.

Riggins, S. (1985) 'The Semiotics of Things: Toward a Sociology of Human-Object Interaction', *Semiotica*, 5(1): 69–77.

Riggins, S. (1990) 'The Power of Things: The Role of Domestic Objects in the Presentation of Self'. In: Riggins, S. (ed.) *Beyond Goffman: Studies on Communication, Institution, and Social Interaction*. Berlin: Mouton de Gruyter: 341–367.

Riggins, S. (ed.) (1994) *The Socialness of Things: Essays on Socio-Semiotics of Objects*. Berlin: Mouton de Gruyter.

Sartre, J.-P. (1943) *Being and Nothingness: A Phenomenological Essay on Ontology*. New York: Philosophical Library.

Sartre, J.-P. (1943) *L'être et le néant*, Paris: Gallimard. Translated as *Being and Nothingness*, London, Routledge [1959].

Schultz, S. et al. (1989) '"These Are a Few of My Favorite Things": Towards an Explication of Attachment as a Consumer Behavior Construct', *Advances in Consumer Research*, 16(1): 359–366.

Simon, H. (1969) *The Science of the Artificial*. Boston: MIT Press.

Sudjic, D. (2008) *The Language of Things*. London: Allen Lane.

Tisseron, S. (1999) *Comment l'esprit vient aux objet*. Paris: Aubier.

Tisseron, S. (2000) *Petites mythologies d'aujourd'hui*. Paris: Aubier.

Trentmann, F. (2017) *Empire of Things*. London: Penguin.

Verdier, Y. (1979) *Façons de dire, façons de faire: la laveuse, la coutirière, la cuisinière*. Paris: Gallimard

Verdier, Y. (1990) *Façons de dire, façons de faire: la laveuse, la couturière, la cuisinière*. Paris: Gallimard.

Warnier, J.-P. (1999) *Construire la culture matérielle. L'homme qui pensait avec ses doigts*. Paris: PUF.

Woodward, I. (2007) *Understanding Material Culture*. London: Sage.

24

The War on Cash[1]

Brett Scott

Several months ago I stayed in an offbeat Amsterdam hotel that brewed its own beer but refused to accept cash for it. Instead, they forced me to use the Visa payment card network to get my UK bank to transfer €4 to their Dutch bank via the elaborate international correspondent banking system.

I was there with civil liberties campaigner Ben Hayes. We were irritated by the anti-cash policy, something the hotel staff took for annoyance at the international payments charges we'd face. That wasn't it though. Our concern was an intuitive one about a potential future world in which we'd have to report our every economic move to a bank, and the effect this could have on marginalised people.

'Cashless society' is a euphemism for the 'ask-your-banks-for-permission-to-pay society'. Rather than an exchange occurring directly between the hotel and me, it takes the form of a 'have your people talk to my people' affair. Various intermediaries message one another to arrange an exchange between our respective banks. That may be a convenient option, but in a cashless society it would no longer be an option at all. You'd have no choice but to conform to the intermediaries' automated bureaucracy, giving them a lot of power, and a lot of data about the microtexture of your economic life.

Our concerns are unfashionable. Without any explicit declaration, the War on Cash has begun. Proponents of digital payment systems are riding upon technology-friendly times to proclaim the imminent Death of Cash. Sweden leads in the drive to reach this state, but the UK is edging that way too. London buses stopped accepting cash in 2014, but do accept MasterCard and Visa contactless payment cards.

Every cash transaction you make is one that a payments intermediary like Visa takes no fee from, so it has an interest in making cash appear redundant, deviant and criminal. That's why, in 2016, Visa Europe launched its 'Cashfree and Proud' campaign, to inform cardholders that 'they can make a Visa contactless payment with confidence and feel liberated from the need to carry cash'.[2]

The company's press release declared the campaign 'the latest step of Visa UK's long term strategy to make cash "peculiar" by 2020'.

There you have it. An orchestrated strategy to make us feel weird about cash. Propaganda is a key weapon of war, and all sides present themselves as liberators. Visa comes across like a paternalistic commander when assuring us that we – like a baby taking first steps – will feel a sense of achievement at liberating ourselves from the burden of cash dependence. Visa's technology offers freedom without dependence or dangers.

Visa is joined by other propagandists. In 2014 Penny for London arrived, an apparently altruistic group set up by the Mayor's Fund for London and Barclaycard, using charity as a hook to switch people to contactless cards on the London Underground. PayPal plastered cities with billboards claiming that 'new money doesn't need a wallet', along with a video proclaiming: 'New money isn't paper, it's progress'. Astroturfing campaigns like No Cash Day are backed by American Express, highlighting such anti-cash themes as the environmental impact of banknotes. Other tactics include pointing out that criminals use cash, that it fuels the shadow economy, that it's unsafe, and that it facilitates tax evasion.

These arguments have notable shortcomings. Criminals use many things that we keep – like cars – and fighting crime doesn't take priority over maintaining other social goods like civil liberties. The 'shadow economy' is a derogatory term used by elites to describe the economic activities of people they neither understand nor care about. As for safety, having your wallet cash stolen pales in comparison to having your savings obliterated in a digital account hack. And if you care about tax justice, start with the mass corporate tax avoidance facilitated by the formal banking sector.

The peculiar feature about this war, however, is that only one side is fighting. Very few media champions defend cash. It is like a taken-for-granted public utility, whereas digital payments platforms are run by private companies with an incentive to flood the media with their key messages. When they fight this war, their target is our cultural belief in cash, and the belief that its provision should be a public right.

The UK government does not plan to maintain that right, and is siding with the payments industry. Their position is summed up by economist Kenneth Rogoff in his new book *The Curse of Cash*. He argues that, apart from facilitating crime and tax evasion, cash hampers central banks from setting negative interest rates. In the absence of cash, everyone must keep their money in the form of digital bank deposits. During recessions central banks could then use the banking system to deliberately corrode people's deposits via negative charges, 'inspiring' them to spend rather than hoard.

The emergent consensus among economic and political elites is that this is the direction to go in, but to manufacture consent for this requires a drip-drip erosion of public resistance. Hearts and minds must be shown that the change represents inevitable and desirable progress.

Anyone defending cash in this context will be labelled as an anti-progress, reactionary and nostalgic Luddite. That's why we must not defend cash. Rather, we should focus on pointing out that the Death of Cash means the Rise of Something Else. We are fighting a broader battle to maintain alternatives to the growing digital panopticon that is emerging all around us.

THE TWO MODES OF MONEY

To understand this conflict, we must step back. A monetary transaction involves specific goods or services being exchanged for tokens giving access to general goods and services from others. The pub landlord hands me beer at night if I transfer tokens that allow him to get cigarettes from a shopkeeper in the morning.

There are two ways to implement this though.

The first is to give the tokens a physical form. In this scenario, 'getting rich' means accumulating those physical things and 'making a payment' means handing them over to someone else. They are bearer instruments, which means nobody keeps a record of who owns them. Rather, whoever holds them owns them. This is your wallet with notes in it. This is cash.

Alternatively, you can use a ledger. Someone sets up a database with spaces allotted to different people. This is then used to keep a record of who has tokens. These tokens have no physical form, but are written into existence. They are 'data objects', and they are 'moved around' by editing the record. The keeper of the ledger thus maintains an account of what money is attributable to you, 'keeping score' of it for you. In this system, 'getting rich' means accumulating a high score on your account. 'Making a payment' involves identifying yourself to the keeper of the ledger via a communications system, and requesting that they edit your account, and the account of whoever you are paying.

Does this sound familiar? It is your bank account.

Old banks used actual books to maintain these account ledgers, but modern banks use digital databases housed in huge datacentres. You then interact with them via your internet banking portal, your phone app, or by going into a branch. This is not a minor part of the monetary system. Over 90 per cent of the UK's money supply exists nowhere but on bank databases.

It is upon this underlying infrastructure that payment card companies like Visa build their operations. They deal with situations in which someone with one bank account finds themselves in a shop owned by someone else with another bank account. Rather than the pub landlord giving me his bank details for a manual transfer, my card sends messages through Visa's network to automatically arrange the editing of our respective accounts.

Many fintech – financial technology – start-ups specialise in finding ways to augment, gamify or streamline elements of this underlying infrastructure. Thus, I might use a mobile phone fingerprint reader to authorise changes to the bank databases. Much fintech 'disruption' merely involves putting slicker clothes on the same old emperor.

The use of high-speed communications systems to rearrange binary code information about who has what money might be new, but ledger money is as old as any bearer form. The Rai stones of the island of Yap were huge and largely unmovable stones that, while seeming like physical tokens, were a form of ledger money. Rather than being physically moved – like cash would – a record of who owned the stones was kept in people's heads, stored in their communal memory. If the owners wished to 'transfer' a stone to another, they 'edited the ledger' of who possessed the tokens by merely informing the community. Why physically roll the stone if you can just get everyone to remember that it has 'moved' to somebody else? The main reason that we struggle to recognise this as a form of cashlessness is that the ledger is invisible and informal.

Cashless society, though, is presented as futuristic progress rather than past history, a fashionable motif of futurists, entrepreneurs and innovation gurus. Nevertheless, while there are real trends in behaviour and tastes to be spotted in society, there are also trends in behaviour and taste among trend-spotters. They are paid to fixate upon change and so have an incentive to hype minor shifts into 'end of history' deaths, births and revolutions. Innovation communities are always at risk of losing touch within an echo chamber of buzzwords, amplifying one another's speculations into concrete future certainties. These prediction factories always produce the same two unprovable sentences: 'In the future we will …' and 'In the future we will no longer …'. Thus, in the future we will all use digital payments. In the future we will no longer use cash.

This is the utopia presented by the growing digital payments industry, which wishes to turn the perpetual mirage of cashless society into a self-fulfilling prophecy. Indeed, a key trick to promoting your interests is to speak of them as obvious inevitabilities that are already under way. It makes others feel silly for not recognising the apparently obvious change.

To create a trend you should also present it as something that other people demand. A sentence like 'All over the world, people are switching to digital payments' is not there to describe what other people want. It's there to tell you what you should want by making you feel out of sync with them. Fintech investor Rich Ricci, for example, invokes the spectre of millennials, with their strange moral power to define the future.[3] They are – according to the digital payments industry – repulsed by the revolting physicality of cash, and feel all warm towards fintech gadgets. But these are not, on the whole, real people. They are a weapon in the arsenal of marketing departments used to make older people feel prehistoric. We're not pushing this. We're just responding to what the new generation demands.

And so we get Visa's Cashfree and Proud campaign. If people really were ashamed of cash, they wouldn't need ads to tell them. Visa must engineer that shame to teach you that what you want is the same as what they want. And if you don't want it, just remember that cashless society is inevitable. Don't get left behind.

But this system will leave many behind. It is hardwired to include only those with access to a bank account; and bank accounts are hosted by profit-seeking corporations that operate at scale. They have no time for your individual idiosyncrasies. They cannot make profit off anyone who cannot easily be categorised and modelled on a spreadsheet.

So, good luck to you if you find yourself with only sporadic appearances in the official books of state, if you are a rural migrant without a recorded birthdate, identifiable parents or an ID number. Sorry if you lack markers of stability, if you are a rogue traveller without permanent address, phone number or email. Apologies if you have no symbols of status, if you're an informal economy hustler with no assets and low, inconsistent income. Condolences if you have no official stamps of approval from gatekeeper bodies, like university certificates or records of employment at a formal company. Goodbye if you have a poor record of engagements with recognised institutions, like a criminal record or a record of missed payments.

This is no small problem. The World Bank estimates that there are two billion adults without bank accounts, and even those who do have them still often rely upon the informal flexibility of cash for everyday transactions. These are people bearing indelible markers of being incompatible with formal institutional space. They are often too unprofitable for banks to justify the expense of setting them up with accounts. This is the shadow economy, invisible to our systems.

The shadow economy is not just 'poor' people. It's potentially anybody who hasn't internalised the correct state-corporate narrative of normality, and anyone seeking a lifestyle outside of the mainstream. The future presented by self-styled innovation gurus has no scope for flexible, unpredictable or invisible people. They represent analogue backwardness. The future is a world of endless consumer choice built upon an inescapable digital uniformity of automated rules, a matrix outside which you can neither exist nor think.

THE FINANCIAL PANOPTICON

Back in Amsterdam I hang out with Ancilla van de Leest of the Netherlands Pirate Party. She only visits establishments that accept cash, true to her political belief in individual privacy from prying eyes.

It would be wrong to assume, however, that Ancilla's primary concern involves surveillance by a Big Brother-style bogeyman. It's true that your spending patterns reveal much about how you actually live, and the privacy implications of having these recorded in searchable database format are only starting to be uncovered. We know that targeted individual surveillance of payments occurs by the likes of the FBI and the NSA, but routinised mass surveillance could become a norm. Imagine automatic flagging systems triggered by anyone engaging in a combination of transactions deemed subversive. Tax authorities are bound to be building systems to flag discrepancies between your spending patterns and your declared profits.

It's also true that at London fintech gatherings the excited visions of cashless society now occasionally come with a disclaimer that we should think about the power granted to those who control the system. Not only can payments intermediaries see every time you buy access to a porn site, but they have the ability to censor your transactions, like Visa, PayPal and MasterCard attempting to choke WikiLeaks by refusing to process people's donations. We could imagine some harsh sci-fi scenario in which a theocratic regime issues decrees to payments processors to block anyone buying books deemed sexually deviant. Such decrees could be automatically enforced via code, with subroutines remotely triggering smart locks to place the offending miscreant under house arrest while automatically deducting a fine from their account.

Such automated dystopias should ideally be avoided, so a dose of paranoia about digital payments systems is a healthy impulse, even if it might be unwarranted.

But that isn't really the point. What's more important to Ancilla and me is the looming sense of an external watcher that 'assists', 'guides' or 'helps' you in your life, tracking and logging your moves in order to influence you. The watcher is not a single entity. It's a collective array being incrementally built in stages by start-ups and companies around the world as we speak. We feel it seeping deeper into our lives, a mesh of connected devices, cookies and sensors. Whether we visualise it as the benevolent eyes of a parent, or the menacing eyes of a tyrant doesn't matter. The point is that the eyes have the potential to monitor you, all the time.

The proclaimed Death of Cash is thus an episode in the broader drama that is the Death of Privacy, the death of breathing room, and the death of informal, non-measured, unaccounted-for behaviour. Every action you take must forever be attached to your digital persona, dragging with it a data trail extending back to the day you were born. We face creating an entire generation of people who do not know what it feels like to not be monitored.

PREPARING FOR THE WAR ON CASH

For many economists, the War on Cash will be resolved by their favourite mystical demigod, the market. This guiding force prevails when utility-maximising producers and consumers go around making rational choices with perfect information about their options, and with total freedom to choose whether or not to exercise those options. If digital payment transaction costs are lower, then cash will rightly die.

The pristine realm of market theory is unfit to assess the dynamics of this situation. Our sense of what constitutes a legitimate choice does not form in a vacuum. We are born into social power structures that tell us what normality is, and that shame us for not choosing 'correctly'. You might be a rebel who challenges prevailing cultural norms, but those norms are conditioned by those with the greatest financial and media clout. At this moment the blaring of propaganda extolling the short-term conveniences of digital payment is dulling our critical impulses to rearrange our cultural DNA. Who is thinking about the longer-term implications of building our lives around these systems, and thereby locking ourselves into dependence upon them?

Unlike a battle fought using violence, hegemony is the assertion of power by getting people to believe in it, to see it as inevitable, unassailable and normal. Visa's four-year plan is one such exercise, and once we've internalised it, we'll choose to build their power. We'll feel strangely comforted by the MasterCard billboard endorsed by the Mayor of London. We'll find ourselves downloading ApplePay like a dazed child accepting a gift.

So, let's prepare for the War on Cash. Remember, this is not about romanticising the £10 notes with the Queen on them. This is about maintaining alternatives to the stifling hygiene of the digital panopticon being constructed to serve the needs of profit-maximising, cost-minimising, customer-monitoring, control-seeking, behaviour-predicting commercial bureaucrats. And fear not, the Germans are onside,[4] along with the criminals, the homeless, the street-side buskers and an army of people whose lives will never get a five-star rating on a mainstream reputation scoring system. We will forge alliances with purveyors of non-bank alternative currency systems like Bitcoin; and yes, we will maintain the option to use our payment cards. Because what we fight for is precisely that. The option.

Notes

1 Originally published by Brett Scott as *The War on Cash* in The Long+Short, 19th August 2016, http://thelongandshort.org/society/war-on-cash. Republished here under Creative Commons Attribution 4.0 International License (CC BY 4.0).
2 Retrieved from https://www.visa.co.uk/newsroom/visa-europe-launches-cashfree-and-proud-campaign-1386958?returnUrl=%2fnewsroom%2fcash-free-and-proud-video-female-22806.aspx
3 http://uk.businessinsider.com/barclays-rich-ricci-says-fintech-is-fundamental-shift-2016-5
4 http://qz.com/262595/why-germans-pay-cash-for-almost-everything/?utm_source=qzfbarchive

FURTHER READING

Economist Kenneth Rogoff has emerged as an anti-cash champion. His argument is sketched out in his book *The Curse of Cash* (2016), but for a shorter piece see: Kenneth Rogoff (2015) 'Costs and Benefits to Phasing out Paper Currency', *NBER Macroeconomics Annual* Vol. 29, No. 1 (January 2015), pp. 445–456: https://www.jstor.org/stable/10.1086/680657

Visions of a 'cashless society' are not new. For some historical views, see:

Bátiz-Lazo, Bernardo, Thomas Haigh and David L. Stearns (2014) 'How the Future Shaped the Past: The Case of the Cashless Society', *Enterprise and Society*, Volume 15, Issue, pp. 103–131: https://www.cambridge.org/core/journals/enterprise-and-society/article/div-classtitlehow-the-future-shaped-the-past-the-case-of-the-cashless-societydiv/C043B7864C290051B7210F1BA168EDC7

Bátiz-Lazo, Bernardo, Thomas Haigh and David L. Stearns (2016) 'Origins of the Modern Concept of a Cashless Society, 1950s–1970s', in Bernardo Bátiz-Lazo and Leonidas Efthymiou (Eds) *The Book of Payments: Historical and Contemporary Views on the Cashless Society*, Springer: http://link.springer.com/chapter/10.1057/978-1-137-60231-2_10

Bennett, Roger C. and Roger A. Strang (1978) 'Bankers and the Cashless Society', *Business Horizons*, Volume 21, Issue 3, pp. 38–45: http://www.sciencedirect.com/science/article/pii/0007681378900897

Chaudhuri, Sushil and Markus A. Denzel (Eds) (2008) *Cashless Payments and Transactions from the Antiquity to 1914*, Franz Steiner Verlag: http://www.steiner-verlag.de/titel/56851.html

Hollow, Matthew (2016) 'Pre-1900 Utopian Visions of the "Cashless Society"', in Bernardo Batiz-Lazo and Leonidas Efthymiou (Eds) *The Book of Payments: Historical and Contemporary Views on the Cashless Society*, Springer: http://link.springer.com/chapter/10.1057/978-1-137-60231-2_2

It is hard to generalise about the use of cash across countries. For some country-specific views, see:

Bartzsch, Nikolaus and Franz Seitz (2016) 'Cash Holdings in Germany and the Demand for "German" Banknotes: What Role Is There for Cashless Payments?' in Jakub Górka (Ed.) *Transforming Payment Systems in Europe*, Springer: http://link.springer.com/chapter/10.1057/9781137541215_4

Bayero, Musa Abdullahi (2015) 'Effects of Cashless Economy Policy on Financial Inclusion in Nigeria: An Exploratory Study', *Procedia – Social and Behavioral Sciences*, Volume 172, 27 January 2015, pp. 49–56: http://www.sciencedirect.com/science/article/pii/S1877(2015)042815003717

Del Angel, Gustavo A. (2016) 'Limits to Cashless Payments and the Persistence of Cash: Hypotheses About Mexico', in Bernardo Batiz-Lazo and Leonidas Efthymiou (Eds) *The Book of Payments: Historical and Contemporary Views on the Cashless Society*, Springer: http://link.springer.com/chapter/10.1057/978-1-137-60231-2_12

Mamonov, M., A. Pestova and O. Solntsev (2011) 'The Cult of Cash in Russia: How Can It Be Dethroned and to What Will This Lead?', *Problems of Economic Transition*, Volume 54, Issue 8, pp. 36–67: http://www.tandfonline.com/doi/abs/10.2753/PET1061-1991540803

For a view on the UK, see:

Tom Fish and Roy Whymark, 'How has Cash Usage Evolved in Recent Decades? What Might Drive Demand in the Future?' *Bank of England Quarterly Bulletin*, 2015, Q3: http://www.bankofengland.co.uk/publications/Documents/quarterlybulletin/2015/q3prerelease_1.pdf

Furthermore, acceptance and uptake of digital payment differs:

Pelilli, David (2008) 'Electronic Money Use: Evidence from Survey Data', in Philip Molyneux and Eleuterio Vallelado (Eds) *Frontiers of Banks in a Global Economy*, Springer: http://link.springer.com/chapter/10.1057/9780230590663_10

Szmigin, Isabelle and Gordon Foxall (1999) 'Styles of Cashless Consumption', *The International Review of Retail, Distribution and Consumer Research*, Volume 9, Issue 4, pp. 349–365: http://www.tandfonline.com/doi/abs/10.1080/095939699342462

There is much uncritical celebration of an imagined cashless society, but there is scepticism too:

de Putter, Eric (2016) 'Cashless Society – Really?', *Journal of Payments Strategy & Systems*, Volume 10, Number 3, pp. 245–252: http://www.ingentaconnect.com/search/article?option1=tka&value1=cashless&pageSize=10&index=2

Erling, Ghita (2013) 'Cash is Dead, Long Live Cash', *Journal of Payments Strategy & Systems*, Volume 7, Number 1, pp. 43–49: http://www.ingentaconnect.com/search/article?option1=tka&value1=cashless&pageSize=10&index=16

VISA. 'Visa Europe launches "Cashfree and Proud" campaign', Accessed on September 20, 2017. Retrieved from https://www.visa.co.uk/newsroom/visa-europe-launches-cashfree-and-proud-campaign-1386958?returnUrl=%2fnewsroom%2fcash-free-and-proud-video-female-22806.aspx

PART VI

The Politics of Consumer Culture

25

Consumer-Citizens: Markets, Marketing and the Making of 'Choice'

Stefan Schwarzkopf

INTRODUCTION: THE FETISHISM OF CHOICE AND THE SECRET THEREOF

Arguably, large parts of Western social and political systems, and increasingly their counterparts in emerging economies, too, are being restructured around people's 'right to choose' and their choice-making capabilities. This observation makes it all the more surprising to note that there is relatively little philosophical and historical reflection on the concept of choice as such. Although the notion of choice is at the heart of empirical research in marketing, micro-economics and consumer psychology today, this literature often merely researches the content and structure of actual choices made by consumers. Normative investigations are then limited to questions of whether these choices are efficient in terms of resource allocation and whether more or less choice *per se* is either good or bad for citizens and consumers (Ariely, 2008; Markus and Schwartz, 2010; Offer, 2005; Rosenthal, 2006; Salecl, 2010; Schwartz, 2005; Sen, 1988). All of this literature accepts that choices have to be made and that in order to understand choice, visible choice outcomes need to be registered, classified and measured. Just as Karl Marx said of the commodity form, choice seems for most people a very trivial thing, and easily understood. In this chapter we will see that choice is in fact a very queer thing, abounding in metaphysical subtleties and theological niceties.

In order to understand how choice became reified as a social policy aim in its own right, we need to construct a much wider genealogy of the concept that allows us to map the historical, cultural and political circumstances of this reification. This will also require us to move away from studies of what I would call 'small-c' choice, namely the content and structure of individual choices and choice-making processes. Instead, a proper genealogy of choice will have to look at the concept with a capital 'C' as it were. This perspective allows us to study when, why and how the mundane idea of choice became a political-economic concept with such an enormous power to mobilise people. As William Davies, Matthew Eagleton-Pierce, John Clarke, Don Slater and others have pointed out, the idealisation of freedom of choice has been promoted by the rise of neoliberal politics since the 1980s (Clarke, 2006; Cockett, 1995; Davies, 2014: 22–30; Eagleton-Pierce, 2016: 20–23; Fox, 2009: 89–107; Slater, 1997: 36–38). The remarkable career of this ideal however has roots that go well beyond the familiar story of the public influence of Chicago-style free-market philosophy.

WHAT ACTUALLY IS 'CHOICE'?

To choose, and 'to have' a choice means (a) to recognise available options, (b) to reflect on them, and then (c) to make decisions according to standards and expectations of outcomes (reward, utility, cost, negative repercussions, fear of regret, etc.). It is important to differentiate and identify this term in this way so as to avoid confusion with two far-better researched concepts and ideas, namely 'decision' and 'free will'. As defined here, the concept of choice understands a person in terms of a duality, that is in their active *and* passive role as chooser. As choosers, we are making active choices but the choice of choice that we have is not always produced by us, nor do we always desire to be in the position of having to choose (e.g. between pension plans, schools, hospitals, etc.). Hence, despite the constant promise of 'empowerment' that the proponents of the choice-agenda in public services and in marketing continuously peddle, one can only be a chooser if one already accepts a set of choices, such as an assortment of brands or a set of healthcare providers. The make-up and consistence of this set of choices is usually outside the remit of those who are then asked to navigate within this set. In other words, as choosers we are never fully proactive, knowing and empowered decision-makers, but by definition always passively exposed to choice-situations and assortments of options. This sense of being exposed and potentially overwhelmed is at the heart of much critical research which shows that having too many options ('choice overload', 'paradox of choice') often leads to suboptimal outcomes even for individuals who prefer a wider array of choices (Greenfield, 2012; Reed et al., 2011).

It is therefore necessary to differentiate between 'choice' and the more action- and *acteur*-oriented term 'decision'. Choice involves decision-making, but should not be reduced to it. The latter term is studied by management science, organisation science, marketing and neuroscience and denotes resource allocation in management, consumers' allocation of time and financial resources, and so on. A second reason for why it is necessary to differentiate between 'choice' and 'decision' is that the latter term is often defined in such a way that it involves a horizon of alternatives that becomes dissolved by the *act* of the decision. An employee gets hired (or fired), an investment is being made, a product-line is discontinued: decisions solve/dissolve the situation that has given rise to the horizon of options. By looking at public and

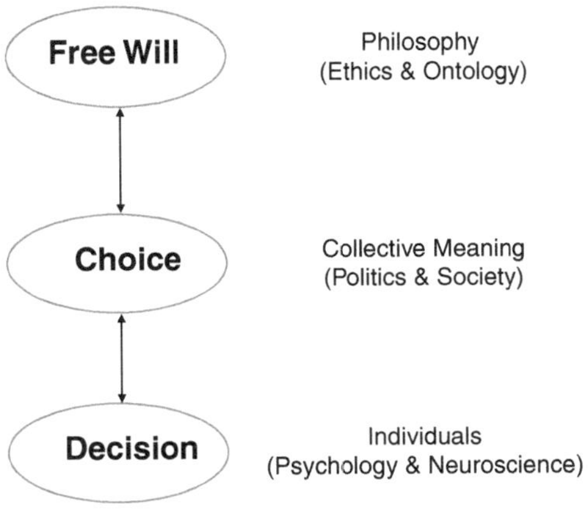

Figure 25.1 Choice as a median-level concept

private decisions through the angle of 'choice', however, it is clear that this horizon of alternatives does not get dissolved once a choice is made. Choices have consequences, and if one makes any type of choice one alters the alternatives available for others in society. Choosing one's car instead of public transport to go to work is likely to act as a signal to government departments to increase spending on roads and reduce spending on public transport, resulting in less attractive public transport options. Decision science and decision theory rarely acknowledge that making a choice structures everybody else's choice options further on. Pure decision science therefore individualises the problem of choice, which is always one of collectives and groups too. In addition, the choices we make between alternatives always stay with us and inform our next choices (path dependence). Hence 'choice' is a term in its own right, and to talk of choices and choice within a socio-political context is not the same as talking of individual decisions.

'Choice' acts as a median-level concept between mere individual decisions and the much larger problem-context around the idea of personal will and the question of whether a 'free' will exists in human beings (Figure 25.1). Given the tremendous importance of the notion of free will for debates on whether citizens and consumers can be good choosers, it is somewhat unsettling to acknowledge how irrelevant the debates around the free will have become for the socio-political problem of whether one should conceive of society as the aggregate outcome of masses of free and utility-oriented individual choices. The relative disconnect between discussions about free will on the one hand, and debates about politics and society on the other, is particularly surprising when contrasted with the political-social relevance of the free will debate during the eighteenth century (Harris, 2007: 4–13, 35–40; Kane, 2011). Despite the obvious link between philosophical debates about free will and debates about people's ability to make informed and optimal choices, there seems to be little evidence that advances in research on free will have informed the reconstruction of society around people as choosers of private goods and services.

CHOICE: A REMNANT OF POLITICAL THEOLOGY IN A SECULAR WORLD

Given the concept's intermediate position between free will and individual decision, there is the possibility of identifying a unique genealogy for the concept of choice. This genealogy shows that although choices and options are seemingly the most obvious thing in a person's life, the way we have come to understand the concept of choice is the outcome of a deliberate and highly politicised invention. We will also see that the concept of choice was constructed for reasons that transcend the profane realm of resource allocation and utility maximisation.

This assertion raises the question as to how the idea of choice can be an invention and a social construction. Whether one is a fifth-century Chinese peasant, a fourteenth-century Italian market trader, or a twenty-first-century commuter on a suburban rail: choices, options, decisions and their consequences provide the most basic structure of all social life. Yet, many seemingly obvious and unproblematic concepts like 'friendship' and 'childhood' are precisely such inventions and constructions. They are socially shared and culturally embedded conventions that have been talked into existence by groups of people with a specific interest in the propagation of these social concepts. That does not mean that friends and children did not exist before these concepts adopted their modern meaning. But the fact, for example, that we look at children as requiring specific protection and specific spaces of development is due to the invented nature of the idea of childhood. In most parts of the Western world, we send our children to kindergartens (literally: 'children's gardens'), and their accessibility and affordability is one of the key issues of policy debates. The reasons for the existence of this particular set of institutions (kindergarten buildings, kindergarten teachers, kindergarten toys and curricula, special food for children, etc.) is the invented idea that childhood constitutes a special phase in one's life, a phase during which a person is still closer to the original nature of man, the one enjoyed by Adam and Eve in Paradise.

As historians of European ideas have shown, ideas such as paternal and family love, childhood, fatherhood and motherhood were deliberately designed by the rising bourgeoisie as political counter-concepts against the ideals of 'fatherhood' and 'family' propagated by the absolutist *ancien régime*. In order to rebel against a morally corrupt, absolutist king, his public image as the 'father of the nation' had to be undermined. How better to do this than through propagating the middle-class idea that each family had its own father and that society was constituted of such families who did not need the supervision of a promiscuous and brutal king. Enlightenment ideas about childhood, fatherhood and family – the most natural things on earth one would imagine – were thus once part of a subversive political counter-culture, which later became naturalised and normalised (Bellingham, 1988).

While it might be the case that apples, apple trees, farmers, apple sellers and apple eaters have existed for thousands of years, the specific social arrangement and set of institutions around markets for apples and choices between (nowadays branded) apples that we have come to accept as normal is a social invention. It is therefore worth delving deeper into the long history of the idea of choice. This history shows that the concept provided a much more important stabilising and destabilising factor than merely that of governing and structuring the marketplace. The concept of choice has for at least three thousand years acted as a revolutionising idea that ushered in entirely new forms of human consciousness.

At the beginning of the very idea of selfhood in Western thought stood the idea of choice; but at this stage, 'choice' was conceptualised as passive and as a one-off act of grace conferred upon people as subjects. The 12 tribes of Israel fashioned themselves as the 'chosen people' whose fate was based on and directed by a covenant with God. This covenant and their status as 'chosen' gave the Israelites a key advantage: even if their temples were burned down and they were enslaved, they had God with them in the Ark of the Covenant and were thus able to 'carry' God around with them. The existence of the Ark meant that God was with them at all times and their collective actions were justified. This idea of justification, which monotheistic religions like Judaism provided for the first time in the history of human consciousness, cannot be separated from the very idea of choice. The idea of choice, here in the sense of 'being chosen', for the first time became politicised in the millennium before Christ (BC) since it provided a mode of socialisation and legitimised this socialised group's claim to statehood and sovereignty (*Exodus*, 25: 10–22; Sloterdijk, 2009: 24–27, 106).

Towards the end of that first millennium BC, Greek philosophers began to afford the problem of decision (κρίσις: krisis), election (ἐκλογή: eklogé) and choice (as in having to conclude the process of deliberation of options meaning επιλογή: epilogé; as in making voluntary and conscious choices meaning προαίρεσις: prohairesis) a central position in their approach to ethics. In Aristotle's *Nicomachean Ethics*, we have for the first time in the history of Western ideas a coherent account of what it means to have agency, to have a will to pursue goals, to perceive freedom of choice, and to consciously reflect that both free will and a range of options actually exist. For Aristotle, choice existed as prohairesis (προαίρεσις), translated as 'deliberate desire' or 'moral purpose'. This definition combined the freely-willed *desire* to achieve a goal (an outcome, reward, state of existence) and the cognitive process of *deliberating* over it (Chamberlain, 1984; Nielsen, 2011).

The Aristotelian definition of choice was to have a profound effect on the history of Western thought. At this moment, the making of choices became closely connected to cognitive capacities of deliberation, the existence of desire and emotions, and the concept of the reflective and conscious self. After Aristotle, children and animals were incapable of choosing. They acted voluntarily, but their behaviour was 'thoughtless' and directed by habits and instincts. Adult human beings of course hardly ever come near this description of the deliberating and agonising chooser since the majority of our daily choices are also guided by thoughtless impulses, habits and unreflected traditions and institutions. Yet, with Aristotle, choice as an *exceptional* situation became now understood as the norm against which all human behaviour had to be judged. One could argue with Carl Schmitt that the modern worship of man as sovereign chooser thus originated in the moment when life became de-habituated and exposed to the logic of exception, since looked at normatively, 'decision emanates from nothingness' (Schmitt, 1985: 32).

The fruitful encounter between Greek philosophy, with its emphasis on the idea of the freely deliberating individual, and Christian thought about God's election modified the emphasis on choice and further internalised and activated it. The status of being among the chosen was now opened up to all members of the human race, whether Jewish or not. All were chosen by God to be part of a coming heavenly kingdom. Crucially, this required the individual to turn around, leave the old ways of living and thinking behind, and *actively choose* to be among the chosen few who enter heaven. This emphasis on the self and on the internalised obligation to choose liberated the human consciousness, but it also caused tremendous anxiety. As shown by Esther Cohen, when twelfth-century theologians and philosophers in Europe began once again to discuss very intensely the existence of free will and its justification, this was accompanied by a spread of moral panic among ordinary monks in monasteries all over Europe, who felt unable to cope with the new-found freedom to choose and the idea of free will. It was within this context that the trope 'the devil made me do it' emerged (Cohen, 2012). A few centuries later, as argued by Max Weber, the Protestant ideal of the choosing and confessing individual created yet more such anxieties to perform and to conform (Weber, 2014: 270–276).

The current millennium is very likely to be characterised by the spread of the principle of choice all over the globe, even into geographical areas whose cultural developments were largely unaffected by the choice-centred philosophies of the Greek and Christian-Judeo heritage. This development is often summarised using the labels of 'individualisation' and 'marketisation'. Simultaneously, we are also observing the spread of the principle of choice and the obligation to choose into areas of social life in which the application of choice-based principles causes anxiety and confusion among consumers and citizens.

THE SECULARISATION (ESCALATION) OF CHOICE

This very brief discussion of the meanings and origins of the concept of 'choice' (the Latin *electio*) has shown that the concept is indeed very different from related concepts like decision (in Greek κρίσις: krisis; in Latin *decisio*) and free will (Latin: *voluntas*). Unlike the idea of prohairesis, the term krisis was also often associated with the context of military leadership: on a battlefield, difficult decisions often had to be made precisely because there are few or no other choices left. Given its continued use within a political-theological context during the Middle Ages, the concept was laden with emotions, promising recognition, freedom, empowerment and sovereignty. Choice as a concept was always religiously determined in ways that separated it from its more philosophical cousins, the decision and the will. But how did this transformation of a profoundly religious term into a term of social-political organisation precisely take place? A study of the concept's use between the seventeenth and the mid-nineteenth centuries, a period identified by German historian Reinhart Koselleck (1994) as crucial for the formation of European politics, will reveal how and why the term became so laden with expectations, and how these expectations ended up providing a dominant governance- and legitimacy-structure for market societies.

The first time that we find the term 'choice' being used in English in its current form is around the early fourteenth century. Imported and adapted from the French verb 'choisir', it came to be used in the sense of 'tasting', 'trying', 'sampling', 'testing' and 'picking out'. The late-medieval usage of the term to denote 'testing' and 'trying out' continued the earlier use of the term in the passive-religious sense of the 'chosen', that is the 'tried' and 'tested' people. At the same time, all late-medieval European languages had a more proactive form of this word which expressed the 'selecting' of something and the 'electing' of somebody. What the Latin knew as *eligere* (to choose, to elect, to select) was known in Old English as 'cyre', in thirteenth- and fourteenth-century German as 'kür' (hence the term 'Kurfürst' for the noblemen who elected the German emperor), and in Old Norse as 'kjósa' (to vote, to choose). The Swedish know this verb as 'utkora', and the Germans as 'küren'. By the sixteenth and seventeenth centuries, we find the use of the word 'choice' in English also as an adjective, denoting something that is preferred, preferable to be chosen, and the best of its kind, such as a 'choice selection of poems' (Fountaine, 1654; Hinton, 1650).

It is in this rather aesthetic form that English literature continued to use the term until well into the early-modern period. Around the turn of the seventeenth century, two political and theological developments came together that provided the background for a changed usage of the term in the English language. On the one hand, Arminianism and its emphasis on the existence of a free will began to get the upper hand over Calvinism and over the insistence of orthodox Puritans on predestination. Promoted by King James VI and I (1566–1625) and the Church of England (Laudianism), Arminian theology heightened the attention of religious, political and intellectual elites all over Europe with regard to the problem of choice, free will and individual responsibility for salvation. Simultaneously, King James began to pursue a strategy of building up the Church of England as the nationally dominant form of religion in order to curb any remaining influence of Roman Catholicism in England, Wales and Scotland. Seeing himself as a king selected by God to rule over his subject (divine king), he demanded an Oath of Loyalty from all his Catholic subjects. This oath of course brought Catholics into a conflict of interest and into a situation where a profound choice had to be made.

The first time we find the term 'choice' being applied in the context of political democracy is in 1603, when King James I sent out pamphlets to 'direct' his people in the choice of members of Parliament. With the increasing competition for power between Crown and Parliament, this logic escalated from the 1630s onwards, which is reflected in more and more pamphlets, sermons and books being published that advise Englishmen to get their (political) choices right (Bellamy, 1645; By the King, 1603; *Memorandums*, 1644; The Parliament, 1646). During the 1630s, the existential logic of choice also became reflected in publications that directed and advised the same populace as to their choice of religion, with Jesuit priests like John Floyd and Puritan firebrands like Jeremiah Burroughs being positioned at the extremes of the religious spectrum of those who competed for souls (Burroughs, 1641; Digby, 1638; Floyd, 1639).

James's son, Charles I (1600–1649), continued to reign in the belief that a king had been chosen by God to rule over his subjects. His demands for absolute obedience drove him into conflict with Parliament, ultimately resulting in a brutal and divisive Civil War (1642–1651). All over Europe, similar political-religious conflicts raged during the early and mid-seventeenth century, causing the concept of choice – between religious denominations as much as between political allegiances – to change its denotation and connotation. During the early seventeenth century, the concept of 'choice' changed its meanings from *being chosen* (e.g. elected Emperors in the German Reich; God's chosen people), and signalling something that should *be preferred* (a 'choice selection of poems'), to denoting a vital and active selection. Within the circumstances of a brutal fight for power between Catholicism and Protestantism, and between Parliament and King, choices had to be made by each and every person. 'Choice' was now understood to be an act, a mode of behaviour related to an active chooser and decision-maker who *brings about* their own state of righteousness and salvation by choosing the right religion, and thus the right type of political interpretation of Christ.

After nearly three decades of religious-political upheaval between the 1620s and the 1640s, Thomas Hobbes summarised the new understanding of the concept of choice in an image of tremendous influence. His idea that a polity was brought about and legitimised by freely contracting individuals who chose to give up certain powers in return for peace introduced the Leviathan as the outcome of those myriad choices being made by innumerable individuals. The image of the Leviathan arising out of the people and protecting their land and livelihood visualised what Western market societies today believe themselves to be: a way of remoulding dispersed sovereignty into a greater unit, embodied in political and economic democracy.

The restoration of the monarchy in England between the 1660s and the 1680s brought back renewed efforts to promote tolerance between the various religious denominations. This, however, made it even more necessary that subjects had to be informed about what kind of religions there were, and what the pitfalls were of being surrounded by people who had the right to choose but perhaps failed to make the true one. From the middle of the seventeenth century right into the eighteenth century, we therefore find a flourishing literature in England that connected the concept of choice to the two aspects of life which the Leviathan resided over, 'civil' and 'ecclesiastical'. From the late 1650s to the 1790s, English readers had access to a copious amount of reading material in form of books and frequently reprinted pamphlets which taught them how to choose members of parliament, aldermen and wardens (representatives in local authorities), and also how to choose a religion for themselves (Tempest, 1658).

The overt politicisation of the term, which had first taken place at the beginning of the seventeenth century, continued to have an impact on the literature and, hence, the use of the term in the English language (Clayton, 1679; Defoe, 1694; Penn, 1680; The King, 1661; The Parliament, 1658). The climate of moderate levels of religious tolerance after the 1660s in turn influenced the language of choice in such a way that a burgeoning market for literature on religious choice and competition emerged in Britain (Gother, 1734; Le Clerk, 1711; Ponteus, 1697). Everything, it seemed, even the most intimate questions regarding someone's spiritual destiny, was now open to that very same person's choice. One publication in 1796 even asked (rhetorically) whether Christianity was still the right choice in an age of reason (Philalethes, 1796). This totalised concentration on individual choices was also enabled by the renewed interest of seventeenth- and eighteenth-century philosophy in Stoicism and the Stoic concept of 'conduct of life' (Foucault, 2007: 191–207; Pomfret, 1701). Stoicism strongly influenced John Locke, whose concern for property and rights ('privacy') led him to value individual liberty above all else (Nuovo, 2008). From Locke's position it was a small step to that of the American clergyman and philosopher Jonathan Edwards, who during the second half of the eighteenth century skilfully argued that liberty and choice were practically synonymous (Edwards, 1797: 41).

From the early eighteenth century, a remarkable widening of the use of the term choice set in. The widening of the usability of the term once again brought about a change in the connotations that surrounded this concept. Having emerged as a precarious issue in the early and mid-seventeenth century (choice between King and Pope; choice between various denominations within Protestantism; choice between King and Parliament), a century later these types of choices were beginning to be understood as rights to be protected by a sovereign and neutral king, and later by constitutional documents such as the ones drawn up during the 1770s and 1780s in the North American colonies and in France. Before choices could become rights, however, the applicability of the term had to be widened into more mundane areas of life and thus become 'civilised'. The English language civilised the formerly life-threatening issue of choice by beginning to discuss mundane economic issues of work, trade, products and prices through the lens of choice and choices. As England began to fashion itself into a free-trade nation, builders and land-surveyors had to be chosen (Gerbier, 1663), food and beverages had to be chosen (Maynwaring, 1672), drink manufacturers needed to know how to choose ingredients (*A Guide to Gentlemen*, 1727), doctors had to be chosen (Philomedicus, 1676), students had to know which books to choose (Barlow, 1699), country squires needed to know how to choose horses and hunting rifles (Page, 1770; *The Gentleman Farrier*, 1732), parents needed to know which profession and trade to choose for their children (*A General Description*, 1747; Collyer, 1761), consumers needed to know how to choose tea (*The Tea Purchaser's Guide*, 1785), and settlers needed to know how to choose emigration opportunities (Holditch, 1818).

'Civilising' the concept of choice here literally meant to integrate the concept fully within the realm of eighteenth-century polite and civil society. While before the 1700s the term was used almost exclusively within a context characterised by gun-powder plots, warfare, statecraft and religion, the early and mid-eighteenth-century secularised and civilised the term by using it to describe the buying and selling of commercial goods of any kind. This civil and commercial use should not be confused with the previously developed adjective use of the term, which continued to be in fashion until the early twentieth century. The Romantic period renewed interest of polite society all over Europe in 'choice collections of songs', 'choice collections of sermons' etc., meaning selections of widely preferred and high-quality works of art and culture.

Yet, masses of middle-class readers were now beginning to be introduced into the art of preferring and the art of making choices themselves, the art of training the eye to make calculated, goal-oriented and value-conscious decisions in a market. Adam Smith's *Inquiry into the Nature and Causes of the Wealth of Nations* (1776) used the term in both ways, as adjective and noun. Smith knew the difference between 'choice and coarse pieces' of beef, but he also referred to the choices that banks made about whom and whom not to lend money to; the choices made by ordinary workers between different types of employment; and to the fact that the relative scarcity of gold and silver in the North American colonies was the outcome of the choice that people made between different forms of exchange, in this case they preferred the use of paper bills and barter trade (Smith, 1904/1776: Vol. I: 136, 152, 300; Vol. II: 425). For Smith, unlike the mercantilists he despised so much, it was human choices that defined the form and outcome of economic exchanges in a national economy, not royal decrees and other forms of 'planning'.

This widening of the use of the term choice, and its introduction into the economic and the social sphere meant that all parts of life could now be interpreted as structured by choices and their consequences. Books appeared that advised young ladies on their choice of husbands, and young men on their choice of company (D'Urfey, 1685; *The West-Country Counsellor*, 1670). Yet other books advised farmers on the choice of crops and animals. Mathematicians and statisticians became obsessed with determining logical patterns even in areas where informed choices seemed futile, such as those observed in gambling. By the mid-eighteenth century, rapidly growing and expanding societies like England and France needed more and more selection- and choice-based processes in order to make places like London and Paris governable. Choices began to determine more and more aspects of local political life with English local democracy expanding considerably, especially during the early nineteenth century. There was no better place to observe how a human being's fate was now determined not only by conscious decisions, but also by random processes of choice and selection, than at London's Foundling Hospital for abandoned children, founded in 1739. Here, mothers who had to give up their children would themselves determine which of the babies left at the orphanage's doorsteps would be accepted by randomly choosing coloured balls: if a mother drew a white ball her child was admitted (Cruickshank, 2009: 256).

What had started with Martin Luther some two hundred years earlier as a problem of the individual conscience now became a problem of what Lutherans would have called 'the world': everything was choice, in every part of life, all the time (Schwarzkopf, 2012). It was not before the early nineteenth century that this change came to be fully reflected by philosophers in a more coherent form. Writing from a deeply Protestant (but also anti-clerical) perspective, Søren Kierkegaard argued that really nothing in life made any sense if it was not seen through the perspective of individual commitment and reflective self-positioning (Kierkegaard, 1988). For Kierkegaard, the choices that human beings faced were not merely options of decisions that could have either this or that outcome. Having to make choices and facing the ubiquity of choice, acknowledging the *Either/Or* in every part of life, was the only way through which a human being could create and enact a sense of self at all. Kierkegaard's perspective thus turned the aesthetical and ethical question of what and how to choose into an existential and thus anthropological question. Kierkegaard, and with him a generation of early nineteenth-century philosophers like John Stuart Mill and Alexis de Tocqueville, directly connected the anthropological (not merely ethical) problem of 'choice' to discussions about social organisation.

Common to all these authors was the suspicion that although 'choice' made modern society governable, its reification as an organising principle created the danger of crowd rule and a tyranny of the majority. For John Stuart Mill, people's choices should govern society because only people themselves were able to assess the utility of a certain selection. Because 'people decide according to their personal preferences', individual independence ('liberty') as to the establishment of these preferences had to be an absolute (Mill, 1859: 8). For precisely this reason, however, political safeguards against the tyranny of a majority that decided on the forms and content of everybody's happiness had to be instituted. In the same vein, Alexis de Tocqueville argued that governance of society through choice and choices created its own forms of dependencies and the danger of political tyranny. Tocqueville also forewarned of the eroding effects that such a system had on the human character. Democracy had no source of legitimacy other than the single voice, the single vote and the individual choice. As a way of life, political democracy therefore threw man 'back forever upon himself alone and threatens in the end to confine him entirely within the solitude of his own heart' (Tocqueville, 2007/1835: 56).

Thus, by the mid-nineteenth century, the idea of choice had largely been taken out of its initial religious context and successfully turned into a secular concept pertaining to private life and public governance. In France, Britain and the United States in particular, philosophical discussion was rife about choice antecedents, consequences, advantages and disadvantages. Through the re-appropriation of the concept within a secular-political context, the liberal bourgeoisie had created a new type of moral universe in which man was self-dependent and able to guide himself/herself in life (Foucault, 2007: 48–49).

CHOICE AS CORNUCOPIA AND THE CONSUMER AS 'ROLE'

Nevertheless, throughout much of the nineteenth century, choice remained understood as a precarious and problematic part of life, as one in which selfhood – or its squandering in perennial aesthetic deliberation – got decided. Remnants of Lutheran theology still held sway in the sense that the idea of choice was connected to questions of selfhood and ethics. At the beginning of the twentieth century, the concept of choice was about to undergo yet another connotative transformation as it became connected to the experience of visible plenitude. 'Having choice' and having to choose no longer meant that as a human being one had to wake up to the fact that one ought to be a self. Now, the term choice simply became synonymous with comfort and good life. By offering choice, this time in a quantitative and not in an existential-anthropological sense, makers of consumer goods and retailers rendered 'choice' a concept that conjured up the image of plenty. Key to this shift in understanding was the commercial profanation of the religious myth of 'cornucopia', or horn of plenty. Before the early twentieth century, the horn of plenty was most often depicted within a religious or quasi-religious context: paintings showed cornucopias in the hands of cherubs, satyrs and nymphs, or being held by the Roman goddess of plenty, Abundantia (Clinton, 1992: 96–107; Rosenthal, 2005: 95–105). From around 1900 onwards, the divine personification of plenty, the goddess Abundantia and her cornucopia, began to adorn advertisements for department stores and the front page of the Sears Roebuck catalogues, which were also called 'Consumer Guides'. In 1924, General Motors developed the advertising slogan 'A Car for Every

Purse and Purpose' and stressed the wide range of choice between different designs and colours so as to distinguish itself from the more austere and product-oriented marketing philosophy of the Ford Motor Corporation and its 'Model T' that was only available in black (McCraw and Tedlow, 1997).

At the same time, the political systems of Great Britain and the United States began to legitimise themselves more and more through the idea of offering choice. According to the British journalist and author on constitutional matters Walter Bagehot, it was due to the fact that people could choose between different political parties that both the despotism of pure monarchical rule and the terror of pure people's rule could be avoided. The House of Commons, itself living in a constant 'state of potential choice' between these two rulers, thus provided political stability for the British (Bagehot, 1963/1867: 59). Late nineteenth-century political theory began to argue that the fact that there was discussion between parties, which in turn enabled voters to make informed choices at the ballot box, was the defining feature of a modern democracy. Discussion and choice, and not any longer the more intangible notion of 'liberty', were now presented in themselves as constituting the prime advantage of a democracy over all other forms of political organisations.

Bagehot famously claimed that modern man had entered 'an age of discussion', which lifted him out of the 'rule of custom' and prepared him for 'the use of choice' and 'the age of choice' (Bagehot, 1872: 88–89; see also Wallas, 1908: 4–5, 52, 79–80, 94). Eighteenth-century and early nineteenth-century notions of 'liberty' had always entailed a sense of being protected *from* something, mainly violations of one's own body and property by either a tyrannical monarch or a revolutionary crowd (Skinner, 2002). Choice, by contrast, carried a more empowering and proactive meaning: having choice and being offered a choice promised much more than merely having one's liberty protected from outside powers.

Within this context, having choice now obviously meant something very different. During the early twentieth century, the language that surrounded the concept of choice began to incorporate the idea that choice in itself was a right. It is no coincidence that at the same time female citizens all over the Western world demanded their right to take part in elections and thus have free choice in matters political (women's suffrage). During the US Presidential election campaign of November 1909, future President William Howard Taft gave a speech in Birmingham, Alabama, in which he directly connected market-based choices with voting rights. Speaking in front of an all-female audience, Taft said that he 'desired all young women to be in a position of independence to be able to make a free choice in the matrimonial market'. In order to achieve that aim, more independence and 'avenues of self-support' had to be given to women, and suffrage (the vote) had to be part of that strategy (*The Times*, 1909). Between 1900 and 1940, Western thought on choice came under the sway of the idea that democracy and access to choice were practically synonymous. The ascent of women in public life as voters, employees, shoppers and home-makers was vitally important for the emergence of this synonymy (Asquer, 2012; Cohen, 2004: 125–126; McGovern, 2006: 67–88; Schwarzkopf, 2011a; Sneeringer, 2004).

It was within this context of political enfranchisement and widened access to a burgeoning consumer market that the quasi-theological aura which had always surrounded the concept of choice became bestowed upon practices of choice as they took place within very new social settings of mass democracy. Without acknowledging this political-theological link, it is impossible to understand why a new set of economists and political philosophers associated with 'Austrian' and 'Chicago' economics (William Harold Hutt, Friedrich Hayek, Ludwig von Mises, Israel Kirzner and Milton Friedman) succeeded in crowning the choosing consumer as the new sovereign king of a free market society (Schwarzkopf, 2011b). This new king, the sovereign consumer, then began to attract adoration in the form of a particularly framed 'belief' and 'faith' in freedom, choice and open trade (Friedman, 2002/1962: 87; Friedman and Friedman, 1990: 51). The expansion of the semantic code of choice and choosing from the religious realm to virtually all other sectors of public and private life meant that liminal spaces and experiences of 'humanness' like sexuality/gender, family planning, birth and death were made governable by exposing them to the logic of choice. Matters of life and death have their sting taken out if a child's sex can be chosen, one's own gender, too, and everything else from treatment options to one's own way and time of death (Salecl, 2009). Thanks to choice, everything and everybody can be changed (*1 Corinthians*, 15: 51–55).

The semantic field of choice with all the hopes it offers is being held together by the now widely shared assumption that all parts of social and private life are situations that require a chooser. But this assumption must not be taken for granted. Sociological role theory helps us understand how consumers and citizens as choosers came to be *assigned* the capacity and capabilities necessary to actually make choices. As argued by John W. Meyer and others, social roles like 'being a consumer' do not naturally exist or emerge by themselves. Societies have to create, and assign the capability to enact specific social roles to, specific groups (Meyer and Jepperson, 2002). In the British context, for example, it was the institutional changes associated with the 1911 National Insurance Act which for the first time created the notion of 'free choice of doctor' in the English language (*The Times*, 1911). Before this moment of institutional change, the language of unfettered choice would not have made sense within the context of illness, health and medical treatment. The choosing consumer, thus, is not *per se* existent, but has to be talked into existence through discourses that move within semantic parameters, which in turn enable and delimit what we accept as sensible or not.

CONCLUSION: CHOICE AND THE HORIZON OF NEOLIBERALISM

Reading the development and escalation of the concept of choice through the lens of social role theory might also protect us from the overly optimistic claims made by neuroscientists and behavioural economists as regards the possibility of editing public and private choice architectures in such a way as 'to nudge' people into making better life choices. Although consumer neuroscience is well placed to explode the myth of the capable, reflective and rational chooser, the research itself is also a social act that further embeds that very same set of role projections. Neuropsychological research, 'Behavioural Insight Teams' and 'Nudge Units' therefore symbolically only strengthen the power assigned to 'the consumer' in the public policy arena (Leggett, 2014; McMahon, 2015; Thaler and Sunstein, 2008).

Conceptual denotations and connotations can be talked into existence, but the reverse is true as well. While it was once considered obvious that benign and popular monarchs provided the best form of government, consumers' democracy eventually replaced the *ancien régime* (Breen, 2004). Yet the same fate that befell the crowned heads of Europe might just await 'King Consumer', too. Widely-read and thoughtful books that made an evidence-led and not populist or resentment-filled case against choice- and vote-based democracy would have been almost unthinkable only twenty years ago. Recent work by well-known political scientists and philosophers such as Bryan Caplan (2008), Jason Brennan (2016) and Christopher Achen and Larry Bartels (2016) signals the possibility of a shift in attitudes towards choice and vote as the one and only, sacred default option to create legitimacy in matters of public policy. These and other recent publications allow us to debate again whether reflective, deliberative individual choice is the fountain spring of virtue and the basis of strong democratic societies, or indeed Tocqueville's high road to collectively shared solitude (McCloskey, 2006: 355–357; Trentmann, 2016: 288–290, 548–561).

REFERENCES

A General Description of all Trades, Digested in Alphabetical Order: by which Parents, Guardians, and Trustees, may Make Choice of Trades agreeable to the Capacity, Education, Inclination, Strength, and Fortune of the Youth under their Care (1747) London.

A Guide to Gentlemen, Farmers, and House-keepers, for Brewing the finest Malt-liquors, Much Better, and Cheaper, than hitherto Known: Shewing, what Care is to be taken in the Choice of Water, Malt, and Hops, and in What Proportions they are to be Mixed (1727) Dublin.

Achen, C.H. and Bartels, L.M. (2016) *Democracy for Realists: Why Elections Do Not Produce Responsive Government*. Princeton, NJ: Princeton University Press.

Ariely, D. (2008) *Predictably Irrational: The Hidden Forces that Shape Our Decisions*. New York: Harper.

Asquer, E. (2012) 'Domesticity and Beyond: Gender, Family, and Consumption in Modern Europe', in F. Trentmann (ed.) *The Oxford Handbook of the History of Consumption*. Oxford: Oxford University Press, pp. 568–584.

Bagehot, W. (1872) *Physics and Politics or, Thoughts on the Application of the Principles of 'Natural Selection' and 'Inheritance' to Political Society*. London: Henry S. King.

Bagehot, W. (1963/1867) *The English Constitution*. London: Collins.

Barlow, T. (1699) Αντοσχεδιασματα, *de studio theologiae: or, Directions for the Choice of Books in the Study of Divinity*. London.

Bellamy, J. (1645) *A Plea for the Commonalty of London, or, a Vindication of their Rights in the Choice of Sundry City Officers*. London: George Miller.

Bellingham, B. (1988) 'The History of Childhood Since the "Invention of Childhood": Some Issues in the Eighties', *Journal of Family History*, 13(1): 347–358.

Breen, T.H. (2004) *The Marketplace of Revolution: How Consumer Politics Shaped American Independence*. New York: Oxford University Press.

Brennan, J. (2016) *Against Democracy*. Princeton, NJ: Princeton University Press.

Burroughs, J. (1641) *Moses – His Choice, With His Eye Fixed Upon Heaven*. London: Thomas Egglesfield.

By the King (1603) *A Proclamation Directing the People in the Choice of Fit Persons to Serve in Parliament*. London.

Caplan, B. (2008) *The Myth of the Rational Voter: Why Democracies Choose Bad Policies*. Princeton, NJ: Princeton University Press.

Chamberlain, C. (1984) 'The Meaning of Prohairesis in Aristotle's Ethics', *Transactions of the American Philological Association*, 114: 147–157.

Clarke, J. (2006) 'Consumers, Clients or Citizens? Politics, Policy and Practice in the Reform of Social Care', *European Societies*, 8(3): 423–442.

Clayton, R. (1679) *London's Choice of Citizens to Represent them in the Ensuing Parliament*. London.

Clinton, K. (1992) *Myth and Cult: The Iconography of the Eleusinian Mysteries*. Stockholm: Swedish Institute in Athens.

Cockett, R. (1995) *Thinking the Unthinkable: Think-Tanks and the Economic Counter-Revolution, 1931–1983*. London: HarperCollins.

Cohen, E. (2012) 'The Devil Made Me Do It'. Paper read at the Centre for the History of Emotions, Queen Mary University of London, January 19.

Cohen, L. (2004) *A Consumers' Republic: the Politics of Mass Consumption in Postwar America*. New York: Vintage Books.

Collyer, J. (1761) The Parent's and Guardian's Directory, and the Youth's Guide, in the Choice of a Profession or Trade. London.

Cruickshank, D. (2009) *London's Sinful Secret: The Bawdy History and Very Public Passions of London's Georgian Age*. New York: St Martin's Press.

Davies, W. (2014) *The Limits of Neoliberalism: Authority, Sovereignty and the Logic of Competition*. London: Sage.

Defoe, D. (1694) *The Englishman's Choice and True Interest in a Vigorous Prosecution of the War against France, and Serving K. William and Q. Mary, and Acknowledging their Right*. London.

Digby, K. (1638) *A Conference with a Lady about Choice of Religion*. London.

D'Urfey, T. (1685) *Advice to the Ladies of London in the Choice of their Husbands*. London.

Eagleton-Pierce, M. (2016) *Neoliberalism: The Key Concepts*. London: Routledge.

Edwards, J. (1797) *A Dissertation Concerning Liberty and Necessity*. Worcester, MA.

Floyd, J. (1639) *A Famous and Prudent Choice of Beliefe. Written by a Student of Divinity*. London.

Foucault, M. (2007) *Security, Territory, Population. Lectures at the Collège de France, 1977–1978*. Basingstoke: Palgrave Macmillan.

Fountaine, E. (1654) *Melancholy's Bane: or, Choice, Pleasant, and Profitable Recreations*. London.

Fox, J. (2009) *The Myth of the Rational Market: A History of Risk, Reward, and Delusion on Wall Street*. New York: HarperBusiness.

Friedman, M. (2002/1962) *Capitalism and Freedom*. Chicago: Chicago University Press.

Friedman, M. and Friedman, R. (1990) *Free to Choose: A Personal Statement*. Orlando, FL: Harcourt.

Gerbier, B. (1663) *Counsel and Advise to all Builders; for the Choice of their Surveyours and other Work-men*. London.

Gother, A. (1734) *The Sincere Christian's Guide, in the Choice of Religion*. London: Thomas Meighan.

Greenfield, K. (2012) *The Myth of Choice: Personal Responsibility in a World of Limits*. New Haven, CT: Yale University Press.

Harris, J. (2007) *Of Liberty and Necessity: The Free Will Debate in Eighteenth-Century British Philosophy*. Oxford: Oxford University Press.

Hinton, E. (1650) *Eighteen Choice and Usefull Sermons*. London.
Holditch, R. (1818) *The Emigrant's Guide to the United States of America; Containing the best Advice and Directions respecting the Voyage, Preservation of Health, Choice of Settlement*. London: W. Home.
Kane, R. (2011) 'The Contours of Contemporary Free Will Debates', in R. Kane (ed.) *The Oxford Handbook of Free Will*. Oxford: Oxford University Press, pp. 3–36.
Kierkegaard, S. (1988/1834) *Either/Or*. Princeton, NJ: Princeton University Press.
Koselleck, R. (1994) 'Some Reflections on the Temporal Structure of Conceptual Change', in W. Melching and W. Velema (eds) *Main Trends in Cultural History: Ten Essays*, Amsterdam: Rodopi, pp. 7–16.
Le Clerk, J. (1711) *Against Indifference in the Choice of our Religion*. Amsterdam.
Leggett, W. (2014) 'The Politics of Behaviour Change: Nudge, Neoliberalism and the State', *Policy & Politics*, 42(1): 3–19.
Markus, H.R. and Schwartz, B. (2010) 'Does Choice Mean Freedom and Well-Being?', *Journal of Consumer Research*, 37(2): 344–355.
Maynwaring, E. (1672) *Serious Cautions against Tobacco – Preservating of Health in the Choice of Drinks, and Regular Drinking*. London.
McCloskey, D. (2006) *The Bourgeois Virtues: Ethics for an Age of Commerce*. Chicago: Chicago University Press.
McCraw, T. and Tedlow, R. (1997) 'Henry Ford, Alfred Sloan, and the Three Phases of Marketing', in T. McGraw (ed.) *Creating Modern Capitalism: How Entrepreneurs, Companies and Countries Triumphed in Three Industrial Revolutions*. Cambridge MA: Harvard University Press, pp. 266–300.
McGovern, C. (2006) *Sold American: Consumption and Citizenship, 1890–1945*. Chapel Hill, NC: University of North Carolina Press.
McMahon, J. (2015) 'Behavioral Economics as Neoliberalism: Producing and Governing *homo economicus*', *Journal of Contemporary Political Theory*, 14(2): 137–158.
Memorandums for London in the choice of their Common-Councel-Men (1644). London.
Meyer, J.W. and Jepperson, R.L. (2000) 'The "Actors" of Modern Society: The Cultural Construction of Social Agency', *Sociological Theory*, 18(1): 100–120.
Mill, J.S. (1859) *On Liberty*. London: Longman, Roberts and Green.
Nielsen, K.M. (2011) 'Deliberation as Inquiry: Aristotle's Alternative to the Presumption of Open Alternatives', *The Philosophical Review*, 120(3): 383–421.
Nuovo, V. (2008) 'Aspects of Stoicism in Locke's Philosophy', in S. Hutton and P. Schuurman (eds) *Studies on Locke: Sources, Contemporaries, and Legacy: In Honour of G.A.J. Rogers (International Archives of the History of Ideas, 197)*. Dordrecht: Springer, pp. 1–25.
Offer, A. (2005) *The Challenge of Affluence: Self-Control and Well-Being in the United States and Britain since 1950*. Oxford: Oxford University Press.
Page, T. (1770) *The Art of Shooting Flying, Containing Directions for the Choice of Guns*. Norwich.
Penn, W. (1680) *England's Great Interest in the Choice of this New Parliament, Dedicated to all her Free-holders and Electors*. London.
Philalethes (1796) *Common Sense; or, the Plain Man's Answer to the Question, Whether Christianity be a Religion Worthy of our Choice in this Age of Reason? In two Letters to a Deistical Friend*. London: T. Knott.
Philomedicus, A.H. (1676) *Reason in Season; or a Word in the Behalf of the Non-Collegiate Physicians, and of the Right of the People in the Choice of their Physicians*. London.

Pomfret, J. (1701) *The Choice: A Poem*. London: J. Nutt.

Ponteus, J. (1697) *The Best Choice for Religion and Government in a Conference between Sir Anthony, a Latitudinarian, John Ponteus, Mr Maggot, Mr Mouth and Friend Henry*. London.

Reed, D.D., DiGennaro-Reed, F.D., Chok, J. and Brozyna, G.A. (2011) 'The "Tyranny of Choice": Choice Overload as a Possible Instance of Effort Discounting', *The Psychological Record*, 61(4): 547–560.

Rosenthal, E.C. (2006) *The Era of Choice: The Ability to Choose and Its Transformation of Contemporary Life*. Cambridge, MA: MIT Press.

Rosenthal, L. (2005) *Gender, Politics, and Allegory in the Art of Rubens*. Cambridge: Cambridge University Press.

Salecl, R. (2009) 'Society of Choice', *Differences*, 20(1): 157–180.

Salecl, R. (2010) *The Tyranny of Choice*. London: Profile.

Schmitt, C. (1985/1922) *Political Theology: Four Chapters on the Concept of Sovereignty*. Chicago: University of Chicago Press.

Schwartz, B. (2005) *The Paradox of Choice: Why More is Less*. New York: Harper.

Schwarzkopf, S. (2011a) 'The Consumer as "Voter", "Judge" and "Jury": Historical Origins and Political Consequences of a Marketing Myth', *Journal of Macromarketing*, 31(1): 8–18.

Schwarzkopf, S. (2011b) 'The Political Theology of Consumer Sovereignty: Towards an Ontology of Consumer Society', *Theory, Culture & Society*, 28(3): 106–129.

Schwarzkopf, S. (2012) 'The Market Order as Metaphysical Loot: Theology and the Contested Legitimacy of Consumer Capitalism', *Organization*, 19(3): 281–297.

Sen, A. (1988) 'Freedom of Choice: Concept and Content', *European Economic Review*, 32(2–3): 269–294.

Skinner, Q. (2002) 'A Third Concept of Liberty', *Proceedings of the British Academy*, 117: 237–268.

Slater, D. (1997) *Consumer Culture and Modernity*. Cambridge: Polity Press.

Sloterdijk, P. (2009) *God's Zeal: The Battle of the Three Monotheisms*. Cambridge: Polity Press.

Smith, A. (1904/1776) *Inquiry into the Nature and Causes of the Wealth of Nations*. London: Methuen (2 vols, ed. by Edwin Cannan).

Sneeringer, J. (2004) 'The Shopper as Voter: Women, Politics and Advertising in Post-Inflation Germany', *German Studies Review*, 27(3): 476–501.

Tempest, R. (1658) *A Discourse Touching Choyce of Religion*. London.

Thaler, R. and Sunstein, C. (2008) *Nudge: Improving Decisions about Health, Wealth, and Happiness*. New Haven, CT: Yale University Press.

The Gentleman Farrier; Containing Instructions for the Choice, and Directions in the Management, of Horses (1732). London.

The King (1661) *The Kings Majesties Letter to the Lord Mayor, and Court of Aldermen of the City of London, Concerning the Choice of Common-Council-Men*. London.

The Parliament (1646) *An Ordinance of the Lords and Commons for Keeping of Scandalous Persons from the Sacrament of the Lords Supper, the Enabling of Congregations for the Choice of Elders*. London.

The Parliament (1658) *Some Grave and Weighty Considerations Proposed to the People, to Direct them in the Choice of their Representatives Which are to Sit in the Approaching Parliament*. London.

The Tea Purchaser's Guide in the Knowledge and Choice of Teas (1785). London.

The Times (1909) 'Mr. Taft on Woman Suffrage', November 4: 5, col. C.

The Times (1911) 'Mr. Lloyd George and Doctors', June 2: 7, col. A.

The West-Country Counsellor: or, the Devonshire Damsels Advice to the Lasses of London, in Their Choice of Kind and Loving Husbands (1670). London.

Tocqueville, A. (2007/1835) 'Democracy in America', in C. Calhoun et al. (eds). *Classical Sociological Theory*. Malden, MA: Wiley Blackwell, pp. 55–71.

Trentmann, F. (2016) *Empire of Things: How We Became a World of Consumers, from the Fifteenth Century to the Twenty-first*. London: Allen Lane.

Wallas, G. (1908) *Human Nature in Politics*. London: Constable & Co.

Weber, M. (2014) *Asketischer Protestantismus und Kapitalismus*, in W. Schluchter and U. Bube. Tübingen (eds). *Max Weber Collected Works: Vol. I/9*. Tübingen: Mohr Siebeck.

Are You Neoliberal Fit? The Politics of Consumption under Neoliberalism

Anisha Datta and Indranil Chakraborty

'Being fit' means to have a flexible, absorptive and adjustable body, ready to live through sensations not yet tried and impossible to specify in advance. (Zygmunt Bauman, 2012)

Data is cheaper than atta [wheat flour] (Lalu Yadav [a member of Parliament in India, 2016])

The good life made easy; be strong, be healthy, be happy (Goodlife Fitness [a Canadian fitness corporation])

Pleasure after all is a safer guide than either right or duty (Samuel Butler, 2012)

Man does not strive for happiness, only the Englishman does that (Friedrich Nietzsche, 1998)

INTRODUCTION

Our friend Siddharth aka Sid, an IIT-Bombay graduate and at present working as a hotshot techie for a multinational microchip manufacturer made this sarcastic point the other day over our occasional skype chats: 'You know, my credit rating and my cholesterol – I'm responsible for both and I have to monitor them both. Hey, no worries, I now have an Apple watch to help me!' Sid has internalized the discourse of compulsory individualization of social problems, the root of which can be located in the ideologies of our time such as debt driven consumerism and a heart attack prone 24/7 stressful overworked life.

Rose, a mid-level corporate manager, drives every day close to two hours each way to commute from home to work. She uses a two-cup breast pump to store breast milk for her infant son. Later, her nanny bottle feeds the baby, from that stored breast milk. Rose who has an MBA degree lives in New Jersey with her school teacher partner. She believes in Sheryl Sandberg's 'lean in' feminism that today's women can have it all. Her struggle with time poverty and the depletion of care support in twenty-first-century America did not make her ask the question of why women's emancipation had to forego the social support that the state and businesses would have provided in the immediate post-war period of social democracy. Rose is relatively fortunate, since she can buy commodified care work, but for the low-paid mothers toiling in retail or other minimum wage jobs, the care work has to be done through the unpaid private service provided by family members or friends.

In the 2009 Hollywood movie *Up in the Air*, the male protagonist Ryan Bingham (played by George Clooney) gives a motivational speech called 'What's in your backpack'. In it, he says the slower we move, the faster we die. We are not swans we are sharks. This speech is pregnant with a neoliberal logic – it's not bad to be laid off, rather it's an opportunity! The laid-off worker is required to practice hardball self-entrepreneurship and professional networking to get employed in an economy characterized by jobless growth.

Consider another new sociological phenomenon. The global wellness industry is a $3.4 trillion market, which is 3.4 times larger than the worldwide pharmaceutical industry.[1] The total GDP of sub-Saharan countries according to the World Bank database (2017) is $1.57 trillion.[2] The humongous wellness market, which is sustained by the rich and upper-middle-class consumers' shape the nature of food intake:

> [T]he influence progressive wellness consumers have over food culture is disproportionate. Progressive wellness consumers are paving the way, sharing their enthusiasm and knowledge with mainstream consumers who are hungry for guidance and direction. As shoppers, progressives are no longer thinking about condition management (lowering cholesterol or blood pressure) or dieting (low fat, low carb) but are focused on real quality food, positive nutrition, fresh, less processed foods and beverages and fun. From a purchase and use perspective, this means moving away from products that are fat-free, diet products and 100-calorie portion packs to kale, dark chocolate and quality fats, such as found in nuts, avocados and butter.[3]

In this chapter, the rising consumption of wellness products and services in the neoliberal era of capitalism, will be a core focus. But let us first focus on some basic definitions.

Consumption is the last part of the material cycle – production, distribution and consumption. The purpose of consumption in the first place is to satisfy human needs to survive and to fulfill the primal desires such as hunger. Consumption is an essential part of human production and reproduction that is vital to sustain human civilization and life on Earth. However, it also plays an important role in the functioning of the economy, the market, where money becomes a medium of exchange to buy consumer goods. Thus, it is not enough to be hungry for food, one has to earn money to satiate that hunger. The demand for food essentially means demand backed by money power of the consumer. Hunger is a state of non-availability of food but it also implies that poor people don't have the (money) power to purchase food. Recently an Indian politician remarked that in India 'Data is cheaper than atta [wheat flour]'– 'Will the poor eat data or atta?'[4] A recent study by the British medical journal *Lancet*[5] states that 'the average global intake of fruits and vegetables is less than required levels – defined as at least two servings of fruits and three servings of vegetables per person per day. And affordability is a crucial factor behind the deficient intake'.

If the above examples are not enough to understand the deeper politics of social inequality involved in the process of consumption, here is the other side of the story, which lays bare a massive social contradiction existing in our world today. Adobe, the multinational software vendor in its monthly release of 'Digital Price Index' (DPI) reports that 'Online grocery shopping and in-store pickup were at a record high, while sales of Pokémon branded items grew significantly as well. Prices across nearly all other categories the DPI tracks continued to decline'.[6]

In this chapter, we will also interrogate this perverse distortion existing in the consumer market, where there is enough food to feed but malnutrition is endemic, while the middle and upper middle classes go for online shopping of groceries and fashionable goods that technology provides at a wallet-friendly price. Any discussion of the politics of modern day consumption cannot limit itself only to the phenomenon of the consumption of high-end organic food, Lexus cars or Apple watches, the discussion should also consider the bizarre phenomenon of milk dumping by American dairy farmers to keep their profit margins high.[7] The availability of enough food, from organic vegetables to low-fat diets, for the people who can afford, and no food for 'about 800 million people who go to bed hungry every night, and many more [who] suffer from the "hidden hunger" of malnutrition' (World Bank, 2015, p. 3),[8] is determined by the present political-economic structure of the production of commodities. But this structure is also mediated by the emotions and subjective feelings of self-gratification and the fulfillment of learned 'cultural' desires (e.g., sports cars, fashion brands, cosmetics, smartphones, 'spornosexual'[9] bodies and so on) that consumption provides to the consumers. Therefore, it is not sufficient to discuss the political-economy to understand the phenomenon of the over- and under-fed populations of this world, but we also have to integrate the discussion of the ideology and discourse of consumer culture into this chapter, in order to understand why people fetishize the objects of consumption. The pundits across various social science disciplines define the current economic structure as neoliberal, but 'it has been drawn far beyond its conceptual crib in economic policy, political economy and the states-versus-markets debate, towards issues of power and ideology' (Venugopal, 2015, p. 169). To understand how the consumption of material objects and immaterial services are shaped by the discourse of neoliberalism, we will look at both the factors – the political economy as well as the subjectivity involved in consumerism.

In the next two sections, our endeavor will be to understand: (i) the meanings and implications of consumption through the glut and scarcity created by the market; and (ii) the rising consumerism of self-love, self-care and wellness products, which is symptomatic of the neoliberal phase of capitalism.

THE POLITICS OF CONSUMPTION FROM INDUSTRIAL CAPITALISM THROUGH NEOLIBERALISM

The images of the twentieth-century modern consumer in Euro-American discourse can be divided into two broad categories – *the victim* who has been duped into accepting consumerism, and *the rational actor* who is a clever communicator through his/her consumption. But what kind of politics is involved in consumption. To answer this question, we will undertake a brief review of the existing sociological and cultural studies works on consumption. Following the genre of critical theory, here the term politics will refer to the issues of power, inequality, domination, appropriation, empowerment and exploitation that are generated through the act of consumption.

The modern consumer as a victim of consumerism produced by the mid-twentieth-century industrial capitalism and culture industry, is best examined in the works of Frankfurt school theorists such as Adorno, Marcuse and Horkheimer. In the post-war period of mass production, the economic needs for patriotic, submissive and hardy workers also gave rise to a need for passive consumers, who would spend their earnings to keep the cycle of mass production running. In 'The Culture Industry: Enlightenment as Mass Deception', Horkheimer and Adorno (1982) point out that culture, which is a creative output of human mind, labor and intellect, has been dumbed down to become trivial, feel-good, banal and entertaining. As Marcuse would later argue in his work *One Dimensional Man* (2002), the critical thinking that the nineteenth century modernist culture could produce has been pulverized into entertainment-induced homogenized culture and art in the post-war period of economic boom in America. The culture of easy listening, easy watching ensured the social reproduction of an unreflexive worker-consumer citizen.

Borrowing insights from Marx's theory of labor alienation, these theorists argue that the objectification of labor requires the objectification of the consumer. Liberal economists such as Galbraith in his *The Affluent Society* (1998) made a similar argument by saying that the interconnection between mass production and mass consumption is crucial, and an examination of it sheds light on the artificial manufacturing of endless consumer desires. This endless desire was generated and sustained by the newly founded service sector of advertising, marketing research and public relations in the 1950s. This spirit is best captured in Bill Bernbach's (the advertising guru of the 1960s) comment 'Advertising is fundamentally persuasion and persuasion happens to be not a science, but an art' (Levenson, 1987, p. xvii). The Canadian theorist C.B. MacPherson in his critique of the discourse of 'possessive individualism' (i.e., man as an infinite desirer and accumulator) that underpins the liberal social theories of Hobbes, Locke, Levellers and Adam Smith says that if man is naturally an infinite desirer, why did corporations spend so much money creating 'artificial needs' or consumer demands through persuasive advertisements (MacPherson, 2012, p. 33)?

Since corporations created and satisfied the demand, an almost seamless compatibility was ensured in the system of post-war capitalist production and consumption in North America and Western Europe. Herein lies the political economic dimension of the twentieth-century consumer's desires. In *The Hidden Persuaders* (1981), Vance Packard highlights how during the 1960s advertising firms started using high-end statistical and psychological marketing research methods to increase the level of consumer desire and demand. This is also the time when corporations started competing with each other for a larger share of the market, by creating finely crafted brand images of their products, which were in essence quite similar – for example, the battle between Coke and Pepsi.

During the same period, a feminist critique of post-war consumerism was advanced by Betty Friedan in her work *The Feminine Mystique* (2013). Friedan states that apolitical advertisements prevent women from self-actualization. Furthermore, she argues that the post-war mass-production-based economy required homebound housewives who could be manipulated into channeling their creative energy into buying washing powders and cake mixes. The branded product lines also offered a sense of style and identity to the consumers of the counterculture generation of the 1960s and 1970s. A prime example of this is the cool feminist smoker image that was simulated by the Virginia slims advertising campaigns.

Overall, these writers by emphasizing the political economic angle of mass consumption show us that the authentic human needs have been undermined by the manufactured wants created by the cult of consumerism. In a way, the twentieth-century woman/man has been seduced and conned into becoming a consumption obsessed homogenized or one-dimensional person. In the process, the class divided, patriarchal capitalist society could carry on its business as usual, that is, to keep the elites secured, and to keep the masses distracted by consumerism.

On the other hand, there are authors who marshal critiques against mass consumerism from the angle of culture and symbolic meanings. They attempt to explain why consumers get hooked on consumerism, which is fundamentally driven by the profit motive of corporations. The most notable work from this approach is by the French sociologist Jean Baudrillard. Material cultural objects are imbued with symbolic meanings in every human society. But in capitalism, mass goods which are functionally and materially similar have to be branded to impart them with symbolic imageries and meanings. Baudrillard pioneered in theorizing the rise of the production of social meaning through mass commodities. He says in his classic work *For a Critique of the Political Economy of the Sign* (1981) that in the West, society has passed from a metallurgic into a semiurgic society (i.e., dominated by simulations and hyperreality). A simulacrum is an identical copy without an original. This is the characteristic mode of postmodernity where hyperrealism rules. His focus is to explain how the needs and wants that sustain consumerism are produced. He argues that our desires are disguised manifestations of social and economic differences in a sign system of cultural meanings that is produced through mass commodities such as attire fashions. Thus, Baudrillard moves away from a watertight demarcation between authentic contra false needs, as theorized in the works of Adorno and Marcuse. One of his most insightful theories is that mediated images such as advertisements and live television produce image frames, which are examples of the Baudrillardian hyperreal. The latter is a simulation of the TV image and reality in which the relation between the signifying system and the reality gets ambivalent. The real is now an effect of the television commercial.[10]

Drawing on Baudrillard, the French semiotician Roland Barthes offered a marvelous discourse analysis of ads as modern mythologies, which are composed by commodity signs (*Mythologies*, 2013). In his analysis and others (such as that of Robert Goldman and Stephanie Papson, 1996) that used semiotics to examine the cultural significations of 'commodity signs', the concept of identity emerges as an important aspect of consumption. A good example of how hip consumption can give access to special identities is Thomas Frank's *The Conquest of Cool* (1997). He shows how everything including counter-cultural social values, progressive ideas and symbolic meanings were commodified, packaged and sold to the boomers in America. For instance, the Volkswagen campaign by the advertising agency DDB transformed the

German car from its Nazi ancestry into a Love Bug. DDB, used anti-advertising rhetoric of the 1960s to turn consumption into an aesthetic and emotional practice. As DDB's guru Bernback had once referred to 'difference' as 'the magic cultural formula by which the life of consumerism could be extended indefinitely, running forever on the discontent that it itself had produced' (Frank, 1997: 68).

From a feminist perspective, Susan Bordo (1993) has used Barthes' semiotic analysis technique to offer an excellent deconstruction of the gendered nature of advertisements. According to her, ads reflect patriarchal ideology which tries to maintain control over women's bodies and sexuality. Bordo shows that by psyching out the female consumer, advertisements and marketers teach women to hate their bodies, hunger and desires. In the process, a class-based construction of femininity gets established in popular culture. As Bordo puts it:

> The hungering bourgeois wished to appear, like the aristocrat, above the material desires that in fact ruled his life. The closest he could come was to possess a wife whose ethereal body became a sort of fashion statement of his aristocratic tastes. If he could not be or marry an aristocrat, he could have a wife who looked like one, a wife whose non-robust beauty and delicate appetite signified her lack of participation in the taxing 'public sphere'. (Bordo, 2003, p. 117)

The above critiques on consumption can also be categorized as the study of consumerism as an ideology; an ideology which assists in legitimizing and reproducing different power inequities existing in a capitalist patriarchal society.

The consumer as *a rational actor* (i.e., the model man in Adam Smith who pursues his self-interest of possessive individualism) seeking to communicate an identity is well represented in Veblen's *Theory of the Leisure Class* (2000). His famous concept of 'conspicuous consumption' epitomizes how the new rich in turn-of-the-century America could communicate their socio-economic status through overt and wasteful consumption. Similarly, Pierre Bourdieu (*Distinction*, 1984) offered a similar theorization on how consumption acts as a marker of taste (such as beer versus red wine; or wrestling versus horse riding) and hence social class in modern France. The consumer's taste varied across the class line, and the endowment of cultural capital played an important role in the development of taste. Bourdieu theorized that taste and consumption helped to reproduce class inequality, where elite consumer culture could remain distinct from mass culture.

Bourdieu's works on consumer culture also helps to explain how consumption can reproduce social inequality, and this is a significant aspect of the politics of modern consumption. In the same vain, Ann duCille (1996) shows how the consumption of mass-produced toys constructs and maintains racial hierarchy in the USA. As the toy maker Mattel moved into the lucrative ethnic market, ethnic and black Barbies were created. But the ethnic Barbies still retained the bodies and class status of the normative, that is, white Barbie. As little black girls would say, the white Barbie is the real one.

As social theory took a postmodern turn in the 1980s, some contributions looked at the consumer as a hedonist artist (Campbell, 1987). A modern consumer, instead of seeking pleasure entirely through sensations, seeks out emotional experiences through consumption. Modern consumption (e.g., window shopping at swanky shopping malls) creates dream, imagination and aestheticization of our humdrum life.

If the worker/producer of capitalist economy follows an over-disciplined, tedious and time-bound work life, the arena of consumption allows him/her to relax and become an irresponsible pleasure seeker. Similarly, John Fiske (1989) theorized how modern consumption is a form of liberation in a postmodern world. He argues that shopping, watching TV, listening to rock music are forms of resistance by marginalized groups against the dominant social structures of capitalism. However, critics would point out that shopping as a practice of socio-cultural liberation does not ever undermine the structural basis of a capitalist economy.

Zygmunt Bauman, who wrote that our transition to consumer society has involved a series of displacements: from the community to the individual, from savings to credit, from the classical modern to the liquid modern self. In liquid modernity, life is organized around consumption, guided by 'ever rising desires and volatile wishes' (Bauman, 2012, pp. 76–77). He says that, unlike Fordist style heavy capitalism, light consumer-friendly capitalism can be characterized by the 'shopping around' type of life, in which latching on to an identity is flexible and mobile. Consumers run after pleasurable things as an escape from the agony of insecurity and from the fear of being sloppy. Shopping offers the promise of certainty. But Bauman also points out that the task of self-identification through consumption has disruptive side effects. It can divide human situations and it prompts fierce competition rather than unifying a human condition inclined to generate co-operation and solidarity.

Bauman's work is a nice segue to move into the contemporary scene of the politics of consumption under neoliberalism. In broad terms, Neoliberalism has been conceptualized in three ways: a set of economic and political policies; an ideology; and a mode of governance.[11] Neoliberal policies arising from the crisis in capitalism during the 1970s gave rise to a neoliberal subjectivity. Neoliberal subjectivity thrives on neoliberal consumption, and the latter in turn reproduces the neoliberal subject. The sustenance of a neoliberal subjectivity drives the engine of neoliberal production and consumption. In the following paragraphs, we will try to examine the following four questions: What is the nature of neoliberal consumption? What makes up a neoliberal subject? How has neoliberal restructuring impacted consumer culture? Lastly, what kind of politics is reflected in consumption under neoliberalism?

Neoliberal policies which have gradually eroded the collectivist principles of the post-war social democratic welfare state in advanced capitalist countries, have subjected people to new forms of economic insecurity and social uncertainty. These socio-economic conditions have shaped the meaning of the everyday reality for people, who are now required to refashion their self to cope and survive. The rationale behind the welfare state was grounded on the modern notion of social rights for citizens (Marshall, 1950). Under neoliberal restructuring, the citizen is supposed to take charge of her own life and make responsible choices so that she can emerge as an innovative entrepreneur who can not only make her life but in the process she can also create opportunities for others (e.g., the business model of Airbnb and Uber). The perfect neoliberal subject does not depend on state provided public services such as public sector jobs, public education, socialized healthcare, an old age pension and so on. To turn the inefficient public sector into a profit-making business, neoliberal policies demand the privatization of social services such as health, education, public parks and so on.

In *Elsewhere, U.S.A.* (2009), the sociologist Dalton Conley says that in the twenty-first century, Americans live multiple lives. Their lives are so fast paced and full of multitasking that things often seem to be out of control. With the economic downturn of America, it is much harder to keep the old middle-class standard of living and hence Americans are working longer hours,[12] and in addition they are constantly nagged by a 'not enough feeling'. As another sociologist Richard Sennett (1998) explains, the idea of 'no-long term' dominates the post-Fordist society. An impatient capitalism is hungry for change and more profit, which produces an *uncertain* time for a *disempowered non-unionized* workforce. There is no fixed role, no loyalty as jobs are replaced by projects, and as jobs get outsourced. In fact, there is no virtue in 'long term' – jobs, places, friends, love, relationships, etc. A pervasive feeling of fear, anxiety, and loss of control characterizes the life of a post-Fordist worker (or, as Sennett puts it the worker in New Capitalism), even if s/he belongs to an upper-middle-class income bracket. Life is marked by a surge in work hours, and by a loss of community and friendship. The 'no long term' economy/work/life mantra damages trust, belonging, bonding, commitment, and human agency and action. In turn, these corrode the character and an atomized individual is produced (Sennett, 1998).

Conley (2009) conceptualizes the twenty-first century consumption habits of upper-middle-class American professionals in the following two ways, The first is 'weisure' (instrumental leisure – leisure is work and work is leisure – e.g., the seamless flow from watching a movie online to writing office emails on your laptop, aided by the marvelous ICT). This gadget-dependent leisure intensifies consumerism since most of the content on the net is supported by advertising revenue. The second new phenomenon is convestment (consumption with investment – e.g., buying houses and condos not only to live in them but to flip them often to make profit, which is aided by the low-rate mortgage loans and remortgaging facilities offered by private banks). The 'intravidual', who has multiple selves[13] accentuated by the cybernetics social media, tries primarily to cultivate an entrepreneurial self. This entrepreneurial self believes more in who he knows versus what he knows (e.g., the career networking platform LinkedIn). The intravidual in order to get over the anxiety of an uncertain time resorts to gambling and betting as a form of recreation (e.g., gambling rose from 5% to 25% from the 1970s to the present in the US, notes Conley [2009]). In addition, the entrepreneurial intravidual is fragmented. As Conley puts it: we seem to be everywhere but nowhere (Conley, 2009); there is no authentic self and a lack of social relations; today social relations are based on instrumental rationality and the logic of market; socializing becomes social networking, trust is damaged – the market dominates and penetrates every nook and cranny of the non-market.

Now, neoliberalism is also a discourse on what makes a successful man/woman. The hegemonic ideas of aggressive individualism (e.g., friends for benefit), market efficiency (e.g., education as human capital), innovative entrepreneurship (e.g., Uber and Airbnb), cut-throat competition (a competitive attitude negates the chances of forming substantive social bonds and long-term associations), the digitization and quantification of our everyday life (Apple watch, Fitbit, the digitally monitored Impact factor of academic journals, and Instagram) and the growing financialization and the rising household debt level (e.g., the sub-prime mortgage; the low interest rate line of credit from the banks; 0% interest car financing) produce a neoliberal subject who is engaged in endless self-improvement to meet the goal of 'zero-imperfection' so that s/he can survive as a 'middle-class' person through the rough ride of our neoliberal times. The rough ride is caused by a jobless economic growth, the growth in precarious labor, state and corporate disinvestment from social welfare, the gradual privatization of public goods, and the rapid commercialization and commodification of care. All these lead to new forms of alienation and anomie under neoliberalism.

The neoliberal self is a product of a particular phase of late capitalism. As neoliberal policies shape the everyday reality of folks, a neoliberal subjectivity is formed. For instance, Raewyn Connell (2011) writes about how neoliberal structural and policy changes impinge on family, emotional and social relationships such as parenting and child care (Connell, 2011). She also identifies some recent cultural practices which help to form and consolidate the neoliberal self: an unhealthy narcissistic egotism/self-esteem based on high insecurity, when self-promotion replaces self-deprecation and modesty; the widespread acceptance of the positive psychology discourse which asks clients/customer to be outwardly tougher and inwardly weaker, which further escalates their anxiety; depression triggered by the threat of constant social evaluation stressors; artificially induced shame/sense of lacking (of wealth, a plush house, the latest SUV, expensive vacations, the washboard abdomen, and finally the happy life) leading to conformism and the incessant and compulsive running on life's break neck speed treadmill.

In these circumstances, an easy coping mechanism is available through therapeutic consumption which shoots up consumers' credit card bills. To manage people's state of anxiety, the big pharma companies step in with their cash cow – anti-depressants. In this neoliberal climate, which is characterized by time poverty, long working hours, the two-earner family, the depletion of social connection and substantive friendship, there is a general atmosphere of a crisis of care and the co-option of the social by businesses. For instance, a paid therapist is expected to substitute for a good old bosom friend. These contemporary social practices which are justified by the dominant discourse of neoliberalism, and which are supported by cybernetics-based social media and digital technology contribute to the formation of a neoliberal self.

In sociology, self is seen as our individual subjectivity, our identity. Jim McGuigan (2014) points out that the neoliberal social type can be identified as a product of neoliberal social pressures. He says this is a sociological proposal with psychological implications. Neoliberal ideology and policy reorder the social and they refashion the self. The three major players in today's capitalism – the successful entrepreneur, the sovereign consumer, and the hard working tax payer – are celebrated in advanced capitalist societies. In neoliberal discourse, the wealth creator/entrepreneur is valued since privatization means efficiency and public services imply wastefulness (McGuigan, 2014).

The neoliberal self recasts its identity in terms of compulsory individualization (i.e., the collective principles of a post-war social democracy are despised, *à la* Thatcherism and Reganism), sovereign consumerism (the consumer mode replaces the citizen mode of existence – e.g., education and health services are marketable commodities; and there is a hyper brand aware commodity fetishism), flexibility (the flexi-worker working multiple precarious jobs to eke out a living), high adaptability, instant transformation, constant switching, and self-entrepreneurship in order to cope with rising insecurity, uncertainty and anxiety.

Given the focus of the chapter, we will focus on the rise of a specific kind of consumption under neoliberalism, a consumption practice which helps to sustain the neoliberal self in a substantial way. Consumption plays a vital role in the maintenance of neoliberal conditions through the rising consumption of commodified wellness, happiness and self-care services. To escape the pressure and insecurity of neoliberal work and life conditions, subjects surround themselves with brands, leisure services and self-care activities, which are infused with neoliberal reasons.

In *The Happiness Industry* William Davies (2015) points out that since capitalism cannot be transformed to meet human needs, humans will have to transform themselves to meet capitalist needs. Gurus such as Achor or Zak provide this popular philosophy and their motto is – I changed myself, and so can you. Similarly, in India the well-heeled upper middle class follow Sri Sri Ravi Shankar to bring *shanti* [peace] to their competitive and chaos-ridden busy lives. His Art of Living Institute has a popular stress management program, which attracts consumers by saying – 'Sudarshan Kriya elevates the prana [life] by flushing out more than 90% toxins and accumulated stress, everyday'.[14] The Art of Living movement, which is supposed to cure depression through its trade marked *Sudarshan Kriya*, has branches in 155 countries worldwide.[15]

But how do people internalize the neoliberal logic through the consumption of wellness and self-care services, which are supposed to bring the missing balance to their work and personal lives, in order that they can achieve a happy and 'good life'. A related fundamental question is why are managers increasingly bothered about the well-being and happiness of their workers? Why do they want optimal psychosomatic fitness in their workers? What does it take to make a psychosomatically fit worker, in particular in this neoliberal phase of capitalism? To remain psychosomatically fit what should the worker consume?

Reflect on the following trends:

> A growing number of corporations employ 'chief happiness officers', while Google has an in-house 'jolly good fellow' to spread mindfulness and empathy. Specialist happiness consultants advise employers on how to cheer up their employees, the unemployed on how to restore their enthusiasm to work, and – in one case in London – those being forcibly displaced from their homes on how to move on emotionally. (Davies, 2015, p. 4)

Neuroscience claims to have found the precise parts of the brain which generate positive and negative emotions. Innovation in apps is leading to the emergence of a quantified self, this self can track its mood swings and kilometers walked in a day. Davies writes that as big data on the above accumulates, 'so the field of "happiness economics" grows to take advantage of all this new data, building up a careful picture of which regions, lifestyles, forms of employment or types of consumption generate the greatest mental well-being' (Davies, 2015, p. 5).

Since the 1990s, positive psychology and the happiness and well-being industry have rapidly grown in the advanced centers of capitalism.[16] Global health and wellness sales are on the way to hit a record high of US$1 trillion by 2017.[17] The well-being industry and the discipline of positive psychology try to mask the cracks in our economy, polity, social relations and culture. A person living in a society that is deeply unequal, who works in an insecure economy, who lives without the social support from the state, but who has imbibed the values of being competitive, materialistic, individualistic and self-centric is bound to feel depressed and unhappy most of the time. The World Health Organization caused a stir in 2001 by predicting that mental health issues would have become the world's largest cause of disability and death by 2020. Mental health disorders are estimated to cost 3–4% of GDP in Europe and North America (Davies, 2015: 107).

Classes such as Dr Jim Loehr's 'Corporate Athlete Course', priced at $4900 for 2.5 days, introduce executives to elite energy investment strategies, which will enable them to achieve a high performance level of physical and mental wellness. Davies writes:

> the psychology of motivation blends into the physiology of health, drawing occasionally on insights from sports coaches and nutritionists, to which is added a cocktail of neuroscientific rumours and Buddhist meditation practices. Various notions of 'fitness', 'happiness', 'positivity' and 'success' bleed into one another, with little explanation of how and why. The idea which accompanies all of this is that there is one ideal form of human existence: hardworking, happy, healthy, and above all rich. A science of elite perfectibility is built on the back of this heroic capitalist vision. The flip side of this, and the real driving force behind many executive wellness programmes, is a set of well-researched risks run by highly competitive businessmen, colloquially known as 'burn-out', which includes the higher chance of heart attacks, strokes and nervous breakdowns. (Davies, 2015, pp. 111–112)

Gallup has estimated that employees' unhappiness costs the US economy $500 billion a year in lost productivity, lost tax receipts and healthcare costs. Thus, corporations and the neoliberal state would like the discourse of positive psychology to step in to keep the worker's motivation and efficiency levels high. By psychologizing the problems of our social fabric and economic organization, the agents of neoliberalism (the state and business corporations) keep the cracks covered up by neoliberal myths, which do not let us see that unhappiness is anger turned inwards or that stress is a type of emotional and physical reaction to any excessive demand. Elton Mayo's research from the 1920s has a great influence on management theories even today – his experiments at the Hawthorne plant demonstrated that an unhappy worker was also an unproductive worker, and the unhappiness stemmed from a deep-set feeling of isolation (Davies, 2015, p. 123).

But why would workers feel isolated? What is there about work and personal life under neoliberalism that makes people get detached from their co-operative, reciprocal, gregarious social selves? Are we not more connected by cybernetics and smartphone apps? Didn't Facebook enhance our capabilities to form new and international friendships? Or is the story of friendship under neoliberalism murky?

Referring to Dale Carnegie (the author of the popular book *How to Win Friends and Influence People*) Cutterham writes in his essay 'Just Friends' (2013):[18]

> His audience wasn't composed of sociopaths. When he advised his readers to smile, offer honest compliments, and talk about what interested other people, he wasn't suggesting they should do so only for what they might gain. He was advocating a better world, a friendlier world, one where things ran more smoothly and pleasantly for everyone. That fantasy sold to the tune of 15 million copies and counting. It's just that his vision of friendship – really, a vision of friendliness – couldn't

> escape the bounds set by mid-century corporate capitalism, and those were narrow bounds indeed. (Cutterham, 2013)

A sociological reflection on this crisis of sociability, friendship, care and warmth can be understood as the fallout of a capitalist modernity: self-interest seemed a much better conceptual tool than friendship for grasping and ordering this modern social world. Liberal thinkers such as Adam Smith assumed commercial society would make people more sociable, not less. After all, merchants had to have a basic level of mutual trust in order to do business with one another. To succeed in commerce, it was better to be friendly. Friendship thus drifted into a subordinate status – a by-product of self-interested rational behavior (Cutterham, 2013).

Under neoliberalism, people are often living a life full of 'friendliness' not friendships. In addition, a neoliberal subject has been inculcated to understand his biographical troubles as personal failures and as chemical imbalances in his brain. He looks away from critically reflecting on the socio-economic and structural conditions of his time. The neoliberal subjects are also taught to view themselves as commodities in the social marketplace – dating on Tinder; pictures on Instagram; and peer rating on LinkedIn. In this condition, for a neoliberal subject happiness is a decision and a concrete goal, which needs to be achieved through the consumption of well-being services (therapies, self-help books, gyms, meditation and mindfulness classes, laughing clubs, motivational speeches, mood enhancing drugs and so on). To him happiness is not an outcome or by-product of a good life that is well lived. By medicalizing people's anxieties (which stems from life under neoliberalism), the big pharma goes laughing to the bank. Another exponentially growing sector is Cognitive Behavioral Therapy (CBT). Many people,

> to get them through the (day and) night [consume] CBT, which teaches people to bypass unhelpful thoughts … [u]p to 43% of all therapy courses in Britain are now CBT, and the practice is increasing: around 6,000 new therapists have been trained since 2007 and CBT absorbs much public funding. In 2012, £213m went on a National Health Service programme delivering CBT, while £172m was spent on all other forms of psychoanalysis and psychotherapy … meanwhile the CBT boost has expanded the British therapy industry: since 2007, spending on psychotherapy has moved from 3% to 7% of Britain's mental health budget – the difference mostly spent on CBT … The British therapy boom is also a triumph for consumer choice: a recent survey showed patients preferred therapy to medication by a ratio of three to one.[19]

Under neoliberalism, the neoliberal subject is brainwashed by the discourse (such as compulsory individualization; high adaptability and self-entrepreneurship; and hedonistic and sovereign consumption) to forget to pause from his 24/7 'on' life and to ask – are the dominant cultural ideologies and social values of his time toxic and maleficent?

In *Bright-Sided: How Positive Thinking is Undermining America* (2010), Barbara Ehrenreich asks a simple yet poignant question: Is positive thinking a solution to all our problems? She critiqued the multi-billion dollar positive thinking industry by saying that it has a huge influence on the economy and how business is executed by Wall Street investors. The recently laid off workers struggling with two or more flexible contracts are inspired by the motivational gurus to be a good team player, that is, a positive person who smiles often, does not complain, is not too critical and submits to whatever the authority demands. These folks who are in fact disempowered in today's economy are made to believe in the new age religion of positive thinking such as – take control of your mind since you are infinitely powerful. It's the 'what's in your backpack' attitude that was elaborated in the film *Up in the Air*.

Drawing on Michel Foucault's theory of governmentality and neoliberalism, Nikolas Rose (1990) argues that psychology and the increasingly popular fields of therapy and counselling play a central organizing role in Western European and North American societies by contributing toward the construction of a particular type of subjectivity. Rose calls it the 'psychological self'. He argues that the contemporary psychological self organizes its subjectivity in a way that internalizes the logic of a neoliberal culture. Through the consumption of the therapeutic culture (e.g., self-help books, mindfulness and meditation classes), people engage in a form of self-governance that perpetuates a fast-paced capitalist consumer culture. This therapeutic culture also helps to maintain a social structure that empowers the wealthy elite and disempowers and exploits the poor.

The rise of a therapeutic culture under neoliberalism, which also gives rise to the discourse of positive thinking, makes people practice self-examination, self-regulation and self-construction, or what Foucault calls 'technologies of the self', so that people develop a neoliberal subjectivity, a subjectivity that thrives on self-care and an individualism. This neoliberal subjectivity helps one to commodify one's self as a commodity in a consumer culture. A professional social networking site such as LinkedIn resonates well with the commodification of a neoliberal subjectivity, where the neoliberal subject has to be self-sufficient, self-brandishing, self-branding and actively networking to keep going in an insecure economy, where good jobs are long dead. The neoliberal subject living in a therapeutic culture is conditioned to individualize (we would add spiritualize) and interiorize the source of his/her troubles. She/he also quickly learns to control their emotional reaction in order to be a nice team player in the workplace. It is clear now, why a psychosomatically fit worker will be much wanted by the managers of the new economy.

Furthermore, Nicole Aschoff writes in *The New Prophets of Capital* (2015) that mythmaking is as central to sustaining our neoliberal economy as profit-making, particularly as severe environmental degradation, breathtaking inequality, and increasing alienation among young people push capitalism up against its own contradictions, and the new prophets of capital emerge in the landscape. In this moment of crisis, a new generation of wealthy mythmakers, masquerading as progressive thinkers, has emerged to reinvent the free market as the solution to society's problems. For instance, Oprah rallies the poor to bootstrap their way into the middle class; while the Facebook chief executive Sheryl Sandberg calls on women to 'lean in' to the unequal demands of a sexist society. On the other hand, Bill and Melinda Gates offer the generosity of the 1% as the solution to a systemic inequality. Aschoff argues that these new prophets of capital strengthen the exploitative system, even as the cracks become more visible.

The back cover of Bifo Berardi's *The Soul at Work* (2009) reads:

> capital has managed to overcome the dualism of body and soul by establishing a workforce in which everything we mean by the Soul – language, creativity, affects – is mobilized for its own benefit. Industrial production put to work bodies, muscles, and arms. Now, in the sphere of

> digital technology and cyberculture, exploitation involves the mind, language, and emotions in order to generate value – while our bodies disappear in front of our computer screens.

A prime example of this phenomenon is the commercial profit that is generated through the use of the big data of our social media usage. On social media, folks share their stories, opinions, networks, pictures, likes and dislikes, all of which could be quantified and packaged into lucrative analytics to be lapped up by Manhattan's market researchers and advertisers. Thus, virtual socialization through social media is not precluded from commodification.

In addition, under neoliberalism's insecure climate:

> a new condition of alienation has taken root in which workers commonly and voluntarily work overtime, the population is tethered to mobile phones, debt has become a postmodern form of slavery, and antidepressants[20] are commonly used to meet the unending pressure of production. (Berardi 2009)

But what happens if you cannot ride the rising wave of neoliberal capitalism? What happens to the poor and the underclass of a neoliberal society? Wacquant in his *Punishing the Poor* (2009) shows how neoliberal restructuring is connected with the increase in penal policies. For the outcasts of neoliberalism, the new social reality is the penalization of precariousness, which is best summed up in a quote from George Bush – society itself doesn't cause crime, criminals cause the crime. With the demise of the social democratic state and with the rise of the unrestrained free market, globally a wide gap has been created between the rich and poor. As Wacquant argues in the time of discontinuous wage work – the disciplining and regulation of the working poor rely on the controlling arm of the penal state. He says that the rise of a neo-Darwinist state under neoliberalism erects competition and celebrates the cultural trope of individual responsibility. With the rapid privatization of the American prison system, another neoliberal feature, the poor are increasingly incarcerated on the grounds of their having made 'bad individual choices'. Thus, crime and poverty which are interrelated social problems are individualized and in the process private profits are further accumulated by the consuming elites. The ones with wasted lives, they also desire the Nikes and Hush Puppies of this world, but to them violence and riots remain the only available avenues to fulfill their consumption desires.

In sum, the politics involved in consumption can be broadly divided into three main dimensions: the manufacturing of consumer wants, especially the relative wants which sustain capitalism; the penetration of market values into non-market areas of human social life, leading to extreme insecurity, alienation, anxiety, frustration and unhappiness; and the reproduction of social and structural inequalities through consumption.

THEORETICAL EXPLORATIONS OF CONSUMPTION UNDER NEOLIBERALISM

Consumption in the neoliberal era performs two kinds of function for the economy. First, consumption calibrates the way goods and services are produced, not just to satisfy *real needs* but to fulfill *relative wants*. The relative want of the neoliberal era promotes the omnipresent notion of 'the customer' (Hall, 2011) who is endowed with a 'free choice' to buy products and services at the best price; this choice-making customer is also deemed as being always right in her/his decisions.

The nature of consumption, driven by relative wants, decides what is to be produced by the corporations. The advertisers and the market researchers examine and create the newer and newer relative wants (consumer demands). Recall the old marketing adage – if you can sell a fridge to a Greenlander, you have matured into a sales honcho. Today, more and more resources are allocated for the production of objects and services like life-style choices, which give higher returns on capital employed. Ultimately, the whole purpose of the discourse of consumerism is to engender and disseminate a consumer psyche, which wants the latest commodities, even if the consumer has to mess up his/her credit score.

From the perspective of critical social theory, the question remains – how the fictitious consumerist dream to consume the latest and the best, even at the peril of becoming swamped in debt, would influence the way a person conducts his/her self in the everyday social world? Would it create a new subjectivity, characterized by a commodified self, who has numbed all his cognitive and physical capabilities to resist consumerism? We want to look at these questions from two angles.

First, we will examine consumption as a part of the neoliberal economic structure, which in turn has been founded upon public policies of the state and capital's constant drive to make production more efficient. Sociologically speaking, an individual's subject formation is incubated and embedded within the socio-economic structure of a historical time. Therefore, any resistance from the subject should be primarily directed at the state policies and capital's exploitative practices on the shop floors where goods are produced. The above broadly represents the Marxist understanding of neoliberalism and its relationship with consumption.

The second perspective is derived from Foucault, in particular from his works such as *The Birth of Biopolitics* (2008) and *Society Must be Defended* (2003). Foucault understands neoliberal subjectivity in the following way: the commodities produced in the neoliberal period are not only for consumption, but they are a part of an individual's personification of the self through various means (e.g., the 'fit' body gained by visiting the gym, the youthful look regained through the use of anti-aging products, the calm mind achieved by drinking herbal tea in the afternoon, and the cool attitude maintained amidst toxic office politics by reading self-help books or by visiting the therapist). This results in the creation of a micro-power structure of self-governance and self-regulation by the subject.

We would add here that this micro-power structure, which is instituted through a neoliberal mode of consumption (e.g., the consumption of wellness and self-care products), leads to the consolidation of the ideology of 'possessive individualism'.[21] This individualism is all about self-centrism, competition and accumulation. The substantive values of 'being co-operative, being warm and friendly' as ends in themselves do not resonate well with this ideology. Just like the dog-eat-dog world of competing firms, human beings must compete with each other to optimize and extract their capability, efficiency, energy and resources.

Therefore, in the Foucauldian perspective, the nature of resistance under neoliberalism should not only be directed against the state-led neoliberal policies, but the resistance should also encounter the neoliberal discursive practices (pervasive in today's mediated messages and corporate-funded advertisements) that form and sustain the neoliberal subjectivity.

The Marxist perspective sees the emergence of the neoliberal ideology as a part of the political program of the new capitalists of the phase of financialized capitalism which began around the oil crisis of the 1970s. To the Marxist theorists, the opposition to neoliberalism should start by interrogating the politics of the neoliberal state. Whereas, from Foucault's perspective, the self-regulating, self-examining, individualized and competitive subject of neoliberalism is all about 'the quotidian experience of buying and selling commodities from the market which is then extended across social spaces' (Read, 2009, p. 26), for example buying wellness services, reading self-help books, and commodifying and externalizing care work. This neoliberal subject has to resist the micro-structure of power by questioning his/her micro-level experience. From this perspective, the neoliberal human existence is like a deadend tunnel, it is mired in hopelessness and futility. In the next few paragraphs, we will discuss these two different theoretical perspectives regarding what they say about the rationale and social impact of consumption under neoliberalism.

The starting point for a materialist understanding of the spectacle of consumerism in the neoliberal era is Marx's contention that production and consumption are intertwined as 'the individual produces an object and, by consuming it, returns to himself, but returns as a productive and self-reproducing individual. Consumption thus appears as a moment of production' (Marx, 2003, p. 94). The synchronization of the operation of production and consumption is a part of the inherent dynamic nature of capitalism, which is constantly revolutionizing the productive forces, whereby, 'all that is solid melts into air, all that is holy is profaned' (Marx, 1848). The continuous creative destruction[22] of the mode of production means not only new ways of producing commodities but also a perpetual churning out of new and refined consumer goods unknown to human history. One of the ways neoliberal capitalism is different from the liberal capitalism of the nineteenth and twentieth centuries is its ability, mediated by digital technology, to accelerate the production-consumption process. The 'political economic practices'[23] (Harvey, 2005, p. 2) of neoliberalism has practically eliminated the time-space differences not only within the production system but also between production and consumption through the acceleration in the circulation of commodities in the product's life-cycle. The various financialization programs (e.g., 0% interest for buying a new car),[24] hyper accelerate this process, which 'speeds commodities through the process of exchange, increasing capital's turnover, the rate at which it changes from commodity into money and then back into the labour process that creates yet more commodities' (Dyer-Witheford, 2015, p. 82).

Therefore, any understanding of consumption has to start with the political economy of the production of commodities and the latter's link with the realization of the surplus value accumulation through the path of consumerism, where a human being is only seen as a *demand creator machine*. The machine's only purpose is to have more and more consumption in order to 'Accumulate, accumulate! That is Moses and the prophets! (Marx, 1867). One of the root causes of the crisis of capital accumulation of the 1970s 'affected everyone through the combination of rising unemployment and accelerating inflation' (Harvey, 2007, p. 27). The discourse of 'individualized entrepreneurship and consumerism' were touted against the 'inefficiency' of the welfare economy in order to drum up support for the ideology of freedom of choice and self-aggrandizement. While the economic crisis of the twentieth-century state-led welfare capitalism, has triggered the emergence of neoliberal capitalism, the Manhattan-Street-driven aggressive consumer culture was seen as a derivative of commodity production, that is, the relentless drive of capital to extract surplus value after every round of production-consumption cycle. After all what is produced has to be sold, and one of the ways to do this is through the 'manipulation' of the human mind by creating artificial human needs (e.g., the TV dinner, perfumed garbage bags, eye lash extensions, the skinny latte, the foundation cream to produce pore-less porcelain faces and so on).

The theoretical postulates of treating production and consumption under neoliberalism as a political-economic project, that Peck refers to as a macroinstitutionalist path (Peck, 2013, p. 141), has been questioned in recent times by critical scholars of various persuasions (Brown, 2015; Lazzarato, 2014; Oksala, 2015; Read, 2009). These scholars draw on Foucault's theory of the difference between classical liberalism and neoliberalism (Foucault, 2008), and Antonio Negri's theory of the production of neoliberal subjectivity (Negri, 1989), under conditions when factories are no longer the centers of subject formation. Rather, capital has crossed the spatial boundaries of factories and entered into our 'life process', obliterating the differences between work place and home, state and civil society, production and social reproduction. There has been a change of the spatial configuration '... the relations of capitalist exploitation are expanding everywhere, not limited to the factory but tending to occupy the entire social terrain ... the dialectic between productive forces and the system of domination no longer has a determinate place' (Hardt and Negri, 2000, p. 209).

The influential critical academic works on media, information and technology seldom use the concept of class or mode of production as a tool of analysis to explain the restructuring of the global economy in terms of the contestation between capital's offensive to subordinate living labor by machines (fixed capital) for surplus appropriation, and the working class's push back for survival. Rather, globalization and neoliberalism are explained (e.g., Brown, 2015; Oksala, 2015) as 'technological enframing' of human relations, where the subject's position is defined by being 'market actors – consumers, individual investors and entrepreneurs – across several dimensions of their lives' (Oksala, 2015, para 17). This forms the neoliberal subject in the cybernetics world, where acceleration of production processes and financialization have turned subject-agency into fragments of multiple identity defined by the consciousness of 'homo oeconomics' (Brown, 2015).

In Foucault's understanding, while liberalism posits human beings as an economic subject ('homo economics'), in neoliberalism this subject position is extended to the governance of the individual to a particular manner of living. Here, consumption plays the most vital role through self-caring and the search for an 'individualized' wellness. This leads to, as Negri (1989) put it, the production of a subjectivity that is more than a political program managed by the state and the corporations; rather society as a whole becomes a marketplace of commodities satisfying the consumer needs of the individual created through an effective control of information and communication about the products. So consumption is not restricted to consuming a pizza produced at a pizza factory, but first of all it is the consumption of information about the taste, size, thickness, toppings, price, ingredients, coupons, apps and websites that will meet the individual's customized criteria of satisfaction. 'The consumer is no longer limited to consuming commodities (destroying them in the act of consumption). On the contrary, his or her consumption should be productive in accordance to the necessary conditions and the new products' (Lazzarato, n.d.). Under neoliberalism and cybernetics, consumption is first of all a consumption of information. Consumption is no longer only the 'realization' of a product, but a real and proper social process that for the moment is defined with the term communication (Lazzarato, n.d.). The information systems associated with the production of a commodity are not produced within the factory space as a part of material production. They are part of '"immaterial" production: audiovisual production, advertising, fashion, the production of software, photography, cultural activities, and so forth', created and produced across the society beyond the factory space (Lazzarato, n.d.).

Lazzarato defines immaterial labor as 'the labor that produces the informational and cultural content of the commodity' (Lazzarato, 1996, p. 133). The proliferation of the service sector and knowledge-based work can be classified as immaterial work. The separation of material labor from immaterial labor has been questioned in a few academic works (Camfield, 2007; Dyer-Witheford and Sharman, 2005; Gill and Prat, 2008). The main argument against this separation is that there is no clear-cut distinction between material and immaterial work. As Camfield notes, for the hospital workers who do both affective labor as well as manual work such as cleaning bedpans, the distinction vanishes (Camfield, 2007, p. 3). For Lazzarato:

> From a strictly economic point of view, the cycle of reproduction of immaterial labor dislocates the production-consumption relationship as it is defined as much by the 'virtuous Keynesian circle' as by the Marxist reproduction schemes of the second volume of *Capital*. Now, rather than speaking of the toppling of 'supply and demand,' we should speak about a redefinition of the production-consumption relationship. (Lazzarato, n.d.)

In this redefinition, Lazzarato thinks that we have to include communication as this is already inscribed in the commodity from the beginning of production. 'Consumption is no longer only the "realization" of a product, but a real and proper social process that for the moment is defined with the term communication' (Lazzarato, n.d.). The communication inscribed in commodities creates its own subjectivity of defining the self – the consumer. It is not enough to just talk about production and consumption, rather we have to look at the entire information ecosystem to understand the process of neoliberal consumption.

On the other hand, Wendy Brown views the neoliberal economy as creating its own zone of the discursive practice of 'neoliberal reason'. In Wendy Brown's recent book *Undoing the Demos: Neoliberalism's Stealth Revolution*, neoliberalism is not construed 'as a set of state policies, a phase of capitalism or an ideology that set loose the market to restore profitability for a capitalist class' (Brown, 2015, p. 29). But as Brown says, 'I join Michel Foucault and others in conceiving neoliberalism as an order of normative reason that, when it becomes ascendant, takes shape as a governing rationality extending a specific formulation of economic values, practices and metrics to every dimension of human life' (Brown, 2015, p. 30). From this she concludes that 'This governing rationality involves … "economization" of heretofore noneconomic spheres and practices, a process of remaking the knowledge, form, content, and conduct appropriate to these spheres and practices' (Brown, 2015, pp. 30–31).

The commodification of every aspect of life's activity is best represented through the memoir of Elizabeth Gilbert's *Eat, Pray and Love* (*EPL*) (2006). *EPL* is a memoir of an unhappy marriage, suffering from depression and the subsequent search for spiritual emancipation, all documented in Gilbert's hugely popular book and movie.[25] Ironically, the search for *nirvana* away from the daily grind of meeting expectations surrounded by glamour and the material comfort of food, gadgets and entertainment, often ends up in people consuming more products, which are more often than not very expensive (e.g., spiritual tourism, therapy classes, gem stones with healing powers, exotic organic food and branded workout gear). The neoliberal individuality spills over into the spiritual realm, where the individual's search for a peaceful and tranquil life, away from the harsh material reality, ends up doing the same thing that Gilbert was unhappy with. *EPL* does not only narrate Gilbert's sincere quest for a spiritual journey away from the consumptive drudgery of life, it also showcases the brands that surround Gilbert in her pleasure travel, experiencing food in Italy, prayer in India and peace in Bali. As Ruth Williams notes:

> Products that bear the Eat, Pray, Love (EPL) brand (both officially and unofficially) range from perfume, tea, yoga gear, prayer beads, and jewelry to EPL-themed travel tours that include spa treatments, visits to temples, and copious amounts of yoga and meditations – all activities Gilbert herself partook in as she wrote her book. (Williams, 2014, p. 613)

The example of the mix of spiritual journey with materiality is something that clearly shows how consumption is connected with today's material and immaterial production processes.

EPL is an example of how 'neoliberal reason' that creates a consummative subjectivity is related to the macro aspects of production, distribution and marketing of commodities. Negri, Lazzarato and Brown look at the micro-level relationships between the individual and the commodified fetish objects, through the prism of neoliberal subjectivity, whereas, Harvey's contention is that the 'political-economic practices' of the state play an important role in the construction of a neoliberal subjectivity by implementing neoliberal policies to satisfy capital's relentless need for surplus value extraction. If any one of the above two theoretical perspectives replace the other, we will lose the totality in our analysis of the politics of consumption under neoliberalism. In our understanding, we should neither forget the forest to count individual trees, nor should we miss that the forest is populated by numerous trees.

CONCLUSION

A recent report says:

> Gen Z already makes up 23 percent of the U.S. population. This generation moves seamlessly between digital behaviors and real life. They are already highly proactive participants in health

> and wellness: Gen Z knows a lot (or think they do), and they think a lot about being 'balanced'. More so than any other generation, Gen Z looks to exercise as a way to treat or prevent illness, and it is particularly relevant for emotional and stress-related issues. For Gen Z, technology is fun, entertaining and useful. These young consumers are learning about what is healthy from their parents and from school ... Outside of direct family, Gen Z is more likely than all other generations to look to their online social networks for advice on health and wellness.[26]

Take another related social trend from a different geography – twenty-first century India. Gauri Pathak notes that since the 1990s, when neoliberal reforms started taking place in India, a new socio-cultural environment has set in. 'Economic growth, globalizing discourses, and new consumer choices have driven desires for new global-yet-Indian identities. An emerging consumer agency has allowed for the embodiment and performance of these identities at the site of the body, even as [sic] new spaces of consumption has necessitated new bodily dispositions and practices' (Pathak, 2014, p. 314). Pathak shows how physical appearance and the notion of exercising consumer agency to be 'presentable' are microcosms through which the creation of neoliberal subjects in India can be delineated.

These examples highlight how the consumption of products and services from the wellness and self-care sector is forming and sustaining neoliberal subjects in developed and rapidly developing centers of capitalism. These neoliberal subjects in turn drive the movement of the cycle of production-consumption in the phase of financialized capitalism. Instead of interrogating the unjust structure of the political-economy, which leads to growing precariousness, overwork, stress, anxiety, indebtedness and depression among the workers, the neoliberal subjects individualize the social problem, and they resort to buying commodified wellness, self-care and therapeutic products. They start believing that 'only those who are at peace within themselves, can bring peace to the world'.[27] They fail to wear their *sociological bifocals*, which would endow them with the vision of sociological imagination.[28] This imagination helps one to see how one's personal troubles under neoliberalism are deeply connected with the structural problems of the time, which affect the working majority, the collectivity.

The neoliberal subject, who suffers from long hours of work, the crisis of care, time poverty, social depletion, rising household debt, insatiable relative wants, is not even free from the clutches from consumerism when she wants to unwind and relax, since leisure activities with gadgets and cybernetics are saturated with shrill calls for consumption. Ultimately, consumption under neoliberal capitalism imposes new forms of homogeneity in our personhood and subjectivity, which undermines our capabilities of critical interrogation and of transformative collective action. In contrast, the neoliberal subjects remain isolated, atomized and fragmented by the dominant ideologies of compulsory individualism, competition, entrepreneurship, self-care, and the individualization and interiorization of social problems. In other words, the erstwhile idea of collective responsibility in finding solutions to macro-social problems is destabilized and seduced by the consumption of self-care and wellness products under neoliberalism.

Let us not forget that any discussion of the politics of consumption under neoliberalism has to consider the bizarre phenomena of over-consumption and hunger that divide our world even today. Since, consumption is an integral part of the political-economic structure of neoliberal capitalism, we still need to ask the following questions. How has development (in the underdeveloped regions) become the password for imposing a new kind of dependency, for enriching the already rich world and for shaping other societies to meet its commercial and political needs (George, 1977, p. xvii)? Why do some 795 million people in the world not have enough food to lead a healthy active life (that is about one in nine people on earth) (World Food Program, 2015)? Why does the hunger of 800 million co-exist another mind-blowing fact – that one billion people on this planet are overweight (Patel, 2007, p. 1).

But how to produce a counter-narrative to neoliberal subjectivity and consumption? Jamie Hakim, writes that the joylessness in the pursuit of wellness services can lead to resistance by the neoliberal subject (Hakim, 2015, p. 193). The individualization and interiorization of social pathologies that are demanded by our contemporary consumer culture of self-care and therapy need to be critiqued and discarded before we can grasp and fight against rising relative poverty, precarious employment, pervasive intolerance and violence, global poverty, war mongering, ecological degradation and the destruction of a cosmopolitan civil society.

Socrates wrote that an unexamined life has no meaning. In our insecure neoliberal times, the anxiety-ridden relentless consumption of material objects and immaterial services, ranging from anti-wrinkle face creams, post-workout protein shakes to therapy and mindfulness sessions, search for endless self-improvement to fit in, and to outshine the Janes and the Johns. In the process, the neoliberal subject's life becomes over-examined by the expertise of therapy and mindfulness practices. Ironically, this over-examination and self-care is so thoroughly co-opted by the marketing logic of 'remain dissatisfied to buy more' that it undermines the development of a reflexive, truly confident and poised subject. We need to ask why for people living under neoliberalism even being happy is a matter of decision. Why cannot they be happy by the virtue of living a happy life in a good society? Why cannot they enjoy the reality of '*Sat-Chit-Ananda*' (existence-consciousness-bliss) as outlined in an ancient philosophical text *The Upanishads*?

Notes

1 http://www.globalwellnessinstitute.org/press-room/statistics-and-facts/
2 http://databank.worldbank.org/data/download/GDP.pdf
3 http://www.forbes.com/sites/thehartmangroup/2015/11/19/consumer-trends-in-health-and-wellness/#72e58ce94be7
4 Lalu Prasad Jadav – http://indianexpress.com/article/india/india-news-india/narendra-modi-reliance-jio-ad-lalu-prasad-yadav-3011910/
5 http://www.livemint.com/Opinion/tCa2Zby4s6BWTONQJDqj3O/Most-people-cannot-afford-fruits-and-vegetables-says-Lancet.html
6 http://news.adobe.com/press-release/digital-marketing/adobe-reports-falling-consumer-goods-prices-six-consecutive
7 http://www.bloomberg.com/news/articles/2015-07-01/milk-spilled-into-manure-pits-as-supplies-overwhelm-u-s-dairies
8 http://documents.worldbank.org/curated/en/700061468334490682/pdf/95768-REVISED-WP-PUBLIC-Box391467B-Ending-Poverty-and-Hunger-by-2030-FINAL.pdf
9 See Mark Simpson, The Metrosexual is Dead: Long Live the Spornosexual, 10.6.14: http://www.telegraph.co.uk/men/fashion-and-style/10881682/The-metrosexual-is-dead.-Long-live-the-spornosexual.html

10 For an application of Baudrillard's theory of simulacra to Indian advertising and gendered body work see Anisha Datta (2014).
11 See the next section titled 'Theoretical Explorations of Consumption under Neoliberalism' for elaboration.
12 See Juliet Schor (1993). Also see Hermann (2015).
13 Check for example, José van Dijck (2013).
14 Founded in 1981 by Sri Sri Ravi Shankar, The Art of Living is an educational and humanitarian movement engaged in stress management and service initiatives. The organization operates globally in 155 countries and has touched the lives of millions of people. More information can be found at https://www.srisriravishankar.org/sudarshan-kriya/ [retrieved Oct. 16, 2017]
15 http://www.artofliving.org/ca-en/about-us
16 Strong recovery of the global health and wellness market is on the way, with sales recording 6.5% value growth (fixed exchange rates) in 2011. Products offering specific health benefits or those renowned for their natural health properties drove value sales, with rates above 7%. Growth was further fueled by the developments in the emerging markets, as China and Brazil alone contributed US$15 billion in new sales that year. Steady real-term growth of 7.2% (current prices) is expected to continue to 2017, with global health and wellness sales on the way to hit a record high of US$1 trillion by 2017. http://blog.euromonitor.com/2012/11/health-and-wellness-the-trillion-dollar-industry-in-2017-key-research-highlights.html
17 Check the link above.
18 http://thenewinquiry.com/essays/just-friends/
19 http://www.economist.com/news/britain/21623773-popularity-cbt-freezing-out-more-traditional-forms-therapy-expanding-shrinks
20 Anti-depressant use is high among Canadians: http://www.macleans.ca/authors/amanda-shendruk/infographic-canadians-and-antidepressants/
21 On possessive individualism see MacPherson (2012).
22 Joseph Schumpeter popularized this concept in economics by drawing on Marx's theory of Historical Materialism.
23 According to Harvey, the 'political economic practices' are: (1) an ideology that strives for the efficiency of the market through privatization of state services; (2) a mode of governance with least state interference; (3) a policy package consisting of work flexibility, casualization of the workforce, and accumulation through dispossession of poor peasants from the land, particularly in developing societies like China and India; (4) the financialization of money markets; and (5) the adoption of cybernetics-centered technology in the production and distribution of commodities (Harvey, 1992, 2005).
25 [T]he book has spent, as of December 3, 2010, 199 weeks on the *New York Times* paperback non-fiction bestseller list, with conservative estimates projecting at least US$15 million in earnings for the book's publisher, Penguin. Book sales received a bump in August 2010, with the release of a long-awaited film adaptation of *Eat, Pray, Love* starring Julia Roberts. Currently, box office sales for the film total more than US$180 million, with additional dollars expected from showings in international venues.
26 http://www.forbes.com/sites/thehartmangroup/2015/11/19/consumer-trends-in-health-and-wellness/#336757d34be7
27 A quote from Sri Sri Ravi Shankar, the founder of the Art of Living.
28 The concept of sociological imagination comes from C. Wright Mills (1959).

REFERENCES

Aschoff, Nicole. (2015). *The New Prophets of Capital*. New York: Verso Books.
Barthes, Rolland. (2013). *Mythologies*. New York: Farrar, Straus and Giroux.

Baudrillard, Jean. (1981). *For a Critique of the Political Economy of Sign*. St Louis, MO: Telos Press.
Bauman, Zygmunt. (2012). *Liquid Modernity*. Cambridge, UK. Polity Press.
Berardi, Franco 'Bifo'. (2009). *The Soul at Work: From Alienation to Autonomy*. Los Angeles: Semiotext(e).
Bordo, Susan. (1993). *Unbearable Weight: Feminism, Western Culture, and the Body*. Berkeley: University of California Press.
Bordo, Susan. (2003). *Unbearable Weight: Feminism, Western Culture, and the Body*. Berkeley, Calif: University of California Press.
Bourdieu, Pierre. (1984). *Distinction: A Social Critique of the Judgement of Taste*. Cambridge, MA. Harvard University Press.
Brown, Wendy. (2015). *Undoing the Demos: Neoliberalism's Stealth Revolution*. New York: Zone Books.
Butler, Samuel. (2012). *The Way of All Flesh*. MA, USA: Courier Corporation.
Camfield, David. (2007). The Multitude and the Kangaroo: A Critique of Hardt and Negri's Theory of Immaterial Labour. *Historical Materialism*, 15(2), 21–52.
Campbell, Collin. (1987). *The Romantic Ethic and the Spirit of Modern Consumerism*. Oxford: Blackwell.
Conley, Dalton. (2009). *Elsewhere, U.S.A.: How We Got from the Company Man, Family Dinners, and the Affluent Society to the Home Office, BlackBerry Moms, and Economic Anxiety*. New York: Pantheon Books.
Connell, Raewyn. (2009). *Gender: In World Perspective*. Cambridge, UK. Polity Press.
Connell, Raewyn. (2011). The Neoliberal Parent: Mothers and Fathers in Market Society. In *Confronting Equality – Gender, Knowledge and Global Change*. Cambridge, UK: Polity Press.
Cutterham, John. (2013). Just Friends. *The New Inquiry*, 23. Retrieved from http://thenewinquiry.com/essays/just-friends/
Datta, Anisha. (2014). The Unfairness of Being Fair. In P. Chakravarty (Ed.), *Shrapnel Minima: Writings from Humanities Underground*. London: Seagull Books.
Davies, William. (2015). *The Happiness Industry*. New York City: Verso.
duCille, Ann. (1996). *Skin Trade*. Cambridge, MA. Harvard University Press.
Dyer-Witheford, Nick. (2015). *Cyber-Proletariat: Global Labour in the Digital Vortex*. London. Pluto Press.
Dyer-Witheford, Nick and Sharman, Zena. (2005). The Political Economy of Canada's Video and Computer Game Industry. *Canadian Journal of Communications* 30(2), 187–210.
Eagleton-Pierce, Mathew. (2016). *Neoliberalism: The Key Concepts*. London: Routledge.
Ehrenreich, Barbara. (2010). *Bright-sided: How Positive Thinking Is Undermining America*. London. Picador.
Euromonitor International. (2012, Nov 29). *Health and Wellness the Trillion Dollar Industry in 2017: Key Research Highlights*. http://blog.euromonitor.com/2012/11/health-and-wellness-the-trillion-dollar-industry-in-2017-key-research-highlights.html
Expanding the shrinks. *The Economist* (2014, Oct 11). Retrieved from http://www.economist.com/news/britain/21623773-popularity-cbt-freezing-out-more-traditional-forms-therapy-expanding-shrinks
Fiske, John. (1989). *Reading the Popular*. Boston: Unwin Hyman.
Foucault, M. (2003). *Society Must be Defended: Lectures at the Collège de France, 1975–76*. (David Macey, Trans.). New York: Picador.
Foucault, M. (2008). *The Birth of Biopolitics: Lectures at the Collège de France, 1978–1979*. London: Palgrave Macmillan.

Forbes. (2015, Nov. 19). *Consumer Trends in Health and Wellness*. Retrieved from http://www.forbes.com/sites/thehartmangroup/2015/11/19/consumer-trends-in-health-and-wellness/#336757d34be7

Frank, Thomas. (1997). *The Conquest of Cool*. Chicago. The University of Chicago Press.

Friedan, Betty. (2013). *The Feminine Mystique*. New York: W.W. Norton & Company.

Galbraith, J.K. (1998). *The Affluent Society*. New York: Houghton Mifflin Company.

George, Susan. (1977). *How the Other Half Dies: The Real Reasons for World Hunger*. Montclair: Allanheld, Osmun & Co. Publishers.

Gilbert, Elizabeth. (2006). *Eat, Pray, Love: One Woman's Search for Everything Across Italy, India and Indonesia*. London: Penguin Books.

Gill, Rosalind and Prat, Andy. (2008). In the Social Factory? Immaterial Labour, Precariousness and Cultural Work. *Theory and Society*, 25(7–8), 1–30.

Goldman, Robert and Papson, Stephanie. (1996). *Sign Wars*. New York: Guilford Press.

Hakim, J. (2015). 'Fit is the New Rich': Male Embodiment in the Age of Austerity. *Soundings*, 61, 84–94.

Hall, Stuart. (2011). The Neoliberal Revolution. *Cultural Studies*, 25(6), 705–728.

Hardt, M. and Negri, A. (2000). *Empire*. Boston: Harvard University Press.

Harvey, David. (1992). *The Condition of Postmodernity: An Enquiry into the Origins of Cultural Change*. Malden, MA: Wiley.

Harvey, David. (2007). *A Brief History of Neoliberalism*. Oxford. Oxford University Press.

Hermann, Christoph. (2015). 'Neoliberalism and the Surge in Work Hours'. In *Capitalism and the Political Economy of Work Time*. New York: Routledge.

Horkheimer, Max and Adorno, Theodore. (1982). The Culture Industry: Enlightenment as Mass Deception. In *Dialectic of Enlightenment*. New York. Continuum.

Lazzarato, M. (1996). Immaterial Labour. In Paolo Virno and Michael Hardy (Eds) *Radical Thought in Italy: A Potential Politics* (pp.132–146). Minnesota: University of Minnesota Press.

Lazzarato, M. (2014). *Signs and Machines* (Joshua David Jordan, Trans.). Los Angeles. Semiotext(e).

Lazzarato, M. (n.d.). *Immaterial Labour*. Generation-Online.org. Retrieved from http://www.generation-online.org/c/fcimmateriallabour3.htm

Levenson, Bob. (1987). *Bill Bernbach's Book: A History of the Advertising that Changed the History of Advertising*. New York. Villard Books.

MacPherson, C.B. (2012). Democratic Theory: Ontology and Technology. In *Democratic Theory: Essays in Retrieval* (pp. 24–38). New York: Oxford University Press.

McGuigan, Jim. (2014). The Neoliberal Self. *Culture Unbound*, 6, 223–240.

Marcuse, Herbert. (2002). *One Dimensional Man*. New York: Routledge.

Marshall, T.H. (1950). *Citizenship and Social Class: And Other Essays*. Cambridge, UK: Cambridge University Press.

Marx, Karl. (1848). *Manifesto of the Communist Party.* Marxists Internet Archive, Communist Manifesto (Chapter 1). Retrieved from https://www.marxists.org/archive/marx/works/1848/communist-manifesto/ch01.htm

Marx, Karl. (1867). *Conversion of Surplus-Value into Capital*. Marxists Internet Archive, Capital Volume One, Chapter 24. Retrieved from https://www.marxists.org/archive/marx/works/1867-c1/ch24.ht

Marx, Karl. (2003). *Grundrisse* (Martin Nicolaus, Trans.). London: Penguin Books Ltd.

Mills, C. Wright. (1959). *The Sociological Imagination*. New York: Oxford University Press.

Negri, Antonio. (1989). *The Politics of Subversion: A Manifesto for the twenty-first century*. Cambridge, UK: Polity Press.

Nietzsche, Friedrich. (1998). *Twilight of the Idols, or, How to Philosophize with a Hammer*. New York: Oxford University Press.

Oksala, Johanna. (2015). *Foucault, Marx and Neoliberal Subjects*. Retrieved from http://theoryculturesociety.org/johanna-oksala-on-foucault-marx-and-neoliberal-subjects/

Packard, Vance. (1981). *The Hidden Persuaders*. New York: Pocket Books.

Patel, Raj. (2007). *Stuffed and Starved: The Hidden Battle for the World's Food System*. Toronto: Harper Collins.

Pathak, Gauri. (2014). Presentable: The Body and Neoliberal Subjecthood in Contemporary India. *Social Identities*, 20(4–5), 314–329.

Peck, Jamie. (2013). Explaining (with) Neoliberalism. *Territory, Politics, Governance*, 1(2), 132–157.

Read, Jason. (2009). A Genealogy of Homo-Economicus: Neoliberalism and the Production of Subjectivity. *Foucault Studies*, 6, 25–36.

Rose, Nikolas. (1990). *Governing the Soul: The Shaping of the Private Self*. London: Routledge.

Sandberg. Sheryl. (2013). *Lean In: Women, Work, and the Will to Lead*. New York: Knopf Doubleday Publishing Group.

Schor, Juliet. (1993). *The Overworked American: The Unexpected Decline of Leisure*. New York: Basic Books.

Sennett, Richard. (1998). The Corrosion of Character: The Personal Consequences of Work in the New Capitalism. New York. W.W. Norton.

Shendruk, Amanda. (2013, Nov 23). Anti-Depressant Use High Among Canadians. *Macleans*. Retrieved from http://www.macleans.ca/authors/amanda-shendruk/infographic-canadians-and-antidepressants/

The Upanishads. (1969). London: Penguin Books. [Translated from Sanskrit by Juan Mascaro].

van Dijck, José. (2013). 'You Have One Identity': Performing the Self on Facebook and LinkedIn, Media, *Culture & Society*, 35(2), 199–215.

Veblen, Thorstein. (2000). *The Theory of the Leisure Class*. London: Transaction Publishers.

Venugopal, Rajesh. (2015). Neoliberalism as Concept. *Economy and Society*, 44(2), 165–187.

Wacquant, Loic. (2009). *Punishing the Poor: The Neoliberal Government of Social Insecurity*. Durham: Duke University Press.

Williams, Ruth. (2014). Eat, Pray, Love: Producing the Female Neoliberal Spiritual Subject. *The Journal of Popular Culture*, 47(3), 613–633.

World Bank. (2015). *Ending Poverty and Hunger by 2030: An Agenda for the Global Food System*. World Bank Group. Retrieved from http://documents.worldbank.org/curated/en/700061468334490682/pdf/95768-REVISED-WP-PUBLIC-Box391467B-Ending-Poverty-and-Hunger-by-2030-FINAL.pdf

World Bank. (2017). World Development Indicators database, World Bank. Retrieved from http://databank.worldbank.org/data/download/GDP.pdf

World Food Programme. (2015). Hunger Statistics, from *State of Food Insecurity in the World*, FAO. Retrieved from https://www.wfp.org/hunger/stats

Yadav, Lalu Prasad. (2016). Lalu Prasad Yadav takes a dig at Reliance Jio advertisement, says 'data is cheaper than atta'. Retrieved from http://economictimes.indiatimes.com/news/politics-and-nation/lalu-prasad-yadav-takes-a-dig-at-reliance-jio-advertisement-says-data-is-cheaper-than-atta/articleshow/53996682.cms

27

Sustainable Consumption, Consumer Culture and the Politics of a Megatrend

William Kilbourne, Pierre McDonagh and Andrea Prothero

INTRODUCTION

Three things must be clarified before we can proceed with the examination. These are the terms sustainability, politics and megatrend. Unfortunately, all three are ambiguous and few disciplines have arrived at a consistent definition for any of them. While we will not resolve the ambiguity to everyone's satisfaction, we will attempt to achieve an extensional bargain (Rappaport, 1953) through which we develop an understanding of how we are using the terms. First, sustainable development became a construct in 1987 through the Brundtland Report (Brundtland, 1987) and has remained ambiguous ever since. This is where we begin our examination of sustainable consumption. Megatrend, as a phenomenon, has been defined in a multitude of ways over the past thirty-five years. In this chapter, we adopt the criteria set forth by Mittelstaedt et al. (2014) for categorising megatrends, but will use a broader interpretation of what constitutes megatrends. Finally, our use of the term political will be broader than the more common use of the term relating to legal structures, laws or agencies, and include the underlying institutions that frame the more micro aspects of politics. This approach is necessary because of the scale of sustainability and megatrends in both time and space.

Using this broad, institutional-based approach, the authors consider the swing in popularity of sustainability and the various solutions provided to the extent that there is discussion of sustainability as megatrend. We ask what changes have occurred in the past and how they affect the politics surrounding sustainable consumption that might enable humanity to feel confident and competent to now offer up solutions to the challenge of sustainability. But before this can be accomplished, it is critical to have a better understanding of the institutional underpinnings of the politics and economics of sustainability: how we got where we are now and what the prospects for the future are. There is no apparent consensus on whether sustainability is a megatrend or even what that means. Mittelstaedt et al. (2014) argue from the perspective of paradigms that sustainability is the new megatrend, while Scott, Martin and Schouten (2014), arguing from the perspective of growing materialism, are not as convinced. This is an anomalous result if one considers that materialism is contained within the Western paradigm (Kilbourne, Dorsch et al., 2009). Varey (2012) offers a third, and more prescient point in terms of the relationship between sustainability and megatrends. He argues that sustainability is larger than a megatrend in its impact and evolution.

To better understand the varying conclusions about sustainability and its prospects, we develop an historical perspective of the changing patterns of economic and political structures (these are considered inseparable) and the evolution of the underlying institutional structures that are firmly in place. This constitutes the Dominant Social Paradigm (DSP) of Western societies (Kilbourne, McDonagh and Prothero, 1997) that includes the political, economic and technological perspectives that constitute its worldview. It is against this backdrop that sustainability as a megatrend will be examined.

The approach to be taken here falls in the general area of the New Political Economy (NPE) that treats economic institutions as the relevant phenomena to be explained by political economy. NPE is said to examine economic doctrines to better understand their political content. It examines economic ideas and behaviour as beliefs and actions that must themselves be explained and that are not taken-for-granted behaviours that are self-evidently rational and, as a result, do not need further analysis (Bauman, 1998). This we hold to be the essence of being immersed in a prevailing structure, or in the DSP of society. In Western industrial societies it is the institutions of the DSP, whatever those may be, that initiate, direct and reward economic beliefs and behaviours. These come to be so prevalent that they become so self-evidently true to the extent that behaving in any other way becomes irrational. Or as Marcuse (1963) states it, beliefs become 'irrational in their rationality'. Our approach in constructing this framework is a synthesis of Kilbourne, McDonagh and Prothero's (1997) use of the DSP and the NPE emphasising the theory of Antonio Gramsci (1971). Thus, the focus will be on the sustainability of consumption as it is currently practised relating to both its quality and quantity, and, in doing this, we will attend both to the genesis of what may be called cultures of consumption (Featherstone, 2007) and the role that consumption can play in ameliorating its own condition through market actions such as, for example, the political consumer (Connolly and Prothero, 2008; Trentmann, 2007).

Here we examine sustainability to determine its position within the prevailing historical context that might be called late modern capitalism. We provide a brief historical assessment of the development of the relevant institutions, and then we provide some likely scenarios that might develop in the future depending on whether sustainability is a new megatrend, or if its internal logic is insufficient to change the direction of globalisation, consumption and the future. What this suggests is that, if current modes of consumption are not globally sustainable, as has been frequently pointed out in recent years (O'Connor, 1994), then there is an inevitable conflict between the culture of consumption and nature, or a conflict between sustainably minded consumers who want to consume less and producers who must produce more.

MEGATRENDS

Since Naisbitt's (1982) first book on megatrends, many others have embarked on the search for megatrends. Foremost among them are the major global consulting firms including Price Waterhouse Coopers, Ernst and Young, KPMG, Frost and Sullivan, and Arthur D. Little. Other public policy organisations such as the Mowat Centre, Konrad-Adenauer-Stiftung and the Council of State Governments have entered the field as well. However, there has not arisen as yet a formal definition of megatrends that is used by everyone. There is a consensus on the general idea of a megatrend that we will adopt for this chapter, and it is that provided by Frost and Sullivan (2017) as, 'Megatrends are global, sustained, macroeconomic forces of development that affect business, economies, societies, cultures, and personal lives. In essence, these trends—such as urbanization, connectivity and convergence—will define our future world'.

While the definition is sufficiently broad to take in most of what are considered megatrends today, it is not sufficiently precise as not to be ambiguous. We could not, for example apply this definition to a particular trend and determine whether or not it is a 'mega' trend. This reduces us to making a subjective judgement and suggests that there might be different opinions on a particular trend regarding the precise meaning of macro, sustained or global. But this is an inherent difficulty of all definitions: they are ambiguous at the margins, and this is acknowledged by the authors. The ambiguity is reflected in the identification of megatrends by the organisations that study them on a regular basis (those mentioned above). We now provide a synthesis of megatrends that have been developed by the above organisations. We also categorise the trends in a general classification scheme presented in Table 27.1.

Each of the megatrends in Table 27.1 was mentioned by one or more of the organisations studying them. While the list is not exhaustive, it provides exemplars of what the organisations consider global megatrends. It can also be seen that some megatrends can fall in different categories, and some may question whether a particular trend is a megatrend.

Of particular note in Table 27.1 is that while resource shortages and climate change are mentioned, sustainability is not. Why this is the case is uncertain, but we can speculate on the possibilities. The first is simply that the term sustainability is not yet sufficiently widespread to be in the vocabulary of those doing the judging. Sustainability is, as will be shown in the next section, still not clearly understood. It also has meanings beyond those concerned with nature; being a sustainable entity for example could refer to an organisation's green credentials or its economic

Table 27.1 Classification of megatrends

Demographic	*Economic*	*Political*	*Technological*	*Ecological*	*Globalisation*
Urbanisation	Poverty	Participation	Information	Climate	Power Centre
Aging	Power Shift	Inequality	Health	Resources	Markets
Middle Class	Integration	Interventions	Energy	Eco-Energy	Brain Drain
Gender	New Models	Nationalism	Biotechnology	Conflict	World Trade
Population	Prosumption		Privacy		

viability. Within marketing, sustainability was frequently used interchangeably with environmentalism, although in recent years there has been a focus on sustainable marketing. All of the megatrends mentioned by the organisations above are mentioned in the context of business opportunities rather than problems. As we will argue later, sustainability is probably not an opportunity for achieving long-term competitive advantage but is, instead, an imperative that will impose itself on all business activity in the not too distant future. This is where the ambiguity of time enters the megatrend discussion.

There is no definite time frame included in any of the megatrend studies. They simply refer to 'long run' changes in strategies and objectives. From the megatrends in Table 27.1, it can be inferred that some will last longer than others, and that during the period, product offerings and consumer demands will change. What is important in this is the nature of the changes wrought by the megatrend, and the changes will certainly vary according to context. Most will involve changing cost structures for firms and prices for consumers. In addition, methods of distribution and marketing communications will likely change to reorient consumption practices. While the Internet of Things has only recently been discussed in any depth, Rifkin's (2015) book is about an emerging megatrend that might have tremendous consequences for the business model. The title, *The Zero Marginal Cost Society*, is self-explanatory. When the marginal cost of production approaches zero, the ramifications for marketing and consumption will be large indeed. But these are strategic changes within the normal course of business activities. The major question with which we are concerned is the ramifications for sustainable consumption. If the price of consumer goods reflects the marginal cost, then prices will necessarily decline and consumption of those goods will increase, further exacerbating the problem of sustainable consumption unless the ecological cost of goods diminishes commensurably. This question can be inferred from Varey's (2013) term, mega-megatrend. Is sustainability a megatrend requiring adaptation (McDonagh and Prothero 2014a) or is it something greater that will require a fundamental shift in the institutional structure of the consumer society? To address this question, we must first establish an extensional bargain on what constitutes sustainability.

SUSTAINABILITY

Because sustainability has been a substantive issue in consumer research for almost thirty years now, it would seem that its meaning would have been established with some consistency by this time. Such is not the case however, and it appears that the term has become more confused than at its original conception in 'Our Common Future' (Brundtland, 1987) (also known as the Brundtland Report). The most often quoted definition of sustainable development is 'development that meets the needs of the present without compromising the ability of future generations to meet their own needs' (p. 43). While it has been acknowledged over the years that this definition is somewhat ambiguous and, therefore, can't be used as a tool or measure, its implications can be used as a conceptual guideline. O'Connor (1994), for example, suggests a triple meaning from the definition of 'sustain' itself. He argues that it implies a system that stays on course, provides the necessities of life for people around the globe, and endures over time in the face of challenges.

It can be inferred from this description of sustainability generally, that it would impose significant restraints (challenges) on firms, consumers and governments. But the magnitude of these restraints can only be discussed if we clarify the different degrees of sustainability being referred to. Unfortunately, within the past twenty years or so, the term sustainable has remained opaque. To help alleviate this ambiguity, we propose a continuum of sustainability rather than different terms. We see sustainability activities as a continuum flowing between strong and weak sustainability. Buying greener products for environmental reasons would be weak sustainability while incorporating eco-rationality into one's daily behaviour would be stronger sustainability. Deep ecology as proposed by Naess (1973) would be strong sustainability. Such an environmental continuum was originally proposed by Kilbourne (1995).

Making the production and/or distribution process more eco-efficient is characteristic of weak sustainability because it implies doing what we have always done, but doing it better and more eco-efficiently. It means reducing the throughput in the system while maintaining or increasing the output (getting more for less). But it does not require fundamental changes in consumption practices. The question then becomes, if we use this approach exclusively, will it eventually achieve strong sustainability? The answer is a resounding 'probably not'. But if such activities as voluntary simplicity (Rudmin and Kilbourne, 1995), adopting the anti-consumption perspective (Black and Cherrier, 2010), or political consumption (Connolly and Prothero, 2008) spread significantly, then the probability is greater because it adds the consumption perspective to the problem. Sustainability generally and sustainable consumption specifically are multidimensional problems and will require multidimensional solutions.

There is no shortage of uncertainty in the eventual outcome, however, because it relates to a complex interaction of production and consumption. We are referring here to the underlying assumptions under which the complete consumption process is carried out from beginning to end as an integrated system. Production and consumption in this view are an inseparable duality that underlies cultures of consumption. While a thorough discussion of each assumption is beyond the scope of this chapter, it is important that significant ones be addressed.

The first, and probably most controversial, is the limits to growth thesis. This dimension of the economic process, including production and consumption, was addressed most formally in Meadows and Randers (1972), in which they concluded that there were definite limits to consumption and that Western industrial societies were rapidly approaching them. This was supported by Daly (1991), who postulated the impossibility theorem stating that infinite growth in a finite system is prima facie impossible. While there was, and still is, contentious debate (Cole, Freeman and Jahoda, 1973; Simon, 1981) on the limits to growth thesis, its basic premise is still worthy of consideration. In support of the limits to growth thesis, more recent and independent research on the ecological footprint (Wackernagle and Rees, 1998) indicates that many nations in the industrial West are already exceeding their bio-capacity limits. That is, resources (sources) are being used at a rate that exceeds their regenerative capacity and waste deposits (sinks) are exceeding the earth's assimilative capacity. This suggests that the current approach to marketing, economics, etc.

will not be sustainable in the long term unless some currently unknown and unpredictable change in the basic structure of our world occurs. Conversely, Porritt (1988) suggests that the situation in which we find ourselves has resulted from our unwillingness to address the underlying causes of environmental destruction, choosing to focus instead on symptoms such as pollution and ozone depletion. These symptoms manifest themselves as a consequence of over-consumption of the wrong types of products that tax both resource availability and the assimilation capacity of the planet. This assessment, which is not universally accepted yet, does have significant implications for the culture of consumption because it ties it directly to the sustainability of current consumption patterns.

Smith (1998) argues that the current situation is related to the underlying rationality of Western industrial societies, particularly the USA, that have been captured by a productivist discourse. This discourse operates as a suture through which the flaws of its role in the sustainability discourse are hidden. The flaws are also hidden by the counter-entropic logic of perpetual economic growth through which inequality in the distribution of goods and ecological 'bads' is perpetuated in a process of economic reductionism that transforms political choice (who we want to be) into economic preferences (what we want to have). In this process, the productivist narrative is conflated with matching consumer and environmental narratives to create the meta-narrative of capitalism. The fundamental problem in this hegemonic process (Gramsci, 1971) is that strong sustainability is incompatible with the prevailing meta-narrative that demands unlimited economic growth in a finite system. The end result of the hegemonic process is that a new myth about sustainability in the culture of consumption is created that factualises fictions (growth in consumption is the ultimate good) and fictionalises facts (current consumption practices are unsustainable). As both Marcuse (1963) and Gramsci (1971) argue, facts contrary to the major societal narrative are absorbed into the narrative rendering them impotent by transforming critique into naive acquiescence.

When this hegemonic process is successful, the narrative of capitalism is reinforced and reproduced in its original form with only minor changes. While the narrative is challenged somewhat by the sustainability discourse, its logic is also reinforced. This is, for example, the case for sustainable consumption generally. Sustainable consumption as a term was first introduced at the 1992 Rio Earth Summit and was an important element of the Agenda 21 programme. It was discussed by the United Nations Environment Programme in 1999 and included such factors as consuming less, consuming differently, consuming more efficiently, and quality of life.

There are disagreements within the various definitions of the term, particularly in relation to consuming less (Jackson, 2014). Meanwhile, recognising the importance of the full life-cycle of a product, the United Nations Environment Programme (2009), building on the earlier work of the Oslo Symposium held in 1994, defines sustainable consumption and production (SC&P) as follows:

> the use of services and related products, which respond to basic needs and bring a better quality of life while minimizing the use of natural resources and toxic materials as well as the emissions of waste and pollutants over the life-cycle of the service or product so as not to jeopardize the needs of further generations. (UNEP, 2009, p. 8)

Switching the emphasis from consumption to production allows a shift of focus from consumption to 'resource productivity issues' (Jackson, 2014), and, while it is clear that to achieve sustainability requires both consumption and production changes, it is important that the emphasis on production should not be at the expense of questioning the role of consumption. As Jackson (2014, p. 282) reminds us: 'Questioning consumption and consumer behaviour quickly becomes reflexive, demanding often uncomfortable attention to both personal and social change. To make matters worse, arguments to reduce consumption appear to undermine legitimate efforts by poorer countries to improve their quality of life'. While there appears to be no clear acceptance of a definition, and indeed some arguments amongst academics and policy makers surrounding the term, particularly in relation to the thorny issue of questioning consumer ideology and consuming less, there is acceptance that both consumption and production must play a part in engendering changes to consumption practices. There have been many global initiatives to achieve such changes, and some of these can be summarised by focusing on the initiatives developed following Rio+20, the most recent United Nations Conference on Sustainable Development.

SUSTAINABLE CONSUMPTION AND PRODUCTION INITIATIVES

Rio+20, built on the success of the 2003 Marrakech process, identified various SC&P needs and priorities that led to numerous initiatives. The UNEP then produced a report (UNEP, 2012) focusing on global and regional SC&P activities and providing 56 case studies from across the globe that address SC&P priorities. Examples are taken from government, business and civil society. At the government level, for instance, is the example of The Montreal Protocol, a global initiative which focuses on substances that deplete the ozone layer. By 2009, over 98% of the chemicals being controlled were totally eliminated. At the business level, various initiatives are considered, ranging from those undertaken by individual companies like Unilever's successful Sustainable Sourcing Initiative, to examples of businesses coming together, both within and across industry sectors to tackle SC&P issues. For example, the Global Reporting Initiative (GRI) produces reports in which businesses document their sustainability performance following the guidelines laid down by the GRI. At the civil society level, organisations, including NGOs, community and indigenous groups, have also played a significant role in affecting change at the SC&P level. Two examples include the FLO, a fair trade labelling scheme now available for 15 product groups, and the success of the Forest Stewardship Council (FSC) in certifying sustainable forest products. While there is criticism of all three bodies, there is also a general acceptance that since the first UN Rio Conference in 1992 much has been accomplished in relation to SC&P and this has been as a result of a global recognition of the need to tackle the depletion of the earth's resources and the role consumption plays therein.

While it is clear that many initiatives have been proposed with success on the production side, much remains to be done regarding the future of the productivist discourse as it relates directly to consumption. Unfortunately, the essence of the relationship between production and consumption will be deferred until a later time as space does not permit a thorough examination. For more recent assessments of production approaches, many can be found in studies of the ecological footprint, such as those by Waggoner and Ausubel (2002) and York, Rosa and Dietz (2003). Instead, we focus the remainder of the chapter on the consumer aspects of the sustainability problem.

The ideology of consumption is maintained within the DSP, in that, while it may advocate weak sustainability, the necessity for continuous growth in production and consumption is maintained intact if not increased through a sustainability backlash effect, suggesting that if people consume better, they can then consume more. Because the current phase of the DSP is so well engrained and its separate narratives so well integrated, especially in the USA, it is opaque to both critics and adherents. Its logic is self-evident, requiring no justification (Kilbourne, McDonagh and Prothero, 1997), and that logic repairs the fracture created by the contradiction between sustainable consumption and expansionary economics. The political nature of sustainability is subverted as it is incorporated into the dominant discourse of economics and markets, as will be discussed later in the chapter.

The second factor that the dominant discourse on sustainability relates to is the time frame, which is admittedly imprecise. But this is not too difficult to deal with if we avoid the standard treatment in neoclassical economics that uses discounting methods to value the future. The rationale here is that the farther into the future we try to imagine, the more likely we are to be wrong, so there are time frames beyond which it is not fruitful to venture. We cannot know what future consumers will value, what technological changes will have occurred, or what the state of the environment will actually be. This is the domain for predicting megatrends and their consequences. But, while it is certainly true that we cannot predict these characteristics with great accuracy, that should not disqualify the endeavour altogether. One of the favoured pastimes within econometrics is making those types of predictions. While Galbraith may have disparaged the discipline in his characteristically witty style with his quip that economic forecasting makes astrology respectable, we must continue to improve our skills. And while it is true that long-term forecasting of social trends is difficult, we can do some 'what-if' assessments that help us frame the possible scenarios.

One approach that has been used in the past, albeit not in studies of consumer culture, is the Ehrlich equation, I = PAT (Ehrlich and Holdren, 1971). The equation, which is really an identity, cannot be used for predicting, but it can be used to gain insight into how a system operates. The actual identity says that environmental impact, I; is a function of the product of population, P; affluence, A; and technology, T. Affluence is defined as per capita consumption (GDP/Population) and technology is defined as the environmental impact per unit of GDP (Impact/GDP). Speth (2008) provides an example of how the equation can be used to enhance one's perspective about change over time. He shows that if the current population growth rate remains at about 3% and the current growth rate in affluence remains at about 3%, how must technological impact change over the next 50 years to maintain the current ecological impact of consumption behaviour? When the problem is solved it shows that for constant impact, the T factor must be reduced by approximately 95%. This becomes reduced to a probability estimate of the likelihood that this dramatic improvement in technology will occur.

This approach to studying sustainability has been improved in the last decade by converting it to an actual predictive equation referred to as STIPAT (York, Rosa and Dietz, 2003). In this formulation, many different factors (for examples see Wei, 2011) such as production of CO_2 or consumer spending, can be included to determine their contribution to the ecological footprint generally. This allows for an assessment of the impact of consumer culture and its ecological impact on sustainability.

In this brief examination of sustainability, the intent was to provide a characterisation of sustainability. It is considered here as a continuum from weak sustainability (making limited sustainability choices – e.g. buying recycled toilet paper) to strong sustainability (incorporating eco-rationality into both consumption and production decisions). We argue that sustainability embedded in the productivist logic rooted in neoclassical economics is an incomplete and flawed construct as it is the product of economic reductionism in which the essential political content has been removed. The missing political content is at two levels: (1) the political consumer embedded in consumer culture; and (2) production embedded in the DSP of Western industrial societies. Our task is now to reintroduce the political in the form of the New Political Economy. From this we will then frame sustainability in a more appropriate and comprehensive way than it is currently considered.

POLITICAL/ECONOMY APPROACH (FROM THE NEW POLITICAL ECONOMY)

Traditionally, within marketing generally and consumption specifically, consumer choices have been taken as an economic phenomenon. It has been viewed through the lens of neoclassical economic theory (NCE), and reduced to an act of choice guided by a singular, all-inclusive consumer (economic) preference function (see Schwarzkopf in this volume). Fundamental to this is that consumers do not make interpersonal comparisons of their respective preferences and that preferences are exogenous and do not change as a result of the market activity in which the consumer is embedded. In short, economic preference functions answer the question, 'What do I want to have?' The difficulty in this is that it is becoming more frequently argued that this is not the end of the question. NCE argues that it is because market actors are perfectly rational and capable of reducing all their disparate roles into the one all-encompassing economic preference function. As a result the confluence of all types of preferences other than economic is realised. The question to which we turn is whether this represents actual reality or is simply a necessary condition for simplicity in the theory underlying it.

DEPOLITICISATION

Kassiola (1990) argues that this position reflects a depoliticisation of society in which all values (including consumption choices) can be reduced to a set of economic choices. As a product of economic imperialism, this effectively removes political choices regarding many aspects of the life one chooses to live. This condition has been examined for several decades going back at least to Hirschman (1970) who argued that such depoliticisation reflects a transition from voice (expressing one's views through discourse) to exit (expressing one's view by exiting the situation). The latter is the market (economic) approach in which consumers express their views through (non)purchase behaviour: If I like your offering I will purchase it, and if not, I will not. The former is concerned with the reasons behind one's choices which are reflected through unadulterated discourse (political).

The primary difficulty with the economic approach is that it is likely that individual tastes and preferences are conditioned by cultural institutions such as advertising to the extent that they do not truly intercede between the consumer and his/her preferences. Samuelson (1947) describes Western man as a 'hodgepodge of beliefs stemming from diverse and inconsistent sources' (p. 226). Deferring to the market as the sole arbiter of all values then becomes highly problematic. This has not gone unnoticed throughout modern history.

In the philosophy of Rousseau (1975) we find a similar distinction that he refers to as the will of all versus the general will. This suggests that there are two types of will residing in the same person, and they reflect different beliefs and preferences. Specifically, the will of all is the sum of individual wills, which includes their individual self-interest in personal choices. The general will is that part of the will of all with self-interest removed. This reveals what the individual would choose as the best for everyone collectively. The first reflects what each individual wants for themselves, and the second reflects their choice for the common good. More recently, this distinction has emerged in O'Neill (1993) who expresses it as want regarding principles versus ideal regarding principles, where the former express that which I want to have and the latter expresses who I want to be. The first is economic and the second political. This same distinction is brought to the fore by Sagoff (2007), who argues that the two types of preference function are generally in conflict with each other, particularly in public finance. Thus, he argues that there are clear distinctions between consumer and citizen where the choices of the former are reflected in the economic preference function, and the choices of the latter are reflected in the political preference function. He further argues:

> Analysts who attempt to shuffle citizen judgements and personal preferences into the same ordering commit a logical mistake. They confuse *judgment* with *preference*, that is to say, beliefs about what we should do with expressions of what I want or prefer (p. 55, italics in the original).

Finally, as clear and distinct an expression as we have found for the difference between consumer and citizen is that provided by Musgrave (1959). He also sets the stage for the approach we will be adopting for the remainder of the chapter. Speaking of the roles of citizen and consumer, he states: 'In the latter situation the voter acts as a private individual determined by self-interest and deals with his personal wants; in the former, he acts as a political being guided by his image of a good society' (pp. 87–88). In this passage, Musgrave ascribes the roles of citizen and consumer to the same person, who reflects one set of values as citizen and a different set as consumer. However, he describes the consumer as a voter, but one who votes in a different way than as a citizen. As a consumer, the individual expresses his/her beliefs with money in the market rather than in political discourse. But Musgrave also suggests that, in some sense, the consumer is voting using exit rather than voice as a strategy. As indicated earlier, the concept of the consumer/voter re-emerged in the marketing literature through Dickinson and Hollander (1991) and has been reiterated by Trentmann (2007). We propose to combine both strategies by reuniting the political and the economic through the mechanism of the New Political Economy proposed earlier.

NEW POLITICAL ECONOMY

Galbraith (1997) argues that within the more affluent countries of the world, consumer goods are produced in such abundance that large sums of money must be allocated to the cultural apparatus to cultivate the wants that the system provides. But he further argues that the preoccupation with consumer satisfaction will someday lead to undesirable consequences that will become more critical in the future. But there is a powerful political agenda carried out through market activities that is managed by those who are engaged in the productive process. The problem we deal with in this chapter is that, while we now begin to see the consequences as they are manifested through the natural environment, we also assent to the system because there are no plausible alternatives to be found within the DSP. Galbraith further argues that dissenting political organisations no longer offer the dissent they did in the past. This suggests the prevalence of the NCE philosophy in advanced market societies, that is, cultures of consumption.

Our use of the New Political Economy (NPE) in assessing the political aspects of sustainable consumption is predicated on Galbraith's conclusion about the tacit assent to the NCE framework in high consumption cultures. To better understand this condition, it is necessary to examine some of the institutions that underlie the NCE system and its encroachment on and absorption of the political element of the original classical economic model, or what Kassiola (1990) referred to as depoliticisation. Maier (1987) describes the distinctive element of NPE as disclosing the sociological and political premises contained in NCE and takes them, not as an established framework, but as 'beliefs that must themselves be explained'. This exposes the normative assumptions that underlie the NCE framework, not as self-evident conditions, but as conditions that themselves require political debate. Besley (2004) states that, '… the new political economy is re-engaging with the art of political economy as envisaged by the classical economists' (p. 5). It further considers seriously the Aristotelian position that one may set aside their individual interest in favour of the common good. This is echoed by Rousseau (1975) who states, 'There is often a great difference between the will of all and the general will. The latter looks only to the common interest, while the former looks to private interest and is only the sum of individual wills' (p. 27). This becomes reduced to the conclusion of Hirschman (1977) that, from Adam Smith on, the self-interested, individual will has been separated from the political, general will. One of the goals of the NPE is to reunite the two to achieve a comprehensive understanding of the political element in economic theory. Myrdal (1954) criticises the confluence of politics and economics in liberalism as well when he observes:

> Presumably 'economic interest' means the desire for higher incomes and lower prices and, in addition, perhaps stability of earnings and employment, reasonable time for leisure and an environment conducive to its satisfactory use, good working conditions, etc. But even with these qualifications, political aspirations cannot be identified with those interests. People are also interested in social objectives. They believe in ideals to which they want their society to conform. (p. 199)

All of the foregoing suggests that economics alone cannot provide an adequate description of human behaviour generally or consumption behaviour specifically. As the emerging field of Socio-Economics suggests, economics is embedded in the larger social and political field and, while it provides essential information in consumer choices, it must be united with other fields to achieve more complete understanding of the multi-faceted cultures of consumption. Simply stated, there are economic preferences (what we want to have) and there are political preferences (who we want to be). These represent different but interactive modes of choice and the most prescient recognition of this is provided by Fromm (1976) whose book, *To Have or To Be?* is aptly titled. This is the essence of consumer culture theory. The question to which we now turn relates to the particular model of NPE that lends itself best to an analysis of sustainability within cultures of consumption.

RELATIONSHIP TO GRAMSCI

Kilbourne, McDonagh, and Prothero (1997) were the first to examine the idea of sustainable consumption, as the term is used here, within the marketing literature. They did so within the context of the DSP of Western industrial societies. One of the difficulties within this approach has been incorporating paradigm change into the model as it was originally developed by Kuhn (1970). He argued that scientific paradigms (the context of his work) do not change smoothly, but rather they transform dramatically when conditions are right for the transformation. That is, they do not change gradually by incorporating changes at the margins of the paradigm into the mainstream, or core, of the paradigm. While this may be true, or at least arguable, within scientific paradigms, it is problematic within social paradigms as described by Dunlap and Van Liere (1978), Cotgrove (1982), Milbrath (1984), and Pirages and Ehrlich (1974). Because they are much more complex than scientific paradigms, social paradigms consist of multiple institutional structures interrelated in a complex and dynamic system that is continuously in flux. Because the idea of the DSP is still in its developmental stages, its improvement as a conceptual model of social development and transition is necessary. Among the changes that would be useful is a better explanation of its dynamic character. Gramsci (1971) provides a good starting point for this explanation.

GRAMSCIAN PERSPECTIVE

While the primary constructs articulated by Gramsci are very diverse, covering a wide range of political/economic activity, two are particularly relevant for this chapter. These are hegemony and passive revolution that can lead to the evolution of the static concept of the DSP, making it more consistent with social, political and economic change. The critical aspect of Gramsci's framework is that it serves to explain the absence of dramatic transitions in the socialist trajectory of Marx. In doing so, it also serves to explain how social paradigms change without the revolutionary component suggested in Kuhn's (1970) *The Structure of Scientific Revolutions.* In this sense, Gramsci's theory argues that changes in paradigms can be evolutionary as well as revolutionary, and our focus is on this aspect of social change. This raises the fundamental question to which this chapter is directed. What are the politics of sustainable consumption and how do we get there from here?

To begin this process, we have adopted Gramsci's (1971) interpretation of hegemony. This approach is useful because, unlike the more static view of the scientific paradigm, hegemony is a dynamic process rather than an end state (Smith, 1998). As such, hegemony adds to rather than replaces the concept of the DSP. The concept of hegemony is an interpretation of political power that explains how the political, cultural and moral values of a dominant class become dominant. How is it that the belief system of the dominant class becomes self-evidently true for the rest of society without the coercion usually associated with elite control? Hegemony is a process through which consent by subaltern classes is achieved more by acquiescence than by coercion. While dominant groups in more advanced societies do have access to coercive power, its exercise is seldom necessary. This is because, when successful, hegemony results in the subordinated classes accepting the extant power relations as the natural order of things. They accept the status quo because they believe that prevalent social relations are as they should be. This is what Gramsci (1971) refers to as '... hegemony protected by the armour of coercion' (p. 263), but he also reasons that, in more advanced societies, the coercive function of the political could wither and become unnecessary in maintaining dominance. This trajectory from coercion to consent was alluded to by Thomas Paine 1776 in his assertion (2017, Introduction, p. 6), 'a long habit of not thinking a thing WRONG, gives it a superficial appearance that it is RIGHT, and raises at first a formidable outcry in defence of custom. But the tumult soon subsides'. It is interesting that the Paine statement is found in the pamphlet entitled *Common Sense* because 'common sense' is taken by Gramsci (1971) to mean '... the uncritical and largely unconscious way of perceiving and understanding the world that has become "common" in any given epoch' (p. 322).

We conclude from this that hegemony differs from mere domination in that while coercion is an alternative, the preferred approach to social control is through the assent of the subaltern classes. Next we briefly examine how, within Gramsci's perspective, assent is achieved. This is similar to asking how it is that the DSP of a society can change from within rather than through coercive political activity and become dominant. This entails an examination of the evolution and structure of macro institutions within civil (as opposed to state) society. In this case we view 'the' DSP, not as a static arrangement of institutions but a phase through which it is passing in the process of dynamic equilibrium.

How this process unfolds is described by Gramsci (1971) as passive revolution. While a complete analysis of the concept of passive revolution is beyond the scope of this chapter, the basic process will be addressed as it relates to consumer culture and sustainability. Callinicos (2010) describes passive revolution as the process through which domination by a particular class is achieved or maintained gradually through compromise and concession rather than the punctuated equilibrium and destruction found in the American and French revolutions. Gramsci (2007) argues that the outcome results from a process through which:

> 'progress' occurs as the reaction of the dominant classes to the sporadic and incoherent rebelliousness of the popular masses – a reaction consisting of 'restorations' that agree to some part of the popular demands and are therefore 'progressive restorations' or 'revolutions-restorations', or even 'passive revolutions'. (p. 252)

This does not suggest that passive revolutions are the product of irrational demands from the subaltern classes, but they can result from contradictions in social relations and crises that occur within the DSP. These crises may first have the character of structural contradictions (described by Kuhn [1970] as anomalies) which are 'sticky' problems to which the dominant class seeks resolution from within hegemonic relations. These are referred to as restorations because, once implemented, the status quo ante is resumed. Gramsci (1971) argues, however, that anomalies of exceptional duration reveal intransigent crises, the solutions of which the dominant class will not accede to, and it is on this ground that the oppositional forces will organise to push their positions. Callinicos (2010) argues that at the conclusion of this 'passive revolution', the elements of dissent initiating the conflict are absorbed by the dominant class, but demands of the subaltern classes are at least partially fulfilled while the dominant class remains dominant. This moves the hegemonic relations to a 'new and improved' phase that is then maintained by the same processes through which it arrived. The DSP after the restoration is both different and the same. The counter-hegemonic project manages the structural contradiction of the existing paradigm but does not achieve a paradigm shift of the kind referred to by Kuhn (1970).

THE COUNTER-HEGEMONIC ELEMENT IN CONSUMER CULTURE

> 'Political consumers respond to corporate policies and products reflecting, expressing, and promoting political, social, and normative values beyond those of consumer price, taste and quality of goods', and political consumerism is defined as 'consumer choice of producers and products with the goal of changing objectionable institutional or market practices'. (Micheletti, Follesdal and Stolle, 2004, p xiv)

These authors also remind us that political consumers have existed for many centuries and are not a recent phenomenon. The National Negro Convention, for example, called for a boycott of slave-produced products in the 1800s. For the purposes of this chapter we will focus on consumers who make political consumption choices based on their concern for the environment – sustainable consumers (in the past also called, for instance, green consumers, environmentally friendly consumers, environmentally conscious consumers, but for the purposes of this chapter we stick with a generic label of sustainable consumers, recognising that this term can have different meanings). There have been a number of reviews of the sustainability marketing literature (Kilbourne and Beckmann, 1998; Leonidou and Leonidou, 2011; McDonagh and Prothero, 2014b), and literature with specific reference to sustainable consumption is assessed here.

In terms of political sustainable consumers, the literature has focused on a wide range of issues spanning over half a century. Much of the early research provided profiles of sustainable consumers and the reasons behind their green purchasing behaviour (Balderjahn, 1988; Granzin and Olsen, 1991; Kinnear, Taylor and Ahmed, 1974). Later research though moved away from an emphasis on buying greener products to consider consuming differently (Jackson and Michaelis, 2003), and in some instances non-consumption (Dobscha and Ozanne, 2001). There has been an emphasis on both individual and collective forms of sustainable actions (Connolly and Prothero, 2008); while there is also a recognition that making sustainable choices is difficult. In Connolly and Prothero (2008) consumers emphasise 'I know that I should and could do something, but I don't know which is the right thing to do' (p. 133). While there have been disagreements with the political consumer literature as to whether or not political consumerism can be successful, we have witnessed similar arguments, specifically in relation to sustainable consumer practices.

What has become clear in recent years is a recognition that much of the early sustainability research which focused on small incremental changes to consumption (buying recycled toilet paper for example) will not be enough to tackle the environmental crisis, and thus, research which reflects this is warranted. To that end Kilbourne and Mittelstaedt (2012) highlighted the need for two strands of sustainable consumption research – the first would pay specific attention to the environmental impact of our consumption practices and the second would focus on the more systemic and fundamental issue of lowering total consumption – both strands tackle the institutional and market-based practices highlighted by Micheletti, Follesdal and Stolle (2004) above. This second avenue therefore poses important questions from political, economic and cultural perspectives because it questions growth – which, of course, occurs against the backdrop of buying more stuff. The ideology of consumption therefore plays an important role in understanding sustainable consumption. This is not a new finding, and something that Fisk (1973) acknowledged many years ago. In focusing on the ideology of consumption issue, McDonagh and Prothero (2014b) ask 'how do we get everyone to consume less?'

CONSUMER CULTURE AND SUSTAINABILITY: MEGATREND OR PASSIVE REVOLUTION

While we posit that sustainability is yet to be widely confirmed as the megatrend, or as Varey (2013) suggests, a mega megatrend, it does appear logical to assume that, for humanity's survival, it is the megatrend. This is because, if left unaddressed, it will have the most serious consequences, such as species extinction and resource depletion.

The rise of consumer culture and its inculcation into development and civilisation (market societies) permits a dynamic DSP to effect both change and restoration. It is notable that many of the very same companies that initiated unsustainable consumption are now presenting themselves as newly improved and offer their products and services to consumers, calling themselves 'solution providers'. In this way consumption levels continue to grow through newly marketed 'sustainable brands'. A key issue here is whether or not this offers too little, too late, but this is open to wide debates. Furthermore, the logic of consumption as articulated within the dynamic of the DSP after restoration is seductive from a consumer point of view. To know that trusted companies and brands have the situation in hand is reassuring, and to see some change occurring supports the premise of a passive revolution unfolding. This is, however, analogous to the people of nations being told to 'Keep calm and continue shopping' during times of intense aggression between states at war.

The counter-hegemonic element then has to once again return to the question 'What is to be done to get from here to there?' And, for the purposes of this chapter we are asking if a Gramscian approach focusing on hegemony and passive revolution might be a part of the answer. Can a move towards strong sustainability, focusing on sustainable consumption, be achieved via acquiescence, compromise and concession? If so, what will this mean for consumer culture? It would appear that the general will is pivotal at this juncture. The need to shift measurements of output for the productivist discourse (indicators of progress such as GDP) towards those more suited to conditions of strong sustainability within consumer culture is apparent. At this stage we now know that these may include the capacity to feed and provide water to a population, provide improved air quality, minimise toxicity and lower risk to personal health, provide cleaner energy supplies and repair polluted resources (the seas, rivers, fish stocks, etc.) all of which require increased capacity for scrutiny. The biggest hurdle for sustainability is its own ambiguity in a conceptual sense, as this delimits the capacity for the counter-hegemonic element to inform political consumers of the best alternatives to move towards sustainable consumption. Passive revolution is an on-going and contradictory project given that what needs to change has taken centuries to emerge and will not be easily altered. This should not, however, be a distraction because Green (1993) reminds us that any form of emancipatory politics involves '... a protracted and fundamental process of counter-hegemonic cultural contestation' (p. 175).

CONCLUSION

Consumer Culture Theory (CCT) is now a well-established research field within the broader consumer research field, and, as illustrated above, sustainable consumption has been an important (but limited) strand of research. In their ten-year review of CCT research Arnould and Thompson (2005) emphasised how 'the politics of consumption' has become a key pillar of CCT research and 'politically engaged theory and practice' will grow in importance in the future. Building on the current trend of assemblage theory in CCT, the authors argue for a future focus on power relations (as well as a specific focus on resistance); this, in conjunction with an emphasis on the politics of consumption, is centrally important if one begins to further theorise sustainable consumption through a hegemonic, passive revolution lens. This requires building on earlier sustainability research which has an institutional, societal and systems perspective (see, for example, Kilbourne, 2004; Prothero et al., 2011) and studies that have questioned the ideology of consumption (see, for example, Dolan, 2002; Kilbourne, Beckmann and Thelen, 2002; Prothero et al., 2011).

There is also further scope for consumer culture research to examine the appropriation of resistance (see Desmond, McDonagh and O'Donohoe, 2000) into what is becoming popularly communicated as corporate sustainability, and a need to unpack this by those seeking meaningful ecological change (McDonagh and Prothero, 2015). This is quite problematic given the power relations at play. It is feasible that large conglomerates can invest heavily in convincing the general public to endorse their improved market offerings under the banner of 'corporate sustainability' as this legitimises their right to continue in business. An analogous situation might be how the US government prior to the first Iraq war hired a public relations firm, Hill and Knowlton, to fabricate 'atrocity stories' about what was happening in Iraq, with the desired result being the public endorsement of an invasion of that country. Therefore, for some people, the emergence of corporate sustainability might be seen as a form of appropriation of sustainability issues that should be resisted. In this respect passive revolution requires even closer scrutiny than before as the DSP after restoration might best be critiqued as an intelligent system which is self-serving. As a result, the politics of resistance on grounds of sustainability may fragment first across a number of issues and second, depending upon whether or not there is weak or strong sustainability at stake, over some types of resistance perhaps being viewed as much more authentic than others.

REFERENCES

Arnould, E. and Thompson, C. (2005) 'Consumer Culture Theory (CCT): Twenty Years of Research', *Journal of Consumer Research*, 31(4), 868–882.

Balderjahn, I. (1988) 'Personality Variables and Environmental Attitudes as Predictors of Ecologically Responsible Consumption Patterns', *Journal of Business Research*, 17(1), 51–56.

Bauman, Z. (1998) *Globalization: The Human Consequences*. New York: Columbia University Press.

Besley, T. (2004) *The New Political Economy. Lecture*. London and Cambridge, UK: Keynes Lecturers.

Black, L.R. and Cherrier, H. (2010) 'Anti-Consumption as Part of Living a Sustainable Lifestyle: Daily Practices, Contextual Motivations and Subjective Values', *Journal of Consumer Behaviour*, 9(6), 437–453.

Brundtland, G.H. (1987) 'Our Common Future'. World Commission on Environment and Development.

Callinicos, A. (2010) 'The Limits of Passive Revolution', *Capital and Class*, 34(3), 491–507.

Cole, H.S., Freeman, C. and Jahoda, M. (1973) *Models of Doom: A Critique of the Limits to Growth*. London: Universe Publishing.

Connolly, J. and Prothero, A. (2008) 'Green Consumption: Life-politics, Risk and Contradictions', *Journal of Consumer Culture*, 8(1), 117–145.

Cotgrove, S. (1982) *Catastrophe or Cornucopia*. New York: Wiley.

Daly, H.E. (1991) *Steady-State Economics*. New York: Island Press.

Desmond, J., McDonagh, P. and O'Donohoe, S. (2000) 'Counter-Culture and Consumer Society', *Consumption Markets & Culture*, 4(3), 241–279.

Dickinson, R. and Hollander, S.C. (1991) 'Consumer Votes', *Journal of Business Research*, 23(1), 9–20.

Dobscha, S. and Ozanne, J.L. (2001) 'An Ecofeminist Analysis of Environmentally Sensitive Women Using Qualitative Methodology: The Emancipatory Potential of an Ecological Life', *Journal of Public Policy and Marketing*, 20(2), 201–214.

Dolan, P. (2002) 'The Sustainability of "Sustainable Consumption"'. *Journal of Macromarketing*, 22(2), 170–181.

Dunlap, R.E. and Van Liere, K.D. (1978) 'The "New Environmental Paradigm"', *The Journal of Environmental Education*, 9(4), 10–19.

Ehrlich, P.R. and Holdren, J.P. (1971) 'Impact of Population Growth', *Science*, 171(3977), 1212–1217.

Featherstone, M. (2007) *Consumer Culture and Postmodernism*. Thousand Oaks, CA: Sage.

Fisk, G. (1973) 'Criteria for a Theory of Responsible Consumption', *Journal of Marketing*, 37(2), 24–31.

Fromm, E. (1976) *To Have or To Be?* London, UK: Bloomsbury Publishing.

Frost & Sullivan (2017) 'Mega Trends', New York: Frost & Sullivan. Retrieved from https://ww2.frost.com/index.php/consulting/key-client-issues/mega-trends

Galbraith, J.K. (1997) 'Preface', *New Political Economy*, 2(1), 5–9.

Gramsci, A. (1971) *Selections from the Prison Notebooks of Antonio Gramsci* (Q. Hoare and G.N. Smith, Trans.). New York: International Publishers.

Gramsci, A. (2007) *Prison Notebooks, Vol. 3*. (J.A. Buttigieg, Trans.). New York: Columbia University Press.

Granzin, K.L. and Olsen, J.E. (1991) 'Characterizing Participants in Activities Protecting the Environment: A Focus on Donating, Recycling, and Conservation Behaviors', *Journal of Public Policy and Marketing*, 10(2), 1–27.

Green, C. (1993) 'Advanced Capitalist Hegemony and the Significance of Gramsci's Insights: A Restatement', *Social and Economic Studies*, 42(2/3), 175–207.

Hirschman, A.O. (1970) *Exit, Voice, and Loyalty*. Cambridge, MA: Harvard University Press.

Hirschman, A.O. (1977) *The Passions and the Interests*. Princeton, NJ: Princeton University Press.

Jackson, T. (2014) 'Sustainable Consumption'. In *Handbook of Sustainable Development* by Giles Atkinson, Simon Dietz, Eric Neumayer and Matthew Agarwala. Edward Elgar Publishing: 279–290.

Jackson, T. and Michaelis, L. (2003) *Policies for Sustainable Consumption*. London, Sustainable Development Commission.

Kassiola, J.J. (1990) *The Death of Industrial Civilization*. Albany, NY: SUNY Press.

Kilbourne, W. (1995) 'Green Advertising: Salvation or Oxymoron', *Journal of Advertising*, 24(2), 7–20.

Kilbourne, W. (2004) 'Sustainable Communication and the Dominant Social Paradigm: Can They Be Integrated?' *Marketing Theory*, 4(3), 187–208.

Kilbourne, W.E. and Beckmann, S.C. (1998) 'Review and Critical Assessment of Research on Marketing and the Environment', *Journal of Marketing Management*, 14(6), 507–512.

Kilbourne, W. and Mittelstaedt, J. (2012) 'From Profligacy to Sustainability: Can You Get There from Here?' In D. Mick, J. Ozanne, and C. Pechmann (eds) *Transformative Consumer Research for Personal and Collective Well-Being* (pp. 283–300). New York: Routledge.

Kilbourne, W.E., Beckmann, S.C. and Thelen, E. (2002) 'The Role of the Dominant Social Paradigm in Environmental Attitudes: A Multi-National Examination', *Journal of Business Research*, 55(3), 193–204.

Kilbourne, W.E., Dorsch, M.J., McDonagh, P., Urien, B., Prothero, A., Grünhagen, M. and Bradshaw, A. (2009) 'The Institutional Foundations of Materialism in Western Societies: A Conceptualization and Empirical Test', *Journal of Macromarketing*, 29(3), 259–278.

Kilbourne, W., McDonagh, P. and Prothero, A. (1997) 'Sustainable Consumption and the Quality of Life: A Macromarketing Challenge to the Dominant Social Paradigm', *Journal of Macromarketing*, 36(1), 54–67.

Kinnear, T.C., Taylor, J.R. and Ahmed, S.A. (1974) 'Ecologically Concerned Consumers: Who Are They?', *Journal of Marketing*, 38(2), 20–24.

Kuhn, T. (1970) *The Structure of Scientific Revolutions*. Chicago, IL: University of Chicago Press.

Leonidou, C.N. and Leonidou, L.C. (2011) 'Research into Environmental Marketing/Management: A Bibliographic Analysis', *European Journal of Marketing*, 45(1/2), 68–103.

Maier, C.S. (1987) *In Search of Stability: Explorations in Historical Political Economy*. Cambridge, UK: Cambridge University Press.

Marcuse, H. (1963) *One Dimensional Man*. London, UK: Routledge.

McDonagh, P. and Prothero, A. (2014a) 'Introduction to the Special Issue: Sustainability as Megatrend I', *Journal of Macromarketing*, 34(3), 248–252.

McDonagh, P. and Prothero, A. (2014b) 'Sustainability Marketing Research: Past, Present and Future', *Journal of Marketing Management*, 30(11/12), 1186–1219.

McDonagh, P. and Prothero, A. (2015), 'Unpacking corporate sustainability: sustainable communication, waste and the 3Rs in network society'. In K. Ekstrom (ed.) *Waste Management and Sustainable Consumption: Reflections on Consumer Waste* (pp. 166–183). London and New York: Routledge.

Meadows, D. and Randers, J. (1972) *The Limits to Growth*. New York: Universe Books.

Micheletti, M., Follesdal, A. and Stolle, D. (2004) *Politics, Products, and Markets: Exploring Political Consumerism Past and Present*. London, UK: Transaction Publishers.

Milbrath, L. (1984) *Environmentalists: Vanguard for a New Society*. Albany, NY: SUNY Press.

Mittelstaedt, J., Kilbourne, W., Shultz, C. and Petersen, M. (2014) 'Sustainability as Megatrend', *Journal of Macromarketing*, 34(3), 253–264.

Musgrave, R.A. (1959) *The Theory of Public Finance: A Study in Public Economy*. New York: McGraw-Hill.

Myrdal, G. (1954) *The Political Element in the Development of Economic Theory*. Cambridge, MA: Harvard University Press.

Naess, A. (1973) 'The Shallow and the Deep, Long-Range Ecology Movement: A Summary', *Inquiry*, 16(1–4), 95–100.

Naisbitt. (1982) *Megatrends: Ten New Directions Transforming Our Lives*. New York: Warner.

O'Connor, M. (1994) *Is Capitalism Sustainable? Political Economy and the Politics of Ecology*. New York: The Guilford Press.

O'Neill, J. (1993) *Ecology, Policy and Politics: Human Well-Being and the Natural World*. London, UK: Routledge.

Paine, T. [1776] (2017) *Thomas Paine: Collected Writings: Common Sense/The Crisis/Rights of Man/The Age of Reason*, CreateSpace Independent Publishing Platform (22 Feb).

Pirages, D.C. and Ehrlich, P.R. (1974) *Ark II: Social Response to Environmental Imperatives*. New York: Viking Press.

Porritt, J. (1988) *Seeing Green: The Politics of Ecology Explained*. London, UK: Basil Blackwell.

Prothero, A., Dobscha, S., Freund, J., Kilbourne, W.E., Ozanne, L.K. and Thøgersen, J. (2011) 'Sustainable Consumption: Opportunities for Consumer Research and Public Policy', *Journal of Public Policy and Marketing*, 30(1), 31–38.

Rappaport, A. (1953) *Operational Philosophy*. New York: Harper and Brothers.

Rifkin, J. (2015) *The Zero Marginal Cost Society*. New York: Macmillan.

Rousseau, J.J. (1975) *The Essential Rousseau* (L. Blair, Trans.). New York: Meridian Books.

Rudmin, F. and Kilbourne, W. (1995) 'The Meaning and Morality of Voluntary Simplicity: The History and Hypotheses on Deliberately Denied Materialism'. In R. Belk, N. Dholakia and A. Venkatesh (eds) *Consumption and Marketing: The Macro Dimensions*. Cincinnati, OH: South-Western College Publishing.

Sagoff, M. (2007) *The Economy of Earth*. New York: Cambridge University Press.

Samuelson, P.A. (1947) *Foundations of Economic Analysis*. Cambridge, MA: Harvard University Press.

Scott, K., Martin, D. and Schouten, J. (2014) 'Marketing and the New Materialism', *Journal of Macromarketing*, 34(3), 282–290.

Simon, J.L. (1981) *Population: The Ultimate Resource. Princeton*, NJ: Princeton University Press.

Smith, T.M. (1998) *The Myth of Green Marketing: Tending Our Goats at the Edge of Apocalypse*. Toronto, CA: University of Toronto Press.

Speth, J.G. (2008) *The Bridge at the Edge of the World*. New Haven, CT: Yale University Press.

Trentmann, F. (2007) 'Citizenship and Consumption', *Journal of Consumer Culture*, 7(2), 147–158.

UNEP/CDG (2000) Sustainable Consumption and Production. Creating opportunities in a changing world: Report of the 4th International Business Forum, Berlin 1999, in UNEP and Consumers International (2002), Tracking Progress: Implementing Sustainable Consumption Policies, http://webdocs.unep.org/bitstream/handle/20.500.11822/7865/-Tracking%20Progress_20Implementing%20Sustainable%20Consumption%Policies%20%20%20%A%20Global%20Review%20of%20Implementation%20of %20the%20United%20%nations%20Guidelines%20for%20Consumer%20Protection-2002156.pdf?sequence=3&isAllowed=y (accessed August 24th, 2017)

United Nations Environment Programme (2009) 'Frequently asked questions: The Marrakech process – towards a 10 year Framework of Programmes on Sustainable Consumption and Production. http://www.unep.fr/scp/marrakecj/about.htm. (retrieved February 22nd 2016)

United Nations Environment Programme (2012) Global Outlook on Sustainable Consumption and Production Policies – Taking action together. http://www.unep.fr/shared/publications/pdf/DTIx1498xPA-GlobalOutlookonSCPPolicies.pdf (accessed online, February 22nd, 2016)

Varey, R. (2012) 'The Marketing Future Beyond the Limits of Growth', *Journal of Macromarketing*, 32(4), 424–433.

Varey, R. (2013) 'Marketing in the Flourishing Society Megatrend', *Journal of Macromarketing*, 33(4), 354–368.

Wackernagle, M. and Rees, W. (1998) *Our Ecological Footprint: Reducing Human Impact on the Earth*. New York: New Society Publishers.

Waggoner, P.E. and Ausubel, J.H. (2002) 'A Framework for Sustainability Science: A Renovated IPAT Identity', *Proceedings of the National Academy of Sciences*, 99(12), 7860–7865.

Wei, T. (2011) 'What STIRPAT Tells about Effects of Population and Affluence on the Environment', *Ecological Economics*, 72, 70–74.

York, R., Rosa, E. and Dietz, T. (2003) 'Footprints on the Earth: The Environmental Consequences of Modernity', *American Sociological Review*, 68(2), 279–300.

Buying into the Nation: The Politics of Consumption and Nationalism

Eleftheria J. Lekakis

INTRODUCTION: THE POLITICS OF CONSUMPTION AND NATIONALISM

This chapter undertakes a study of the politics of consumption which places the nation at the heart of the examination of consumer culture. Consumption is a form of identification; as such, it can allude to one's national positioning, preference or politics. It can pronounce pride through the conspicuous consumption of a recognised national brand, as it might in the case of a national sports team. It can also pronounce the preference of a fashion symbol that signifies a fellow nation. Additionally, it can promote a politics through the rejection of and campaign against a specific nation. Yet, because nations are individually and collectively imagined constructs, a consumer politics is directed against states. In approaching the relationship between the politics of consumption and different variations of the nation (nationalism, national culture, national identity),[1] it is evident that consumption crosses the boundaries between the private and the public sphere. Consumption also becomes a vehicle for constructing and communicating one's identity (Jackson, 1999). From thinking of consumption as a personal act for the purpose of survival or satisfaction to thinking about consumption as a tool for political expression or for fighting against injustice, a convoluted version of the nation and national belonging can be found. The politics of consumption can range significantly; whether the nation is constructed and communicated as a brand or contested due to the violation of human rights, its exploration remains relevant on the approach used to make sense of it.

In approaching the relationship between nationalism and consumption, there are four key areas of study: *ethnocentric consumption*; *economic nationalism*; *consumer nationalism*; and *commercial nationalism*. Ethnocentric consumption interrogates consumer behaviour in terms of preference or lack of preference towards products on the basis of their country of origin ('made in') and is situated within marketing literature. Economic nationalism concerns the use of consumer culture by the state to promote ethnocentric consumption ('buy national' campaigns) and is mostly studied in history and sociology. A similar phenomenon, explored from various disciplines is consumer nationalism, concerning citizens' exhibition of patriotism or nationalism in the marketplace. Commercial nationalism, then, refers to processes of nation branding and the commodification of the nation by both state and market interests. The rise of the latter in particular resonates with what Kania-Lundholm (2014) calls the 'economization of the social' in the context of neoliberal globalisation, arguing that national identity is increasingly mediated and articulated in commercial terms, whether by corporations or by states. The evolution of scholarly work on this area demonstrates that there is a transformation of consumption *for* the nation towards consumption *of* the nation. The nation is increasingly continuously reified through different state and/or market-driven campaigns, promoted not only as a destination, but as a business partner or educator, or relationship with fellow inhabitants of its borders.

There are some tensions in the unravelling of these manifestations of nationalism in consumer culture. The first concerns the power dynamics between the state and/or market actors on the one hand and citizens on the other. The second concerns the power asymmetries between campaigners of consumer activism for and against a cause. The third concerns the binary treatment of forms of consumer politics as either good or bad. Recent literature on the use of consumer politics against forms of everyday racism has been significant in highlighting the colonial histories and controversies that can often be found in consumer practices.

ETHNOCENTRIC CONSUMPTION AS CALCULATED CONSUMER CHOICE: COUNTRY-OF-ORIGIN, CONSUMER ETHNOCENTRISM AND BRAND ORIGIN

The study of Country-of-Origin (COO) effects has become a sub-field of marketing scholarship. The literature on COO and its branch of consumer ethnocentrism (CE) have been understood in terms of three historical periods: (a) origin of COO research strand (mid 1960s–early 1980s); (b) increase of COO research and examination in terms of other factors that impact upon consumer preference (early 1980s–early 1990s); and (c) updating of COO scholarship vis-à-vis branding (early 1990s–mid 2000s) (Dinnie, 2004). The first period is annexed by Schooler's (1965) seminal piece whose research in Guatemala suggested that the country of origin label influences consumer choice. His survey also indicated that the type of influence stems from attitudes towards people and governments of different countries. The sub-field has broadened to include a number of different considerations impacting upon consumer preference in the COO paradigm (e.g. product evaluations, visuals, national labelling). The second period is characterised by challenging and forging a more complex understanding of consumer effects regarding national origin. For instance, during this period, the consumer ethnocentric tendencies scale (CETSCALE) was developed (Shimp and Sharma, 1987) for the calculation of consumer ethnocentrism; 'from the perspective of ethnocentric consumers, purchasing imported products is wrong because, in their minds, it hurts the domestic economy, causes loss of jobs, and is plainly unpatriotic' (ibid., p. 280). The CETSCALE is constructed with American consumers in mind, presenting 17 items intended to measure ethnocentric tendencies.[2] The third period embraces the role of image (Papadopoulos and Heslop, 1993) and branding in the field of COO (Thakor and Kohli, 1996; Kotler and Gertner, 2002). There are attempts to continue engaging with the CETSCALE (Acharya and Elliott, 2003; Lee et al., 2003), but also to move away from a Western understanding of consumer effects such as COO and CE (Batra et al., 2000; Balabanis et al., 2001; Wang and Chen, 2004). Furthermore, there is a broadening of COO to include the study of services as well as products. In what might be conceptualised as a fourth period, scholarly attention from marketing has continued to update the CETSCALE (Sharma, 2015), while it has also widened its focus to study preference for local consumption (Parsons et al., 2012), as well as regional ethnocentrism (Seidenfuss et al., 2013).

This chronology allows for understanding the development of a field in which the relationship between consumers and consumption can be measured in terms of feelings of loyalty towards a nation (such as nationalism and patriotism).[3] However, it remains normative in the way in which it treats the impact of perceived national origin on consumers, while it also disregards the role of political players in the formation of consumer identity as national identity. The methodological approach of this type of scholarship typically involves surveys, thereby quantifying ideologically charged concepts such as patriotism, nationalism and internationalism. In its attempt to measure the impact of national identity – the CETSCALE includes a series of statements such as 'a real American should always buy American-made products' – this literature fails to account for the complex relationship between everyday nationhood and consumption which can often involve dimensions of consumer culture beyond material consumption, such as rituals and media consumption (Billig, 1995; Fox, 2006). Consumer ethnocentrism has been a key concern of marketing, but its study has also extended into the social sciences and the humanities, where historical and cultural appraisals of economic nationalism can highlight how the nation has been constructed in parallel with the state.

MAKING CONSUMERS, MAKING THE NATION: ECONOMIC NATIONALISM AND BUY NATIONAL CAMPAIGNS

There is a wealth of literature in this area, from a variety of disciplinary approaches, all of which focus on the way in which the relationship between the state and citizens is mediated by consumer culture (Constantine, 1987; Frank, 1999; Tejapira, 2002; Gerth, 2003, 2008; Hopkins and Powers, 2007; Saffu et al, 2010; Schulze and Wolf, 2012; Thackeray and Toye, 2012; Kilic, 2013; Lekakis, 2015). Historical approaches have explored the way in which consumer culture and the public culture of modern nations were constructed alongside one another. A significant contribution in terms of understanding the history of consumer politics is Lawrence Glickman's (2013) differentiation between consumer activism, consumer regimes and the consumer movement; consumer activism refers to bottom-up processes by non-state actors, consumer movement addresses advocacy attempts to protect the consumer interest, while consumer regime refers to attempts made by the state to engage in the politics of consumption. While Glickman's approach is based in the specific context of the US, it is relevant more broadly in terms of its outlining of the agents of consumer politics that play a part in the constitution of the nation. The politics of consumption can be examined through the framework of economic nationalism. Economic nationalism is an argument constructed by the state suggesting that the national citizenry is to benefit from engaging in the ferocious nationalistic consumption of goods and services. Therefore, it is also akin to consumer regimes.

The theory of economic nationalism has been articulated by economic science approaches, which, similarly to marketing approaches, aim to understand the normative manifestations of citizens' consumer choices. For example, Harry G. Johnson (1965) constructs a theoretical model of economic nationalism based on an economic theory of democracy; in this model, he regards the power of nationalism over economic development policy as detrimental to the economic growth of the nation, due to the prioritising of the symbolic value of the nation over its economic value. This theory is based on three manifestations of economic nationalism: as discrimination (Becker, 1957), as democratic governance (Downs, 1957), as nationalism (Breton, 1964). Additionally, political scientists have constructed a theoretical model for understanding economic nationalism. Takeshi Nakano (2004) offers a systematic theory for understanding the role of nationalism in political economy. Through Emile Durkheim's political sociology of the state and economic sociology of industrial capitalism, Nakano explores the way in which national power is articulated as 'the positive relationship between nationalism, democracy and economic development' (Nakano, 2004, p. 221). Economic nationalism, then, highlights 'the reciprocal relationship between the political power and economic power of the nation-state' (ibid., p. 226). This tightly knit relationship between the economic and political power of the nation-state demonstrates that economic nationalism is not concerned with autarky, but the cohesion, dominance and increase of national power, and economic nationalist policies can often side with free trade, if it aids that.

Historically, the politics of consumption can often precede the constitution of modern nations. For example, an important contribution in the field of economic nationalism has been Dana Frank's *Buy American* (1999) which charts the construction of the US as an 'economic nation', as well as the ways in which US citizens have understood, adapted to and challenged the nation. For Frank, 'a Buy American campaign gave birth to the United States of America' (1999, p. 4); this is the story of American colonialists (such as the Boston Tea Party) boycotting British products to undercut the British Crown's authority. This movement, originally named 'nonimportation', 'nonconsumption' or 'nonintercourse' yielded the economic independence of the colonies from Great Britain, two years before political independence was granted through the Declaration of Independence. Hence, Frank's thesis highlights an important argument also echoed by Liah Greenfeld (2001); a history of economic nationalism illustrates the economic construction of contemporary nations at the core of their polity. Furthermore, Frank (1999, p. 21) argues, the early 'buy American' campaign was a useful 'nationalist smokescreen through which to increase one's profit rate, as prices rose in response to shortages'. Similarly, Greenfeld (2001, p. 33), tracing the origin of economic nationalism in England in the nineteenth century, suggests that it was 'a refraction of national consciousness in the consciousness of particular – economically active – strata'. Echoing Nakano (2004), then, while consumption is an everyday practice in the context of the nation, it can also be used as a tool for the state to promote itself as well as for nationalist exclusion.

Economic nationalism manifests as early as the construction of modern states, if not earlier (Foster, 1999). A global picture of modern nations reveals both similarities and differences in the way in which 'making consumers' became an integral part of 'making the nation'. In the case of the US, two years before the signing of the Declaration of Independence (1776), the Continental Association was created in order to ban trade between America and Great Britain (1774); thus, the economic independence of the US preceded its political independence. The trend of connecting citizenship and consumption in the US continued on to the twentieth century; Lizabeth Cohen (2003) documents the construction of the 'citizen consumer' at the turn of the century in *A Consumer's Republic*. The case of China is similar. Karl Gerth (2003, p. 17) argues that the Chinese nation and 'Chinese products' 'evolved together'. In one of his influential works, *China Made*, he demonstrates that in early twentieth-century China 'consumerism played a fundamental role in defining nationalism and nationalism in defying consumerism' (Gerth, 2003, p. 3). He has also outlined how the National Products Movement represented the state's attempt to promote Chinese nationalism (Gerth, 2008). The exploration of various global examples, thus, demonstrates that consumer cultures have been forged alongside the political construction of modern nations.

Modern nations demonstrate specific histories of colonialist relations. For example, important work has focused on the role of the Empire Marketing Board (EMB) (Constantine, 1986a, 1986b; Biccum, 2010; Kothari, 2014a, 2014b). The Board was set up in 1926 by the Secretary of State for the Dominions and its creation was

> symptomatic of the considerable political interest at this time in attempts to develop British Empire resources and to increase the flows of intra-imperial trade, so as to assist Britain's own domestic economic recovery and safeguard her long-term economic future. (Constantine, 1987, p. 47)

Uma Kothari (2014a), in her visual analysis of the EMB poster campaign (1926–1933) highlights how consumption was constructed as integral to progress and humanity and how the campaign attempted to positively stereotype empire goods and produce consumer culture that operated to legitimate the very existence of Empire. This process of state legitimation can also be traced in modern nations.

One of the core elements of economic nationalism is to be found in buy national campaigns. This is identified in numerous histories around the world, ranging from the US, Britain, Slovakia and Greece to China, South Korea and Thailand, among others (Constantine, 1987; Tejapira, 2002; Hopkins and Powers, 2007; Boehme, 2008; Saffu et al., 2010; Insch et al., 2011; Schulze and Wolf, 2012; Thackeray and Toye, 2012; Kilic, 2013; Lekakis, 2015). For example, when the kingdom of Siam became the nation of Thailand in 1938 with the rise to power of Pibulsongkram, several cultural mandates (*Rattha Nyiom*) were passed to inculcate

> a greater sense of nationalism among the Thais ... "Thais buy Thai" became a standard slogan which proved so effective that certain members of Parliament were reported to have voluntarily shaved their heads to avoid the use of combs which had to be imported at the time. (Numnonda, 1978, p. 235)

Dragged out of the past, buy national campaigns are often brought back in the face of a financial crisis. A campaign similar to the 'Thais buy Thai' campaign was revived in the late 1990s when the country went through a devastating economic crisis, the response to which came in the form of IMF-induced austerity policies (Numnonda, 1978; Tejapira, 2002). Similarly, in 1931, a Buy British campaign was launched aiming to 'persuade British consumers to buy, the British traders to sell, products made in Britain or in the British empire overseas at the expense of foreign suppliers' (Constantine, 1987, p. 44). This was not the first time a buy national campaign was launched in Britain; previously there had been the All-British Shopping Movement, which organised an 'All-British Shopping Week' in 1911, and industrialist entrepreneur Sir Williams Morris's[4] Buy British campaign in 1924 (ibid). The framing of the 1931 campaign was important in the context of the economic crisis in which it appeared and the Empire Marketing Board gave it the motto 'Buy British – From the Empire at Home and Overseas'. This campaign was exemplary of a consumer regime, as it was '"the biggest campaign ever undertaken by a Government in peacetime", according to one minister' (ibid., p. 45). Furthermore, in 1968, economic hardship was behind the launch of the I'm Backing Britain campaign,[5] which exhibited 'a neglect of the (post)imperial economy' (Thackeray and Toye, 2012). The revival of buy national campaigns is not uncommon in times of crisis.

When looking closely at the comeback of buy national campaigns, there is a change in the core narrative. If economic nationalism's contention used to be that the nation can be built through patriotic consumption, it now means that it should be saved through the same route. In the early 1980s when Greece came out of the military junta and a democratic state was being set up, the campaign 'I Insist on Greek' (*ο Επιμένων Ελλη-νικά*)[6] was launched to construct the citizen consumer. The very same campaign was re-launched after the first years of the financial crisis in Greece, making use of a video which was part of the campaign in 1984 (Lekakis, 2015). The reappearance of the video featured an annotation at the beginning which read '30 years ago we had prophetically sounded the alarm'.[7] The first time the buy national campaign is presented as a civic duty. The second time around it is represented as reprimanding. The global crises of the late 2000s have brought forward progressive and regressive waves of civic action, inclusive of economic nationalism as a structural adjustment of consumer spending directed towards nation-building. Economic nationalism is a phenomenon in which nationalism becomes manifest and communicated through the economic sphere. In the context of crisis, economic nationalism is promoted as ethnocentric consumption and demonstrates a close and dangerous relationship with extreme forms of nationalism (Lekakis, 2015). Stillerman (2015, p. 169) underscores that in the early twenty-first century 'it is common for public officeholders to exhort individuals to consume more to bolster economic activity'. This is evident in George W. Bush's statement after 9/11 urging Americans to resume normality by consuming in an attempt to fulfil their patriotic duty (Paterson, 2005; Banaji and Buckingham, 2009). Yet, theories of economic nationalism focus on the production and dissemination of the historical construction of the citizen as consumer and on buy national campaigns, but often do not focus on their understanding and negotiation by citizens.

FIGHTING (FOR) THE NATION: CONSUMER NATIONALISM, CONSUMER ACTIVISM AND POLITICAL CONSUMERISM

In parallel to many manifestations of consumer regimes, as discussed above, within nations struggles for social justice and emancipation also have significance in terms of the politics of consumption. In nineteenth-century England there were boycotts linked to anti-slavery campaigns (Gabriel and Lang, 2006; Soper and Trentmann, 2008). Over the course of a century, the intensification of trade relations and the constant remix of global consumer culture have culminated in the presence of sophisticated and all-encompassing forms of participation. In discussing consumer activism in relation to the nation, it is important to outline cases ranging from consumer nationalism to consumer activism. A difference between them is that the first 'provides a symbolic victory to the public' (Wang, 2006, p. 202), while the second aims at social change (Friedman, 1999; Forno, 2015; Micheletti and Stolle, 2015; Stolle and Micheletti, 2015). Yet, the terms are similar in the sense that they reflect bottom-up approaches to understandings of the relationship between nationalism and consumption, unlike economic nationalism which is concerned with the top-down approach to the making of a nation.

Consumer nationalism is concerned with the study of ethnicity and nationalism where through the practice of consumption, collective consumer identities are invoked 'based on their nationality to accept or reject products perceived of certain other countries' (Wang, 2006, p. 187). Consumer nationalism has been studied widely (Yoshino, 1999; Hooper, 2000; Jackson, 2004; Ozkan and Foster, 2005; Wang, 2006). However, it is not always distinct from economic nationalism. As Gerth (2013, p. 431, emphasis added) suggests:

> consumption and nationalism have intersected with efforts by nation-states, business leaders, patriotic students, and other figures to define buying and *use as a political statement* through the non-consumption of things from other countries and the consumption of one's own nation's goods and services.

Consumer nationalism is a perspective which can manifest positively through 'buy national' campaigns or negatively through boycott campaigns against 'foreign' products. Therefore, it is directly related to the politics of consumption. Forms of participation in public life that embrace formations of consumer activism have been described by political scientists as political consumerism (Micheletti et al., 2004). This is a phenomenon ranging from boycotts and buycotts to discursive political consumerism and lifestyle politics (Stolle and Micheletti, 2015). The first two have to do with the material act of consumption (avoiding or preferring the purchase of a product or service) while the latter two refer to discursive cultures of consumption (e.g. subvertising, culture jamming), and lifestyle commitments to consumer politics (e.g. freeganism, veganism).

The nation can become the target of political consumerism campaigns which often intersect with labour conditions, product safety and other elements, as outlined in different histories of consumer activism (Lekakis, 2012). However, often consumer nationalism is linked to public culture and affective national identity. Wang (2006, pp. 202–203) outlines the relationship between consumer nationalism and media discourse in the case of the Toshiba 'incident'[8] in 1999 when the company settled a lawsuit in the US but did not resolve the issue in China, concluding that it represents 'empowerment, as it is another platform for the public to express and contest identity and solidarity'. When consumer nationalism intersects with the two first types, it manifests as fighting for the nation or fighting the nation. Consumer activism, correspondingly, can manifest as positive (buycotts) or as negative (boycotts).

Firstly, buycotts targeting the nation are evident in terms of buy national campaigns, as discussed in the previous section, in which case approaches of economic nationalism coincide with those of consumer nationalism. Significant works in this area are Laura Nelson's (2000) study of consumer nationalism in South Korea, Li's (2008, 2009) work on China, and Roza Meuleman's (2014) study of the Netherlands. When exploring a global picture of economic and consumer nationalism, it is also important to discern between consumer cultures of frugality rather than excess as they have manifested in East Asia and in the West respectively (Nelson, 2000; Garon and Maclachlan, 2006). For example, Laura Nelson (2000) demonstrates how the concept of excessive consumption (*kwasobi*) is central to political activism in South Korea; 'Buy Korean' campaigns in the early 1900s were concerned with supporting limited consumption, savings and the purchase of South Korean products. For Gerth (2013, p. 432), the study of branding as the intersection of nationalism and consumption is 'a productive area of research for the foreseeable future'. Research on 'brand nationalism' which concerns the cross-fertilisation of economic and consumer nationalism through processes of branding has been emerging (Iwabuchi, 2015; Pike, 2015).

Secondly, boycotts targeting the nation concern cases of perpetration through colonialism, repression or violation of human rights.[9] Two cases stand out in particular here. The politics of consumption manifest historically in the case of the international boycott against the apartheid regime in South Africa, but also in the more recent example of the boycott against the state of Israel 'until it complies with international law and universal principles of human rights' (the Boycott, Divestment and Sanctions – or BDS – movement).[10]). Both of these cases represent social justice campaigns against institutional racism, social segregation and state violence, and with Archbishop Desmond Tutu (2013, p. xiii) states stating that the experience of the South African apartheid 'bears such remarkable parallels with the struggle of the Palestinian people for their freedom from the oppression and injustice imposed on them by successive Israeli governments'. BDS is a global movement which calls for a boycott of Israeli commodities produced in the occupied territories, but also an academic, tourist, sports and cultural boycott (Rose and Rose, 2008; Bakan and Abu-Laban, 2009; Wiles, 2013; Ananth, 2013; Di Stefano and Henaway, 2014; McMahon, 2014). For Micheletti and Stolle (2015, p. 484) this case highlights 'how individual and institutional consumers (e.g. universities) globally can be drawn into complex international issues'. Yet, while the BDS has achieved high visibility, it is not uncontested, not least because of the argument that it is a case of anti-Semitic/anti-Jewish racism. On the contrary, however, as Bakan and Abu-Laban (2009, p. 32) argue:

> the effectiveness of such a civil society initiative, as a strategy of resistance and cross-border solidarity, can be usefully framed as an anti-racist movement that contests a post-second world war hegemonic construction of state ideology, in which Zionism plays a central role and serves to enforce a racial contract that hides the apartheid-like character of the state of Israel.

The BDS is a movement against colonialism and racism. Yet, during at the time of writing, the British state is seeking to ban publically funded institutions from supporting the BDS movement.[11] Future research can build a rights-based approach at an interdisciplinary level, including the study of law, cultural studies and political science. Stolle and Micheletti, referring to political consumerism, also state about political consumerism that 'it can also be *a tool for supporting nationalism, intolerance, exclusiveness, or other types of hatred*.' (2015, p. 39, emphasis added). They go on to suggest that 'one important example that is completely understudied is what is called here *undemocratic political consumerism*' (ibid., p. 267, emphasis in original).

The politics of consumption have historically addressed ethnic/racial injustice, in the form of state apartheid or segregation. Historically, this is documented in the U.S., through the famous case of the Montgomery bus boycott of 1955 (Cohen, 2003; Stillerman, 2015). Still, Austin (1994, p. 226) documents ongoing service discrimination against black people in the U.S., as well as the construction of black consumption 'as a form of deviance'. She also connects the critique of forms of racialized consumption with the importance of linking production and consumption (cf. Seidman, 2007). Brown (2015, p. 239) extends this argument by exploring racialised political consumerism, a term which refers to instances where:

> (1) race is invoked to help encourage, describe, or explain consumption patterns and experiences, and
>
> (2) marketplace sites of consumerism are used or targeted for some political purpose that is designed to influence how resources are allocated toward a specific racial group.

Through the exploration of the case of the Black Star Line (BSL), a business initiative by the Universal Negro Improvement Association (UNIA), Brown (2015, p. 245) concludes that while offering opportunities for engagement and the operations of consumerism, 'racialized political consumerism can be effective in mobilizing groups while also being unsuccessful in leading to sustained improvement for those groups within a white capitalist context'. Her contribution is important in terms of exploring the relationship between the politics of consumption at its intersection with race and goes beyond the passing references to struggles for recognition and against oppression.

COMMERCIAL NATIONALISM: NEOLIBERAL REGIMES OF NATION BRANDING

Beyond commodity consumption, the notion of consuming the nation through images and brands also deserves critical attention. Nation branding is an obvious intersection between nationalism and consumption, yet it is important as a neoliberal consumer regime evoking the nation and national identity. Through the work of British branding strategists Simon Anholt and Wally Ollins, nation branding became a tool for public diplomacy and economic development. The definitions of nation branding converge on its harnessing of promotional communication of the nation; for

Aronczyk (2013, p. 15), it refers to 'the creation and communication of national identity using tools, techniques and expertise from the world of corporate brand management', while for Kaneva (2011b, p. 118) it is 'a compendium of discourses and practices aimed at reconstituting nationhood through marketing and branding paradigms'. There is growing scholarship exploring processes of nation branding (Iordanova, 2007; Jansen, 2008; Huang, 2011; Kaneva, 2011a, 2011b; Kaneva and Popescu, 2013; Valaskivi, 2013; Jordan, 2014; Bolin and Stååhlberg, 2015; Dinnie, 2016). Among these, *Branding the Nation* by Melissa Aronczyk (2013) has become a seminal book in which she outlines the collaboration between the commercial and public sectors for the purposes of increasing competitiveness and foreign direct investment. An important issue in this literature concerns issues around representation in terms of the national body and multiculturalism. Different nation branding campaigns exemplify the tendency to promote the nation as a battlefield of sameness, through often failed or non-existent attempts to communicate diversity (Aronczyk, 2013).

A related strand in the literature on media, communications and cultural studies has highlighted the rise of the phenomenon of commercial nationalism (Volcic, 2009; Volcic and Andrejevic, 2011; Volcic and Erjavec, 2012; Quail, 2015; Sanín Santamaria, 2015; Volcic and Andrejevic, 2015). Commercial nationalism refers to the process of symbolic commercial construction of a version of national identification. It is a process through which commercial entities promote national identity through their products or services, and as such, it is connected to the evolution of the study of COO and CE, as discussed earlier in this chapter, which seeks to measure the commercial impact of national identity on consumer behaviour. As Volcic and Andrejevic (2011, p. 613) state:

> The selling of nationalism – which has become a common theme in populist commercial outlets globally in a number of countries – represents a reflexive form of national identity building: the choice to consume a particular version of national identification. We see this development as a complementary one to nation branding: On the one hand, commercial entities sell nationalism as a means of winning ratings and profits, while on the other, the state markets itself as a brand. Such is the double logic of commercial nationalism.

The relationship, thus, between nationalism and consumption is also burdened by attempts to 'transpose politics into the register of sales and promotion' (ibid., p. 607). Hence, it is important to account for processes that develop from consumer regimes to neoliberal consumer regimes.

CONCLUSION: BUYING INTO THE NATION AND NATIONALISM

When addressing the politics of consumption, its relationship with nationalism manifests in different ways, each of which is mobilised by different entities and is appropriated by different agencies, but where the nation is almost always at the heart of the struggle. This chapter has highlighted different articulations of nationalism in consumption in the forms of *ethnocentric consumption*, *economic nationalism*, *consumer nationalism* and *commercial nationalism*. Ethnocentric consumption is rooted in a history of COO and CE literature which focuses on consumers' perceptions of product attributes, but it represents a normative way of conceptualising the convoluted relationship between nationalism and consumption and regards positive consumer choice as the main target. As such, it is similar to commercial nationalism, which is concerned with nation branding and co-branding with the nation to achieve economic success. Both these forms of nationalism in the marketplace demonstrate a neoliberal consumer regime whereby the nation and national identity are undergoing processes of commodification which can be accepted, appropriated or rejected by citizens. Economic nationalism is a phenomenon evident in the construction of nations where the citizen consumer is also forged as a key figure in the new national marketplace, and it manifests through 'buy national' campaigns, which often can and do make a comeback in times of crisis. Consumer nationalism, similarly, is a phenomenon where citizen consumers are acting in the marketplace with their national identity in mind. Therefore, while studied in different disciplines and rarely conversing, these phenomena spell out histories which can offer important contextual understandings of public cultures around the world.

Some of the areas for future development and critical issues arising will form the concluding remarks of this piece. Firstly, the nation is neither the state nor the individuals which inhabit it. The nation is discursively constructed and susceptible to both banal nationalism but also neoliberal globalisation. Yet, it is also formed by different races/ethnicities, each of which formulates a national identity on the basis of complex negotiations. Secondly, and importantly, as neoliberal globalisation is already in crisis, the way in which certain racialised/ethicised discourses around consumption emerge is often hidden or halted; the politics of consumption cannot merely concern the choice of a faceless, classless, genderless and raceless consumer, but individuals and groups who are situated within specific social positionings and which might or might not negotiate their national identities within neoliberal consumer regimes.

Notes

1 The nation is a geo-political construct, addressing 'imagined communities' (Anderson, 2006) and presenting borders and legal systems for access or non-access to the provisions of the state. Nationalism can describe a phenomenon of ideological, organisational and mobilisational character, as it can evoke sentiments and direct actions, include or exclude from its bureaucracy and muster resources and support for its diplomacy or military activities. National identity is a concept which deals with the additional complexity of emotional attachment and rationality in the configuration of civic agency. It concerns the experience and negotiation of belonging in the nation.

2 These include a series of statements ranging from statements about American-made products, imports and the perceived effects of purchasing the former versus the latter and vice versa.

3 There is a fine line between nationalism and patriotism. Some authors distinguish between the two; 'patriotism is commitment – a readiness to sacrifice for the nation – while nationalism is commitment plus exclusion of others, a readiness to sacrifice bolstered by hostility towards others' (Druckman, 1994: 47). Importantly, both are tools of the state to reaffirm a national identity upon its subjects; 'patriotism is precisely the ideas and feelings as a whole which bind the individual to a certain State' (Durkheim, 1992: 73), but also 'the patriotic card represents a particular political strategy, but it does not constitute the whole genus of nationalism within contemporary democratic politics' (Billig, 1995: 103).

4 Sir William Morris was the owner of the Morris Motor Company and a British philanthropist who donated to medical research and Nuffield College, University of Oxford.

5 The campaign was launched following the decision of five Surbiton secretaries to work for an extra half hour every day without receiving pay in order to boost productivity. I'm Backing Britain was backed by the government which faced a series of financial issues such as devaluation in the interior and diplomatic pressures in the exterior.
6 This generally translates to s/he who insists wins, but the word 'wins' becomes the word 'Greek' when a few more letters are attached to the front of it. So, the campaign carries the message s/he who insists on Greek, but effectively also wins.
7 https://www.youtube.com/watch?v=fAZzz8NalhI [accessed 1 March 2016].
8 The 'incident' concerned Toshiba's sale of computers with faulty floppy disk drives. Whereas in the US the corporation settled out of court for $1.05 billion, it did not compensate for the sale of its unreliable products in China, leading to a public outcry based on national pride and dignity in the Chinese media.
9 Some historical examples include anti-U.S. boycotts in China (Wong, 2001; Gerth, 2003), and anti-Japanese boycotts by Chinese immigrants in the U.S. during the invasion of China (Frank, 1999).
10 The BDS movement is a global movement brought into action in 2005 by different groups of the Palestinian civil society. For more information, see http://www.bdsmovement.net/ [accessed 1 March 2016]. The call for BDS also elaborates on what compliance with international law will mean: (1) Ending its occupation and colonisation of all Arab lands and dismantling the Wall,; (2) Recognising the fundamental rights of the Arab-Palestinian citizens of Israel to full equality; and (3) Respecting, protecting and promoting the rights of Palestinian refugees to return to their homes and properties as stipulated in UN resolution 194.
11 http://www.aljazeera.com/news/2016/02/anger-uk-moves-ban-israeli-settlement-boycott-160215164105804.html [accessed 1 March 2016].

REFERENCES

Acharya, C. and Elliott, G. (2003) 'Consumer Ethnocentrism, Perceived Product Quality and Choice – An Empirical Investigation', *Journal of International Consumer Marketing*, 15(4): 83–112.

Anderson, B. (2006) *Imagined Communities: Reflections on the Origin and Spread of Nationalism*. [revised edition]. London: Verso.

Aronczyk, M. (2013) *Branding the Nation. The Global Business of National Identity*. New York: Oxford University Press.

Austin, R. (1994) '"A Nation of Thieves": Consumption, Commerce and the Black Public Sphere', *Public Culture*, 7(1): 225–248.

Bakan, A.B. and Abu-Laban, Y. (2009) 'Palestinian resistance and international solidarity: the BDS campaign', *Race & Class*, 51(1): 29–54.

Balabanis, G., Diamantopoulos, A., Mueller, R. and Melewar, T. (2001) 'The Impact of Nationalism, Patriotism and Internationalism on Consumer Ethnocentric Tendencies', *Journal of International Business Studies*, 32(1): 157–175.

Banaji, S. and Buckingham, D. (2009) 'Civic Sell: Young People, the Internet, and Ethical Consumption', *Information, Communication and Society*, 12(8): 1197–1223.

Batra, R., Ramaswamy, V., Alden, D., Steenkamp, J.B., and Ramachander, S. (2000) 'Effects of Brand Local and Nonlocal Origin on Consumer Attitudes in Developing Countries', *Journal of Consumer Psychology*, 9(2): 83–95.

Becker, G.S. (1957) *The Economics of Discrimination*. Chicago: University of Chicago Press.

Biccum, A. (2010) *Global Citizenship and the Legacy of Empire: Marketing Development*. London and New York: Routledge.

Billig, M. (1995) *Banal Nationalism*. London: Sage.
Boehme, O. (2008) 'Economic Nationalism in Flanders before the Second World War', *Nations and Nationalism*, 14(3): 542–561.
Bolin, G. and Ståăhlberg, P. (2015) 'Mediating the Nation-State: Agency and the Media in Nation-Branding Campaigns', *International Journal of Communication*, 9: 3065–3083.
Breton, A. (1964) 'The Economics of Nationalism', *Journal of Political Economy*, LXXII: 376–386.
Brown, N.M. (2015) 'Freedom's Stock: Political Consumerism, Transnational Blackness and the Black Star Line', *Critical Sociology*, 41(2): 237–248.
Cohen, L. (2003) *A Consumers' Republic: The Politics of Mass Consumption in Postwar America*. New York: Vintage Books.
Constantine, S. (1986a) *Buy and Build: The Advertising Posters of the Empire Marketing Board*. London: PRO.
Constantine, S. (1986b) '"Bringing the Empire Alive": The Empire Marketing Board and Imperial Propaganda, 1926–33,'. In J. M. MacKenzie (ed) *Imperialism and Popular Culture*. Manchester: Manchester University Press, pp. 191–231.
Constantine, S. (1987) 'The Buy British Campaign of 1931', *European Journal of Marketing*, 21(4): 44–59.
Di Stefano, P. and Henaway, M. (2014) 'Boycotting Apartheid from South Africa to Palestine', *Peace Review*, 26(1): 19–27.
Dinnie, K. (2004) 'Country-of-Origin 1965-–2004: A Literature Review', *Journal of Customer Behaviour*, 3(2): 165–213.
Dinnie, K. (2016) *Nation Branding: Concepts, Issues, Practice*, 2nd edition. London: Routledge.
Downs, A. (1957) 'An Economic Theory of Political Action in a Democracy', *Journal of Political Economy*, 65(2): 135–150.
Druckman, D. (1994) 'Nationalism, Patriotism and Group Loyalty: A Social Psychological Perspective', *International Studies Quarterly*, 38(1): 43–68.
Durkheim, E. (1992) Professional Ethics and Civic Morals. [trans by Cornelia Brookfield]. London and New York: Routledge.
Forno, F. (2015) 'Bringing Together Scattered and Localized Actors: Political Consumerism as a Tool for Self-organizing Anti-mafia Communities', *International Journal of Consumer Studies*, 39(5): 535–543.
Foster, R.J. (1999) 'The Commercial Construction of "New Nations"', *Journal of Material Culture*, 4(3): 263–282.
Fox, J. (2006) 'Consuming the Nation: Holidays, Sports, and the Production of Collective belonging', *Ethnic and Racial Studies*, 29(2): 217–236.
Frank, D. (1999) *Buy American: The Untold Story of Economic Nationalism*. Boston, MA: Beacon Press.
Friedman, M. (1999) *Consumer Boycotts: Effecting Change Through the Marketplace and the Media*. New York: Routledge.
Gabriel, Y. and Lang, T. (2006) *The Unmanageable Consumer*. London: Sage.
Garon, S. and Maclachlan, P.L. (2006) 'Introduction'. In S. Garon and P. L. Maclachlan (eds) *The Ambivalent Consumer: Questioning Consumption in East Asia and the West*. Ithaca and London: Cornell University Press, pp. 1–15.
Gerth, K. (2003) *China Made: Consumer Culture and the Creation of the Nation*. Cambridge, MA: Harvard University Press.
Gerth, K. (2008) 'Consumption and Politics in Twentieth-century China'. In K. Soper and F. Trentmann (eds) *Citizenship and Consumption*. Basingstoke: Palgrave, pp. 34–50.

Gerth, K. (2013) 'Consumption and Nationalism: China'. In F. Trentmann (ed) *The Oxford Handbook of the History of Consumption*. Oxford: Oxford University Press, pp. 418–433.
Glickman, L.B. (2013) 'Consumer Activism, Consumer Regimes, and the Consumer Movement: Rethinking the History of Consumer Politics in the United States'. In F. Trentmann (ed) *The Oxford Handbook of the History of Consumption*. Oxford: Oxford University Press, pp. 399–417.
Greenfeld, L. (2001) *The Spirit of Capitalism: Nationalism and Economic Growth*. Cambridge, MA: Harvard University Press.
Hooper, B. (2000) 'Globalisation and Resistance in Post-Mao China: The Case of Foreign Consumer Products', *Asian Studies Review*, 24(4): 439–470.
Hopkins, R.A. and Powers, T.L. (2007) '"Buy National" and Altruistic Market Segments', *Journal of Global Marketing*, 20(4): 73–87.
Huang, S. (2011) 'Nation-branding and Transnational Consumption: Japan-mania and the Korean Wave in Taiwan', *Media, Culture & Society*, 33(1): 3–18.
Insch, A., Prentice, R.S. and Knight, J.G. (2011) 'Retail Buyers' Decision-making and Buy National Campaigns', *Australian Marketing Journal*, 19(4): 257–266.
Iordanova, D. (2007) 'Cashing in on Dracula: Eastern Europe's Hard Sells', *Framework: The Journal of Cinema and Media*, 48(1): 46–63.
Iwabuchi, K. (2015) *Resilient Borders and Cultural Diversity: Internationalism, Brand Nationalism and Multiculturalism in Japan*. Lanham, MD: Lexington Books.
Jackson, P. (1999) 'Consumption and Identity: The Cultural Politics of Shopping', *European Planning Studies*, 7(1): 25–39.
Jackson, P. (2004) 'Local Consumption Cultures in a Globalizing World', *Transactions of the Institute of British Geographers*, 29(2): 165–178.
Jansen, S.C. (2008) 'Designer Nations: Neo-liberal Nation Branding – Brand Estonia', *Social Identities*, 14(1): 121–142.
Johnson, H.G. (1965) 'A Theoretical Model of Economic Nationalism in New and Developing States', *Political Science Quarterly*, 80(2): 169–185.
Jordan, P. (2014) 'Nation Branding: A Tool for Nationalism?' *Journal of Baltic Studies*, 45(3): 283–303.
Kaneva, N. (2011a) *Branding Post-Communist Nations: Marketizing National Identities in the New Europe*. London: Routledge.
Kaneva, N. (2011b) 'Nation Branding: Toward an Agenda for Critical Research', *International Journal of Communication*, 5: 117–141.
Kaneva, N. and Popescu, D. (2013) '"We are Romanian, not Roma": Nation Branding and Postsocialist Discourses of Alterity', *Communication, Culture & Critique*, 7(4): 506–523.
Kania-Lundholm, M. (2014) 'Nation in Market Times: Connecting the National and the Commercial: A Research Overview', *Sociology Compass*, 8(6): 603–613.
Kilic, N.P. (2013) 'Fight against the Economic Crisis: Communication Campaign Samples in Turkey', Paper presented at *IAMCR Conference*, Dublin, 25–29 June.
Kothari, U. (2014a) 'Visual Representations of Development: The Empire Marketing Board Poster Campaign, 1926–1933'. In D. Lewis, D. Rodgers and M. Woolcock (eds) *Popular Representations of Development: Insights from Novels, Films, Television and Social Media*. Abingdon: Routledge, pp. 151–173.
Kothari, U. (2014b) 'Trade, Consumption and Development Alliances: The Historical Legacy of the Empire Marketing Board Poster Campaign', *Third World Quarterly*, 35(1): 43–64.
Kotler, P. and Gertner, D. (2002) 'Country as Brand, Products, and Beyond: A Place Marketing and Brand Management Perspective', *Journal of Brand Management*, 9(4/5): 249–261.

Lee, W.-N., Hong, J.-Y. and Lee, S.-J. (2003) 'Communicating with American Consumers in the Post 9/11 Climate: An Empirical Investigation of Consumer Ethnocentrism in the United States', *International Journal of Advertising*, 22(4): 487–510.

Lekakis, E.J. (2012) 'Will the Fair Trade Revolution Be Marketised? Commodification, Decommodification and the Political Intensity of Consumer Politics', *Culture & Organization*, 18(5): 345–358.

Lekakis, E.J. (2015) 'Economic Nationalism and the Cultural Politics of Consumption under Austerity: The Rise of Ethnocentric Consumption in Greece', *Journal of Consumer Culture*. DOI: 10.1177/1469540515586872.

Li, H. (2008) 'Branding Chinese Products: Between Nationalism and Transnationalism', *International Journal of Communication*, 2: 1125–1163.

Li, H. (2009) 'Marketing Japanese Products in the Context of Chinese Nationalism', *Critical Studies in Media Communication*, 26(5): 435–456.

McMahon, S. (2014) 'The Boycott, Divestment, Sanctions Campaign: Contradictions and Challenges', *Race & Class*, 55(4): 65–81.

Meuleman, R. (2014) 'Consuming the Nation: Domestic Cultural Consumption: Its Stratification and Relation with Nationalist Attitudes', PhD Thesis, Utrecht University.

Micheletti, M. and Stolle, D. (2015) 'Consumer Strategies in Social Movements'. In D. della Porta and M. Diani (eds) *The Oxford Handbook of Social Movements*. Oxford: Oxford University Press, pp. 478–493.

Micheletti, M., Follesdal, A. and Stolle, D. (2004) *Politics, Products, and Markets: Exploring Political Consumerism Past and Present*. London: Transaction Publishers.

Nakano, T. (2004) 'Theorising Economic Nationalism', *Nations and Nationalism*, 10(3): 211–229.

Nelson, L. (2000) *Measured Excess: Status, Gender, and Consumer Nationalism in South Korea*. New York: Columbia University Press.

Numnonda, T. (1978) 'Pibulsongkram's Thai Nation-Building Programme during the Japanese Military Presence, 1941–1945', *Journal of Southeast Asian Studies*, 9(2): 234–247.

Ozkan, D. and Foster, R.J. (2005) 'Consumer Citizenship, Nationalism, and Neoliberal Globalization in Turkey: The Advertising Launch of Cola Turka', *Advertising & Society Review*, 6(3).

Papadopoulos, N. and Heslop, L. (1993) *Product and Country Images: Research and Strategy*. New York: The Haworth Press.

Parsons, A.G., Ballantine, P.W. and Wilkinson, H. (2012) 'Country-of-Origin and Private-label Merchandise', *Journal of Marketing Management*, 28(5/6): 594–608.

Paterson, M. (2005) 'Shut Up and Shop! Thinking Politically about Consumption'. Available at http://www.globalpolicy.org/globaliz/econ/2005/0105shop.pdf (accessed 1 March 2016).

Pike, A. (2015) *Origination: The Geographies of Brands and Branding*. Chichester: Wiley Blackwell.

Quail, C. (2015) 'Anatomy of a Format: So You Think You Can Dance Canada and Discourses of Commercial Nationalism', *Television & New Media*, 16(5): 472–489.

Rose, H. and Rose, S. (2008) 'Israel, Europe and the Academic Boycott', *Race & Class*, 50(1): 1–20.

Saffu, K., Walker, J.H. and Mazurek, M. (2010) 'The Role of Consumer Ethnocentrism in a Buy National Campaign in a Transitioning Country: Some Evidence from Slovakia', *International Journal of Emerging Markets*, 5(2): 203–226.

Sanín Santamaria, J.D. (2015) 'Branding Australia: The Commercial Construction of Australianness', PhD thesis, Monash University.

Schooler, R.D. (1965) 'Product Bias in the Central American Common Market', *Journal of Marketing Research*, 2(4): 394–397.

Schulze, M.S. and Wolf, N. (2012) 'Economic Nationalism and Economic Integration: The Austro-Hungarian Empire in the Late Nineteenth Century', *Economic History Review*, 65(2): 652–673.

Seidenfuss, K.-U., Kathawala, Y. and Dinnie, K. (2013) 'Regional and Country Ethnocentrism: Broadening ASEAN Origin Perspectives', *Asia Pacific Journal of Marketing and Logistics*, 25(2): 298–320.

Seidman, G.W. (2007) *Beyond the Boycott: Labor Rights, Human Rights, and Transnational Activism*. New York: Russell Sage Foundation.

Sharma, P. (2015) 'Consumer ethnocentrism: Reconceptualization and cross-cultural validation', *Journal of International Business Studies*, 46(3): 381–389.

Shimp, T.A. and Sharma, S. (1987) 'Consumer Ethnocentrism: Construction and Validation of the CETSCALE', *Journal of Marketing Research*, 24(3): 280–289.

Smyczek, S. and Glowik, M. (2011) 'Ethnocentrism of Polish Consumers as a Result of the Global Financial Crisis', *Journal of Customer Behaviour*, 10(2): 99–118.

Soper, K. and Trentmann, F. (eds) (2008) *Citizenship and Consumption*. Basingstoke: Palgrave.

Stillerman, J. (2015) *The Sociology of Consumption: A Global Approach*. Cambridge: Polity.

Stolle, D. and Micheletti, M. (2015) *Political Consumerism: Global Responsibility in Action*. Cambridge: Cambridge University Press.

Tejapira, K. (2002) 'Post-Crisis Economic Impasse and Political Recovery in Thailand: The Resurgence of Economic Nationalism', *Critical Asian Studies*, 34(3): 323–356.

Thackeray, D. and Toye, R. (2012) 'From "Empire Shopping" to "Buying British": The Public Politics of Consumption, 1945–63'. Paper presented at the *Annual Conference of the Economic History Society*, St Catherine's College, University of Oxford. Available at http://www.ehs.org.uk/dotAsset/facc80e7-e1ce-499a-acc5-82ee2533cb51.pdf [accessed 1 March 2016].

Thakor, M.V. and Kohli, C.S. (1996) 'Brand Origin: Conceptualization and Review', *Journal of Consumer Marketing*, 13(3): 27–42.

Tutu, Archbishop D. (2013) 'Preface'. In R. Wiles (ed) *Generation Palestine: Voices from the Boycott, Divestment and Sanctions Movement*. New York: Pluto Press, pp. xii–xiv.

Valaskivi, K. (2013) 'A Brand New Future? Cool Japan and the Social Imaginary of the Branded Nation', *Japan Forum*, 25(4): 485–504.

Volcic, Z. (2009) 'Television in the Balkans: The Rise of Commercial Nationalism'. In G. Turner and J. Tay (eds) *Television Studies after TV: Understanding Television in the Post-Broadcast Era*. London: Routledge, pp. 115–124.

Volcic, Z. and Andrejevic, M. (2011) 'Nation Branding in the Era of Commercial Nationalism', *International Journal of Communication*, 5: 598–618.

Volcic, Z. and Andrejevic, M. (2015) *Commercial Nationalism: Selling the Nation and Nationalizing the Sell*. Basingstoke: Palgrave.

Volcic, Z. and Erjavec, K. (2012) 'Commercial and Sexualized Nationalism on Serbian Reality TV', *International Journal of Cultural Studies*, 16(6): 597–614.

Volcic, Z. and Andrejevic, M. (2015) *Commercial Nationalism: Selling the Nation and Nationalizing the Sell*. Basingstoke: Palgrave.

Wang, C.L. and Chen, Z.X. (2004) 'Consumer Ethnocentrism and Willingness to Buy Domestic Products in a Developing Country Setting: Testing Moderating Effects', *Journal of Consumer Marketing*, 21(6): 391–400.

Wang, J. (2006) 'The Politics of Goods: A Case Study of Consumer Nationalism and Media Discourse in Contemporary China', *Asian Journal of Communication*, 16(2): 187–206.
Wiles, R. (ed) (2013) *Generation Palestine: Voices from the Boycott, Divestment and Sanctions Movement*. New York: Pluto Press.
Wong, S.-K. (2001) 'Die for the Boycott and Nation: Martyrdom and the 1905 Anti-American Movement in China', *Modern Asian Studies*, 35(3): 565–588.
Yoshino, K. (ed) (1999) *Consuming Ethnicity and Nationalism: Asian Experiences*. Richmond: Curzon Press.

29

The Politics of Consumption

Alan Bradshaw

INTRODUCTION

The character of the consumer is subject to a number of contestations that arguably fail to trigger what might boldly be claimed as a *politics proper*. With particular reference to two new books that point towards an alternative reckoning of how a politics of consumption might be engaged, *The Politics of Everybody* by Holly Lewis (2016) and *On the Commodity Trail* by Alison Hulme (2015), and via brief explorations of contemporary questions of homeownership and the privatisation of communication on social media, this chapter argues for, first, a politics of consumption grounded on rejecting the idea of a consumer class and second, a commitment to studying the politics of consumption as a question of who owns the mechanisms for reproducing social relations.

At one far poll, which we can caricature[1] as *stridently leftist*, we see the consumer as a dupe who is all-too amenable to the false claims of hidden persuaders; as a reified reproducer of mass-manufactured identities and therefore a person who has failed to realise a subjectivity proper; as an overweight alcoholic porn-obsessed addict of social media's false news; as the atomised hyper-individualised narcissist who bowls alone, as an id-like fool committed to toxic instant gratification; as a subject of his/her own stupid desire rather than rational reflection; as an un-reflexive reproducer of all manners of gender, class, age and race outrages; as a post-political subject oblivious to his/her own cruel conservativism; as an opprobrious polluter who carelessly generates trails of smoking fossil fuels; and as an unapologetic asshole who lacks basic awareness of the ethics of shared space and yells 'I'm on a train' into their mobile phone.

At the opposite poll, which we might term *boisterously neoliberal*, is the celebrated consumer who is a creative chameleon, whose endless play with markers of identification is a rich mode of cultural expression in its own right, whose consumerism is a form of social enterprise that carves new practices of communal being and value, who is so empowered by their consumption choices that they might as well be an energy grid for a small city, whose banana consumption will rescue the global South, and who re-organises and transcends gender, race, class and age norms each time they gloriously hit the high street.

In between lies, arguably, the falsest position of all, the *enlightened liberal*, who, following prolonged in-depth interviews and longitudinal participant engagement, reports back from their exotic anthropological field that this special species known as 'consumer' is actually constantly negotiating between these hysterical poles and whose consumption should be interpreted as remarkably sensible solutions to conundrums of mythical proportions. Accordingly, one does not simply eat a sandwich, one sutures grand narratives and ideological injunctions, though it typically requires an interview with a consumer researcher for this real meaning of sandwich eating to register.

A separate contestation of 'the consumer' considers this subject's dialectical relationship with the producer. Rather than accept the consumer as the person who merely consumes and wastes away objects, the consumer is understood as actively participating in a sort of tango dance with the producer, where who gets to lead the dance shifts between both partners in the co-production of a mesmerising spectacle.[2] The consumer, hence, is an immaterial labourer who adds value to the object during consumption and therefore is not the logical other of the producer. Here terms like co-creation, prosumer and service-dominant logic abound.

Both Lewis and Hulme present arguments that perhaps, from a politics of consumption perspective, posit all of the above as false positions. As Lewis (2016) puts it, 'neoliberal political thought, whether progressive or conservative, acknowledges two great classes in the world: not capitalists and proletarians, but producers and consumers' (p. 10). In other words, these are false categories that serve to mystify and naturalise broader class antagonisms. Lewis, rightfully, insists that consumption and consumerism are not the causes, but consequences, of exploitation and therefore any categorical split between producers and consumers is a misnomer. Our focus must instead be directed, away from the consumer good as a 'thing' that is to be understood in terms of how a person or set of people consume it, but instead to understand the commodity as 'concretised' through invisible processes. 'Each of us', Lewis reminds us,

> has a network of invisible caretakers scattered across the globe, fulfilling tasks once performed within the community. People we don't know stitch together our underwear, mine the metals used to make the machines that make our bicycles and pots, harvest our grain, grind the sand to make our drinking glasses. Sometimes our invisible caretakers live in town: lifting boxes from pallets, grading our term papers, preparing food in the backs of restaurants, cleaning our shit off public toilets. (p. 10)

The point is not to identify a shamefully parasitic relation of a consumer class to a worker class because it is not simply the wealthy who get to consume. The point, Lewis propounds, is to develop a politics that

> addresses global subjects and asserts that there is commensurability between them. In other words, the only way to confront the system is to develop solidarity between those who must

> labour – including those who are unable to labour – in this enormous network of mines, factories, schools, stores and transport centres: solidarity between the visible and the invisible, the waged and the unwaged. (p. 11)

This is all to say that a politics of consumption should not concern itself with arriving at an endpoint of either critique or appreciation of the consumer (a concern with normative affects), but rather to consider how our consumption might allow us to understand ourselves as networked to an invisible global army of caretakers and to understand this constellation in terms of capitalist accumulation and reproduction (a concern with structural effects).

By contrast, Hulme (2015) argues that the choice between the 'consumer-as-dupe vision' and 'consumer-as-creative-agent' vision, or indeed some kind of compromise between the two, is a false question because it emphasises consumption as a matter of personal desires between available products. Instead, Hulme argues that the question of the consumer and consumer choice should be recognised at the broader level of the state in which consumer spending is invoked for different purposes. For example, in contemporary China, Hulme argues, consumption is linked to the notion of the 'trickle-down effect', whereby the enrichment of the upper income levels will benefit poorer members of society by improving the economy as a whole. In contrast, post September 11 USA, consumption was encouraged as a means of exhibiting defiance to terrorists who apparently were motivated by their great hatred of American consumer freedom. By examining these broader political projects that contextualise consumerism, Hulme argues that we can identify that the idea of consumer agency is bounded by the subject's relationship with the state, which in turn is framed in terms of being a citizen with rights, when in reality it is about being a subject with responsibilities: as Hulme puts it, 'obligatory consumer societies, by their very nature, require subjects who take their responsibility to consume seriously. The era of obligatory consumerism changed the structure of the subject's position to the State and strategic relation to his or her own consumption as far as the State is concerned' (2015, p. 105). In other words, the identifications that we make with our own consumption, and with our status as consumers, whether it be in the capacity of being actual consumers or indeed academic consumer researchers, is to obscure how this consumption is framed by a far broader instrument of power. This is also to remind us that being a consumer is not a matter of personal choice but an obligatory subjectivity.[3]

THE COMMODITY FETISH

Both Lewis and Hulme address how we should conceive politically of the relationship we have with these global 'invisible caretakers' that facilitate our consumption. Such politics might well begin with wondering how the exploitation that facilitates our consumption becomes invisible, because, from a Marxist perspective, this moment of disappearance is critical for the formation of class stratification. The term given to this moment is the 'fetish', which Harvey (2014) defines as the 'various masks, disguises and distortions of what is really going on around us' (p. 4). Geras (1983) explains, the fetish is the moment when 'material objects have certain characteristics conferred on them in virtue of the prevailing social relations, and are regarded as if such characteristics belonged to them by nature' (p. 190). The fetish is recognisable in our inability to recognise labour as a social process. Instead, this social relation between workers is only effected in the form of a relation between their products, the commodities they buy and sell – this is because the social character of labour only appears *indirectly* in the values of these commodities so that value seems inherent in the commodity, indeed as natural to the commodity, rather than a reflection of a division of labour. The commodity itself is the bearer of a 'historically specific social characteristic' (p. 190). As Marx (2017) famously put it:

> Could commodities themselves speak, they would say: Our use value may be a thing that interests men. It is no part of us as objects. What, however, does belong to us as objects, is our value. Our natural intercourse as commodities proves it. In the eyes of each other we are nothing but exchange values.

The significance of this point is of major consequence for Marx's analysis and indeed is the very starting point of his analysis; after all the first two sentences of *Das Kapital* read: 'The wealth of societies in which the capitalist mode of production prevails appears as an "immense collection of commodities": the individual commodity appears as its elementary form. Our investigation therefore begins with the analysis of the commodity' (Marx, 2017). Marx explains that the value of any object becomes relativised by the value of other commodities during exchange so that a general form of value emerges in which, famously, 20 yards of linen = 1 coat. The logic of the emergent capitalist exchange relies on the labour necessary for producing these objects finding their social expression in the commodity itself. As Fine (1983) puts it, 'the social relationship between tailor and carpenter appears as a relationship between coat and table in terms of the ratio at which these things exchange with each other rather than in terms of the labors embodied in them' (p. 102). This is all a matter, for Marx, of the 'fetishism of the commodity and its secret', where the secret is the social character of the labour that produced the commodity. It is important to add that there is an affective dimension to the fetish – as Ahmed (2014) argues, the commodity fetish might also be understood as a type of affective value because feelings come to reside in the objects but only through the erasure of the history of the object's production and circulation. To this end, we might say that forms of marketing such as branding and advertising inject affective content into the commodity so to fill the void left by rendering the social relations of production itself invisible (Fuchs, 2017).

Consumption, therefore, must be understood as a moment when systemic blindness happens. Notably, Marx identifies the active hand of the consumer. It is not the capitalist, the rentier, nor other agents of state, who puts the labourer *out of sight, but the consumer*. Yet as Marx also acknowledges, when we consume objects, we also bring into existence the object's use-value because simply 'without consumption there is no value'. Intriguingly Marx acknowledges that these objects – that carry with them a secret – have a 'phantomlike', and 'unsubstantial character'; namely that human labour remains contained within them. In other words the commodity may not always succeed in maintaining its secret, and here lies the possibility of a different form of politicising our consumption.

'FOLLOW THE THING'

Harvey (2014) tells us that we constantly encounter fetishes:

> The supermarket is riddled with fetishistic signs and disguises. The lettuce costs half as much as half a pound of tomatoes. But where did the lettuce and the tomatoes come from and who was it that worked to produce them and who brought them to the supermarket? And why does one item cost so much more than another? Moreover, who has the right to attach some kabalastic sign like $ or € or £ over the items for sale and who puts a number on them, like a $1 a pound or £2 a kilo? Commodities magically appear in the supermarkets with a price tag attached such that customers with money can satisfy their wants and needs depending upon how much money they have in their pockets. We get used to all this, but we don't notice that we have no idea where most of the items come from, how they were produced, by whom and under what conditions, or why, exactly, they exchange in the ratios they do and what the money we use is really all about. (pp. 6–7)

To politicise our consumption we should constantly question the social distribution of labour and particular forms of exploitation that brought the object into our lives, and question the relationship between the object's value and the people whose labour the object depends upon. At stake, for Harvey, is the political project of de-fetishising the object by exposing the social process of its production and allowing the object to reveal everyday exploitations and our reliance upon concealed networks of helpers.

By 'following the thing', to invoke the challenge set by Appadurai (1988), a number of substantial insights may be generated. Notably Mintz (1986), in his landmark study of the global network that linked West Indies sugar farmers and British tea drinkers, brings an entire colonial model into focus that reveals much about how imperialistic domination functions while the shifting tastes for sugar consumption reveal much by way of class dynamics. By demonstrating the global commodity chain of sugar, Mintz evidences a direct link between slave labour and commodity consumption which should prompt us to wonder how much of our everyday consumption links us to contemporary forms of slavery and exploitative working conditions. More recent examples of the 'follow the thing' genre include Cook and Harrison's (2007) study of hot pepper sauces. Here the authors trace relations between a north London family cooking fishcakes on a Friday night with Jamaican sugar cane farmers. Between the two is revealed a 'constellation of people, plants, bugs, diseases, recipes, politics, trade agreements and histories, whose multiple, complex entanglements and disjunctures animate this "thing" and its travels' (p. 40). To be sure, Cook and Harrison's study is moving and evokes sympathetic awareness of and identification with various agents along the constellation.

It is within this field of study that Hulme (2015) invokes phantasmagorical wonder by re-imagining Walter Benjamin's *Arcades Project*, this time tracing bargain goods. Providing a set of memorable imagery, Hulme outlines a commodity trail that links a peddler pushing an old cart of cardboard boxes through abandoned parts of Shanghai, a wholesale buyer comparing goods at huge markets, a port employee who uses a computer to move crates, a south east London pound shop owner who bulk loads his shelves with bargain trinkets and a domestic consumer lovingly placing gnomes in a suburban garden. In each case, the exercise is to establish broader identifications based on recognising the conditions of labour and production. Such a task might well serve to restore Marxism as what Ahmed (2014) describes it to be, a 'philosophy of wonder' that serves to teach us to see differently what appears before consciousness, or to generate an 'affective opening up of the world through the act of wonder, not as a private act, but as an opening up of what is possible through working together' (p. 181).

Yet as Hulme (2015) reminds us, in matters of politics, varying forms of response emerge. For some, influenced by Harvey, the consequence is to merely 'shop differently' and hence ethical consumption emerges as a preferred solution. Hulme is clear; 'shopping differently is a rather weak version of the outcomes Harvey's thought could potentially lead to and [I] wanted to apply his theory in a way that did not simply berate terrible working conditions and profiteering practices, but tried to place a commodity chain within a wider vision of spaces and operations globally' (Hulme, 2015: xiii). Accordingly, market solutions to market problems whereby all one has to do is 'shop differently' are to be problematised in as much as they do not confront underlying antagonisms of accumulation and exploitation. This is a reminder that we ought to consider the link between ideology and the fetish because, for Marx, ideology is that which naturalises domination and exploitation and we must understand this naturalisation as just as immanent to the commodity as commodity fetishism (Fuchs, 2017). Accordingly, the idea that a solution is arrived at by shopping differently is already to naturalise commodity exchange, even if it entails degrees of defetishisation.

For example, Fair Trade consumerism emerges as such a solution for problems of ethical consumerism and it invokes a spirit of planetary mutuality and shared empowerment that links labourers and consumers. While Fair Trade might appear to have succeeded in partially de-fetishising obscured global commodity chains, it would be more accurate to say that it has re-appropriated the fetish and did so by creating a new kind of symbolic value that sometimes romanticises and exoticises global South producers and their labour for the benefit of consumers in the north (see Littler, 2008). Hence advertising images that depict indigenous farmers hard at work uncomfortably resonate with Victorian discourses of the 'noble savage', the 'deserving poor' and in some cases, the 'negro goddess'. At stake, in other words, may be a false and patronising form of solidarity that reproduces colonial tropes. Further, such promoted forms of 'consumer citizenship' that depend upon cosmopolitan concerns about the distant other and individualised types of action imagined as collective, can end up undoing the work and symbolic efficiency of more traditional modes of political action (Lekakis, 2013). Such acts might be understood as instantiating what Dean (2009) terms 'communicative capitalism' – that is, the 'materialization of ideals of inclusion and participation in information, entertainment and communication technologies in ways that capture resistance and intensify global capitalism' (p. 2).

Further analysis of the particular ideological content of the commodity fetish of socially enterprising goods is presented by Žižek. For Žižek, there is a fundamental irony in how Starbucks, for example, offer consumers redemption from the sin of consuming Starbucks because they promise to donate a sum from each purchase to developing contexts (Žižek, 2011). This gesture, he argues, contains a logic of disavowal because buying coffee that promises to solve the problems created by buying coffee is an erasure of real politics. Capitalism, therefore, often functions like a 'chocolate laxative' (Žižek, 2011), in that it represents itself as the object of its own containment – it is this double take of commodity fetishism that constitutes how ideology is often inscribed into the commodity. From a politics of consumption perspective, if the radical task succeeds and the fetish is uncovered, Žižek reminds us that the dialectical materialist's work is not yet finished. A defetishisation may serve for a re-appropriation of the fetish, as per Fair Trade, or for the consumer to move into a self-referential relationship with the fetish in which 'knowing' about the fetish appears as an end in its own right and facilitates a disavowal that

> enables you to fully participate in the frantic pace of the capitalist game while sustaining the perception that you are not really in it, that you are well aware how worthless this spectacle is – what really matters to you is the peace of the inner Self to which you know you can always withdraw. (Žižek, 2001, p. 15)

The consequence of Žižek's important intervention is to ensure that we must understand the supplemental relationship between the fetish and ideology.

THE HOME

A powerful example of why a politics of consumption cannot simply depend upon observing how people consume certain objects is presented by a broader analysis of the home. The home is arguably the most important object that anybody will consume in terms of how much of our lives are given to both consuming, and indeed paying for it, how much essential components of the life such as protection, security and health are bound to it, not to mention the more banal fact of how physically big a home tends to be relative to any other consumer object a person is ever likely to possess, and thus it becomes clear what Miller meant when he stated that 'basically homes are the elephants of stuff' (Miller, 2010, p. 81).

As Harvey (2014) tells us, despite the centrality of the use value of our homes (as sources of accommodation, security, the place of family reproduction, etc.), it is the exchange value that tends to dominate, because in most Western countries, housing is built speculatively as a commodity, meaning that it is the potential exchange value that tends to matter most, especially when the state declines to subsidise affordable housing. Such are the stakes of home ownership that the maintenance and improvement of housing asset values, as well as questions of access and exclusion, have become important political objectives for large segments of the population. Given the degree of speculation on house prices, much economic instability ensues with the obvious damage to the global economy of the various bursting house price bubbles. When prices collapse, disaster ensues – for example, four million Americans lost their homes to foreclosure during the recent property market crash (Harvey, 2014). When house prices rise, a different type of disaster also ensues: 'growing social housing waiting lists, rising rents and house prices, insecure tenancies, overcrowding, declining quality and the rapid gentrification driving the less well-off out of cities' which overall attest to the context of housing today in many countries as 'a major source of inequality, social division and deteriorating living standards' (Robertson, 2017, p. 195).

Homeownership, therefore, presents an excellent example of Hulme's commitment to understanding the idea of consumption with reference to the fetishised relationship between the consumer and the state. For example, as argued by Robertson (2017), the domination of use value by exchange value for homes is best demonstrated in circumstances where housing consumption is organised around the principle of homeownership as a means of capturing ground rents. In countries like the UK, this is a consequence of a deliberate government neoliberal strategy to restructure the relationship between the individual and society away from collectivist models of welfare provision towards an individualist model grounded in asset investment (Robertson, 2017). Where our relationship to home becomes so financialized that the asset role of the home dominates over its role as a form of shelter (Robertson, 2017), the circumstances of inequality quickly become extreme. Robertson (2017: 204) outlines the consequences:

> ... there is a world of difference, for example, between a young family getting heavily into debt in order to acquire a starter home and wealthy foreign investors buying property in London, often without ever having seen it or intending to occupy it ... [they are] driving up prices for would-be homeowners or those further down the housing ladder. A similar source of inequality among owner-occupiers emerges because some are able to leverage their properties to acquire more houses, thus giving them greater access to the value accumulating on residential land ... Even more notable is the inequality between those who are on the property ladder and those who are not. Given that everyone needs housing, the nature of housing wealth is such that a rise in house prices is essentially a redistribution towards homeowners away from renters. As mortgage credit has been channeled into residential values, homeowners become wealthier, but the housing costs of those who do not own a home go up ... There is a generational dimension to this inequality because it tends to be older generations – particularly the baby boomers and those who bought during the first wave of the Right to Buy – who acquired a windfall from house price inflation over the last three decades, while younger generations are left to face higher housing costs.

Once our lives become dominated by the exchange value of a home, not only do we have to commit our working lives to servicing credit or paying rent, but for some home owners their whole live becomes a form of asset maintenance. For example, Zwick and Ozalp (2011) studied condominium and loft buyers in transitional Toronto neighbourhoods, and noticed that the sellers decreasingly emphasise the traditional use value of the property (e.g. the number of bedrooms) and instead emphasise 'the dwelling's symbolic, emotional, communal, and affective potential for facilitating the production of specific forms of life and subjectivities aspired to by the buyers of the product' (p. 236). Of course these abstract assets tend not to materially exist in these transitional neighbourhoods because it is yet to be seen if they are to become vibrant creative or 'hipster' districts. But what is clear is that if the neighbourhoods are to succeed, and will therefore justify the high home prices that buyers are asked to pay, then this will require the active participation and life-style performativity of the new urban dwellers because lifestyles and consumption practices and affective attachments are reconfigured as necessary forms of investment in home prices and community development. As Zwick and Ozalp (2011) put it, the sellers seek to 'sell the value generated by the consumers to the consumers through their collective production of social communication, lifestyle, social relationships, community, and so forth' (p. 236). The tacit injunction, then, is that 'while you own a dwelling, you do not dwell', because the value of this future labour has already been appropriated by the seller within the sale price.

From a Marxist perspective, we must consider how such commodity fetishism can come into view for politicisation. Should the Toronto hipsters succeed in staging a trendy lifestyle that regenerates the entire neighbourhood, valorising it for a further round of gentrification and thereby ensuring rising home prices, it can be easy to miss that this lifestyle was never a natural spontaneous cultural occurrence, but a lifestyle existence that is intelligible in terms of a less visible imperative of home prices grounded in state policy. From a historical materialist perspective, we can see that much of the consumption activities in neighbourhoods, including the sense of class structure, is contingent upon specific modes of commodity speculation entailed in the property market. As Miller (2010) attests, home dwelling is often a matter of thwarted desire because the dwellers are subject to 'powerful forces which are by no means under their control' (p. 80), immediately incurring the interest of the state, landholders, local councils, financial institutions, meaning that

> against these forces, any desire by us, the mere people who dwell in houses, to engage in a certain relationship to them can find us way down any pecking order of power. Sometimes these powers manifest themselves in quite extraordinary and unexpected ways, hidden within genres of material culture where we do not perceive them as power. (p. 81)

Further, given the enormous costs of home ownership, the usual consumer ideology of freedom of choice is necessarily limited because it is simply an illusion for most people to imagine that they can choose to leave their home and get a new one as a matter of instantly gratified consumer decision-making, or at all. Given the enormous disruption and expense involved with moving home, most people will simply adapt themselves and modify their lifestyle until they can achieve a degree of familiarity and security in their home (Miller, 2010).

This contrived feeling of familiarity combined with security, clearly deeply compromised, reminds us of Ahmed's (2014) analysis of the affective dimension of erased emotions. Home dwelling necessarily entails, for most consumers, erasing the affective dissonance of having to work hard to pay rent for a landlord to live off simply by virtue of their primitive accumulation (that is they privatised a scarce asset before the person who needs it could access it), or having to commit to servicing a thirty-year mortgage in order to avoid being a renter and all for a building which may be actually quite disappointing if one were to linger on the issue. These moments of erasure that obscure the possibility of an alternative form of politicising the home partially constitutes the fetish itself. But most of all, what the fetish conceals is the broader question of why we should continue to live in circumstances where the use value of our homes can be dominated by such an all-consuming quest for exchange value that immiserates the many and creates huge instability for global economies? That is to say, why do we permit a regime of private property for home ownership and why do we permit a constant escalation of property prices? That it appears entirely natural that any home at all is a commodity and that a house price directly reflects a value of the house itself, demonstrates the actuality of the fetish.

SOCIAL MEDIA

A further example of the commodity fetish resides in the question of ownership of communication. To the extent that many people increasingly perform their communicative capacity and maintain relationships via social media, it is important to note that their personal communication is privatised for the purpose of surplus extraction. As Arvidsson (2016) notes, Facebook operates in such a way as to reconfigure our social relations so that they become fit for financialisation; we are constantly being sorted and valued on the basis of our communicative expressions and it is mostly our affective dispositions that are of great interest to Facebook's algorithm (and Facebook must be understood as in the business of surveillance). As Fuchs (2017) rightly argues, our participation in online forums, like Facebook, is fetishistic because our immediate experience is the sociality in which we engage, and because we do not pay, this sociality masks Facebook's commodity form. The term 'social media' is therefore a misnomer for Fuchs because Facebook, Google and other organisations are private enterprises and therefore are expressions of possessive individualism.

More pressingly, whether one might agree or disagree that Facebook suitably provides value for its users to the extent that this is not a case of genuine exploitation, the core political question, again, must revolve around the idea of private ownership. To agree that our communication should be privatised in such a way that it can be valorised for commodification is a political question. That this is precisely the question that rarely gets asked reveals commodity fetish at play. By contrast Fuchs (2017, p. 65) insists: 'True social media can only exist in a commons-based participatory democracy. Marx's works are key intellectual tools for the inspiration of struggles for a commons-based society and commons-based media'.

CONCLUSION

This chapter concludes with two arguments. The first is that analysing the politics of consumption should entail revealing obscured constellations of labourers; the 'hidden helpers' whose work produces and circulates the commodities. The purpose of this defetishisation of the commodity trail is not to demonstrate the shameful decadence of privileged Western consumers, but instead to show how we are networked together in ways which might provide a basis for solidarity. To be sure, imagining how a solidarity might form between the Yiwu factory workers who manufacture trinkets and the customers of a south east London pound shop, as per Hulme's (2015) study, remains exceptionally difficult to conceive, let alone strategise for. However, it is important from a politics of consumption perspective not to invoke such disparities between different consumer groups with a view to declaring that there is a basic incommensurability between the class experiences that necessarily entails an unavoidable antagonism between a consumer class and a labourer class because the distinction is a categorical misnomer. Indeed, by focusing on such contexts as a pound shop, Hulme reminds us that there is a near universality at stake; a sort of hyper availability of products for all the people.

Invoking a commodity trail, therefore, is to invoke a politics of everybody that does not obscure the vast differences of quality of life, but rather pulls it into focus in a context of a network of interdependency. It provides the basis for, in other words, a politics of everybody that forms a political commitment and a militant commitment to an inclusion that does not deny antagonism (Lewis, 2016). As Lewis argues, this is different from a capitalist invocation of 'everybody' which is in reality a political euphemism to deflect responsibility from systemic processes onto consumers who cannot control them (for example, '*everybody* in Ireland overspent and caused the financial crash' or 'environmental devastation is *everybody's* fault'). Rather, it is an everybody that is politically productive because it seeks to undo the ideological individualism of capitalism.

The political error then, is to conclude that first-world consumers are the agents that actively exploit and violently dominate third-world labourers. This repeats the neoliberal invocation of 'everybody' inasmuch as 'everybody is to blame' and leads to more handwringing. However, as Lewis (2016) argues, this perspective misses the point, namely 'the majority of the world proletariat may be outside the wealthy regions of the global North; still, the vast majority of people even in the global North own no means of production and have nothing to trade for survival but their own labor' (p. 201). This is to say, as Lewis does, that a politics of class begins with an understanding of economies as deeply structured so that one subset of people can extract surplus value from another, and will produce an extensive system that ensures the reproduction of this exploitative class arrangement. This typically Marxist position accepts the principle of collaboration between diverse people, whose labour, in circumstances that will vastly differ in terms of actual experiences of exploitation, is necessary to reproduce this profitable circulation of consumer goods, and argues that they must find the grounds for cooperation and solidarity, as extremely difficult as this might be.

To accept otherwise is to accept that material social relations cannot go beyond specific intersecting points – that there is a basic incommensurability that exists between different profiles of class, race, gender, age, sexuality, disability, etc., and that real solidarity is limited to those who share certain characteristics; characteristics that are actually materially static, insurmountable antagonisms. From a Marxist perspective, what each of these groups share is that they are all locked into capitalist reproduction in varying ways and, further, each of these sources of distinction – race, class, gender – are mutually conditioning components of material social relations; in other words they are symptoms and not causes. A Marxist approach must immediately clarify that this does not mean that the appearance of these class experiences is false. It exists, but the appearance conceals the relationship between the producers. As Marx (2017) himself put it: 'the relations connecting the labor of one individual with that of the rest appear, not as direct social relations between individuals at work, but as what they really are, material relations between persons and social relations between things'.

Therefore, a politics of consumption should insist that consumption, with its various violent iniquities, is a symptom and not a cause of class. Accordingly, each different class experience will reproduce material social relations in ways that reflect and amplify and therefore concretise and normalise the political economic structure.

But to then focus on how certain class profiles are particularly unreflexive and disappointing in their social reproduction, or as Lewis (2016) puts it, 'worrying about whether or not individuals desire assimilation' is to swap a 'concern about normative affects with actual anti-capitalist struggle' (p. 227), and this moment of swapping, at worst, can create a political dead-end based on different groups expressing their resentment and demands for sacrifice against others whilst forgetting that, in capitalism, uneven development is still a combined development. The politics of consumption, therefore, is not a displacement or refusal of these issues – the antagonisms that exist are no less real or concrete nor not in need of urgent reform just because they reproduce and amplify social relations, but it is a question of how to frame these antogonisms within a broader analysis grounded in a politics of everybody.

The second argument is to say that a politics of consumption should never lose sight of the circumstances of whether the consumption takes place in private property or in a commons. This entails not just whether the object is a public good, but also the means of producing this object. Issues of private ownership are seldom static or simply stated – for example, much of the neoliberal project entails deepening the logic of privatisation. The example of home ownership reveals that the matter of a government deciding to instil a national order of home owners did not produce a single discrete period of privatisation but set in motion a systemic reform that, decades later, still demands constant labour. In this regard, the logic of privatisation is often an experience of intensification – for example, whilst British universities may remain public entities, the apparatus of privatisation which includes student tuition fees, league tables, etc. leaves everybody in a constant state of intensifying disruption.

The work of the fetish and its supplemental ideology is to naturalise these states of affairs so that the labour necessary for inculcating regimes of privatisation are rendered both invisible and natural and therefore taken outside the realm of politics. The moment we stop analysing our experience in terms of privatisation, is the moment that we succumb to their naturalisation, and from that point onwards we will be responding to the apparition of things. Whether it be in terms of how our communicative ability is reordered and then valorised for surplus extraction by so-called social media or of how our experience of living in a home and our sense of community is ordered by a governmental commitment to the principle of homeownership, it is important that we engage these topics in terms of questions of private versus commons, and beyond that, that we understand these as questions of materialism which immediately invoke questions of exploitation and oppression, that we remember that at stake is the contestation of the mechanisms for reproducing social life and whether or not we accept as natural the idea that these mechanisms should be concentrated in private hands.

Put differently, the difference between a critical perspective on consumption and a politics of consumption, is that the critical perspective wants to take all representations of consumption with a pinch of salt, whereas the politics of consumption perspective insists that the salt was pinched from everybody and wants to know how everybody can get it back.[4]

Notes

1 As this is a caricature, it is not helpful to cite any particular study as it is not intended as a direct representation of actual studies, rather it is to notice the polls that envelope much analysis.
2 This analogy comes from *Consumer Tribes* by Cova, Kozinets and Shankar.
3 As should become clear as the argument is further pursued, it would be entirely a mistake to read this argument as claiming that the consumer has no agency.
4 I here paraphrase my friend Stephen Dunne.

REFERENCES

Ahmed, Sara. 2014. *The Cultural Politics of Emotion*, 2nd Edition. Edinburgh: University of Edinburgh Press.

Appadurai, Arjun. 1988. *The Social Life of Things: The Commodity in Cultural Perspective*. Cambridge: Cambridge University Press.

Arvidsson, Adam. 2016. Facebook and Finance: On the Social Logic of the Derivative. *Theory, Culture & Society*. 33(6): 3–23.

Benjamin, Walter. 1999. *The Arcades Project*. Cambridge: The Belknap Press of Harvard University Press.

Cook, Ian and Harrison, Michelle. 2007. Follow the Thing: 'West Indian Hot Pepper Sauce'. *Space and Culture*. 10(3): 40–63.

Cova, Bernard, Kozinets, Robert and Shankar, Avi. 2007. *Consumer Tribes*. London: Routledge.

Dean, Jodi. 2009. *Democracy and Other Neoliberal Fantasies: Communicative Capitalism and Left Politics*. Durham: Duke University Press.

Fine, Ben. 1983. Commodity Fetish. In *A Dictionary of Marxist Thought*. Edited by Tom Bottomore, p. 102. London: Blackwell.

Fuchs, Christian. 2017. Marx's *Capital* in the Information Age. *Capital & Class*. 41(1): 51–67.

Geras, Norman. 1983. Fetishism. In *A Dictionary of Marxist Thought*. Edited by Tom Bottomore, pp. 190–192. London: Blackwell.

Harvey, David. 2014. *Seventeen Contradictions and the End of Capitalism*. London: Verso.

Hulme, Alison. 2015. *On the Commodity Trail: The Journey of a Bargain Store Product from East to West*. London: Bloomsbury.

Lekakis, Eleftheria. 2013. A Liquid Politics? Conceptualising the Politics of Fair Trade Consumption and Consumer Citizenship. *Ephemera: Theory & Politics in Organisation*. 13(2): 317–338.

Lewis, Holly. 2016. *The Politics of Everybody: Feminism, Queer Theory and Marxism at the Intersection*. London: Zed Books.

Littler, Jo. 2008. *Radical Consumption: Shopping for Change in Contemporary Culture*. Berkshire: Open University Press.

Marx, Karl. 2017. *Capital Volume 1*. https://www.marxists.org/archive/marx/works/download/pdf/Capital-Volume-I.pdf [accessed: March, 2017].

Miller, Daniel. 2010. *Stuff*. London: Polity.

Mintz, Sidney. 1986. *Sweet and Power: The Place of Sugar in Modern History*. London: Penguin.

Robertson, Mary. 2017. The Great British Housing Crisis. *Capital & Class*. 41(2): 195–215.

Zwick, Detlev and Ozalp, Yesim. 2011. Flipping the Neighbourhood: Biopolitical Marketing as Value Creation for Condos and Lofts. In *Inside Marketing*. Edited by Detlev Zwick and Julian Cayla, pp. 236–253. Oxford: Oxford University Press.
Žižek, Slavoj. 2001. *On Belief*. London: Routledge.
Žižek, Slavoj. 2011. *Living in the End of Times*. London: Verso.

Index

Page numbers in **bold** indicate tables and in *italic* indicate figures. End of chapter notes are indicated by a letter n between page number and note number.

FSC
www.fsc.org
MIX
Papier | Fördert gute Waldnutzung
FSC® C083411

Kolibri 360 GmbH
Ferdinand-Jühlke-Straße 7
99095 Erfurt, Deutschland
produktsicherheit@kolibri360.de